algebraic and arithmetic structures

algebraic and arithmetic structures

A CONCRETE APPROACH FOR ELEMENTARY SCHOOL TEACHERS

developed cooperatively by

MAX S. BELL
The University of Chicago

KAREN C. FUSON
Northwestern University

RICHARD A. LESH
Northwestern University

THE FREE PRESS
A Division of Macmillan Publishing Co., Inc.
NEW YORK

Collier Macmillan Publishers
LONDON

The Free Press
A Division of Macmillan Publishing Co., Inc.
866 Third Avenue, New York, N.Y. 10022

Collier Macmillan Canada, Ltd.

Library of Congress Catalog Card Number: 75-2807

Printed in the United States of America

printing number
1 2 3 4 5 6 7 8 9 10

Library of Congress Cataloging in Publication Data

Bell, Max S
    Algebraic and arithmetic structures.

    Bibliography: p.
    Includes index.
    1. Mathematics--Study and teaching (Elementary)
I. Fuson, Karen C., joint author. II. Lesh, Ri-
chard A., joint author. III. Title.
QA135.5.B43   372.7   75-2807
ISBN 0-02-902270-3

Richard A. Lesh (Ph.D., Indiana University) is an Associate Professor of Mathematics and Education at Northwestern University. Professor Lesh is also Co-Director of the Cognitive Development Division of the University of Georgia Center for Learning and Teaching Mathematics.

Karen C. Fuson (Ph.D., University of Chicago) is an Assistant Professor of Mathematics Education at Northwestern University. Professor Fuson is also associated with Northwestern's Early Childhood Education Program.

Max S. Bell (Ph.D., University of Michigan) is an Associate Professor of Mathematics Education in the University of Chicago's Graduate School of Education.

contents

---

part c underlying mathematical concepts and structures   449

preface

A few years ago at the University of Chicago and at Northwestern University we found that our lectures on mathematics were having only limited success in teaching prospective elementary school teachers. Our students often came to us with deep-seated fears and virtually no self-confidence with respect to mathematics. Yet they were well aware that a year or so hence they would be teaching mathematics. They wanted practical, sure-fire prescriptions for accomplishing what they were sure would be an unpleasant task, and their fears and anxieties often left little tolerance for our excursions into theoretical mathematics, however "simple" and "nice." On our part, we felt it would be unfair to them and their future pupils if they didn't acquire an understanding of mathematics well beyond that contained in the school books they would use.

As we struggled with such dilemmas, we began first to use such things as counters and rods when they could make some obvious contribution to the theory we wanted to teach. Encouraged by the success of this, we began actively to search for ways of illustrating whatever mathematics was at hand by activity-oriented exercises. We soon came to believe that it is possible to find or invent helpful "concretizations" or "embodiments" for practically every concept of elementary mathematics. That is, an activities oriented approach imposed virtually no restrictions on the mathematics content we believe teachers should know. Furthermore, with these activities, adults were willing to tackle once again mathematical topics that had often been mysterious or threatening to them. They saw the activities as suggesting ways to teach similar concepts to youngsters, and this provided additional motivation. Eventually we began to wish to share these rather nice results with our colleagues, and this book is the result.

No particular course or method is likely to suit every student, yet we have found the range of students to whom these materials appeal to be rather surprising. This range has included the usual college age students and mature students returning to college after many years; students with considerable and with little mathematical training; students at relatively "high-power" private universities, and those attending urban commuter universities, and pre-service teachers and in-service teachers. Depending on mathematical expertness and experience, the material in this book either allows a fresh start and gentle guidance in coming to terms with some mathematics, or a reexamination of fundamental concepts which were never difficult for a given teacher but which must now be taught to youngsters who have considerable difficulty.

The material contained herein is an adult level treatment of the arithmetic and algebra of whole numbers, integers, rational numbers, and (briefly) real numbers plus some excursions into theoretical structures involving material on logic, number theory, relations, functions, and modern algebra. The material has no mathematical prerequisites since every topic is started from scratch in quite accessible ways.

In working with those adults who are reconstructing many of their concepts of mathematics (and perhaps their mathematical confidence as well), several things are often mentioned by them as impressions taught by their own school mathematics experience. First, their school experience has often led them to the false belief that mathematics is a completed rather than a growing and developing field of inquiry. Second, they have been given little reason to believe that mathematics is good for anything, except possibly the everyday uses of very simple calculation. Third, they have often come to think of mathematics as tricky symbol manipulation using some sort of magic, in which "correct" results are more a matter of good luck than of good management. They frequently express some anxiety about being urged to work things out first in action oriented, mostly nonsymbolic ways that seem to come from a feeling that it is almost *immoral* not to do things the hard way; or that using concrete materials is an indication that one is too stupid to do it the "right" way.

Such misconceptions about mathematics itself, the usefulness of mathematics, and the variety of respectable ways in which mathematics can be learned (or indeed created) are most unfortunate. This book is motivated principally by the hope of breaking into the circle in which teachers with such misconceptions pass them on to children.

We had help from many sources in preparing this book, our families not least of all. Special thanks are due Barry Hammond for early help and encouragement, Hazel Wagner for assistance in developing some of the materials and Warren Crown, Sandy Kerr, Michael Mahaffey, and Lauren Woodby for helpful criticism of various drafts. Thanks also go to our typists and to Robert Garfield, Michael Harkavy, and Ellen Simon of The Free Press.

Chicago and Evanston, Illinois
December 1975

KF
RL
MB

introduction

0.1.
ASSUMPTIONS INFLUENCING THE CONTENT OF THIS BOOK

1. We are convinced that in spite of years of exposure to school mathematics, many adults (perhaps the majority) have negative feelings toward the subject and are often unable to *use* mathematics comfortably. This means to us that mathematics education has failed for far too many people. It seems to us that the most likely way to change this state of affairs is to provide a much better mathematics experience in the early school years. In order to do this, elementary school teachers must be much better prepared—and prepared in a new way—for teaching mathematics.

2. To us, better teacher preparation means at least two things. First, teachers must become much more expert in mathematics itself; hence, our selection of content in this book comes from good solid mathematical ideas and structures. Second, teachers need to consider deeply and carefully how they can help children build for themselves durable mathematical intuitions, concepts, and skills.

3. With possible (but rare) exceptions, mathematics cannot simply be poured into a person's head in its purest and best symbolic form; most people must build it for themselves, starting from considerable concrete experience. If that is so, the way in which mathematics is learned assumes importance along with what is learned. Hence, although this is a course in mathematics, it illustrates some important "methods" by which good mathematics can be taught.

4. We believe that nearly all of school mathematics is (or should be) "useful" mathematics, but that this usefulness is often obscured or ignored in school instruction. Hence, as you go through this book we encourage you to keep asking, in effect, "Why bother? Who needs it?" [1]

5. Contrary to the impression one might get from much school instruction, mathematics is much more than computation. What we ultimately want is an understanding of mathematical operations and structures along with considerable flexibility and ingenuity in using mathematics.

---

[1] You should come to expect answers of two sorts to such a question. The first involves a need for new mathematical tools to cope with the actual real world. For example, fractions are needed as soon as one must cope with measures. The second involves the need to tidy up or extend basic mathematical structures. For example, negative numbers need inventing in order that all subtraction problems will have answers (e.g., $3 - 23 = -20$.) (Negative numbers are also useful in the real world, of course.)

This book, then, aims at an understanding of computation, but even more it is designed to help each person build a sure intuitive feel for numbers and operations ("number sense"); build an equally secure "measure sense"; build an understanding of the several uses of variables; and combine these into the problem-solving skills that allow one to look at a new situation, size it up, and *do* something with it.

6. *Some part* of a person's mathematical knowledge does involve computation. In this respect, we believe that an understanding of what the various operations do, and how they behave, is a distinct issue from consideration of the sometimes complicated algorithms of arithmetic (e.g., long division). For example, one might know that for a given problem dividing 375 by 23 is the appropriate thing to do without being able to carry out the algorithmic process to get an answer. And, of course, one can be a whiz at the long division algorithm but understand little about division itself.[2] Hence, the first third of this book is about number systems and what the operations mean in each; the middle third of the book deals with algorithmic processes, which we believe are interesting and important in their own right; and the final third of the book deals in a more general way with underlying algebraic ideas that were considered in the other two-thirds of the book. The net result is an adult-level, relatively advanced consideration of arithmetic and algebra that uses activities and applications in most of the learning sequences.

0.2.
MATHEMATICS
AND REAL WORLD LINKS

Such beliefs as those outlined above have led to consistent emphasis throughout the book on several major themes: applications of mathematics; "embodiment" or "concretization" of theoretical mathematics by actions on concrete materials; mathematical structures. All these touch in one way or another on links and interrelationships between the "world of mathematics" and the "world of reality." The range of possibilities is indicated by the diagram on the facing page.

Neither "mathematical models" nor "embodiments" of mathematics have been emphasized in mathematical instruction in the past, and even now there is little in the preparation of teachers that would help them

[2] For example, William H. Burton reported in *The Guidance of Learning Activities* that a child with good standardized test computation scores but unable to solve problems was asked what she did: "I know what to do by looking at the examples. If there are only two numbers, I subtract. If there are lots of numbers, I add. But if there are just two numbers and one is littler than the other, then it is a hard problem. I divide to see if they come out even, but if they don't, I multiply." (3d ed., Appleton-Century-Crofts, Inc., New York, 1962.

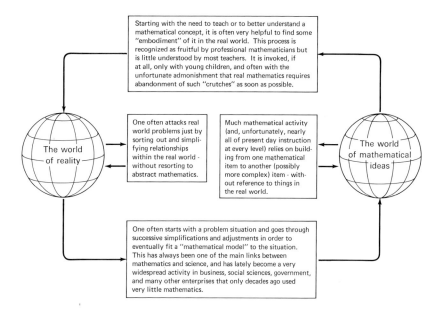

understand such matters. In the next two sections they are treated in more detail as background for the rather frequent reference that is made to them in the remainder of this book.

0.3.
APPLICATIONS
OF MATHEMATICS AND
MATHEMATICAL MODELS

The use of applied mathematics in its relation to a physical problem involves three stages: (1) a dive from the world of reality into the world of mathematics; (2) a swim in the world of mathematics; (3) a climb from the world of mathematics back into the world of reality, carrying a prediction in our teeth.[3]

Starting *thousands* of years ago, man invented numbers, computation, and geometry to help understand and keep track of his world. For the past few *hundreds* of years mathematics has been seen as having "unreasonable effectiveness" in providing equations, formulas, and other mathematical models to help understand real world events related to astronomy and physical sciences. But only in the past few *tens* of years, especially since about 1950, when the first practical electronic computers were built, has mathematics been used extensively in many fields outside the physical sciences. As a result, statements such as these are now commonplace:

[3] J. Synge, quoted in the *American Mathematical Monthly*, October 1961, p. 799.

For economics:

The applied contributions of mathematical economics cover a wide range of areas. It has helped in the planning and analysis of . . . the measures designed to eliminate recessions and inflations. . . . It has helped to promote efficiency and reduce costs in the selection of portfolios of stocks and bonds, and to the planning of expanded industrial capacities and public transportation networks. In economic theory, it has helped us to investigate more deeply the process of economic growth and the mechanism of business cycles. In these and many other areas, the use of mathematics has become commonplace and has helped to extend the frontiers of research.[4]

For biology:

There now exists, at least in outline, a systematic mathematical biology which, in the words of one of its pioneers, is "similar in its structure and aims (though not in content) to mathematical physics." . . . Moreover, this mathematical biology has already greatly enriched the biological sciences.[5]

For business:

The use of mathematical language . . . is already desirable and will soon become inevitable. Without its help the further growth of business with its attendant complexity of organization will be retarded and perhaps halted. In the science of management, as in other sciences, mathematics has become a "condition of progress." [6]

The process by which mathematics becomes useful to workers in these fields is indicated by the quotation at the beginning of this section. The "dive into the world of mathematics" typically results in what is called a "mathematical model" of the real world problem—some bit of mathematics that expresses in abstract terms something about the real situation: a numerical expression, some equations, a geometric diagram, and so on.

---

[4] W. J. Baumol, "Mathematics in Economic Analysis," in T. L. Saaty and F. W. Neyl, *The Spirit and Uses of the Mathematical Sciences,* McGraw-Hill Book Company, New York, 1969, p. 246.

[5] A. Rosen, "On Mathematics and Biology," also in *The Spirit and Uses of the Mathematical Sciences,* p. 204.

[6] A. Battersby, *Mathematics in Management,* p. 11. In this book, whenever the authors make only brief reference to some source, full information about it will be found in Appendix II.

This same process of using abstract mathematical models to express something going on in the world also characterizes everyday uses of mathematics. For example, the counting numbers 1, 2, 3, appear to have been needed, and hence invented, early in human history by virtually every human society that we know about. This "dive into the world of mathematics" was first by way of *spoken* words; written number systems were a later development. Such things as "addition" and "multiplication" of counting numbers were invented to describe something about what happens when sets of things are combined. Fractions may have been invented to express measures.

That is, for centuries man has applied numbers in ways not very different in basic spirit and method from the modern use of mathematical models to solve complicated problems in business, science, government, or social sciences. This method involves examining and simplifying the real world situation until it is possible to describe what you want to know about it in some mathematical terms. One works strictly with the mathematics for a "solution" or answer, then checks this answer to the mathematical problem back in the original real world problem. If the mathematical solution does not fit the real world situation, then one goes through another such round (and perhaps another and another), until an appropriate fit is achieved between some bit of mathematics and some part of the real world.

0.4. EMBODIMENTS OR CONCRETIZATIONS

Many of the activities in this book involve starting the study of a given mathematical concept by dealing with "embodiments" of the concept in actions on real world things. The process is that indicated earlier: Start with a mathematical abstraction and seek to understand it better by acting it out with such things as counters, sticks with graduated lengths, a board with a grid of nails on it, cardboard, string, or whatever works.

Embodiments of mathematics are not mathematics. The ultimate goal is still to be able to understand and work with mathematical symbols and structures. But working with embodiments has proved to be very helpful to children and to adults in achieving this goal. Mathematical "knowledge" for too many people consists of a verbal and symbolic superstructure, much of which lacks meaning. Naturally they find it difficult to use such "knowledge" or teach it to others. We have found that even people with considerable and excellent mathematical training often gain new insights into both mathematics and the teaching of mathematics by putting themselves through the exercise of using concrete materials to act out mathematical abstractions.

For those who are going to teach children, using embodiments of mathematics concepts is especially useful. It is almost certainly true that many children (especially young children) learn mathematics best and come to feel better about it by operating on real objects. For teachers who wish to understand how this sort of learning takes place in children, there is no substitute for going through a similar experience themselves.

One caution is in order, however. This is a course for adults, and over and over again it moves from operations on concrete objects to consideration of patterns of results from these operations, and from there to abstract structures that describe these patterns. The process is similar to what might happen over several years with children, but here it is compressed into a fraction of the time required with children and calls on mature patterns of thinking that may not even be available in young children. Hence, it would almost certainly be hazardous to use the exercises and worksheets in this book directly with children. Still, the experiences outlined here are suggestive of what might be done in teaching mathematics to children, and with suitable adaptation and elaboration many of the "embodiments" and worksheets can become useful teaching resources.

One other remark: Beginning number work in the early school grades does sometimes include concretization by use of counters and counting. But *measure* is the source of numbers to be processed at least as often as is counting. However, the measure motivation for the use of numbers is frequently neglected in instruction of children. Therefore, whenever appropriate, this book has used measure situations as a source of number ideas. Embodiments that reflect measure considerations are given as much prominence as embodiments that reflect counting processes.

0.5. ACTIVITIES AND LABORATORY WORK

The "activities" approach that is used in this book emphasizes that mathematics is as much a process (something one does) as it is a product (something one possesses). Through the use of problem-solving situations, we hope to encourage you to estimate reasonable answers, generate hypotheses, formulate models, investigate regularities, and test and modify hypotheses. Because mathematics is created by people and exists only in their minds, it must be recreated by every person who learns it; this means that some freedom must be allowed for mathematical inquiry. However, allowing freedom for mathematical inquiry does not mean giving no guidance. Indeed, this book provides considerable guidance by the nature of the problem situations that are presented, and the nature of the concrete materials that are used.

We hope that some of the activities in this book will make you want to get involved in *doing* mathematics. To create a balance between giving you a chance to think your own thoughts and forcing you to communicate with (i.e., learn from and teach) other students, many of the activities that we present will encourage you to interact with other students—check your findings with theirs, ask for or give help, talk about any new insights, and so on.

Wherever it is not mathematically misleading, new topics will be presented through the use of simple, concise explanations, together with concrete illustrations and everyday examples. The procedure in most sections will be to introduce concepts in an intuitive fashion before the ideas are gradually refined and formalized.

If advance preparation or special materials are required for a lesson, you can know this ahead of time by looking at the overview to the lesson. Overviews describe what each lesson is generally about and describe the materials that will be needed. If such materials are not available, Appendix I tells how the equipment can be made for inexpensive materials.

Although the use of laboratory materials is rather unusual in mathematics classes, it is common practice in many other subject areas. We believe that the "homemade" materials that are suggested here are the kind that will be useful to you in many teaching and learning situations. Our students have found that by the end of the course they not only have a firm understanding of the major ideas, but they have also accumulated a personal collection of instructional materials that they feel comfortable about using in a wide range of situations.

A criticism that instructors and students sometimes have about activities programs is that concrete problem-solving sessions take time, perhaps at the expense of covering more content. We don't believe that good laboratory activities result in time wasted, but we realize that an activities program requires that efficient use be made of homework assignments. Consequently, some sections of the book are especially suited for in-class laboratory sessions, some for in-class discussions, some for outside reading research assignments, and some for homework or research assignments. These homework assignments frequently ask for thought and analysis with respect to the concepts introduced by the laboratory experience. All these avenues to learning will need to be used, with each of you providing for yourself the links among them.

We have found that an activities-oriented course works best with at least 2-hour class sessions in a room with tables or with movable desks that give space to use materials and opportunities for some work in small groups. But college schedules and room assignments often get in the way of setting up classes in this way. With some ingenuity it is possible to adapt the course to fit whatever scheduling and room conditions are imposed, perhaps even with much of the laboratory activity taking place outside of regularly scheduled "lecture" hours. The "lecture" hours can then be times for discussion and organization of the findings from the outside activities. In such cases there is a much greater burden on you, the student, to take responsibility for your own learning, we hope, by considerable interaction with your fellow students.

0.6. ORGANIZATION OF THIS BOOK

The book is organized in three parts. Part A begins with a thorough treatment of whole numbers, especially of the underlying meaning of the various operations with whole numbers. Here, as elsewhere, there is a stress on applications of numbers—why we need them and how they are used. A series of "extensions" to other number systems then takes place. In each such extension the first question is always, "Why bother? Of what use would the extended system be?" That answered, an extended set of numbers is constructed, the possible new meanings of such relations as "equal" and "less than" are explored, and new definitions and properties of the standard operations are developed, including the various uses to which such operations might be put.

Part B begins with a much more complete investigation of algorithmic processes than is usual in this kind of book. These processes can provide examples of the practical use of "properties" and increased understanding of some of the consequences of various characteristics of our system of numeration. We stress such matters because computational routines and notation are not trivial matters in using mathematics and because, for better or worse, such concerns constitute a very large part of the elementary school curriculum with which teachers must cope. This part of the book also includes a discussion of decimals motivated by the metric system of measurement. Also, the extension of rational numbers to the real numbers gets brief, but honest, treatment.

Part C is perhaps the most self-consciously "mathematical" of the three parts, but its reliance on concrete embodiments is as great as that in the other two parts. It deals in a general way with underlying algebraic concepts (e.g., sets and logic, relations, operations) that occurred throughout Parts A and B.

Since the three series of units are relatively independent, the units in Part A do not have to be completed before Parts B and C are begun. The units are independent enough to allow repeated fresh starts to students who are having difficulties and to allow instructors to modify the sequential presentation of units without destroying the logical themes that run throughout the book. In this way, we hope that the program can be easily adapted to the needs of individual colleges and universities and that instructors will feel free to organize their courses to fit the needs of their students.

Overviews inserted at the beginning of many sections attempt to improve the readability of the book by helping you distinguish the important ideas from the relatively less important ideas as you read through each unit. The overviews also indicate what materials are used in the lesson, including some that may need to be made outside of class prior to the lesson.

In the text itself, there are often footnotes that give further information or give answers to questions so that you can check your work. "Answer" footnotes are printed in blue. Try to resist the temptation to look at "the answer" before really coping with the problem yourself. Problems that are "optional," in the sense of being either relatively less important or more difficult than normal, are marked with an asterisk.

The primary intention of this book is to teach good mathematics. We have included brief "pedagogical remarks" at the end of most units to help you make the transition from learning mathematics yourself to teaching it to children. You should also have a close look at one or more textbook series actually used in schools and read some of the books on the theme of how children learn mathematics that are listed in Appendix II.

Rods and chips and a few other materials are needed in many of the units. Some suggestions about acquiring and managing such materials with a minimum of fuss are in Appendix I.

About one-fourth of this book is a do-it-yourself project. There are many places in which you are asked to write in the results of your investigations or the conclusions that you and your classmates have arrived at as the result of some activity. When you have finished the book by actually filling in these blanks in the lessons, you should have a reference book of considerable value, especially if you are preparing yourself for the exciting task of teaching mathematics to children.

part a
number systems: sets relations operations uses

unit 1
preliminary whole number ideas

1.1
INTRODUCTION
Everything must start somewhere and in this book we will start with the set of "whole numbers." This set begins 0, 1, 2, 3, 4, . . . , and goes on forever.[1] It is possible and interesting to start further back and develop this *set* of numbers, its *relations,* and its *operations* in rigorous mathematical ways from even more basic starting points, but we won't do so in this book.

In this unit we will first consider some of the basic uses of whole numbers that do not involve such operations as adding or multiplying, then consider a few basic ideas about *sets,* and last consider the basic relations for whole numbers: *equals, less than,* and *greater than.* Subsequent units in Part A will deal with the meaning and structure of standard operations with whole numbers, extension of the whole numbers to the integers, and extension of the integers to rational numbers.

In taking the whole numbers as known and as an obvious and easy

---

[1] The set of numbers without the zero—that is, one, two, three, four, . . . , —is called the set of "counting numbers" or the set of "natural numbers" because they appear early and naturally both in human history and in the early learning of children. Zero, on the other hand, developed relatively late in history; even later than fractions, in fact.

3

4 NUMBER
SYSTEMS:
SETS
RELATIONS
OPERATIONS
USES

starting place it must be observed that there is still much to be said about the historical development of this number system as a tool for mankind and about the psychological development of whole number ideas in children. The pedagogical notes at the end of this unit discuss these matters briefly, and in Appendix II there are suggestions for further reading.

As to historical development of our number system, counting-number systems appear to have developed wherever man himself has developed, often only as verbal systems of number names but in some places as symbolic numeral systems. Our own verbal and symbolic numeral system is based on the ten symbols 0, 1, 2, 3, 4, 5, 6, 7, 8, 9 (and corresponding number words) and their elaboration by an efficient "base-ten, place-value" numeration system to express any whole number whatever. A base of ten appears to have been the favored one as numeration systems developed independently in many human societies (no doubt from counting on fingers and thumbs) but several other bases have been reported.

Many societies had only verbal counting systems coupled with calculating devices such as the abacus. Various symbolic numeral systems were eventually invented and some of these supported quite sophisticated arithmetics; for example, the Babylonian system (base sixty) and the Mayan system (base twenty). The very efficient numeral system we use was late in coming, historically speaking. Even the zero that we find so essential was a long time in its invention. This fascinating story is elaborated in Part B, Unit 7, but we are starting here with the end results—the system of whole numbers and our usual base-ten, place-value notation for them.

Some counting systems

Verbal: uno, dos, tres, cuatro, cinco, . . .

Tally: / / / / / / / / / / / /

Improved tally: ╫╫ ╫╫ / /

Roman: I II III IV

Modern: 1, 2, 3, 4, 5, . . . , 904, . . .

1.2
PROBLEM SET:
USES OF WHOLE NUMBERS

Overview: **This problem set asks you to consider ways in which whole numbers are used, most of them *without* the four basic operations of addition, multiplication, subtraction, and division.**

1.2.1
Collecting Uses
of Whole Numbers

1. As a matter of interest and possibly for class discussion, take about ten minutes to list below actual ways in which you have recently used numbers or seen them used.

2. For the next two days, make a log of *every* use of whole numbers that you become aware of outside of your mathematics classes. (You may also list uses of fractions or decimals or negative numbers, but since we are particularly interested right now in whole numbers, keep that log separate from the others.) As you make the two-day log, keep separate lists of those uses that involve calculations and those that do not. Save the former list for future reference. Try to sort your list of non-calculation uses of whole numbers into several general categories.[1]

1.2.2
**Whole Numbers
Used in Gathering and
Recording Data**

1. Important information about the world frequently comes from counting things. Give examples in which actual counting yields useful information.

2. Sometimes a set of things is countable in theory but in practice an actual one-by-one count would be impractical. In such cases, ways of getting approximate counts are devised. List one or more situations described as counts, in which actual counting of everyday objects was probably not accomplished.[2]

3. Important information about the world can come from measuring as well as from counting. For example, many measures such as shoe size, blood pressure, and college entrance test scores are attached to people. Make a list of some names of measures that apply to yourself. Whenever possible also include the actual number that applies to you; for example, shoe size = 8, or weight = 125 pounds. (We are most

---

[1] For example, if during the two days you wanted to order, from a mail-order catalog, a traverse rod for hanging draperies, the index might direct you to pages 1051–1057. You might decide to order the one on page 1055 that projects from the wall $2^{1}/_{2}$ to $3^{1}/_{2}$ inches, adjusts from 84 to 150 inches in length, and has 38 carriers for drapery hooks. On the order blank you would fill in the catalog number (735-2099), the fact that you want two such rods, the mailing weight (6 pounds each, 12 pounds total), the price for each ($10.89), and the total price ($2 \times \$10.89 = \$21.78$). The whole numbers in this experience fall into several different categories; the catalog number, for example, is quite a different thing from the mailing weight or the length of the rod.

[2] Representative examples might be the world population in 1960 and the number of atoms in a gram of uranium.

6 NUMBER
SYSTEMS:
SETS
RELATIONS
OPERATIONS
USES

interested here in whole numbers but measuring often leads to decimals or fractions. In this exercise, save the fractions or decimals on your list for future reference and concentrate discussion on the whole numbers.)

4. The count versus measure distinction is sometimes difficult to make when considering how numbers arise in recording data about the world. For example, there is much news about an energy shortage of millions of barrels of oil with prices of $7 to $22 per barrel. A "barrel" is clearly a measure but the "millions" sound like a count and the price per barrel can be considered either as a measure of the value of oil or as a certain number of dollars. Rather than arguing about assigning such data to a count or measure category, it may be more profitable to recognize a certain amount of ambiguity. List a few more examples of data that could be considered either as counts or as measures, or perhaps as some combination.

5. The information that a citizen needs to process in order to make responsible and intelligent political and social decisions is frequently given in numerical form. The following items using mostly whole numbers are from a few issues of the *New York Times* in 1974. (Uses of operations on whole numbers and uses of fractions from news stories will appear in later units.) Similar information is available any week from newspapers, weekly news magazines, or other sources. Keeping in mind that some ambiguity can be expected, put "C" for "count," "M" for "measure," or "?" for "neither or ambiguous" on each of the numbers that appears in these items.[2] Be prepared to

---

[2] You can expect that your labels will sometimes differ from those of colleagues, which might lead to some interesting discussion. There is ambiguity in nearly every classification scheme. If you can devise a better scheme than we suggest, do so.

discuss with colleagues some ways in which schools can help prepare people to evaluate and use such information.[3]

a. Dried green peas for split pea soup have nearly quadrupled in price over the last year. A pound, which now costs about 65¢, will make about 12 bowls of soup. It is said that low prices over the past few years prompted farming decisions that led to last year's crop being only 250 million pounds, down from 331 million in 1972 and 487 million in 1971. There is said to be as much protein and other food value in split pea soup as in steak.

b. The Ethiopian government reports that more than 700,000 people are suffering from famine caused by drought in the southern provinces in addition to 1,340,000 suffering from famine in the northern provinces. According to the United Nations, about 100,000 people have died from the famine in one northern province alone.

c. At a meeting entitled "Black Capitalism: Myth or Reality" an Atlanta University professor saw hope in the fact that black-controlled banks have grown from 11 institutions with assets of $77 million in 1963 to 53 institutions with assets of about $1 billion. The reporter writing the story observes that this still means that the combined assets of the 53 banks are less than half the assets of the fiftieth largest commercial bank in the United States.

d. Over the next 10 years United States corporations expect to need $2 trillion in new capital, including perhaps $300 billion from new stock issues. Wall Street is worried about where the money will come from. About 300 offerings of stock were withdrawn from the capital market in the first half of 1973 because they were unsalable, and only 99 new stock issues were marketed in 1973, as compared with 568 in 1972. There has been an estimated decline in participation of individuals in the stock market of 800,000 since early 1972.

e. A New York state antidrug law offers $1,000 reward for information leading to a narcotics conviction. Officials say they get 25 to 30 calls per day and that more than 15 arrests have resulted from the tips. No rewards have been paid so far.

f. The Swiss government has raised to 80 miles per hour the 62 mile per hour speed limit imposed last November to save gasoline (formerly there was no limit at all). Tentative figures indicate a substantial drop in traffic deaths (from 1,722 in 1972 to 1,450 in 1973) but no definite conclusions are being drawn from that.

g. Oil companies now pay $7 per barrel in royalties and taxes in

[3] One troublesome issue in this connection is when and to what extent children should be asked in school to deal with such information, considering their social and emotional development as well as their cognitive development.

8 NUMBER
SYSTEMS:
SETS
RELATIONS
OPERATIONS
USES

Mideast producer countries, while on the open market oil has recently been as high as $22 but is presently in the range of $9 to $11. Both royalties and market price have at least tripled within the last year. A number of items in the March 17, 1974, and March 24, 1974, issues of the *New York Times* deal with various consequences of this. For example: (1) American petroleum companies offered 2 million tons of oil at below current market prices in an effort to dissuade governments from entering into long-term agreements with producing countries that would keep prices high. (This is about 14 million barrels or about a seven-day supply for a country such as France.) (2) Saudi Arabia is arguing for reducing oil prices for fear of causing worldwide problems. (3) Saudi Arabia will earn $20 billion this year and by 1980 may have $200 billion in foreign investments and currency reserves. (4) AbuDhabi may earn $40 billion this year, or more than $100,000 for every citizen of the country. (5) Economists argue that the greatly increased Arab oil earnings cannot be absorbed even by all the Arab states combined, including those with no oil, and that much of it will therefore go to investments in the West. There is much more along these lines that may be quite important to understanding how the world is going.

h. The Ford Foundation is giving $250,000 for resettlement of Soviet refugee scholars and writers coming to the United States: 450 refugees in 1972; 1,450 in 1973; and an estimated 4,000 in 1974. Israel, by contrast, absorbed 30,000 refugees in 1973.

i. In a darts tournament the American team beat the British team. A professional set of three darts costs about $40; the board is hung 8 feet away and 5 feet 8 inches off the floor. Championship play is to a preordained total and final points must be made on doubles; that is, if six points are needed they must be made by hitting the "double three" area on the target.

j. During the week ending March 15, 1974, 1,084 of the stocks listed on the New York Stock Exchange advanced in price and 656 declined. New highs were posted by 500 stocks and new lows by 77. Average volume for the week was about 17 million shares per day, with a total volume during the week of 86,812,260 shares and a total for the year of 803,779,459 shares.

1.2.3 The Natural Order of Whole Numbers

The mathematician Philip Davis tells this story:

On a recent trip to New York I got off at Pennsylvania Station. I walked to the taxi platform, but the train had been crowded and soon dozens of people poured out of the station for cabs. Some of them waved and yelled;

some stepped in front of the cabs rushing down the incline; some, who had porters in their employ, seemed to be getting preferential treatment. I waited on the curb, convinced that my gentle ways and the merits of my case would ultimately attract a driver. However, when they did, he was snatched out from under me. I gave up, took the subway, cursing the railroad, the cabbies, and people in general and hoping they would get stuck for hours in the crosstown traffic.

Several weeks later, on a trip to Philadelphia, I got off at the 30th St. Station. I walked to the taxi platform. A sign advised me to take a number. A dispatcher loaded the cabs in numerical order, and I was soon on my way to the hotel. It was rapid, it was pleasant, it was civilized. And this is a fine, though exceedingly simple, way in which mathematics may affect social affairs. . . . The numbers have an order, and can be used to simulate a queue [line of people] without the inconvenience and indignity of actually forming a queue. The numbers are a catalyst that can help turn raving madmen into polite humans.[4]

1. List places where the natural order of the whole numbers and the "take-a-number" system have been used to simulate a queue to make order of service more equitable.

*2. Could the set of fractions be conveniently used in this way? Why or why not?

3. Try to list some other places where the natural order of whole numbers plays a role (games, sequencing work, putting together model kits, etc.).

---

[4] "The Criterion Makers: Mathematics and Social Policy," *The American Scientist,* 50 (Sept. 1962) p. 258A.

10 **NUMBER
SYSTEMS:
SETS
RELATIONS
OPERATIONS
USES**

4. How do such uses of whole numbers differ from counting uses?

5. Can you imagine a situation where strict adherence to numerical order might *not* be warranted in dispensing some service?

1.2.4
**Whole
Number Lines**
In planning a journey, you might use a turnpike map like this one.[5]

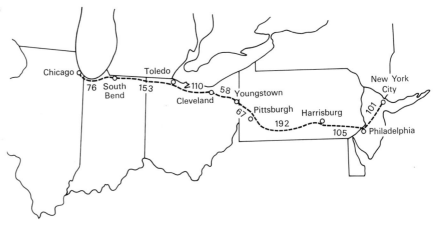

Such a map is a model of your route. It shows some features of your trip and omits others. It is much simpler to study than a movie of the route itself, and for this reason it can be useful in planning a trip. Suppose you were interested in only the distances between cities. This is a mathematical feature; it can be measured. A simple mathematical model of the map of the turnpike route looks like this.

---

[5] This example is adopted from R. Bargen et al., *Algebra I*, Chicago Mathematics Curriculum Project, University of Chicago Laboratory Schools, Multilith, 1970, unit 1, p. 10.

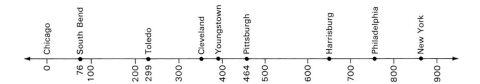

Such a model is called a "number line"; the point labeled 0 is called the "origin."

1. What characteristics are included in the mathematical model but not the map?

2. What characteristics are omitted from the mathematical model that are included on the map?

3. For what practical problems would you find the mathematical model useful?

*4. Try to think of problems that you might encounter in traveling the turnpike for which the mathematical model would *not* be useful?

5. Study the number line above. Numbers have been placed below the names "Chicago," "South Bend," "Toledo," and "Pittsburgh." Why is 229 associated with Toledo? Write an appropriate number below each of the other city names on the number line.

6. List several other uses of number lines, perhaps with both whole numbers and other points marked.[3]

1.2.5
Whole Numbers for Identification or Coding

We generally think of numbers in connection with "counts" or "measures," but whole numbers are also very widely used in indexing, or in various sorts of codes in identifying people or things. Here are some examples and some questions to go with them.

1. List ways that identify you by whole number codes. (Some examples are social security numbers, driver's license numbers, and credit cards.)

2. a. Years ago telephone numbers had just as many digits as were necessary in a local situation. For example, a 3-digit number might do nicely for a small town, while a 6- or 7-digit number might be necessary for a large city. Large city telephone numbers were frequently a combination of letters and numbers, for example, BU 1-2345, with the letters often abbreviations for neighborhoods in the city. Recently telephone companies throughout the United States agreed to assign 7 digits to all local exchange telephone numbers, doing away with letter designations and considerations of the size of town where a phone is located. What are some of the reasons that might have prompted such a decision?

---

[3] Rulers and thermometers are, in effect, number lines.

b. Actually telephone numbers are now identified by a 10-digit code, with the first 3 digits being the "area code." Make some conjectures about the way area codes were assigned. If possible, check the conjectures with a telephone official.

c. For the 7 digits following the area code, what is the largest possible number of telephones that can be included within an area served by one area code?[4]

*d. Actually local telephone numbers never have 0 or 1 as their first two digits. How does this fact change the number of telephones that can be accommodated by 7 digits?[5]

e. Area codes use 0 or 1 as the second digit. Local numbers do not. This is done so that the machinery can detect when an area-code number is being dialed. The first digit is never 0 or 1 and the third never 0 except for the toll-free 800 code. What is the largest possible number of such area codes that telephone companies can assign?

*f. In theory, can more telephones be accommodated by using such a 3-digit area code followed by a 7-digit number or by simply assigning anyone who has a telephone a 10-digit telephone number?

3. Using a United States map that shows the interstate highway systems and the older national highway system, study the numbers on interstate highways and determine whether any particular principles have been used in assigning numbers. For example, is there any signifi-

---

[4] From 0000000 to 9,999,999 is 10 million numbers. Another way to look at this is to observe that there are 10 choices for digits in each place, so that the number of possibilities would be $10 \times 10 \times 10 \times 10 \times 10 \times 10 \times 10 = 10^7 = 10,000,000$ possibilities.

[5] Using the second line of reasoning in footnote 4 and with only eight possibilities in each of the first two places, there are $8 \times 8 \times 10 \times 10 \times 10 \times 10 \times 10$ or 6,400,000 possibilities.

14 NUMBER
SYSTEMS:
SETS
RELATIONS
OPERATIONS
USES

cance to even and odd numbers? To 3-digit versus 2-digit numbers? To the relative sizes of the numbers? Now study the numbers assigned to the older United States highway network and answer similar questions. Try to verify your conclusions from some outside source.

1.2.6
Summary

The purpose of this section has been to sensitize you to the many ways in which whole numbers play a part in the common life of people. The possibilities have certainly not been exhausted and you should continue to be alert to various uses of numbers. Keeping a file of number uses, especially those that are new to you or novel in some way, would be a useful exercise for this course and for your later teaching.

In working through the exercises of this section you have no doubt seen uses of numbers other than whole numbers. Keep track of these for reference in some of the units that follow this one.

1.3
**ACTIVITY:
BASIC SET IDEAS**

Overview: **We will use only very simple set ideas in these early chapters, but the minimum vocabulary and notation outlined below will be used from time to time. The exercises here will enable you to assure yourself that you understand these basic ideas and the notation used.**

Materials needed: An ordinary 52-card deck of playing cards.

Ideas about sets (collections, groups) are pretty basic in mathematics and children's earliest experiences with "number" probably grow out of experience with various sets of objects. We use set ideas quite informally in the early part of this book but some minimum understanding of set ideas and notation is a helpful tool. A few such ideas are outlined in this section: *set, set membership, union, intersection,* and *count of a set.* Part C, Unit 1, deals in more detail with sets and the algebra of sets.

1. Consider these explanations:

Set: A set is well defined provided there is some way of deciding for *any* given thing whether or not it belongs to the set. A set can be specified by listing its membership within braces or by providing a clear enough description. Thus {Bell, Fuson, Lesh}, {1, 2, 3, 4, 5, 6}, and "The set of Justices of the United States Supreme Court" all designate sets.

Set Membership: One often designates a set by giving it a capital letter name, and designates set membership with the Greek letter epsilon (ϵ). Thus if $A = \{$a, e, i, o, u, y$\}$ (the set of vowels in the English alphabet), then we can also write a ϵ A, e ϵ A, etc., to say that "a is an element of the set A," "e is an element of the set A," and so on.

Empty Set: It is easy to give clear descriptions of sets that have no members; for example, the set of purple cows or the set of real live unicorns. Whenever this happens we have the empty set, which is symbolized either by empty braces, { }, or by a zero with a slash through it, $\emptyset$.

With a playing card deck, form each of the following sets (if possible) by pulling out and displaying the appropriate cards. If the set is not well defined, say so; if it is empty, say so. Check your responses with others in your class or group.

$E = \{$entire deck$\}$
$R = \{$red cards$\}$
$B = \{$black cards$\}$
$H = \{$hearts$\}$
$D = \{$diamonds$\}$
$F = \{$face cards$\}$
$X = \{$one-eyed face cards$\}$
$L = \{$lucky cards$\}$
$Q = \{$queens$\}$
$J = \{$happy kings$\}$
$S = \{$smiling queens$\}$
$T = \{$cards with values less than 5$\}$ (Ace counts 1.)
$Y = \{$black hearts$\}$

2. Just as addition of two numbers gives a third number, there are operations on two sets that give new sets:

The *union of two sets* A and C (written as $A \cup C$) is a new set containing the combined membership of those two sets. That is, whatever is in *either* of the two sets is in the union. For example,

$$\text{if } A = \{0, 1, 2, 3, 4\}$$
$$\text{and } C = \{3, 4, 5, 6\}$$
$$\text{then } A \cup C = \{0, 1, 2, 3, 4, 5, 6\}$$

16 NUMBER
SYSTEMS:
SETS
RELATIONS
OPERATIONS
USES

Notice that overlapping membership is listed only once in the union.

The *Intersection of two sets A and C* (written as $A \cap C$) is a new set containing only the overlapping membership of those two sets. That is, for the two sets listed above, only elements that are in *both* sets are in the intersection.

$A \cap C = \{3, 4\}$

Using the sets of playing cards from above, complete each of the following statements either by the letter name of a set (for example, $R \cup B = E$) or by a listing of elements (for example, $H \cap T = \{ace,$ two, three, four of hearts$\}$) or by a description (for example, $H \cup B =$ all cards except the diamonds).

a. $H \cup D =$

b. $F \cap X =$

c. $H \cup R =$

d. $B \cup D =$

e. $H \cap B =$

f. $Q \cap X =$

3. The *count of a set* is simply the number of distinct objects included within the set. The notation used for the count of set A is $n(A)$.

Considering the sets formed in 1 and 2 above, complete each of the following (the first three are done for you).

a. $n(E) = 52$

b. $n(R \cup B) = 52$

c. $n(R \cap B) = 0$

d. $n(H \cup D) =$

e. $n(E \cap B) =$

f. $n(Q \cap X) =$

g. $n(X) =$

h. $n(T) =$

1.4
ACTIVITY: RELATIONS
FOR WHOLE NUMBERS:
"IS EQUAL TO," "IS LESS
THAN," "IS GREATER THAN"

Overview: You are asked to think about ways of dealing with "is equal to," "is less than," and "is greater than" with respect to sets of objects and without counting. The same relations with respect to measures are explored briefly. Some general properties of these relations are listed in symbolic form and you are asked to act out their meaning with chips and rods.

Materials needed: Chips, rods.

Basic notions about relations between two counting numbers probably come from experience with finite sets. If the elements of two sets are paired off one by one and they "come out even," then the sets are "the

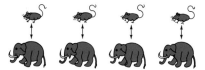

same size," even if we are comparing a set of mice and a set of elephants. In that case, we say that they are "matched sets."

If set *A* runs out of elements before set *B*, we say that *A is less than B* or, equivalently, that *B is greater than A*. Such one-to-one pairings can take place without attaching any counts to the sets.

In a similar vein, it is often possible to determine "is equal to," "is less than," or "is more than" with respect to measures by some sort of direct comparison independent of numbers. For example, youngsters might decide who is the tallest, or who has the longest stick of candy or the most root beer, by direct comparison.

Eventually, counts are assigned to sets and this experience carries over to relations between counting numbers, as follows. If for any two finite sets *A* and *B,* counts are assigned so that $n(A) = a$ and $n(B) = b$, then one of three things happens[6]:

1. In the one-to-one pairing of elements, set *A* matches set *B*. In that case, $n(A) = n(B)$, or in other words, $a = b$.

2. In the pairing, set *A* is less than set *B*. In that case, $n(A) < n(B)$ or $a < b$.[7]

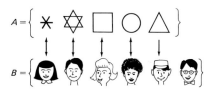

---

[6] The "count" of the empty set is zero.

[7] Note that the shape of the "is less than" symbol ($<$) suggests which number is smallest — the point of the symbol is by the smaller number, the open part by the larger. Observe that this also holds for the "is greater than" symbol ($>$).

18 NUMBER
SYSTEMS:
SETS
RELATIONS
OPERATIONS
USES

3. In the pairing, set A is greater than set B. In that case, $n(A) > n(B)$ or $a > b$.

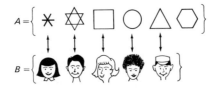

These basic ideas probably developed in you so naturally and so long ago that you have forgotten how they developed. The exercises in section 1.4.1 are intended to remind you what that process of development might have been.

1.4.1
Learning to Count

These exercises are optional and are best done outside class.

1. Try to work individually for a few minutes with each of several young children. Have each count aloud for you as far as he can go (or until it is clear that he can go further than you want to listen to). Have each count sets of objects. With younger children there is often little relation between the set and the counting; objects may be skipped or counted more than once, etc. Make notes on this experience and share findings with your colleagues.

2. For many children, counting may be only a memorized ritual so that "one, two, three, . . . ," is the "right" way to count for much the same reasons as "A, B, C, D, . . . , Z" is the "right" way to say the alphabet. A child may only be able to answer "What comes after seven?" by counting from one through eight, just as many people can answer "What comes after the letter N?" only by reciting part or all of the alphabet. Check this out with a few children.

*3. In what ways do numerical "order" and alphabetical "order" differ from each other? In what ways are they the same?

4. Watch several "Sesame Street" television programs and pay special attention to the number skits. Write a critical review of the number work, perhaps considering such questions as the following: Exactly what ideas about counting numbers do these skits aim to convey? What misconceptions, if any, are possibly conveyed? Consider that similar skits are played on each program; taken as a whole, do they convey all that needs to be said to young children about counting numbers (short of operations such as addition and multiplication)? If not, what important ideas are left untouched? On the whole, would you rather your children watch the number parts of the program or not? Why? How would you improve the treatment of numbers if you were hired as a consultant?

**1.4.2
Comparing Sets
Without Counting[6]**

Sometimes the subtle underlying mathematical issues in something already very familiar can be retrieved by pretending to be a smart child or a member of a prenumber society who has not learned as much as you "know." Such simulation is sometimes difficult to get into, both because of reluctance of adults to play such games and because of questions about how much to assume—how far back to go. Still, we suggest occasionally that you do such pretending, without giving you exact guidance about it. We rely on your common sense to find the appropriate level of pretense. For the exercises below, pretend you do not know

[6] Some of these problems are adapted from M. S. Bell, et al., *A Brief Course in Mathematics for Elementary School Teachers,* School Mathematics Study Group, Stanford California, 1963, p. 3.

20 NUMBER
SYSTEMS:
SETS
RELATIONS
OPERATIONS
USES

how to count, then using poker chips, bottle caps, or other counters to represent candies, people, goats, etc., act out the situations. As you do these exercises, consider how ideas about *equal, more,* and *less* may develop in young children. These exercises will probably work best if you do them with one or several of your colleagues.

1. Grab a handful of chips, then a second handful. Which hand has more?

2. You and a friend each have a handful of candies. How can you find out who has more and then fix it so that you and your friend share equally?

3. Suppose you are interested in finding out whether there are more 6-year-olds than 7-year-olds in a large room. What might you do?

4. There are two pastures of cattle separated by a river. The two herdsmen want to know which has more cattle. They have a raft which will transport one of them but will not transport the animals. What might they do?

5. You own a set of tools that is so large that you cannot remember all that are in the set. Try to devise a scheme by which you can keep track of each tool. Could you solve this problem differently if you had

number symbols to work with? If so, would the number solution be any improvement on the one without numbers?[8]

6. You have as many textbooks as there are desks in your schoolroom. The principal of the school notifies you that there will be as many children in your class as there are desks. What conclusions can you make concerning textbooks, desks, and children?

7. You have a friend who speaks no English and you do not speak his language. How can you use sets to convey to him the idea of the number five?

1.4.3
Comparing
Measures

1. The need to *measure* generates as many uses of numbers as does the need to *count*. Of the many sorts of measure (length, area, etc.) this book relies primarily on embodiments[7] of length, especially on colored

---

[7] The term "embodiment" is discussed in the Introduction to this book. In brief, it means concrete materials used in such a way as to represent in actions mathematical concepts or abstractions. For example, numbers are abstract but can be "embodied" or made concrete by appropriate sets of counters or by sticks of given lengths in terms of an agreed-on unit length. The abstract operation of adding two numbers can be embodied by combining appropriate sets of counters or placing two appropriate sticks end to end.

[8] A system actually used in many toolrooms is to paint the outline of each tool on the board where the tools are hung up. It is immediately obvious at the end of the day what tools are missing. Many systems using numbers could be devised; for example, numbering each tool and then turning over a correspondingly numbered tag whenever that tool is taken out.

rods.[8] If you haven't worked with such materials, you should take some time before you work the exercises below to engage in "free play" with the materials. (Build towers; make designs; see what relationships you, as an adult, notice.) Essentially everyone who advocates using such materials insists that such unstructured play with the materials is necessary for children before putting them to specific tasks, and it is probably equally necessary for adults unfamiliar with them.

2. It is sometimes possible to establish measure relations such as "is equal to" or "is less than" by direct comparison, without the intervention of numbers. Rods are a measure embodiment and most programs that use them prescribe considerable prenumber work with them, exploiting a *code* for the colors such as the one below, which can be used for rods produced by several companies. (If you are using rods with other colors, replace this code by an appropriate one.) Keep before you the code and a "stairway" of the rods arranged in order as you do the exercises. Notice that the code is sometimes the first and sometimes the last letter that names the color.

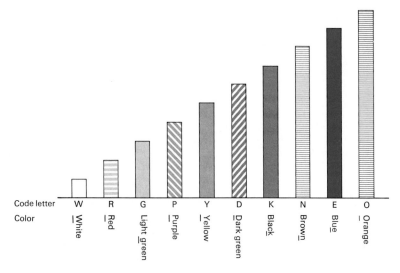

| Code letter | W | R | G | P | Y | D | K | N | E | O |
| Color | White | Red | Light green | Purple | Yellow | Dark green | Black | Brown | Blue | Orange |

Use the rods and code to illustrate the following *equations* and *inequalities* and record your results. In each case, you are looking for

---

8   Sets of rods in graduated lengths (usually from a unit length up to 10 times that length) with each length a different color are available from several sources and are a widely used teaching aid. Commercially produced versions made of wood and brightly colored are nice to use, but much cheaper and quite satisfactory versions are available in cardboard or can be homemade. See Appendix I for suggestions.

what will give a "true" result if put in the boxes. The main rule is that in a given expression the same thing must go in each similarly shaped box; if there are two kinds of boxes they may or may not have the same thing in them. As you act these out, try to assess what the value of similar work (with rods and codes rather than numbers) might be for children, and discuss this with your colleagues. (If there is more than one correct answer, list all the possibilities.)

a. $\square < Y$

b. $R + Y = \square$

c. $\triangle + \triangle + \triangle = D$

d. $K + \square = 0$

e. $G > \square$

*f. $0 < \square$

*g. $\triangle + \square = K$

3. When working with chips, a single chip counts as the unit; that is, as 1. In number work with the rods, the unit must be assigned. When using a set of rods such as illustrated above, the white rod is usually designated as this unit length and in this case red is 2, purple is 4, and so on. A red rod could be designated as the unit length, and in that case white would be ½ and purple would be 2. For the following problems first use counts with chips and then use rods, with white considered as the unit to "solve" each equation. Note any differences you see in solving these by "counts" and by "measures" and compare your notes with those of your colleagues.

a. $3 + 4 = \square$

b. $6 + \square = 10$

c. $3 \times 3 = \square$

d. $7 - 3 = \square$

*e. $8 \div 4 = \square$

24 NUMBER
SYSTEMS:
SETS
RELATIONS
OPERATIONS
USES

*1.4.4
Properties
of Relations

There is nothing surprising about the properties that follow, and with your long experience with numbers they may seem trivial. This is fair enough and if they are very familiar to you, so much the better. However, one important stage in the learning of mathematics is eventually stating properties in more or less abstract language and studying their applicability over a variety of situations.

In order to indicate that properties hold for *any* whole numbers, they are stated using letters such as *a, b, c, . . .* , or "frames" such as □, ○, ◇, . . . , that can be replaced by any whole numbers that fit the statement.

Some of the properties that follow are not trivial for young children, and so it is worth thinking about how they develop as concepts. Some that seem "obvious" with whole numbers are less so for negative numbers and for fractions. In any case, do two things both individually and in group discussion for each of the following "properties": (1) Try to add examples of common life situations where these properties are used, and (2) act out a few illustrative examples with rods and a few with chips.

1. *Symmetric property of "is equal to": For any whole numbers a and b, if a = b then b = a.* This really is "obvious"—so much so that it is hard to act out—but the fact remains that many people do not exploit this reversability. For example, everyone knows that $2 + 2 = 4$ but few think of breaking 4 down into $2 + 2$. Many people who can reduce ²/₄ to get ½ still don't see that in a given situation ½ might be profitably changed to ²/₄. In an algebra problem like $7 = x + 3$, many people go to some trouble to get the *x* on the left side because $x = 4$ looks OK to them, while $4 = x$ is somehow "wrong."

2. *Transitive property of "is equal to": For any whole numbers a, b, or c, if a = b and b = c, then* _____.[9] (Finish the statement.) For example, if James is exactly as tall as Mary, and Mary is exactly as tall as Richard, then we know without measuring that James is exactly as tall as Richard. Try to think of some other instances of this transitive property.

3. *Addition property of "is equal to": For any whole numbers a, b, and c, if a = b then a + c = b + c.* A common image here is to think of a balance scale in balance; if something additional is put on one side then exactly that same amount is needed on the other side to bring things back into balance. An example familiar to parents or teachers of young children is the action of giving two children some root beer carefully measured out so that each has the same amount. If more is

[9] $a = c.$

then poured in one glass, there may be a demand to put the same amount in the other glass; otherwise it's "not fair!"

4. *Additive cancellation property of "is equal to": For any whole numbers a, b, and c, if $a + c = b + c$, then $a = b$.*[9] For example, if each of two youngsters has $4 + 3$ candies and they both gobble up 3 candies, each still has the same amount. (In this example, 4 replaces a and b, and 3 replaces c in the statement of the property.) Try to imagine at least one more such common life situation and write it in the space below. The main mathematical use of this property is in solving equations that have been set up as mathematical models of problem situations. For example, if $x + 3 = 10$ and this is thought of as the equivalent $x + 3 = 7 + 3$, then we know that $x = 7$ says the same thing.

5. *A definition of "is less than": For any whole numbers a and b, $a < b$ provided that for some whole number c other than zero, $a + c = b$.* For example, we know for sure that $4 < 7$ because we need to add 3 to 4 in order to have 7; or in the words of this property, $4 < 7$ because there is a whole number, 3, such that $4 + 3 = 7$. (Here 4 replaces a, 7 replaces b, and 3 replaces c in the definition.)

Act out with chips and rods the following situations and find what number c is needed to fit the definition.

a. Is it true that $3 < 6$? If so, what is c? _____

b. Is it true that $7 < 10$? If so, what is c? _____

c. Is it true that $7 < 7$? If so, what is c? _____

d. Is it true that $7 < 5$? If so, what is c? _____

6. *Transitive property of "is less than": For any whole numbers a, b, and c, if $a < b$ and $b < c$, then $a < c$.* A mistaken argument similar to this property that is often used in common life goes like this:

---

[9] This is the converse proposition for that stated in property 3; that is, the "if" phrase and the "then" phrase have been reversed. A converse to a true statement may or may not be true. An example of a converse that is *not* true would be the converse to "If I stand in the rain, then I get wet." (State the converse and you will see that it isn't necessarily true.)

26 NUMBER
SYSTEMS:
SETS
RELATIONS
OPERATIONS
USES

"Snead got a lower score than Palmer in Los Angeles, and Palmer got a lower score than Nicklaus in Las Vegas. Therefore, Snead is sure to get a lower score than Nicklaus in Chicago." Such a chain of events might make you more willing to bet on Nicklaus, but would be far from a guarantee that you would win the bet. A valid use of the property would require numbers all in the same context. Think of an example of a valid use of the property from common life, and write it below.

7. *Addition property of "is less than": For any whole numbers a, b, and c if a < b then a + c < b + c.* (Example: If you have more money than I and if we both earn $10, you still have more than I.) Find at least one more example and write it below.

8. *The converse of property 7 above: For any whole numbers a, b, and c, if a + c < b + c, then a < c.* This is a sort of "additive cancellation property" for "is less than" and it happens to be true. Convince yourself of the truth of the statement by either trying some numbers in place of letters or acting out some situations with chips or rods. Find a common situation that illustrates this property and write it below.

9. *"Is less than" on a number line: Once a number line is started and the "positive" direction established, then a < b if b is "farther out" in the positive direction on the number line than a.* Several possible

whole number lines are indicated below. See how properties 6 and 7 would be interpreted on a number line and discuss this with your colleagues.

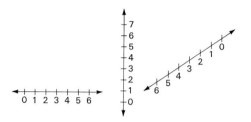

10. *We know for sure that for any two whole numbers a and b, if a is greater than b, then b is less than a.* (Got that?) How could this be used to save us the trouble of stating properties for the "is greater than" relation?

1.5
**SUMMARY AND
PEDAGOGICAL REMARKS**

This unit has considered some whole number ideas that precede consideration of such operations as addition, subtraction, multiplication, and division. An effort was made to consider a variety of uses of whole numbers; to consider some preliminary ideas about sets; to consider how sets might be related to whole number concepts; and to discuss the usual relations between pairs of whole numbers (equals, less than, greater than).

From their early life experience children somehow give meaning to thousands of spoken sounds such as "yes," "red," "egg," "big," and "love." In school (or sometimes before) they attach these sounds to printed words, and hence printed words become associated both with actual objects and with more abstract ideas. How all that happens is clearly too complicated to go into here, but it is probable that much the same sort of process also gives meaning to verbal counting-number names (one, two, three, and so on), then to the symbols for counting numbers, and in the fullness of time to words and symbols for zero, fractions, decimals, and negative numbers.

The historical development of numbers as tools for mankind appears to have at least a superficial resemblance to the development of number ideas in children. All human societies have invented counting systems. In the beginning, number words may be closely associated with particular things and many words survive in various languages showing this at-

28 NUMBER
SYSTEMS:
SETS
RELATIONS
OPERATIONS
USES

tachment to specific sets; for example, *Brace, span, yoke,* and *pair* as names for various sets of two things.[10] The great discovery in the development of number systems is the recognition of "twoness" as a common property of all such sets, "threeness" as a property of another collection of sets, and so on. Having invented specific words to express the numerousness of such relatively small sets, counting systems develop that use the smaller numbers in some patterns to count and record larger numbers (e.g., "sixty" for "six tens"). That is, *immediate* perception of exactly "how many" is not possible for larger sets, but the faith persists that every set has some unchanging count and ways to attach a count are found.[11]

Both in the historical development of counting systems and in young children, development of counting numbers seems to be intimately connected with experience with finite sets of things. Some mathematician-philosophers express this connection by saying that the number 2 somehow *is* a certain collection of sets, 3 *is* another collection of sets, and so on. With a subtle change of emphasis, others prefer to say that 2 is a property shared by each set in a certain collection of sets that otherwise might have little or nothing in common, 3 is a property common to each set in another collection of sets, and so on.

Children frequently can count to five or ten and sometimes beyond before the number words have much meaning; that is, the words are not attached to anything in particular. Many counting nursery rhymes reflect this. (Do you know any such rhymes?) At some point the counting words begin to get attached to sets as the child points to each object in turn and says, for example, "One, two, three, four, five; there are five pennies!" In doing this a child may make mistakes by skipping objects, counting some twice, or in other ways failing to suit the action to the words. In any case, awareness that many sets have *threeness* or *fiveness* as a property, as opposed to counting any particular set, probably comes still later in a child's number development. Willingness and ability to work with number symbols as things in themselves come still later.

All this merely indicates that even "simple" and "obvious" things are

---

[10] In all languages there are names of specific groups of animals or other things that do not suggest any particular number of things. A charming book by J. Lipton called *An Exaltation of Larks* gives several hundred of these along with many of their derivations. Some are well known—school of fish, bevy of beauties, and pride of lions. There are also many that are less well known—murder of crows, skulk of foxes, drift of hogs, gaggle of geese (on water), and skein of geese (in flight). (See Appendix II for reference.)

[11] Immediate perception of the "numerousness" of a set is limited to small sets. For example, for sets larger than six or so, few people can *immediately* attach the correct number without some counting. If the objects are patterned so that smaller sets can be recognized within the larger set, the immediate perception appears to extend to larger sets.

probably more complex than we often realize. The development of number concepts has been the subject of considerable inquiry. Our personal favorite theories are those of Jean Piaget and others associated with him, but respectable non-Piagetian theories also exist.[12]

Because the origins of number ideas are so closely tied to experience with sets and because the use of sets is a pervasive theme in many areas of basic and advanced mathematics, most recently published school books make some fuss about sets as such. Any treatment that goes beyond quite informal use of set ideas and language can get out of hand, especially if the special vocabulary and symbolism are stressed as things to be learned in themselves. In this unit we included an outline of some of the rock-bottom ideas of sets and a bit of symbolism; however, we advise caution and good judgment in deciding how much explicit teaching about sets as such is appropriate in early school learning. We also advise making sure that any such early work is closely tied to sets of actual things.

Just as *red* is an abstract property expressed in a variety of ways[13] a number such as 2 is expressed in a variety of symbolic ways, for example II, 2, $1 + 1$, $4/2$, $105 - 103$, $\sqrt{4}$, $-(-2)$, and so on. That is, there is a distinction to be made between *numbers* as abstract properties and *numerals* as names or symbols used to express those properties. (The distinction between actual things and names for those things is an important one in language generally, of course, not merely in mathematics.) It may be worth observing the number-numeral distinction with youngsters

$$2 = 1 + 1 = 2 + 0 = \frac{4}{2} = 2 \times 1 = \frac{8}{2} - 2 = \frac{1}{2} \times 4$$

by way of such exercises as "List a lot of names for the number 2" or "Which is bigger, 4 or 7?" or "Make an 8 out of two zeros" (answer: 8). As with many other things, what is worth noting in a lighthearted way as a matter of interest may not be worth running into the ground with insistence on day-to-day consistency in usage. In any case, to be consistent all the time in the "proper" use of *number* and *numeral* is difficult, and we don't claim even to have tried in this book.

It is important to sensitize children so that they will *notice* the pervasive use of numbers in their environment, even if at a given time they don't fully understand all the uses. Parents and others help young children notice counting, but measuring as a use of numbers gets less attention, and the uses of numbers as coordinates, addresses, codes, identification numbers, and in other ways suggested by the examples in this

---

[12] Several of the references in Appendix II discuss such inquiries. At least one author, Copeland, has undertaken an attempt to sort out the pedagogical implications of Piaget's research.

[13] *Red* as a word is *rouge, rojo, rosso,* and *rot* in French, Spanish, Italian, and German, respectively; to a physicist it is a certain range of frequencies in the electromagnetic spectrum; and so on.

30 NUMBER
SYSTEMS:
SETS
RELATIONS
OPERATIONS
USES

unit get little attention in most early schoolwork. This sensitization to numbers should be done gently. It would be easy to overdo an insistence on categorizing various uses of numbers—counts, measures, ordering, codes, and so on—if only because uses sometime overlap and assigning them to specific categories would be difficult.

There is a genuine distinction to be made between whole numbers used as *cardinal numbers,* to designate counts of sets, and whole numbers used as *ordinal numbers,* to designate relative order in a sequence. Number words sometimes suggest the difference: "one of," "two of," "three of," etc., for cardinal number uses versus "first," "second," "third," etc., for ordinal number uses. There are many applications of the ordinal use of numbers, but here again there are ambiguities and it may not be worthwhile to insist that children make such distinctions. For example, one can regard a number line marked with whole numbers as indicating a series of lengths, hence tied to measures; or as imposing a certain order; or as an aid to counting by hopping along in one-unit steps.

It must be said that it is possible to use manipulative materials in ways that are just as stereotyped and devoid of meaning as are many purely symbolic drill and skill procedures. For example, some children supposedly using rods with the letter codes talked of earlier in this chapter have in effect learned an operation code or table for the code letters themselves, so that $R + R = P$ is a memorized response that has nothing to do with making a train of two red rods and finding that the total length is the same as that of a purple rod, just as $2 + 2 = 4$ can be completely without meaning. There are, in other words, no panaceas; one can only keep working in as nice a variety of sensible ways as possible to try to give real meaning to the mathematics learning experience.

In clipping examples of uses of whole numbers from newspapers and other sources to use in this unit, we were impressed with how often such whole numbers as 2 billion, 12 million, and 80 billion were used. It may well be that the language of informed citizenship is largely in such terms, with millions and billions the modern "units" that must then be related to everyday quantities such as merely thousands or tens of thousands. If that is so, there are educational tasks that we have scarcely even thought about in giving meaning to such units and in helping people understand and evaluate the decisions that are made in terms of them. We were also impressed, by the way, with how frequently these same news stories used percents. Though more has been done in schools with percents than with millions and billions, it is still unlikely that the average citizen has the facility with them that the news stories would so often demand.

It is certainly true that children develop number ideas at very different rates with respect to each other, and in sometimes zigzag ways for each individual, though a general sequence and trend may be identifiable "on the average" for large groups of children. It may be that things that are important and well understood at earlier ages get displaced and forgotten later, even though they are still important. For example, for preschool and early school children the direct attachment of counts to particular sets of things may be strong—each number is an adjective describing something. The child may then learn the symbols (numerals) for those numbers and learn that the symbols can be manipulated abstractly to give answers, without reference to particular sets of objects. The number may then become a thing in itself. For efficiency this is very useful, but many children somehow lose the links between the real situation and the symbols, and hence are blocked whenever any particular "number fact" or symbolic procedure is forgotten. The trick is probably to keep children able to regard numbers both ways—as descriptions or mathematical models[14] for common life events, and as things amenable to efficient manipulation in their own right. The ideal to aim for is children who can operate comfortably in both the common world and the mathematical world, and who have many ways of establishing links between the two.

[14] As explained in the introduction to this book, a mathematical model is the mathematical symbolism for the real situation. For example, $2x + 7 = 43$ might be the equation needed to express the relationships in some real world problem. If so, it would be a mathematical model of that situation.

unit 2
addition of whole numbers

2.1
INTRODUCTION The next few units will take you through a rather comprehensive analysis of the basic meaning and properties of the various operations with pairs of whole numbers: addition, multiplication, subtraction, division. You can approach this analysis from either of two points of view, or perhaps a mixture of the two. If you know all this material well (in your bones!), play the role of a child who is encountering it for the first time and try to imagine how it feels to come to terms with the meanings and complexities of the whole number operations. If you are somewhat unsure about some parts of this material, these exercises will give you a fresh chance to rebuild your understanding and confidence. In either case act out things whenever possible with the chips, rods, and other embodiments of concepts that the exercises suggest. As you do this, try to put aside your skills with symbol manipulation and instead construct these ideas as nearly as possible from scratch. That is, try *not* to use what you already know to understand the manipulative materials. Your own knowledge will unavoidably get in the way sometimes. Many teacher trainees have remarked that children seem to understand and cope with experiences using embodiments more easily than teachers do. Perhaps this is because children do not need to make the experience fit

32

preconceived notions, which are not always correct, as adults try to do.[1] Once you have tried to come to terms simply with the manipulation of materials, the next step is to be more "intellectual" and "analytical" in summarizing in symbolic ways the concepts and structures that have been embodied using concrete materials.

Remember that this is a course for adults. The issues confronted are those with which children eventually must cope and the materials used are suggestive of some of those appropriately used in teaching children. However, you are going through things much more rapidly than most children could be expected to, and in abbreviated form. You are also moving to consideration of symbolic and abstract issues more quickly and in more depth than would usually be the case with children.

For yourself and for the youngsters you teach, the addition operation should be linked to everyday experience and our need to keep track of things around us. If the *addends* come from counting sets of objects, the *sum* gives the count of the *union* of these sets. If the addends are measures, the sum gives the total measure of combined quantities.

2.2
ACTIVITY: THE
MEANING OF ADDITION
OF WHOLE NUMBERS

Overview: Since addition is needed both in combining counts and in combining measures, addition problems will be acted out using both count and measure embodiments. Addition on the number line is also considered.

Materials needed: Chips, rods, ruler marked in centimeters, two strips of poster board or folded paper about 1 by 11 inches (or about 3 by 25 centimeters).

2.2.1
Addition of
Whole Number Counts

1. Try to record some recent instances in which you have made use of addition of whole numbers. If you are working in a group, share some of these instances and have the group as a whole record about six such uses.

---

[1] Those familiar with Piaget's writings will recognize that you are being asked to pretend that you are at either the late preoperations or at the concrete operations stage while acting out problems with rods, chips, and number lines. You should then shift your thinking to something like Piaget's symbolic operations stage in order to analyze the experience and its results. With such role playing we believe adults can sample the various stages in the learning process and perhaps gain more insight not only into the mathematics itself—which is the main aim of this book—but also into the learning of mathematics.

34 NUMBER
SYSTEMS:
SETS
RELATIONS
OPERATIONS
USES

2. There are many problems such as this one: "Amy had 8 gerbils. Then one of the females had a litter of 4. How many gerbils does Amy have now?" The obvious embodiment is to let chips (or any other counters) represent gerbils, count out a set of 8 and another set of 4, push the sets together (form the union), then count the resulting combined set. The process can be diagramed like this:

Real World Situation	Embodiment	Mathematical Model

$$8 + 4 = 12$$

In the mathematical model, the 8 and the 4 are called "addends" and 12 is called the "sum." In set language, if we have two nonoverlapping sets A and B, then $n(A) + n(B) = n(A \cup B)$.

Fill in the blank spaces in the following display with a brief outline of a situation, an equation, or a sketch of the embodiment in chips as appropriate. Act out the situation with actual chips and record the answer. (Additions involving zero require some special adjustments; think of the set of no chips.) The first one is done for you.

Situation from Common Life	Embodiment	Mathematical Model
a. Jamie has 5¢ and Mom gives her 3¢.	○○○○○ ○○○	$5 + 3 = \boxed{8}$
b.	○○○○ ○○ ○○○○ ○○○○	
c.		$3 + 5 = \square$
d.		$13 + 0 = \square$

3. Zero was invented late in history and it may offer special difficulties in learning mathematics. Counting starts with "one" (rather than "zero") because *something* is usually being counted, and yet nearly every situation that counts something invites thinking about what happens if there is nothing instead. Briefly outline situations from common life where zero would be involved in a sum, and indicate ways to make sure it is somehow "visible," even though nothing is there, in the embodiments of those situations with chips.[2]

---

[2] One way this is sometimes done is to put loops of string or yarn around sets of objects. In that case putting a single loop around what had been shown as two sets can indicate the "sum" and an empty loop can embody zero.

2.2.2
Addition of Whole Number Measures Using Rods

Counting situations dominate school instruction, but reality has us operating with measures as often as with counts. For example: "If a pint of milk is poured into a pitcher that already contains 3 cups of milk, how much milk is then in the pitcher?" "How long to supper? Well, I'll need 15 minutes to mix this up, then it must cook 25 minutes. . . ." "Jack is 36 inches tall and Jill 40 inches tall; are both combined taller than their dad, who is 68 inches tall?"[3]

The rods we use to embody measure situations really embody only length, but they still serve quite well to illustrate how measure and count situations differ. For example, to embody $7 + 2 = \Box$, make a "train" by placing the 7-rod and the 2-rod end to end, and then find a rod equivalent to the total train:

9-rod	
7-rod	2-rod

$7 + 2 = 9$

(In some cases, such as $9 + 4 = \Box$, you will need one or more 10-rods and one other rod to find the total measure.)

Zero again poses a special problem because while it is easy to imagine addition situations with one of the measures zero (as in pouring milk into an empty pitcher), it is harder to see how to embody such situations with trains of two rods. One way is to cut 1- by 1-centimeter squares from clear acetate, or simply from paper, and use them on edge in the train; such a "clear rod" adds so little to the length that it can be seen as embodying zero. Its letter code could be C. If you can think of another way to solve this problem, outline it and share it with your colleagues.

1. As before, fill in the display as appropriate by indicating briefly some common life measure situation, diagraming the train of rods that embodies the situation (not necessarily to scale), or writing the appropriate equation. In each case actually act out the solution with rods and fill in the frame in the equation. The first one is done for you.

---

[3] In all these uses the whole is the sum of its parts, but where that isn't true, addition of measures is *not* appropriate. For example, a cup of sugar added to a cup of hot water does *not* make 2 cups of syrup.

36 NUMBER
SYSTEMS:
SETS
RELATIONS
OPERATIONS
USES

Common Life Situation	Embodiment	Mathematical Model
a. Three cups of water poured into an empty bottle	(clear rod)→ 3-rod	$0 + 3 = \boxed{3}$
b.	4-rod 9-rod	
c. Jane needs to buy a board long enough to get a 2-foot and a 4-foot piece from it. . . .		

2.2.3

**Addition of
Whole Number Measures
Using Number Lines**

1. Mark and fold lengthwise a standard sheet of paper (8½ by 11 inches) as shown below to leave a 1-centimeter-wide slot to hold rods.

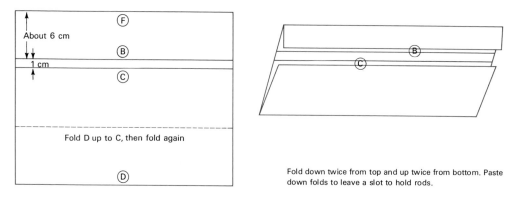

Fold down twice from top and up twice from bottom. Paste down folds to leave a slot to hold rods.

Use a ruler marked with centimeters to mark it from 0 to 25 centimeters. The result should look like this:

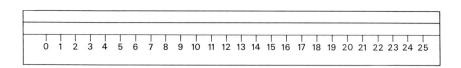

Now, do the problems below, or some of your own invention, by forming trains in the slot starting with zero and reading the "sum" at the other end of the train.

a. $2 + 4 = \square$ **c.** $7 + 6 = \square$

b. $6 + 7 = \square$ **d.** $8 + 0 = \square$

*2. What is the maximum number of rods that could be used to embody problem 1a above? What is the minimum number of rods in a train that shows both addends? Which shows the use of *measures* best (rather than *counts*)?

*3. Strictly speaking, a number on a number line is represented by a *length,* but much schoolwork considers each whole number on the number line as a certain number of "steps" away from zero, which suggests counting in order to get a measure. Which of the possibilities in problem 2 goes with each of these ways of using the number line? Think about ways of emphasizing the measure aspect of number lines.[4]

2.2.4
Counts
or Hops on the
Number Line

Number lines can be used for addition without rods by counting steps or hops. For example, $7 + 8 = \square$ could be found either by starting with zero, counting 7 hops, and then counting 8 more; or simply by starting at 7 and counting 8 hops. (Do it both ways now for $7 + 8 = \square$ on the same number line you made for adding rods.) A hazard is that one must count the *spaces,* not the *points* on the number line; take a moment to see why it might make a difference. (A way to handle that hazard is to make the hops with your pencil or finger and always count while the pencil or finger is in the air.)

1. Do the problems below by hops on the number line.

a. $6 + 3 = \square$ **c.** $13 + 0 = \square$

b. $3 + 6 = \square$ **d.** $5 + 9 = \square$

*2.2.5
Addition with
Slide Rule Made from
Number Lines

1. First make a slide rule: Get two strips of cardboard or poster board about 1 by 11 inches (or fold sheets of paper to make strips of similar dimensions). Put their edges together as shown and mark both at once up to 20 with a ruler that indicates centimeters.

---

[4] One would not necessarily have to abandon counting by steps as one way of doing things; for example, going by "two-steps" to approach the number faster might still keep measure ideas in the picture. Also, one aspect of measure is "how many units" are in the length in question.

38 NUMBER
SYSTEMS:
SETS
RELATIONS
OPERATIONS
USES

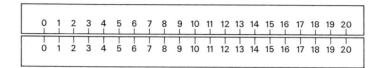

Add two numbers by physically adding lengths; for example, $7 + 4$ is pictured below:

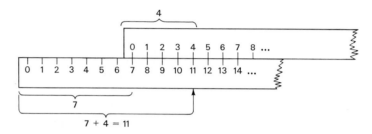

$$7 + 4 = 11$$

2. Use your slide rule to fill in the sums below, and as many more as you care to do.

a. $5 + 8 = \square$ **c.** $15 + 4 = \square$

b. $8 + 5 = \square$ **d.** $8 + 0 = \square$

3. List below some advantages and disadvantages to this embodiment of addition. Talk them over with your colleagues.

Overview: These exercises focus on such properties of whole number addition as closure, uniqueness of sums, equivalence classes of sums, zero as the additive identity, commutative property, associative property, and a "do-as-you-please" property.

Materials needed: Rods, chips.

2.3
ACTIVITY:
PROPERTIES OF ADDITION
OF WHOLE NUMBERS

However "obvious" it might be to you that $7 + 6$ has the same answer no matter who does it or that adding 6 to 7 gives the same result as adding 7 to 6, such things may not be obvious to many first graders (or some older children). Abstraction of such properties and explicit statement of them as applying in general to *all* numbers was a relatively late development in the history of mathematics. Recognition of them as usable general principles also develops rather slowly in children.

The properties of whole number addition that are worked through below have already appeared implicitly in earlier exercises. The idea here is to pull these basic properties together in one place and embody each of them a few more times with concrete materials such as chips and rods.[5]

2.3.1
Closure

An operation with whole numbers is *closed* provided doing that operation with *any* whole numbers *always* leads to a whole number answer. Is addition of whole numbers closed? Is subtraction of whole numbers closed?[1]

2.3.2
Uniqueness
of Sums; equivalence
classes of sums

1. Closure tells us that addition of whole numbers gives a whole number sum, but it is still not stated for sure that a given addition could not lead to, say, a different answer on Sundays than on the other days of the week. An operation gives "unique" results if this doesn't happen; for example, $113 + 93$ gives the same result (if correctly done) no matter how, when, where, or by whom it is done. Does addition of whole numbers give unique results? Does subtraction of two whole numbers give a unique whole number if it gives one at all?[2]

2. On the other hand, the same whole number might be the sum, from several different addition problems. For example, pick out a 10-rod (it would be orange in the usual rod set, but make appropriate adjustments here and below if you have different colors in your set). See how many different trains using exactly two rods (including the zero or clear rod) you can make that will be exactly equal in length to the 10-rod. Complete the list below. (There is no help for the fact that O as a code for the orange rod looks like 0 as the whole number zero.)

[5] It may be useful to repeat previous reminders: Though it is useful for you as an adult to work with number system properties and structures stated in general and symbolic ways, we do *not* necessarily regard the same sort of activity as appropriate for young children.

[1] Addition of whole numbers is closed, but it is easy to write a problem involving subtraction of whole numbers that does not have a whole number answer: for example, $10 - 13 = \square$ or $1 - 3 = \square$. Hence subtraction of whole numbers is *not* closed.

[2] The answer is "yes" in both cases.

40 NUMBER
SYSTEMS:
SETS
RELATIONS
OPERATIONS
USES

Rod Equation	Number Equation
Y + Y = O	5 + 5 = 10
R + B = O	2 + 8 = 10
B + R = O	8 + 2 = 10
O + null rod = O	10 + 0 = 10

3. In any situation such as the one in exercise 2, where a number of things that look different come down to essentially the same thing, you very likely have what is called an "equivalence class." In the case above there are many different ways of expressing the number 10, and any of these could be used in place of any other. This sort of thing is very useful in mathematics. You may not have thought of it in connection with addition of whole numbers, but you are probably familiar with the same sort of thing in fractions where, for example, $\frac{2}{4}$, $\frac{3}{6}$, $\frac{4}{8}$, and many other fractions can be used instead of $\frac{1}{2}$ as the occasion demands.

   a. Count out a set of 13 chips and systematically separate this set into two sets as many times as necessary (including a set of 13 chips and the empty set) to get all the addition problems for which 13 is the answer. Record your results by completing the following list:

$$13 + 0 = 13$$
$$0 + 13 = 13$$
$$12 + 1 = 13$$

b. In some children's games the total number of children playing remains the same but the number on each of two teams keeps shifting back and forth; indicate briefly the name or rules of any such games you know and share this with colleagues. (If the total number of children playing were 13, the list you made in exercise 2 would, of course, contain all possible moment-to-moment outcomes of such a game.)

*c. How many examples did you get in exercise 2? How many for the addition combinations of 10? How many would you get for 6? Can you find a general way to predict how many such examples will result for any given whole number? [For such a problem it helps some people to think of pairs of numbers instead of equations. For example, (1, 5), (2, 4), (3, 3), (4, 2), and so on are pairs of numbers that add up to 6.]

2.3.3
Zero as the Identity for Addition of Whole Numbers Such results as $13 + 0 = 13$ and $0 + 1 = 1$ have appeared frequently in the exercises of this unit. Presumably your experience convinces you by now of the validity of the following general statement: For any whole number a, $a + 0 = a$ and $0 + a = a$. It is difficult to make much of a fuss about anything so "obvious" as this, and yet the particular role that zero plays in addition (it lets you get back whatever you started with) is important in sorting out many mathematical systems. Whatever element (if any) plays that role is called the "identity element" for the system; hence zero is the *additive identity* for whole numbers.

42 NUMBER
SYSTEMS:
SETS
RELATIONS
OPERATIONS
USES

1. Unit 3 deals with multiplication in more depth, but it is appropriate to ask here: What whole number plays the same role for multiplication as zero does for addition? That is, what whole number used as one of two factors in a multiplication problem lets you get back the other factor as the answer to the problem?[3] Write several examples to illustrate your answer.

2. A tricky matter in teaching is to rid youngsters of the notion that "zero is nothing," or that "zero makes no difference," or even that "zero isn't a number." Indeed, many adults use such phrases. The phrases themselves don't matter very much, but the people who use them sometimes do arithmetic problems that have zero in them as if the zero were not there; for example:

$$
\begin{array}{cc}
23 & 101 \\
\times\,10 & \times\;\,23 \\
\hline
23 & 23 \\
& 23 \\
\hline
& 253
\end{array}
$$

       or

a. Think back to the discussion in Unit 1 of sets, the counts of sets, and the empty set. What is the role of zero in that context?[4]

b. What is the role of zero in our ordinary system of writing numbers? That is, can it be said of 50, 5,000, 505, and so on that "zero is nothing" or that "zero is not a number"? How does the role of zero in writing such numbers reflect its status as the count of the empty set?[5]

---

[3] The number 1 acts this way; for example, $1 \times 3 = 3$, $101 \times 1 = 101$.

[4] Zero is the count of the empty set, that is, it tells how many things the empty set contains. The empty set really is a set, by the way. It has the peculiarity that it is a set with no members, but it is very necessary in rounding out the total picture of sets. A colleague who read an early version of this book suggested that we say "Zero is *not* nothing, but it stands for something which *contains* nothing." If you see that this makes good sense, you probably have both zero and the empty set well in mind.

[5] Remember that in our place-value system of writing whole numbers the place on the far right indicates the number of ones, the next place the number of tens, and so on. Then, the zero in 505 tells us that there are no tens—that the set of tens is empty.

*c. A youngster (or an adult) who says that "zero doesn't matter" might be moved to think things over if he were then offered 5¢ in place of 50¢. What other ways can you think of to demonstrate that zero is an honest-to-goodness and important number even though in addition all it does is give you back what you started with? Make notes on these demonstrations, and share them with your colleagues.

*d. One important use of zero that you may or may not have listed in problem c is its role in marking the starting place on the number line. List some other places in which zero plays a similar role.

*2.3.4
Whole Numbers Have No Additive Inverses

One way of looking at zero in such an addition as $0 + 5 = 5$ is to think of having no money, then earning \$5. If there were some way of reversing that process *by addition,* we would be able to start with \$5 and by *adding* something get back to having no money at all. That is, the equation $5 + \square = 0$ would have an answer. Clearly there is no *whole number* answer to such a problem. But in some systems that you will cope with in this book, such equations as $a + \square = 0$ and $\square + a = 0$ do have answers no matter what number is represented by a. In such systems whatever answer works in the boxes for $a + \square = \square + a = 0$ is called the *additive inverse* of whatever number a represents. Do you know of any system of numbers where every number has an additive inverse?[6]

2.3.5
The Commutative Property of Addition of Whole Numbers

It takes time but children are eventually persuaded, after much experience and many examples, that the order in which two numbers are added makes no difference in the result; for example, $8 + 6$ and $6 + 8$ both give 14. But examples never *prove* anything for certain. Here is a sort of concrete proof: On a piece of paper, place chips to show $3 + 6$ with a pile of three chips first, then a pile of six chips next to it. If you turn this paper a half turn (180°) without disturbing the piles it becomes an embodiment for $6 + 3$, and yet the number of chips is "obviously" not changed. This would be true for *any* $a + b$ embodied as sets of chips. Try to find other ways to demonstrate that for *any* two whole numbers a and b, $a + b = b + a$.[6] Make brief notes on any ideas you have along these lines, and share them with your colleagues.

---

[6] How could you use rods, for example?

---

[6] One such system is the system of integers, which will be taken up in Part A, Unit 6. With integers, for example, $5 + (-5) = 0$; $(-13) + 13 = 0$.

44 NUMBER
SYSTEMS:
SETS
RELATIONS
OPERATIONS
USES

2.3.6
**The Associative
Property of Addition
of Whole Numbers**

Preliminary exercise: Find the sum of $51 + 7 + 3$. Then before you read on, reflect for a moment on how you got the answer.

Addition is a "binary operation," which means that it can only work with two numbers at a time. In an addition problem involving three numbers the procedure is to add two of them to get a single number, and then add that number to the third number. With $51 + 7 + 3$, for example, this could be done in either of two ways:

$$51 + 7 + 3 = (51 + 7) + 3 = 58 + 3 = 61$$

or

$$51 + 7 + 3 = 51 + (7 + 3) = 51 + 10 = 61.$$

Since there is more than one way to pair three numbers in order to do the addition, it would be confusing indeed if different ways of pairing led to different final results. The fact that this does not happen is expressed in general terms like this:

The associative property of addition: For any three whole numbers a, b, and c, $(a + b) + c = a + (b + c)$.

Once this property is stated for three numbers in a sum it can be extended to apply to sums involving more than three addends. In such sums any pairing of adjacent addends gives the same result as any other pairing. (This can be "proved" to be true if we accept the associative property involving only three addends, but we won't do so here.) For example, the sum $5 + 4 + 2 + 7$ could be worked out by pairing the addends in any of the following ways, as you should verify:

$(5 + 4) + (2 + 7)$
$[(5 + 4) + 2] + 7$
$[5 + (4 + 2)] + 7$
$5 + [(4 + 2) + 7]$
$5 + [4 + (2 + 7)]$

For five or six or more addends it is clear that the number of ways of pairing addends would be even larger than for four addends. (You might try listing all the possibilities for, say, a sum with five addends.) It obviously makes arithmetic much easier to know that all such pairings of adjacent addends give the same result.

Strictly speaking, "the associative property" is assumed to be true for just three addends so the more general result that follows from it might be called a *generalized associative property of addition—GAPA* for short.

1. Show with parentheses the two ways allowed by the associative property for working out $7 + 13 + 8$ and verify that both give the same sum.

*2. One way of pairing adjacent numbers to get the sum of $2 + 3 + 4 + 5$ is shown below. Show two other ways that would be allowed by the generalized associative property.

$$2 + 3 + 4 + 5 = [2 + (3 + 4)] + 5 = (2 + 7) + 5 = 9 + 5 = 14$$

$$2 + 3 + 4 + 5 =$$

$$2 + 3 + 4 + 5 =$$

2.3.7
A "Do-As-You-Please" Property for Addition of Whole Numbers

Preliminary exercise: Find the sum of $7 + 6 + 3 + 4$ in your head as quickly as you can. Think about how you did it, especially if you rearranged the order to make it easier.

By combining the commutative property (which lets you reverse pairs) and the generalized associative property (which lets you pair any two adjacent addends) it becomes legitimate when adding many numbers to pick pairs in any way one likes, so long as each addend is used just once.

It is somewhat tedious (and not necessarily recommended for children) to "prove" that this is so with step-by-step application of these two properties, but it can be done. Exercise 1 below shows in step-by-step fashion that $7 + 6 + 3 + 4$ is the same as $(7 + 3) + (6 + 4)$, which might be more convenient for mental calculation than adding in the original order. In exercise 2, see if you can show how $9 + 27 + 3 + 11$ is the same as $(9 + 11) + (27 + 3)$.

1. Equivalent Expressions	Property Used to Get This from the Previous Expression
$7 + 6 + 3 + 4$	(Given)
$[7 + (6 + 3)] + 4$	GAPA
$[7 + (3 + 6)] + 4$	Commutative property
$[(7 + 3) + 6] + 4$	GAPA
$(7 + 3) + (6 + 4)$	GAPA

2. Equivalent Expressions	Property Used to Get This from the Previous Expression
$9 + 17 + 3 + 11$	(Given)

46 NUMBER
SYSTEMS:
SETS
RELATIONS
OPERATIONS
USES

3. For each of the following sums, try to see how judicious use of the do-as-you-please property of addition of whole numbers (it is *not* a property of all operations) would simplify mental calculation of the sums. That is, find each sum without pencil and paper if you can. Compare your procedure with procedures used by your colleagues.

a. $11 + 12 + 39 + 18 = \square$

b. $6 + 23 + 19 + 4 + 7 + 11 = \square$

c. $19\cent + 2\cent + 11\cent + 38\cent = \square$

2.4
SUMMARY
AND PEDAGOGICAL
REMARKS

Teaching addition of whole numbers to children has several main responsibilities: It should provide links to reality both by showing how addition is used in solving problems from common life and by using concrete materials to embody the operation. It should foster genuine understanding and sound intuition about addition as a process. It should develop certain addition reflexes ("number facts"). It should eventually develop efficient computational procedures—a matter not covered in this unit but explored at length in Part B, Unit 1. Other important matters are to note the main structural properties of addition (such as the commutative property and the role of zero as an additive identity) and to deal with certain symbolic and notational conventions.

From your work in this unit, you may have developed a feeling for some of the difficulties in learning about addition, and your experience here may suggest some materials and procedures that can be adapted for use with children. But you have gone through in a few days material that might take several years to mature in children, and the exercises and embodiments you have used here are very far from exhausting the possibilities. Additional experience with such things as weight, volume, and liquid measures will be needed in working with children.[7]

It is essential to encourage children to make shrewd guesses, to approximate answers, and in other ways to get a good feeling for what is a likely and appropriate answer in a given situation. Indeed, the common picture of mathematics as demanding a single and precise answer in every situation is very wrong, and probably also very harmful to the learning of mathematics in order to *use* mathematics. In nearly every sit-

---

[7] Z. P. Dienes insists that a child learning mathematics should be exposed to "multiple embodiments" of essentially every concept he is expected to master. That is, something different about addition is learned from counting out chips than from making trains of rods, and something still different might be learned from pouring water into containers, putting weights on a scale, or other experiences. Works by Dienes are listed in Appendix II, if you want to follow up on his ideas.

uation an approximation in order to check whether you are "in the right ball park" is useful, and as often as not, such an approximation serves about as well for practical purposes as does an exact answer. Acting out problems with materials may help develop such a "number sense." For example, a child should feel that something has gone wrong if his calculations result in an answer in tens when hundreds would be appropriate.

On the other hand, symbol manipulation is also important. If one must add up a column of ten numbers it is certainly more efficient to be able to combine the symbols properly than to act out the addition with rods or chips. In teaching it is important to find the links and the easy stages from concrete experience to efficient symbol manipulation. One such link might consist in using numerals to record the *results* of having done an operation with concrete materials. That is, a child can accumulate many results by recording with symbols what is happening with the manipulation of materials and then look for patterns in these accumulated results as one way of finding out how the symbols are combined and used. The important thing to realize is that symbol manipulation as a reading and writing task may be something quite different from an understanding of what addition means and what it does. That is, a child might be able to write $2 + 4 = 6$ or even fill in the box for $2 + 4 = \square$ without necessarily understanding what is meant by those symbols.

It is not possible or appropriate in this book to specify at length how to arrange the learning experience for children—the sequencing of experiences, what concepts are emphasized at given times and in given order, the proper mix of work with symbols and work with embodiments, and so on. (Some of the references in Appendix II, including some "methods" books for teachers, deal with some such issues. However, we are very far from having complete understanding of such matters.) As a rough guide the learning of addition might go something like this: Children might begin with situations from their own life that indicate "addition" as the way to get answers. They might act these out with concrete embodiments to get those answers, using numerals and other symbols to keep track of these transactions. They might then get considerable practice acting out addition problems, only some of which come from actual life situations. In that process each child should become very familiar with (and eventually memorize) the 100 results of adding two single-digit numbers.[8] This happens more quickly for some than for

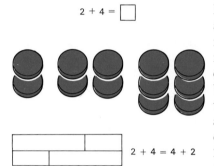

$2 + 4 = \square$

$2 + 4 = 4 + 2$

[8]   Actually there are only 55 such basic facts if $a + b = b + a$ is known and exploited. Check this out by looking at an addition table showing the results of adding the digits 0 through 9. Ten of these 55 facts are disposed of by the fact that $0 + a = a$, and many of the remaining facts are very easy—adding 1 or 2 to another number, for example. Only a few are difficult to learn and remember.

48 NUMBER
SYSTEMS:
SETS
RELATIONS
OPERATIONS
USES

others and we think a person (of any age) should *never* be made ashamed of resorting to counting out objects, counting on his fingers, consulting a table, or using other methods to find a result not known or forgotten.[9]

Although addition is a "binary" operation (an operation with pairs of numbers only) the child learns that more than two numbers can be added by combining any pair of addends into a single number, pairing that with another addend to get a new sum, and so on, using some sort of do-as-you-please property to make this more efficient. The child eventually learns to exploit the base 10 place value numeration system with exchanges of 10 ones for 1 ten, 10 tens for 1 hundred, and so on. ("Carrying" is the usual label for this exchange process.) The child learns that by using this system *any* two numbers no matter how large can be added, using only the basic addition facts for single digit numbers. This symbolic handling of addition (which is taken up in detail in Part B, Unit 1) requires that the child know basic addition facts as nearly instantaneous "reflexes." Relatively few children fail to learn how to add at the level of being able to get a correct answer to a given example but there are many who don't understand very well what they are doing.

Understanding of addition of whole numbers is an important matter in further learning of arithmetic, because it has some role to play in all the other operations. It has been suggested that addition is not really understood until its inverse operation, subtraction, has been dealt with; and this may well be true. Addition is perhaps the most accessible of any of the operations, and given plenty of appropriate experience and time to build that experience into sound intuition and understanding, few children should have difficulty with it.

[9] Every teacher has seen children secretly "counting on their fingers" and has seen reactions ranging from sheepishness to guilt at having been "caught" doing so. We have also seen children unable to find such a sum as 3 + 4 because of their adamant refusal to count on their fingers since they feel it is *wrong* to do so. Why teachers (and parents?) so effectively amputate these natural and accessible calculating devices is beyond our understanding.

unit 3
multiplication of whole numbers

3.1
INTRODUCTION
This unit continues the analysis of the basic meaning and properties of operations with pairs of whole numbers. In most school instruction multiplication of whole numbers is presented as repeated addition but this is only one of the ways of looking at multiplication and exclusive emphasis on it is probably harmful in the long run. For example, repeated addition is seldom appropriate in multiplication of fractions and even with whole numbers there are multiplication situations that are best thought of in other than repeated-addition ways.

Here we deal only with the basic meaning and properties of multiplication of whole numbers. As with previous work you should put aside your memorized facts and your skills with symbol manipulation and reconstruct the ideas through the concrete embodiments suggested by the work sheets. In this way you can experience some part of what youngsters may go through in encountering these ideas in school — and you may even sweep out some cobwebs in your own understanding.

Before you begin this unit, consult the log of everyday uses of numbers that you made in response to an assignment in Unit 1 (and that you may have kept up since) and see if any of those uses involved multiplication of whole numbers. If so, share them with your colleagues; if not, try to find some such uses now in your own everyday world.

49

50 NUMBER
SYSTEMS:
SETS
RELATIONS
OPERATIONS
USES

3.2
**ACTIVITY: THE
MEANING OF MULTIPLICATION
OF WHOLE NUMBERS**

Overview: **Various interpretations of multiplication are worked through, including repeated addition, arrays, and several manifestations of Cartesian products. As usual, counts, measures, and other embodiments are used.**

Materials needed: Chips, rods. Graph paper or dot paper may also be helpful.

Even though you know how to do these problems symbolically, act them out in concrete materials as suggested and record your results. Work with others from your class, watch what they are doing, and compare results and impressions. If your experience gives you any new insights into numbers and the multiplication operation, keep track of these insights for discussion with others in your class.

3.2.1
**Multiplication of Counts
Using Repeated Addition**

1. Using chips, count out this problem: "How many children are there in three reading groups of five children each?" A mathematical model of this problem is $3 \times 5 = \square$, where 3 and 5 are *factors* and the result is a *product*. Just to have a uniform way of talking about things, let us agree that in such situations the first factor indicates the number of sets and the second factor the size of each set. To get the answer, you might think of $3 \times 5 = \square$ as an addition problem: $5 + 5 + 5 = \square$; or you might simply count by fives: five, ten, *fifteen*.

2. Fill in Table 3.2.1 as appropriate, either with a problem from common life to go with the mathematical model given or with various versions of the mathematical model. The first one is completed for you. You should also act each problem out once with chips and put the answer in the frames in the equation.

3.2.2
**Multiplication
with Measures Using
Repeated Addition**

Consider a problem such as this: "What minimum amount of ribbon should I buy in order to have 3 pieces, each exactly 6 inches long?" Using the convention of letting the first factor indicate "how many" and the second factor indicate "how much in each," the mathematical model might be $3 \times 6 = \square$. Note that the two factors have slightly different roles; the first is a count but the second is a measure. Acted out with rods, this becomes a train of three 6-rods. Then we find the equivalent train of 10-rod(s) and some other rod that will give the total length.

1. Fill in Table 3.2.2, as indicated by the first example. Act out each problem with rods, with the first factor the number of rods and the second factor the length of each rod, and then fill in the boxes in the equations.

Mathematical Models

Table 3.2.1	Problem from Common Life	Product	Repeated Addition	Count by *m*
	a. How many people are there in four committees of six people each?	$4 \times 6 = \square$	$6 + 6 + 6 + 6 = \square$	six, twelve, eighteen, *twenty-four*
	b.		$3 + 3 + 3 + 3 + 3 + 3 = \square$	
	c.	$1 \times 7 = \square$	Not very applicable	Not very applicable
	d. How many oranges are there in seven empty orange boxes?[1]			
	*e. [2]	$0 \times 7 = \square$	Not applicable	Not applicable

Table 3.2.2	Problem from Common Life	Mathematical Model
	a. How much medicine is in two 9-ounce bottles of medicine?	$2 \times 9 = \square$
	b.	$9 \times 2 = \square$
	c.	$1 \times 7 = \square$
	d. How much root beer is in seven empty bottles?[3]	
	e. [4]	$0 \times 7 = \square$

---

[1] $7 \times 0 = \square$; $0 + 0 + 0 + 0 + 0 + 0 + 0 = \square$; 0, 0, 0, 0, 0, 0, 0. Repeated addition of zero or counting by zero would seldom be used, of course, but they do illustrate how zero as a second factor (the number of things in each set) could be interpreted.

[2] A situation might be "How many oranges would I have if there existed bags of seven oranges each, but I didn't have any of these bags?" No repeated addition model can be displayed, and similarly there is no count-by-*m* model, which may be some part of the reason why multiplication by zero is confusing to many people.

[3] Writing the mathematical model for this isn't so bad ($7 \times 0 = \square$) but acting it out with rods might be troublesome. The trouble may be that even though you use the "clear rods" made of squares of paper or acetate, a few of them piled up amount to something, not nothing, and it is difficult to visualize a "train" of seven "rods" with zero length.

[4] A problem might be: "How much lumber do I have if 7-foot boards exist, but I have none of them?" Such problems often sound a little farfetched. The difficulty with acting out such problems as $0 \times 7 = \square$ with rods may be even greater than with $7 \times 0 = \square$, since one must visualize a "train" of *no* 7-rods—a pretty abstract sort of "embodiment."

52 NUMBER
SYSTEMS:
SETS
RELATIONS
OPERATIONS
USES

*3. As soon as one gets beyond pairs of small numbers to such problems as 5×73 or 9×17 it seems clear that using repeated addition or counting by m would at least be tedious. Still, some variations on such procedures might be useful for mental arithmetic. For example, 5×73 might become $70 + 70 + 70 + 70 + 70 + 3 + 3 + 3 + 3 + 3 = 365$ and 9×17 might be $15 + 15 + 15 + 15 + 15 + 15 + 15 + 15 + 15 + 2 + 2 + 2 + 2 + 2 + 2 + 2 + 2 + 2 = 153$ (or even $20 + 20 + 20 + 20 + 20 + 20 + 20 + 20 + 20 - 3 - 3 - 3 - 3 - 3 - 3 - 3 - 3 - 3 = 153$). These are, of course, the counterparts of $5 \times 73 = (5 \times 70) + (5 \times 3) = 350 + 15$, and $9 \times 17 = (9 \times 15) + (9 \times 2)$. Try to invent similar repeated addition or combination addition-subtraction ways to get answers to these problems.

a. $4 \times 199 = \square$

b. $8 \times 26 = \square$

c. $7 \times 55 = \square$

d. $14 \times 11 = \square$

3.2.3
Multiplication Using Arrays

1. An array is a regular rectangular pattern. Here, for example, is an array with three rows of five stars each (or, more generally, one could say an array of three rows and five columns). It represents the product 3×5.

★ ★ ★ ★ ★
★ ★ ★ ★ ★
★ ★ ★ ★ ★

Arrays are found in common life in such examples as the number of windows on the side of a large building or the number of acoustical tiles on a ceiling. Take 3 minutes to list some more examples, and then share your examples with colleagues.

2. To assure that everyone gets the same array for a given problem, let us agree that the n in $n \times m$ will indicate the number of rows and the m, the number in each row (this is also the number of columns). Using poker chips, form an array to represent each of the problems below, and fill in the missing number in the equation by finding the number of chips in the array.

a. $4 \times 5 = \square$ **c.** $1 \times 8 = \square$

b. $5 \times 4 = \square$ **d.** $5 \times 0 = \square$

e. For one of the equations above, give a common life situation for which the equation would be a mathematical model and for which an array would be a suitable embodiment.

3. Once an array is formed, you must still figure out how many items are in it. Take a few minutes to reflect on the problems you just acted out. In finding how many, once you had formed the array, did you rely on your multiplication reflexes (for example, $4 \times 5 = 20$) or count one by one, or use repeated addition (for example, $5 + 5 + 5 + 5 = 20$) or count by the number in each row (for example, five, ten, fifteen, *twenty*)? Or perhaps you used some other method; if so, indicate below what it was. Find out whether some of your colleagues used a different method from yours.

4. How many such arrays would need to be made and counted in order to fill in an ordinary multiplication table from 1×1 up to 10×10? Do you think this would or would not be a good exercise for children? Talk about it with your colleagues.

*5. An array can give a sort of "picture" of a product. It would be tedious to picture large products as arrays, but with graph paper or dot paper it isn't very hard to picture such products as $15 \times 17 = \square$. A diagram of such a picture is shown below. In finding how many dots are in such an array, a fairly natural shortcut is to isolate any 10×10 parts of the array, then any 1×10 rows and 10×1 columns, then deal with whatever is left, perhaps even by groupings of tens. It is possible that by using such a visual method of seeing products and a count method of getting answers, even first graders could find the answers to a much richer variety of common life problems than they can solve by using their usual skills. Work out $13 \times 23 = \square$ in this way.

54 NUMBER
SYSTEMS:
SETS
RELATIONS
OPERATIONS
USES

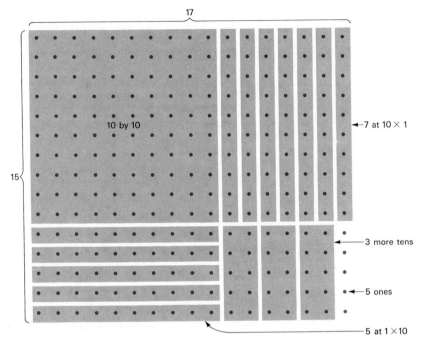

An array picture of the product $15 \times 17 = 100 + 50 + 70 + 30 + 5$.

6. Two possible ways of embodying measure (rather than count) ideas of multiplication using arrays of rods are illustrated for the product $3 \times 6 = \square$.

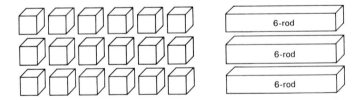

The one on the left, using unit cubes, resembles the count model, but if the cubes are pushed in close, the embodiment bears a closer resemblance to an *area* problem—such as finding the number of square feet in a ceiling by counting the number of ceiling tiles—so many rows with so many in each row.[1]

Some manuals on using colored rods advocate a picture of mul-

---

[1] One might get the same effect with fewer rods by marking the units off on the rods—say with a water-base marker.

tiplication something like the picture on the right above. For a product such as 3 × 6, 6-rods are put side by side with a 3-rod across them at right angles to measure how many there should be, as pictured here:

Act out each of the products in exercise 2 by using rods in any or all of these ways.

3.2.4
Cartesian Products; Combinations

1. Another category of real situations that lead to multiplication is illustrated by this problem: "Suppose a person has three different pairs of slacks (say red, blue, and twill) and four different shirts (say white, checked, dotted, and plaid). How many *different* slack and shirt outfits does the person have?"

a. Trace the slacks and shirts below (or make your own) and cut them out, then actually make as many different outfits as you can. Keep a record of the outfits as you make them, by listing the combinations of slacks with shirts using pairs of the letters; for example, (R, D) for red pants with dotted shirt or (T, C) for twill pants with checked shirt. How many outfits are possible? Compare your results with the results of your classmates.

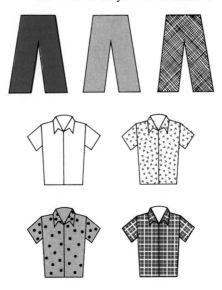

56 NUMBER
SYSTEMS:
SETS
RELATIONS
OPERATIONS
USES

b. A pictorial way of representing the combinations is shown below:

Therefore $3 \times 4 = 12$

Make a similar picture showing the number of combinations possible with four pair of slacks and three shirts, and from the picture find the answer to $4 \times 3 = \square$.

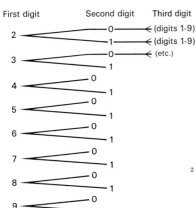

c. It is only a short step from the pictures above to the "tree diagrams" (p. 57) fairly common in applications of mathematics.[2] Here is one that represents a situation such as that shown above. (For uniformity, let the first factor in a product be represented by the "big limbs" and the second by the "branches." In that case, this diagram represents the products $3 \times 4 = \square$.)

---

[2] Applied problems, especially in probability or statistics, frequently ask in how many ways a certain thing can happen. Tree diagrams can frequently help sort that out. For example, in Unit 1 you were asked about telephone area codes; a diagram such as the one at the left helps us see how many possibilities there are.

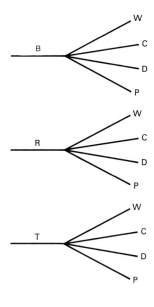

d. Pair off with someone else in your class. Imagine three more "combinations" problems (not necessarily about clothes). Diagram each of these as a tree diagram and write the multiplication equation that would be a mathematical model of the situation.

e. Draw a tree diagram for the number of different shoe, dress, scarf outfits that can be made from two pairs of shoes, three dresses, and four scarves, and use it to find the answer to $2 \times 3 \times 4 = \Box$.

2. A related motivation for multiplication comes from forming ordered pairs of sets of objects. Suppose $A = \{$John, Kelly, Lem$\}$ (therefore $n(A) = 3$), a set of three boys; and $B = \{$Aretha, Betty, Diana, Christina$\}$ (therefore $n(B) = 4$, a set of four girls. Complete this list of possible boy, girl pairings:

(John, Aretha), (John, Betty), (John, Diana), (John, Christina); (Kelly, Aretha),

58 NUMBER
SYSTEMS:
SETS
RELATIONS
OPERATIONS
USES

One gets $3 \times 4 = 12$ such pairs. (If you got a different result, check again and talk over your results with class members.) The set of ordered pairs you get by taking first elements from a set A and second elements from a set B is a useful way of sorting out certain situations in real life. In mathematics such a set is called a "Cartesian product" and designated by the symbol $A \times B$.[3] Note that in this case $n(A \times B) = 3 \times 4 = 12$. Write out the complete Cartesian product set of ordered pairs for each of the following problems and verify that if $n(A) = \triangle$ and $n(B) = \bigcirc$ then $n(A \times B) = \triangle \times \bigcirc$.

a. How many ways are there for a party of five Germans to shake hands with a party of three Frenchmen? $G = \{I, J, K, L, M\}$ $F = \{A, B, C\}$

b. For the sets L and M below, invent a plausible story for which forming the Cartesian product $L \times M$ would make sense.

$L = \{a, b\} \qquad M = \{c, d, e, f, g, h, i\}$

*c. Given three sets, ordered triples can be formed by first forming ordered pairs in the usual way (first elements in first set, second elements in second set) and then associating each pair with each element in the third set. As it turns out, the number of such triples is the product of the counts of the three sets. Verify this by forming the triples suggested by this problem: "Suppose a lunchroom always has the same menu available, with milk and a sandwich for 59¢. The possibilities are: ham, cheese, salami, or corned beef on rye bread, wheat bread, or white bread with either regular or chocolate milk. How many days can I get a lunch there without having the same lunch twice?"

---

[3] At least one popular elementary school mathematics textbook series uses Cartesian products in one of its approaches to multiplication of whole numbers. This may or may not be a good idea, perhaps depending on where it comes and how successfully it is tied in to some imaginable real life situation or acted out with concrete materials.

Cartesian product is named in honor of René Descartes (1596–1650), French philosopher and mathematician, who is credited with the invention of analytic (or coordinate) methods in geometry (while in the army and hardly ever getting out of bed, yet!). Descartes is interesting in many ways and it would be worth your while to read something about him—perhaps in an encyclopedia or in E. T. Bell's colorful book *Men of Mathematics*, Simon & Schuster, New York, 1937.

1. Another motivation for multiplication might come from such a story as this: "A certain town wants to put a single traffic light at each of the downtown intersections of seven east-west streets with nine north-south streets; how many traffic lights are needed?" An easy diagram is to mark the intersections of seven horizontal and nine vertical "lines":

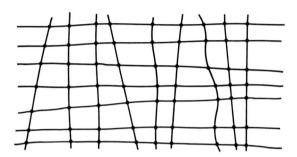

The number of such intersections is, of course, $7 \times 9 = 63$. This problem suggests another sort of activity for motivating and giving a picture of multiplication of pairs of numbers. The lines can be slanting, or wavy, or can have any other shape, so long as each horizontal does not intersect another horizontal, each vertical does not intersect another vertical, and each horizontal intersects each vertical exactly once. For each of the following problems, draw a picture and complete the equation.

a. $3 \times 6 = \square$ **b.** $7 \times 2 = \square$ **c.** $5 \times 1 = \square$

*d. Discuss with class members whether such a notion could be extended to three factors, say $5 \times 6 \times 3 = \square$.

2. If you look only at the marked intersections in the street example in exercise 1 above, it resembles a 7×9 array. A Cartesian product interpretation arises from considering the intersections as so-called whole number lattice points on a coordinate graph like the one pictured at the top of page 60:

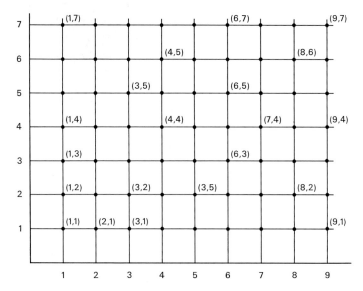

Each point is named by an ordered pair; the first "coordinate" in the ordered pair shows "how far over" (to the right) the point is, and the second coordinate shows "how far up" the point is. Some of the points in the diagram above are named by their coordinates; mark all the other points with their coordinates. The complete set of ordered pairs is, of course, the same as the Cartesian product $A \times B$ for sets $A = \{1, 2, 3, 4, 5, 6, 7, 8, 9\}$ and $B = \{1, 2, 3, 4, 5, 6, 7\}$. Considered as a Cartesian product, there are 9×7 such pairs of numbers because there are 9 elements in set A and 7 elements in set B. Considered as an array, there are 7 rows of 9 points each, or 7×9 points; or if the page were turned sideways, it would look like an array of 9 rows with 7 points each, or 9×7 points. Set A could have been paired with set B by a tree diagram, and again the result would have been 9×7 or 7×9, depending on how you formed the diagram. That is, all such combination embodiments seem to be somewhat similar.

*3. An interesting and striking teaching device for showing arrays or intersections of lines is to make up a series of cards similar to the ones on page 61 but larger—say 8 by 8 inches. The parts shown shaded in this illustration must be cut out when you make the cards. Two cards are needed for each of the numbers 1, 2, . . . , 9 so that all possible combinations can be shown, including such products as 6×6. To show, for example, 3×2, just put the 3-card at right angles across the 2-card (see p. 61), and there will be an array of 6 holes showing; or, if you prefer, the number of intersections of 2 lines with 3 lines will show.

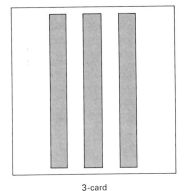

3-card

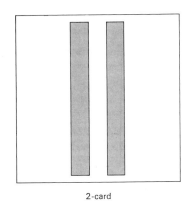

2-card

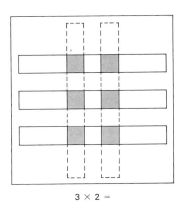

3 × 2 =

The effort involved in making these cards is worthwhile, for they are surprisingly effective with children.

What would a "0-card" look like? Using a 0-card, how would $0 \times 7 = 0$ be embodied? How about $7 \times 0 = 0$? Would these embodiments illustrate pretty much the "right" concepts with respect to multiplication with 0 as a factor?

3.3
ACTIVITY: PROPERTIES
OF MULTIPLICATION OF
WHOLE NUMBERS

Overview: **This section focuses on structural properties of multiplication of whole numbers: closure, 1 as multiplicative identity, multiplication property of zero, commutative property, associative property, a "do-as-you-please" property, and the distributive property of multiplication over addition.**

Materials needed: Chips as a minimum; other embodiments depending on the wishes of the class or the individual.

Throughout this section, array models are suggested whenever embodiments seem appropriate. If the activity is done in a small group other embodiments should also be considered, perhaps by designating members of the group as "specialists." For example, there can be a repeated-addition-of-counts specialist, a repeated-addition-of-measures specialist, and an arrays specialist. Alternatively, the class might have a variety of materials close at hand and pool their efforts to illustrate each property in several ways. If you are working alone, on the other hand, you should select a couple of properties and illustrate them in as many ways as you can.

62 NUMBER
SYSTEMS:
SETS
RELATIONS
OPERATIONS
USES

3.3.1

**Closure, Uniqueness,
Equivalence Classes of Products**

1. Remember that an operation on whole numbers is closed if doing the operations on whole numbers *always* yields a whole number answer (and not, for example, a fraction or negative number answer). Is multiplication of whole numbers closed?

2. An operation gives "unique" results if for each problem there is no more than one possible answer. For example, if multiplication is unique, then 13×134 should always result in the same answer when correctly done. Is multiplication unique? Take some time to discuss with class members how you might help such ideas to develop in youngsters.

3. On the other hand, a number such as 12 can be the "answer" to several different multiplication problems. Take 12 poker chips and see how many different rectangular arrays can be formed. Record the multiplication equations for each. (As an array, 3×4 looks different from 4×3 and should be counted as two "different" combinations.)

Similarly, make arrays and write corresponding multiplication equations (with two factors) for each of the following numbers.
a. 10
b. 7
c. 24
d. 11

As noted in the discussion of properties of addition, when things that look different generate the same result, there are very likely "equivalence classes" in the picture. In this case, all the products that give 24 as a result belong to one equivalence class, all those that give 20 as a result belong to another equivalence class, and so on. These choices are sometimes quite useful in working out problems. Another way to express this is to say that each whole number can have several "multiplication names." A "mapping"[4] diagram can show where pairs of numbers go under a multiplication operation:

[4] Loosely speaking, a *mapping* associates with each member of a given set some definite member of a second set. In a mapping diagram such as the one here, the arrows show what goes where.

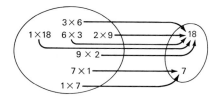

3.3.2

**The
Identity Element for
Multiplication**

Notice in your work above that two of the arrays for every number are single-row or single-column arrays, for example:

○ ○ ○ ○
$4 = 1 \times 4$ and $4 = 4 \times 1,$ ○
○
○
○

This experience indicates that if 1 is factor in a multiplication example then it "duplicates" or "makes a copy of" whatever the other factor is. This is similar to the role of zero as one addend in addition problems.[5] To express this idea in symbols, we say that for any whole number a, $1 \times a = a \times 1 = a$. Thus, 1 is labeled as the "identity element" for multiplication.

What experiences with concrete materials or with common applications might help children see this special role of the number 1 in multiplication problems? Respond to this and then discuss it with colleagues.

*3.3.3

**Whole Numbers Have
No Multiplicative Inverse**

1. Multiplying by 2 has the effect of "doubling" whatever is represented by the other factor. If there were some way of reversing this *by multiplication*—of "undoubling"— then the net effect of the two operations would be the same as a single multiplication by 1, which is no effect at all. In that case, there would be an answer to the equation $2 \times \square = 1$. We know there is no such whole number; but is there any number at all that could go in the box so that $2 \times \square = 1$ would have a solution.[5]

---

[5] Curiously enough, when zero acts this way in addition it tempts people to say that "zero is nothing" or doesn't change anything, but the exactly analogous role of the number 1 in multiplication doesn't seem to elicit similar nonsense.

[5] **Yes, the number 1/2.**

64 NUMBER
SYSTEMS:
SETS
RELATIONS
OPERATIONS
USES

We bring this up because in many systems it is possible to find an answer in the equation $a \times \square = 1$ for almost every number. When that is the case, each such number a has a "multiplicative inverse" which acts as a "reverser" or "undoer" of the effect of multiplying by a. This is one of the nice things that you do *not* have if you work only with whole numbers.

3.3.4
**Multiplication
Property of Zero**

1. Zero in multiplication acts as an "eliminator." Can you make an array with 0 as a factor? Try it in stages by completing the following arrays and equations:

   a. Start with a 4×5 array of poker chips. $\qquad 4 \times 5 = \square$
   b. Remove one row to get a 3×5 array. $\qquad 3 \times 5 = \square$
   c. Remove another row to get a 2×5 array. $\qquad 2 \times 5 = \square$
   d. Remove another row to get a 1×5 array. $\qquad 1 \times 5 = \square$
   e. Remove another row to get a 0×5 "array." $\qquad 0 \times 5 = \square$

   Think about and discuss some other embodiments that may help children to come to terms with the fact that for any n, $0 \times n = 0$.

2. 5×0 as an array would be a "nonarray" of 5 rows with no elements in each row, and so the result would clearly be zero. Can you imagine more satisfactory ways to embody the equation $n \times 0 = 0$?[6]

*3. Start over with a 4×5 array of white chips, go through the sequence of steps a to e in problem 1 above, and think of each play as losing 5 chips. Then continue losing by "going into the red" (literally, by using red chips). Continue the sequence by regarding a subtracted row below zero as negative and the total number of chips in the array as a "debt" represented by a negative number. That is, complete the following:

$$4 \times 5 = \boxed{}$$

$$3 \times 5 = \boxed{}$$

$$2 \times 5 = \boxed{}$$

$$1 \times 5 = \boxed{}$$

$$0 \times 5 = \boxed{0}$$

[6] How many combinations of scarf and shoes would be possible with 5 scarves, no shoes? How many intersections of 5 east-west streets with no north-south streets would be possible?

$$-1 \times 5 = \boxed{-5}$$

$$-2 \times 5 = \boxed{}$$

$$-3 \times 5 = \boxed{}$$

This exercise, of course, is an intimation of how multiplication of a positive number by a negative number behaves.

3.3.5
Commutative
Property of Multiplication
of Whole Numbers

Children eventually learn by experience that the order in which two whole numbers are multiplied makes no difference in the result; for example, 6×8 and 8×6 both give 48. But individual examples can never "prove" that something *always* happens. Here is a proof of sorts: Set up a 5×9 array of chips on a piece of cardboard or something else movable. Rotate it by 90 degrees so that it becomes a 9×5 array. Note that the number of chips involved "obviously" hasn't changed. This would be true for *any* $n \times m$ array, and so $n \times m = m \times n$. Can you show with any of the other embodiments of multiplication by some *general* method (one that will work for all examples) that the order in which things are multiplied makes no difference?

3.3.6
Associative
Property of Multiplication
of Whole Numbers

1. Multiplication can be performed with two numbers at a time; that is, it is a *binary operation*. Given a problem such as $2 \times 5 \times 3 = \square$ (such as from a three-level tree diagram), you first combine one of the pairs into a single number and then use that single number with the third number. Hence, $2 \times 5 \times 3 = (2 \times 5) \times 3 = 10 \times 3 = 30$; or, alternatively, $2 \times 5 \times 3 = 2 \times (5 \times 3) = 2 \times 15 = 30$. By pairing adjacent numbers in all possible ways, verify with the examples below that the pairs you choose make no difference in the final product.
a. $2 \times 3 \times 4 = \square$

b. $4 \times 2 \times 3 = \square$

2. Try to figure out ways to embody the product of three factors, such as $2 \times 3 \times 4$ in both of the two ways in which pairs of factors can be formed.[7]

---

[7] Say as a 2×3 array taken four times, then a 3×4 array taken twice. Or a 2×3 array of piles of 4 chips versus a 3×4 array of pairs of chips. Discuss other possibilities in your group. Perhaps with rods you could represent a three-dimensional box in two different ways.

66 NUMBER
SYSTEMS:
SETS
RELATIONS
OPERATIONS
USES

Multiplication would be a very confusing operation if different ways of pairing factors led to different results. The fact that this does not happen is expressed in general terms like this:

The associative property of multiplication: For any three whole numbers *a, b,* and *c,* $(a \times b) \times c = a \times (b \times c)$.

3. As with addition, the associative property is stated as an assumption for three factors but can be extended to any number of factors. Show all the possible pairings for the product $5 \times 4 \times 3 \times 2$ and verify that each gives the same result.

3.3.7
The "Do-as-You-Please" Property of Multiplication

By combining and generalizing the power to reverse the order of pairs in multiplication (commutative property) or to pair adjacent numbers any way you like (associative property), it becomes legitimate to use the factors in a multiplication in any order you like. This can be a convenience in mental arithmetic or in rearranging expressions into more convenient forms. For example, $3 \times 2 \times 13 \times 5$ might be easier as $(2 \times 5) \times (3 \times 13)$.

1. It is tedious to do each single exchange and pairing that would arrange $3 \times 2 \times 13 \times 5$ as $(2 \times 5) \times (3 \times 13)$, but it is worth doing once in order to see the legitimacy of such changes. Follow through the example below and fill in any blanks.

Problem	Property Applied to Previous Expression to Get This Result
$3 \times 2 \times 13 \times 5$	(Given)
$3 \times [2 \times (13 \times 5)]$	Associative property (for four factors)
$3 \times [2 \times (5 \times 13)]$	Commutative property
$3 \times [(2 \times 5) \times 13]$	_____
$[3 \times (2 \times 5)] \times 13$	_____
$[(2 \times 5) \times 3] \times 13$	_____
$(2 \times 5) \times (3 \times 13)$	Associative property

2. The do-as-you-please property turns some problems into a form that you can do in your head, and simplifies many others. Use it to rearrange each of the following into a form that might be easier to do.
a. $6 \times 5 \times 4 \times 3 \times 2 \times 1$

b. $25 \times 14 \times 4 \times 2$

c. $125 \times 7 \times 3 \times 8$

3.3.8

The Distributive Property of Multiplication Over Addition

To celebrate its thirteenth year in business a variety store has a "lucky 13 sale" with many items priced at (you guessed it) 13¢. Extra cashiers have been hired to handle the crowds; each has a sheet taped to his cash register that reads like this:

Number of Items	Total Price
1	$ .13
2	.26
3	.39
4	.52
5	.65
6	.78
7	.91
8	1.04
9	1.17
10	1.30
11	1.43
12	1.56
13	1.69

The supervisor notices that the line of one new cashier moves much more slowly than the others and then sees that this cashier is ringing up items as follows: 5 pads of paper at 13¢, ring up 65¢; 7 toothpastes at 13¢, ring up 91¢; then find the total. The supervisor advises the cashier to first find the total number of 13¢ items and *then* look at the table; the cashier follows his advice and thereafter his line moves faster. Symbolically: $(5 \times 13) + (7 \times 13) = (5 + 7) \times 13 = 12 \times 13$.

The supervisor then notices several clerks in trouble and finds that many people are purchasing more than 13 of a certain popular item. Since the table provided only goes up to 13, some clerks are doing multiplication on paper sacks while others are entering the items one by one on the cash register. In this case, the supervisor tells them that if, for example, there are 19 items purchased all together, they should use the table to ring up the price of 10 of them, then the price of 9 of them, and let the machine give the total. Symbolically: $19 \times 13 = (10 + 9) \times 13 = (10 \times 13) + (9 \times 13)$.

This supervisor is having his clerks use variations of the so-called distributive property that links multiplication and addition and makes

68 NUMBER
SYSTEMS:
SETS
RELATIONS
OPERATIONS
USES

much of arithmetic possible. Acted out with arrays, an example might look like this:

$$5 \times 13 = 5 \times (10 + 3) = (5 \times 10) + (5 \times 3) = 50 + 15 = 65$$

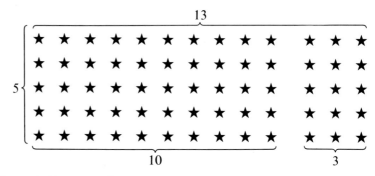

In a similar way, illustrate each of the following (with chips or with a drawing):

1. $4 \times 8 = 4 \times (6 + 2) = (4 \times 6) + (4 \times 2)$

2. $3 \times 14 = 3(10 + 4)$

The units in Part B that deal in detail with computation algorithms will exploit the distributive property again and again. (For example, $7 \times 137 = (7 \times 100) + (7 \times 30) + (7 \times 7)$; do you see why?) The distributive property is nearly indispensable in the symbol manipulation that makes up much of the work of high school mathematics. Yet this property gives youngsters considerable difficulty, especially in algebra. It must be taught with attention to embodiments and many applications from common life in the pre-high school years. Watch for it in the units that follow, and in real situations.

3.4
SUMMARY AND PEDAGOGICAL REMARKS

In teaching multiplication we insist as usual on the importance of establishing solid links with the real world in two ways: (1) by using multiplication as the appropriate mathematical model for solving problems from real life, and (2) by working with concrete embodiments of symbolically stated multiplication examples. To the extent that schoolwork includes links to the real world, teachers tend to focus too often on repeated addition of counts and not enough on measure or on other sources of multiplication as outlined in this unit.

The typical school curriculum guide probably does not suggest very much explicit work on multiplication in kindergarten or first grade, and very little even in second grade. Work with multiplication of small single-digit numbers may begin early in third grade, and by late third grade or early fourth grade mastery of the "multiplication tables" may be expected, along with multiplication of several-digit numbers by single-digit numbers. From then on the size and complexity of the multiplication problems escalate rapidly, and complete mastery of the rather complicated algorithm for multiplying *any* two whole numbers may be expected by the end of fifth grade. The difficulty experienced by many students with this rapid escalation suggests that they did not have enough concrete experience with simple multiplication. Such work could probably begin earlier than it usually does in schools.

Judging from the problems many adults have in coming to terms with multiplication in which one of the factors is zero, we are quite sure that this skill is inadequately taught in schools. It is a deceptively simple matter since there is only one result to learn (if any factor is zero, the product is zero). It seems that anyone should be able to remember *that*. Indeed, many probably do "remember," but the suspicion lingers that something strange is going on. That is, they don't understand or trust the result that they remember.

Problems such as $5 \times 0 = 0$ can be considered, for example, as "five zeros," or "repeated addition of zero five times," or "an array with five empty rows." If it is ever put to a person in these ways (as it may not have been), he may be able to accept the result quite well. But problems such as $0 \times 5 = 0$ are more troublesome. The corresponding explanations are, for example, "no fives," "five added to itself zero times," or an array of no five-element rows" and for many people these explanations do not "obviously" suggest zero as the result. In any case, teachers should watch for difficulties with zero in youngsters and deal with them again and again from as many points of view as possible.

In talking with teachers about laboratory approaches to teaching or about trying to link arithmetic to common life situations and to embodiments, we usually encounter this question in one form or another: "All this is fine *but* will the kids learn their tables and learn how to calculate?" Hence, this may be as good a place as any to make some remarks

70   NUMBER
SYSTEMS:
SETS
RELATIONS
OPERATIONS
USES

about "learning the tables" and other such reflex responses. First we state emphatically that having such reflexes eventually is quite important to nearly everyone. Such reflexes are important in coping with simple numerical problems presented by common life, in making rough-and-ready approximations in many sorts of decision making, and for efficiency in using various computation algorithms.

Granted that "learning the tables" is important, there is often too much anxiety surrounding the task. Anyone of any age who happens to have forgotten a particular result should not be ashamed to resort to whatever he finds is helpful in order to retrieve that result, including manipulation of concrete materials, making an array of dots, looking at a multiplication table, or counting on his fingers. As a general rule we see little point to the many pages of drill in books and the thousands of drill sheets duplicated by teachers. There are easy ways for youngsters to generate their own practice problems or to test each other. For example, with a deck of playing cards children can generate a large number of multiplication combinations in a few minutes by turning up pairs of cards.[6] Spinners, dice, and other such devices can also generate practice examples and can be "rigged" to present more examples of the practice a child happens to need. Children should experience all the basic combinations in a variety of embodiments while they are being asked to memorize the results. They should always be encouraged to feel good about acting out any result that gives them trouble.

It is probable that the need to do laborious pencil and paper calculations will considerably diminish as small electronic calculators become more and more available. Knowing what is appropriate to do, knowing how to set up a problem, and knowing whether the answer given by the machine makes sense will then be more important than actually slogging through the algorithm.[7] But the need to make quick approximations in a wide variety of situations will not diminish, and being able to calculate quickly with easy numbers and with powers of 10 is a great asset to such approximation. For example, to see if you can afford to carpet a room about 11 by 14 feet, it is sufficient to round off to 4 yards by 5 yards and figure that at $20 a square yard the cost will be about $400 and at $15

11 × 8 = ☐

6   A deck of cards can be "rigged" in many ways to increase the occurrence of desired combinations. Face cards can be taken out, counted all as tens, counted all as zeros, or kept at the usual values (11, 12, and 13) depending on what the children need to practice. Extra sevens or eights or nines can be put in the deck to increase the probability that difficult combinations will be learned. To add an element of competition, such games as "war" can be adapted by having each child turn up pairs of cards (highest product wins).

7   This does not necessarily mean that the schools will be able to stop teaching algorithmic processes. No one really knows what contribution the learning of algorithms makes to development of a solid understanding of numbers and operations. It may well be a considerable contribution.

per square yard about $300. If exact calculation changes those figures by a few dollars, it won't really make much difference in the basic decision. Similarly, you can save yourself considerable problems sometimes by being able to estimate quickly that the television set offered at $18.23 per month for 2 years will cost over $400.

An aspect of multiplication that was not covered in this unit is its role in "transformations" and especially in uniform expansion or shrinking transformations. Materials that exist for use in the middle school years serve to illustrate the essential idea.[8] These materials construct an elaborate fantasy about a "stretch-and-shrink" factory where, for example, a customer can bring in an item and have it put through a 3-stretch machine, and it comes out 3 times as long as it was. Such a continuous transformation doesn't fit any of the multiplication notions considered in This unit; the item is not added to itself 3 times, nor is it an array, nor is it a Cartesian product. Such words as *doubling, tripling,* and *quadrupling* (as compared with *two of, three of,* and *four of*) come close to conveying the idea.[9]

The role of multiplication in such size transformations is neglected in schoolwork, just as it was in this unit. There are some difficulties that may be hard to handle in early schoolwork; one of these is indicated by the pictures below.

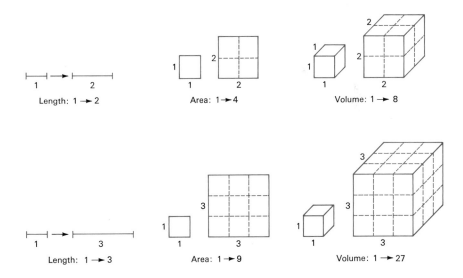

Length: 1 → 2   Area: 1 → 4   Volume: 1 → 8

Length: 1 → 3   Area: 1 → 9   Volume: 1 → 27

[8] University of Illinois Committee on School Mathematics, *Stretchers and Shrinkers.*

[9] A useful embodiment might be a number line made of nails driven into a board. An elastic stretched from 0 to 3 would be a 3-length, and "doubling" or making a "2-stretch" would involve stretching the rubber band to twice its former length, not using two 3-lengths.

72 USES
NUMBER
SYSTEMS:
SETS
RELATIONS
OPERATIONS

Uniform expansion by some factor has the normal multiplication properties for one dimension, but the effects escalate rapidly for two dimensions and three dimensions. (The growth is proportional to the square of the expansion factor for areas; to the cube of the expansion factor for volumes.)[10] Where and how this role of multiplication should be brought into schoolwork needs thinking about. Perhaps by the middle school years the interesting and significantly different effects of expansion on linear dimensions, areas, and volumes could get some attention.[11]

Another very common use of multiplication is in "formulas" that serve as mathematical models for many phenomena in science and elsewhere. For many people the main occupational use of mathematics is concerned with the use of formulas, and in many of these, multiplication either defines the main relationships or plays some role. This is too large a subject to be taken up here, but some references are given in Appendix II.[12]

Finally, those who subscribe to the findings and theories of the Piagetians believe that neither multiplication nor division is fully understood until both are understood. There is good reason to believe that this is probably true.

---

[10] A fascinating and easy-to-follow discussion of such effects in biology is given by J. B. S. Haldane, "On Being the Right Size," in J. R. Newman, ed., *The World of Mathematics,* Simon & Schuster, New York 1956, pp. 1001–1046.

[11] D. Huff's *How to Lie with Statistics* has some nice examples of how such effects can be (and are) used to present misleading impressions in informational graphs in propaganda—and even in advertising and news magazines.

[12] For example, M. Bell, *Mathematical Uses and Models in Our Everyday World,* chap. 4.

unit 4
subtraction of whole numbers

This unit continues the analysis of the meaning and properties of whole number operations by considering subtraction. As usual, we begin by asking what real situations lead to subtraction problems. This approach soon shows that subtraction has complications not present in addition. For one thing, at least two quite different sorts of situations lead to subtraction as a mathematical model. For another, it is possible to set up problems that have no answers; for example, $7 - 10 = \square$ can have no answer if only whole numbers are available.

The material in this unit will be somewhat different in format from previous units, and so some explanation is in order before you proceed. The units up to this point, and many to follow, have been written so that at the option of yourself or your instructor much of the learning can take place with individuals or small groups working on the activities worksheets. We feel that such activity is too often neglected in both school and college. But an entire class working together can also be effective. In our work with such courses as this one we have found that subtraction presents a number of issues that may be best sorted out in an activity-discussion session led by the instructor. You may already have had such a session about subtraction during which the class and the in-

74 NUMBER
SYSTEMS:
SETS
RELATIONS
OPERATIONS
USES

structor worked through activities, discussed results, then moved on to the next point. The material that follows assumes that such a session has taken place, that several students were assigned as observers and notetakers, and that these students collaborated on a set of notes describing the session. The notes are included in sections 4.2 and 4.3.

Some users of this book will be working through it on their own; some instructors may decide not to have an activity-discussion session; and some users may feel the need to go through this material again. Hence work sheets parallel to those for previous units are given in section 4.4.

4.2 CLASSROOM NOTES: THE MEANING OF SUBTRACTION OF WHOLE NUMBERS

Overview: **Subtraction in school classrooms usually means "take away," but in fact at least two quite different situations lead to subtraction problems. The search for tidiness in the mathematical world provides still another way of getting at subtraction by linking it to addition.**

Explanatory Note (From the Classroom Notetakers)

During the session each of us had rods and chips within reach. The professor (hereafter referred to as "Prof") posed questions and situations for us (hereafter referred to as "Us" or "We") to act out or think about, then Prof and We together summarized some conclusions, then Prof presented some new situations, and so on. The format of these summary notes is to describe first the problems or activities and then the conclusions.

4.2.1 "Take-away" Situations with Counts or with Measures

Prof suggested We do the appropriate counts and take-aways using chips for such story problems as this: "Susan has 12 candies and gives 7 of them away to friends. How many does she have left?" After a few of these Prof asked for similar stories from Us, including some resulting in problems such as $9 - 9 = \square$ and $11 - 0 = \square$. Prof asked Us to consider how the starting set, the removed set, and the remainder set of chips relate to corresponding addition problems where two sets are combined into a single set instead of the whole set being pulled apart.

Prof then directed attention to measure problems for which counting out chips seems inappropriate, such as this one: "Maria saws 6 feet off a 10-foot board. How much is left (ignoring the 1/16 inch or so lost in the saw cut)?" Short of sawing up a 10-rod, this can't be acted out literally but Prof suggested starting with a 10-rod, covering part of it with a 6-rod as shown, then trying the other rods in turn to see what is left. Prof asked Us to make up similar take-away stories about lengths and act them out, using trains of several rods to represent any whole numbers that exceed 10. Prof asked Us to observe

how the final rod situation resembles addition with rods. We showed subtraction in several ways; for example, with $10 - 6 = \square$ all these emerged:

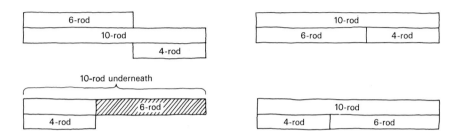

Some of these showed subtraction more clearly, some showed the relationship between addition and subtraction more clearly. Prof asked for measure stories not involving length take-aways. One suggestion was filling a 7-ounce glass from a 12-ounce can of pop; how much is left in the can? Prof suggested We consider how such problems could be acted out by children.

Finally, Prof stated a few problems that sounded like subtraction but for which We couldn't get answers with the rods or chips. For example, Judy has 13 pennies and owes 17¢ to Paul. How much does she still have to pay him if she gives him all her pennies? Prof also gave Us more problems where zero is subtracted, and We talked about the difficulties in acting out such problems. We recalled the use in earlier units of a square of paper or clear acetate as 0-rod and an empty loop of yarn as indicating zero chips, but even so "take-away" with zero seems a little phony.

Some Conclusions

1. Take-away problems involve a full set or a full measure from which a portion is actually removed and the "remainder" is counted or measured. As a mathematical model, the appropriate equations have the form $a - b = \square$, where a is the number attached to the whole set or measure, b is the number attached to the part removed, and $\square$ is the number attached to what remains.

2. It is easy to think of taking away "nothing," which corresponds to subtracting zero, but it is a bit tricky to see how to embody this either with chips or with rods.

3. Count situations and measure situations are quite different, with perhaps more scope for thinking up really different sorts of situations for measures.

4. There are perfectly reasonable situations where one would subtract a larger number from a smaller one, but as long as We are restricted to whole numbers, such problems have no answers. This is as good a way as any to anticipate the need for and use of negative numbers.

76 NUMBER
SYSTEMS:
SETS
RELATIONS
OPERATIONS
USES

5. From the variety of examples We explored some of the main properties of the subtraction operation; these will be pulled together in a later section of these notes.

*6. One of Us asked if subtraction was linked up with sets in any way comparable to the link between addition of whole numbers and unions of finite sets. Prof explained briefly that for counts such a link could be made by considering a set A with $n(A) = a$ and a set B that is a subset of set A with $n(B) = b$. Then the "difference set," sometimes written as $(A \sim B)$ consists of all those elements of A that are *not* in B, and $a - b = n(A \sim B)$. For details Prof referred Us to Begle, *The Mathematics of the Elementary School*[1] and observed that he doubted that it would be useful to stress with youngsters the notation or details of this link with sets. In any case, Prof observed, the main features of a "difference set" interpretation are implicit in actions with sets of chips or other embodiments of subtraction of counts.

7.,8., . . . [Add any conclusions you came to that the reporters missed in the above summary.]

4.2.2
**"Comparison" Situations
with Counts and Measures**

Again We had chips and rods within reach. Prof asked Us to set up the following situation with white chips for Susan and red for Jerry: "Susan has 12 pieces of candy and Jerry has 7; how many more does Susan have than Jerry?" Most of Us set up a line of 12 chips and underneath it a line of 7 chips, then matched them one for one and counted the unmatched white chips. All agreed that this is quite a different situation from take-away (where Susan actually gives away some candy). For one thing, there is a total of 19 pieces of candy somewhere in the situation. We also agreed that the mathematical model—the subtraction equation $12 - 7 = \square$—looks just like the model for the comparable take-away situation in spite of the differences in the real life situation.

Prof asked for other examples, and We supplied some and acted them out. Some examples were elicited that led to such equations as $13 - 0 = \square$ and $17 - 17 = \square$. Prof asked us how the equation would look if the problem were "Susan has 12 and Jerry 7; how many more does Jerry have than Susan?" With some reluctance We concluded this would be $7 - 12 = \square$, that this problem has no answer if only whole numbers are available, and that a negative number answer didn't sound quite right ("Jerry has negative five more than Susan"???).

[1] McGraw-Hill Book Company, New York, 1975, pp. 55–58.

Prof then asked Us to set up rods to work out such length situations as
"Steve has 10 inches of ribbon and Ruth 7 inches: How much longer is Steve's
ribbon?" It was suggested that we set up the rods side by side like this:

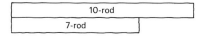

instead of concealing part of the longer rod as we did in the take-away situation. Then we looked for a rod to fill out the equivalent train. Once we had
done this, it was immediately apparent that there are strong links between
subtraction and addition, for the resulting display looks just like a completed
addition train. Prof asked for a few more length situations, and We supplied
them and worked them out with rods, including some involving zero both as
something to be subtracted and as a result. We again used a square of paper
as a 0-rod.

Prof asked Us for measure situations involving comparison for which the
rods would not be as obviously appropriate as they are for embodying
measures as lengths. We offered these examples: "Rob is 7 years old and Will
is 3: How much older is Rob?" "How much taller is Rob at 42 inches than Jill at
37 inches?" "How much more is in a full quart bottle of soft drink than in
another common size that contains 1 pint 12 ounces?" Prof asked Us for
ambiguous situations that could be considered either as take-away or as
comparison. We offered these: "Billie Jo is headed for Flitsville, 100 miles
away from her starting point. How much farther will she have to go when she
gets to Claytown, which is 65 miles from where she started?" (The assumption, of course, is that Claytown is on the way to Flitsville, on the same road,
etc.) "The gas tank of Ralph's automobile holds 15 gallons when full but is
now down to 6 gallons. How much is needed to fill it?"

Some Conclusions

1. Comparison situations seem quite different from take-away situations,
   even though they can lead to identical subtraction equations. Such situations involve two distinct quantities and both remain in the situation;
   nothing is given away, taken away, or otherwise lost (or indeed "subtracted") from the situation.
2. There is actually more in a comparison situation than appears anywhere
   in the subtraction equation. For example, if 13 is compared to 8 resulting
   in an equation $13 - 8 = \square$, the number 21 is somehow concealed in the
   situation as a total count or measure. Query: Does this confuse children?
3. Count situations and measure situations are again quite different. For
   comparisons you find the answer in a count situation by matching one
   for one, then counting those not matched. You find the answer in a
   measure situation by some sort of direct comparison of the measures,

78 **NUMBER
SYSTEMS:
SETS
RELATIONS
OPERATIONS
USES**

then asking how much more is needed to make the smaller measure equal to the larger.

4. It isn't easy to think of reasonable comparison situations that would lead to trying to subtract a larger number from a smaller one; that is, take-away seems to lead more naturally to consideration of negative numbers than does comparison.

5. Some of the basic properties of subtraction were considered, but these will be pulled together in a later section of these notes.

6.,7., . . . [Add any conclusions you or your class came to that are not included in these notes.]

**4.2.3
Number
Lines in Subtraction**
Prof had asked Us in advance to bring to class the number line we made for Unit 2, or to make a new one. Using the rods We did a number of subtraction problems such as the one pictured here for $15 - 8 = \square$: Put the right end of the 8-rod at 15 and read the answer at the left end of the rod.

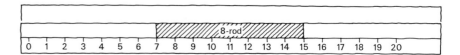

Working further with this, We found that of the three numbers in a subtraction situation, symbolized as $a - b = c$, the number a is represented as the starting length on the number line, and to represent the other two numbers either one rod or two can be used. We decided that problems where We put the b-rod coming back from the starting length (as in the drawing above) were take-away problems. On the other hand, in "comparison" problems, the b-rod starts from zero and we look for another rod to fill out the total length, as in the diagram below:

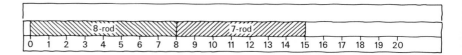

Prof advised Us to do some of the same problems without the rods by using "hops" or "trips" on the number line; for $15 - 8 = \square$ start at 15 and count back eight spaces, which is something like "lose 8 spaces" in certain games. Some of Us got confused by counting points instead of spaces. We talked about ways to avoid this and the extent to which similar errors would confuse youngsters working on the number line.

Prof asked Us, as usual, to consider how subtraction with rods and with hops embody measures and counts and what the relation is in each case to the addition problems that correspond to these subtraction problems. Also as usual, some of the problems We worked on forced Us to consider the role of zero both in subtraction itself and in these embodiments of subtraction.

Some Conclusions

1. Of the three numbers present in a subtraction situation, one number is usually represented as a number line length (though rods could be used), and the other two numbers can be represented either by two rods or by one rod and another number line length.
2. Take-away number line embodiments show quite clearly that subtraction can be thought of as a sort of reverse operation for addition. We go forward on the number line for addition, but backward for subtraction.
3. Using rods on a number line reinforces measure notions in connection with subtraction. It is easy to see, for example, that We are not restricted to whole number lengths. We merely measure back from one number to find another, and some (as yet unnamed) point can be found even if the measures are not whole numbers.
4. The various properties of subtraction emerged again (these are summarized later).
5., 6., . . . [Record here any other conclusions you or your class reach.]

**4.2.4
Addition-
Subtraction Links**

All through the session Prof had kept asking Us to notice how the subtractions We were embodying could be associated with corresponding addition problems and situations. Prof observed that the sorting out of such links is an important mathematical activity and waxed eloquent about the "niceness" of making an already known operation or structure serve an apparently very different purpose.

Prof had asked Us to make an addition table for sums up to $10 + 10$ at home. In class We were asked to find several subtraction answers using *only* this table (for example, to do $15 - 7 = \square$ you find a 15 in the 7 row and run your finger up the column to see what was added to 7 in order to get 15 as the sum). Prof observed that Piaget and others believe they have shown that a child fully understands neither addition nor subtraction until he has the links between them well in mind. Prof also observed that there are other respectable opinions that would deny this.

80 NUMBER
SYSTEMS:
SETS
RELATIONS
OPERATIONS
USES

Some Conclusions

1. It would be possible to *define* subtraction using only what is known about addition:

   Definition: $a - b = \square$ if and only if $\square + b = a$.
   (From the properties of addition, $\square + b = a$ could also have been written as $b + \square = a$, $a = b + \square$, or $a = \square + b$.)

2. Though each subtraction equation leads to a single addition equation (or obvious variations of it), an addition equation can lead to two different subtraction problems. That is, such a problem as $a + b = \square$ can become either $\square - a = b$ or $\square - b = a$.

3. By using the definition given in 1, above, some of the properties of subtraction can be "proved" by reference to already known properties of addition. For example, we know for sure that $a - a = 0$ because $0 + a = a$.

*4. Though it was not taken up in class, some of Us remembered the addition slide rule given as an option in Unit 2 and wondered how it could be used for subtraction. (To understand what follows you will need to have such an addition slide rule at hand.) One way to do such a problem as $15 - 8 = \square$ is to reverse the top scale to measure back from 15. Another way is to keep the scales just as in addition, set the 8 on the top scale over the 15 on the bottom scale, then look back under the 0 on the top scale to see what 8 had been added to to give 15. There are other possibilities and this is an investigation We recommend.

5.,6., . . . [Write in any other conclusions you or your class reached.]

4.3
CLASSROOM NOTES:
PROPERTIES OF WHOLE
NUMBER SUBTRACTION

The notetakers summarize here the properties of subtraction that emerged during the session. Prof had reserved a place on the blackboard to record these properties in symbolic form as they emerged.

4.3.1
Subtraction
of Whole Numbers
Is *Not* Closed

Such a problem as $80 - 100 = \square$ has no whole number answer. (But situations leading to such problems do arise; e.g., "Joe has an $80 balance in his checking account and writes a $100 check. . . .")

4.3.2
Uniqueness;
Equivalence Classes
of Differences

For whole numbers a and b and the subtraction $a - b = \square$, the answer is unique (if it exists). However, many different subtraction problems could lead to the same whole number, that is, there are equivalence classes of subtraction expressions. For example, here are four problems that give 7 as an answer and hence belong to the same subtraction equivalence class:

$$12 - 5 = \boxed{}, \; 13 - 6 = \boxed{}, \; 8 - 1 = \boxed{}, \; 7 - 0 = \boxed{}$$

4.3.3
Zero Is a Right
Identity, but Not a Left
Identity, for Subtraction. Used on the right (as the number being subtracted) zero qualifies as an identity because what goes into the subtraction comes out intact. For example, $11 - 0 = 11$; $3 - 0 = 3$; and in general, for any whole number a, $a - 0 = a$. The situation is quite different for zero used on the left, as in $0 - 3 = \square$. Not only is it not the case that the 3 comes out intact, but there is no whole number answer to such an equation.

*4.3.4
For Subtraction,
Every Whole Number Is
Its Own Inverse We were reminded that whole numbers do not have additive inverses since for nonzero whole numbers the equations $a + \square = 0$ and $\square + a = 0$ have no whole number solution. In other words, there is nothing you can add to bring a sum back to zero, the additive identity. Similarly, whole numbers do not have multiplicative inverses because for $a \neq 1$ there is no whole number solution for $a \times \square = 1$ and $\square \times a = 1$. That is, for multiplication of whole numbers there is nothing by which you can multiply a number greater than 1 to bring the product back to 1, the multiplicative identity.

If the same sort of equations are set up for subtraction, remembering that zero is at least in part an identity for subtraction, they look like this: $a - \square = 0$ and $\square - a = 0$. For the first time, such equations do have a whole number solution, namely a itself (because $a - a = 0$). Subtraction of whole numbers lacks many properties that addition and multiplication have, but it has one new property that they don't have.

4.3.5
Subtraction
of Whole Numbers Is
***Not* Commutative** In general, $a - b \neq b - a$. In fact, the only cases where subtraction is "commutative" is where $a = b$; for example, $5 - 5 = 5 - 5$ or $0 - 0 = 0 - 0$.

4.3.6
Subtraction
of Whole Numbers Is
***Not* Associative** Subtraction, like addition and multiplication, is a binary operation (i.e., deals with just two numbers at a time). Unlike addition and multiplication, if there are more than two numbers, an indication of how the pairs are formed *must* be given: e.g., for $8 - 5 - 3$, $(8 - 5) - 3 = 3 - 3 = 0$, but $8 - (5 - 3) = 8 - 2 = 6$. That is, in general $(a - b) - c \neq a - (b - c)$.

4.3.7
There Is *Not* a
"Do-as-you-Please" Property for
Subtraction of Whole Numbers Such a property comes from combining commutative and associative properties, and neither of these properties holds for subtraction of whole numbers.

82 NUMBER
SYSTEMS:
SETS
RELATIONS
OPERATIONS
USES

4.4
**WORK SHEETS
ON SUBTRACTION OF
WHOLE NUMBERS**

Overview: These work sheets cover the same ground as in sections 4.2 and 4.3. They can serve for review or additional practice or as an alternate to the suggested activity-discussion session.

Materials needed: Rods, chips, slotted number line (as used in Unit 2), addition slide rule.

4.4.1
**Take-away
Situations with Counts**

1. Act out the following situation by substituting chips for marbles: "Joe had 12 marbles and lost 7 of them in a game; how many did he have left?" (Or Joe had $12 and spent $7, . . . ; or other such examples.) Finish this equation: $12 - 7 = \square$. Similarly, make up simple take-away stories that might lead to the following equations, and act them out with chips.

Equation	**Take Away Story**
a. $17 - 8 = \square$	
b. $17 - 9 = \square$	
c. $7 - 7 = \square$	
d. $6 - 0 = \square$	

*2. Consider how the subtraction embodiments with chips relate to or resemble embodiments of addition.[1]

[1] For such a subtraction problem as $12 - 7 = 5$:

The subtraction starts

with one set: and ends with two sets:

   Total   Those left   Those taken away

The addition $5 + 7 = 12$

starts with two sets: and ends with one set:

Addend   Addend   Total

Both the total and the partition into two sets are the same in both cases.

4.4.2
Take-away
Situations with Measures

1. Consider this problem: "Joe has a 12-foot board and cuts 7 feet off it; about how much is left (ignoring the 1/16 inch or so lost in the saw cut)?" This is hard to act out with rods short of having a 12-rod and cutting it. The usual compromise is to exhibit a 12-train,

| 10-rod | 2-rod |

, hide part of it with a 7-rod,

| 7-rod |

, and measure what is left (perhaps by trial and error) with a 1-rod, 2-rod, 3-rod, 4-rod, 5-rod (aha! that's it!).

Such a solution becomes a bit farfetched for acting out a measure problem such as "Joe fills a 7-ounce glass from a full 12-ounce can of pop; about how much is left in the can?"

For each of the following examples, record a simple but plausible take-away measure situation that would lead to that equation and then act it out either with rods or with some embodiment more appropriate to the situation you have specified.

Equation	Take-away Measure Situation
a. $13 - 3 = \Box$	
b. $5 - 5 = \Box$	
c. $9 - 0 = \Box$	
d. $25 - 9 = \Box$	

4.4.3
Comparison
(How Much More)
with Counts

Such situations as this are quite common: "Jean has 12 marbles and John has 7 marbles. *How many more marbles does Jean have than John?*" Here one needs to display Jean's marbles (say with white chips) and John's marbles (say with blue chips), then pair off blues and whites on a one-for-one basis, then see what the excess of whites is. It is clear that the underlying situation here is quite different from the take-away situation (where somebody actually loses marbles), but exactly the same subtraction equation ($12 - 7 = \Box$) serves as a mathematical model. Imagine a plausible comparison situation leading to each of the following problems, act them out by comparing sets of chips, and record the answers.

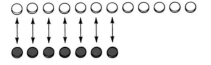

84 NUMBER
SYSTEMS:
SETS
RELATIONS
OPERATIONS
USES

Equation	Comparison Situation
a. $15 - 7 = \square$	
b. $15 - 8 = \square$	
c. $7 - 7 = \square$	
d. $7 - 0 = \square$	

4.4.4
**Comparison
(How Much More)
with Measures**

1. Many sorts of measures exist, but the rod embodiment is most appropriate for comparing lengths. A length comparison might come from such a problem as this: "Mary is 50 inches tall and Joe 42 inches tall; how much taller is Mary?" For many common life problems, embodiments that involve measures of volume or weight would be appropriate. For each of the following problems, consider that you are comparing lengths and act out the problem with rods. Record your answers.

a. $13 - 5 = \square$ **c.** $10 - 10 = \square$
b. $13 - 8 = \square$ **d.** $4 - 0 = \square$

*2. Work with other class members to make up plausible measure-comparison situations that might lead to the above subtraction problems. Specify an appropriate way of embodying each in concrete materials—not necessarily rods.

*3. How do such comparisons embodied with rods resemble corresponding addition embodiments?

4.4.5
Number Lines and Rods Used for Subtraction

1. Whatever the source of a given subtraction problem, a number line can be used to embody it. Use the rod number line you made for Unit 2. One way to use this number line for such a problem as $12 - 7 = \square$ is to lay a 7-rod in the slot with the right end point at 12 on the number line, and read off the answer at the left end point. Similarly, embody each of the following problems with the number line and write in the answers.

a. $18 - 5 = \square$
b. $18 - 13 = \square$
c. $13 - 4 = \square$
d. $8 - 8 = \square$

(For other ways to handle subtraction on this number line, see section 4.2.3.)

*2. How do the above problems resemble and/or not resemble the corresponding number line embodiments of addition problems?

*3. Subtraction by counting on a number line is also possible — and is popular in school textbooks. For $12 - 5 = \square$, start with 12 and then take 5 hops backwards (like "lose 5 spaces" in certain games). Try this with each of problems *a* to *d* above and talk over with other class members the differences in what might be learned from this approach versus the rod embodiments.

4.4.6
Addition-Subtraction Links

From having been asked many times in school to "check" your subtraction answers by adding, you no doubt know that subtraction can be defined in terms of addition in the following way:

Definition: $a - b = \square$ if and only if $\square + b = a$.[2]

Among other things, this means that the mathematics student need *not* memorize "subtraction facts" provided he already knows all the results in an addition table. For example, how would you find the answer to $17 - 8 = \square$ using *only* an addition table?[2] It warms a mathematician's

---

[2] The Piagetian findings may suggest that youngsters fully understand *neither* subtraction nor addition until they have this link well in mind (see R. W. Copeland, *How Children Learn Mathematics,* p. 101). Remember, however, that this is not a unanimous opinion; a behaviorist, for example, might well have a different opinion.

[2] **Find 17 in the 8-row, and follow up that column to find what was added to 8 to get 17.**

86 NUMBER
SYSTEMS:
SETS
RELATIONS
OPERATIONS
USES

heart (and, we hope, yours?) whenever something previously learned can be exploited to solve an apparently different problem.

1. For each of the following subtraction equations write a corresponding addition equation:

Subtraction	Addition
a. $17 - 8 = 9$	
b. $9 - 9 = 0$	
c. $9 - 0 = 9$	
d. $93 - 79 = 14$	

2. For each of the following addition equations, write *two* corresponding subtraction equations. (The first one is done for you as an example.)

Addition	Subtraction
a. $9 + 4 = 13$	a. $13 - 4 = 9$
	a'. $13 - 9 = 4$
b. $8 + 6 = 14$	b.
	b'.
c. $9 + 0 = 9$	c.
	c'.

*3. If you used an "addition slide rule" with whole number addition, see how each of these *subtraction* problems can be done using that slide rule. (Several different ways are possible; compare your procedures with the procedures used by other class members.)

a. $15 - 6 = \square$ c. $11 - 7 = \square$
b. $8 - 3 = \square$ d. $13 - 13 = \square$

4. Take the time now to review how subtraction using each of the embodiments is related to addition using that embodiment. Talk this over with other students.
Note: If you are doing the work sheets *instead of* reading the notes and conclusions earlier in this unit, you should turn back now to section 4.3, which summarizes the properties of subtraction.

4.5
SUMMARY AND
PEDAGOGICAL REMARKS

It is clear that, in teaching subtraction, problems should come from the real world. Children should begin by acting out the problems using concrete embodiments, with both counting and measuring situations illustrated. But with subtraction (and division) there are a number of rather tricky complications that do not appear with addition (or multiplication). Some of these are indicated below.

For beginning work with $a - b$, you consider only cases where b is less than a, but this prohibition must not be so strongly learned that there will be reluctance later to accept results like $8 - 11 = -3$. That is, most teachers do *too* good a job of teaching that $8 - 11$ has no answer, thus leaving a lasting suspicion of perfectly legitimate negative number results. In your own teaching of subtraction we think you should in a casual way always include a few subtraction *situations* in which negative results are plausible: "Joe's hot dog stand took in $25 last Monday, but he paid out $30 in expenses. Poor Joe." "At eight P.M. it was 5°F above zero, but by midnight the temperature had dropped 10°. How do *you* like below-zero weather?" It is also useful to show instances in which the first *must* be bigger than the second, "Joe has a 7-foot-long board and wants to cut a 9-foot shelf from it."

Subtraction for most teachers means take-away, but as you have seen, at least two common and quite different types of situations lead to such problems as $12 - 7 = 5$. The first can be called "take-away" situations and the second "comparison" or "how much more" situations. It should be made clear to children that the underlying situations are quite different, that one occurs about as often as the other, and hence that the same subtraction equations (as mathematical models) can come from quite different sources.

Unlike addition and multiplication, for subtraction you do *not* make a table of basic facts about combining the numbers 0 through 9. A table of "subtraction facts" could be made, but it would look a little strange and is not needed. Instead, you exploit the fact that $\square - \triangle = \bigcirc$ if and only if $\bigcirc + \triangle = \square$ ($12 - 7 = 5$ because $5 + 7 = 12$). Hence, in effect, the addition-facts table also contains the subtraction facts.

The words used in describing subtraction operations are more ornate, less standardized, and much less helpful than those used in addition (*addends* and *sum*) or multiplication (*factors* and *product*). This is because in subtraction a distinction must be made between the two numbers—hence *minuend* and *subtrahend* with the result a *difference* (possibly from comparison situations) or a *remainder* (possibly from take-away situations). Few people ever remember which number is the minuend and which the subtrahend, and the usefulness of teaching these words is questionable. To the extent that subtraction becomes addition, so that $12 - 7 = \square$ means $7 + \square = 12$, the "difference" can be spoken of as a *missing addend* and some school books do this.

88 NUMBER
SYSTEMS:
SETS
RELATIONS
OPERATIONS
USES

Such words and phrases as *minus, take away, how many more, plus how many,* and *difference between* often signal subtraction situations, especially in the tidy world of "word problems" in school books. Children are often taught, implicitly or explicitly, to look for these words and phrases and act accordingly (i.e., subtract). However, to follow such teachings blindly, as people so often do, may be hazardous in a real world situation, in part because habits can't substitute for a good sense of what operation is right in a particular situation, and in part because it is easy to make the same phrases signal other sorts of problems. For example (to stretch the point quite a bit), this problem should signal addition: *"The difference between you and me is that I've traveled 5,000 miles to deliver this airplane and you came 3,550 miles to take away the airplane. I don't know how many more miles you have to fly it, but up to this point, how far have we traveled together to accomplish this delivery?"*

In *doing* subtraction, two different ways of thinking about things are commonly taught. In different places and among most groups of people there will be some who think of it one way, some the other. These are the rough algorithm equivalents of take-away and comparison. For $12 - 7$ some will say "12 take away 7 is 5," having perhaps memorized many subtraction facts. Others will say "What must I add to 7 to get 12?" relying on addition facts. In the United States most schools would teach the former, whereas abroad most might teach the latter; but even in the United States both approaches are common.

Properties of subtractions are quite different than those of addition. There is no commutative property: $7 - 5 \neq 5 - 7$. If there are three or more numbers it *does* make a difference how they are grouped: $(7 - 4) - 2 \neq 7 - (4 - 2) \neq (7 - 2) - 4$. Zero is a right identity; $7 - 0 = 7$ (but $0 - 7 \neq 7$); and any number minus itself is zero: $7 - 7 = 0$. There is no way to handle the problem of subtraction using three or more numbers (such as $7 - 4 - 2$) without getting into parentheses or other means of grouping things. Parentheses are often studiously avoided by books and teachers, but you should not hesitate to introduce such grouping symbols in your classes when they can be helpful.

Since the ultimate aim of teaching mathematics is for students to be able to *use* what they know, teachers should not dodge the combinations of actual uses that involve count, measure, take-away, number lines, and so on.

unit 5
division of whole numbers

5.1
INTRODUCTION "Long division" appears on the school scene about fifth grade and is troublesome for countless youngsters. Part of the reason lies in the fact that the long division algorithm *is* long and complicated and demands a number of separate skills, including one (approximation) that is very much neglected in schools. However, it is also true that the meaning of division itself is often little understood by many youngsters, and hence the algorithm for accomplishing it merely adds to the confusion.

In this unit we do *not* deal with the algorithm for doing division (which is covered in Part B, Unit 4). Instead we concentrate on the meaning of the operation, the sorts of problems it solves, and some of its properties and peculiarities.

5.2
ACTIVITY: THE
MEANING AND SOURCES OF
DIVISION OF WHOLE NUMBERS

Overview: As with the other operations, division arises sometimes in dealing with counts and sometimes in dealing with measures. As with subtraction, a couple of quite different sorts of situations lead to division problems. Dividing one whole number by another may not give a whole number answer, and so remainders must be dealt with.

Materials needed: Chips, rods, a few yards (meters) of string.

89

90 NUMBER
SYSTEMS:
SETS
RELATIONS
OPERATIONS
USES

5.2.1
Exploration of Division

The work outlined by this activity will be most effective if several people work together as a group, talking about results and checking with each other. Most of the work will be done in the count mode with chips, but measure embodiments will also be used.

1. Working alone, act out with chips the problem $15 \div 3 = \square$, using whatever you know about what division means. Leave whatever you have done with the chips visible on the table, and look at everyone else's chip display. With any luck, there will be several different sorts of displays; if so, the class members whose displays are different should explain how the problem is embodied in their displays. (A number of possibilities will be explored below; watch to see how many of them came up in your class.)

2. Examine your own display and that of several classmates to see if they suggest any links between multiplication and division. Record any such links you see, and share them with your colleagues.

3. Use 28 chips to embody the problem $28 \div 4 = \square$, preferably in a different way than the one you used for the first problem. Examine other class members' displays and see whether any new methods have emerged on this second round. Discuss whether the displays that result suggest any links between division and multiplication.

4. Count out 19 chips and act out the problem $19 \div 3 = \square$. Leave your display visible and look at other people's displays. Discuss the various solutions to this problem and the various ways of handling the "remainder."

5.2.2
Sources of Division

Given the total and the number of sets, find the size of each set.

1. One of the sorts of situations that lead to division is illustrated by this example: "Michael's mom gives him 15 cookies to be shared equally among himself and four friends. How many cookies should each get?" Get out 15 poker chips and work out this problem concretely, perhaps by imagining five people and passing out the cookies ("One for you, and one for you, and . . .") until they are all dealt out. Finish the equation $15 \div 3 = \square$. The result, of course, is 5 sets of 3 cookies

each; you knew the number of sets and the total and you were looking for the number in each set.

2. As you acted this out, did you end up with 5 piles of 3 chips each, or with a 3×5 array of chips, or with some other arrangement? Did others in the group get different-looking displays?

3. In the problems below, make up and record a simple situation of the same sort as the cookie sharing (a certain number of things to be allocated equally into a certain number of sets; find out how many are in each set). Then act out the problem with chips and fill in the answer. For future reference, draw a diagram of at least one of your chip layouts.

Equation	Situation (Size of Set Not Known)
a. $18 \div 3 = \square$	
b. $18 \div 6 = \square$	
*c. $21 \div 5 = \square$	

Diagram of a chip layout:

5.2.3 Given the total and the size of each set, find the number of sets.

Sources of Division

1. A different sort of situation leading to division is illustrated by this example: "A teacher has 24 children and she wants them to work on a certain project in committees of 6 children each. How many such committees will there be?" With 24 chips, act out the situation and then complete this equation: $24 \div 6 = \square$.

The answer, of course, is that there are 4 such 6-person committees. You knew the size of each set and the total and you were looking for the number of sets. If different sorts of displays appeared among class members, discuss the differences.

2. A common way of stating such a problem as the one just illustrated is "How many sixes in 24?" For example, the problem "How many 5¢

92 USES
NUMBER
SYSTEMS:
SETS
RELATIONS
OPERATIONS

apples can I buy for 35¢?" essentially asks "How many fives are there in 35?" The equation would be $35 \div 5 = \square$.

3. For each of the following problems, imagine a common situation of the sort discussed above and briefly record it. Act out the problem with poker chips and fill in the answer. For future reference, make a diagram of at least one of your chip layouts.

Equation	**Situation (Number of Sets Not Known)**
a. $21 \div 3 = \square$	
b. $21 \div 7 = \square$	
*c. $29 \div 9 = \square$	

Diagram of a chip layout:

5.2.4
Sources
of Division with
Measures

Given the total amount and the number of equal pieces, find the size of each piece.

The two sorts of situations indicated above that lead to division also arise with measures. For the first, you might have a youngster making an even split among four tall glasses from a quart bottle (32 ounces) of pop; how much pop would he put in each glass? The equation would be $32 \div 4 = \square$. To act out such a situation would clearly be a trial-and-error procedure, pouring a bit in each glass until they are all the same level—something like the "One for you, and one for you, and . . ." of the count situation.[1]

---

[1] Here the calculation by arithmetic of $32 \div 4$ would no doubt give more exact results than the actual trial-and-error solution.

1. Act out this problem by actually measuring out a 20-centimeter length of string or ribbon, cutting it up, and measuring the pieces: "How long is each of 4 equal pieces cut from a 20-centimeter-long ribbon?" Complete the equation $20 \div 4 = \square$.

2. "A boy needs to cut three equal boards from a 12-foot board; how long will each piece be, ignoring the loss from saw cuts?" To act this out with rods, you might set up a 12-length (say with a 10-rod and a 2-rod) and then, by trial and error, see what length rod works for a train of 3 equal rods equivalent to the 12-length: $12 \div 3 = \square$.

3. Using rods, string, or ribbon, act out each of the following situations and complete the equation:
  a. What is the length of each of 7 equal pieces cut from stock 14 units long? $14 \div 7 = \square$
  b. What is the length of each of 3 pieces cut from stock 27 units long? $27 \div 3 = \square$

5.2.5 Sources of Division with Measures

Given the total amount and the size of equal pieces, find the number of pieces.

1. A measure situation illustrating a second source of division problems might be this: "How many 3-inch lengths of ribbon can I get from a yard (36 inches) of ribbon?" The division problem is $36 \div 3 = \square$. Here there is no trial and error; you cut off one piece, then another, then another, till the ribbon is gone; then you count the pieces. With rods, you might act out $36 \div 3 = \square$ by starting with a 36-length (three 10-rods and a 6-rod) and building a train of 3-rods above it, and then counting how many 3-rods are in the train. Similarly, act out the following problems with rods:

  a. $28 \div 7 = \square$
  b. $28 \div 4 = \square$
  c. $35 \div 7 = \square$

5.2.6 "Remainders" in Division

You will recall that in order for subtraction to have a whole number answer the first number must be at least as large as the number being subtracted from it; for example, $15 - 7 = \square$ has a whole number answer, but $7 - 15 = \square$ does not. Similarly, for division to have a whole number answer, the total must be at least as large as the number dividing it. For example, $4 \div 8 = \square$ will *not* give a whole number answer. (If 8 friends share 4 cookies, the cookies must crumble.) Additional complications come from the fact that reasonable situations of any of the kinds

94 USES
NUMBER
SYSTEMS:
SETS
RELATIONS
OPERATIONS

considered earlier might lead to equations such as $16 \div 3 = \square$ or $26 \div 4 = \square$. These do not have uncomplicated whole number answers even though 16 is larger than 3, and 26 is larger than 4.

1. Act out $26 \div 4 = \square$ with chips. Write the answer first as a whole number considered as "How many fours in 26 (and how much left over)?" and then as "If $26 is split four ways, how many *dollars* are in each share, and how many *dollars* are left over?" If you now divide the leftover dollars into equal shares and complete this transaction, how big is each share?

2. Consider the equation $16 \div 3 = \square$ as the mathematical model for this question: "How many 3-unit lengths are there in 16 units, and how much left over?" Act this out with rods and leave the display intact while you do problem 3.

3. Consider the equation $16 \div 3 = \square$ as the mathematical model for this situation: "If you cut an object 16 units long into 3 exactly equal pieces, how long is each piece?" Act out the situation with a piece of string. In what ways are the result and the action leading to the result different here from the previous problem? Could this problem be easily acted out with rods? (Try it with rods and see what some of the difficulties are.)

4. Consider the equation $16 \div 3 = \square$ as the mathematical model for this situation: "What is the largest whole number length contained in a 16-length exactly 3 times, and how much of the 16-length remains?" Would this be best acted out with string or with rods? Act it out and consider how, if at all, it differs from the previous two problems.

5. Consider the equation $16 \div 3 = \square$ as the mathematical model for this situation: How many packages of 3 chocolate rabbits each can be made from 16 rabbits? Act this out and consider how it differs from the problems above.

6. How to deal with whole number division in practical situations that do *not* come out even depends on the situation and common sense. If you are really dealing with counts of things that are not to be cut up, the only thing to do is settle for a whole number and indicate the remainder—how much is left over.

   Similarly, if you want 3-foot pieces from a 10-foot board, you get three such pieces and a scrap. If the things in question can be divided up, you go to fractional parts; the 10-year-old has no difficulty in assuring that he and his two friends get the same share from a 16-ounce bottle of pop with no remainder. There is no difficulty for an older child in seeing that each of these shares is $5\frac{1}{3}$ ounces. (Most schoolwork starts by using *only* remainders and later allows *only* quotients worked out to fractions or decimals. The former may be necessary; the latter is certainly silly if the situation from which the division problem comes doesn't sensibly permit fractions.)

For each of the following problems, imagine a situation in which stating a quotient and remainder would make sense and a second situation in which splitting up the remainder equally (thus getting fractions in the quotient) would make sense. Discuss these situations with class members.

Equation	Remainder and Fraction Situations
a. $19 \div 6 = \square$	
b. $21 \div 4 = \square$	

**5.3
PROBLEM SET:
LINKS BETWEEN DIVISION AND
MULTIPLICATION OF
WHOLE NUMBERS**

Overview: Multiplication and division are closely related in much the same sense that addition and subtraction are related. The division process can be considered as finding a "missing factor" in a multiplication or as finding the number of rows in an array or as repeated subtraction (versus repeated addition in multiplication) or in other ways.

Materials Needed: Chips

**5.3.1
"Checking"
Division by Multiplying**

Just as children are told to "check" a subtraction by doing the appropriate addition, they are also told to "check" a division that "comes out even" by multiplying the quotient times the divisor. Thus in $63 \div 9 = \square$, the number 7 goes in the box because $7 \times 9 = 63$; or, if you like, because $9 \times 7 = 63$. Hence any division equation of the sort $p \div n = \square$ can be rewritten as either of two (equivalent) multiplication equations: $n \times \square = p$ or $\square \times n = p$.

1. Rewrite each of the following equations in both possible multiplication ways:

96 NUMBER
SYSTEMS:
SETS
RELATIONS
OPERATIONS
USES

Division Equation	Multiplication Equations
a. $36 \div 12 = \square$	a. $\square \times 12 = 36$
	a'.
b. $36 \div 3 = \square$	b.
	b'.
c. $48 \div 8 = \square$	c.
	c'

**5.3.2
Checking
When There Are Remainders:**
$p = (n \times q) + r$

We have already observed that a division with two whole numbers resulting from a real situation is not likely to "come out even." If fractions are avoided, the division usually leads to a *pair* of whole numbers: a *quotient* and a *remainder*. Thus a child might do $30 \div 7 = \square$ in this form:

$$\begin{array}{r} 4 \\ 7\overline{)30} \\ \underline{28} \\ 2 \end{array}$$

and give the answer as "4 R2," meaning a quotient (as far as it goes) of 4 and a remainder of 2. In this case, checking the answer is more complicated. For $30 \div 7 = \square$, the child's answer of "4 R2" is correct if $30 = (4 \times 7) + 2$.

In general, any division problem $p \div n = \square$ (n can't be zero) gives rise to a quotient q and a remainder r such that $p = (n \times q) + r$. If the division comes out even, the remainder is zero; for example, $72 \div 8 = \square$ leads to $q = 9$ and $r = 0$, and sure enough, $72 = (8 \times 9) + 0$.

1. Act out each of the following division problems with chips to find the q and r, and write the "check" equation in the form $p = (n \times q) + r$. The remainder should be less than the divisor, that is, r should be less than n.

	Problem: $p \div n = \square$	q	r	$p = (n \times q) + r$
a.	$19 \div 6 = \square$			
b.	$13 \div 7 = \square$			
c.	$12 \div 4 = \square$			
* d.‡	$7 \div 8 = \square$			

‡Hint: Let the "quotient" be zero.

*5.3.3
Multiplication-
Division Links: Arrays, Repeated
Addition, and Repeated Subtraction

Note: It is assumed in this section that all division problems come out even, in order to explore links between whole number divisions and corresponding whole number multiplications.

Recall the work in section 5.3.1 which showed that any division (that comes out even) can be rewritten as a multiplication in two ways. On the other hand, any multiplication can be regarded as concealing two division problems. For example, $8 \times 7 = 56$ could become either $56 \div 7 = 8$ or $56 \div 8 = 7$. In general, $n \times s = p$ can become either $p \div n = s$ or $p \div s = n$.

1. Rewrite each of the following multiplication equations in its two possible division forms:

Multiplication Form	**Division Forms**
a. $9 \times 7 = 63$	*a.*
	a'.
b. $4 \times 12 = 48$	*b.*
	b'.
c. $1 \times 113 = 113$	*c.*
	c'.

2. Remember that in the multiplication activities given in Unit 3 the *n* in $n \times s = p$ was consistently regarded as giving the number of sets (or number of rows in an array), while the second factor, *s*, was regarded as giving the size of each set (or size of a row in an array). Hence the rewriting of $n \times s = p$ as $p \div n = s$ could be seen as coming from one of the interpretations of division, namely, given the total quantity and the number of equal sets, how many are in each set?

Here is an example in which the total and the number of sets are known: "If 24 cookies are to be shared equally among 6 friends, how many cookies will each get?" An equation is $24 \div 6 = \square$. Act this example out with chips by starting 6 rows, then putting another chip in each row, then another, and so on till all 24 are used. Note that the division problem evolves into a 6×4 array when it is acted out in this way.

3. Similarly, if the *s* in $n \times s = p$ is the size of each of *n* sets, the corresponding division problem $p \div s = n$ means that the total amount and the size of each set are known and the problem is to find the number of such sets.

An example that resembles that in problem 2 and yet reflects this different situation might be: "Twenty-four cookies are to be put up by the half dozen into bags. How many such bags of cookies will there be?" Act this out by counting out a row of 6 chips (to represent one bag of cookies), then another row of 6, and so on till the 24 chips are

98 NUMBER
SYSTEMS:
SETS
RELATIONS
OPERATIONS
USES

all used. Note that when it is acted out in this way the division problem evolves into the same array that embodies the corresponding multiplication problem.

4. Problem 3 could also be acted out by repeated subtraction. In effect the question is, "How many sixes in 24?" Act this out by starting with 24 chips and proceeding as follows:

Action	How Many Sixes So Far?	Remainders
Start with 24 chips	0	24
Take out 6	1	−6
		18
Take out another 6	2	−6
		12
Take out another 6	3	−6
		6
Take out the final 6	4	−6
There are 4 sixes in 24.		0

The link with multiplication comes from remembering the repeated-addition interpretation of multiplication and by considering subtraction as the operation that, in some sense, reverses the operation of addition. Just as multiplication and division reverse each other, so do repeated addition and repeated subtraction.[2]

5.3.4
Using a
Multiplication Table to
Do Division

One of the nicest things about the links between multiplication and division is that nobody needs to learn "division facts" if he already knows his multiplication table.

1. Finish filling in this multiplication table, and then use it to find the answers to the problems given below the table by turning each division problem into a "missing-factor" multiplication problem. (Actually use the table, even if you already know the answers. This allows you to see the possible difficulties children might have in using tables.)

[2] As a matter of fact, many calculating machines operate by doing many repeated additions for multiplication and many repeated subtractions for division. That is, calculators (and computers, for that matter) are often just super adders and super subtractors. The power of calculators and computers comes from the fact that essentially all mathematical operations, including some pretty fancy ones, can be broken down into a series of single basic operations—addition, subtraction, multiplication, and division—and from the great speed with which such machines can do single operations. (Electronic computers can perform *millions* of operations every second.)

×	0	1	2	3	4	5	6	7	8	9	10
0	0	0			0			0	0		
1	0		2	3	4					9	10
2				6		10		14	16	18	
3		3			12		18		24		
4	0	4	8			20	24				
5			10	15		25				45	50
6		6			24		36	42	48		60
7	0		14						56	63	
8			16	24		40					
9		9			36					81	90
10	0		20		40		60				

a. $81 \div 9 = \square$ **d.** $42 \div 6 = \square$

b. $80 \div 10 = \square$ **e.** $0 \div 2 = \square$

c. $49 \div 7 = \square$ **f.** $72 \div 9 = \square$

5.3.5 Division by a Whole Number Versus Multiplication by a Fraction Even at first- or second-grade level many children are quite at home with simple fractions such as "half of," "one-third of," and so on, provided they arise in contexts very familiar to them. ("Give me half of your candy bar and I'll give you half of my marbles." Notice, by the way, that both a measure and a count are involved in this transaction.) Strictly speaking, such fractions do not belong in a section on whole numbers. However, at the level of real world actions, taking half of something and dividing something by 2 look very much the same. A symbolic rendering of this link between division and multiplication looks like this:

$$p \div n = p \times \frac{1}{n}$$

This symbolic rendering won't seem strange to you if you stick to numerical examples: ⅓ of 24 means dividing 24 three ways; ¼ of 24 means dividing it 4 ways, and so on.[3]

1. Fill in the blanks in the chart (p. 100), and act out each problem

---

[3] Some important special cases are those that result in 1 as an answer: $2 \div 2 = 1$ and ½ × 2 = 1; $5 \div 5 = 1$ and ⅕ × 5 = 1; and so on.

100 NUMBER
SYSTEMS:
SETS
RELATIONS
OPERATIONS
USES

with chips until you have a good feeling for how multiplication by a fraction can amount to the same thing as division by a whole number.

Division Problem	Fraction Problem
a. $14 \div 2 = \square$	a.
b.	b. ⅓ of $12 = \square$
c. $16 \div 4 = \square$	c.

5.4
PROBLEM SET:
PROPERTIES OF DIVISION OF
WHOLE NUMBERS

Overview: **The same properties already examined for addition, multiplication, and subtraction will be considered with respect to their validity or nonvalidity for division. These include closure, uniqueness, equivalence classes, commutativity, associativity, identity element, and inverses. Some properties special to division are discussed, including the important fact that division by zero is impossible.**

Materials needed: Chips.

5.4.1
Closure
Property

1. Remember that an operation is closed with respect to a set of numbers if doing the operation with those numbers *always* yields one of those numbers. Does division of whole numbers always yield a single whole number as quotient? If not, list a couple of examples where it does not.[4]

*2. If $p \div n = \square$ does give a whole number answer, we say that "*n* divides *p*" or that "*p* is *divisible* by *n*."
a. List three examples where the division $p \div n = \square$ *does* give a

---

[4] In testing a proposition, trying out many examples that give positive results certainly increases your confidence in the truth of the proposition, but examples can never prove for sure that something *always* happens. On the other hand, a *single* negative result is enough to prove the falseness of a proposition by showing that something doesn't always happen. Such a negative result is sometimes called a *counterexample*. A problem such as $3 \div 4 = \square$ is a counterexample that proves that division of whole numbers is *not* closed since the answer is not a whole number.

whole number (hence p is divisible by n) and three examples where it does not.

b. Does the fact that $0 \div 2 = 0$ show that 0 is divisible by 2?

5.4.2
**A Substitute
for "Closure" of Division
of Whole Numbers**
We cannot be sure that a given division will give a whole number quotient, but every division $p \div n$ with whole numbers does give a *pair* of whole numbers, namely a quotient (call it q) and a remainder (call it r) with r less than q. For that q and r, it is *always* true that $p = (n \times q) + r$; indeed, this is the way schoolchildren are told to check their division results.

A concrete test for whether or not $p \div n = \square$ has a whole number answer is to take p chips and try either to form an array with n rows exactly filled out with none left over or to see if a certain number of groups of n can be formed with none left over. (In either case, if any are left over, that is the remainder.)

For each of the following, use chips to find the pair of whole numbers that give the largest possible quotient and a remainder less than the divisor. Fill in all the columns of the table as indicated by the first two examples, which are done for you.

Division Problem: $p \div n$	q	r	Verify $p = (n \times q) + r$
a. $9 \div 2 = \square$	4	1	$9 = (2 \times 4) + 1$
b. $16 \div 8 = \square$	2	0	$16 = (8 \times 2) + 0$
c. $27 \div 5 = \square$			
d. $23 \div 6 = \square$			
e. $14 \div 7 = \square$			
*f. $3 \div 6 = \square$ (Hint: q is zero.)			

5.4.3
**Uniqueness;
Equivalence Classes
of Quotients**
1. If a whole number quotient exists (with zero remainder), then it is unique. On the other hand, any given whole number can be the quotient for many different problems.

Two division problems that yield the quotient 3 are given. Make up

102 NUMBER
SYSTEMS:
SETS
RELATIONS
OPERATIONS
USES

five more division problems that give the quotient 3 and write them below.

$$6 \div 2 = 3$$
$$18 \div 6 = 3$$

In the language we have used in talking about other operations, there are *equivalence classes* of quotients. One such class contains all the problems that give 3 as quotient; another such equivalence class contains all those that give 10 as quotient; and so on.

2. Similarly, if a division problem leads to a quotient and a remainder, it should give the same quotient and the same remainder no matter when, how, or by whom it is done (provided it is done correctly and carried on until the remainder is less than the divisor.) On the other hand, there may be many different division problems that yield the same quotient and remainder. Two problems that yield 3 as quotient and 2 as remainder are given and checked below. Add three more examples.

Problem Giving Quotient of 3 and Remainder of 2	Check
a. $14 \div 4 = 3$ R2	$(3 \times 4) + 2 = 14$
b. $11 \div 3 = 3$ R2	$(3 \times 3) + 2 = 11$
c.	
d.	
e.	

5.4.4
The
Number 1 as a Right
Identity
It is easy to see that $1 \div 13$ has a very different meaning from $13 \div 1$. In general, for any whole number p, $p \div 1 = p$, but $1 \div p$ has a whole number answer only if p itself is 1. In the language used for the other operations, this means that 1 acts as an *identity element* on the right but not on the left. What number plays a similar role for subtraction?

5.4.5
Inverses
Think about and discuss the concrete meaning of such problems as $5 \div 5 = \square$ and $13 \div 13 = \square$. In general, convince yourself that for any whole number $p \neq 0$, $p \div p = 1$ is always true. In the language used for the other operations this means that to the extent that 1 is an identity for division, every whole number p (except zero) has an "inverse" – namely p itself.

5.4.6
Commutativity

1. If division were commutative, then for *every* two numbers a and b, it would be true that $a \div b = b \div a$. Convince yourself that this is not the case by writing three more counterexamples in addition to the one given below.

    a. $4 \div 2 \neq 2 \div 4$

    b.

    c.

    d.

2. There may be special cases where for *some* a and b, $a \div b = b \div a$. See if you can find some, and list examples below if you do.[1]

5.4.7
Associativity

1. In order for division of whole numbers to be associative, it would have to be true for any a and any non zero b or c that $(a \div b) \div c = a \div (b \div c)$. Convince yourself that this statement is *not* always true, and supply three more counterexamples below.

    a. $(8 \div 4) \div 2 \neq 8 \div (4 \div 2)$ because $2 \div 2 \neq 8 \div 2$

    b.

    c.

    d.

2. The fact that division is not associative doesn't exclude the possibility that there may be special cases where for *some* a, b, and c, $(a \div b) \div c = a \div (b \div c)$. Try to find at least one such special case and list it below.[2]

---

[1] For whole numbers, this can only happen for a number divided by itself; for example, $5 \div 5 = 5 \div 5$.

[2] Some examples would be $(1 \div 1) \div 1 = 1 \div (1 \div 1)$ or $(4 \div 2) \div 1 = 4 \div (2 \div 1)$. What is special about such examples?

104 NUMBER
SYSTEMS:
SETS
RELATIONS
OPERATIONS
USES

5.4.8
Division of
Zero by a Nonzero
Whole Number

Think about what some of the interpretations of $0 \div 3 = \square$ might be and what should go in the box. Try to formulate a general conclusion about the answer to $0 \div a = \square$ for *any* $a \neq 0$.[3]

5.4.9
Division by
Zero: Impossible!

1. One of the most persistent myths fostered by the usual school mathematics experience is that one can *always* get an answer to any arithmetic problem. Even the fact that division and subtraction of whole numbers are not closed presents only temporary difficulties that are cleared up merely by expanding the number set to include fractions and negative numbers. But there is no way to expand the set of numbers to get an answer to such a problem as $5 \div 0 = \square$.

Take a few minutes to run through various interpretations of such a division as $5 \div 0 = \square$ and try to convince yourself that there can be no numerical answer to such a problem. (It might help you to keep in mind the contrast with such a problem as $5 \div 1 = \square$.) Discuss these interpretations in class and also discuss which of them, if any, would be really convincing to a child or to an adult skeptic in showing that indeed $5 \div 0 = \square$ cannot have an answer.[4]

*2. The usual reasoning that for any nonzero number p, $p \div 0 = \square$ cannot have any number as its answer (because no answer would "check" in $0 \times \square = p$) breaks down for zero divided by zero. Consider $0 \div 0 = \square$. Many people would say that 1 goes in the box because for all $p \neq 0$, $p \div p = 1$. This proposed answer does check, since $1 \times 0 = 0$. To see the difficulty with this approach, check by multiplication each of the following proposed answers to $0 \div 0 = \square$. (The first two are done for you.)

Equation	Check
a. $0 \div 0 = \boxed{1}$	$1 \times 0 = 0$
b. $0 \div 0 = \boxed{10}$	$10 \times 0 = 0$
c. $0 \div 0 = \boxed{100}$	
d. $0 \div 0 = \boxed{13,147}$	
e. $0 \div 0 = \boxed{42}$	

[3] Any such quotient must be zero, of course, because if you are instructed to check the answer to $0 \div a = \square$ by the multiplication $\square \times a = 0$, the only thing that would work in the box would be a 0.

[4] A persuasive *logical* argument is to observe that for any multiplication by zero, the product is

Thus it seems that *any* number would work as an answer, and this is just as troublesome as having *no* answer that works. Hence, it is always understood whenever division is in the picture that zero is absolutely excluded as a possible divisor.

5.5 SUMMARY AND PEDAGOGICAL REMARKS

As usual, division problems should be seen as coming from real situations. A number of complications appear that are not present with addition or multiplication, and that parallel the complications with subtraction: division of whole numbers is not closed, not commutative, and not associative. However, division, like subtraction, does have a right identity and each number is its own inverse. An additional sticky point for many people is that division by zero is impossible.

In school, the teaching of division often seems to be ignored through the first grade, developed in a very leisurely way through fourth grade, and accelerated quite suddenly about fifth grade with considerable stress on the long division algorithm with all its complications, using quite difficult examples. But during the fifth and sixth grades there is also an escalation in teaching about symbolic manipulation of fractions and decimals. Hence, for many children there may be an overload of new and fairly abstract processes to be learned during those years. The results seem to be depressingly predictable. Many children don't understand what is going on, even if they learn to perform the symbolic manipulations, and these may be the years during which far too many people simply give up on trying to understand mathematics.

Our feeling is that the division process has little meaning even by grade five for many students. For these students, the ornate and complicated long division algorithm, which demands skill with subtraction, multiplication, and approximation (a very neglected skill) merely adds to the confusion. The role of the primary school teacher should be to give meaning to division and to tie it securely to its companion operation, multiplication. Algorithmic concerns can be safely neglected for some time, except maybe to show the standard forms for displaying division problems (for example, $5 \overline{)275}$). Even without the division algorithm there are many issues to be considered and infiltrated into the child's experience.

---

zero; for example, $114 \times 0 = 0$. Then, since the multiplication "check" for $5 \div 0 = \square$ would be $\square \times 0 = 5$, it is clear that there is no number that could go in the box, because for *any* number put in the box the product would be zero and not 5. That is, once you accept that multiplication with a zero factor *always* gives a zero product, you must also accept that division of a nonzero number by zero cannot give any number at all as the quotient.

106 NUMBER
SYSTEMS:
SETS
RELATIONS
OPERATIONS
USES

Three numbers are in the picture: the total you start with (in school books, the *dividend*), the number you divide by (the *divisor*), and the answer (the *quotient*). In early work the divisor is never larger than the total, but that shouldn't be put *too* strongly because later on it doesn't matter. An extra complication is that there may be "remainders" in dealing with whole numbers. All these complications can get confusing, but if the teacher has a light touch and sticks close to acting out actual applications, they need not cause troubles.

At least two quite different everyday situations lead to division. It is more difficult to describe them in words than to act them out. Both apply to counts or to measures. In the first, one has p things to be shared equally in n groups; how many end up in each group? (Example: "With 12 pennies and six children, how many pennies does each child get?") For the second type of situation, one has p things and wants to form groups each of size s; how many such groups can be formed? (Examples: "If 12 donuts are packaged by fours, how many packages will there be?" "How many 6-inch ribbons can be cut from a yard of ribbon?")

The choices for acting out any such situation all recall the work with multiplication. One choice is via arrays: For such a count situation as 12 pennies, 4 children, the allocation goes "One for A, one for B, one for C, one for D; then two for A, two for B, . . . ," until there are 4 piles of 3 pennies each or, probably better, an array with 4 rows of 3. For 12 donuts in packages of 4, put down 4 chips, then another 4, then another 4 — again either in piles or as an array of 3 rows of 4 each.

Another choice is via repeated subtraction, the inverse of repeated addition in multiplication. In the problem of dividing up 12 pennies among 4 children, each takes a penny, then each takes another penny, etc.; how many times do the 4 kids each pick up a penny? For the donuts, subtract enough for one package, then for the next, etc.

"How many fours in 12?" is another common way of phrasing $12 \div 4$. This again recalls multiplication by asking for a missing factor ("What times 4 gives 12?"). Similar remarks apply to measure situations, with the added caution that since measures themselves are always approximate, the results from any calculation are approximate. (*About* and other such words should be used liberally in connection with measure problems.)

To the extent that the primary school teacher goes beyond acting out division situations to teaching symbolic operations, it may be best to stick to links with multiplication. That is, instead of drill for a lot of division facts such as $12 \div 3 = \square$, ask instead "3 times what is 12?". A "division table" would be ridiculous, but using a multiplication table to find a missing factor makes good sense. To motivate this, one can exploit the usual school instruction to check division by multiplying.

In most schoolwork, the fraction notation for division is neglected until it can't be avoided, and we think this is a mistake. In fact, $\frac{12}{3}$ is one of the ways of writing "12 divided by 3" (along with $12 \div 3$ and $3\overline{)12}$) and for later work in mathematics it becomes the main way. Even such a fraction as $\frac{1}{2}$ is usefully thought of as division: one thing (or group) divided into two equal parts (or two equal groups).

Proponents of Piaget's findings insist that neither multiplication nor division is fully understood by a child until he understands the links between them. Although this may be too extreme a view, the links between multiplication and division certainly are helpful in learning both operations. As a matter of fact, links among all the basic operations are needed in order to really understand division. This is true because repeated subtraction (and hence repeated addition) is in the picture. In doing a division problem with the standard algorithm and then checking the answer, all four operations are used. This may be why long division is so difficult for so many youngsters, but it also presents a fine opportunity to pull together and solidify many computation concepts and skills.

unit 6

extension of the whole numbers to the integers

6.1
INTRODUCTION Negative numbers are avoided in most elementary school teaching, perhaps because of teachers' memories of such mysteries as $-(x - 6) = 6 - x$ or $(^-2)(^-4) = {}^+8$ or $6 - (^-2) = {}^+8$ from high school algebra. But a child's life is not so obliging as to avoid the situations that negative numbers fit: temperatures are reported as "below zero," children hear of gains and losses both in games and in money affairs, they perhaps see negative numbers in print (in stock market quotations, for example). In many classrooms children see number lines with unnumbered space to the left of zero and are told that a problem such as $2 - 6 = \square$ *"just can't be done."* They may wonder in both cases why that should be so.

There are some rather difficult manipulations with negative numbers, but there are also uses of them that are natural and convenient to most people. There is probably no more reason to avoid such uses with children than to withhold basic readers because Shakespeare is also in print. Certainly adults who work with children should understand both the elementary and the relatively difficult aspects of negative numbers in order to sort out what children can do with them at given times and in order to know what children will eventually be asked to learn.

108

This unit begins with a couple of work sheets with embodiments of integers and their sometimes peculiar behavior. If you have forgotten about integers since you were in school, use these work sheets to see how much you can recall; if you remember all about them, work through the materials and try to judge how effective such embodiments might be in sorting out various issues for someone who doesn't have your knowledge.

6.2 ACTIVITY: BLUE AND WHITE NUMBERS[1]

Overview: **Addition, subtraction, multiplication, and division of integers will be examined using a count embodiment.**

Materials needed: Chips that are white on one side and blue on the other.

Although numbers have no color, the title of this activity is as good a way as any of describing this count embodiment of "integers" (whatever they are). The "rules" that are given are guaranteed to give "correct" results, and so you should read them carefully and follow them precisely even if for a while you don't quite understand the "why" of what you are doing. The idea is to get a number of results, then figure out what is going on from the pattern of the results.

6.2.1 The Basic Rule for Equivalence

Chips that are blue on one side and white on the other can be made by spray painting one side of white chips with blue paint, or vice versa; marking a blue cross with a felt pen on one side of white chips; putting white self-stick labels on one side of blue chips; or in other ways. Each chip can be part of a white number (W) or a blue number (B) depending on which side is showing. For example, here are some such "numbers" symbolized by chips:

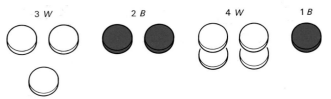

3 W   2 B   4 W   1 B

---

[1] In this section and in section 6.3 we have included quite a lot of work with embodiments of integers before defining explicitly what integers are. The reason for doing this is to give you a chance to discover or recall some of the rather curious properties of integers without relying very much on symbols and definitions. A more symbolic treatment of the integers as an "extension" of the whole numbers begins with section 6.4, and some may prefer to work through that section first. We see no harm in that.

110 NUMBER
SYSTEMS:
SETS
RELATIONS
OPERATIONS
USES

Equivalence or "equals" is defined as follows:

Equivalence Rule: Any number of *BW* pairs (consisting of one *W* and one *B*) may be added to or taken from a number without changing the number. For example, 2*W* can be represented in any of these ways, and many more.

As another example, the display shown below is really equivalent to 3*B*. (Verify this statement.)

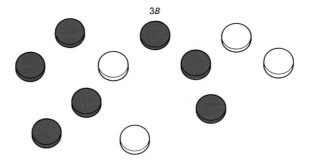

1. Use chips to represent each of the numbers below in the simplest way. (The simplest way is that which uses the least number of chips.)

a. 7*B*

b. 1*W*

c. 1*B*

d. 4*W*

*e. 0[1]

2. Put crosses to represent "blue" on chips in each display below so that the total display represents the number given above it.

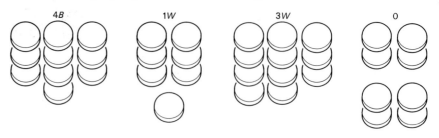

---

[1] Zero can be a *BW* pair or no chips at all.

3. From your previous experience with fractions, you may remember that each fraction comes in many equivalent versions; for example, $\frac{1}{2} = \frac{2}{4} = \frac{3}{6} = \cdots$. Each B number also comes in many equivalent forms. Fill in the blanks in the table below so that if each were displayed as chips, it would be $5B$:

	Number of Whites	Number of Blues	Equivalent *BW* Number
a.		6	$5B$
b.	6		$5B$
c.	0		$5B$
d.		10	$5B$
e.			$5B$ (your choice)

6.2.2
Addition
of *BW* Numbers

Addition Rule: Make a pile of chips representing the first number and add to it chips representing the second number. Symbolize the answer *using chips of one color only* (you may have to use the equivalence rule to get the answer in one color form). For example, follow through this example with actual chips:

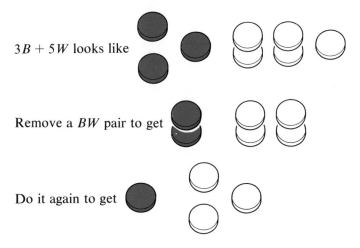

$3B + 5W$ looks like

Remove a *BW* pair to get

Do it again to get

112 NUMBER
SYSTEMS:
SETS
RELATIONS
OPERATIONS
USES

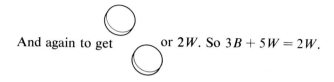

And again to get _____ or $2W$. So $3B + 5W = 2W$.

1. Try these addition problems with the chips.[2]

a. $1W$ b. $3B$ c. $3W$ d. $7B$ e. $5W$ f. $4B$ g. $4W$
    $+3W$ $+2B$ $+2B$ $+4W$ $+8B$ $+7W$ $+2W$

h. $3B$ i. $6W$ j. $7B$ k. $2W$
    $+4B$ $+3B$ $+5W$ $+5B$

2. We would like to find a pattern with small numbers so that we can use this pattern to do addition with large numbers. Obviously we do not want to do $375W + 279B$ with chips. First sort the problems above into two types: (*a*) with the addends the same color and (*b*) with the addends not the same color. Examine problems of each type and see if you see a pattern. If possible, do the problems below using that pattern; if not, do them with chips.[3]

a. $4W$ b. $9W$ c. $2B$ d. $3B$ e. $4B$ f. $9W$
    $+8B$ $+6B$ $+6W$ $+8B$ $+6W$ $+2B$

g. Make up five more problems and do them:

*3. With children, and sometimes with adults, it is often one thing to see what is going on well enough to do it correctly, but quite another thing to put it into words. Try to formulate a verbal rule in two parts as indicated below for dealing with addition of any two *BW* numbers. (Assume you already know about operations with ordinary whole numbers.)[4]

[2] a. $4W$, b. $5B$, c. $1W$, d. $3B$, e. $3B$, f. $3W$, g. $6W$, h. $7B$, i. $3W$, j. $2B$, k. $3B$.

[3] a. $4B$, b. $3W$, c. $4W$, d. $11B$, e. $2W$, f. $7W$.

[4] The rule involves the color of the answer and the operations you do on the whole number of chips of each color.

a. Addends the same color:

b. Addends different colors:

6.2.3
**Subtraction
of *BW* Numbers**

Subtraction Rule: Make a pile of chips representing the first number and take from it chips representing the second number. Symbolize the answer *using chips of one color only.* (In some cases you must use the equivalence rule to supply chips of the right color to "take away" from the pile.) For example, for $4W - 2B$, start with $4W$:

Then add two neutral *BW* pairs to get *B*'s to take away:

then take away $2B$, leaving $6W$:

Hence $4W - 2B = 6W$.

1. Try these subtraction problems with the chips.[5]

a.	**b.**	**c.**	**d.**	**e.**	**f.**	**g.**
$6W$	$5B$	$7W$	$2W$	$3B$	$3W$	$2W$
$-4W$	$-3B$	$-2W$	$-7W$	$-5B$	$-1B$	$-3B$

h.	**i.**	**j.**
$5W$	$3W$	$2B$
$-2B$	$-6B$	$-3W$

[5] a. $2W$, b. $2B$, c. $5W$, d. $5B$, e. $2W$, f. $4W$, g. $5W$, h. $7W$, i. $9W$, j. $5B$.

114 NUMBER
SYSTEMS:
SETS
RELATIONS
OPERATIONS
USES

2. From the results above try to find patterns by which you can get correct answers for these problems without using chips, but use chips if you need to.[6]

a. $4W$ b. $2B$ c. $3B$ d. $5W$ e. $4W$ f. $5B$ g. $4B$
   $-8W$ $-4B$ $-6B$ $-7W$ $-9W$ $-2W$ $-3W$

h. $6B$ i. $3B$ j. $9W$
   $-2W$ $-5W$ $-2B$

*3. See if you can formulate a subtraction rule as a two-part statement involving the colors and operations with whole numbers:[7]
a. Chips the same color:

b. Chips different colors:

*4. With whole numbers, for every subtraction problem there is a corresponding addition problem. From the results in exercises 1 and 2 above try to formulate a single rule for subtraction of *BW* numbers that converts subtraction of *BW* numbers to addition of *BW* numbers.

6.2.4 The rule for multiplication is a bit strange, but it does give the "correct"
Multiplication answers.
of *BW* Numbers

Multiplication Rule: In $\square \times \bigcirc$, first look only at the *whole number* part of the first number. This tells you the *number* of piles of chips to make; *each* such pile is to have the *number* of chips and the *color* of chips

---

[6] a. 4B, b. 2W, c. 3W, d. 2B, e. 5B, f. 7B, g. 7B, h. 8B, i. 8B, j. 11W.

[7] Look at those examples with same color numbers—both *B* or both *W*. See what happens to the whole number parts and the color of the answer. The color probably depends on whether the top or bottom is larger. Now have a look at what happens in those examples with two colors. (No wonder youngsters sometimes have a hard time "explaining" things in words!)

given by the second number. After you have made the piles, look at the *color* that goes with the first number. If it is blue (*B*), all the chips must be turned over; that is, they all change color. If it is white (*W*) nothing more is done. The product is the number and color of the result.

That is admittedly a pretty complicated rule. Follow the rule through the examples below, using your own *BW* chips:

Example 1: $3W \times 2B$
First make 3 piles with $2B$ chips in each pile:

Then, since the first number is a *W* number, do *not* turn the chips over.
Therefore, $3W \times 2B = 6B$.

Example 1: $3W \times 2B$
First make 3 piles with $2B$ chips in each pile:

Then, since the first number is a *B* number, turn over all the chips.

Therefore, $4B \times 2W = 8B$.

1. Do these problems with your chips.[8]

a. $2W \times 3W = \square$ **d.** $2B \times 3B = \square$ **g.** $3W \times 3B = \square$ **j.** $3B \times 4W = \square$
b. $3W \times 4W = \square$ **e.** $2B \times 4B = \square$ **h.** $4W \times 3B = \square$ **k.** $4B \times 2W = \square$
c. $4W \times 3W = \square$ **f.** $3B \times 5B = \square$ **i.** $7W \times 2B = \square$ **l.** $2B \times 6W = \square$

2. Do you see a pattern in these results for multiplication of *BW* numbers? If so, describe it.[9]

---

[8]   a. 6*W*, b. 12*W*, c. 12*W*, d. 6*W*, e. 8*W*, f. 15*W*, g. 9*B*, h. 12*B*, i. 14*B*, j. 12*B*, k. 8*B*, l. 12*B*.

[9]   **Hint: Look at the colors of the factors and at the color of the answer.**

6.2.5

Division of *BW* Numbers

Division Rule: For $\square \div \bigcirc$ or $\dfrac{\square}{\bigcirc}$ make a pile representing the first (or top) number. Then let the whole number part of the second (or bottom) number be the number of smaller and equal piles you make from the total pile. If the second number is blue, all the chips must be turned over before the answer is recorded. The size and color *of each pile* is the quotient. Do these examples, using your own chips.

Example 1: $8B \div 2W$
$8B$ chips separated into 2 equal piles

Since the second number is W, do *not* turn all the chips over. Therefore, $8B \div 2W = 4B$.

Example 2: $\dfrac{10W}{5B}$

$10W$ chips separated into 5 equal piles

Since the second number is B, turn all the chips over:

Therefore, $\dfrac{10W}{5B} = 2B$.

1. Try these problems with your chips.[10]

a. $15W \div 5W = \square$ **d.** $6B \div 2B = \square$ **g.** $12W \div 3B = \square$ **j.** $14B \div 7W = \square$

b. $10W \div 2W = \square$ **e.** $8B \div 2B = \square$ **h.** $9W \div 3B = \square$ **k.** $12B \div 2W = \square$

c. $\dfrac{8W}{4W} = \square$ **f.** $\dfrac{12B}{4B} = \square$ **i.** $\dfrac{18W}{9B} = \square$ **l.** $\dfrac{15B}{5W} = \square$

2. Do you see a pattern for division of *BW* numbers? If so, describe it.

[10] a. 3*W*, b. 5*W*, c. 2*W*, d. 3*W*, e. 4*W*, f. 3*W*, g. 4*B*, h. 3*B*, i. 2*B*, j. 2*B*, k. 6*B*, l. 3*B*.

6.3
ACTIVITY: A
MEASURE EMBODIMENT
OF INTEGERS WITH
DIRECTED RODS

Overview: **Addition, subtraction, multiplication, and division of integers will be examined with a length embodiment.**

Materials needed: For each person, a set of rods, and two different-color water-base marking pens (so marks will show on all colors of rods).

6.3.1
Making
the Embodiment

With the marking pens put a small arrow on an end of two rods of each color, as shown in the examples below (looking down on the tops of marked rods):

5-rod   7-rod

These arrow rods give us two kinds of numbers. If the arrow is pointing to the right, the number is an *R* number. If the arrow is pointing to the left, the number is an *L* number. Assume the smallest rod is 1. Each rod has two characteristics: length, which gives it a number (from 1 to 10), and direction, which gives the rod a letter (*R* or *L*).

1 R   3 L   3 R

10 R

6.3.2
Addition

Select a rod that represents the first number. Place a rod representing the second number with the tail (nonarrow end) of the second rod touching the arrow end of the first. The answer will be the rod that reaches from the *tail* of the *first* rod to the *arrow* of the *second* rod.

Addition problems with rods going in opposite directions look different from problems with rods going in the same direction. But they both come from the above definition of addition. Here are three examples:

Example 1:

2 L + 5 L

Tail of second rod touches
arrow end of first rod

2 L + 5 L = 7 L

118 NUMBER
SYSTEMS:
SETS
RELATIONS
OPERATIONS
USES

Example 2:

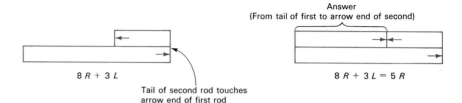

Answer
(From tail of first to arrow end of second)

$8R + 3L$

$8R + 3L = 5R$

Tail of second rod touches
arrow end of first rod

Example 3:

$4L + 6R$

Tail of second rod touches
arrow end of first rod

$4L + 6R = 2R$

Answer
(From tail of first to arrow end of second)

1. Try these problems with your rods. Be on the lookout for patterns.[11]

a.	**b.**	**c.**	**d.**	**e.**	**f.**	**g.**
4L	2R	6R	3L	9R	7L	1R
+2L	+3R	+3L	+1R	+5L	+2R	+6L

h.	**i.**	**j.**	**k.**
2R	3L	5L	2L
+5L	+5L	+7R	+7R

2. If you have found a pattern, use it; otherwise keep using rods.[12]

a.	**b.**	**c.**	**d.**	**e.**	**f.**	**g.**
4R	8R	7L	4L	2L	5L	10R
+3R	+9L	+2R	+3L	+5R	+8R	+ 6L

h.	**i.**	**j.**	**k.**
7R	12L	14R	15L
+5R	+ 7R	+ 6L	+ 7R

*3. Try to put into words some pattern in the addition results. (You
might want to consider separately problems with addends going in

---

[11] a. 6L, b. 5R, c. 3R, d. 2L, e. 4R, f. 5L, g. 5L, h. 3L, i. 8L, j. 2R, k. 5R,

[12] a. 7R, b. 1L, c. 5L, d. 7L, e. 3R, f. 3R, g. 4R, h. 12R, i. 5L, j. 8R, k. 8L.

the same direction and problems with addends going in opposite directions.)

6.3.3 Follow these directions:

Subtraction

a. Select an arrow rod for the first number.
b. Select an arrow rod for the second number.
c. Reverse the direction of the second rod.
d. Place the reversed rod with its tail touching the arrow of the first rod.
e. Just as with addition, the answer will be the rod (or rods) that reaches from the tail of the first rod to the arrow of the second rod.

1. Try these subtraction problems with your rods. Watch for patterns.[13]

	a.	**b.**	**c.**	**d.**	**e.**	**f.**	**g.**
	$3R$	$5R$	$9R$	$6L$	$4L$	$1R$	$6R$
	$-2R$	$-3L$	$-3R$	$-2L$	$-2R$	$-5R$	$-2L$

	h.	**i.**	**j.**	**k.**
	$5L$	$9L$	$2R$	$5L$
	$-7L$	$-4L$	$-6L$	$-2R$

2. Use a pattern if you have discovered one; otherwise continue using the rods.[14]

	a.	**b.**	**c.**	**d.**	**e.**	**f.**	**g.**
	$3R$	$7L$	$1L$	$2R$	$8L$	$6R$	$7R$
	$-7L$	$-3L$	$-5L$	$-6L$	$-12L$	$-9R$	$-2L$

	h.	**i.**	**j.**	**k.**
	$12L$	$4R$	$11R$	$9L$
	$-4R$	$-9R$	$-5R$	$-3R$

*3. Try to express in words whatever patterns you see in the above subtraction problems.

---

[13] a. 1R, b. 8R, c. 6R, d. 4L, e. 6L, f. 4L, g. 8R, h. 2R, i. 5L, j. 8R, k. 7L.

[14] a. 10R, b. 4L, c. 4R, d. 8R, e. 4R, f. 3L, g. 9R, h. 16L, i. 5L, j. 6R, k. 12L.

120 NUMBER
SYSTEMS:
SETS
RELATIONS
OPERATIONS
USES

*4. There is one pattern that describes all subtraction problems with *LR* numbers in terms of addition of *LR* numbers. Try to put this pattern into words.[15]

6.3.4 Multiplication

The whole number part of the first number in the product □ × ○ tells how many rods you have. The second number is the size and direction of the rods you use. If the first number is an *L* number, reverse the direction of all the rods that represent the second number before you find the answer train. The answer is given by the length and direction of the resulting train of rods. Here are two examples:

Example 1:
$2R \times 3R$:

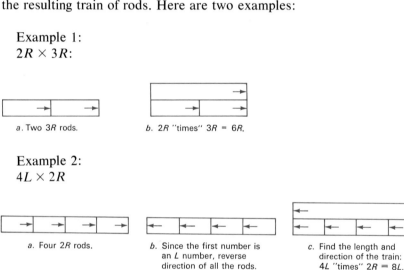

a. Two 3*R* rods.

b. 2*R* "times" 3*R* = 6*R*.

Example 2:
$4L \times 2R$

a. Four 2*R* rods.

b. Since the first number is an *L* number, reverse direction of all the rods.

c. Find the length and direction of the train: 4*L* "times" 2*R* = 8*L*.

1. Try these multiplication problems with your rods. Watch for patterns. (You may need to draw arrows on more rods.[16]

a. $3R \times 5R = \square$ **d.** $2R \times 4L = \square$ **g.** $4L \times 2R = \square$ **j.** $3L \times 6L = \square$
b. $2R \times 7R = \square$ **e.** $5R \times 2L = \square$ **h.** $3L \times 5R = \square$ **k.** $4L \times 2L = \square$
c. $5R \times 3R = \square$ **f.** $3R \times 4L = \square$ **i.** $2L \times 4R = \square$ **l.** $5L \times 4L = \square$

2. If possible, describe in words the patterns you see in multiplication of *R* and *L* numbers.

---

[15] Hint: See how subtraction is related to addition.

[16] a. 15*R*, b. 14*R*, c. 15*R*, d. 8*L*, e. 10*L*, f. 12*L*, g. 8*L*, h. 15*L*, i. 8*L*, j. 18*R*, k. 8*R*, l. 20*R*.

6.3.5 Division

In $\bigcirc \div \triangle$ or make a train of rods for the first (or top) number. Make a train of as many rods representing the second (or bottom) number as are needed to equal the length of the first train. The whole number part of the quotient is given by *how many* such rods are needed. If these rods must then be reversed in order to make the second train go the same direction as the first, the quotient is an *L* number. If the rods do not need to be reversed, the quotient is an *R* number. Here are two examples:

Example 1:
$6L \div 2R$

8 L ÷ 4 L:

The two 4 *L* rods were not reversed, and so the answer is an *R* number:
8 *L* ÷ 4 *L* = 2 *R*

Example 2:
$8L \div 4L$

6 L ÷ 2 R:

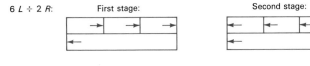

The three 2*R* rods were reversed to match the 6 *L* train, and so the answer is an *L* number:
6 *L* ÷ 2 *R* = 3 *L*.

1. Try these division problems with your rods. Look for patterns.[17]

a. $12R \div 2R = \square$ d. $10R \div 5L = \square$ g. $6L \div 3R = \square$ j. $15L \div 5L = \square$

b. $14R \div 7R = \square$ e. $8R \div 2L = \square$ h. $18L \div 6R = \square$ k. $12L \div 3L = \square$

c. $\dfrac{18R}{9R} = \square$ f. $\dfrac{10R}{2L} = \square$ i. $\dfrac{12L}{6R} = \square$ l. $\dfrac{9L}{3L} = \square$

2. Attempt to write a rule for division of *R* and *L* numbers from the results above.

[17] a. 6*R*, b. 2*R*, c. 2*R*, d. 2*L*, e. 4*L*, f. 5*L*, g. 2*L*, h. 3*L*, i. 2*L*, j. 3*R*, k. 4*R*, l. 3*R*.

122 NUMBER
SYSTEMS:
SETS
RELATIONS
OPERATIONS
USES

6.4
PROBLEM SET:
EXTENDING THE SET OF
WHOLE NUMBERS
TO THE INTEGERS[2]

Overview: **As we move from whole numbers to consideration of a new set of numbers, it is fair to ask, "Why bother with integers?" It is possible to answer that question by appealing both to common life usage and to the requirements of mathematics itself.**

6.4.1
Uses of Integers
in common life

In common life we have temperatures that are above and below zero, elevations above and below sea level, gains and losses in business transactions, and other situations that lend themselves to description using positive and negative numbers and, of course, zero. Indeed, positive and negative numbers are useful in any situation where it is convenient to set an arbitrary starting point (zero point) and then consider counts or measures in opposite directions from that starting point.

1. From an almanac or other source find the highest and lowest dry land elevations in the United States and in the world.

Find out what the lowest elevation would be if the seas were drained; that is, how deep is the deepest point in the oceans?

2. All such elevations are recorded from "mean sea level" as the zero point, which is a little tricky since the seas themselves fluctuate in height according to tides and other influences. How might such a zero point be determined? How might a reference line around a lake, say to measure property lines from, be determined?

3. If you were on an airplane coming into New York at an altitude of 5,000 feet you would be justified in feeling pretty safe. Now suppose you are approaching Denver at an "altitude" of 5,000 feet; what might some interpretations of that be?

---

[2] Throughout this unit negative numbers will be designated with a superior dash; for example, $^-3$, $^-43$, $^-1098$. This is to avoid confusion with the subtraction symbol and the notation for the "opposite" of a number. Strictly speaking, the integers include positive numbers, negative numbers, and zero rather than negative numbers and whole numbers. Hence every integer except zero ought to have either a positive or a negative symbol: $^+3$, $^-7$, $^+1115$, etc. But since the positive integers and zero act in every way like whole numbers, use of the positive sign is not essential. In this book we sometimes do and sometimes do not use it.

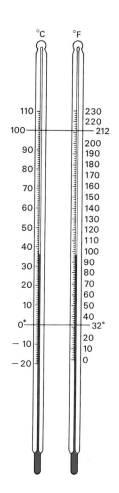

	°F	°C	Comment
a.	68		(Room temperature)
b.	32		(Water freezes at sea level)
c.	0		
d.	98.6		(Body temperature)
e.	212		(Water boils at sea level)
f.	⁻10		
g.	10		
*h.		⁻273	(Absolute zero—theoretically the coldest possible temperature. The thermometers pictured don't register this low; if you can't figure out a way to get at least an approximate °F equivalent, don't worry about it.)

4. In temperature scales, the zero point shifts depending on the scale used. On the Celsius (centigrade) scale used in science and in countries using the metric system of measures, 0°C is the temperature at which water freezes and 100°C is the boiling temperature of water. On the Fahrenheit scale used in reporting weather in the United States, the freezing point of water is 32°F and so 0°F is 32°F below the freezing point of water. (The 0°F point may have been set as the coldest liquid temperature that could be obtained with a saturated salt, ice, and water mixture—which should suggest to you why a salt and ice mixture freezes ice cream in an old-fashioned ice cream freezer.) Thermometers using the two scales are pictured side by side. Using this picture, convert some of these common °F temperatures to the approximately equivalent °C measure that will be used in a few years when the United States has made the transition to the metric system.

5. Stock market quotations in newspapers often show negative numbers in plenty, though they are positive and negative fractions rather than integers. Look at such a stock market quotation page and see if you can tell at a glance whether the market has had a good day or a bad day.

124 NUMBER
SYSTEMS:
SETS
RELATIONS
OPERATIONS
USES

6. In traditional accounting practice there is an analogy to *BW* numbers in the use of "red ink" to record losses or deficits in a ledger. "In the red" as a description of a business in trouble is standard terminology in America. Nowadays, however, accounting firms get annoyed with clients who use red ink in ledgers, because once a ledger is photocopied, you can't tell the red ink from the black ink. With copying machines so much a part of our lives, this turns out to be a serious problem. Suggest some ways including but not restricted to the use of positive and negative numbers by which accounting ledgers can indicate deficits and losses without the use of red ink.

6.4.2
**Uses of
Integers in Mathematics**
As the number system is extended, there is increasing reliance on motivations that relate to mathematical consistency, although common life uses should never be ignored. In the case of the integers, there are at least three ways in which invention of negative numbers ties up some mathematical loose ends that are left when only whole numbers are available.

1. It is known that the whole numbers are "closed" under the operation of addition; that is, if you add two whole numbers you always get a whole number as an answer. But this is *not* the case for whole number subtraction, as illustrated by such examples as $7 - 10$ or $101 - 103$. With the invention of integers any problem using subtraction of whole numbers has an answer. Verify this statement by completing the examples below.

a. $7 - 10 = \Box$ **d.** $5 - \Box = {}^-5$

b. $101 - 103 = \Box$ **e.** $13 - 13 = \Box$

c. $10 - 7 = \Box$ **f.** $\Box - 4 = 4$

2. In contemporary elementary school mathematics textbooks, "equations" like those that were once reserved for high school algebra are often used, but with "frames" instead of letters used to indicate missing numbers. Such equations as $7 + \Box = 10$ and $7 + 3 = \Box$ have obvious meanings. But what about such equations as $7 + \Box = 5$ or $5 + \Box = 0$, which have no answers if only whole numbers are allowed? They do have answers if integers are used: $7 + \boxed{{}^-2} = 5$ and

$5 + \boxed{^-5} = 0$. Complete the following equations by filling in each frame with an appropriate whole number or integer.

a. $5 + \square = 1$ ***d.** $(2 \times \square) + 5 = 15$

b. $\square + 3 = {}^-1$ ***e.** $(2 \times \square) - 6 = 0$

c. $13 - \square = {}^-4$

3. The use of "neutral" *BW* pairs (one white and one blue chip) in section 6.2 proved to be useful in simplifying certain sums or in getting extra blue or white chips on the scene for certain subtraction problems. If $1W$ represents $^+1$ and $1B$ represents $^-1$, then a neutral *BW* pair simply expresses the fact that $^+1 + (^-1) = 0$. More generally, we would like any number to have an "opposite" or "additive inverse" so that the sum of the number and its opposite is zero. Thus, $5 + (^-5) = 0$, $(^-17) + 17 = 0$, and in general, $a + (-a) = (-a) + a = 0$. This "additive inverse property" is the main thing that distinguishes the mathematical structure of the integers from that of the whole numbers. To make sure this is clear to you, fill in the frames in the equations below.

a. $10 + \square = 0$ **d.** $0 + \square = 0$

b. $103 + {}^-103 = \square$ ***e.** $5 + \square + 8 = 8$

c. $^-5 + \square = 0$

6.4.3
Extension of the Whole Numbers to Integers on the Number Line

In this book, wherever we have pictured a whole number line there has been unnumbered space to the left of zero (a practice we recommend in number line work with children):

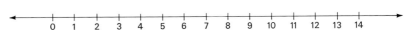

Since a line goes as far in one direction as it does in the other—in fact infinitely far in both directions—there ought to be labels for the points to the left of zero just as there are for the points to the right of zero. With the invention of the integers this becomes the case. Every whole number becomes a positive number that has a negative number paired with it exactly as far from zero as it is:

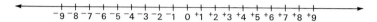

Another way to look at this is to think of all the whole numbers reflected across the zero point, picking up a negative sign as they cross to the other side. The picture looks like this:

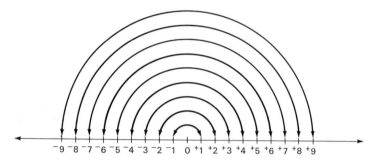

With such a picture it is clear that this is a two-way street; the opposite of every positive number is a negative number; and the opposite of every negative number is a positive number. This point is discussed in more detail in the next section.

1. Recall the original introduction to the number line in Unit 1, which had an idealized mathematical model of an expressway map that showed mileages from Chicago to various cities along the way. It looked like this:

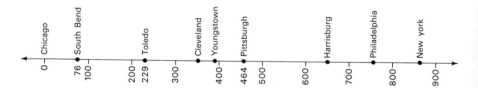

Now suppose that a motorist who lives in Pittsburgh chooses to call Pittsburgh the zero point on the number line and to designate the easterly direction as positive. Put new numbers on the number line (p. 127) to reflect easterly distances from Pittsburgh as positive numbers and westerly distances as negative numbers. (The distance itself is always a positive number; the positive and negative symbols give extra information with respect to direction as well as distance.)

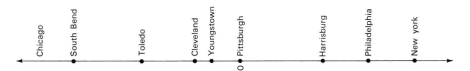

2. A thermometer can be regarded as an integer number line (if we ignore fraction temperatures), even though it often goes up and down instead of right to left. As a matter of fact, the direction chosen as positive is entirely arbitrary. All but one of the number lines pictured below are quite all right; circle the one that is not.

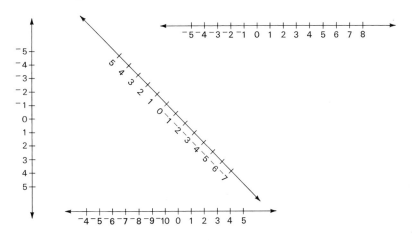

6.5
PROBLEM SET:
RELATIONS AND OPERATIONS
WITH THE INTEGERS

Overview: **The work of this section deals with the relations "is less than," "is greater than," and "is equal to" for integers; with two new operations on single numbers, the "opposite of" and the "absolute value of"; and with the integer versions of the familiar binary operations of addition, subtraction, multiplication, and division. In every case the "new" relations and operations are defined in terms of the "old" relations and operations.**

Numbers are symbolic inventions that serve the needs of human beings. The numbers we count with are so much a part of our experience that they seem somehow natural and inevitable. (Indeed the counting numbers without zero are usually called the "natural numbers.") However, in extending the whole numbers to integers, rational numbers, and real numbers, mathematical inventions become more prominent and sometimes seem artificial. Ties to common life are not always so direct, and there tends to be more reliance both on symbols and on rules for

128 NUMBER
SYSTEMS:
SETS
RELATIONS
OPERATIONS
USES

manipulating the symbols. (We believe, however, that for all school mathematics the ties to common life exist and should be emphasized.) Thus several of the answers to the question "Why bother with integers?" had to do with mathematical rather than common life "necessities" and some of the discussion here of relations and operations will have that same flavor.

6.5.1
The
"Is Less Than"
Relation

The state of affairs with respect to "is less than" and "is greater than" can be pretty much summarized as follows: For two positive integers, things are the same as they were for whole numbers. Any negative number is smaller than any whole number. For two negative numbers, the more negative it is, the smaller it is. For the usual number line with positive numbers extending to the right, "is less than" means "to the left of" on the number line. Some people are uncomfortable about regarding a number like $^-1,089$ as less than the number $^+2$, but a reference to common life such as "$1,089 in debt" makes it clear that such a person is worse off than one who is $2 ahead. Fill in the appropriate symbol ($=$, $<$, or $>$) in the frames below:

a. $^-100$ ☐ $^+10$ **c.** $^+7 + (^-5)$ ☐ $^+2$

b. $^-2$ ☐ $^-5$ **d.** $^+10$ ☐ $^-100$

6.5.2
The
"Opposite of"
Operation

Up to now the operations we have dealt with are "binary" operations that combine a pair of numbers into a single number by addition, subtraction, multiplication, or addition. The "opposite of" operation turns a positive number into a negative number and a negative number into a positive number.

1. If the opposite of a number n is called $opp(n)$ then, for example, $opp(5) = ^-5$; $opp(^-14) = 14$; and $opp[opp(3)] = 3$. $Opp(0)$ is just zero because zero is neither negative nor positive. Fill in the frames below:

a. $opp(5) =$ ☐   **d.** $opp\{opp[opp(5)]\} =$ ☐

b. $opp(\ ) = 5$ **e.** $opp(opp\{opp[opp(5)]\}) =$ ☐

c. $opp(0) =$ ☐

2. Perhaps unfortunately, the usual sign for *opp* is the same sign used to denote the subtraction operation; that is, −*a* means the same as *opp*(*a*). This means that −*a* (read "the opposite of *a*") can be either negative or positive depending on what number is used for *a*. Complete the table below.

	a	−*a*
a.	4	
b.	⁻4	
c.		3
d.		⁻1
e.	0	

3. The "opposite of" operation has the effect of switching the "direction" of a quantity—from positive to negative or negative to positive. For the *BW* embodiment with chips, was it the *B* or the *W* that signaled the switching in subtraction, multiplication, and division? For the *RL* rods, did the *R* or the *L* play this role?

6.5.3
The
"Absolute Value of"
Operation

In working with integers, so that both a quantity and a direction are expressed, it sometimes becomes useful to ignore the direction and work only with the quantity. The operation that accomplishes this is the "absolute value of" operation. The absolute value of a number *a*, expressed as |*a*|, is either the number itself or its opposite, depending on which of these is positive. For example, in multiplying with *BW* chips, to do such a problem as $2B \times 3W$ we first took 2 piles of $3W$ chips, which in effect means we were working with the absolute value of $2B$, then used *B* to designate the "opposite of" as we turned over the chips.

1. Complete this table (the first one is done for you):

a	*opp*(*a*)	|*a*|
⁻10	10	10
3	⁻3	
⁻7		
	⁻11	

130 NUMBER
SYSTEMS:
SETS
RELATIONS
OPERATIONS
USES

*2. Since distance or length is always positive, the absolute value is often useful in expressing a distance. For example, such a mathematical sentence as $|a| \leq 3$ (read as "all integers whose absolute value is less than or equal to 3") means all those integers at a distance of three or less from zero on the number line (since we work only with integers). This means those points marked below on the number line:

This can be verified by substituting each of the marked numbers for a in the inequality $|a| \leq 3$, as follows:

$|^-3| \leq 3$ (True since $|^-3| = 3$)	$|1| \leq 3$ (True)
$|^-2| \leq 3$ (True)	$|2| \leq 3$ (True)
$|^-1| \leq 3$ (True)	$|3| \leq 3$ (True)
$|0| \leq 3$ (True)	

But if other points are substituted, the inequality is no longer "true." For example, $|^-4| = 4$ which is *not* less than or equal to 3; $|5| = 5$ which is *not* less than or equal to 3; and so on.

The sentence $|a - 3| \leq 4$ means all those integers within a 4 unit distance from the number 3. Marked on the number line, it comes out like this:

Again, if the numbers associated with each marked point are substituted into $|a - 3| \leq 4$, they all make the sentence "true," but no other integers make it true. For example, for $a = ^-1$, $|a - 3| = |(^-1) - 3| = |^-4| = 4$, and so for $a = ^-1$, $|a - 3| \leq 4$ is true. Similarly, for $a = 6$, $|a - 3| = |6 - 3| = |3| = 3$ and $3 < 4$. But for $a = ^-3$, $|a - 3| = |(^-3) - 3| = |^-6| = 6$, which is *not* less than or equal to 4.

Mark on the number line the integer points that make each of the following sentences true, and check out each of them in the sentence itself just to make sure.

a. $|a| \leq 5$

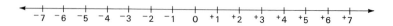

b. $|a - 2| \leq 5$

6.5.4
Addition
of Integers

1. Addition of integers is quite simple and is well motivated by situations in the real world. As you perhaps discovered with the *BW* chips and *RL* rods, if the two addends have the same sign, you take the sum of absolute values and give that sign to the answer. That is, things get more positive or more negative. If the two addends have different signs, you take the excess of the one absolute value over the other, and attach the sign of the addend that is largest in absolute value.

Note that working with absolute values means working with whole numbers, so the "new" addition operation is done using "old" operations along with some way of attaching "positive" or "negative" to the result. Addition of integers as accumulating or taking the excess fits many situations in common life; think about that and make sure you understand it fully. Briefly note at least one such common life situation below.

2. Complete these sums:

a. $(^+3) + (^+5) = \square$ **d.** $(^+3) + (^-5) = \square$

b. $(^-3 + {}^-5) = \square$ **e.** $(^-5) + (^+3) = \square$

c. $(^-3 + {}^+5) = \square$ **f.** $(^-5) + 0 = \square$

6.5.5
Subtraction
of Integers

Subtraction may be the hardest of the four operations with integers to really get a good feeling about. The easiest way to handle the matter is suggested by the *BW* chip and *RL* rod embodiments: change the subtraction problem to an addition problem instead. That is, subtraction can be defined in this way: $a - b = a + opp(b)$ or in other words, $a - b = a + (-b)$ where the dash in $a - b$ means "subtract" and the dash in $a + (-b)$ means "the opposite of" whatever number b is.

1. Rewrite each subtraction problem as an addition problem or vice versa. The first one is done for you.

132 NUMBER
SYSTEMS:
SETS
RELATIONS
OPERATIONS
USES

Subtraction Version	Addition Version	Answer
$a.\ ^+3 - (^+5) = \square$	$3 + (^-5) = \square$	$^-2$
$b.\ ^+3 - (^-5) = \square$		$^+8$
$c.\ ^-3 - (^+5) = \square$		$^-8$
$d.$	$^-3 + 5 = \square$	$^+2$

2. The University of Illinois Committee on School Mathematics in the 1950s invented "postman stories" to motivate addition and subtraction of integers. Such a story might have a man sitting in his office while a postman makes rather frequent mail deliveries of payments (positive) and of bills (negative). To get subtraction into the picture, it turns out that this is an inept postman who misdelivers rather frequently and has to come back and take away bills or payments already delivered. For example, the day starts with $50 in the till and the postman delivers a payment of $5: $50 + 5 = 55$. Then a bill for $20 comes in: $55 + (^-20) = \$35$. Another bill for $40: $35 + (^-40) = ^-5$. Now, fortunately, the postman discovers that he misdelivered the bill for $20 and so comes and gets it: $(^-5) - (^-20) = 15$. And so on. Extend the story to require at least three more transactions with integers, by completing the following table:

Situation	Expression
$a.$ The postman delivers a bill for $10.	$a.\ 15 + \quad =$
$b.$	$b.\ 5 + (^-10) = ^-15$
$c.$	$c.\ (^-15) - (^-10) = ^-5$

6.5.6
The
Multiplication
Operation

For a product $a \times b$ where the numbers replacing a or b can be either positive or negative integers, there are clearly four possibilities that must be attended to in one way or another: positive times positive, positive times negative, negative times positive, and negative times negative. When both numbers are positive, this simply amounts to ordinary multiplication of whole numbers. Each other case can be "explained" either by a situation from common life or by a pattern or, as we will show later, by a mathematical proof.

1. For such a problem as $3 \times (^-4)$, you can think of the factors in the usual way as the first factor giving the number of things and the second the "size" of things. Thus three things, each with value "negative four" must give a product of "negative twelve." In common life this might be three debts of $4 each or a loss of 4 yards each on three successive football plays. Make up such a common life story for each of the products below.

   a. $2 \times (^-12) = \square$

   b. $4 \times (^-3) = \square$

2. Other multiplication situations from common life involve rates and times. For example the product $4 \times (^-3)$ could come from this situation: "If I run a film *backward* at the rate of 3 feet per second for 4 seconds, what is the result relative to my starting point?" One may also think of pumping water into or out of a tank, or automobile travel or other situations. Make up a rate-time story for each of these products:

   a. $2 \times (^-12) = ^-24$

   b. $3 \times (^-4) = ^-12$

3. A positive number times a negative number gives a negative number as product. A pattern motivating this result starts as shown below; carry it on enough further to see the pattern clearly.

134 NUMBER
SYSTEMS:
SETS
RELATIONS
OPERATIONS
USES

$$5 \times 3 = 15$$
$$5 \times 2 = 10$$
$$5 \times 1 = 5$$
$$5 \times 0 = 0$$
$$5 \times {}^-1 = \square$$
$$5 \times {}^-2 = \square$$
$$5 \times {}^-3 = \square$$

4. For a negative number times a positive number such as $({}^-3) \times 4$, the usual convention of having the first factor show the number of things and the second the size of each thing breaks down because "the number of" can't really be given by a negative number. But common life situations that involve rates and times can be used. For example, the product $({}^-3) \times 4$ could come from such a situation as this: "If I am running a film forward at the rate of 4 feet per second, where were we in the film *3 seconds ago?*" The product $({}^-5) \times ({}^+20) = \square$ fits this problem: "For an hour or so I have been filling a tank at the rate of 20 gallons per minute; what was the situation 5 minutes ago?" Write down a brief rate-time story or other plausible situation for each of the following problems, and fill in the results.

   a. $({}^-2) \times ({}^+5) = \square$

   b. $({}^-10) \times ({}^+15) = \square$

5. A negative number times a positive number gives a negative number as product. Complete the pattern begun below, and comment on the extent to which it helps make that plausible.

$$4 \times 5 = 20$$
$$3 \times 5 = 15$$
$$2 \times 5 = 10$$
$$1 \times 5 = 5$$
$$0 \times 5 = 0$$
$${}^-1 \times 5 = \square$$
$${}^-2 \times 5 = \square$$
$${}^-3 \times 5 = \square$$

Comment:

6. That a negative number times a negative number gives a positive number as product must seem mysterious to many people. Having had this result pushed down their throats in school may have left them with a lasting suspicion that mathematics is not sensible. Such multiplication situations do not come up frequently in common life. Indeed it is mainly the wish for completeness, for rounding out the multiplication of integers, that moves mathematicians to inquire about the situation at all. Different things persuade different folks. Here is a pattern motivation; complete it until you get the "right" result. Comment on the extent to which you find this demonstration convincing.

$$4 \times {}^-5 = {}^-20$$
$$3 \times {}^-5 = {}^-15 \qquad \text{Comment:}$$
$$2 \times {}^-5 = {}^-10$$
$$1 \times {}^-5 = {}^-5$$
$$0 \times {}^-5 = 0$$
$${}^-1 \times {}^-5 = \square$$
$${}^-2 \times {}^-5 = \square$$
$${}^-3 \times {}^-5 = \square$$

7. Stories where the mathematical model is the product of two negative numbers tend to be a bit farfetched, but they can be fabricated. To motivate $({}^-3) \times ({}^-4)$, for example, we could have water being pumped out of a tank at a rate of 4 gallons per minute, then ask what the status of the water level was 3 minutes ago. (It was, of course, 12 gallons *higher* than it is now, or 12 gallons *more positive*.) To fabricate such stories there must be three different elements: the first factor must represent something that allows for an arbitrary zero and for positive and negative directions from zero (*time* in the example above); the second factor must be a different situation with the same characteristic (*rate in* or *rate out* in the example above); while the product must be still a third situation with the same characteristic (*water level* with respect to some arbitrary starting level in the example above). Try to write several such stories to motivate problems in which a negative number is multiplied by a negative number. Share them with others in your group.

136 NUMBER
SYSTEMS:
SETS
RELATIONS
OPERATIONS
USES

8. "Double negatives" in common speech must be interpreted as positive statements. While this really has nothing to do with multiplication of two negative numbers (and it is dishonest to use it as if it did), judicious reminder of it might help students to come to terms with multiplication of two negative numbers. One teacher gets cheers when he first announces that he "never never gives homework" until a few suspicious souls in his class stop to think about it. To get at negatives in common speech another teacher uses "A friend of a friend is a friend"; "A friend of an enemy is an enemy" and so on. Complete the sequence. Make up other examples of double negatives, or, better still, find some that are perhaps inadvertent in some published source, or from a conversation.

6.5.7
**The
Division Operation**

For division of integers, you work with absolute values and hence reduce each problem to division of whole numbers, then at the end attach a positive or negative sign to the quotient as appropriate. Division is closely linked to multiplication; indeed, every division has a corresponding multiplication version, and the results are much the same as for multiplication. That is, if total and divisor are both positive or both negative, the quotient is positive. If one is positive and the other negative, the quotient is negative.

1. To make sure you understand division with integers, complete the following division problems. In order to see the link between multiplication and division results, write a multiplication equation that is related to each division problem.

Division	Multiplication
a. $(^+12) \div (^+3) = \boxed{4}$	*a.* $^+3 \times {}^+4 = {}^+12$
b. $(^-12) \div (^-3) = \square$	*b.*
c. $(^+12) \div (^-3) = \square$	*c.*
d. $(^-12) \div (^+3) = \square$	*d.*
e. $\dfrac{^-6}{^+2} = \square$	*e.*
f. $\dfrac{^-15}{^-3} = \square$	*f.*

6.6
PROBLEM SET:
THE PROPERTIES OF INTEGERS

Overview: The properties of integers that are the same as for whole numbers are reviewed and new properties are explored.

6.6.1
Introductory
Remarks

It should be recognized that when a set of numbers is extended by adding new numbers to those present before, such relations as "is equal to" and "is less than" and the operations of addition, subtraction, multiplication, and division may take on quite different meanings than they had before, even though the same symbols ($=$, $<$, $>$, $+$, $-$, $\times$, $\div$) are used. Since the operations and relations are "different," such properties as the commutative property need reexamination.

It is possible to extend the whole numbers to the integers in a rigorously correct mathematical way, but the intricate symbol manipulation needed to do so would require algebraic techniques that are beyond the scope of this book. Whether it is done rigorously or informally, what must be done is first to extend the set of numbers, then to redefine all the relations and all the operations in ways that use only numbers, relations, and operations from the "old system" of whole numbers. Before carrying out such a program, the meaning of the "absolute value of" operation on single numbers must be established, in order to turn any negative numbers into whole numbers so that the old relations and operations can be exploited.

Another operation on single numbers, the "opposite of" operation, is also needed. This operation turns positive numbers into negative numbers, turns negative numbers into positive numbers, and leaves zero unchanged.

This explanation has been given simply to let you know that the summary here does *not* set up a rigorous and logically consistent system. It "fudges" by relying on intuition from your experience with such things as the *BW* chips, *RL* rods, and the number line, none of which could have a place in a symbolic, tightly reasoned algebra.

To get a brief picture of what it might mean to do a rigorous symbolic extension of whole numbers to integers, consider the problem of defining addition of integers. The verbal rule for adding any two particular integers is long but presents few difficulties: If both are positive, add just as for whole numbers. If both are negative, add absolute values and make the sum a negative number. If one is positive and the other negative, take absolute values, subtract the smaller absolute value from the larger absolute value and make the answer positive or negative depending on which has the larger absolute value. Note that this procedure changes all addition of integers to addition and subtraction of whole numbers.

To express a symbolic rule for $a + b$ where either a or b can be posi-

138 NUMBER
SYSTEMS:
SETS
RELATIONS
OPERATIONS
USES

tive, negative, or zero requires stating a number of separate cases that cover all the possibilities:

Case 1. If $a \geq 0$, $b \geq 0$,   Example: $10 + 3 = 13$
then $a + b$ is whole number
addition.

Case 2a. If $a \geq 0$, $b < 0$, $|a| > |b|$,   Example: $10 + (^-3) = 7$
then $a + b = |a| - |b|$.

Case 2b. If $a \geq 0$, $b < 0$, $|a| < |b|$,   Example: $3 + (^-10) = ^-7$
then $a + b = -(|b| - |a|)$.

Case 3a. If $a < 0$, $b \geq 0$, $|a| > |b|$,   Example: $(^-10) + 3 = ^-7$
then $a + b = -(|a| - |b|)$.

Case 3b. If $a < 0$, $b \geq 0$, $|a| < |b|$,   Example: $(^-3) + 10 = 7$
then $a + b = |b| - |a|$.

Case 4. If $a < 0$, $b < 0$,   Example: $(^-3) + (^-10) = ^-13$
then $a + b = -(|a| + |b|)$.

It is apparent that this is a pretty complicated definition and to use it to "prove" such things as the commutative property of addition of integers, or even worse the associative property, would be a tedious, though possible, exercise. Hence, contrary to our practice in earlier chapters, we will not go through each property in detail. Instead we urge you to review the content of the sections of this unit and note the various properties implicit in them. First we somehow get the negative integers themselves, perhaps by naming points to the left of zero on the number line or perhaps by naming differences $a - b$ of two whole numbers, where a is smaller than b. These along with the whole numbers compose the set of integers. As for relations, we take the meaning of "is equal to" as obvious, while the "is less than" and "is greater than" relations are outlined in section 6.5.1. The "opposite of" operation and the "absolute value of" operation are defined as indicated in sections 6.5.2 and 6.5.3.

The addition operation is defined in section 6.5.4. Furthermore, addition of integers is closed, commutative, and associative, and zero acts as the additive identity. If this were all, addition of integers could not be distinguished from addition of whole numbers, mathematically speaking, because its structure would be exactly the same. In fact, however, this is not the case because with integers there is one new property: For any integer a, there exists exactly one integer $-a$ (the opposite of a) such that $a + (-a) = (-a) + a = 0$.

Multiplication of integers behaves as indicated in section 6.5.6. Products of two integers are positive if both factors are positive or both factors are negative, zero if zero is a factor, and negative otherwise. The operation is closed, commutative, and associative, and 1 is the multiplicative identity. The distributive property of multiplication over addition is true with integers; that is, multiplication for integers has the same structural properties as does multiplication of whole numbers.

Since subtraction and division with integers can be defined in terms of addition and multiplication, no additional properties need be listed for them.

The discussion above can be summarized as follows:

Properties of Addition and Multiplication of Integers

For all integers a, b, c:

	Addition	**Multiplication**
Closure	$a + b$ is an integer	ab is an integer
Commutativity	$a + b = b + a$	$ab = ba$
Associativity	$(a + b) + c = a + (b + c)$	$(ab)c = a(bc)$
Identity	$a + 0 = 0 + a = a$	$a \cdot 1 = 1 \cdot a = a$
Inverse	For every a, $-a$ exists such that $a + (-a) = 0$. (This is *the* new property for integers.)	(In general, integers do not have multiplicative inverses.)

Distributive Property: $a(b + c) = ab + ac$

Definitions of Subtraction:

1. $a - b = a + (-b)$
2. $a - b = c$ if and only if $a = c + b$

Definition of Division:

$a \div b = c$ if and only if $a = bc$

**6.6.2
Some
Useful "Theorems" About
the System of Integers**

If we "agree to agree" on the above properties, they allow us to "prove" other properties that are sometimes useful in work with integers. Or, put another way, if you accept the statements above, you are compelled by logic to accept certain other statements. A few of these are given below. It is not expected that you would be able to put together such proofs from scratch (especially since a couple of them involve pretty fancy maneuvers that hardly anyone would naturally think of doing). But you should try to follow each of them through the steps given, try to under-

140 NUMBER
SYSTEMS:
SETS
RELATIONS
OPERATIONS
USES

stand each individual step, and also try to understand the progression from one step to the next.

1. Theorem: $a \cdot 0 = 0$. (The product of zero and *any* integer is zero.)

Proof: We know for sure that $a \cdot 1 = a$, and that zero is the additive identity. The proof below exploits those facts:

$a \cdot 1 = a$
$a \cdot (1 + 0) = a$, since $1 + 0$ can be substituted for 1.
$a \cdot 1 + a \cdot 0 = a$, by the distributive property,
Hence $a \cdot 0$ is acting as the additive identity, and so $a \cdot 0 = 0$.
(Also, $0 \cdot a = 0$ either by a similar proof or just by using the commutative property.)

2. Theorem: $(^-1) \cdot a = -a$. (The opposite of any integer is the same as the product of $^-1$ and that integer.)

Proof: We know for sure that $a + (-a) = 0$. If we can show that $(^-1) \cdot a$ acts in just this same way, then $(^-1) \cdot a$ must be just another name for $-a$. Here is the way that is done:

$0 \cdot a = 0$, as proved in the previous problem.
$[1 + (^-1)] \cdot a = 0$, since $[1 + (^-1)]$ can be substituted for 0.
$1 \cdot a + (^-1) \cdot a = 0$, by applying the distributive property.
$a + (^-1) \cdot a = 0$, since $1 \cdot a = a$.

Therefore $(^-1) \cdot a$ is another name for the additive inverse of a, and so $(^-1) \cdot a = -a$.

3. Another general way of showing that $(-a)(-b) = ab$ (where either a or b can be positive, negative, or zero) is shown below by a numerical example on the left and in general terms on the right. This argument convinces some youngsters better than stories or patterns. Keep track of your own reactions as you read through the proof.

Consider $2 \cdot 3 + (^-2)(3) + (^-2)(^-3)$.
By the associative property,
$[2 \cdot 3 + (^-2)(3)] + (^-2)(3)$
$\qquad = 2 \cdot 3 + [(^-2)(3) + (^-2)(^-3)]$
Working out the left side,
$\quad [2 + (^-2)](3) + (^-2)(^-3)$
$= 0 \cdot 3 + (^-2)(^-3)$
$= \quad 0 + (^-2)(^-3)$
$= \qquad (^-2)(^-3)$

Consider $ab + (-a)b + (-a)(-b)$.
By the associative property,
$[ab + (-a)b] + (-a)(-b)$
$\qquad = ab + [(-a)b + (-a)(-b)]$
Working out the left side,
$\quad [a + (-a)]b + (-a)(-b)$
$= \quad 0 \cdot b + (-a)(-b)$
$= \quad 0 + (-a)(-b)$
$= \qquad (-a)(-b)$

Working out the right side,
$$2 \cdot 3 + (^-2)[3 + (^-3)]$$
$$= 2 \cdot 3 + (^-2)(0)$$
$$= 2 \cdot 3 + 0$$
$$= 2 \cdot 3$$

Since one way yields $(^-2)(^-3)$ and the other yields $2 \cdot 3$ it must be true that $(^-2)(^-3) = 2 \cdot 3$.

Working out the right side,
$$ab + (-a)[b + (-b)]$$
$$= ab + (-a)(0)$$
$$= ab + 0$$
$$= ab$$

Since one side of the associative property equation gives $(-a)(-b)$ and the other side gives ab, it must follow that $(-a)(-b) = ab$, no matter what integers are represented by a and b.

4. The definition of subtraction, $a - b = a + (-b)$, and the "theorem" $-a = (^-1)a$ can be used to sort out and simplify many algebraic expressions that are otherwise somewhat confusing. An example of this is worked out below; study it and then try your hand at the remaining examples. In each case the task is to write the expression without parentheses and simplified as much as possible.[18]

a. $-(b + 3) - (3 - b) = {}^-1(b + 3) + (^-1)[3 + (-b)]$
$$= (-b) + (^-3) + (^-3) + b = (-b) + b + (^-3) + (^-3) = {}^-6$$
b. $^-3(m - 7 + x)$
c. $a - (x + 3) - 3$
d. $-(a - 3)$

6.7
**Pedagogical
Remarks**
The extension of whole numbers to the integers is the first of several extensions of the number system in this book. The reason for making this first extension is to allow the next extension (the extension to fractions) to include all positive and negative rational numbers. But in schoolwork the first extension of the whole numbers is normally to positive fractions. As a matter of fact, negative numbers of any sort are usually avoided by teachers even if they happen to appear in the book. While we can give no particular advice about whether negative numbers or fractions should be introduced first, we believe it is a mistake to avoid negative numbers altogether in elementary schools.

As a matter of fact, the *set* of integers as descriptive of common life situations such as temperatures below zero, gains and losses, or opposite

[18] b. $(^-3) [m + (^-1)(7) + x] = {}^-3[m + (^-7) + x] = -3m + 21 + (-3x) = -3m + 21 - 3x$
c. $a + [(^-1)(x + 3)] + (^-1)(3) = a + [(-x) + (^-3)] + (^-3) = a + (-x) + (^-6) = a - x - 6$
d. $(^-1)(a - 3) = (^-1)[a + (^-3)] = (-a) + 3 = 3 + (-a) = 3 - a$

142 NUMBER
SYSTEMS:
SETS
RELATIONS
OPERATIONS
USES

directions from some starting point can appear on the scene quite early—perhaps as early as kindergarten. Once that step has been taken, few children have difficulty with addition of positive and negative numbers if the task is approached in a fairly lighthearted way in the context of common life situations. In this early exposure there should not be much reliance on symbol manipulation or much demand to verbalize the rules.

On the other hand, subtractions, multiplications, and divisions involving negative numbers seem to involve a considerable escalation in difficulty and are probably best left alone until late elementary school. (However, if a given child gets curious about these operations it can surely do no harm to indulge his curiosity as far as it naturally leads him, preferably with the use of concrete embodiments and whenever possible with problems tied to common life.)

One of the best ways of keeping open the possible existence of negative numbers is to be sure that in number line work there is always ample space left empty on the other side of zero not occupied by whole numbers. With such space left some children may wonder why only some of the points are numbered when the line goes *both* ways. For similar reasons, all the number lines pictured in this book have arrows at both ends to indicate that the line continues both directions; we suggest that teachers also do this in number line work with children.

Rulers used in schools nearly always begin the measures exactly at the left end, without even a zero shown. Hence they are relatively poor embodiments of the number line. We would like to see rulers made for work in primary school with the zero point clearly marked and some empty space to the left of zero. Perhaps primary school teachers could construct such rulers, or have the children make them.[3]

We feel that the eventual difficulties that beset so many people in dealing with negative numbers come mainly from two sources. The first is that attention to negative numbers is delayed so long that they are made to seem artificial and unreal as compared with whole numbers and nonnegative fractions. We have already suggested ways to lessen this difficulty. The second difficulty comes not so much in dealing with expressions involving actual numbers but in being asked to manipulate

[3] We have seen a so-called "New Math Ruler" (Sterling Plastics Company) with a zero on all scales and with a scale marked as an integer number line, with zero in the middle.

expressions that contain variables, where any such variable can represent either a positive or a negative number. For example, most people regard such a symbol as $-b$ as representing a negative number, but if, for example, the number $^-10$ replaces b, then $-b$ (the opposite of b) is of course the number $^+10$. Similarly, most people would say that $|-b| = b$, but again if b is replaced by $^-10$ this would mean that $|-(^-10)| = ^-10$ which couldn't be true because the absolute value of a number is always positive.

At best, working with variables requires careful thought and considerable understanding. Appropriate and relaxed work throughout elementary school with equations, frames, and negative numbers should go a long way toward building that understanding.

In sum, negative numbers are respectable and useful numbers. You should become very comfortable with them and then not avoid them in your work with children.

unit 7

extension of the integers to the rational numbers

7.1 INTRODUCTION

For most children fractions are at the same time familiar and confusing. They are familiar because children cope with such expressions as "Give me half of . . ." about as often as "Give me two of . . ." but confusing because the symbol manipulation in doing standard operations with fractions seems to many youngsters strange and unpredictable. (For example, there are probably few who really understand what they are doing when they use the "invert and multiply" rule in order to divide one fraction by another.) It may be that these "mysterious" manipulations, usually not accompanied by the concrete embodiments that might give them meaning, are as responsible as anything else for the feeling we so often encounter that mathematics is impossible to understand and that getting "correct" results is a matter of good luck rather than good management.

Fractions also seem confusing to many people because the results from the operations often run counter to what people expect from dealing with whole numbers. For example, many children feel that multiplication *is* repeated addition, but such a notion has little meaning for multiplication of two fractions. From whole number work children expect that the product of two numbers will be larger than either factor, but this is often not true for fractions, for example, $\frac{1}{2} \times \frac{1}{4} = \frac{1}{8}$. Similarly, "dividing" can lead to a quotient much larger than the dividend (the total being divided), for example $\frac{2}{3} \div \frac{1}{24} = 16$. With such hazards, fractions require careful teaching. We believe that solid grounding in work with embodiments in physical materials and close ties to actual real life uses are required.

There is a semantic difficulty that must also be dealt with for purposes of this course, though not perhaps with young children. Contrary to common usage, *fraction* does not mean the same as *rational number*. Anything written in the form $\frac{a}{b}$ is called a *fraction* in mathematics, although it is customary to require that b (the *denominator*) cannot be zero. Hence $\frac{3}{2}$, $\frac{\sqrt{4}}{3}$, $^{47.5}\!/_{36.9}$, $\frac{\pi}{2}$ and $\frac{1/2}{1/3}$ are all fractions, but only some of them are rational numbers.

In other words, *fraction* in mathematics means a certain sort of symbol that may or may not represent a rational number. A *rational number* is defined to be any number that *can be* written as a fraction $\frac{a}{b}$ with the requirement that a (the *numerator*) be some integer (positive, negative, or zero) and b be some nonzero integer. This describes what most people think of as fractions, but it also describes such nonfractions as 50 percent (which *can be* written as $^{50}\!/_{100}$ or as $\frac{1}{2}$), -3 (written as $^{-3}\!/_1$), and 0.13 (written as $^{13}\!/_{100}$). Of the fraction examples given above, $^{-3}\!/_2$, $\frac{\sqrt{4}}{3}$ (written as $\frac{2}{3}$), $^{47.5}\!/_{36.9}$ (written as $^{475}\!/_{369}$), and $\frac{1/2}{1/3}$ (written as $\frac{3}{2}$) are all rational numbers. However, the fraction $\frac{\pi}{2}$ is not a rational number because, even though in practical work with circles we use some "rational approximation" for π such as $^{22}\!/_7$ or 3.1416, the fact is that the decimal representation for π, and hence for $\frac{\pi}{2}$, goes on forever without a pattern ever establishing itself. Hence it is completely unpredictable beyond any point already figured out, and fractions involving it could never be expressed as one integer over another. (See Table 7.1 showing the first 4,000 digits of the number π.) We call such a number an "irrational number." This topic will be discussed in more detail in Part B, Unit 6.

In this unit we will be dealing only with rational numbers that are already expressed as fractions. (Rational numbers expressed as decimals will be taken up in Part B, Unit 5.) Whenever it is used in this unit the

146 NUMBER
SYSTEMS:
SETS
RELATIONS
OPERATIONS
USES

Table 7.1   **Four Thousand Decimals of π^a**

3.14159	26535	89793	23846	26433	83279	50288	41971	69399	37510
58209	74944	59230	78164	06286	20899	86280	34825	34211	70679
82148	08651	32823	06647	09384	46095	50582	23172	53594	08128
48111	74502	84102	70193	85211	05559	64462	29489	54930	38196
44288	10975	66593	34461	28475	64823	37867	83165	27120	19091
45648	56692	34603	48610	45432	66482	13393	60726	02491	41273
72458	70066	06315	58817	48815	20920	96282	92540	91715	36436
78925	90860	01133	05305	48820	46652	13841	46951	94151	16094
33057	27036	57595	91953	09218	61173	81932	61179	31051	18548
07446	23799	62749	56735	18857	52724	89122	79381	83011	94912
98336	73362	44065	66430	86021	39494	63952	24737	19070	21798
60943	70277	05392	17176	29317	67523	84674	81846	76694	05132
00056	81271	45263	56082	77857	71342	75778	96091	73637	17872
14684	40901	22495	34301	46549	58537	10507	92279	68925	89235
42019	95611	21290	21960	86403	44181	59813	62977	47713	09960
51870	72113	49999	99837	29780	49951	05973	17328	16096	31859
50244	59455	34690	83026	42522	30825	33446	85035	26193	11881
71010	00313	78387	52886	58753	32083	81420	61717	76691	47303
59825	34904	28755	46873	11595	62863	88235	37875	93751	95778
18577	80532	17122	68066	13001	92787	66111	95909	21642	01989
38095	25720	10654	85863	27886	59361	53381	82796	82303	01952
03530	18529	68995	77362	25994	13891	24972	17752	83479	13151
55748	57242	45415	06959	50829	53311	68617	27855	88907	50983
81754	63746	49393	19255	06040	09277	01671	13900	98488	24012
85836	16035	63707	66010	47101	81942	95559	61989	46767	83744
94482	55379	77472	68471	04047	53464	62080	46684	25906	94912
93313	67702	89891	52104	75216	20569	66024	05803	81501	93511
25338	24300	35587	64024	74964	73263	91419	92726	04269	92279
67823	54781	63600	93417	21641	21992	45863	15030	28618	29745
55706	74983	85054	94588	58692	69956	90927	21079	75093	02955
32116	53449	87202	75596	02364	80665	49911	98818	34797	75356
63698	07426	54252	78625	51818	41757	46728	90977	77279	38000
81647	06001	61452	49192	17321	72147	72350	14144	19735	68548
16136	11573	52552	13347	57418	49468	43852	33239	07394	14333
45477	62416	86251	89835	69485	56209	92192	22184	27255	02542
56887	67179	04946	01653	46680	49886	27232	79178	60857	84383
82796	79766	81454	10095	38837	86360	95068	00642	25125	20511
73929	84896	08412	84886	26945	60424	19652	85022	21066	11863
06744	27862	20391	94945	04712	37137	86960	95636	43719	17287
46776	46575	73962	41389	08658	32645	99581	33904	78027	59009

147 EXTENSION
OF THE
INTEGERS
TO THE
RATIONAL
NUMBERS

94657	64078	95126	94683	98352	59570	98258	22620	52248	94077
26719	47826	84826	01476	99090	26401	36394	43745	53050	68203
49625	24517	49399	65143	14298	09190	65925	09372	21696	46151
57098	58387	41059	78859	59772	97549	89301	61753	92846	81382
68683	86894	27741	55991	85592	52459	53959	43104	99725	24680
84598	72736	44695	84865	38367	36222	62609	91246	08051	24388
43904	51244	13654	97627	80797	71569	14359	97700	12961	60894
41694	86855	58484	06353	42207	22258	28488	64815	84560	28506
01684	27394	52267	46767	88952	52138	52254	99546	66727	82398
64565	96116	35488	62305	77456	49803	55936	34568	17432	41125
15076	06947	94510	96596	09402	52288	79710	89314	56691	36867
22874	89405	60101	50330	86179	28680	92087	47609	17824	93858
90097	14909	67598	52613	65549	78189	31297	84821	68299	89487
22658	80485	75640	14270	47755	51323	79641	45152	37462	34364
54285	84447	95265	86782	10511	41354	73573	95231	13427	16610
21359	69536	23144	29524	84937	18711	01457	65403	59027	99344
03742	00731	05785	39062	19838	74478	08478	48968	33214	45713
86875	19435	06430	21845	31910	48481	00537	06146	80674	91927
81911	97939	95206	14196	63428	75444	06437	45123	71819	21799
98391	01591	95618	14675	14269	12397	48940	90718	64942	31961
56794	52080	95146	55022	52316	03881	93014	20937	62137	85595
66389	37787	08303	90697	92077	34672	21825	62599	66150	14215
03068	03844	77345	49202	60541	46659	25201	49744	28507	32518
66600	21324	34088	19071	04863	31734	64965	14539	05796	26856
10055	08106	65879	69981	63574	73638	40525	71459	10289	70641
40110	97120	62804	39039	75951	56771	57700	42033	78699	36007
23055	87631	76359	42187	31251	47120	53292	81918	26186	12586
73215	79198	41484	88291	64470	60957	52706	95722	09175	67116
72291	09816	90915	28017	35067	12748	58322	28718	35209	35396
57251	21083	57915	13698	82091	44421	00675	10334	67110	31412
67111	36990	86585	16398	31501	97016	51511	68517	14376	57618
35155	65088	49099	89859	98238	73455	28331	63550	76479	18535
89322	61854	89632	13293	30898	57064	20467	52590	70915	48141
65498	59461	63718	02709	81994	30992	44889	57571	28289	05923
23326	09729	97120	84433	57326	54893	82391	19325	97463	66730
58360	41428	13883	03203	82490	37589	85243	74417	02913	27656
18093	77344	40307	07469	21120	19130	20330	38019	76211	01100
44929	32151	60842	44485	96376	69838	95228	68478	31235	52658
21314	49576	85726	24334	41893	03968	64262	43410	77322	69780
28073	18915	44110	10446	82325	27162	01052	65227	21116	60396

[a] From a table of π to 10,000 decimals, calculated on the IBM 704 by Cie IBM, France, Institut de Calcul Scientifique. Limited space does not permit the presentation of the entire table.

SOURCE: Reprinted by permission from Phillip Davis, *The Lore of Large Numbers,* Random House, Inc., New York, 1961, pp. 72–73. Copyright 1971 by Random House, Inc.

148 NUMBER
SYSTEMS:
SETS
RELATIONS
OPERATIONS
USES

word *fraction* will mean one of those sorts of fractions that also happen to be rational numbers. But keep in mind that not all rational numbers are expressed as fractions (though all of them *can be* so expressed) and that not all fractions are rational numbers.

Fractions were developed in prehistoric times, no doubt in response to such human needs as the need to have more adequate "measures" of various things than could be accommodated by whole number units. Ancient documents show symbols equivalent to such "unit fractions" as ½, ¼, ⅓, ⅛, and the Egyptians used sums of unit fractions for more complicated fractions; for example, ½ + ¼ for ¾.[1] Even in modern times such unit fractions can suffice for the common life needs of many people.

This unit will follow our usual pattern by first asking the question "Why bother to extend the number system to include fractions; what are they good for?" After answering this question, we will deal in turn with the meanings of fraction symbols, relations such as "is equal to" and "is less than," the standard operations, and the properties of these operations.

7.2
**PROBLEM SET:
WHY BOTHER WITH
FRACTIONS? SOURCES
AND USES**

Overview: **"One-half of" and similar phrases have clear meaning to most people and in schools are the main motivation for fractions. But the fraction notation is also used in everyday life to express ratios and scales, as an "operator," and as another notation for division problems. Added to these uses are certain requirements of mathematics that dictate the invention of fractions (or, more accurately, rational numbers). Each of these motivations will be dealt with in this section.**

7.2.1
**Various
Motivations for
Fractions**

The fraction form $\frac{a}{b}$, with a and b whole numbers (or, sometimes, integers) has a number of different interpretations. For each of the uses outlined below (except possibly use 5), try to supply at least one example from your own recent experience and write it down for discussion with your colleagues.

1. $\frac{a}{b}$ as taking a of b equal parts of some unit:

In this interpretation the denominator b indicates how many equal

---

[1] The story of the historical development of fractions is a fascinating one. Part of that story is told in B. L. Van Der Waerden, *Science Awakening,* Oxford University Press, Fair Lawn, N.J., 1961, and also in other books.

149 EXTENSION
OF THE
INTEGERS
TO THE
RATIONAL
NUMBERS

parts something has been divided into and the numerator *a* indicates how many of these parts we are considering. Thus "⁷⁄₈ of . . ." means 7 of 8 equal parts of something. It is important in this interpretation to define what the "unit" is; half a 12-ounce can of root beer is quite a different matter from half a gallon, and half an inch is quite a different matter from half a mile. Once a unit is defined, there is no difficulty in talking in terms of such fractions as ⁴⁄₄ or ³⁄₂ as meaning all of something or more than one of something.

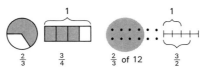

Some pictures of fractions

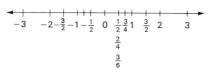

2. Fractions used for filling in a number line and in linear measure: On a number line marked only with whole numbers there are vast spaces left unmarked. With fractions, each of these spaces can be divided into equal intervals and appropriate fractions can be used to name the points. In doing this, some points are named in many ways—which begins to get at the business of equivalent fractions. This use is a variant on the first use above, but it is important in its own right. Whenever you use a ruler, a graduated beaker, a measuring cup, or many sorts of dials, this use is visible.

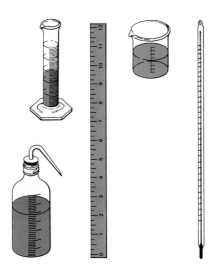

3. Fractions used to express ratios:
Another way in which fractions are used is to express what we call "ratios"—comparing almost anything with almost anything else. For ex-

150 NUMBER
SYSTEMS:
SETS
RELATIONS
OPERATIONS
USES

ample, $\frac{2}{20}$ could mean that 2 out of 20 people in a class got A grades; or that it takes 2 gallons of gas to go 20 miles; or that it takes $2 to buy 20 candy bars; or that 2 out of 20 people think arithmetic is more fun than anything; and so on. There are many special uses of ratios—too many to sort out here. One frequent example is ratios used to indicate relative size. For example, a dictionary picture to $\frac{1}{30}$ scale means every linear measure in the picture is $\frac{1}{30}$th of the measure of the actual object; a similarity ratio in ordinary geometry or a map with a scale of $\frac{1}{25,000}$ has that same sort of meaning. Ratios are sometimes expressed as, for example, 1:25,000. Such a curious use of the equals mark as $\frac{1}{4}$ inch $= 1$ foot, often seen on building plans or maps, can be converted to a scale ratio; in this case $\frac{1}{48}$.

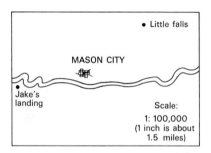

Proportions are equations involving two ratios, usually in the form $\frac{a}{b} = \frac{c}{d}$. They open up still more uses of fractions as ratios, since explicit or implicit use of proportions as mathematical models of common life situations is frequent.

4. $\frac{a}{b}$ as a way of representing a divided by b:

The notation $a \div b$ virtually disappears beyond elementary school with $\frac{a}{b}$ replacing it, and meaning precisely the same thing.

5. Fractions used to help tidy up mathematical structures: (Note: You are not likely to find real life examples of these uses.)

Here are several examples of this use of fractions.

a. With only whole numbers, division is not "closed"; for example, $13 \div 8$ has no whole number answer. Extending the number system to include fractions attends to this, and $13 \div 8 = {}^{13}/_8$ or $1{}^5/_8$.

b. For various mathematical reasons, it is nice if every number used in multiplication has an "inverse" or "reciprocal" so that multiplication of a number and its inverse gives the "identity"—the number 1—as product. With fractions every number (except zero) has a multiplicative inverse: $3 \times {}^1/_3 = 1$, $7 \times {}^1/_7 = 1$, ${}^7/_8 \times {}^8/_7 = 1$, etc. (This use will be further discussed below.)

c. Equations such as $2n = 1$ or $13m = 47$ do not have solutions if only integers are being used, but with fractions, solutions can be found. For $2n = 1$, the solution is ${}^1/_2$ (since $2 \times {}^1/_2 = 1$); for $13m = 47$, the solution is ${}^{47}/_{13}$.

7.2.2
Fractions as Used in the Common World
Consider each of the uses of fractions indicated by the following examples and see if you can identify the general uses outlined above. (You may want to use the following symbols: *PW* for parts of a whole, *M* for measure or number line, *R* for ratio or rate, *Q* for quotient.) Since more than one use sometimes seems to be in the picture, don't worry about getting an unambiguous decision; nor should you be concerned if there is disagreement among you and your colleagues about what to call the various examples. In some of the items, questions are asked. You can try to answer these questions if you want to, but the main purpose of this exercise is just for you to consider a number of ways in which fractions are used in common life.[2]

1. *1001 Questions Answered about Trees*[3] tells us that a bamboo tree resembles certain grasses in its structure (the scientific name of bamboo, *dendrocalalamus,* means "tree reed") and that you can almost see a thriving bamboo tree grow—as much as 18 inches in a single day. What is the average growth per hour of a bamboo tree growing at that rate?

2. Much of the land in the United States is surveyed and divided into mile-square "sections"; these in turn are divided into quarter sections, then quarter-quarter sections, then into square blocks (see diagram). Hence there are 8 blocks along a 1-mile side of a section.

---

[2] The first eight examples are taken from M. S. Bell, *Mathematical Models and Uses in Our Everyday World.*

[3] R. Platt, *1001 Questions Answered about Trees,* Grossett & Dunlap, New York, 1959, p. 39.

152 NUMBER
SYSTEMS:
SETS
RELATIONS
OPERATIONS
USES

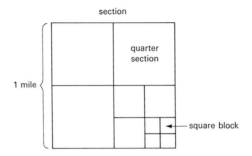

(See if this is the case for your city.) If there are 8 blocks per mile, how many feet per block are there (5,280 feet per mile)? How many yards per block? About how many football field lengths or 100-yard-dash track lengths per block? If you run hard for a block, have you done a 100-yard dash or a 220-yard dash or a 440-yard dash or what? Notice how many times the word "per" is used in the few sentences above; this word frequently indicates ratio or rate expressions.

3. One common use of ratios is to express "scale" on such things as building plans and maps. For example, a frequently used ratio in architectural drawings is $\frac{1}{8}$ inch to 1 foot. Using this scale, for how large a building could you draw a plan on a page the size of this book, leaving reasonable margins and space for title and explanations? What scale would be appropriate if you were going to draw a floor plan of your mathematics classroom on a similar page? What scale would be appropriate for drawing an entire floor of your school on the same size page?

4. The book *Mapping*[4] tells us that the scale of a map is often expressed as a "representative fraction" which tells exactly how much the map is "shrunk" with respect to the actual ground it represents. For example, a representative fraction of $\frac{1}{5,280}$ would tell us that 1 foot of the map would represent 1 mile of actual distance (a mile is 5,280 feet). If, as is fairly common, a map you are looking at has 1 inch "equal" to a mile, what would the representative fraction be? That is, how many inches are there in a mile? At a scale of 1 inch per mile how wide would a map have to be to represent the United States, excluding Alaska and Hawaii, coast-to-coast (about 3,000

---

[4] D. Greenhood, *Mapping,* The University of Chicago Press, Chicago, 1964.

153 EXTENSION
OF THE
INTEGERS
TO THE
RATIONAL
NUMBERS

miles)? How long would the map be? If your school has a flat roof, is it large enough to accommodate such a map?

5. *Mapping* tells us that the purpose of a map is often defined by its scale. For example, maps with representative scales of 1:1,000,000 and smaller are usually atlas maps giving general views of the earth's surface, shapes of continents, boundaries of countries, and so on. Maps between 1:1,000,000 and 1:10,000 allow more detail about a given region. Maps of a larger scale than 1:10,000 are usually used to show real estate divisions and surveys. We are told that the nickname for maps with 1:1,000,000 scale is a "million map." Such a million map may be part of a large map-making project, "The International Map of the World," which many nations throughout the world are cooperating on. In this scale about how many miles are there to an inch?

6. According to *The Physics of Music*,[5] "horsepower" as a unit of power was defined when mine operators began to replace horses with steam engines; it was the *rate* at which an average horse could do work over an average working day. It is now defined as the power required to lift 550 pounds 1 foot per second. A watt is about $1/746$ of a horsepower; or in other words, 746 watts are about 1 horsepower.

7. *The Odd Book of Data*[6] notes that small amounts of wear from friction can have large effects; for example, just a pound or two of material worn from the bearings could consign a large truck to the scrap heap. Suppose a truck weighing 5 tons is made unusable by loss of 1 pound of metal by wear on its moving parts. What fraction of the weight is this 1-pound loss?

8. A link between the system of weights during the Middle Ages and the modern-day system is the designation of gold as being "14 carat," "18 carat," etc. According to *Realm of Measure*,[7] there was an old coin called a "mark" that had a mass of 24 carats, with a carat equal to half a pennyweight, or 12 grains. But without strict standards it would be easy to cheat by, for example, making a 24-carat

[5] A. Wood, *The Physics of Music,* Dover Publishers, Inc., New York, 1961, p. 61.

[6] R. Houwink, *The Odd Book of Data,* Elsevier Publishing Co., Amsterdam, 1965, p. 69.

[7] I. Asimov, *The Realm of Measure,* Fawcett World Library, New York, 1967, p. 66.

1975 High	1975 Low	Stocks and Div. in Dollars	P/E	Sales 100s	High	Low	Last	Net Chg
2 3/8	7/8	CCI Corp	...	5	1 3/4	1 3/4	1 3/4	......
39 1/2	25 7/8	Celanse 2.80	8	58	38 3/4	38 1/2	38 3/4	+ 1/8
11 1/2	5	Centex .12	23	65	8 7/8	8 1/2	8 7/8	+ 1/4
18 7/8	12 1/2	CenHud 1.72	7	4	16 7/8	16 5/8	16 5/8	− 3/8
17 3/8	11 1/4	CenIllLt 1.60	8	x20	16 1/8	16	16	− 1/8
48	43 3/4	CnILt pf4.50	...	z30	45	44 1/2	44 1/2	− 2
13 1/2	9 3/8	CenIIPS 1.20	8	72	12 3/4	12 1/2	12 3/4	+ 1/4
20 1/8	14 1/8	CenLaE 1.28	7	11	17 3/8	17 3/8	17 3/8	+ 1/8
15	10 7/8	CeMPw 1.34	10	17	13 1/2	13 1/8	13 1/2	+ 1/8
18 1/4	13 3/8	CenSoW 1.16	8	49	14 3/4	14 1/2	14 5/8	......
16	10	CenSoya .60	11	57	15	14 3/4	14 3/4	− 1/8
22 1/8	16 1/2	CenTel 1.20	8	39	18	17 5/8	17 5/8	− 1/8
25	6 1/2	Centrn Data	10	55	17 1/8	16 3/8	17	− 1/8
17 1/2	11 3/8	Cerro 1.20	7	50	14 3/8	14	14	− 3/8
13 1/2	6 3/4	Cert-teed .60	...	20	11 1/8	11	11	+ 1/8
20 1/4	11 7/8	CessnaAir 1	6	3	16 7/8	16 7/8	16 7/8	......
18 1/4	10 1/2	ChampInt 1	8	127	16	15 5/8	15 3/4	− 1/8
19 1/4	12 7/8	Chml pf1.20	...	17	17	16 3/4	17	......
14	9	ChamSp .60	9	x105	10 7/8	10 5/8	10 5/8	......
6 1/2	4 3/4	Charter Co	3	131	5 1/8	4 7/8	5	− 1/8
27 1/2	18 3/4	Chartr NY 2	5	12	24 3/8	24 1/8	24 1/8	......
9 1/8	7	ChaseFd .60	...	7	7 1/4	7 1/4	7 1/4	......
38 3/4	26 1/2	ChaseM 2.20	4	139	33 1/8	32 1/2	32 3/4	+ 1/4
8 5/8	3	ChasT 1.73e	...	151	3 1/4	2 7/8	3	......
7	5 1/8	Chelsea .40a	9	21	6 1/4	6	6 1/4	+ 3/8
45 1/8	22 1/8	ChemIn 1.10	4	183	37 1/2	36	36	− 3/8
43 5/8	29 1/2	ChmNY 2.88	5	41	36 3/4	36 3/8	36 3/8	− 1/8
38	28	CheVa 1.80a	5	4	33 3/4	33 3/4	33 3/4	......
67	37 1/8	Chesbg 1.36	20	92	57 1/4	56 3/4	57 1/8	+ 1/8
37 7/8	26	Chessie 2.10	6	57	32 1/2	32 1/8	32 1/8	− 1/4
16 7/8	10 1/4	ChiEasIl .65	5	6	13 1/2	13 1/2	13 1/2	− 1/8
11 1/4	5 3/8	ChiMilw Cp	...	24	5 3/4	5 1/2	5 1/2	− 1/4
15	10	Chi Milw pf	...	1	9 7/8	9 7/8	9 7/8	− 1/2
31 1/2	23 1/4	ChiPneuT 2	7	15	26 3/8	26 1/8	26 1/4	......
4 7/8	2 1/8	ChkFull .19t	...	6	3 7/8	3 7/8	3 7/8	− 1/8
6	2 1/8	Chris Craft	...	169	5 1/8	4 7/8	5 1/8	+ 1/4
13 1/2	5 1/2	ChCft cvpf	...	1	9 5/8	9 5/8	9 5/8	− 7/8
13	8 1/8	Chromal .70	5	19	11 7/8	11 5/8	11 7/8	......
14 1/2	7 3/8	Chrysler	...	437	11 1/8	10 3/4	10 3/4	− 3/8
2 3/8	1 1/4	Chrysler wt	...	17	1 3/8	1 1/4	1 1/4	......
3 1/8	1	CI Mtg Gp	...	29	1 5/8	1 1/2	1 1/2	......
4 7/8	2 1/2	CI Rlt Inv	....	14	3 3/4	3 3/4	3 3/4	− 1/8
21 1/8	18 3/8	CinBell 1.60	7	12	20 1/8	20	20	− 3/8
18 1/2	14 3/4	CinnGE 1.64	8	59	16 1/2	16 1/8	16 3/8	+ 1/4
104 3/4	94 1/2	CinG pf9.30	...	z40	101	101	101	......
53 1/8	44	CinG pf4.75	...	z130	50	49 1/2	50	......
48 1/2	40 3/4	CinGE pf 4	...	z70	43	42 1/4	42 1/4	− 3/4
25 1/2	16 3/8	CinMila 1.40	7	x15	18 3/8	18	18 3/8	+ 5/8
37 1/2	30 1/2	CIT Fin 2.20	7	59	30 5/8	30	30 1/4	− 3/8
39	28 3/8	Citicorp .88	12	505	32 3/4	32 1/8	32 1/4	− 1/8
50 1/2	36 1/4	CitiesSv 2.40	8	81	45 3/8	44 1/2	44 1/2	− 1/4
6	2 1/2	CitzSR 1.17e	...	32	2 5/8	2 1/2	2 5/8	+ 1/8
4 3/8	1 5/8	Citizns Mtg	...	3	2	2	2	......
9 1/4	4 3/4	CityInvst .66	17	128	7 1/8	7	7	......
19 1/2	11 3/4	CityIn pf B2	...	25	16 7/8	16 5/8	16 7/8	+ 1/8
2 5/8	1 5/8	City Strs	...	14	2 3/8	2 1/4	2 3/8	+ 1/4
34 1/4	22 3/8	ClarkE 1.60	7	19	28 3/4	28 1/2	28 5/8	− 1/8
14 1/2	7 3/8	ClarkOil .50	...	12	11	10 3/4	11	+ 3/8
7	2 7/8	CLC Am .24	5	5	4 5/8	4 5/8	4 5/8	......
103 1/2	66 1/8	ClvClif 2.60a	11	5	99 1/2	99 1/8	99 1/2	+ 3/4
28 3/8	23 3/8	ClvElIll 2.48	7	50	25 1/2	25 1/4	25 1/4	+ 1/8
81	68 1/2	ClElIl pf7.40	...	z200	75	74	75	− 1
13 1/2	6 1/8	CloroxCo .52	12	257	10 7/8	10 1/4	10 1/4	− 1/4
8	3 1/4	CluetPea .30	...	286	5 5/8	5 1/2	5 5/8	+ 1/8
11 5/8	7 3/8	CluettP pf 1	...	5	10 1/8	10 1/8	10 1/8	......
13 5/8	6 3/8	CMIInv Cp	...	25	8 1/2	8 1/4	8 3/8	......
7 7/8	2 3/4	CNA Finl	...	20	6	6	6	......
13 1/4	6 1/4	CNA pfA1.10	...	14	11 7/8	11 5/8	11 5/8	......
12	9 1/2	CNA I 1.08a	...	4	10 3/4	10 3/4	10 3/4	......
1 7/8	1/2	CNA Larw	...	8	1 3/8	1 1/4	1 1/4	......
11 7/8	6 1/4	CNAL pf2.10	...	24	7 1/2	7 1/4	7 1/4	......
11 5/8	5 3/4	CoastSt Gas	3	323	8 3/8	7 7/8	8	− 1/8
20 7/8	15 3/8	CstSG pf1.83	...	2	18 1/2	18 3/8	18 1/2	+ 1/8
93 1/2	53 1/4	CocaCol 2.30	23	116	78 1/4	76 1/8	76 3/8	− 1 1/4
9 7/8	4 3/4	CocaBtlg .40	16	152	6 5/8	6 3/8	6 1/2	+ 1/4
14	6 1/2	ColdwBk .36	8	3	10 1/4	10 1/8	10 1/8	+ 1/8
4 3/8	1 1/2	Coleco Ind	...	11	3 1/8	3	3	......
34 7/8	22	ColgPal .68	15	202	27 7/8	27 3/8	27 1/2	− 1/4

SOURCE: © 1975 by the New York Times Company. Reprinted by permission.

coin half gold and half copper; that is, containing only 12 carats of gold. Hence, it became the custom to call such a coin a 12-carat coin, and strict penalties were exacted for violating standards. Nowadays, any object, regardless of its total weight, is marked 14 carat if it is $^{14}/_{24}$ gold. Find out what the present price of gold is on the world market and then compute what 1 ounce of 14-carat gold and 1 ounce of 18-carat gold would be worth. ("Ounce" here means troy ounce, not our ordinary ounce.)

9. Over the next few years the United States will finally join most other industrialized countries by changing over to the metric system of measurement. One of the useful things to know at that time will be that a kilometer is about $^{6}/_{10}$ mile. A useful but less accurate conversion factor is to regard a kilometer as $^{5}/_{8}$ mile (which is pretty close to $^{6}/_{10}$) because that would tell us that a kilometer is about 5 city blocks in cities that have 8 blocks to the mile.

10. The stock market quotations use fractions in several implicit and explicit ways. The fractions in the price of the stock are fractions of dollars, and so the closing price of one share of Coca-Cola on the quotations to the left is \$76.375. The P/E column gives a price-earnings ratio—a rounded-off number obtained by dividing the closing price of one share of stock by the most recent yearly earnings per share. Can you find out why stock prices are expressed in fractions of dollars instead of dollars and cents?

11. Here are some items taken from the *New York Times* of March 17, 1974:

a. The U. S. Defense Department plans fighting forces adequate for $1^{1}/_{2}$ wars (meaning a major conflict in Europe or Asia and a limited war elsewhere). Considering this figure as a fraction ($1^{1}/_{2} = ^{3}/_{2}$) do you suppose $1^{1}/_{2}$ wars is equivalent to 3 half-wars? (The news item reports controversy about this concept and our overseas military commitments generally.)

b. Nine out of ten ($^{9}/_{10}$) college athletic budgets are "in the red" because costs have doubled within the past decade.

c. In an experiment in Japan, Holstein cows are being fed $4^{1}/_{2}$ pounds of newsprint each day—about $^{1}/_{6}$ of their food—and are yielding good milk.

155 EXTENSION
OF THE
INTEGERS
TO THE
RATIONAL
NUMBERS

12. Over the next couple of days look through at least one daily newspaper or weekly newsmagazine and keep notes on all uses of fractions you find. Also record other uses of fractions you encounter during this time and bring them to class for comparison and discussion.

7.3
ACTIVITY: PAPER
STRIPS AS EMBODIMENTS OF
(RATIONAL) FRACTIONS

Overview: With 24-centimeter-long strips as "units," fractional lengths will be created by folding. The meaning of the "is less than" and the "is equal to" relations will be explored, and you will begin to form equivalence classes of fractions. The meaning of operations with fractions will be briefly explored; the strips are especially effective in embodying multiplication. There are aspects of fractions that don't easily emerge from work with strips, and these aspects are brought out in activities with other embodiments.

Materials needed: Several dozen paper strips 24 by 1½ centimeters; construction paper; glue or rubber cement.

As indicated in the previous section, the fraction notation is used for a variety of purposes. You and the youngsters you teach should become conscious of different interpretations and flexible in switching among them as appropriate in given situations. The rules and properties that govern relations and operations for fractions are the same, whatever the interpretation of the fraction symbol itself. For fractions used as ratios, equivalence is the key issue and it is rarely necessary to add or multiply two ratios. For other interpretations, the standard operations are sometimes used.

Z. P. Dienes insists on the necessity for multiple embodiments of the ideas we try to teach, because, he says, different concrete embodiments bring out different things. As you work through the activities that follow, try to determine what pieces of the rather complicated fraction ideas come through best from each of the embodiments you are asked to use. Also keep track of any new insights or solidified understandings that you gain from the work.

7.3.1
The Set of
Rational Fractions Embodied
by Paper Folding

1. Fold a paper strip (24 by 1½ centimeters) into two equal parts (halves). Fold another strip to show fourths, and another to show eights. Experiment to find a good way of getting thirds, and then, with other strips, get sixths and twelfths. See how well you can do for fifths, then get tenths. Mark the folds and save the strips for the next exercise.

156 NUMBER
SYSTEMS:
SETS
RELATIONS
OPERATIONS
USES

2. On a piece of colored construction paper turned sidewise, mark a line about ½ inch from the left margin. At the top of the construction paper, starting at the line, paste a paper strip that has not been folded. Then paste the strips you folded and marked in exercise 1 onto the construction paper under the first strip, starting each strip at the line. This will give you a poster picture of the unit length (the top strip), halves, thirds, fourths, fifths, sixths, tenths, twelfths, and as many others as you want to make. Label the strips appropriately.

7.3.2
Relations:
"Is Equal To," "Is Less Than,"
"Is Greater Than"

1. With the same unit length folded to represent a number of different fractions, it becomes possible to compare size of fractions by direct comparison of lengths. Using the display of fraction strips completed in section 7.3.1, fill in the proper symbol ($<$, $>$, or $=$) between each pair of fractions below:

a. $\frac{1}{3}$ ☐ $\frac{2}{6}$

d. $\frac{8}{12}$ ☐ $\frac{2}{3}$

b. $\frac{3}{4}$ ☐ $\frac{5}{6}$

e. $\frac{2}{3}$ ☐ $\frac{5}{6}$

c. $\frac{7}{12}$ ☐ $\frac{3}{4}$

f. $\frac{1}{4}$ ☐ $\frac{2}{4}$

2. Referring to the display of fraction strips you made earlier and by placing a ruler vertically on the fold marked ½ on the second strip, see what other names there are for this same length on other strips. Record them here:

(Partial) equivalence class for ½: ½,

Using a similar procedure, fill in other equivalence classes on page 157, using only evidence from the folding strips. Compare your work with that of other students.

157 EXTENSION
OF THE
INTEGERS
TO THE
RATIONAL
NUMBERS

(Example) ½, ²/₄, ³/₆, ⁴/₈, ⁶/₁₂, ⁵/₁₀

⅓, _____   ²/₅, _____

¼, _____   ¾, _____

⅕, _____   ¾, _____

⅙, _____   ⅚, _____

⅛, _____   ³/₈, _____

⅔, _____

3. From the results you got in exercise 2 above, try to formulate a general numerical way of creating fractions equivalent to any given fraction.[1]

7.3.3
Multiplication of
Fractions Using Paper Strips

1. Repeated addition is the standard motivation for multiplication of whole numbers and can conceivably be used for such problems as $3 \times ½$, but it has little meaning for the likes of $½ \times ⅓$. Another way of expressing such a whole number multiplication as 2×6 is a phrase such as "two (groups) of six." The word *of* seems to convey clearly what is meant by multiplication of fractions: $½ \times ⅓$ is $½$ *of* $⅓$. Starting with a unit strip, fold it to get $⅓$; then, leaving it folded, again fold it in half and mark $½$ of $⅓$. Open up the strip, and you will see that $½$ of $⅓$ is $⅙$ of the unit strip.

Fold some fresh strips to get answers to each of these problems:

a. ¼ of ½ = ☐   **d.** $⅓ \times ½$ = ☐

b. ¾ of ½ = ☐   **e.** $½ \times ¾$ = ☐

c. ⅔ of ¼ = ☐   **f.** $⅔ \times ¾$ = ☐

[1] One rule that works in the creation of equivalent fractions is to multiply the numerator and denominator by the same whole number: $\dfrac{a}{b} = \dfrac{n \cdot a}{n \cdot b}$ (Here and later when "variables" are used to state a rule we will use a center dot instead of a multiplication sign to denote multiplication because in algebraic work the letter x is sometimes confused with the multiplication sign.) This rule is nicely embodied by folding strips of paper because, for example, in folding ½ to get ²/₄, you change both the number of equal parts of the unit (the denominator) and the number of equal parts being considered (the numerator), each by a factor of 2.

158 NUMBER
SYSTEMS:
SETS
RELATIONS
OPERATIONS
USES

2. Examine the results recorded above and try to formulate a general rule for accomplishing the multiplication of two fractions.[2]

7.3.4
Multiplicative
Inverse; Reciprocals

We observed earlier that one of the motivations for inventing fractions is to tidy up the mathematical world. With (rational) fractions we have this new mathematical property:

Multiplicative inverse property: Given any nonzero number, there exists a number to multiply it by (called the "inverse" or "reciprocal") so that the product is the multiplicative identity 1.

1. For whole numbers, the inverses are obvious: $\square \times 7 = 1$ has $1/7$ as the answer, $\square \times 13 = 1$ has $1/13$ as answer, and, in general for $b \neq 0$,

$\square \times b = 1$ has $\dfrac{1}{b}$ as the answer. To see about inverses of fractions, act out the problem $\square \times 1/4 = 1$ using the paper strips. To do this, fold to get a $1/4$-length strip, and then see how many of these fit into the unit-length strip. Hence, $\square \times 1/4 = 1$ has 4 or $4/1$ as the answer. How many $3/4$ strips fit the unit length? That is, what goes in the box in the equation $\square \times 3/4 = 1$? Evidently it is 1 and some fraction; find out what fraction (by folding paper strips). Then go one step further and record your answer in the box as a fraction rather than as a mixed number.[3]

2. Using the strips in a similar way, try to fill in the frames below:

a. $\square \times 1/5 = 1$ **d.** $\square \times 4/5 = 1$

b. $\square \times 1/8 = 1$ **e.** $\square \times 3/5 = 1$

c. $\square \times 2/3 = 1$ ***f.** $\square \times 2/4 = 1$

*3. Try to formulate a general rule for finding multiplicative inverses by filling in the frames in this statement: Given any rational number $\dfrac{a}{b}$ (except zero), there exists a rational number $\square$ such that $\dfrac{a}{b} \times \square = 1$.

---

[2] One such rule is $\dfrac{a}{b} \cdot \dfrac{c}{d} = \dfrac{a \cdot c}{b \cdot d}$. In other words, multiply numerators to get the new numerator, denominators to get the new denominator. This may not result in an answer that is in "lowest terms" (that is, with no common factors in numerator and denominator) but don't let this both you. If the answer is needed in lowest terms or any other equivalent form, you can make the appropriate selection from the equivalence class.

[3] It takes $1 1/3$ strips $3/4$ unit long to make a unit length. Record this as $4/3$. The equation looks like this: $\dfrac{4}{3} \times \dfrac{3}{4} = 1$.

7.3.5
Division of Fractions Using Paper Strips

1. For a whole number division problem such as $18 \div 2 = \square$, one approach is to ask "How many twos in 18?" Similarly, such a problem as $\frac{1}{2} \div \frac{1}{4} = \square$ can be expressed as "How many one-fourths in $\frac{1}{2}$?" This can be acted out by seeing how many $\frac{1}{4}$-lengths make a $\frac{1}{2}$-length. Going one step beyond this, notice that a $\frac{1}{2}$-length can also be named $\frac{2}{4}$ (since $\frac{1}{2}$ and $\frac{2}{4}$ are in the same equivalence class). The question then becomes "How many one-fourths in two-fourths?" which has a nearly obvious answer. Do the problems below by using your display of strips (to get equivalent fractions), along with the suggestions above.

a. $\frac{3}{4} \div \frac{1}{4} = \square$ **e.** $\frac{5}{10} \div \frac{1}{2} = \square$

b. $\frac{1}{2} \div \frac{1}{8} = \square$ **f.** $\frac{3}{4} \div \frac{1}{2} = \square$

c. $\frac{8}{12} \div \frac{1}{6} = \square$ **g.** $\frac{1}{6} \div \frac{1}{2} = \square$

d. $\frac{3}{4} \div \frac{3}{8} = \square$

2. Try to formulate a general rule, which exploits common denominator fractions selected from equivalence classes, for getting an answer for any division problem $\frac{a}{b} \div \frac{c}{d} = \square$.

3. Think about and discuss whether problems **1** and **2** above give any basis for understanding the standard "invert and multiply" rule for dividing fractions; that is, the rule that $\frac{a}{b} \div \frac{c}{d} = \frac{a}{b} \cdot \frac{d}{c}$.

7.4
ACTIVITY: FRACTIONS WITH NUMBER LINE AND ROD EMBODIMENTS

Overview: **Equivalence classes of fractions; the relations "is equal to," "is less than," and "is greater than"; and the division operation will be stressed again. However, the operation of multiplication will be neglected. Addition and subtraction will be considered at length in this activity, although they were neglected in the folding of paper strips.**

Materials needed: A folded paper number line for rods; rods; a few 24-centimeter-long paper strips like those used in the previous activity.

There are many things to be learned about fractions, some of which are

[4] Select from the equivalence classes for $\dfrac{a}{b}$ and $\dfrac{c}{d}$ fractions such that $\dfrac{a}{b} = \dfrac{\ell}{m}$ and $\dfrac{c}{d} = \dfrac{n}{m}$ (i.e. fractions with the same denominator). Then $\dfrac{a}{b} \div \dfrac{c}{d} = \dfrac{\ell}{m} \div \dfrac{n}{m} = \dfrac{\ell}{n}$.

160 NUMBER
SYSTEMS:
SETS
RELATIONS
OPERATIONS
USES

better brought out by certain embodiments than by other embodiments. Folding paper strips appears to be effective in embodying such things as the role of a "unit" in fraction discussions; in explaining $\frac{a}{b}$ as meaning a out of b parts of a unit; in showing equivalence classes of fractions; and for showing multiplication of fractions. In this activity we will use rods on a number line. This embodiment effectively shows some of the same things as do the paper strips, but not all of them. On the other hand, the use of rods on the number line brings out things about fractions that are not dealt with at all, or are dealt with poorly, by paper strips.

7.4.1
**Making
and Using the
Number Line**

1. Make a number line for rods similar to the ones you have made before for whole number work, but with the following changes (indicated by the diagram below): Fold the paper lengthwise; fold up only once from the bottom (to leave room to write in the fraction labels for points), and mark a 24-centimeter-long space between 0 and 1 as the unit length to refer fractions to.

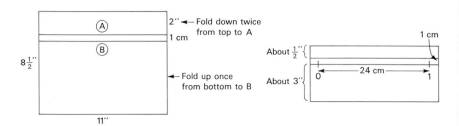

2. Take a 24-centimeter paper strip, fold it in half, and use it to mark the points $\frac{0}{2}$, $\frac{1}{2}$, and $\frac{2}{2}$ on the number line. (It is better to have or make special 12-centimeter-long rods to embody a $\frac{1}{2}$-length here, but the paper strip or an appropriately cut piece of cardboard will do. Whatever you use, mark it $\frac{1}{2}$ and save it for later in this activity.)

3. Starting with the longest rods and using only one color at a time, try to make one-color trains that *exactly* fit from 0 to 1 on the number line. If a train does not work out, put aside all rods of that color. If a train does fit exactly the unit length, count the number of rods and then *carefully* mark the end of each rod on the edge of the slot and give each such mark an appropriate fraction name. For example, with one popular set of rods, four dark green rods fill in the unit exactly; in that case, mark the left end point as $\frac{0}{4}$, and the other end points as $\frac{1}{4}$, $\frac{2}{4}$, $\frac{3}{4}$, $\frac{4}{4}$, respectively.

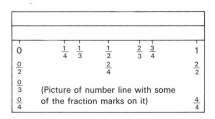

Write each new name just below the previous one. Work carefully and write small to make room for a considerable amount of information, for by the time you finish, some points will have many fraction names. Keep out two rods from each train that works and mark them with the fraction length they represent in this situation, using a soft lead pencil or a water-base marking pen.[5]

7.4.2 Equivalence Classes of Fractions

1. Your number line now displays some equivalence classes of fractions. (Each such equivalence class has many more members than you have listed, of course.) Show three of these below by copying down columns of names for three of the points marked on the number line. Then add to each such list two more fractions that are *not* marked on your number line but that do belong to that equivalence class.

Named on Number Line	Not Yet Named, but in the Equivalence Class.
a.	
b.	
c.	

2. In working with the paper strips, you found that one way to get a fraction equivalent to a given fraction is to multiply numerator and denominator by the same nonzero whole number; in symbols, $\frac{a}{b} = \frac{n \cdot a}{n \cdot b}$. Pick out pairs of fractions that are equivalent by this rule, and complete the table on page 162. The first one is done for you.

[5] With Cuisenaire or similar rods, you will have trains for brown, dark green, purple, light green, red, and white rods and whatever you used for halves. From those you will have marked thirds, fourths, sixths, eighths, twelfths, twenty-fourths, and halves. Don't forget to mark the 0 and 1 end points with appropriate names in every case; ⁰⁄₆ and ⁶⁄₆, for example.

162 NUMBER
SYSTEMS:
SETS
RELATIONS
OPERATIONS
USES

$\dfrac{a}{b}$	$\dfrac{n \cdot a}{n \cdot b}$	What n?
a. $\frac{1}{3}$	$\frac{4}{12}$	4
b. $\frac{5}{6}$		
c.	$\frac{9}{18}$	
d.		5

3. We know for sure that $\frac{3}{6} = \frac{4}{8}$, and yet there is no whole number n that would produce either of these fractions from the other by the rule $\dfrac{a}{b} = \dfrac{n \cdot a}{n \cdot b}$. From the equivalence classes shown on your number line, write three other equivalences that could not be obtained by that rule.

   a.

   b.

   c.

4. A general rule for showing whether *any* two fractions are equivalent is as follows: For any two fractions $\dfrac{a}{b}$ and $\dfrac{c}{d}$ ($b \neq 0$, $d \neq 0$), $\dfrac{a}{b} = \dfrac{c}{d}$ if and only if $a \cdot d = c \cdot b$. The rule is called the "cross multiplication rule" and is used in algebraic work and in working with ratios and proportions. Satisfy yourself that it works by trying it on the three equivalences you wrote in exercise 3 above. (If it does *not* work, get help from someone and find out what has gone wrong.)

   a.

   b.

   c.

163 EXTENSION
OF THE
INTEGERS
TO THE
RATIONAL
NUMBERS

Note: Verification of the cross multiplication rule requires symbolic "proof." That is, it does not follow directly from this embodiment. If you are interested in such a verification, go through the next problem. Otherwise go on to section 7.4.3.

*5. The cross multiplication rule for equivalence of fractions is easily verified by using a property that is sometimes called the "multiplication property of equality." This property states that if two numbers are equal, then multiplying both of them by the same number leads to equal products. Below is the verification that $\frac{a}{b} = \frac{c}{d}$ if and only if $a \cdot d = c \cdot b$, with a numerical example on the left and a strictly symbolic treatment on the right.

Numerical Example

a. Start with $\qquad\qquad \frac{3}{6} = \frac{4}{8}$

b. Multiply both numbers $\quad \frac{3}{6} \cdot 6 = \frac{4}{8} \cdot 6$

by 6, and observe that $\quad 3 \cdot \frac{6}{6} = \frac{4 \cdot 6}{8}$

$\frac{6}{6}$ can be replaced by 1. $\quad 3 \cdot 1 = 3 = \frac{4 \cdot 6}{8}$

c. Multiply both these new $\quad 3 \cdot 8 = \frac{4 \cdot 6}{8} \cdot 8$

numbers by 8, and ob- $\quad 3 \cdot 8 = 4 \cdot 6 \cdot \frac{8}{8}$

serve that $\frac{8}{8}$ can be $\quad 3 \cdot 8 = 4 \cdot 6 \cdot 1$

replaced by 1.

d. The result is as $\quad 3 \cdot 8 = 4 \cdot 6$
required by the cross
multiplication rule.

Symbolic Verification

Start with $\qquad\qquad \frac{a}{b} = \frac{c}{d}$ $(b \ne 0, d \ne 0)$

Multiply both numbers by b, $\frac{a}{b} \cdot b = \frac{c}{d} \cdot b$

and observe that $\frac{b}{b}$ $\qquad a \cdot \frac{b}{b} = \frac{c \cdot b}{d}$

can be replaced by 1. $\quad a \cdot 1 = a = \frac{c \cdot b}{d}$

Multiply both of these $\quad a \cdot d = \frac{c \cdot b}{d} \cdot d$

new numbers by d, and $\quad a \cdot d = c \cdot b \cdot \frac{d}{d}$

observe that $\frac{d}{d}$ can be $\quad a \cdot d = c \cdot b \cdot 1$

replaced by 1.
The result is as re- $\quad a \cdot d = c \cdot b$
quired by the cross
multiplication rule.

Since the rule says $\frac{a}{b} = \frac{c}{d}$ *if and only if* $a \cdot d = c \cdot b$, it must also be possible to start with the product $a \cdot d = c \cdot b$ and get the equivalent fractions $\frac{a}{b} = \frac{c}{d}$. This is easy to do by first *dividing* both products by d and then dividing the resulting expressions by b. Carry this out. ("If and only if" means you have a reversible rule.)

164 NUMBER
SYSTEMS:
SETS
RELATIONS
OPERATIONS
USES

*6. Show how the cross multiplication rule helps find the number that should go in the $\square$ in $\dfrac{3}{6} = \dfrac{\square}{14}$.[6]

7.4.3

Using the Number Line to Explore the "Is Less Than," "Is Greater Than," and "Is Equal To" Relations

1. The numbers as they appear in order on the number line show quite graphically what is *less than* or *greater than* or *equal to* what, at least for positive numbers. Look over the display on the number line and get some feeling for these relations. Use the display to put the appropriate symbol ($=$, $<$, or $>$) between each of the pairs below. (The first one is done for you.)

   a. $\frac{1}{2} > \frac{1}{3}$ e. $\frac{3}{6}$ $\frac{6}{12}$

   b. $\frac{4}{6}$ $\frac{5}{6}$ f. $\frac{13}{24}$ $\frac{1}{2}$

   c. $\frac{7}{12}$ $\frac{3}{4}$ g. $\frac{3}{8}$ $\frac{9}{24}$

   d. $\frac{8}{12}$ $\frac{2}{3}$

2. If two positive fractions have the same numerator, how can you tell whether the one is greater than, less than, or equal to the other? What has this to do with the meaning of fractions?[7]

3. If two positive fractions have the same denominator, how can you tell whether the one is less than, greater than, or equal to the other? What has this to do with the meaning of fractions?[8]

*4. In addition to the common denominator test for the relations "is less than" and "is greater than" there is a cross multiplication test. Try to formulate it.

---

[6] After cross multiplying, you have $3 \cdot 14 = 6 \cdot \square$. This is the same as $42 = 6 \cdot \square$, and you know that 7 must go in the box because $6 \cdot 7 = 42$.

[7] With the same numerator, the larger the denominator, the smaller the fraction. This is, of course, because a larger denominator means the unit is cut up into more, and hence smaller, parts.

[8] With the same denominator, the larger the numerator, the larger the fraction. This, of course, is because the unit is cut up into the same size parts, and so the more you have of them, the larger the fraction.

5. Since for rational numbers the numerators and denominators can be either positive or negative, work on the positive number line does not tell the whole story. For every positive fraction on the number line, there is a negative fraction with the same numerator and denominator and the same sort of equivalence class at exactly the same distance on the other side of zero. Make some notes below on how the work done in problems 1 to 3 above could be adapted to determine the relation between *any* two fractions, either of which could be positive or negative. (Zero is a special case, being less than any positive number and more than any negative number.)
Notes:

7.4.4
Addition of Fractions with Rods on the Number Line

1. Many addition problems can be done with the number line you made in 7.4.1 and the two rods you marked for each fraction length. (There are also, of course, many that cannot be done with these materials.) Two procedures are possible:

a. Make a train of appropriate rods starting at the zero, and read the answer at the other end. (You may need to get out more rods; for example, it requires seven of the 1/8-length rods to represent 7/8.) Given two fraction lengths, it could happen that the length that represents the sum would not be marked on the number line, but that won't happen if you stick to the rods used to mark your number line. Thus for $\frac{1}{3} + \frac{1}{2} = \square$, make a train as shown and record any of the names of the end point, say, $\frac{5}{6}$. Do the same for $\frac{1}{6} + \frac{1}{3} = \square$ and fill in the box.

($\frac{1}{3}$-rod) ($\frac{1}{2}$-rod)

0	1/24	1/12	1/8	2/12	5/24	1/4	7/24	1/3	3/8	5/12	11/24	1/2	13/24	7/12	5/8	2/3	17/24	3/4	19/24	5/6	7/8	11/12	23/24	1
0/2		2/24		4/24		2/8		2/6	9/24	10/24		2/4		14/24	15/24	4/6		6/8		10/12	21/24	22/24		2/2
0/3						3/12		4/12				3/6				8/12		9/12		20/24				3/3
0/4						6/24		8/24				4/8				16/24		18/24						4/4
0/6												6/12												6/6
0/8												12/24												8/8
0/12																								12/12
0/24																								24/24

166 NUMBER
SYSTEMS:
SETS
RELATIONS
OPERATIONS
USES

b. Find the point that represents the first addend on the number line and a rod or rods that represent the second addend. Put those rods with the left end at the first addend and read the sum at the right end. Thus for $\frac{1}{2} + \frac{1}{3} = \square$, start a $\frac{1}{3}$-length rod at $\frac{1}{2}$ on the number line, and record as the sum any of the names of the point at the other end of the $\frac{1}{3}$-length rod. Do the same for $\frac{5}{12} + \frac{1}{3} = \square$.

$\frac{1}{3}$-rod

0	$\frac{1}{24}$	$\frac{1}{12}$	$\frac{1}{8}$	$\frac{2}{12}$	$\frac{5}{24}$	$\frac{1}{4}$	$\frac{7}{24}$	$\frac{1}{3}$	$\frac{3}{8}$	$\frac{5}{12}$	$\frac{11}{24}$	$\frac{1}{2}$	$\frac{13}{24}$	$\frac{7}{12}$	$\frac{5}{8}$	$\frac{2}{3}$	$\frac{17}{24}$	$\frac{3}{4}$	$\frac{19}{24}$	$\frac{5}{6}$	$\frac{7}{8}$	$\frac{11}{12}$	$\frac{23}{24}$	1
$\frac{0}{2}$		$\frac{2}{24}$		$\frac{4}{24}$		$\frac{2}{8}$		$\frac{2}{6}$	$\frac{9}{24}$	$\frac{10}{24}$		$\frac{2}{4}$		$\frac{14}{24}$	$\frac{15}{24}$	$\frac{4}{6}$		$\frac{6}{8}$		$\frac{10}{12}$	$\frac{21}{24}$	$\frac{22}{24}$		$\frac{2}{2}$
$\frac{0}{3}$						$\frac{3}{12}$		$\frac{4}{12}$				$\frac{3}{6}$				$\frac{8}{12}$		$\frac{9}{12}$		$\frac{20}{24}$				$\frac{3}{3}$
$\frac{0}{4}$						$\frac{6}{24}$		$\frac{8}{24}$				$\frac{4}{8}$				$\frac{16}{24}$		$\frac{18}{24}$						$\frac{4}{4}$
$\frac{0}{6}$												$\frac{6}{12}$												$\frac{6}{6}$
$\frac{0}{8}$												$\frac{12}{24}$												$\frac{8}{8}$
$\frac{0}{12}$																								$\frac{12}{12}$
$\frac{0}{24}$																								$\frac{24}{24}$

2. Act out the answers for the problems below, using either of the two methods in exercise 1. If the sum goes beyond what is marked, try to make a guess about (or find some way of figuring out) the answer.

    a. $\frac{1}{4} + \frac{2}{4} = \square$

    b. $\frac{7}{12} + \frac{2}{12} = \square$

    c. $\frac{3}{8} + \frac{1}{4} = \square$

    d. $\frac{1}{3} + \frac{1}{6} = \square$

    e. $\frac{1}{8} + \frac{1}{3} = \square$

    f. $\frac{2}{3} + \frac{1}{4} = \square$

3. Look at those problems that have addends with the same denominator in exercise 2. In each such problem, if your answer did not also have the same denominator, look again at your number line and replace your answer with one equivalent to it that has the same denominator as the addends. Look at the results, and fill in the blanks on p. 167 to make a general rule for adding same-denominator fractions, or, as is usually said, fractions with a common denominator:

167 EXTENSION
OF THE
INTEGERS
TO THE
RATIONAL
NUMBERS

For any two fractions $\frac{a}{b}$ and $\frac{c}{b}$ with the same denominator, $\frac{a}{b} + \frac{c}{\Box} = \frac{\Box}{b}$.

4. Find those problems in exercise 2 that do not have the same denominator in the addends. For each of these, look at the column of names for each addend, and replace one or both with equivalent fractions so they *do* have a common denominator. Look at the column of names for the sum and replace the sum you wrote with one that also has this common denominator.

5. The work above suggests that many problems can be turned into common denominator problems; in fact, this is true for *any* problem of addition of fractions, just by appropriate selection from the (infinite) equivalence classes available. To get some additional feel for what this means, first act out each of the problems below directly with rods, than work out its common denominator version. The first two are done for you as examples.

Direct Result	Common Denominator Version
a. $\frac{1}{2} + \frac{1}{3} = \boxed{\frac{5}{6}}$	a'. $\frac{3}{6} + \frac{2}{6} = \frac{5}{6}$
b. $\frac{1}{8} + \frac{3}{8} = \boxed{\frac{1}{2}}$	b'. $\frac{1}{8} + \frac{3}{8} = \frac{4}{8}$
c. $\frac{1}{4} + \frac{1}{2} = \Box$	c'.
d. $\frac{5}{12} + \frac{1}{3} = \Box$	d'.
e. $\frac{2}{3} + \frac{1}{6} = \Box$	e'.
f. $\frac{5}{12} + \frac{1}{2} = \Box$	f'.
g. $\frac{1}{2} + \frac{1}{6} = \Box$	g'.
h. $\frac{2}{6} + \frac{1}{2} = \Box$	h'.
*i. $\frac{2}{3} + \frac{1}{2} = \Box$	i'.

6. There are more direct ways of getting fractions with common denominators than sorting through equivalence classes. But for most fraction problems in common life, the methods suggested above are surprisingly efficient. As a matter of fact, there are not really as many addition-of-fraction problems in most people's lives as the amount of work on this subject in schools would suggest. Schoolwork makes

168 NUMBER
SYSTEMS:
SETS
RELATIONS
OPERATIONS
USES

quite a fuss about getting *least* common denominators, but even this can be accomplished by methodically sorting through equivalence classes. Look at an elementary school textbook and see how it teaches children to find common denominators. Make some notes on the method in that book, and compare it with the one you have used in this section. Write your comments below.

7. As noted above, schoolwork makes quite a fuss about working only with least common denominators. But any common denominator will do and there is an easy way to get a common denominator (though rarely the least one). This method, which leads to a general definition for adding *any* two fractions, is suggested by the examples below:

Problem	Getting a Common Denominator	Common Denominator Version of Problem
a. $\dfrac{1}{2} + \dfrac{4}{3} = \square$	$\dfrac{1}{2} = \dfrac{3 \cdot 1}{3 \cdot 2} = \dfrac{3}{6}$ $\dfrac{4}{3} = \dfrac{2 \cdot 4}{2 \cdot 3} = \dfrac{8}{6}$	$\dfrac{3}{6} + \dfrac{8}{6} = \dfrac{11}{6}$
b. $\dfrac{2}{5} + \dfrac{3}{7} = \square$	$\dfrac{2}{5} = \dfrac{7 \cdot 2}{7 \cdot 5} = \dfrac{14}{35}$ $\dfrac{3}{7} = \dfrac{5 \cdot 3}{5 \cdot 7} = \dfrac{15}{35}$	$\dfrac{14}{35} + \dfrac{15}{35} = \dfrac{29}{35}$
c. $\dfrac{1}{6} + \dfrac{3}{4} = \square$	$\dfrac{1}{6} = \dfrac{4 \cdot 1}{4 \cdot 6} = \dfrac{4}{24}$ $\dfrac{3}{4} = \dfrac{6 \cdot 3}{6 \cdot 4} = \dfrac{18}{24}$	$\dfrac{4}{24} + \dfrac{18}{24} = \dfrac{22}{24}$

With a least common denominator, this would have been $^2/_{12} + {}^9/_{12} = {}^{11}/_{12}$, but, of course, $^{11}/_{12} = {}^{22}/_{24}$. Now, try to fill in the blanks in this general definition of addition of two fractions:

For $\dfrac{a}{b} \times \dfrac{c}{d} = \square$, multiply $\dfrac{a}{b}$ by $\dfrac{d}{d}$ (remembering that $\dfrac{d}{d} = 1$) and $\dfrac{c}{d}$ by $\dfrac{b}{b}$ so that $\dfrac{a}{b} + \dfrac{c}{d} = \dfrac{a\square}{b\square} + \dfrac{bc}{bd} = \dfrac{ad + bc}{\square}.$ [9]

8. The examples given above are with positive fractions. Think about

---

[9] $\dfrac{a}{b} + \dfrac{b}{c} = \dfrac{ad}{bd} + \dfrac{bc}{bd} = \dfrac{ad + bc}{bd}$

what would be done if some fractions were negative. Make some notes below and discuss this with your colleagues.

7.4.5 Subtraction of Fractions with Rods on the Number Line

1. The easy way to act out subtraction on the number line (but not the only way) is to find the first fraction on the number line and a rod (or rods) representing the second fraction. Put the *right* end of the rod(s) at the first number and read the answer at the *left* end. Here is a picture of $5/6 - 1/2 = \square$:

$\frac{1}{2}$ -rod

0	1/24	1/12	1/8	2/12	5/24	1/4	7/24	1/3	3/8	5/12	11/24	1/2	13/24	7/12	5/8	2/3	17/24	3/4	19/24	5/6	7/8	11/12	23/24	1
0/2		2/24		4/24		2/8		2/6	9/24	10/24		2/4		14/24	15/24	4/6		6/8		10/12	21/24	22/24		2/2
0/3						3/12		4/12				3/6				8/12		9/12		20/24				3/3
0/4						6/24		8/24				4/8				16/24		18/24						4/4
0/6												6/12												6/6
0/8												12/24												8/8
0/12																								12/12
0/24																								24/24

Now do $5/6 - 1/3 = \square$ on your number line.

2. Without going into the same detail as for addition, it is clear that there are common denominator ways to accomplish subtraction. It is also clear that a subtraction problem can lead to a negative result. If you were to make a new number line with negative numbers on it as well as positive numbers, you could act out subtraction problems on the number line. With these things in mind, work out the following, both by acting out with rods on the number line (making a sensible guess if the action leads to a point on the negative side of zero) and by formulating and working out the common denominator version.

170 NUMBER
SYSTEMS:
SETS
RELATIONS
OPERATIONS
USES

Direct Result	**Common Denominator Version**
a. $\frac{5}{6} - \frac{1}{3} = \square$	*a′.*
b $\frac{8}{9} - \frac{2}{3} = \square$	*b′.*
c. $\frac{5}{9} - \frac{1}{2} = \square$	*c′.*
d. $\frac{1}{2} - \frac{1}{3} = \square$	*d′.*

3. All this still deals only with subtraction of one *positive* fraction from another *positive* fraction, but since fractions can be either positive or negative, other situations are possible. To cope with those, the rules for subtracting and adding integers are extended. In particular these two rules can be exploited:

$$a - b = a + (-b)$$
$$-a = (-1) \cdot a$$

(It must of course be assumed that the rules work not only for integers but also for rational numbers.) See if this is enough to enable you to get correct answers to the following problems. If not, ask your colleagues or professor for assistance, or perhaps ask for a class session on such problems.[10]

a. $\frac{1}{2} - (^-\frac{1}{3}) = \square$

b. $(^-\frac{1}{4}) - \frac{1}{2} = \square$

c. $\frac{3}{4} - (^-\frac{3}{4}) = \square$

d. $\frac{7}{12} - \frac{5}{12} = \square$

e. $\frac{3}{4} - (^-\frac{1}{2}) = \square$

4. The general rule developed above for adding fractions by taking the common denominator as the product of the two given denominators

[10] a. $\frac{5}{6}$, b. $-\frac{3}{4}$, c. $\frac{6}{4}$ or $1\frac{1}{2}$, d. $\frac{2}{12}$ or $\frac{1}{6}$, e. $\frac{5}{4}$.

171 EXTENSION
OF THE
INTEGERS
TO THE
RATIONAL
NUMBERS

was that $\dfrac{a}{b} + \dfrac{c}{d} = \dfrac{ad + cb}{bd}$. State a similar general rule for subtraction of two fractions.[11]

7.4.6

**Division of
Fractions with Rods on
the Number Line**

1. Such a division problem as $\frac{2}{3} \div \frac{1}{6} = \square$ can be acted out on the fraction number line by asking "How many one-sixths are there in two-thirds?" and then seeing how many $\frac{1}{6}$-rods fit between 0 and $\frac{2}{3}$ on the number line. Act out $\frac{3}{4} \div \frac{1}{8} = \square$ and $\frac{1}{2} \div \frac{1}{6} = \square$ in this way.

2. This approach gets more troublesome if there is not a whole number answer—that is, if it doesn't "come out even" when you try to fit in a train of rods. For example, if you ask, for $\frac{1}{3} \div \frac{1}{2} = \square$, "How many halves in one-third?" it is clear that there is less than one-half in one-third, but what *part* of one-half is in one-third is problematical. If you lay in the $\frac{1}{2}$-rod, you may see that two-thirds of it is "in" the one-third, and in fact $\frac{1}{3} \div \frac{1}{2} = \frac{2}{3}$. Using rods, try to estimate the answers to $\frac{1}{2} \div \frac{3}{4} = \square$ and $\frac{1}{6} \div \frac{1}{3} = \square$.

3. The limits on trying to use the procedures from exercises 1 and 2 above for all problems with division of fractions are pretty clear. The equivalence classes displayed on the number line can help in formulation of a more general method, however. Using them, the problems we have done can be stated with common denominator versions as indicated below:

Problem	Common Denominator Version	Answer
$\frac{2}{3} \div \frac{1}{6} = \square$	$\frac{4}{6} \div \frac{1}{6} = \square$	4
$\frac{3}{4} \div \frac{1}{8} = \square$	$\frac{6}{8} \div \frac{1}{8} = \square$	6
$\frac{1}{2} \div \frac{1}{6} = \square$	$\frac{3}{6} \div \frac{1}{6} = \square$	3
$\frac{1}{3} \div \frac{1}{2} = \square$	$\frac{2}{6} \div \frac{3}{6} = \square$	$\frac{2}{3}$
$\frac{1}{2} \div \frac{3}{4} = \square$	$\frac{2}{4} \div \frac{3}{4} = \square$	$\frac{2}{3}$
$\frac{1}{6} \div \frac{1}{3} = \square$	$\frac{1}{6} \div \frac{2}{6} = \square$	$\frac{1}{2}$

Look at those results and see if you can complete this rule:

[11] $\dfrac{a}{b} - \dfrac{c}{d} = \dfrac{ad - cb}{bd}$ If either of the fractions is negative, make the numerator negative before using the rule $\left(\text{e.g., for } -\dfrac{3}{4} \text{ use } \dfrac{^-3}{4}\right)$.

172 NUMBER
SYSTEMS:
SETS
RELATIONS
OPERATIONS
USES

For division of fractions changed so that both total and divisor have the same denominator, get the quotient by _____

_____ .

In symbols, $\dfrac{a}{b} \div \dfrac{c}{b} =$ ____ .[12]

4. The rule for dividing fractions usually taught in school is, "Invert the divisor and multiply." A more respectable version of this same rule avoids the curious word *invert* (which is not a mathematical operation) and says, "To divide by a fraction, multiply instead by the multiplicative inverse of the divisor.[8] We will not try to justify this rule here but will just say that it does always work. (Justification for the rule is contained in section 7.5.5.) Do each of the following problems in three ways. First act it out with the rods, then use the common denominator version, and finally use the rule of multiplying by the multiplicative inverse of the divisor.

Direct Result	Verification by Common Denominators	Verification by Using $\dfrac{a}{b} \div \dfrac{c}{d} = \dfrac{a}{b} \cdot \dfrac{d}{c}$
a. $\frac{1}{2} \div \frac{1}{6} = \boxed{3}$	*a'.* $\frac{3}{6} \div \frac{1}{6} = 3 \div 1 = 3$	*a".* $\frac{1}{2} \div \frac{1}{6} = \frac{1}{2} \cdot \frac{6}{1} = \frac{6}{2} = 3$
b. $\frac{6}{8} \div \frac{1}{4} = \square$	*b'.*	*b".*
c. $\frac{12}{18} \div \frac{2}{9} = \square$	*c'.*	*c".*
d. $\frac{1}{3} \div \frac{1}{2} = \square$	*d'.*	*d".*
e. $\frac{7}{9} \div \frac{1}{3} = \square$	*e'.*	*e".*
f. $\frac{1}{2} \div \frac{1}{3} = \square$	*f'.*	*f".*
g. $\frac{2}{3} \div \frac{1}{2} = \square$	*g'.*	*g".*

---

[8] Remember that the multiplicative inverse of a number is the thing you multiply it by to get 1. For 3, it is $\frac{1}{3}$ because $3 \cdot \frac{1}{3} = 1$; for $\frac{3}{4}$ it is $\frac{4}{3}$ because $\frac{3}{4} \cdot \frac{4}{3} = 1$; and so on.

---

[12] If both total and divisor have been rigged to have the same denominator, the quotient is the quotient of the numerators. In symbols, $\dfrac{a}{b} \div \dfrac{c}{b} = \dfrac{a}{c}$.

173 EXTENSION
OF THE
INTEGERS
TO THE
RATIONAL
NUMBERS

7.5
PROBLEM SET;
A FRACTION POTPOURRI

Overview: Some additional ways of coping with fractions are briefly outlined. Included are several other ways of thinking about fraction operations, justification of the "invert and multiply" rule for division, and discussion of why division by zero is impossible.

7.5.1
Fractions as
"Operators" on Sets of Objects
or on Measures

Numbers, including fractions, are typically thought of as *describing* some state of affairs or some situation. For example, ⅔ can describe situations where two things are compared to three things or where two of three equal parts of some unit quantity have been taken. But numbers can also be regarded in a more active way as transforming situations. In such a transformation situation, for example, the number 2 might be a command to "double" the quantity or to expand something by factor of 2; ½ might be an order to chop something in half or "shrink" something to half its former size.

1. In some of the writings of Z. P. Dienes, this sort of motivation for fractions is elaborated by acting on sets of objects. The following problems indicate briefly what is involved; for more detail consult Dienes or similar material. Act them out with chips.

   a. 2 of 12 chips = □

   b. ⅓ of 12 chips = □

   c. Do ⅔ of 12 by a two-step operation either as 2 of 12, then ⅓ of the result, or as ⅓ of 12 and then 2 of the result.

   d. ½ of ¾ of 12 = □   **d′.** ⅜ of 12 = □

   e. ⅔ of 12 = □   **e′.** ⁴⁄₆ of 12 = □   **e″.** ⁸⁄₁₂ of 12 = □

   f. (½ of 12) + (¼ of 12) = □   **f′.** ¾ of 12 = □

2. The University of Illinois Committee on School Mathematics exploits the notion of numbers as operators in a textbook for "slow-learning" middle school youngsters called *Stretchers and Shrinkers* (see Appendix II). These books construct an elaborate fantasy about a stretch-and-shrink factory. A considerable simplification of the stories might go as follows: Suppose the factory is initially set up with doubling machines and tripling machines. One day a customer comes in and asks for a 6-stretch; the engineers consult and conclude that

174 NUMBER
SYSTEMS:
SETS
RELATIONS
OPERATIONS
USES

they need not make a new machine but need only do a 2-stretch and then a 3-stretch. But when a customer asks for a shrink instead of a stretch, the engineers invent ½-shrink and ⅓-shrink machines. When a later customer asks for a ¼-shrink, the engineers put it through a ½-shrink twice, and so on. Now, what do the engineers do about a request for a ¾-shrink? What about a 1½-stretch? (Be careful with that last one, and try using the equivalence 1½ = ³⁄₂.) Make up some other problems to bring to the factory, and decide for your problems when the engineers can use existing machines and when they must get new ones.

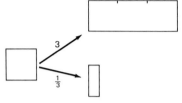

Square transformed by triple one-way stretch
and by one-third one-way compression.

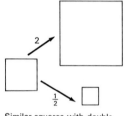

Similar squares with double
expansion and with half shrink.

3. The fraction-as-operator motivation and the embodiments that can be used to understand it touch on some important ideas both for mathematics and for everyday usage. These ideas have to do with various sorts of "transformations"—perhaps with uniform "similarities" (uniform stretch or shrink in all directions at once) like those you may have studied in high school geometry, or perhaps with one-way stretches and compressions. Refer to the illustration for the effects on a square.

7.5.2
**Other Uses
of Rods to Embody
Fraction Work**

In this unit fractions have been embodied with colored rods always with reference to a fixed unit length on a number line. A more common embodiment of fractions with rods keeps changing the "unit-length" rod according to the fraction situation you want to embody. For example, ½ might be shown as a white rod with red rod as unit, or as a red rod with purple rod as unit, or in several other ways. (Take time to show all the possibilities for ½ with whatever rods you are using.) There are obvious limitations in this approach, but the great advantage is that the importance of identifying the unit and the arbitrariness of what is called the "unit length" are embodied over and over again. In acting out such a problem as ½ + ¼ with the rods, you must choose a unit such that both halves and fourths can be shown relative to the *same* unit rod, and this embodies something about the use of common denominators in fraction problems.

Take some time, perhaps working with classmates, to make up and do a few problems with equivalence of fractions and a few with addition of fractions with rods and appropriately chosen units. Doing the other

175 EXTENSION
OF THE
INTEGERS
TO THE
RATIONAL
NUMBERS

operations in this way is also illuminating. There are a number of published materials dealing with this sort of use of colored rods; consult some of them if you wish, and think about how you might use such ideas and materials in your own teaching.[9]

7.5.3
"Addition-Only" Methods for Getting Equivalent Fractions

George Klein has elaborated at some length the use of some addition-only methods of getting at equivalent fractions, and hence at the sometimes troublesome matter of finding common denominators.[10] The examples below illustrate the two main possibilities:

First possibility

$$\frac{2}{3} = \frac{4+4}{4+4+4} = \frac{7+7}{7+7+7}$$

or in other words

$$\frac{2}{3} = \frac{2 \times 4}{3 \times 4} = \frac{2 \times 7}{3 \times 7}$$

Second possibility

$$\frac{2}{3} = \frac{2+2+2+2}{3+3+3+3} = \frac{2+2+2+2+2+2+2}{3+3+3+3+3+3+3}$$

or in other words

$$\frac{2}{3} = \frac{4 \times 2}{4 \times 3} = \frac{7 \times 2}{7 \times 3}$$

This is surprising at first to most people accustomed to working with fractions in more conventional ways. If you want to use these methods with children, you should be prepared to take them far enough (and to supply enough practice) so they will be thoroughly understood. Otherwise you might promote such erroneous uses of addition in fractions as these:

$$\frac{1}{2} + \frac{1}{4} = \frac{1+1}{2+4} = \frac{2}{6} \text{ (No!)} \qquad \frac{1}{3} + \frac{2}{3} = \frac{3}{6} \text{ (No!)}$$

1. A useful embodiment of these addition-only methods for getting equivalent fractions is a horizontal stick of soft wood or plastic with map pins in the top face of the stick representing the numerator and

[9] For example, see materials by Genise listed in Appendix IIB.
[10] *Analytical Arithmetic Problem Books–Fractions;* see Appendix IIA.

pins in the bottom face representing the denominator. The main possibilities are embodied as in these pictures:

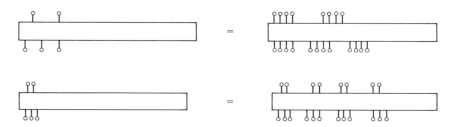

These could also be acted out with sets of chips or other counters above and below a line drawn on a sheet of paper.

2. So that you will understand the addition-only methods, do several problems using them, with or without embodiments. (You may want to work with a classmate.) For more details, consult the Klein materials.

7.5.4
Equivalent Fractions and Multiplication of Fractions by Marking Rectangular Units

A nice picture of fractions that appears in many school books is illustrated by the following:

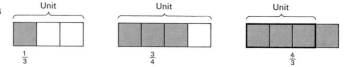

In such pictures it is important to have the unit rectangle clearly outlined, but this necessity to make the unit clear should be quite familiar to you by now. It is especially essential to have the unit clearly shown and used as the ultimate reference in the case of "improper fractions."

Simply as pictures of fractions, the rectangles have little advantage over circles or other shapes that lend themselves easily to division into congruent pieces. The advantage of rectangles appears in picturing such a multiplication as ½ of ⅓ = ☐ as follows:

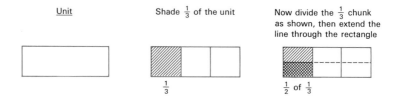

177 EXTENSION
OF THE
INTEGERS
TO THE
RATIONAL
NUMBERS

The resulting double-hatched chunk of rectangle is clearly one-sixth of the unit rectangle.

1. Perhaps working with classmates, make diagrams for the following problems on the unit rectangles given. Do as many more as necessary until you understand this way of working out fractions.

    a. $\frac{2}{3}$ of $\frac{3}{4} = \square$

    b. $\frac{2}{3}$ of $\frac{3}{2} = \square$

2. In the two examples below show the commutative property first with a rectangle unit and then with a square unit. Which do you prefer? When might you use the one or the other with youngsters?

    a. $\frac{1}{2}$ of $\frac{3}{4} = \square$

    $\frac{3}{4}$ of $\frac{1}{2} = \square$

    b. $\frac{1}{2}$ of $\frac{3}{4} = \square$ $\frac{3}{4}$ of $\frac{1}{2} = \square$

7.5.5
Justifying the "Multiply by the Reciprocal of the Divisor" Rule for Division of Fractions

For division of fractions, older books say "invert the divisor and multiply" and newer books usually say "multiply by the multiplicative inverse (or reciprocal) of the divisor." Either rule seems mysterious to many youngsters and causes such confusions as inverting the wrong number in division problems (especially for such problems as $\frac{3}{4} \div 2 = \square$, inverting for operations other than division, and inverting everything in sight. We have tried to suggest several ways of dealing with this problem; here is a strictly symbolic argument that you might find helpful and that might sort things out for some youngsters. It requires that you believe in and understand the following properties, where a, b, and n can be fractions. (As usual, the assumption is that denominators cannot be zero.)

178 NUMBER
SYSTEMS:
SETS
RELATIONS
OPERATIONS
USES

Property 1. $\dfrac{a}{b} = \dfrac{a \cdot n}{b \cdot n}$

Property 2. $\dfrac{a}{b} \cdot \dfrac{b}{a} = 1.$ (The product of a number and its reciprocal is 1.)

Property 3. $\dfrac{a}{1} = a$

Property 4. $a \div b = \dfrac{a}{b}$

Such a problem as $\frac{2}{3} \div \frac{5}{8}$ is then done in several stages as follows:
1. Using rule 4,

$$\frac{2}{3} \div \frac{5}{8} = \frac{\frac{2}{3}}{\frac{5}{8}}$$

This would be neater if the denominator were not a fraction. Using rules 1, 2, and 3, we get:

$$2.\ \frac{\frac{2}{3}}{\frac{5}{8}} = \frac{\frac{2}{3} \times \frac{8}{5}}{\frac{5}{8} \times \frac{8}{5}} = \frac{\frac{2}{3} \times \frac{8}{5}}{1} = \frac{2}{3} \times \frac{8}{5}$$

The $\frac{8}{5}$, of course, was chosen precisely because $\frac{5}{8} \times \frac{8}{5} = 1.$ Therefore, division by $\frac{5}{8}$ ends up as multiplication by $\frac{8}{5}$, the multiplicative inverse (or reciprocal) of $\frac{5}{8}$.

Go through the same process with the following problems, and make up as many more as you need to become convinced that this is an OK way to do things. The first one is done for you.

a. $\frac{3}{4} \div \frac{1}{2} = \dfrac{\frac{3}{4}}{\frac{1}{2}} = \dfrac{\frac{3}{4} \cdot \frac{2}{1}}{\frac{1}{2} \cdot \frac{2}{1}} = \dfrac{\frac{3}{4} \cdot \frac{2}{1}}{1} = \frac{3}{4} \cdot \frac{2}{1}$

b. $\frac{5}{8} \div \frac{3}{4}$

c. $\frac{6}{5} \div \frac{1}{3}$

7.5.6
**More on Why Zero
Denominators or Divisions by
Zero Are *Never* Allowed**
We have stressed many times in this book that division by zero is impossible (within our ordinary number system) and since a fraction can be interpreted as a division problem this also means that zero denominators are never allowable. Now that we have division of fractions, a some-

179 EXTENSION
OF THE
INTEGERS
TO THE
RATIONAL
NUMBERS

times convincing argument can be given for prohibiting zero denominators or division by zero. It proceeds by a series of questions such as these (fill in the missing answers):

Question	Answer
How many ones in 1 $\left(\frac{1}{1}=\Box\right)$?	1
How many tenths in 1 $\left(\frac{1}{\frac{1}{10}}=\Box\right)$?	10
How many hundredths in 1 $\left(\frac{1}{\frac{1}{100}}=\Box\right)$?	
How many thousandths in 1 $\left(\frac{1}{\frac{1}{1000}}=\Box\right)$?	
How many millionths in 1 $\left(\frac{1}{\frac{1}{1,000,000}}=\Box\right)$?	

Clearly, the smaller the denominator, the larger the answer, and as the denominator gets very close to zero, the quotient becomes enormous. If the denominator (divisor) were allowed actually to *be* zero, this sequence of events convinces most people that the quotient would go out of bounds altogether, and indeed it does; there is no number large enough to express it. (You might say that it is "infinity," but that is not expressible as a number.)

7.6
SUMMARY
OF PROPERTIES OF THE
SYSTEM OF RATIONAL
FRACTIONS

7.6.1
General
Remarks

The task in this unit has been to extend the integers by invention of a new set of numbers expressed by a new notation; that is, to extend the integers to rational numbers expressed as fractions. Such an extension can be justified in two ways. The first justification appeals to the requirements of the real world: the old system isn't adequate to deal with certain common life situations. The second justification appeals to the requirements of mathematical tidiness and "niceness": some equations don't have integer solutions; division is not closed for the integers; we would like each number (except zero) to have a multiplicative inverse.

Such an extension requires new inventions and definitions, but not arbitrary ones. We proceed with such guidelines as the following in mind:

180 NUMBER
SYSTEMS:
SETS
RELATIONS
OPERATIONS
USES

1. The extended system should give results consistent with those in the old system. For example, whatever multiplication of rationals is, it should be commutative, associative, etc., just as the integers were.

2. The extended system must be consistent with real world requirements.

3. Since at the start we have only the integers to work with, definitions must reduce the "new" relations and operations for rational numbers to a succession of "old" ones for integers.

In such an extension every relation and every operation are "new" and their properties must be investigated. For example, just because multiplication of integers is "closed" does not guarantee that multiplication of rational numbers is closed. Of course, as indicated above, we try to assure that the old properties will still apply — pretty much by making the new operations a succession of old ones — but this is not automatic and must be checked. Also, we should expect that there will be new properties not applicable to the old system. If there were no new properties, the new system could not be distinguished from the old, mathematically speaking.

This section will be primarily an expository and symbolic summing up of the extension of integers to rational numbers written in fraction form. You should make sure you understand (*really* understand) what is being said throughout. You should also, throughout the section, relate the symbolic version of the definitions and properties to your experience earlier in this unit with embodiments of rational fractions. Finally, you should take the opportunity to begin to sort out how such things can be conveyed to children. Nearly everything here has certain aspects that can be anticipated as early as kindergarten or first grade, as well as implications that probably must wait for development in courses beyond the elementary school.

In this summary, the task is to define the new set, new relations, and new operations in terms of the presumably already known system of integers (which include the whole numbers). As always, assume throughout that no denominators are ever zero and that division by zero is not allowed.

7.6.2
The Set of Rational Fractions

1. **Definition:** A rational number is any number that *can be* written as a fraction $\frac{a}{b}$ with a an integer and b a nonzero integer. The set of rational numbers includes all such numbers and only such numbers.

2. Throughout the rest of this discussion, definitions and properties

will be assumed to hold for all such fractions $\left(\dfrac{a}{b}, \dfrac{c}{d}, \dfrac{m}{n}, \dfrac{km}{kn}, \text{ and so on}\right)$.

7.6.3 Equivalence

1. Basic definition: $\dfrac{a}{b} = \dfrac{c}{d}$ if and only if $ad = bc$ (cross multiplication).

Although this is the basic definition it is not the one used in schoolwork; instead, one or more of the following facts that follow from this definition are used:

2. $\dfrac{a}{b} = \dfrac{ka}{kb}$ for any $k \neq 0$. In schoolwork, k would be a counting number, but it can be any number. This is useful for producing equivalent fractions but not always useful for checking equivalence. For example $\frac{1}{2} = \frac{2}{4}$ and $\frac{1}{2} = \frac{3}{6}$ (using $k = 2$ and $k = 3$, respectively) but if k must be a whole number the rule doesn't help in showing that $\frac{2}{4} = \frac{3}{6}$.

3. $\dfrac{a}{b} = \dfrac{a \div k}{b \div k}$ (used to "reduce" fractions).[13]

4. $\dfrac{a}{b} = \dfrac{c}{d}$ if and only if reducing both to lowest terms makes them identical. $\left(\dfrac{a}{b}\right.$ is in lowest terms if a and b are "relatively prime"; that is, if all factors common to both a and b have been divided out.$\left.\right)$

7.6.4 "Is Greater Than" or "Is Less Than"

Change to fractions with a common denominator. The fraction with the smallest numerator is the smallest number.

7.6.5 Addition

Definitions:

1. $\dfrac{a}{c} + \dfrac{b}{c} = \dfrac{a + b}{c}$ (for fractions with the same denominator).

2. $\dfrac{a}{b} + \dfrac{b}{d} = \dfrac{ad + bc}{bd}$. This definition comes from getting a "common denominator" by multiplying the two denominators. It is the basic and essential definition when doing algebraic and symbolic work with fractions, but it is seldom used in schools because of the fuss made in schools about lowest common denominators.

3. For $\dfrac{a}{b} + \dfrac{c}{d}$, select from the equivalence class containing $\dfrac{a}{b}$ some

---

[13] Both fact 2 and fact 3 can come from use of the multiplicative identity and $\dfrac{k}{k} = 1$;

$$\frac{a}{b} = 1 \cdot \frac{a}{b} = \frac{k}{k} \cdot \frac{a}{b} = \frac{ka}{kb}.$$

182 NUMBER
SYSTEMS:
SETS
RELATIONS
OPERATIONS
USES

fraction $\dfrac{k}{m}$, and from the equivalence class containing $\dfrac{c}{d}$ some fraction $\dfrac{s}{m}$ (m is the common denominator). Then $\dfrac{a}{b} + \dfrac{c}{d} = \dfrac{k}{m} + \dfrac{s}{m} = \dfrac{k+s}{m}$. If m is the "least common multiple" of the denominators b and d, then you have a lowest common denominator. (See Part C, Unit 5, for a discussion of least common multiple.)

7.6.6 Multiplication

Definition: $\dfrac{a}{b} \cdot \dfrac{c}{d} = \dfrac{ac}{bd}$

7.6.7 Subtraction

Much the same definitions are used as for addition, with the subtraction symbol replacing the addition symbol.

7.6.8 Division

Definitions:

1. To divide two fractions, multiply the first by the multiplicative inverse of the second; in symbols: $\dfrac{a}{b} \div \dfrac{c}{c} = \dfrac{a}{b} \cdot \dfrac{d}{c}$. This has the same effect as the "invert and multiply" rule, but by using inverses we can explain what would otherwise be an arbitrary rule.

2. Select appropriately from equivalence classes so that $\dfrac{a}{b} = \dfrac{k}{m}$ and $\dfrac{c}{d} = \dfrac{s}{m}$. Then $\left(\dfrac{a}{b}\right) \div \left(\dfrac{c}{d}\right) = \left(\dfrac{k}{m}\right) \div \left(\dfrac{s}{m}\right) = k \div s$. That is, exploit common denominators.

7.6.9 Properties of Operations with Rational Numbers That Parallel Properties of Operations with Integers

Addition and multiplication of rational numbers are closed, commutative, and associative, and the usual distributive property applies. These are "axioms" for whole numbers but can be "proved" for rational numbers by applying the definitions of addition and multiplication. For example, suppose we want to "prove" the commutative property of multiplication. It might be done like this: $\dfrac{a}{b} \cdot \dfrac{c}{d} = \dfrac{ac}{bd} = \dfrac{ca}{db} = \dfrac{c}{d} \cdot \dfrac{a}{b}$. (The commutative property of multiplication of integers is used to replace ac by ca and bd by db.)

Zero is still the identity for addition and 1 is still the identity for multiplication, and the usual properties of zero and one apply. Every rational number has an additive inverse.

7.6.10
New
Properties

1. *Existence of multiplicative inverses.* The main thing that extension to the rationals accomplishes, mathematically speaking, is to assure that every non-zero number has another number paired with it so that multiplying the two together gives 1 (the multiplicative identity) as the product. For a non-zero integer n, the inverse is $\frac{1}{n}$; for a fraction $\frac{a}{b}$ it is $\frac{b}{a}$ (since $\frac{a}{b} \cdot \frac{b}{a} = \frac{ab}{ba} = 1$). This is the property that sets rational numbers apart from whole numbers, and it is very useful in fraction manipulations.

2. *Density.* There are an infinite number of fractions between each of the integer points on the number line and indeed, there are an infinite number of fractions between any pair of fractions, no matter how close. Among other things, this means that given any fraction, it is impossible to say what the "next" fraction is—which is quite different from the situation with whole numbers or integers. Also, the density of rational numbers opens the way to closer and closer approximation—"as close as you please"—and to other infinite processes that are at the heart of the calculus. The fact that an infinite number of fractions exists between any of an infinite number of pairs of points opens up other interesting mathematical possibilities. Some of these matters are explored further in Part B, Unit 6, and in Part C, Unit 1.

7.6.11
Other
Useful Properties

Below are some useful properties that frequently play a role in manipulations with fractions. In the blank space to the right of each property, write a numerical example that uses that property.

Property 1. $\frac{n}{n} = 1$

Property 2. $n = \frac{n}{1}$

Property 3. $0 = \frac{0}{n}$

Property 4. $a\left(\frac{1}{n}\right) = \frac{a}{n}$

Property 5. $\frac{-a}{b} = \frac{a}{-b} = -\frac{a}{b}$

Property 6. $a\left(\frac{m}{n}\right) = \frac{am}{n}$

184 NUMBER
SYSTEMS:
SETS
RELATIONS
OPERATIONS
USES

7.7
PEDAGOGICAL REMARKS

In most school books, whole numbers are extended first to positive rational numbers in fraction form, and only later are these "numbers of arithmetic" extended to negative numbers. In this book, the extensions were first to integers and then to rational fractions both positive and negative. In either case, the extension to fractions can be rich in mathematical possibilities and also powerful in extending the range of applications of mathematics to common life.

The increased mathematical richness includes the notion of equivalence classes which emerges most strongly with fractions. It also includes the consequences of "density" of fractions on the number line. As to increased richness of application to common life, there are, to begin with, the pervasive uses of fractions to express parts of sets of things and parts of units in measurement. Fractions open up the use of ratios and proportions and with them a host of new ways for using mathematics to cope with the common world. The notation provides $\frac{a}{b}$ as a substitute for $a \div b$. The possibility of considering any fraction in various ways (parts of a unit, ratio, quotient) and of switching one's point of view in this regard (perhaps several times within a single problem) greatly increases the options in formulating and using mathematical models of common life situations. The range of relationships expressible by formulas and functions is also greatly extended by fractions.

Not all these matters can be pursued in detail in this book, although they must of course be developed with care and over a long period of time with school youngsters. You should be aware that extension to rational fractions is one of the most significant advances in the mathematics learning sequence.

The extension to rational numbers could be made by way of "decimals" rather than by way of fraction forms. The decimal system also extends both the applicability of mathematics and its theoretical content. However, the fraction forms themselves are very useful innovations, quite apart from their use in expressing rational numbers. Developing procedures for working with rational fractions gives as a bonus most of the procedures for working with fraction forms as such (for example, $\frac{x}{y}$ in algebra or proportions in geometry or many formulas used in science, business, and skilled trades).

Unfortunately few people ever develop real power and comfort in dealing with fraction forms. It is our conviction that more careful teaching of fractions in the early school years with considerable use of concrete embodiments would ease the problem that most people have in this respect. Learning arbitrary and abstract rules for manipulating fractions doesn't transfer very well to more general uses of fractions, but the gut-level intuition that can result from building your own ideas by acting things out with various embodiments can give considerable power in understanding fraction forms in more abstract situations.

Since this course emphasizes the underlying mathematical structure of school mathematics content, the focus here is on rational numbers as a mathematical system, and on such new mathematical properties as density and the existence of multiplicative inverses. In teaching children, however, the main emphases might be on such "practical" things as the necessity in any discussion for a unit to which to refer fractions; equivalence classes of fractions and ways to exploit the many choices they allow; and the various common life uses of fraction notation. That is, the focus in teaching might properly be on the usefulness and power of fraction forms, with sufficient attention given to structure so that the child will be helped to understand and exploit this power.

In making the extension from integers (or whole numbers) to rational fractions, there is a significant escalation in the sophistication of the notation used. A *pair* of numbers now sometimes represents a single number, in a different sense than $2 + 3$ represents 5 or 3×7 represents 21. This is complicated by the fact that sometimes the same fraction form is not a single number but represents an operation using two numbers, as when $6 \div 3$ is written as $^6/_3$. Furthermore, sometimes a fraction is first one thing and then another, as when you set up a ratio using two numbers but then shift gears and regard it as being a single rational number. Such complexities are probably at the root of many of the difficulties that people have with fractions. But it is also such complexities that give fraction forms their power as mathematical models of situations from common life.

The first task for you as a teacher is to get the complexities of fractions sorted out in your own mind, and then to plan the careful teaching that will help youngsters sort them out. Needless to say, this process must take place over a long period of time and not be dumped on children all at once in a few months or even over merely a couple of years.

Because "half of," "one-third of," and so on are often part of the vocabulary of children and appear to have pretty clear meaning to them, this meaning often becomes the only motivation in school teaching of what the fraction notation means. It is also the case in schools that such terms as "half of" are usually applied to counts of sets of objects. Both restrictions on the meaning and use of fractions are quite unfortunate, as we hope the work of this unit has demonstrated.

Looking not so very far ahead, it may be that calculation with frac-

186 NUMBER
SYSTEMS:
SETS
RELATIONS
OPERATIONS
USES

tions just as numbers will become a nearly obsolete skill. (We hope that this unit has shown that even if this were to become the case, manipulation of fraction forms for such things as formulas, ratios, and proportions would still be important.) Even now an ordinary citizen rarely needs to work with any but simple fractions. Problems such as $7/9 \div 7/13 = \square$, which are common in school books, virtually never come up in the common life of people. Also, decimal rather than fraction data are given in virtually all actual uses of rational numbers, and this will be even more the case when the United States converts to the metric system. Furthermore, computers and inexpensive pocket calculators require decimal inputs and give decimal outputs. These machines will increasingly be the means by which calculations are actually done. What will then be left as essential are the various meanings and uses of the fraction notation itself, the notion of equivalence classes of fractions, and conversion of fractions to decimals in processing by computers or calculators whatever fractions do come up.

It should be remarked here that whole numbers have close ties to everyday experience and the operations with them have close analogs in physical actions. Each extension (to integers, rational numbers, real numbers) puts mathematics further away from this sort of "reality." It is still possible to find real world embodiments, but they sometimes seem contrived. There are still many applications to the common world, but they tend to be more sophisticated than with whole numbers. We increasingly rely on symbolic inventions and on abstract definitions to make the extended number system behave the way it "ought" to behave. Since this is the case, it is not surprising that many children have difficulty learning to operate sensibly with the extended systems of numbers. The object of this book is to make the learning task manageable, and to tie the extended systems firmly to experience with the common world and to already familiar number systems.

part b
algorithms and numeration

unit 1
the algorithm for addition of whole numbers

1.1
INTRODUCTION

1.1.1
Algorithms

An *algorithm* (or *algorism*)[1] is some definite means or system of performing a task, usually with a series of steps that repeats over and over again. Table 1.1 illustrates an "algorithm" for grocery shopping with a list. Notice that this is not a mathematical algorithm because no computation is involved. The grocery shopping algorithm has several features in common with computational algorithms. There is an initial phase that is not repeated, a setting-up or beginning phase (not all mathematical algorithms have this initial phase). There is a series of steps that is repeated if necessary. A decision point, where the shopper decides whether to repeat the series again or to stop, is indicated. At every point, you know exactly what the next step is; there is no ambiguity. The answer in a mathematical algorithm accumulates, just as the groceries accumulate in the grocery cart. The grocery algorithm will accommodate any size of list. It works equally well for a list of 2 items or a list of

[1] According to Howard Eves, *An Introduction to the History of Mathematics,* Holt, Rinehart & Winston, New York, 1969, p. 197, the word algorithm (or algorism) comes from al-Khowârizmî, the Arabic author of a book on the use of Hindu numerals (the numerals we use today). A Latin translation of this book begins, "Spoken has Algoritmi. . . ." Thus al-Khowârizmî became Algoritmi, which became algorithm or algorism.

189

47 items. In fact, it would work for a list of a billion items. The limits on how long a list you would want to use come from the situation, not from the algorithm. Similarly, the limits of a calculation usually come not from a mathematical algorithm but rather from a situation (e.g., time limitations, cost of the calculation, the use to be made of the result). Some algorithms, particularly those involving whole numbers, have built-in stopping places; for example, the whole number long division algorithm usually stops when the remainder is less than the divisor.

* Activity: Make a flow chart similar to that in Table 1.1 showing an algorithm for the addition of two whole numbers that are both greater than ten.

Table 1.1 **Algorithm for Grocery Shopping**

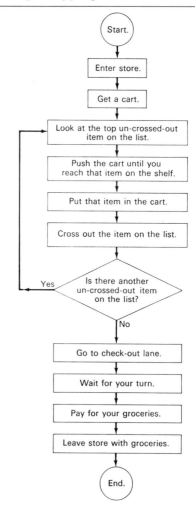

1.1.2
**Brief
Historical Background
of Algorithms**
In most cultures whose history of mathematical development is known, calculation with large numbers was done with the aid of physical objects. Pebbles or shells, often grouped in a helpful way, were used for calculation. Sometimes columns were drawn in sand or on wood, and pebbles in different columns stood for different amounts. Such a computing device is called an "abacus" (Greek *abax,* meaning "counting board"). Some cultures invented a kind of portable abacus that used strings of movable beads. The arrangement and number of beads used varied. Abaci (or abacuses) are still used in parts of Russia, China, and Japan.

Our present Hindu-Arabic numeral system and the symbolic calculation performed with these numerals were disseminated in Europe by a twelfth-century Latin translation of al-Khowârizmî's Arabic work on the subject and by subsequent European works. For the next 400 years, symbolic calculation vied with calculation on the medieval counting board. Only in the late 1500s did symbolic calculation become widely used by merchants, bankers, estate record keepers, and tax collectors. By the eighteenth century little trace of a counting board was found in western Europe.[2] Europeans took their numeral system and the symbolic algorithms for calculation wherever their merchants or armies went. These algorithms are now known all over the world.

The algorithms for addition, subtraction, multiplication, and division of whole numbers as we now know them did not arise instantaneously, however. They evolved slowly, undergoing many small changes of form and arrangement. Long multiplication and long division did not develop until the fifteenth century.[3] Sections 3.6.9 and 4.4.7 give many examples of multiplication and division algorithms used in the past.

Algorithms for addition, subtraction, multiplication, and division were not always part of a child's education. In the Middle Ages, these algorithms were part of the university curriculum. Later they moved into the secondary school, then into the preparatory school for those students who were planning to attend the university. Only in the late 1800s did these algorithms become part of the elementary school curriculum. In the past century, children have spent countless hours trying to learn arithmetic algorithms. To many Americans, mathematics means *only* the algorithms for addition, subtraction, multiplication, and division of whole numbers (with perhaps a bit about decimals and fractions).

The enormous increase in the number of people who are able to use the symbolic algorithms has been dictated largely by the economic situation. In this century, the number of jobs requiring arithmetic calculation has mushroomed. Whole new fields of science have appeared, social sciences have become increasingly important and increasingly mathemati-

[2] Ibid., p. 20.
[3] Ibid., p. 16.

Table 1.2 **Increasing Speed and Capacity of Modern Electronic Computers.***

Author	Machine	Date	Decimal Places of π	Time to Calculate π
Reitwiesner	ENIAC	1949	2,037	70 hours
Nicholson & Jeenel	NORC	1954	3,089	13 minutes
Felton	Pegasus	1958	10,000	33 hours
Genuys	IBM 704	1958	10,000	100 minutes
Genuys	IBM 704	1959	16,167	4.3 hours
Shanks & Wrench	IBM 7090	1961	100,265	8.7 hours

Computers of the 1970's are larger, faster, smaller, and cheaper. The fourth generation family of IBM computers, the 370 series, has a capacity 100 times as large as the 7090 and is 10 times faster. If the present day technology of integrated circuits were used to make the 7090 now, its entire storage capacity would fit into a purse. In 1952, 100,000 multiplications cost about $1.25 on IBM's first large scale computer; today the cost is about $.01 (the decrease in cost would be even greater if inflation were not a factor.).†

* Howard Eves, *An Introduction to the History of Mathematics,* Holt, Rinehart & Winston, New York, 1969, p. 264. π is discussed in section 6.3.5.
† Figures from IBM Data Processing Division, Chicago office.

cal, an affluent society has multiplied the size and complexity of the business world, engineering has entered new fields. The number and complexity of personal accounts and records that must be kept has increased. Another phenomenon has paralleled this unprecedented increase in the need for arithmetic calculation: the invention and dissemination of increasingly sophisticated computing machines.

Also recently available are small "pocket" calculators that add, subtract, multiply, divide, and often do even more difficult operations. These frequently sell for under $25 and are anticipated to become even cheaper. The effect of these calculators may be to decrease greatly an individual's need to be able to do algorithms for operations on large whole numbers, while increasing his need to understand these algorithms and to estimate reasonable answers.

This almost unbelievable increase in computing power has opened new areas of research in many areas, since problems that once required "unreasonable" amounts of calculation now are quite reasonable. Businesses have new methods of keeping accounts. Banks can give interest compounded daily, instead of four times a year. Many jobs in these areas no longer require people who can only compute. The jobs now require people who understand what is involved in the methods of computation so that they can design effective systems of machine use. Positions now require people who can think about new problems and can analyze problems in a mathematical way. New machines of the future will require people who can invent them, service them, and use them effectively to solve a myriad of problems in many different areas. People who have learned only rote performance of algorithms and who do not understand the strengths and the weaknesses of our number system and of other number systems will not be able to fill these needs of the future.

1.1.3
Uses of Addition

For each exercise below, give a mathematical model for finding the solution. Find the solution if you wish.

1. In 1973 in the United States, 57,400,000 tires were installed as original equipment on new cars, and 150,000,000 tires were sold as replacements for old tires. How many tires were sold in 1973?
Mathematical model:

2. What is the total area of the Great Lakes in square miles if the lakes have the following areas (in square miles): Erie, 5,002; Huron, 8,975; Michigan, 22,178; Ontario, 3,033; Superior, 21,118.
Mathematical model:

3. In 1971 fatal United States traffic accidents were of the following types: 13,700 noncollisions, 23,300 collisions with other motor vehicles, 10,600 collisions with pedestrians, 7,100 collisions with fixed objects. How many fatal traffic accidents were there in 1971?
Mathematical model:

4. The 1971 population estimates for various parts of the world:

Continents	Population	Square Miles	Population per Square Mile
North America	270,000,000	9,390,245	29
South America	245,000,000	6,795,000	36
Europe	466,000,000	1,905,799	244
U.S.S.R.	225,000,000	8,649,457	29
Asia	2,104,000,000	10,630,160	198
Africa	354,000,000	11,706,613	31
Oceania	19,800,000	3,285,728	5

What was the total population of the world in 1971? What are the total square miles of earth? (How much is habitable?)
Mathematical models:

5. Here are some data about new housing units started in various parts of the United States:

Area	1960	1965	1970	1971	1972
Northeast	237,000	281,000	224,000	271,000	334,000
North Central	304,000	369,000	301,000	440,000	445,000
South	441,000	588,000	629,000	884,000	1,068,000
East	314,000	271,000	315,000	490,000	532,000

How many units were started in each year? What is the total number of new housing units started in each area since 1960?
Mathematical models:

6. Here is what I ate yesterday:

How many calories and grams of protein did I have at each meal?

Sample Menu	Calories	Grams of Protein
Breakfast		
1 slice of white bread, toasted, with butter and jam	167	2
½ cup of orange juice (frozen)	55	0
1 scrambled egg	110	6
Lunch		
½ cup creamed cottage cheese	120	15
1 apple	70	0
1 doughnut	135	2
1 glass of Pepsi	137	0
Dinner		
¼ pound hamburger	327	28
on a bun	115	3
½ cup frozen peas	34	2
20 pieces French fried potatoes	310	2
1 cup milk (whole)	165	8

A person can utilize only 20 grams of protein in a 5-hour period; the excess is excreted. How many grams of protein were wasted by this menu? A person needs about 20 grams of protein in the morning to "get going" and about 60 grams in a day. How could I have rearranged the food above so that I would have had a more equal 20-20-20 distribution of protein?

7. Cut three newspaper or magazine clippings that use addition of large whole numbers. Share these with your colleagues.

1.1.4
**This Text's
Approach to Algorithms for
Whole Number Operations**

In this text the approach to the use of algorithms for whole number operations is through embodiments. An embodiment is a concrete or tangible representation of a concept. In other words, activities that require the use of objects are provided.

Embodiments are useful for several reasons:

• Embodiments can give meaning to the symbolic algorithms. Most adults who have done these activities have reported that their understanding of the algorithms has increased.
• Embodiments provide a fresh approach to material that you may feel you have already mastered.
• If teachers learn how embodiments work, they can make good decisions about how to use them in teaching the algorithms to children.
• If teachers experience some of the feelings that accompany work with embodiments, they become better prepared to deal with these feelings in children. ("I wish I had more time to work on this. I feel rushed." "Hey! I really see how this addition business works now." "I wish I could understand this more quickly. Sue is ten pages ahead of me already.")

Our number system has a base of ten. The activities for each operation will begin by using embodiments of a base other than ten because:

• In doing the algorithms, the automatic responses to base-ten numbers that you have built up over the years will prevent you from thoroughly reexamining the way these algorithms work.
• Since you do not have automatic responses in bases other than ten, they cannot interfere. For example, what is $2 + 3$ in base four? What is 10×27 in base eight? You will have to think about how to do these problems.

• Because all activities with non-ten bases are with embodiments of these bases, you do not need to know anything about other bases. In fact, any such knowledge may interfere if you try to use it to make the embodiments work rather than trying to approach them afresh.

• The algorithms in other bases work just as the algorithms in base ten do. Work with base-ten embodiments always follows work with non-base-ten embodiments, but the step from the non-base-ten activities to the base-ten activities is a very short one.

Sometimes it takes a prolonged exposure to a non-ten base before you really understand what is happening. For this reason, base four will be used for the algorithms for both addition and subtraction. The reexposure in subtraction can help strengthen the understanding that was beginning to be built during the activities for addition. The same embodiments will also be used for addition and subtraction so that the links between the algorithms for these operations will be clear. Consequently, addition may progress slowly as base four and all the embodiments are worked through, but subtraction will move quickly because a preliminary understanding will have already been established.

Similarly, multiplication and division will each be done first in base eight. This larger base is needed for these operations in order to make the analogy with base ten clear. Base eight was also chosen because it is one of the few non-ten bases actually used: it is used in some computer programming languages. As with addition, multiplication may progress more slowly than division because the embodiments and multiplication shift rules (used in division also) must be figured out before the multiplication can be done.

Although the algorithms are being done in other bases chiefly so that your previous knowledge will not interfere with your reexamination of these algorithms, your experience with other bases will enable you to get a more general picture of characteristics of the base-ten system. Your experiences with base four and base eight will be drawn upon and discussed in section 7.6.

This unit and each of the next three units will begin with activities using embodiments of a non-ten base. Each embodiment shows some aspects of the algorithm more clearly than the other embodiments do. Watch for these strengths and weaknesses. The activities with the non-ten base will be briefly repeated with embodiments of base ten in order to make clear the similarities between the algorithms in the different bases. Analysis of various mathematical aspects of the activities will follow. All analysis is done in base ten.

1.2
ACTIVITY:
THE ADDITION ALGORITHM FOR
BASE-FOUR WHOLE NUMBERS

This section begins with an activity that shows how a base-four system might originate. You are asked to point out the similarity between the number words for base four and the number words for our base-ten system of numeration. Next, you will do some addition with *base-four blocks*. The ability to do this will take some time to develop because the meaning of the blocks must first be established. Addition on a *base-four chip computer* follows. Because this is the second embodiment of base four, it will go more quickly. An optional section on the *base-four rod computer* is last.

There are opportunities for working with your colleagues in this section. You may practice asking questions that can aid other persons in figuring out problems themselves. This takes some skill and practice. Telling someone how to do something is much easier than helping him figure it out for himself.

Base four may seem difficult at first. It is one of the many mathematical concepts which take time to develop. Many teachers who have done the following activities have been in a confused haze for a long time and have worried that they will never understand. Then, suddenly, they do see. A typical remark at this stage is, "But it seems so easy now. Why didn't I understand it before?" The answer is that a certain amount of experience is required before anyone can begin to see the general pattern. This experience cannot be rushed.

Overview: The reading of base-four words will be the first activity. Then the addition algorithm will be done using base-four blocks and the base-four chip computer. Work with the base-four rod computer is optional.

Materials needed: *For each group*—a set of base-four blocks, four sheets of paper (or a table at least 17 by 22 inches in size), and masking tape. *For each person*—chips, one sheet of paper (optional: rods and one extra sheet of paper).

*1.2.1
Base-
Four Words

Here is one way a base-four system might have begun. Suppose that you are in a society in which people count the *spaces between their fingers* (instead of counting their fingers). They count first on their right hand. When it is "full" (i.e., when four spaces have been counted), they record on their left hand the fact that they have 1 four. Thus a full right hand is always changed to one space on the left hand plus an "empty" right hand. The special word to describe one space on the left plus an empty right hand is "quad" (see the illustration). Because these people never keep a full right hand, they have no need for a symbol for four. The only symbols they use are 0, 1, 2, and 3.

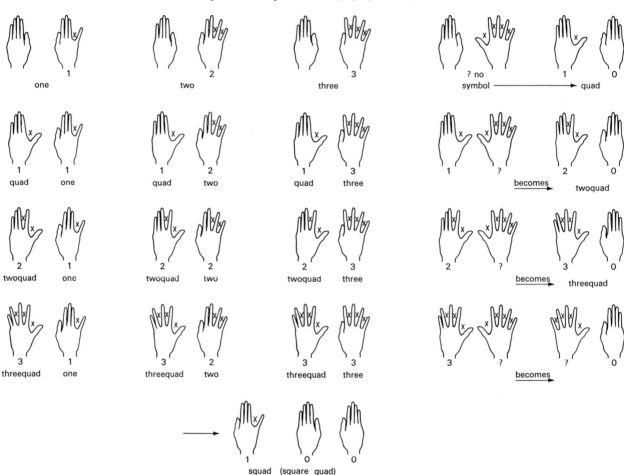

Hold out your hands and try counting as these people would count. Remember to look at the spaces between the fingers, not at the fingers. Start counting from the right on each hand. Check the pictures as you count.

For each of the following base-four words, give the word that we use in base ten for that situation (if necessary, check the symbols to see the similar points).[1]

[1] a. Ten, b. eleven, c. twelve, d. thir*teen*, e. twen*ty*, f. twen*ty*-one, g. twen*ty*-three, h. thir*ty*, i. thir*ty*-two, j. thir*ty*-three, k. one hundred.

    a. Quad: ___   **e.** Two quad: ___   **i.** Threequad two: ___
    b. Quad one: ___   **f.** Twoquad one: ___   **j.** Threequad three: ___
    c. Quad two: ___   **g.** Twoquad three: ___   **k.** Squad: ___
    d. Quad three: ___   **h.** Threequad: ___

What would you call the first space on the fourth hand (1000)?

1.2.2
The Trade Rules for Base-Four Blocks

1. Take two or three minutes to make some designs, or to build some things with the blocks. What observations did you make during these play activities?

2. Take one block of each size. Arrange them by size with the smallest on the right and the largest on the left.

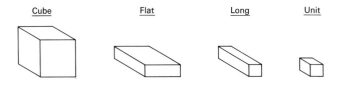

Cube   Flat   Long   Unit

3. Figure out the trade rules for the blocks. Fill in the blanks.

Right-to-Left Trades	*Left-to-Right Trades*
How many units = one long? __	How many longs = four units? __
How many longs = one flat? __	How may flats = four longs? __
How many flats = one cube? __	How many cubes = four flats? __
General rule:	*General rule:*
Trade __ for __.[2]	Trade __ for __.[3]

[2] Trade four for one.

[3] Trade one for four.

Can you justify your answers by making a demonstration and not saying a single word?[4]

4. Make a calculating area as pictured. Use masking tape to form the boundaries on a table *or* fasten together four 8½- by 11-inch sheets of paper and mark them to form a calculating sheet.

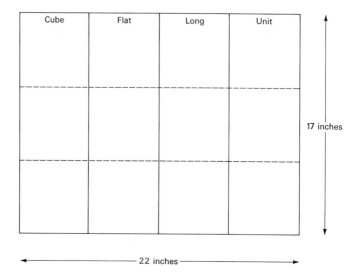

5. *Symbolization:* The symbols used are 0, 1, 2, and 3. The blocks of each kind are counted and a symbol is recorded, in order, for each kind of block. If there are more than three blocks in any column, a trade must be made. Empty columns to the left of the last column that contains blocks do not have to be recorded.

Fill in the symbols for each situation below. (If necessary, set up the calculating sheet and trade.)[5]

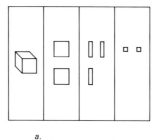

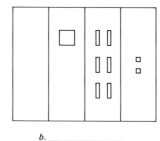

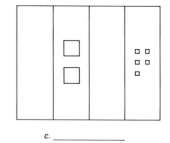

a. _____   b. _____   c. _____

---

[4] Show each trade rule by putting small pieces together to make a larger piece.

[5] a. 1232, b. 222, c. 211, d. 1003, e. 2030, f. 223.

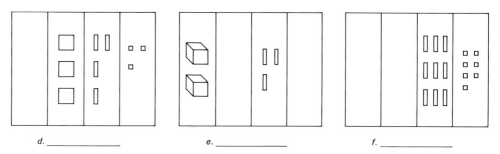

d. _____   e. _____   f. _____

The base-four number 1231 is read aloud as one-two-three-one (*not* "one thousand, two hundred, and thirty"; for those are base-ten words). The number 3022 is read three-oh-two-two (or three-zero-two-two). The number 310 is read three-one-oh (or three-one-zero). This will be difficult to do at first, because base-ten words are so familiar for these symbols. Work with your classmates and try to help each other use the correct terminology. Later you will learn why the terminology is important.

1.2.3
Addition with
Base-Four Blocks

Place blocks for the first number in the top row of the calculating area. Place blocks for the second number in the second row. Begin adding in the units column. Repeat the sequence of steps given below for each column in turn, moving one column to the left each time.

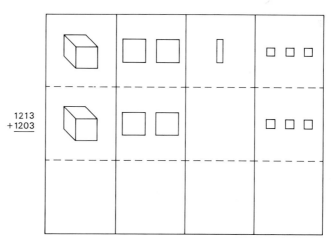

1213
+1203

To Add

Step 1. Push all blocks into the bottom row.

Step 2. Make all possible trades. Put any new larger block at the *top* of its proper column.

Step 3. To solve the problem in numerals, record the number of blocks remaining in the column and record the trade (if any) at the top of the column to the left.

Step 4. If there are blocks in the next column to the left, repeat steps 1 to 3 for that column.

Put blocks on your calculating area for the above problem. Follow the instructions for adding. Your recording should be done as shown below.

| a. | 1
1213
+1203
2 | b. | 1
1213
+1203
22 | c. | 1 1
1213
+1203
022 | d. | 1 1
1213
+1203
3022 |

Try the addition problems below. Remember to record after you do *each column*. The answers may seem funny because these are base-four, not base-ten, problems. Don't worry if you feel you are not understanding what is happening with the symbols. Further experience with base four may be required in order to understand the concept. By the time you have finished other base-four embodiments and have done base-four subtraction, you will feel much more confident.

If you have seen bases other than ten before, try to forget what you know. Do not just do these problems symbolically without using the blocks. Your task right now is to see how the *blocks* work. The symbols should be used *only* for recording data from the blocks. After you have done a problem using the blocks, you may check your answer by adding symbolically if you wish.[6]

| a. | 112
+213 | b. | 331
+1132 | c. | 1213
+1202 | d. | 1033
+1331 | e.[4] | 1223
+2321 |

Try these problems if you want additional practice.

| f. | 1122
+1303 | g. | 1321
+1113 | h. | 1313
+1222 | i. | 3003
+3333 |

---

[4] What did you notice while doing problems *e* and *i*? What shape would you make the block in the fifth column? the sixth column? Some people have suggested that these be called "long cube" and "flat cube."

---

[6] a. 331, b. 2123, c. 3021, d. 3030, e. 10210, f. 3031, g. 3100, h. 3201, i. 13002.

1.2.4
Trade Rules
for the Base-Four
Chip Computer

Make a calculating area, like the one pictured, on a table or on a piece of paper. Label the columns as shown. Your letters may be *on* the paper.

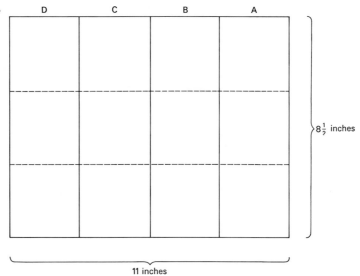

1. In dealing with blocks, you were able to figure out the trade rules for yourself, but the trade rules for the chip computer must be provided:

Right-to-Left Trades	*Left-to-Right Trades*
Four A = one B	One B = four A
Four B = one C	One C = four B
Four C = one D	One D = four C
General rule:	*General rule:*
Trade *four* for *one*.	Trade *one* for *four*.

2. Symbolization for the chip computer is just like that for the blocks. Count the number of chips in each column and record symbols for each column, in order. The symbols are 0, 1, 2, and 3. Trade if there are too many chips in a column to be recorded by the above symbols. Numbers are read aloud just as they are for the blocks.

3. Do not make each column have a different color of chips. That does not make a place value system, e.g., if A is white and B is blue, then

is two-three (2 blue, 3 white). If the values are according to *color*, the chips can be in any order. The position of the chips does not matter. The numeration system we use is a *place-value* system. We want the chip computer to show that aspect.

1.2.5 Place chips for the first number in the top row of the calculating area.
Addition Place chips for the second number in the second row.
with the Base-Four
Chip Computer

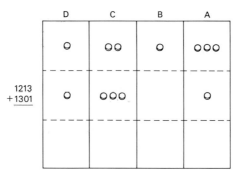

Begin in column A. Repeat the following sequence of steps for each column in turn, moving one column to the left each time.

To Add **Step 1.** Push all chips into the bottom row.

Step 2. Make all possible trades. Put any new traded chip at the *top* of its proper column.

Step 3. To solve the problem in numerals, record the number of chips remaining in the column and record the trade (if any) at the top of the column to the left.

Step 4. If there are chips in the next column to the left, repeat steps 1 to 3 for that column.

Put chips on your calculating area for the problem illustrated, and then follow the instructions for adding. Your recording should be done as shown below.

	1		1		1 1		1 1
a.	1213	**b.**	1213	**c.**	1213	**d.**	1213
	+1301		+1301		+1301		+1301
	0		20		120		3120

Try these addition problems. Remember to record after you do each column. The goal is to learn how the addition algorithm works, not just to get answers to these problems.[7]

a.	303	**b.**	1312	**c.**	2011	**d.**	1032	**e.**	2313
	+212		+ 332		+1232		+1323		+3233

[7] a. 1121, b. 2310, c. 3303, d. 3021, e. 12212.

*1.2.6

Trading and Adding with the Base-Four Rod Computer

1. This rod computer uses only the four smallest rods (W, R, G, P). Make a calculating area on a table or paper as pictured below. (A white rod is 1 centimeter long, red is 2 centimeters, green is 3 centimeters, and purple is 4 centimeters.)

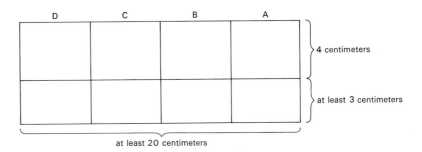

2. The trade rules for the rod computer are as follows (for colored rods; adapt appropriately for other rods).

Right-to-Left Trades	*Left-to-Right Trades*
Purple A = white B	White B = purple A
Purple B = white C	White C = purple B
Purple C = white D	White D = purple C
General rule:	*General rule:*
Trade *purple* for *white*.	Trade *white* for *purple*.

3. The rod computer uses white, red, light green, and purple rods, but it will stop working only when all purple rods have been traded. The white, red, and light green rods are symbolized by 1, 2, and 3 respectively.

 To symbolize the contents of the computer at any given moment, all rods in a given column are formed into a single *vertical* train (the train may consist of only one rod). If the train has length 0, 1, 2, or 3 the correct symbol is recorded for that column. If the train is longer than 3 (the light green rod), a trade must be made. This is done by making beside the first train a second train of length equal to the first. This second train includes a *purple* rod and any remaining rod which will make the second train as long as the first (the remaining rod may be of length 0 if the first train has length four). After the second equal train is made, remove the first train, as it is no longer needed. Now trade the *purple* rod for a *white* rod in the column to the left. The rod remaining in the original column (if any) is now the value of that column.

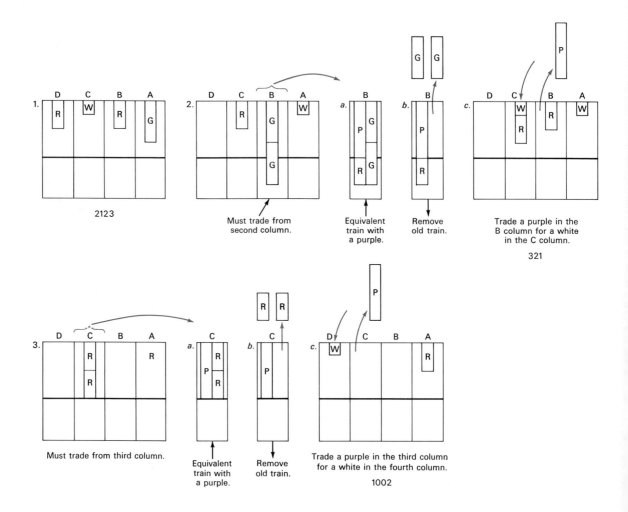

To Add Place rods for the first number vertically touching the top of the sheet. Place rods for the second number just beneath and touching the top rods.

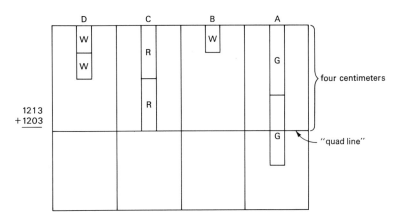

$$\begin{array}{r} 1213 \\ +1203 \\ \hline \end{array}$$

Begin at column A and move to the left.

Step 1. If the vertical train *is longer than a light green rod,* make beside it an equivalent train containing a purple rod. Remove the first train. Trade the purple rod for a white rod in the column to the left. Place the new white rod at the top of the train in that column.

Step 2. If the vertical train *is not longer than a light green rod,* place beside the train the single rod which is as long as the original train. Remove the original train.

Step 3. To solve the problem in numerals, record the rod remaining in the column and record the trade (if any).

Step 4. If there are rods in the next column to the left, repeat steps 1 to 3 for that column.

Put rods for the above problem on your calculating area. Follow the instructions for adding. After you have finished doing each column, check with the notes below to see if you did it correctly.

(You may, if you wish, use a "quad line" on the computing sheet to tell you when to trade instead of using a purple rod. The "quad line" is drawn 4 centimeters from the top of the sheet as shown in the illustration.)

Column A: Since the train in column A is longer than a light green rod, make beside it a train of a purple rod and a red rod (this train is the same length as the original train, and so you haven't changed the problem). Remove the original train (two light greens) because you do not need two identical trains. Now trade the purple rod in column A for a white rod in column B. Add the white rod to the top of the train in column B. Record the red rod and the trade as follows:

$$
\begin{array}{r}
1\\
1213\\
+1203\\
\hline
2
\end{array}
$$

Column B: No trade is necessary. Two whites make a red rod. Record the red rod as follows:

$$
\begin{array}{r}
1\\
1213\\
+1203\\
\hline
22
\end{array}
$$

Column C: The train in column C is longer than a light green rod. Make beside it a train with a purple rod (this time the train contains no rod except the purple rod). Remove the two red rods. Trade the purple rod in column C for a white rod in column D. Record the remaining zero rod and the trade as follows:

$$
\begin{array}{r}
1\ \ 1\\
1213\\
+1203\\
\hline
022
\end{array}
$$

Column D: The train in column D is as long as a light green rod. Replace that train with a light green rod. Record the light green rod as follows:

$$
\begin{array}{r}
1\ \ 1\\
1213\\
+1203\\
\hline
3022
\end{array}
$$

Try these addition problems on the base-four rod computer.[8]

a.	303	b.	232	c.	2031	d.	1022	e.	3132
	+222		+133		+1211		+1332		+1233

[8] a. 1131, b. 1031, c. 3302, d. 3020, e. 11031.

1.3
ACTIVITY:
THE ADDITION ALGORITHM FOR
BASE-TEN WHOLE NUMBERS

The activities done for base four will be repeated in base ten. Remember that the final goal in teaching algorithms is still to have students learn to do algorithms with pencil and paper only. But to make this a feasible and understandable ability, work with concrete materials must precede it. As you do the base-ten activities, think about how they can lead to doing the symbolic algorithm without materials.

Overview: The addition algorithm will be done with base-ten blocks and base-ten chip computer. The base-ten rod computer is optional.

Materials Needed: A set of base-ten blocks for each group, chips for each person, the same calculating area used for base-four blocks, one sheet of paper for each person. Optional: rods for each person.

1.3.1
Addition with
Base-Ten Blocks

1. As with base-four blocks, the blocks are called "units," "longs," "flats," and "cubes." Figure out the trade rules for the blocks and fill in the blanks.

Right-to-Left Trades	*Left-to-Right Trades*
How many units = one long? __	How many longs = ten units? __
How many longs = one flat? __	How many flats = ten longs? __
How many flats = one cube? __	How many cubes = ten flats? __
General rule:	*General rule:*
Trade __ for __.[9]	Trade __ for __.[10]

2. Use the same calculating area for base-ten blocks as you did for base-four blocks.

3. *Symbolization:* As with base four, simply record the number of pieces in a place by one of the following numerals: 0, 1, 2, 3, 4, 5, 6, 7, 8, 9. You may need to trade before you can record. Why do we need the numeral 0? Why is it necessary to have a new numeral for ten? Why are more numerals used for base ten than for base four?

Give symbols for these situations[11]:

---

[9] Trade ten for one.

[10] Trade one for ten.

[11] a. 2085, b. 312, c. 1300.

Give symbols for these situations:

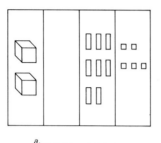 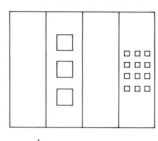 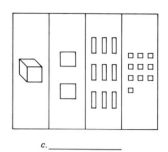

a. _____ b. _____ c. _____

To make the analogy with base four clearer, continue to use the one-two-oh-three (for 1203) verbal reading of numbers. Of course you may now also use the words for four through nine.

4. *Addition:* Addition in base ten is done exactly as it is done in base four (except that the trade rules are different). If you need to, review the instructions for addition given in section 1.2.3.

Try the addition problems below. Remember to record after you do each column. *Do the problems with the embodiments.* (Of course you are able to do them without the embodiments. But this is a new learning experience, not a test of your old calculation skills. You are trying to find out how the blocks work and look and feel.)

a. 47	b. 164	c. 375	d. 1408	e. 1092	f. 2643
75	358	638	327	1955	1887

1.3.2 Addition with the Base-Ten Chip Computer

1. Use the calculating area that you used for the base-four chip computer.

2. The trade rules for the base-ten chip computer are as follows:

Right-to-Left Trades	*Left-to-Right Trades*
Ten A = one B	One B = ten A
Ten B = one C	One C = ten B
Ten C = one D	One D = ten C
General rule: Trade *ten* for *one*.	*General rule:* Trade *one* for *ten*.

3. *Symbolization* for the base-ten chip computer is just like that for the base-ten blocks. The symbols used are 0, 1, 2, 3, 4, 5, 6, 7, 8, and 9.

4. *Addition:* Addition on the base-ten chip computer is exactly like addi-

tion with the base-ten blocks. Read through the instructions in section 1.2.3, substituting chips for blocks, if you are not sure how to add on a base-ten chip computer. Remember that all the trades will be ten for one (right to left) or one for ten (left to right) trades. Try these problems. Record after doing each *column*.

a. 582	**b.** 259	**c.** 1437	**d.** 6208	**e.** 4357	**f.** 2666
+469	+475	+2581	+3375	+4976	+7895

*1.3.3

Addition with the Base-Ten Rod Computer

1. Turn a piece of paper sideways and make a calculating sheet as pictured.

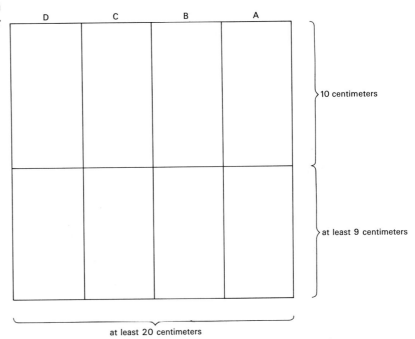

2. The trade rules for the base-ten rod computer are:

Right-to-Left Trades	*Left-to-Right Trades*
Orange A = white B	White B = orange A
Orange B = white C	White C = orange B
Orange C = white D	White D = orange C
General rule:	*General rule:*
Trade *orange* for *white*.	Trade *white* for *orange*.

If you wish, try to find the extension of the base-four rod computer to this base-ten rod computer yourself. Then try some of the problems at the end of exercise 4.

3. *Symbolization:* The base-ten rod computer uses rods of all colors. White is 1, red is 2, . . . , blue is 9. The symbols 0 to 9 are used. The orange rod is used for trading purposes only. To find the value of a given column, find the rod which is as long as the vertical train made by all rods in that column. It will be necessary to trade (orange for white in the column to the left) if the train is longer than a blue rod (9).

4. *Addition:* Addition in base ten is just like addition on the base-four rod computer except that the trades are now orange for white instead of purple for white.

To Add   Place rods for the first number vertically touching the top of the sheet. Place rods for the second number just beneath and touching the top rods (make a vertical train). Begin at column A and move to the left.

Step 1. If the vertical train is not longer than a blue rod, place beside the train the single rod that is as long as the original train. Remove the original train.

Step 2. If the vertical train is longer than a blue rod, make beside it an equivalent train containing an orange rod and one other rod. Remove the first train. Trade the orange rod for a white rod in the column to the left. Place the new white rod at the top of the train in that column.

Step 3. Record the rod remaining in the column and the trade (if any).

Step 4. If there are rods in the next column to the left, repeat steps 1 to 3 for that column.

Try these addition problems on your base-ten rod computer.

a. 347   b. 1482   c. 3875   d. 1485   e. 7532
   +562   +3954   +2168   +5763   +6829

1.4
PROBLEM SET:
ANALYSIS OF THE
ADDITION ALGORITHM

Overview: **Problems concerning alternative symbolic approaches, trading, comparison of embodiments, and analysis of student errors in addition problems are included.**

1.4.1
An Inter-
mediate Form of the
Addition Algorithm

An intermediate form of recording might be used before the one-row form used in all the activities. This intermediate form might also be used with older students as a check on their understanding of the one-row form or as a learning method for students who have difficulty with the one-row algorithm.

In the intermediate form, each sum is written on a separate line. Thus trades do not have to be recorded above the problem, and the sums make clearer the sizes of the numbers being added.

Example:

```
    476        (A)    6      (B)    70      (C)    400
  + 985          +   5         +   80         +   900
    11  A.           11            150           1300
   150  B.
  1300  C.
  1461
```

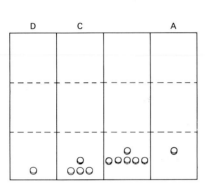

If the same problem were done with manipulatives, the sums in the bottom row would be kept separate to reflect the above process. (See the illustration.) Do each of the following base-ten addition problems using the intermediate form. For at least two of the problems, write out the separate sums to the right, as done in (*A*), (*B*), and (*C*) above.

a. 674
   +818

b. 2704
   +1656

c. 1527
   +5473

d. 789
   +276

e. 3028
   +2685

f. 4546
   +7287

1.4.2
The most difficult step in addition is the trading step. It is necessary to trade because of the way the base-ten numeral system is symbolized. This system has numerals only for sets containing zero through nine elements; thus a set containing more than nine members cannot be symbo-

lized by a *single* numeral. But there can also be only *one* numeral in any given place (ones place, tens place, hundreds place, etc.).

For example, when we add $27 + 15$, we first get twelve ones. But there is no *single* numeral for a set of twelve. To get a set of ones small enough to symbolize by a single numeral, you must trade ones for tens. The base-ten trade rule is "Trade ten for one (when moving left)." Use it to do the following problem:

$$\begin{array}{r} 27 \\ \underline{15} \\ \frac{\text{twelve}}{\text{ones}} = 1 \text{ ten} + 2 \text{ ones} \end{array}$$

We cannot leave the ten in the ones column, and so we add it in with the other tens.

$$\begin{array}{r} 1 \\ 27 \\ \underline{15} \\ 2 \end{array} \qquad \begin{array}{r} 1 \\ 27 \\ \underline{15} \\ 42 \end{array}$$

For each problem below, tell what trades must be made before the sum is symbolized (for example, ten ones for a ten, ten tens for a hundred, etc.) You do not need to work out the problem.

a. $\begin{array}{r} 43 \\ \underline{71} \end{array}$ **b.** $\begin{array}{r} 27 \\ \underline{85} \end{array}$

c. $\begin{array}{r} 454 \\ \underline{666} \end{array}$ **d.** $\begin{array}{r} 8567 \\ \underline{2634} \end{array}$

1.4.3 **a.** Remember that a binary *operation* can only take *two* numbers and assign a *third* number. Thus to do $4 + 2 + 3$, we must add the first two numbers, and then add that sum to the third number.

$$4 + 2 + 3 = (4 + 2) + 3 = 6 + 3 = 9$$

With the above in mind, make a list of all additions and use it to count how many times the operation addition is used in doing this problem (remember to count the addition of the traded numbers).

8594
+7647   Number of addition operations: _____ [12]

Therefore the addition algorithm involves quite a few separate addition operations. Each one of these is a possible source of error. This means that excellent addition reflexes (i.e., knowledge of "number facts") are required for accurate addition of large whole numbers.

+	0	1	2	3
0	0	1	2	3
1	1	2	3	10
2	2	3	10	11
3	3	10	11	12

b. A person whose addition reflexes were insufficient might still get accurate answers through the use of an addition table. Because you have excellent reflexes in base ten, an addition table for base four will be used. In base four you will be in a position similar to that of an upper elementary student in base ten: you have had experiences with manipulative materials in base four and know some of the addition facts ($1 + 2 = 3$), but you probably do not know them all.

To use the base-four addition table to find the sum of two numbers (for example, $2 + 3$), find the *first* number in the first *column,* and find the *second* number in the top *row.* The sum is in the square where the first number's row (the 2 row) and the second number's column (the 3 column) intersect (see the arrows; they intersect in 11: "one-one", *not* "eleven"). Use the table to do the base-four addition problems below. Remember that the answers will not be the same as in base ten. Think about the base-four blocks or chip computer if you get confused.[13]

(1) 1032	(2) 333	(3) 3021	(4) 2231	(5) 11032
+2231	+213	+1223	+1223	+21332

c. Examine the base-ten addition table for patterns. Do you see a pattern that shows commutativity of addition? Do you see any patterns which might make learning the combinations any easier? (Read problem *d* after you have described the patterns.)

Use the table to do the following base-ten addition problems. Try to use it for every step and think about how the algorithm works. Use the intermediate form for at least one problem.

(6) 872	(7) 954	(8) 376	(9) 6805	(10) 9876
+485	+278	+485	+3378	+4787

[12] $4 + 7, 1 + 9, 10 + 4, 1 + 5, 6 + 6, 1 + 8, 9 + 7, 1 + 0$; eight in all.

[13] (1) 3323, (2) 1212, (3) 10310, (4) 10120 (5) 33030.

+	0	1	2	3	4	5	6	7	8	9
0	0	1	2	3	4	5	6	7	8	9
1	1	2	3	4	5	6	7	8	9	10
2	2	3	4	5	6	7	8	9	10	11
3	3	4	5	6	7	8	9	10	11	12
4	4	5	6	7	8	9	10	11	12	13
5	5	6	7	8	9	10	11	12	13	14
6	6	7	8	9	10	11	12	13	14	15
7	7	8	9	10	11	12	13	14	15	16
8	8	9	10	11	12	13	14	15	16	17
9	9	10	11	12	13	14	15	16	17	18

d. The addition reflexes that are necessary to do the addition algorithm are all the combinations of pairs of numbers from 0 through 9 (or in other words, all the entries in the addition table for base ten). There are 100 combinations in all, but commutativity of addition of whole numbers decreases this number to 50. (How?) The ten problems with zero are very simple (zero is the additive identity, i.e., $\square + 0 = \square$). The nine problems with 1 are quite simple, and the eight (only eight because $0 + 2$ and $1 + 2$ are included in the 0 and 1 problems) problems with 2 are also easy. The seven remaining problems with 3 and the six remaining problems with 4 are not difficult. This leaves only fifteen difficult combinations to learn. Write them below:

1.4.4 **a.** To understand the addition algorithm and to use it properly, a person must understand that units are added to units, tens to tens, hundreds to hundreds, thousands to thousands, etc. It must be clear that a ten plus a hundred is still a ten plus a hundred and not two tens or two hundreds. Which embodiment would help the most with this understanding? Defend your choice.

b. In order to understand the trading process, a person must feel that ten units do equal 1 ten, that ten tens do equal 1 hundred, that ten hundreds do equal 1 thousand, etc. Which embodiment would help the most with this understanding? Defend your choice.

c. The symbols in our numeration system are used over and over again in different places. The "2" used in two (2) and in twenty (20) and in two hundred (200) looks exactly the same in all those numbers. It does not, for instance, get larger as its positional value gets larger (2,2 0, 2 00). Which embodiment reflects this uniform appearance of our symbols the best? Defend your choice.

d. Does the addition algorithm enable us only to add numbers with four or fewer places? How large can the numbers be which we can add using the addition algorithm? Which embodiment reflects this aspect of our addition algorithm best? Defend your choice.

e. Each of problems *a* to *d* illustrates an aspect of addition that needs teaching. Which of these would be most important at the beginning of work on the addition algorithm? Why? Which are finer points that could be left to the end? Would this suggest an order you might use the embodiments with children? Comment on this by suggesting an order or by saying why you don't think it would make much difference.

1.4.5   Children need practice in recognizing real situations that require the use of the addition algorithm and in deciding on the correct mathematical model (e.g., 35 + 76) for a given situation. Initially it is helpful if the teacher provides or points out such situations and the students then do all the necessary steps toward finding an answer for the situation.

In the early grades such situations can be pointed out in common school experiences such as these:

Situation 1: If the class is getting 21 white milks and 13 chocolate milks, how many straws should be taken from the cupboard?

Situation 2: Children from two tables are coming to the story corner. Six children were sitting at one table and eight at the other. How many mats are needed for them?

a. Give four situations where use of addition would (or could easily with the help of a question from the teacher) arise in the primary classroom.

b. Give four activities or projects for middle or upper grade children that would require addition of at least three-place whole numbers. (The project might be in a subject area other than mathematics.)

1.4.6   Suppose you noticed children making the kinds of errors illustrated in the problems below. For each such error, tell (1) what the child did, (2) what mathematical concept was probably being misunderstood or was lacking, and (3) what experiences you might provide for the child to help him overcome this type of error.

a.   23   (1)
   +145   (2)
    375   (3)

b.   1 6   (1)
   +4 7   (2)
   513   (3)

     2
c.   27   (1)
   +45   (2)
    81   (3)

d.   23   (1)
   +14   (2)
    36   (3)

e.   38   (1)
   +15   (2)
    43   (3)

f. 102   (1)
       + 34   (2)
         46   (3)

Some errors are merely reflex or careless errors. Other errors are indicative of more serious problems of misunderstanding. A problem may be almost right, with only one small error; or a problem may contain several errors and the answer may be quite far from right. The common practice of marking problems "right" or "wrong" with no indication of how nearly "right" they are does not contribute to the child's understanding. It focuses all the attention on the absolute correctness of the answer rather than on difficulties connected with learning the addition process.

1.4.7 Make a flow chart of the usual addition algorithm. (A flow chart is simply a chart which shows all the steps for a procedure and has arrows connecting these steps). Table 1.1 (in section 1.1) is a flow chart for buying groceries with a list. First try making a chart for the following specific problem: $3,859 + 2,573$. Then see if your chart will work for any problem (e.g., a problem without any trading, a problem with some trading, a problem with two-place numbers). Remember that your chart must show how to stop. If there is a series of repeated steps, you might draw an arrow back to the beginning of the series instead of repeating all the steps over and over again.

Will your flow chart accommodate five-place numbers? _____
Six-place numbers? _____ Seven-place numbers? _____
x-place numbers? _____

1.4.8 Make a calculating sheet with four columns labeled D, C, B, A (left to right). Use one of the embodiments of base ten to do the following problems:

a. Put $2614 + 1253$ on the calculating sheet.
Add the C's, then the A's, then the D's, then the B's: _____
Add the B's, then the C's, then the D's, then the A's: _____

Add the D's, then the B's, then the A's, then the C's: _____
Did you get the same sum each time? _____

b. Will that happen with every pair of numbers? _____
Try a problem with many trades: 1476 + 1825.
Add the C's, then the A's, then the D's, then the B's: _____
Add the B's, then the C's, then the D's, then the A's: _____
Add the D's, then the B's, then the A's, then the C's: _____
Did you get the same sum each time? _____

c. Why does it not matter in what order you add the places? First try an argument using the intermediate algorithm:

Now try an argument using commutativity of addition of whole numbers (for example, 278 + 693 = 200 + 70 + 8 + 600 + 90 + 3):

d. In Europe, a common addition algorithm is similar to ours, but begins at the *left* and moves to the right. What disadvantages does this European algorithm have? (Consider a problem like 1476 + 1825.)

What advantages might the European algorithm have? [Suppose you needed only an approximate answer; with which algorithm could you stop working first? Later on, what about problems involving repeating decimals (.33333 . . . + .99999 . . .)?]

1.4.9 If you had to add 6 + 7 + 4, which two numbers would you add first?
_____ Could you add any two first and then add the remaining one to that sum? _____ Why can you add in whatever order you choose?[14] _____
Add each of the strings below in at least two ways. Tell which way is easier.

a. 4 + 8 + 6

b. 9 + 7 + 1

c. 5 + 8 + 5 + 2

d. 2 + 7 + 8 + 6 + 3

e. 5 + 4 + 7 + 6 + 5 + 3

You might use strategies like this in adding columns of large numbers.

---

[14] Associativity and commutativity of addition of whole numbers. See Part A, section 2.3.7.

1.4.10 Some people find it easy to remember all the combinations that result in ten as a sum (for example, $4 + 6$, $5 + 5$, $3 + 7$, $7 + 3$), but difficult to remember the sums that are greater than ten (for example, $7 + 6$, $6 + 8$). They solve the difficulty by changing all problems of the latter kind to the former by breaking the second number into two parts.

Excess-over-Ten Method

Example 1: $7 + 6 = 7 + \Box + \triangle = 7 + \boxed{3} + \triangle = 10 + \triangle = 13$
$(7 + \Box = 10, \Box + \triangle = 6)$

Example 2: $4 + 8 = 4 + \Box + \triangle = 4 + \boxed{6} + \triangle = 10 + \triangle = 12$
$4 + \Box = 10, \Box + \triangle = 8$

This process is done mentally, so that it does not take as long as it looks. Try to do the following sums in the same way.

a. $9 + 5 = 9 + \Box + \triangle = 10 + \triangle = $ _____

b. $8 + 3 = 8 + \Box + \triangle = 10 + \triangle = $ _____

c. $5 + 7 = 5 + \Box + \triangle = 10 + \triangle = $ _____

d. $6 + 9 = 6 + \Box + \triangle = 10 + \triangle = $ _____

e. $7 + 8 = 7 + \Box + \triangle = 10 + \triangle = $ _____

Some elementary school textbooks stress this method for all children. It is probably a good idea to introduce it, and let children use it if they wish to do so. What manipulatives would you use to introduce this method? Why?

This process can also be done with multiples of 10 (20, 30, 40, etc.). It is a useful technique when adding a long string of numbers.

1: $\begin{matrix} 27 \\ 49 \\ 97 \\ +38 \end{matrix}$ *Think:* $7 + \boxed{3} + 6 = 16$

2: $\begin{matrix} 27 \\ 49 \\ 97 \\ +38 \end{matrix}$ *Think* $16 + \boxed{4} + 3 = 23$

3: $\begin{matrix} 27 \\ 49 \\ 97 \\ +38 \end{matrix}$ *Think* $23 + \boxed{7} + 1 = 31$

4: $\begin{matrix} 3 \\ 27 \\ 49 \\ 97 \\ +38 \\ \hline 1 \end{matrix}$

5: $9 \begin{matrix} 3 \\ 27 \\ 49 \\ 97 \\ +38 \\ \hline 1 \end{matrix}$

6:
Think

$9 + \boxed{1} + \triangle\!\!\!\!8 = 18 <\!\!\begin{array}{c}3\\27\\49\\97\end{array}$

$+\underline{38}$

1

7:
Think

$18 + \boxed{2} + \triangle\!\!\!\!1 = 21 <\!\!\begin{array}{c}3\\27\\49\\97\\\underline{38}\end{array}$

211

Try this technique on the problems below. Write down as many steps as necessary to understand how the process works.

f. 66
47
88
46
+$\underline{75}$

g. 49
46
58
85
+$\underline{56}$

1.4.11 Mechanical calculators make the trades in addition automatically. One way this is done is to have a row of intermeshing gears with ten teeth on each gear. When the ones gear has turned completely around once, it moves the tens gear one place (that is, 10 ones = 1 ten, or 10 A's = 1 B). Similarly, when the tens gear has moved completely around, it moves the hundreds gear one place (10 tens = 1 hundred, or 10 B's = 1 C).

One of the first uses of such gears was in a calculator built in 1642 by Blaise Pascal, a French mathematician, to assist his father in the auditing of the government accounts at Rouen.

A very inexpensive (about $2) hand-operated calculator that has this automatic trading feature is the Dialamatic, manufactured by Sterling Plastics Company and sold to schools and retail stationery stores. Selective Educational Equipment (SEE) distributes a similar calculator that is transparent, allowing you to see the gears work. If either of these calculators is available, try some addition problems on the calculator.

1.4.12 Hassler Whitney[5] has invented a calculator that is easy to make and fun to use. Make a sheet as illustrated on page 223.

[5] Hassler Whitney, "A MiniComputer for Primary Schools," *Mathematics Teaching*, no. 52, pp. 4–7, Fall 1970.

To Add Place markers (white rods or pennies) on the squares for the first number. Place markers on the squares for the second number. For any column, move the pieces *away from* each other, one square at a time (e.g., markers on $5 + 3$ move to $6 + 2$, then to $7 + 1$, then to $8 + 0$), until one marker reaches the top or the bottom. A marker on 0 can be removed. A marker in the top space should be moved to the square in the column to the left containing the same value. The sum has been found when no more than one marker is in each column.

Work through the example below on your calculator.

10,000	1,000	100	10
9,000	900	90	9
8,000	800	80	8
7,000	700	70	7
6,000	600	60	6
5,000	500	50	5
4,000	400	40	4
3,000	300	30	3
2,000	200	20	2
1,000	100	10	1
0	0	0	0

↕ 11 inches

←———— 8½ inches ————→

Example: $263 + 578$:

Place markers on 200, on 60, on 3.
Place markers on 500, on 70, on 8.
Move 8 and 3 away from each other: $8 + 3$ become $9 + 2$, then $10 + 1$. Move the marker from 10 at the top of the ones to the 10 at the bottom of the tens (second column).

There are now three markers in the second column, which means there are several ways to move, depending on which pair of markers you start with. Try it this way: start with the 70 and the 10; they move away from each other and become $80 + 0$. Remove the marker from 0. Now use the 80 with the 60; they move away from each other and become $90 + 50$, and then $100 + 40$. Move the marker from the 100 at the top of the tens (second column) to 100 at the bottom of the hundreds (third column). Now there are three markers in the third column, and so there are several possibilities of moves. Do 100 and 200 first, and then 500. Move $100 + 200$ away from each other. They become $0 + 300$. Remove the marker from 0. Move $300 + 500$ away from each other. They become $200 + 600$, then $100 + 700$, then $0 + 800$. Remove the marker from 0. There now is no more than one marker in each column, and therefore the sum is 841.

Try some addition problems on your calculator. Try to figure out why this calculator works. (Mathematical hint: Equivalence classes are involved.) (Real world hint: Think about a pen of 5 rabbits connected to a pen of 3 rabbits. Suppose one rabbit at a time ran from the second pen to the first pen.)

1.5
**PEDAGOG-
ICAL REMARKS** Children need a progression of learning experiences that lead up to the addition algorithm. Only the final steps in this progression were done in this unit—the addition with embodiments that is analogous to the addi-

tion algorithm. Below is a series of suggested activities for children. They would probably extend from kindergarten through third or fourth grade (or even later, for children who have difficulty with the symbolic addition algorithm).

It is of paramount importance that children understand why we add units to units, tens to tens, hundreds to hundreds, thousands to thousands, etc. It is of equal importance that children understand why we *cannot* add together the numerals for units and tens, or units and hundreds, or tens and hundreds, or any other unlike combination of places. Without this understanding, the addition algorithm remains a useful but mysterious process.

A length embodiment can be of particular help in understanding both of the above points (and has another advantage described later). One such base-ten embodiment is as follows:

D thousand:	C hundred:	B ten:	A unit:
Piece of string ten meters long	A meter stick (or any stick one meter long)	Orange Cuisenaire rod	White Cuisenaire rod

The trade rules are obviously ten for one (right to left) and one for ten (left to right).

Numbers are represented first by "trains": a row of touching pieces ordered from large (left) to small (right). (See Figure 1.1 below)

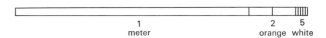

1
meter   2   5
                    orange white

To add two numbers, a train for the second number is placed to the right of and touching a train for the first number. A third "sum" train can be made of equivalent length to the two trains together. (See Figure 1.2)

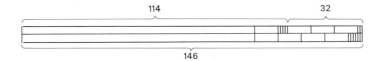

114   32

146

The process of making a third "sum" train is time-consuming and somewhat tedious. Children eventually see that they can merely rearrange the pieces in the two trains (putting all D's on the left, followed by all C's, then all B's, then all A's) and make any necessary trades. In Figure 1.2, children will combine the 4 whites and 2 whites to get 6 whites, then the one orange rod and three orange rods to get 4 orange rods.

This stage then moves into a place-value mode. Children make piles of string, piles of meter sticks, piles of orange rods, and piles of white rods. They trade between the piles when necessary.

With this length embodiment, children themselves discover place value. They see that the more efficient approach is to add units to units (white rods to white rods), tens to tens (orange rods to orange rods), hundreds to hundreds (meters to meters), and thousands to thousands (strings to strings). It is also quite clear that one cannot add 2 units to 3 tens and get 5 units, tens, or anything else (2 white rods and 3 orange rods do not make 5 white rods, or 5 orange rods, or 5 meter sticks, or 5 anything else).

The length embodiment and the blocks also illustrate quite clearly the approximate size differences of units, tens, hundreds, thousands, etc. This is useful in enabling students to approximate answers to real problems (e.g., "In what range will my answer be?"). In real life, an approximation is sometimes as useful as an exact answer.

Give an example of a real situation in which an approximate sum would be all the information you would require.

Knowing the approximate size difference is also useful in preventing silly mistakes such as: $123 + 45 = 573$.

The next stage of experiences for a child is to use in turn many different embodiments of base ten. Children probably need extended experience in adding with one embodiment before they use another embodiment. Experiences with embodiments should be as open as possible. Children can be encouraged to add the columns in any order that they wish. Through experimentation, they may decide that a methodical process has advantages and may devise a process satisfactory to themselves. Some of these processes may be quite interesting, and discussions of the advantages of various processes may be valuable learning experiences.

If this stage begins to turn into an automatic, answer-getting process, questions that will lead children to examine what they are doing should be asked. For example: Can you begin in any column? Can you predict an answer for a column and *then* check it with the materials? How are the embodiments alike? How are they different? If the teacher's emphasis is on what the students are learning and not just on what answers the students are getting, the children's emphasis is much more likely to be on the process of learning also.

The addition algorithm is a repeated pattern of steps: add the two numbers, trade if necessary, add the next column, trade if necessary, etc. It is difficult to see this pattern if you are only doing two-place numbers. In fact, there *is* no pattern for two-place numbers. The patterns of adding and trading are much clearer if children work on problems with three or four places. Embodiments that have different sizes in different places make it quite clear what they are adding at a given time and also make the pattern of repeated actions accessible to children. The usual practice of restricting problems to two places for a long time may actually make addition more difficult for children to understand. Children who understand addition of numbers less than ten can move immediately to four-place numbers *if* they use embodiments.

Many embodiments have different-size pieces for different places. Some examples are: base-ten blocks, the length embodiment described previously, bundles of toothpicks or coffee stirrers or popsicle sticks fastened with rubber bands, plastic bingo chips glued together to make "towers," beads or buttons on strings, a weight embodiment (kilograms, hectogram, dekagram, gram; see section 5.2), beans glued to tongue depressors, tagboard rectangles (in centimeters, for example, 1×1, 2×5, 5×20, 20×50), and egg cartons (with 1, 10, and 100 egg spaces) fastened together. You and your colleagues can probably think of others. All these embodiments share the characteristic of showing that tens are greater than ones, that hundreds are greater than tens and ones, etc. They also clearly show the ten-for-one and one-for-ten trades. Because of this, they would be good embodiments to use in first introducing the addition algorithm to children.

If you were asked, "Which of the above embodiments and the ones you used in class do you like the best? Why?", part of your answer would probably be based on mathematical, pedagogical, and practical (e.g., which is easiest or cheapest to make?) considerations. But part of the answer would be: "I like this one best because I just like it best." There is an arbitrary aspect to manipulative materials. Some embodiments "make sense" to some people, others "make sense" to other people. Your students will also have preferences for particular embodiments. You will want to make sure that they use several embodiments, both because of this difference in appeal and because each embodiment has something different to offer mathematically. But a child's preference for extended work with a particular embodiment can often be humored if it is a strong one.

The process of learning from manipulative materials requires that a person abstract certain general properties from the materials (for example, ten units trade for 1 ten, etc.). If the number of embodiments is small, inappropriate abstractions may be made (e.g., ones are little cubes, tens are always long and skinny, hundreds are flat, etc.). Or a limited number of embodiments may mean that the abstractions desired

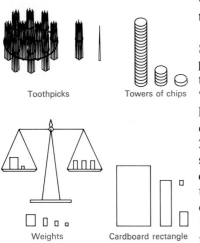

Toothpicks   Towers of chips

Weights   Cardboard rectangle

are never made. Very few people can generalize from one or two cases. Most people need three or four or five or more examples from which to generalize. Multiple embodiments can aid this generalization.

Embodiments that show the trades (i.e., where ten units do actually make 1 ten, where ten tens do make 1 hundred, etc.) should be used first. This type of embodiment shows most clearly the vital point that units are added to units, tens are added to tens, hundreds are added to hundreds, etc. After this point and the concept of trading are quite clear, embodiments that are closer to our numeration system can be used. The chip computer is like our numeration system because a four (four chips on the computer) in one place looks exactly like a four in any other place. The rod computer is like our numeration system in that each rod represents a unique symbol. The color eventually becomes symbolic, and you apprehend immediately the size of a number (blue-red-yellow-purple immediately looks like 9254) instead of having to count the number of chips in a given column. The difficulty with chips can be minimized, however, by arranging the chips in some pattern easily recognized, e.g., rows of three chips. ○ ○○ is 5, ○ ○○ is 8, etc.).

Abacuses of various kinds may also be useful at this stage.

The final stage of experiences with manipulative materials should be analogous to the usual addition algorithm. The activities you did in class belong to this stage. Out of such experiences should grow an understanding of how and why the algorithm works. Recording after addition of each column was emphasized so that the symbols would be very closely associated with the manipulative materials. In this way also the repetitive nature of the algorithm becomes clear. If the answer is made by using extra pieces to "match" the pieces being added, the embodiments parallel the symbolic algorithm almost exactly.

If a student is having difficulty with the algorithm or if you have an older student who does not understand the algorithm, you could have him use the intermediate form for recording from the materials. After the algorithm is clear to him in the intermediate form, he could progress to the usual abbreviated form.

Even though a student may understand the algorithmic process and understand the trading, he needs to have good addition reflexes (4 + 3 should immediately give the response 7, and 8 + 7 should immediately give 15) in order to do the algorithm quickly and accurately. A good deal of experience with many embodiments of simple addition problems (such as those used in Part A, Unit 2) will provide an excellent foundation for such reflexes. The addition reflexes that are necessary in doing the addition algorithm are all combinations of pairs of numbers from 0 through 9 (or in other words, all the entries in the base-ten addition table

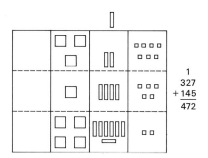

```
    1
  327
+ 145
  472
```

```
     1
  2841
+ 3625
  6466
```

in section 1.4.3, problem *c*). There are 100 combinations in all. But as shown in section 1.4.3, problem *d*, these can be reduced to only fifteen "difficult" combinations. Analysis of patterns in the addition table, practice of ways to find a forgotten answer (8 + 9: "Let's see; that is eight plus four plus five, or eight plus two plus seven, or . . ."), and more practice on these difficult combinations with manipulative materials can aid the development of these reflexes.

Symbolic practice is also necessary to help cement understanding. The most usual difficulty with symbolic practice is that it is often done before a student has any blocks of understanding to cement together. Such practice cannot be expected to produce a lasting edifice. But if a student does possess understanding of how and why the algorithm works, practice can help bring this understanding to a polished and skilled state.

It should be mentioned again that the whole point of spending so much time on the addition algorithm is to enable a person to *use* it. This means that a person must recognize real situations where the useful mathematical model is addition of large whole numbers. Recognizing such situations and being able to extract the correct mathematical model to use for them requires practice. The teacher must devise situations that will allow students to gain such experience. (See sections 1.4.5 and 1.1.3.)

A final note on bases other than ten is in order. We used base four to force you to reexamine the addition algorithm. Such a reexamination is obviously unnecessary for children who do not already know the addition algorithm. Opinion about the use of bases other than ten with children is mixed. Such experience might be interesting and valuable for older or brighter children. In any case, such work should be done with manipulative materials and not just with symbols. Otherwise it often seems to be mysterious hocus-pocus. Any such work should be done entirely within a given base with no translating back and forth from base ten. The value of experience with non-ten bases lies in the analogy such experience has with base ten. Arithmetical practice in changing from one number base to another cannot provide a broad understanding of what a base system of numeration is. (For other comments on number base systems, see the pedagogical notes in Section 7.7.)

unit 2
the algorithm for subtraction of whole numbers

2.1
INTRODUCTION The same embodiments used in Unit 1 are used in this unit, to enable you to become more familiar with the embodiments and to see more clearly the relationships between addition and subtraction of whole numbers. As before, base-four embodiments will be used first. You can thus reexamine your knowledge of the subtraction algorithm by being forced out of the usual base-ten situation. The subtraction algorithm is essentially the same in base four as in base ten, with only the trade rules differing. If you do not quite understand base four as yet, the extra experience in this unit will help.

As with addition, three different embodiments are used in each base. Each embodiment shows some aspects of the subtraction algorithm more clearly than the others. Watch for these aspects as you use the various embodiments.

Brief work with base-ten embodiments follows the base-four activities. Analysis in base ten of the subtraction algorithm is presented next.

2.1.1
Uses of Subtraction For each problem below, give a mathematical model for finding the solution. Find the solution if you wish.

1. In March 1974, on the first "bargain-rate" Sunday, 558,860 persons rode the Chicago Transit Authority buses and trains. On the same Sunday a year before, 353,959 persons rode the CTA. How many more people rode the CTA on the 1974 Sunday?
Mathematical model:

2. Here are some 1973–1974 and some 1974–1975 tuition figures for some universities in the Chicago area:

	Loyola	University of Chicago	North-western	DePaul	Roosevelt
1973–1974:	$1,850	$2,625	$3,000	$1,800	$1,830
1974–1975:	$1,950	$2,850	$3,180	$1,890	$1,950

What were the increases for each institution? What is the difference between the largest and the smallest increase? How much less would it have cost to go to DePaul instead of to Northwestern?
Mathematical models:

3. Goodyear reported 1973 sales of $4,675,300,000 and 1972 sales of $4,071,500,000. How much more was the sales figure for 1973?
Mathematical model:

4. Amtrak reported total ridership in January 1974 of 1,423,188 as compared to 1,109,078 in January 1973. What was the increase? Is this a significant increase?
Mathematical model:

5. A total of 4,364,000 people were unemployed in December 1973, and 4,732,000 people were unemployed in January 1974. How many more were unemployed in January than in December?
Mathematical model:

6. In 1973 the number of United States births was 3,141,000 and the number of deaths was 1,977,000. How many people were added to the total United States population in 1973 (disregarding immigration and emigration)?
Mathematical model:

7. People in the United States average 3300 calories per day. People in Bolivia average 1760 calories per day. What is the difference in calorie consumption in these two countries?
Mathematical model:

8. Find three newspaper or magazine clippings that involve subtraction of large whole numbers. Share these with your colleagues.

2.2
ACTIVITY: THE SUBTRACTION ALGORITHM FOR BASE-FOUR NUMBERS

Overview: **The subtraction algorithm will be done with base-four blocks and with the base-four chip computer. Work with the base-four rod computer is optional.**

Materials Needed: For each group — a set of base-four blocks and a calculating area for the blocks.
For each person — chips and a calculating area for chips (optional: rods and a calculating area for the rod computer). (Instructions for making the calculating areas are given in Unit 1.)

2.2.1
Subtraction with Base-Four Blocks

For addition, the blocks on the sheet were gathered together to make the answer. For subtraction, blocks not used in designating the problem will be needed to make the answer.

Example:

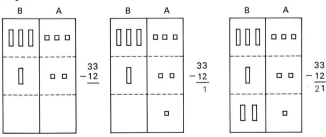

To Subtract

Step 1. Place blocks for the *first* number in the *top* row of the calculating sheet and blocks for the *second* number in the *second* row. (In the example shown, put 3 longs and 3 units in the top row, and put 1 long and 2 units in the second row.)

Step 2. Perform the following procedure for each column in turn, moving from right to left (that is, begin with the units in column A).

   a. Look at the blocks in the column and ask either of the following questions:

     (1) The blocks in the second row *plus* how many more blocks will equal the blocks in the top row? (In the example, $2 + \square = 3$?)

     (2) The blocks in the top row *minus* the number of blocks in the second row will equal how many blocks? (In the example, $3 - 2 = \square$?) [It may be necessary to trade blocks in the top row to make the questions reasonable (i.e., if the top digit is less than the bottom digit, the questions do not have whole number answers). If you do trade, record the trade in the symbolic (numerical) problem.]

   b. Place the number of blocks that you got as the answer to your question in the bottom row. (In the example, put 1 unit in the bottom row.)

   c. To solve the problem in numerals, record the number of blocks placed in the bottom row. (In the example, record 1.) Remember also to record any trades.

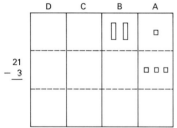

$$\begin{array}{r} 21 \\ -\ 3 \\ \hline \end{array}$$

In column A, the question "3 plus how many more = 1?" makes no sense. We need more units in the top row.

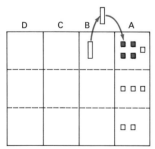

Trade one long for four units in the top row. Now the question makes sense and the answer is 2.

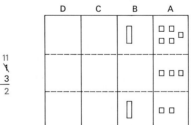

$$\begin{array}{r} 1\ 11 \\ \not{2}\ \not{1} \\ -\quad 3 \\ \hline 2 \end{array}$$

Record the trade[1] and the first column answer.

Ask the questions for column B. "1 minus 0 = 1." Put the block in the bottom row.

$$\begin{array}{r} 1\ 11 \\ \not{2}\ \not{1} \\ -\quad 3 \\ \hline 1\ 2 \end{array}$$

Record the answer for column B.

Try the following subtraction problems with the blocks. For each problem, ask yourself both questions: ("Plus how many more?" and

---

[1] You traded 1 long for 4 units. That gave you a total of five units. But there is no symbol for five in base four. Therefore, in the units place you have what looks like an eleven (11). Actually, however, it is the original 1 unit plus the 1 long (written in base four as 10) traded from the second column. It would be read aloud as one-one.

"Minus?"). Remember that the answers will look "funny" because they are base-four, not base-ten, answers.[1]

a. 3 3 1 **b.** 3 0 0 **c.** 1 1 2 3 **d.** 3 0 3 0 **e.** 3 0 3 0
−2 1 3   −1 2 3   − 3 3 1   −1 3 3 1   −1 0 3 3

**2.2.2
Subtraction
with the Base-Four
Chip Computer**

Subtraction on the chip computer is done exactly as it is done with the base-four blocks. If necessary, reread the instructions, substituting "chips" for "blocks" as you read.

The trades are one for four (left to right) and four for one (right to left). Be sure that any trading is done in the top row.

To check that you are recording properly (especially the trades) place the following problem on the chip computer. Do the problem and check your recording at each step with the steps given below.

Example:

```
                            3              3              3
             2 10       2 10 11       2 1̶0̶ 11       2 1̶0̶ 11
a.  3 0 1  b. 3̶ 0̶ 1  c. 3̶ 0̶ 1̶  d. 3̶ 0̶ 1̶  e. 3̶ 0̶ 1̶
   −1 2 3    −1  2 3    −1  2 3    −1  2 3    −1  2 3
                              2        1 2        1 1 2
```

Try these base-four subtraction problems on your chip computer. For practice, ask yourself both questions ("Plus how many more?" and "Minus?") for each problem.[2]

a. 3 3 2 **b.** 3 2 1 2 **c.** 2 0 0 3 **d.** 3 0 2 1 **e.** 1 2 0 3 1
−1 2 3   −2 1 2 3   −1 2 1 2   −1 2 1 3   −3 2 2 2

***2.2.3
Subtraction with
the Base-Four Rod Computer**

Subtraction with the rod computer looks different from subtraction with the other two embodiments. The rods are placed side by side in each column, with the "number being subtracted from" or sum (the top number in a vertical problem) on the *left* and the "number being sub-

---

[1] a. 112, b. 111, c. 132, d. 1033, e. 1331.

[2] a. 203, b. 1023, c. 131, d. 1202, e. 2202.

tracted" or addend on the *right*. The answer in each column is the rod that makes the right-hand rod as long as the left-hand rod.

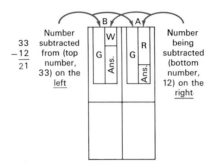

Sometimes the left rod in a column is not the longest rod. Then a trade must be made *among left rods* to make that rod as long as or longer than the rod being subtracted on the right. This trade will be a white rod for a purple rod (one for four).

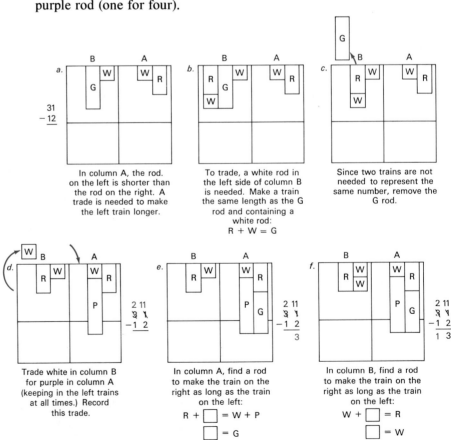

a.
$$31$$
$$-12$$

In column A, the rod on the left is shorter than the rod on the right. A trade is needed to make the left train longer.

b.

To trade, a white rod in the left side of column B is needed. Make a train the same length as the G rod and containing a white rod:
$$R + W = G$$

c.

Since two trains are not needed to represent the same number, remove the G rod.

d.

$$\begin{array}{c} 2\ 11 \\ \cancel{3}\ \cancel{1} \\ -1\ 2 \end{array}$$

Trade white in column B for purple in column A (keeping in the left trains at all times.) Record this trade.

e.

$$\begin{array}{c} 2\ 11 \\ \cancel{3}\ \cancel{1} \\ -1\ 2 \\ \hline \ 3 \end{array}$$

In column A, find a rod to make the train on the right as long as the train on the left:
$$R + \Box = W + P$$
$$\Box = G$$

f.

$$\begin{array}{c} 2\ 11 \\ \cancel{3}\ \cancel{1} \\ -1\ 2 \\ \hline 1\ 3 \end{array}$$

In column B, find a rod to make the train on the right as long as the train on the left:
$$W + \Box = R$$
$$\Box = W$$

Do these subtraction problems with a rod computer.[3]

	a.	b.	c.	d.	e.
	3 2	3 1 2	2 0 0	3 0 2 1	1 2 3 2 1
	−2 3	−2 2 2	−1 3 2	−2 1 1 3	−3 2 3 2

**2.3
ACTIVITY: THE
SUBTRACTION ALGORITHM FOR
BASE-TEN WHOLE NUMBERS**

Do only as many problems in each section as necessary to understand how subtraction with the base-ten embodiment works. As you do these activities, watch for advantages and disadvantages of each embodiment.

Overview: **The base-ten subtraction algorithm is done using base-ten blocks, the base-ten chip computer, and the base-ten rod computer.**

Materials Needed: For each group—a set of base-ten blocks and a calculating area. For each person—chips and a calculating area. (Optional: rods and a calculating area for each person.)

**2.3.1
Subtraction
with Base-Ten Blocks**

The subtraction process with base-ten blocks is done according to the same instructions as the process with base-four blocks. However, the blocks are a different size, and the trades with them are all ten for one (right to left) and one for ten (left to right). The trades are recorded as follows (illustrate this problem with your blocks):

a.	b.	c.	d.
	1 13	1 13	1 13
2 3	2̶ 3̶	2̶ 3̶	2̶ 3̶
− 8	− 8	− 8	− 8
		5	1 5

Try these subtraction problems. For each problem, ask both questions ("Plus how many more?" and "Minus?"). Be sure to do the problems with the blocks. The goal for this activity is to understand how the subtraction algorithm works, not just to get a bunch of answers to base-ten problems.[4]

	a.	b.	c.	d.	e.
	4 1 6	7 0 2	1 2 1 5	3 1 4 2	3 1 4 2
	−2 3 5	−5 8 9	−3 4 8	−1 3 5 4	−1 7 8 8

**2.3.2
Subtraction with
the Base-Ten Chip Computer**

Subtraction on the base-ten chip computer is done exactly as it is with the base-ten blocks. Reread the subtraction instructions if you need to. The trade rules for the base-ten chip computer are ten for one (right to left) and one for ten (left to right).

[3] a. 3, b. 30, c. 2, d. 302, e. 3023.

[4] a. 181, b. 113, c. 867, d. 1788, e. 1354.

As you do these subtraction problems, ask yourself both questions ("Plus how many more?" and "Minus?").[5]

	a.	**b.**	**c.**	**d.**
	8 2 4	7 0 0	7 4 3 1	2 3 7 4 2
	−6 5 3	−5 2 6	−2 9 5 2	−5 6 6 7

*2.3.3
Subtraction
with the Base-Ten
Rod Computer

Subtraction on the base-ten rod computer is done exactly as on the base-four rod computer except that all the trades are white for orange (one for ten, left to right) instead of white for purple. Review the base-four instructions in section 2.2.2 if necessary.

Use your base-ten rod computer to do these problems.[6]

	a.	**b.**	**c.**	**d.**
	4 8 6	8 0 3	5 4 2 7	4 5 0 2 5
	−2 1 9	−5 7 6	−3 6 7 3	−7 3 6 6

*2.3.4
Take-away
and Comparison Methods of
Using Embodiments for the
Subtraction Algorithm

1. In Part A, Unit 4, take-away and comparison sources of subtraction problems were discussed.

Take-away
I have 5 and lose 3.
a. ○ ○ ○   **b.** ○ ○
    ○ ○   ○ ○
How many do I have then?

Comparison
I have 3 and she has 5.
   ○ ○ ○
   ○ ○ ○ ○ ○
How many more does she have?

Take-away and comparison suggest two different ways to do the subtraction algorithm with embodiments. Use chips and a calculating sheet to see if you can figure out a take-away and a comparison way to do subtraction of large numbers. Each method has advantages and disadvantages. List some of these. (A description of each method follows in exercise 2. Check this description after you have figured out your method, if you wish.)

Describe advantages and disadvantages of these methods of doing the subtraction algorithm: take-away, comparison, three-numbers-

[5]   a. 171, b. 174, c. 4479, d. 18075.
[6]   a. 267, b. 227, c. 1754, d. 37,359.

represented "Minus?" and three-numbers-represented "Plus how many more?" Consider the ease of doing a problem, the closeness to symbolic notation, the representativeness of real life problems (look at 2.1.1), physical representations of all numbers involved, clearness of subtraction as an inverse operation to addition, and any other criteria you consider important.

2. Three methods of doing the subtraction algorithm are described below.

a. Take-Away Method

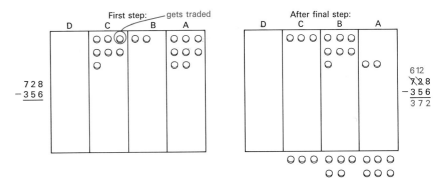

Place only pieces for the larger number on the calculating sheet. Beginning on the right, remove the pieces specified by the smaller number, one column at a time. It may be necessary to trade pieces on the sheet in order to get enough pieces to remove. Record the number of pieces remaining in a column after pieces in that column have been removed.

b. Comparison Method

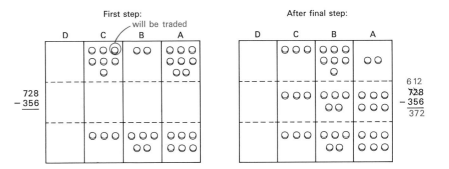

Put pieces for the first (larger) number in the top row of the calculating sheet.

Put pieces for the second number in the bottom row.

Beginning in column A, *use pieces from the top row* to make in the second row a set containing the same number of pieces as are in the bottom row. You may need to trade to get enough pieces in the top row (all trades involve pieces in the top row only).

Record the number of pieces remaining in the top row after you have made the set in the second row and record the trade, if there was one.

Continue the previous step for each column, moving to the left.

In this method you simply partition the larger number into two parts: one equal to the subtracted number and one equal to the answer.

c. Three-Numbers-Represented Method

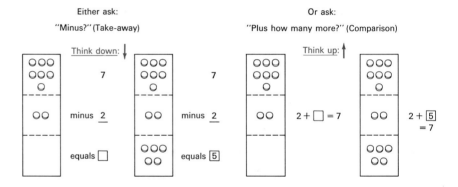

In the method used in the activities in sections 2.2 and 2.3, all three numbers were represented by the embodiments. The sum was in the top row, the given addend was in the second row, and the unknown addend or difference was in the bottom row. When filling in the bottom row, either of two questions could be asked: "Plus how many more?" or "Minus?" "Plus how many more?" is really a *comparison* question, and "Minus?" is really a *take-away* question. That is, in using this method you may adopt a take-away approach or a comparison approach to find the third set.

2.4

**PROBLEM SET:
ANALYSIS OF THE
SUBTRACTION ALGORITHM**

You have had experiences with embodiments for the subtraction algorithm in two bases. Because you are more familiar with base ten and because that is the base you will be teaching to children, all the analysis of the subtraction algorithm will be in base ten.

Overview: The following problems deal with various aspects of the subtraction algorithm. Alternative approaches, both with materials and with symbols, the inverse relationship of addition and subtraction, and difficulties of trading are covered.

2.4.1 Trading (or "borrowing") is a difficult aspect of subtraction. It occurs when a digit in the sum is smaller than the corresponding digit in the number being subtracted (the known addend). In this case it is necessary to "get more" for the digit in the sum. With the symbols it may not be clear from where the "more" should come. With embodiments, particularly those with pieces of different size for different places, it seems natural to trade a larger piece to get more smaller ones.

Once the idea of trading is well established, the problem of how to record the trade arises. It may be easier to do the recording first in a layout that is strongly linked to the embodiments, such as:

Hundreds	Tens	Ones		Thousands	Hundreds	Tens	Ones
4	12			5	10	3	11
5	2	6		6	0	4	1
1	8	3		2	3	1	5
3	4	3		3	7	2	6

With such a recording layout, "12 what?" is not a problem. It is clear that it is 12 ones, or 12 tens, or 12 hundreds, or whatever. Depending on the embodiment being used, you might also (or instead) want to label the columns "Cubes," "Flats," "Longs," "Units" for blocks, or use some other helpful labels.

Elementary school books do a great deal with "expanded notation." This means writing out the place names in words:

548 is 5 hundreds, 4 tens, 8 ones
2,067 is 2 thousands, no hundreds, 6 tens, 7 ones

The column layout above is easier for children to write, is closer to the way the symbolic algorithm works, and is probably as clear as writing out the expanded notation. When the meaning of the symbols is clear, the children can move to the standard symbolic form of the algorithm.

At least initially, it is probably clearer if the old number involved in the trade is crossed completely out, and the new value written on top:

$$
\begin{array}{r}
5\ 13 \\
\cancel{6}\ \cancel{3} \\
-1\ \ 6 \\
\end{array}
$$

It actually is a fortunate accident that in our number system, trading to the right can be recorded by putting a 1 to the left of a number: i.e., that 5 7 means 4 (17). This is a result of the trade rules for our system: a piece in a column to the left is worth 10 pieces in the column to its right.

The same symbolic process works in base four or in any other base. For example, in base four:

$$
\begin{array}{rl}
31 & \text{We trade one long} \\
-12 & \text{for four units:}
\end{array}
\qquad
\begin{array}{c}
2\ 11 \leftarrow \\
\cancel{3}\ \cancel{1} \\
-1\ \ 2
\end{array}
\qquad
\begin{array}{l}
10 + 1 = 11 \\
\underbrace{} \\
\text{one} \\
\text{long}
\end{array}
$$

If children do not understand that one piece in a column is being traded for ten (10) pieces in the column to the right, many different kinds of mistakes can result. For each problem below, tell the error the student made and what experiences you might provide to help him to avoid the error in the future.

Example:

$$
\textbf{a.}\quad
\begin{array}{r}
1 \\
6\ 2 \\
-3\ 5 \\
\hline
3\ 7
\end{array}
\qquad
\textbf{b.}\quad
\begin{array}{r}
4\ 17 \\
\cancel{5}\ \cancel{7}4 \\
-2\ \ 3\ 1 \\
\hline
2\ \ 4\ 3
\end{array}
\qquad
\textbf{c.}\quad
\begin{array}{r}
4 \\
\cancel{5}1\ 1 \\
\cancel{6}0\ 2 \\
-3\ 4\ 7 \\
\hline
1\ 6\ 5
\end{array}
\qquad
\textbf{d.}\quad
\begin{array}{r}
4\ 1\ 2\ 9 \\
-1\ 3\ 6\ 7 \\
\hline
3\ 4\ 8\ 2
\end{array}
\qquad
\textbf{e.}\quad
\begin{array}{r}
4\ 1\ 2\ 9 \\
-1\ 3\ 6\ 7 \\
\hline
3\ 2\ 4\ 2
\end{array}
$$

2.4.2 Addition and subtraction are inverse operations. That is,

$$x \text{ (add } y \text{ then subtract } y) = x$$
$$5 \text{ (add 3 then subtract 3)} = 5$$
$$5 + 3 - 3 = 5$$
$$32 \text{ (subtract 17 then add 17)} = 32$$
$$32 - 17 + 17 = 32$$

Another way of saying this is that subtraction "undoes" addition and addition "undoes" subtraction. This is an important and useful relationship. It has many implications, including:

a. Subtraction reflexes are related to addition reflexes. If this relationship is exploited, children can use their addition reflexes to help build their subtraction reflexes.

Reinterpret $12 - 7 = \boxed{}$ as $7 + \boxed{} = 12$

and $\qquad 14 - 8 = \boxed{}$ as $8 + \boxed{} = 14$

The relationship between addition and subtraction greatly reduces the number of reflexes that must be built.

b. A table of addition facts can be used for subtraction. To find the difference between two numbers (for example, $11 - 2$) by using a base-four addition table like the one given here, find the row containing the smaller number (2). Look in that row for the larger number (11) and follow up the column containing the larger number to find the difference (3). (Note the arrows on the table.) The table uses the following relationship: if $2 + \square = 11$, then $11 - 2 = \square$. Work the following base-four subtraction problems using the addition table. Record any necessary trades.[8]

+	0	1	2	3
0	0	1	2	3
1	1	2	3	10
2	2	3	10	11
3	3	10	11	12

(1) 1 2
  − 3

(2) 1 0
  − 2

(3) 3 1
 −1 2

(4) 1 3 2
 −1 2 3

(5) 1 0 2
  − 2 1

(6) 1 0 2
  − 2 3

+	0	1	2	3	4	5	6	7	8	9
0	0	1	2	3	4	5	6	7	8	9
1	1	2	3	4	5	6	7	8	9	10
2	2	3	4	5	6	7	8	9	10	11
3	3	4	5	6	7	8	9	10	11	12
4	4	5	6	7	8	9	10	11	12	13
5	5	6	7	8	9	10	11	12	13	14
6	6	7	8	9	10	11	12	13	14	15
7	7	8	9	10	11	12	13	14	15	16
8	8	9	10	11	12	13	14	15	16	17
9	9	10	11	12	13	14	15	16	17	18

[8] (1) 3, (2) 2, (3) 13, (4) 3, (5) 21, (6) 13.

Now try some base-ten problems using the base-ten addition table.

(7)	4 3	(8)	1 2 6	(9)	4 0 6 3
	−1 8		− 4 2		−2 3 1 7

c. Addition can be used to check a subtraction calculation and subtraction can be used to check an addition calculation. Do and then check each of the following (base-ten) problems using the inverse relationship of addition and subtraction.

$$
\begin{array}{cc}
3498 & 7408 \\
+5821 & -4239 \\
\hline
\end{array}
$$

*d. Which methods of subtraction (take-away; comparison; three-numbers-represented: "Plus how many more?"; three-numbers-represented: "Minus?") show the inverse relationship of addition and subtraction clearly?

e. Suppose one of your students said, "I just figured out a new way to subtract. Watch me subtract 315 from 479."

Step 1	Step 2	Step 3	Step 4	
	4	64	164	**Answer:**
315	315	315	315	315 from 479 is 164.
479	479	479	479	

Can you figure out what she did?[9]

You would want to help the student extend his invention as far as possible. You might say "Your method works when no trading is necessary. I wonder if it will work when you have to make trades. Why don't you try 925 − 647?" Extend the student's method to this problem.

$$
\begin{array}{c}
647 \\
\hline
925
\end{array}
$$

What are the advantages of this method? (What does it show about the relationship between addition and subtraction? If you were not already used to the method with the largest number on the top, would this method be any more difficult to learn?)

[9] Hint: The subtraction problem is in an addition layout.

2.4.3 Subtraction problems with trading are more difficult for two major reasons. First, a student may have difficulty with the trading (see section 2.4.1). Second, problems with trading require reflexes for numbers greater than 10 (for example, $16 - 9$, $12 - 7$). Reflexes for these larger numbers are generally more difficult to acquire than those for smaller numbers.

a. If a student's addition reflexes are good, he may use them for finding the subtraction answers. But if addition reflexes are weak, a method similar to that used in section 1.4.10 can be used for subtraction: a number is broken up into a ten part and the remainder.

$$7 + \square = 12 \text{ becomes } \underbrace{7 + \triangle}_{10} + 2 = 12 \qquad \triangle = 3$$
$$\square = 3 + 2 = 5$$

"Minus" mode:
$$12 - 7 = 2 + (10 - 7) = 2 + 3 = 5$$

$$8 + \square = 15 \text{ becomes } \underbrace{8 + \triangle}_{10} + 5 = 15 \qquad \triangle = 2$$
$$\square = 2 + 5 = 7$$

Minus mode:
$$15 - 8 = 5 + (10 - 8) = 5 + 2 = 7$$

b. You may want to try the above examples with colored rods. Try doing these subtraction reflexes using both the plus and the minus modes.

(1) $17 - 9$
(2) $13 - 5$
(3) $14 - 6$
(4) $16 - 7$
(5) $12 - 7$

c. In mechanical calculators the trading is done automatically. If the gears are turned counterclockwise instead of clockwise, whenever one gear hits 0 and needs to continue (that is, it needs to have more there from which to subtract), pushing the gear past 0 to 9 will move the gear in the column to the left back one space.

If you have a transparent Dialamatic (see Appendix I for the address of SEE, the distributor), try these problems and watch what happens when trading is necessary to get a larger number on the top.

(1) 34	**(2)** 257	**(3)** 704	**(4)** 5002	**(5)** 4112
−18	− 79	−326	−2678	−2345

2.4.4 The embodiments and problems in this unit are all aimed at increasing the understanding of the mathematical model "subtraction of large whole numbers." But if the student does not know *when* and *how to use* the mathematical model (for example, 275 − 149), the understanding of the model itself is useless. Links between a real situation and the mathematical model need to be pointed out by the teacher, and children need to practice translating real situations into the mathematical models describing those situations. This process can become a game: "That's a subtraction situation! And the mathematical model for it is 35 − 17."

For this to happen, a teacher must become sensitive to the many subtraction situations present in the classroom. Complete *a* and *b* and share your answers with your colleagues.

a. Describe four subtraction situations that might arise in a classroom, *not* during the mathematics work. (Include at least one take-away and one comparison situation.)

b. Describe four activities or projects for middle-grade children that require subtraction of at least three-place whole numbers. (The project might be in a subject area other than mathematics.)

2.4.5 Work on a calculating sheet with columns labeled D, C, B, A (D on the left). Use one of the embodiments of base ten to do the following:

a. Put 8473 − 4251 on the calculating sheet.

Answer:

Subtract the C's, then the A's, then the D's, then the B's: _____

Subtract the B's, then the C's, then the D's, then the A's: _____

Subtract the D's, then the B's, then the A's, then the C's: _____

Did you get the same difference each time? _____

b. Try a problem with trades: 6235 − 4476.

Subtract the C's, then the A's, then the D's, then the B's: _____
Subtract the B's, then the C's, then the D's, then the A's: _____
Subtract the D's, then the B's, then the A's, then the C's: _____
Did you get the same difference each time? _____
What difficulties did you encounter in doing the problem in different ways?

2.4.6 A subtraction algorithm that was widely taught in the United States years ago increased the bottom number instead of decreasing the top number whenever a trade was made. This increase was usually done mentally.

Why does this algorithm work?

Examplc 1:   72   Think: "I made the 2 a 12; 12 minus $8 = 4$."
            -58 Think: "I had to make 2 a 12, and so I need
             14   to increase the 5 to a 6; $7 - 6 = 1$."

Example 2:   837   Think: "I had to increase the 3 to a 13, and so
            -564 I must increase the 5 to a 6; $8 - 6 = 2$."
             273

Do you think it is easier or more difficult than our usual algorithm? Explain why.

2.4.7 Get out the Hassler Whitney computer you used in addition (section 1.4, exercise 12). As usual, subtraction can be done in at least two ways: by a take-away mode and a comparison mode. Each of these modes on the Hassler-Whitney computer uses a different mathematical property to make the computer work. Both involve equivalence classes of names for a given number. As you do the problems below, try to figure out what equivalence classes are being used. In subtraction, you need markers of two different colors. For uniformity, we will use bronze markers (pennies) for the larger number and silver (nickles, dimes) for the smaller number. You will be asked to do subtraction of three- and four-place numbers eventually, but the initial examples will be in a single column.

Take-away mode

For $8 - 5$, put a bronze marker on 8 and a silver marker on 5. How can you move the markers (without changing the problem) so that the 5 marker is taken off the sheet and the 8 marker ends on 3? (Remember that you can only take markers off 0 and put markers on 0; any other moves change the problem)[10]

Now try $12 - 5$. Put bronze markers on the 10 and on the 2 in the tens column and put a silver marker on the 5. How can you legally remove the marker for 5?[11]

Now try $61 - 45$. Put bronze markers on 61 and silver markers on 45. You need a larger bronze marker in the Ones column to make the silver marker disappear. The only way to get a large bronze marker is to get a marker on 10. To do that, you need a bronze marker on the 10 in the Tens column. How can you get it there?[12] Now finish the problem.[13]

Work these subtraction problems in the take-away mode. The goal is to *take off* the silver (second-number) markers.

a.	518	b.	427	c.	1534	d.	6027	e.	5000
	-309		-153		-1265		-4553		-2974

[10] $8 - 5 = 7 - 4 = 6 - 3 = 5 - 2 = 4 - 1 = 3 - 0$. That is, move the markers in the same direction until the silver marker reaches 0. It may then be removed. The bronze marker is then on 3. (The above list is just some of the members of the equivalence class for 3; i.e., they are different names for 3.)

[11] Move the $5 - 2$ to $4 - 1$ to $3 - 0$. Remove the marker from 0. Now move the bronze marker from the 10 in the Tens column to the 10 in the Ones column. Move the $10 - 3$ to $9 - 2$ to $8 - 1$ to $7 - 0$. Remove the marker from 0. The answer is then 7. (This involved the following members of the equivalence class for 7: $12 - 5$, $11 - 4$, $10 - 3$, $9 - 2$, $8 - 1$, $7 - 0$.)

[12] Put a bronze marker on the 0 in the Tens column. Then $60 + 0 = 50 + 10$ (bronze markers on 50 and 10).

[13] Do the Ones column first (it doesn't matter which you do, but this is closer to the way we do the subtraction algorithm). Move from $5 - 1$ to $4 - 0$. Remove the bronze marker from 0. You now still need to get the silver marker off. Move the bronze marker from 10 in the Tens column to 10 in the Ones column. Now move $10 - 4$ to $9 - 3$ to $8 - 2$ to $7 - 1$ to $6 - 0$. Remove the silver marker from 0. The answer is 6. Now in the Tens column move from $50 - 40$ to $40 - 30$ to $30 - 20$ to $20 - 10$ to $10 - 0$. Remove the silver marker from 0. The answer is 10. The total answer is $10 + 6 = 16$.

Comparison Mode

As in all comparison modes, the goal is to partition the first number into two sets, one of which is the second set and the other of which is the difference set. Put a bronze on 8 and a silver on 5. *Do not* move the 5 marker. The goal is to move (legally—you may only add markers on 0) the bronze marker on 8 so that you get two bronze markers: a marker on 5 and a marker on the difference between 8 and 5 (the answer). How can you get another marker the same color as the 8 marker?[14] (What is the only legal way to add in new markers?)

How will you then move these markers to get a bronze marker on 5?[15] You should get one marker on 5 and one marker on 3.

Try $12 - 7$ by the comparison mode: (Try to get bronze markers on 7 and on another square; that square will be the answer.)[16]

Now try $61 - 45$ using the comparison mode.[17] (You will have to trade a 10 in the Tens column for a 10 in the Ones column to get two bronze markers to move toward each other.) Do *not* move the markers on 45; they simply mark your goal.

Try these subtraction problems using the comparison mode. For takeaway you tried to move the silver markers off the sheet, leaving only

---

[14] Add a bronze marker on 0.

[15] Toward one another: $8 + 0 \rightarrow 7 + 1 \rightarrow 6 + 2 \rightarrow 5 + 3$. You now have partitioned 8 into 5 and 3. The difference between 8 and 5 is 3.

[16] You need a bronze marker to move toward the 2. Trade the 10 in the Tens column for the 10 in the Ones column. Move the 10 and the 2 toward each other: $10 + 2 \rightarrow 9 + 3 \rightarrow 8 + 4 \rightarrow 7 + 5$. You now have partitioned 12 into 7 and 5. The difference between 12 and 7 is 5.

[17] Assume 61 is bronze and 45 is silver. Put a bronze on 0 in the Tens column to get a marker to move toward the silver 40. Move: $60 + 0 \rightarrow 50 + 10 \rightarrow 40 + 20$. Stop since you have a marker on 40, your goal. Now you need another bronze marker in the ones column. A 0 will not help, since you need always to "pinch" the silver between two bronzes. So you need a 10. To get a 10 in the Tens column, put a bronze on the 0 in the Tens column, and move the 20 and the 0 toward each other: $20 + 0 \rightarrow 10 + 10$ (you do not want to move the 40; that is why you move the 20). Trade one 10 in the Tens column for a 10 in the Ones column. Now move the bronze 10 and 1 toward each other; $10 + 1 \rightarrow 9 + 2 \rightarrow 8 + 3 \rightarrow 7 + 4 \rightarrow 6 + 5$. Stop, since you have reached your goal—a bronze marker on 5. You have now partitioned 61 into two sets: 45 and 16. The difference between 61 and 45 is 16.

bronze markers. For the comparison mode, you do not move the silver markers. You move bronze markers (adding in extras on the 0, if necessary) until you have a bronze marker on every silver marker.

f. 456	**g.** 739	**h.** 3451	**i.** 8402	**j.** 5000
-128	-572	-1287	-5715	-2026

Notice that the solution (given in the footnote) for $61 - 45$ started from the left and moved right. Does it matter which column you do first on this computer? That is, will you always get the right answer no matter what order you do the columns in? Is it as convenient to do them in any order?

What kinds of members from the equivalence classes for numbers did you use for the take-away approach?[18] (Give an example.)

What kinds of members from an equivalence class for a number did you use for comparison?[19] (Give an example.)

This agrees with the earlier analysis of take-away as a "minus?" kind of subtraction and comparison as a "Plus how many more?" kind of subtraction.

2.5
PEDAGOGICAL REMARKS

The addition and the subtraction algorithms for whole numbers are very closely related. In addition, there is "too much" to record in a given column, and you must trade to the left to get rid of the excess. In subtraction, you sometimes do "not have enough" in a given column, and must trade to the right to get more. However, the embodiments used, the symbols used, and the concepts involved in these algorithms are the same. Thus many of the points made in the pedagogical remarks about addition are relevant here. Rather than repeat these points, we will discuss a few with their special relevance to subtraction. You might reread section 1.5 with the subtraction algorithm in mind.

---

[18] Pairs of numbers being subtracted; for example, 5: $10 - 5 = 9 - 4 = 8 - 3 = 7 - 2 = 6 - 1 = 5 - 0$.

[19] Pairs of numbers being added; for example, 8: $8 + 0 = 7 + 1 = 6 + 2 = 5 + 3$.

The length embodiment described for addition in section 1.5 can be equally helpful in bringing students to see a place-value arrangement for subtraction. This embodiment is:

D	C	B	A
thousand:	**hundred:**	**ten:**	**unit:**
A piece of string ten meters long	A meter stick (or any stick one meter long)	An orange rod	A white rod

Numbers are represented by "trains"; each train consists of a row of touching pieces ordered from large (left) to small (right).

To subtract two numbers, a train for the second number is placed adjacent to the train for the first number, with both trains either starting or ending at the same place. The "difference" train is the train that will make the second train as long as the first train.

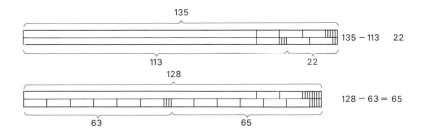

As in addition, the process of making trains eventually becomes tedious. Children see that for the problem $478 - 321$ they need 1 meter stick, 5 orange rods, and 7 white rods. They then begin to make piles of string, piles of meter sticks, piles of orange rods, and piles of white rods. Subtraction is then done by any of the three methods (take-away, comparison, or three-numbers-represented), using piles of similar pieces as blocks and chips were used. Trades arise in some cases, but they are now done from pile to pile (1 orange for ten whites, etc.) instead of within a train.

The notion of trading (or "borrowing"; can you think of a better name for it?) is essential for subtraction. As with addition, the embodiments that get larger for larger places illustrate trading quite well. Later use of more abstract embodiments such as the chip computer, which have the same size piece in each place, can indicate that the subtraction algorithm does work in the same way for each place and that the algorithm continues in the same manner for all new places.

The various methods of the subtraction algorithm discussed in section 2.3.4 (take-away, comparison, and three-numbers-represented-"plus how many more?" and three-numbers-represented—"minus?") have relative advantages and disadvantages. The take-away method involves the fewest pieces and is more intuitively obvious to some people. The comparison method illustrates the links between subtraction and addition clearly. The method with all three numbers represented (the one used in sections 2.2 and 2.3) is the closest to the symbolic algorithm. The needs of a particular group of students should dictate which of the methods to use. Probably the three-numbers-represented methods should be used by everyone at some time because it parallels the symbolic algorithm so closely.

The addition and subtraction algorithms will benefit by being done one immediately after the other. Many of the concepts involved in the algorithms are similar—the relative size of each base-ten place, trading (though addition and subtraction require trades in the opposite directions), the repetitive nature of the processes, and the embodiments used for the algorithms. The reflexes necessary for the symbolic algorithms are closely related, and practice and experience with addition reflexes will carry over into subtraction reflexes and vice versa. Checking problems by using the inverse operation (subtraction for addition, and addition for subtraction) is one way to practice reflexes while stressing the links between addition and subtraction.

Children need practice in analyzing real situations in order to decide what mathematical model is suitable. Teachers and students can point out or create take-away and comparison subtraction situations involving large whole numbers. These frequently involve situations that occur outside the mathematics area.

Estimation skills are also important. Such questions as "Will this check overdraw my account?" and "Do I have enough money to buy this steak in addition to my other groceries?" are usually answered by estimation, not by exact computation. Estimation can also allow the discovery of the "silly" mistakes that are so often made in computation.

Estimation skills can be improved in at least two ways. Estimation requires you to stop for a moment before plunging into the computation process, and to consider the approximate size of the numbers involved. A standard procedure of having students estimate the answer before doing any problem would serve the double purpose of beginning to inculcate this useful habit and providing practice in estimating.

unit 3
the algorithm for multiplication of whole numbers

As with addition and subtraction, activities will first be done in a base other than ten. The rationale for using non-ten bases in this text is in Part B, section 1.1.4; read that if you have not yet read it. Base eight was chosen here because it is a large enough base to have many multiplication combinations, as does base ten, and because it is a base that is often used in computer languages. You are not expected to know multiplication combinations in base eight. Activities are presented in a base other than ten primarily so that your knowledge will not get in the way of a reexamination of the multiplication algorithm. Work in a base where you have few reflexes may also enable you to appreciate difficulties students may have.

Activities with materials in base ten will follow those in base eight. Analysis of multiplication algorithms will be done in base ten.

The basis of multiplication processes with large numbers is a set of shift rules. These rules tell how to multiply by 1, by 10, by 100, by 1000, and by larger powers of the base. From this basic set of rules, any multiplication algorithm may be developed. Because these shift rules are so important, four different ways to arrive at them are given. Each has advantages and differing appeal.

251

Three different multiplication algorithms will be described: the copy algorithm, the intermediate place-value algorithm, and the compact place-value algorithm. The copy algorithm uses only the shift rules and addition; it is a good introduction to the idea of multiplication of large whole numbers. Both place-value algorithms require the shift rules, multiplication, and addition. The compact place-value algorithm is the usual "long multiplication" taught in schools.

The development of these ideas is not difficult, but it does take many short, focused activities. If the activities are completed by individuals or groups working from work sheets, the project tends to become long and drawn-out. If the activities are led by the teacher and performed by everyone at once, they advance more briskly and coherently.

Thus, the activities in sections 3.2, 3.3, 3.4, and 3.5 are a summary written by a student of results of work completed in one classroom. They are intended to be read as a review of the activities done in your class.

Teachers have reported that these activities are interesting and helpful in aiding them to understand the multiplication algorithm. You may not have time to do all of them in class. Therefore, each section ends with practice problems. These may be done either if you feel you need a bit of additional practice or if that section was not covered in class and you wish to check your understanding after reading it.

Materials used in this unit are chips and base-eight multiplication pieces (see Appendix I). Base-ten multiplication pieces are optional.

3.1.1 Uses of Multiplication

For each problem below, give a mathematical model for finding the solution. Find the solution if you wish.

1. Striking San Francisco workers (March, 1974) average about $850 a month. What is their average yearly salary?
Mathematical model:

2. If California highway patrolmen spent 5,900 hours waiting in gas lines during February, 1974, at a cost of about $11 per hour, how much altogether did this cost the state?
Mathematical model:

3. If there were 3,141,000 births in the United States in 1973 and if each baby uses an average of 45 diapers a week, how many diapers were changed by the time these babies were one year old? How many diapers were changed by the parents of just one of these children?
Mathematical models:

4. The largest brick company in the world, the London Brick Company, produces 17 million bricks and equivalents every week. How many does it produce in a year?
Mathematical model:

5. Between 1962 and 1970 John Lennon and Paul McCartney together wrote 30 songs which sold more than 1 million single records each. If each record sold for 89¢ and sold exactly 1 million copies, what was the total dollar amount of sales for these Lennon-McCartney songs?
Mathematical model:

6. If tolls on the Illinois state tollways were $8,849,000 for the first two months of 1974, what would you estimate the total for the year to be? (What factors did you use in your estimate?)
Mathematical model:

7. Cut out three newspaper articles that involve multiplication of large whole numbers. Share your clippings with your colleagues.

3.2
ACTIVITY:
DEVELOPMENT OF THE SHIFT
RULES WITH BASE-EIGHT
MULTIPLICATION PIECES

Overview: **Rules for multiplying a number by 1, 10, and 100 will be developed from activities with base-eight multiplication pieces first by multiplying a number as a whole entity and then by multiplying a number place by place.**

Materials needed: For each group—a set of base-eight multiplication pieces. (See Appendix I for instructions about making them.)

These notes were written by class observers as in Part A, Unit 4; you may wish to reread the explanation in section 4.1.

3.2.1
How the
Multiplication
Pieces Work

1. We decided on the following names for the pieces:

Huge   Fat long   Thin long   Square   Long   Unit

2. By putting together small pieces to make the next larger piece, we found the trade rules to be:

Eight units = one long
Eight longs = one thin long or one square
Eight thin longs or eight squares = one fat long
Eight fat longs = one huge

3. We decided that each piece would be symbolized as follows:

Huge	Fat long	Thin long and square	Long	Unit
10000	1000	100	10	1
(one-oh-oh-oh-oh)	(one-oh-oh-oh)	(one-oh-oh)	(one-oh)	(one)

We were a bit puzzled about having two different pieces (the square and the thin long) the same size (each is equivalent to eight longs). The reason for having them both is given in note 5.

4. To symbolize a collection of pieces, just count the number of pieces of each size and record that number in the correct place. Sometimes a trade must be made before a collection can be recorded (symbolized). Because this is base eight, only the symbols 0, 1, 2, 3, 4, 5, 6, and 7 can be used. For example:

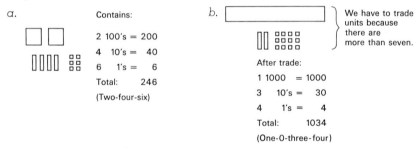

a.

Contains:

2 100's = 200
4 10's = 40
6 1's =   6

Total: 246

(Two-four-six)

b.

We have to trade units because there are more than seven.

After trade:

1 1000 = 1000
3   10's =   30
4   1's =   4

Total: 1034

(One-0-three-four)

5. To multiply with the multiplication pieces, you make rectangles. The *factors* are the lengths of adjacent sides of the rectangle, and the *product* is all the pieces making the rectangle. To be sure that the pieces showing the lengths of the sides of the rectangle are not counted in as part of the rectangle, pieces of a different color are used for the sides (blue will be used in these notes).

Because the sides are embodied by lengths, they can have a width of only one unit. This is the reason for having two different shapes for 100 pieces. The *thin long* 100 piece must be used when 100 is in a *factor*. Both the thin long and the square 100 pieces are used in the product.

The multiplication pieces are closest to the symbolic algorithms when they are laid out in the following pattern:

Horizontal train: largest on left, smallest on right

Vertical train:
smallest at top, largest at bottom

(Fill in pieces in all this space to make the product of these two trains.)

For the sake of consistency, we agreed that the horizontal train is the number being multiplied (the top or second number) and the vertical train is the multiplier (the bottom or first number). The problem laid out above is symbolized as:

Yes: No:

$$35 \times 142 \qquad \text{or} \qquad \begin{array}{r} 142 \\ \times\ 35 \\ \hline \end{array}$$

The upper-left-hand corners touch at only one point. If the pieces were flush, one side would be one unit too short.

6. Other observations from your class session:

Practice Problems[1]:

Symbolize each of these collections (you may need to trade):

a.   b.   c.

Write how you would read each of the following:

d. 472   **e.** 32006   **f.** 3207

[1] a. 2142, b. 1140, c. 10106, d. Four-seven-two, e. Three-two-oh-oh-six, f. Three-two-oh-seven.

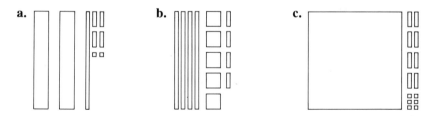

g.   h.   or   i.

(or 4 thin longs)

j.   k.

Draw a collection of pieces for each of the following:

g. 53 **h.** 102 **i.** 2407

Draw a horizontal train for each of these multiplied numbers.

j. 41 **k.** 235 (remember to use the thin longs)

3.2.2
**Shift Rules:
Total Approach with the
Multiplication Pieces**

1. Multiplying a number *by 1* just makes a *single copy* of the number:

2. Multiplying a number by 10 (one-oh) means using a Long as the vertical train. Recording the results of each problem symbolically helped Us to see that the *result* in each case of multiplying a number *by 10* (one-oh) was to *shift* the number over one place to the *left* (and consequently a zero was needed on the right).

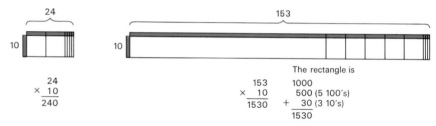

$$\begin{array}{r} 24 \\ \times\ 10 \\ \hline 240 \end{array}$$

$$\begin{array}{r} 153 \\ \times\ 10 \\ \hline 1530 \end{array}$$

The rectangle is

$$\begin{array}{r} 1000 \\ 500 \ (5\ 100\text{'s}) \\ +\quad 30 \ (3\ 10\text{'s}) \\ \hline 1530 \end{array}$$

3. Multiplying a number by 100 (one-oh-oh) means using a Thin Long as the vertical train. Again, recording the results symbolically led Us to agree that multiplying a number *by 100* just *shifts* the number *two places* to the *left*.

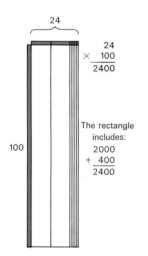

$$\begin{array}{r} 24 \\ \times\ 100 \\ \hline 2400 \end{array}$$

The rectangle includes:

$$\begin{array}{r} 2000 \\ +\ 400 \\ \hline 2400 \end{array}$$

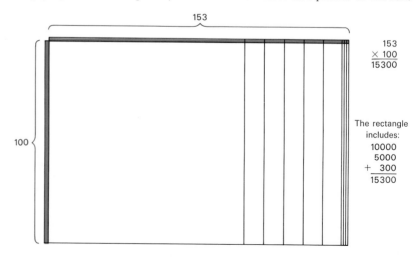

$$\begin{array}{r} 153 \\ \times\ 100 \\ \hline 15300 \end{array}$$

The rectangle includes:

$$\begin{array}{r} 10000 \\ 5000 \\ +\quad 300 \\ \hline 15300 \end{array}$$

4. If we were going to multiply by 1000 using the pieces, a piece one unit wide and eight times as long as the thin long would be needed. We guessed that the effect of multiplying a number by 1000 would be to shift it three places to the left. We could check this guess when We used the chip computer.

5. Other observations from your class session:

Practice Problems[2]:

Draw a sketch (graph paper with tiny squares is helpful) for each problem below, and then record the results symbolically.

a.	246	**b.**	37	**c.**	205	**d.**	136
	× 1		×10		×100		×100

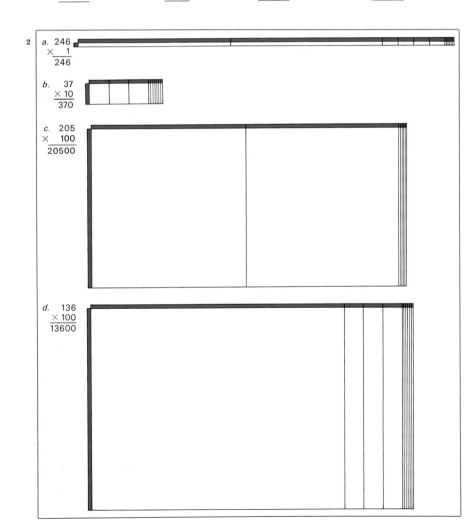

2 | a. 246
   ×   1
   246

b.   37
  × 10
   370

c. 205
× 100
 20500

d. 136
 × 100
 13600

3.2.3

**Shift Rules:
Piece-by-Piece Approach with
the Multiplication Pieces**

1. Using the pieces, We decided that:

Unit × unit = unit	Unit × long = long	Unit × thin long = thin long
or: $1 \times 1 = 1$	$1 \times 10 = 10$	$1 \times 100 = 100$

Thus multiplying by 1 just copies a piece of each size. Because every number is made up of 1s, 10s, and 100s, multiplying any number by 1 must just make a copy of it.

126
× 1

2. Long × unit = long   Long × long = square   Long × thin long = fat long
   $10 \times 1 = 10$ $10 \times 10 = 100$ $10 \times 100 = 1000$

That is, multiplying by 10 makes each piece one size larger, or symbolically, moves the symbols for each piece one place to the left. Because each number is made up of 1, 10, and 100 pieces, the effect of multiplying by 10 is to make each piece in the number one size larger; or symbolically, the effect is to shift the number one place to the left.

3. Thin long × unit = thin long   Thin long × long = fat long
   $100 \times 1 = 100$ $100 \times 10 = 1000$

   Thin long × thin long = huge
   $100 \times 100 = 10000$

Multiplying a piece by 100 makes a piece two times as large. Symbolically this moves each piece two places to the left. As with the other multipliers, because each number is made up of 1, 10, and 100 pieces, multiplying by 100 makes each piece two sizes larger. Symbolically, this moves the digit in each place two places to the left.

4. Other observations from your class session:

Practice Problems[3]:
Draw sketches and give symbolic answers for these problems:
a. Long × long = _____   **b.** Long × thin long = _____

c. Thin long × long = _____   **d.** Thin long × thin long = _____

3.3
ACTIVITY:
DEVELOPMENT OF SHIFT
RULES WITH THE BASE-
EIGHT CHIP COMPUTER

Overview: **Shift rules for multiplying by 1, 10, 100, 1000, 10000, etc., will be developed on a base-eight chip computer. First, numbers will be multiplied as complete entities, and then they will be multiplied place by place.**

Materials needed: For each group or for each individual — chips and 2 to 4 sheets of paper.

3.3.1
How
the Base-Eight Chip
Computer Works

1. A calculating area with six or eight horizontal columns was needed. Two sheets can be used to make a calculating sheet for an individual, and four sheets for a large group calculating sheet. Some groups drew six columns on the back of the calculating sheets used for blocks in Part B, Units 1 and 2. The columns were labeled so that We could talk about them. We chose letters.

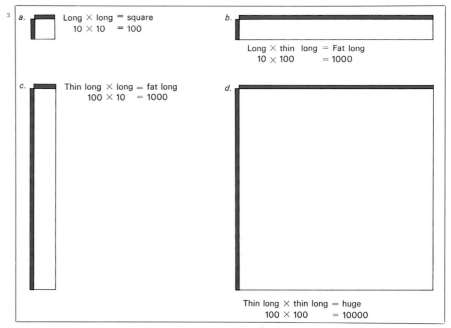

3

a. Long × long = square
    10 × 10 = 100

b. Long × thin long = Fat long
    10 × 100   = 1000

c. Thin long × long = fat long
    100 × 10 = 1000

d. Thin long × thin long = huge
    100 × 100   = 10000

17 or 22 inches

F	E	D	C	B	A

11 or 17 inches

2. We decided that, if this were a base-eight chip computer, the trade rules would all have to be eight for one (right to left) and one for eight (left to right). For example,

Eight chips in A = one chip in B.
Eight chips in B = one chip in C.
Eight chips in C = one chip in D.

3. Symbolizing is done as on a base-four or a base-ten chip computer: Count the number of pieces in each column, trade if necessary, and record the number in each place. Base eight uses symbols 0, 1, 2, 3, 4, 5, 6, and 7. Each place is symbolized as follows:

F	E	D	C	B	A
100000	10000	1000	100	10	1

142

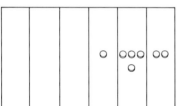

6275

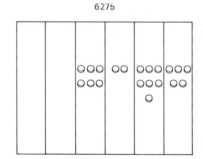

3025

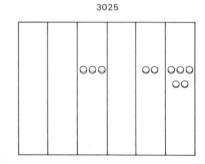

4. Other observations from your class session:

Practice Problems[4]:
Symbolize each of the following problems (you may need to trade):

a.

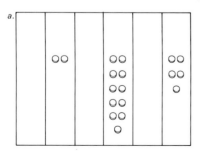

b.

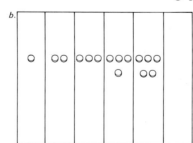

c.

[4] a. 21305, b. 123450, c. 1121142.

3.3.2
Shift Rules:
Total Approach on the
Base-Eight Chip Computer

1. One interpretation of multiplying is making copies:

   2×3 means make 2 copies of 3:

   5×4 means make 5 copies of 4:

   Therefore, multiplying by 1 just means making a single copy of a number.
   Multiplying by 10 means making 10 (one-oh) copies of a number. Because this is base eight, making 10 (one-oh) copies means making eight copies [one 10 (one-oh) chip trades for eight 1 chips]. To multiply a number by 10 (one-oh) on the chip computer, you make eight copies of that number, make any necessary trades, and record the results.

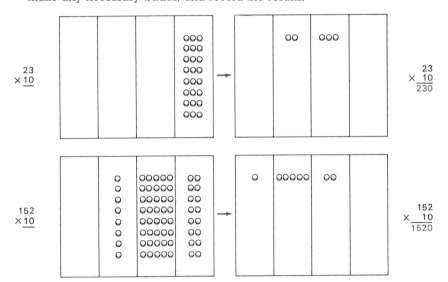

   Results: Multiplying a number by *10 shifts* the number one place to the *left.*

2. One 100 (one-oh-oh) chip = sixty-four 1 chips, but no one wanted to make sixty-four copies of anything. We decided that $100 = 10 \times 10$ (i.e., a 10 (one-oh) chip moved one place to the left is a 100 (one-oh-oh) chip). Therefore to multiply by 100, just multiply by 10 twice.

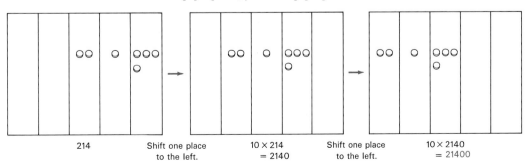

| 214 | Shift one place to the left. | 10×214 $= 2140$ | Shift one place to the left. | 10×2140 $= 21400$ |

Results: Multiplying a number by *100 shifts* the number *two* places to the left.

3. With the chip computer, multiplying by 1000 (one-oh-oh-oh) could be done. We decided that $1000 = 10 \times 10 \times 10$, because if we put a chip on 1, it would take three shifts one place to the left (or $10 \times 10 \times 10 \times 1$) to get the chip in the 1000 place. So multiplying by 1000 is the same as multiplying by 10 and then by 10 again and then by 10 again.

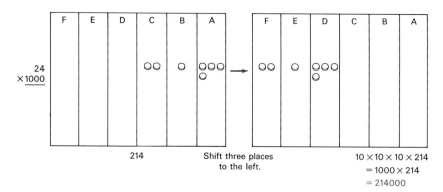

Results: Multiplying a number by *1000* has the effect of *shifting* the number *three places to the left.*

4. Similarly, We decided that $10000 = 10 \times 10 \times 10 \times 10$ because it would take four applications of the 10 shift rule to move a chip from the units place to the 10000 (one-oh-oh-oh-oh) place. Therefore multiplying by 10000 is the same as multiplying by 10 four times in succession.

Results: Multiplying a number by *10000* has the effect of *shifting* the number *four places to the left.*

5. This process could go on and on with the chip computer. We arrived at a general shift rule:

General shift rule for powers of 10: To multiply a number by 100 . . . 0 (where there are *n* 0s), shift the number *n* places to the left.

That general shift rule works because $100 \ldots 0 = \underbrace{10 \times 10 \times \ldots 10}_{n \text{ 10's}}$ and so the 10 shift rule is used *n* times.

6. Other observations from your class session:

Practice Problems[5]:
Do each of the following problems by making eight copies of the number
and then trading. Record your answers.

a. 52
  × 10
  ‾‾‾‾‾

b. 304
  × 10
  ‾‾‾‾‾

3.3.3
Shift Rules:
Place-by-Place
Approach on the Base-
Eight Chip Computer

1. Some people in the class could see that the shift rule for multiplying by 10
(one-oh) worked, but they didn't understand why it worked. It seemed more
mysterious on the chip computer. This was particularly true for people who
had made eight piles of 3, or 5, or whatever. Prof suggested that We look at
the trades in this way:

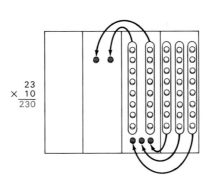
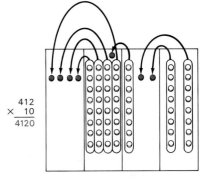

If you think of 10 (one-oh; in base eight this means eight) copies *of each
chip*, then it is easier to see that a number will always shift one place to the
left.

2. Similarly, making 100 (= 10 × 10) copies *of each chip* means moving each
chip one place to the left and then one place to the left again. That is, each
chip is moved two places to the left. Because this will happen to the chips
in each column, the whole number gets moved two places to the left.

3. Similarly for 1000 (= 10 × 10 × 10), 10000 (= 10 × 10 × 10 × 10), etc.: Making
that many copies of each chip means moving *each chip* to the left the
appropriate number of places. Thus the *whole number* moves to the left.

4. Other observations from your class session:

[5] **a.** 52
  × 10
  ‾‾‾‾‾
  520

 b. 304
  × 10
  ‾‾‾‾‾
  3040

3.4
ACTIVITY: THE
COPY MULTIPLICATION
ALGORITHM FOR BASE EIGHT

Overview: **The copy multiplication algorithm is done with the base-eight multiplication pieces, with the base-eight chip computer, and with a base-eight addition table.**

Materials needed: base-eight multiplication pieces, chips, calculating areas for the chip computer.

3.4.1
**The Copy
Multiplication Algorithm with
Base-Eight Multiplication Pieces**

1. Multiplying by 2, 3, 4, 5, 6, or 7 just means making that many single copies of a number.

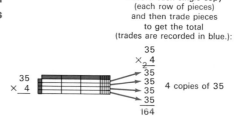

2. Multiplying by 20, 30, 40, 50, 60, or 70 just means making 2, 3, 4, 5, 6, or 7 size 10 (one-oh) copies of a number; that is, 2, 3, 4, 5, 6, or 7 copies of the number shifted one place to the left.

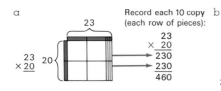

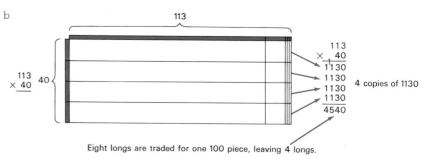

Eight longs are traded for one 100 piece, leaving 4 longs.

3. Similarly, multiplying by 200, 300, 400, 500, 600, or 700 just means making that many 100 copies of a number. That is, the number is shifted two places to the left and *x* copies are made of it.

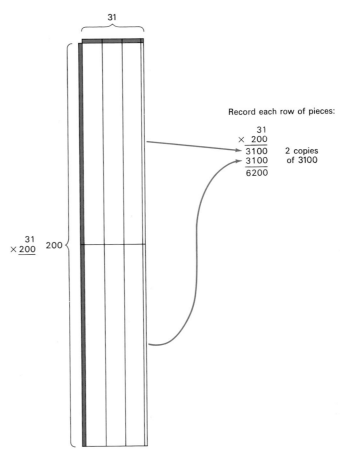

Record each row of pieces:

$$\begin{array}{r} 31 \\ \times\ 200 \\ \hline 3100 \\ 3100 \\ \hline 6200 \end{array}$$

2 copies
of 3100

$$\begin{array}{r} 31 \\ \times\ 200 \end{array}$$ 200

4. The number in each place tells how many copies, and the place (1, 10, 100) tells the size of copy to make. Together, these two pieces of information tell how to multiply by a number.

24×31 We estimated the answer would be 650.

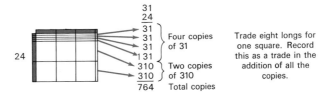

$$\begin{array}{r} 31 \\ 24 \\ \hline 31 \\ 31 \\ 31 \\ 31 \\ 310 \\ 310 \\ \hline 764 \end{array}$$

Four copies of 31

Two copies of 310

Total copies

Trade eight longs for one square. Record this as a trade in the addition of all the copies.

After such trades the rectangle is no longer a rectangle. But the rectangle is only needed originally to find the size of the product. Trading in order to symbolize the product doesn't change the value of the product.

142×123:   We estimated 14500 for the answer.

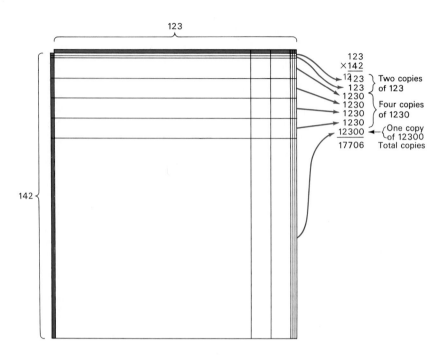

5. In the copy algorithm, each row of pieces is recorded as a separate number. The pieces in a row are added up to tell what number to record. A row may be a 1 copy, a 10 copy, or a 100 copy of the number being multiplied.

6. Other observations from your class session:

Practice Problems[6]:
Draw sketches for these problems. Record the results in symbols using the copy algorithm.

a.   15
    ×32

b.   145
    ×134

3.4.2
**The Copy
Multiplication Algorithm on the
Base-Eight Chip Computer**

1. We wanted the number being multiplied to be visible so that it would be easy to make copies of it. We decided to put chips for the number being multiplied *above* the calculating sheet.

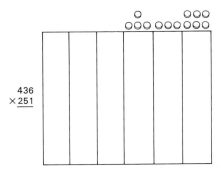

436
× 251

When We made 10 copies of a number, We would shift the top chips over one place (because that is the effect of multiplying by 10).

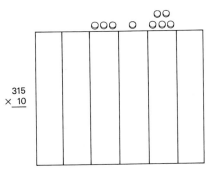

315
× 10

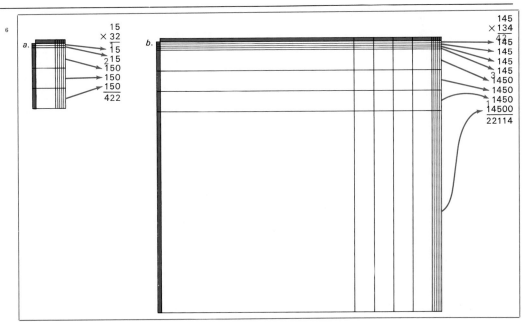

Similarly, We would shift the top chips over when multiplying by 100 or 1000 or etc.

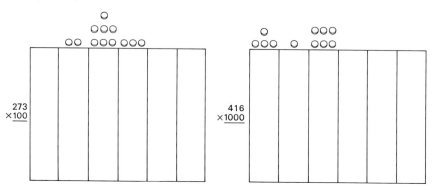

2. The number in each place tells how many copies to make and the place (1, 10, 100, 1000, etc.) tells what size of copy to make (copy shifted no, one, two, three, etc., places to the left). Each row of chips is recorded separately. After all the copies (rows) have been made and recorded, trades are made to get the total answer. A trade on the chip computer means a trade (or "carry") in the symbolic problem.

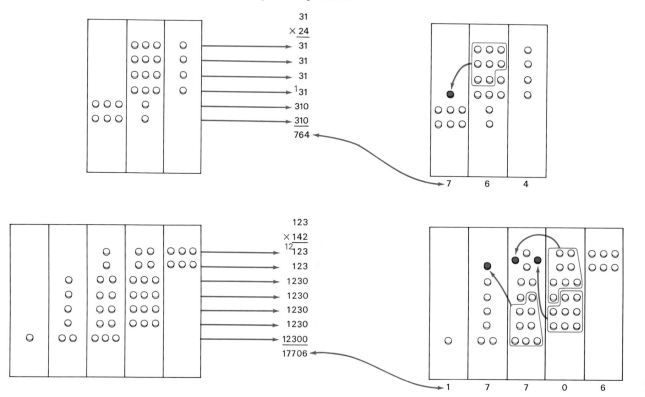

Practice Problems[7]:

Do these problems on a base-eight chip computer. Draw a sketch of your computer after all copies are made. Record each row of chips as it is made.

a.   42
   ×35

b.   216
   ×342

3.4.3
The Copy
Multiplication Algorithm
Symbolically

1. The copy algorithm for base eight requires only the shift rules and addition. Because We have poor addition reflexes in base eight, a base-eight addition table helped Us to add the totals in base eight. We usually only needed to use the table in cases that involved a "carry."

Base-Eight Addition Table

+	0	1	2	3	4	5	6	7
0	0	1	2	3	4	5	6	7
1	1	2	3	4	5	6	7	10
2	2	3	4	5	6	7	10	11
3	3	4	5	6	7	10	11	12
4	4	5	6	7	10	11	12	13
5	5	6	7	10	11	12	13	14
6	6	7	10	11	12	13	14	15
7	7	10	11	12	13	14	15	16

To use the table, look up one of the addends in the far left column and the other addend in the top row. Follow those rows and columns together until the point of intersection is found. Example: $4 + 6 = 12$ (See arrows.)

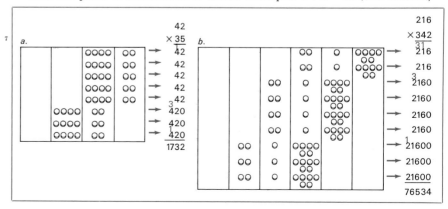

```
     421
  ×  352
     421 ⎫
  2  421 ⎬ 2
     4210⎫
     4210⎪
     4210⎬ 5
     4210⎪
  13 4210⎭
     42100⎫
     42100⎬ 3
     42100⎭
   174612
```

Multiplying by 352 means:

Make 2 single copies of 421.

Make 5 10 copies of 421 (=5 copies of 4210).

Make 3 100 copies of 421 (=3 copies of 42100).

(The addition was a bit difficult in base eight, but We realized that it would have been quite easy in base ten.)

```
     314
  ×  432
     314 ⎫
     3314⎬ 2 single copies of 314
     3140⎫
     3140⎬ 3 10 copies of 314 or
  12 3140⎭ 3 copies of 3140
     31400⎫
     31400⎪ 4 100 copies of 314 or
     31400⎬ 4 copies of 31400
     31400⎭
   160270
```

2. Other observations from your class session:

Practice Problems[8]:

Use the copy algorithm to do the following base-eight problems. (You may need the addition table.)

a.   52
   ×34

b.   312
   ×243

3.5
ACTIVITY:
THE PLACE-VALUE
MULTIPLICATION ALGORITHM
FOR BASE EIGHT

Overview: An intermediate place-value algorithm will be done with the chip computer and will also be done symbolically using a base-eight multiplication table. The compact place-value algorithm will be done symbolically using a base-eight multiplication table.

```
[8]  a.    52      b.     312
        ×  34          ×  243
           52             312
           52             312
           52            2312
      23  52             3120
          520            3120
          520            3120
          520         12 3120
         2230            31200
                         31200
                        100236
```

3.5.1
**The Intermediate
Place-Value Algorithm on the
Base-Eight Chip Computer**

1. The copy algorithm is easy to understand and requires no knowledge of multiplication facts. But it is slow and cumbersome when the multiplier contains large numbers like 5, 6, and 7. Instead of making copies of the number being multiplied using the number all together, the number can be multiplied place by place. This allows you to use multiplication facts if you know them.

213		Do with the chips:
× 35		
17	5 × 3	Make 5 copies of 3 and trade.
50	5 × 10	Make 5 copies of 10.
1200	5 × 200	Make 5 copies of 200 and trade.
110	30 × 3	Use 10 shift rule: 3 copies of 30 and trade.
300	30 × 10	Use 10 shift rule: 3 copies of 100.
6000	30 × 200	Use 10 shift rule: 3 copies of 2000.
7677		

The first six steps on the chip computer are:

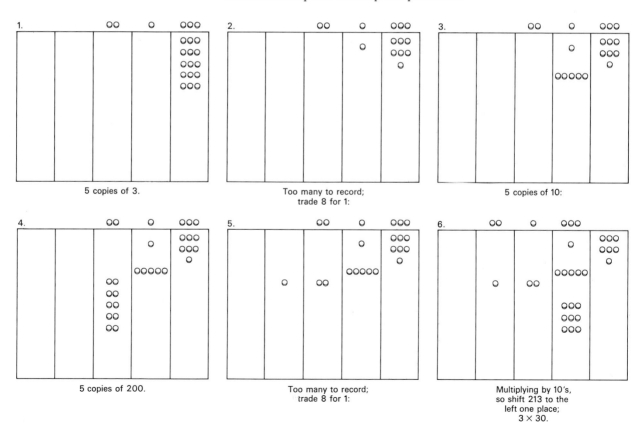

1. 5 copies of 3.

2. Too many to record;
trade 8 for 1:

3. 5 copies of 10:

4. 5 copies of 200.

5. Too many to record;
trade 8 for 1:

6. Multiplying by 10's,
so shift 213 to the
left one place;
3 × 30.

Notice that you no longer make copies of the whole number 213. Now you makes copies of it place by place.

475		Do on chip computer:
×576		
₁36	6 × 5	Make 6 copies of 5 and trade.
₁520	6 × 70	Make 6 copies of 70 and trade.
3000	6 × 400	Make 6 copies of 400 and trade.
430	70 × 5	Use 10 shift rule: 7 copies of 50 and trade.
₂6100	70 × 70	Use 10 shift rule: 7 copies of 700 and trade.
34000	70 × 400	Use 10 shift rule: 7 copies of 4000 and trade.
3100	500 × 5	Use 100 shift rule: 5 copies of 500 and trade.
₁43000	5 × 70	Use 100 shift rule: 5 copies of 7000 and trade.
240000	500 × 400	Use 100 shift rule: 5 copies of 40000 and trade.
354406		

The computer just before the final addition looked like the illustration at the left.

This method is called the intermediate place-value algorithm.

2. Other observations from your class session:

Practice Problems[9]:

Do these base-eight problems on the chip computer using the intermediate place-value algorithm.

a. 215
    × 46

b. 127
    ×325

[9]

a. 215	**b.** 127
× 46	×325
36	₁43
₁₁60	120
1400	500
240	160
400	₂400
10000	2000
12356	2500
	₁6000
	30000
	44143

3.5.2
The Intermediate Place-Value Algorithm Using Base-Eight Tables

1. There are at least three ways to find the answers in each row of the intermediate place-value algorithm. If you need 5×3, you can *know* the answer (i.e., have that reflex), you can *use chips* to find the answer (make 5 threes), or you can *look up* the answer in a *table*. We don't have many base-eight reflexes (which puts Us in the position of upper-grade students trying to learn multiplication algorithms when they don't know the multiplication facts). We used chips to find products in the last section. Now We'll use base-eight tables to fill in the rows for the intermediate place-value algorithm.

Base-Eight Addition Table

+	0	1	2	3	4	5	6	7
0	0	1	2	3	4	5	6	7
1	1	2	3	4	5	6	7	10
2	2	3	4	5	6	7	10	11
3	3	4	5	6	7	10	11	12
4	4	5	6	7	10	11	12	13
5	5	6	7	10	11	12	13	14
6	6	7	10	11	12	13	14	15
7	7	10	11	12	13	14	15	16

Base-Eight Multiplication Table

×	0	1	2	3	4	5	6	7
0	0	0	0	0	0	0	0	0
1	0	1	2	3	4	5	6	7
2	0	2	4	6	10	12	14	16
3	0	3	6	11	14	17	22	25
4	0	4	10	14	20	24	30	34
5	0	5	12	17	24	31	36	43
6	0	6	14	22	30	36	44	52
7	0	7	16	25	34	43	52	61

(See section 3.4.3 to learn how to use these tables.) At first We found it useful to write the products We were finding out at the side of a problem. This helped with deciding which shift rules to use.

$$
\begin{array}{rl}
367 & \\
\times\ 54 & \\
\hline
34 & 4 \times 7 \\
{}_1300 & 4 \times 60 \\
1400 & 4 \times 300 \\
430 & 50 \times 7 = 5 \times 70 \\
{}_13600 & 50 \times 60 = 5 \times 600 \\
\underline{17000} & 50 \times 300 = 5 \times 3000 \\
24164 &
\end{array}
$$

$$
\begin{array}{rl}
275 & \\
\times 643 & \\
\hline
1\,17 & 3 \times 5 \\
{}_2250 & 3 \times 70 \\
6600 & 3 \times 200 \\
240 & 40 \times 5 = 4 \times 50 \\
{}_23400 & 40 \times 70 = 4 \times 700 \\
10000 & 40 \times 200 = 4 \times 2000 \\
3600 & 600 \times 5 = 6 \times 500 \\
{}_152000 & 600 \times 70 = 6 \times 7000 \\
\underline{140000} & 600 \times 200 = 6 \times 20000 \\
240527 &
\end{array}
$$

We decided that this was a helpful way to approach the place-value algorithm, but that some more efficient method was needed after this one was understood. This compact method is described in the next section.

2. Other observations from your class session:

Practice Problems[10]:
Do these problems using the base-eight tables and the intermediate place-value algorithm.

a. 63
   ×45

b. 746
   ×302

c. 634
   ×725

3.5.3
The Compact Place-Value Algorithm

1. All the products of a given number can be written on the same line. Trades from multiplying are usually written above the original problem.

```
 43
 64
 53        53        64        43
475       475       475       475
×576      ×  6      × 70      ×500
3556      3556      42530     306100
42530
306100
354406
```

The numbers in blue are the trades or "carries." On a chip computer, this problem would be done as the intermediate place-value algorithm is done except that all the products of a given number (above: 6, 70, and 500) are found before the total is recorded. These products are all on the same row.

[10]

a.	63	b.	746	c.	634
	×45		×302		×725
	₁17		14		₁24
	₁360		1100		₂170
	140		1600		3600
	3000		₁2200		100
	3537		14000		2 600
			250000		14000
			270114		3400
					25000
					520000
					571314

The base-eight tables can again be used for those multiplication combinations We don't know.

2. The compact place-value algorithm has quite a complex layout, and a good deal of understanding is required to use it correctly. But after such understanding has been reached through the use of embodiments and intermediate symbolic recording steps, the algorithm is extremely efficient.

3. Other observations from your class session:

Practice Problems[11]:
Do these problems using the base-eight tables and the compact place-value algorithm. Do at least one of the problems by writing the extra steps out at the side.

a.	b.	c.
36	437	356
×45	× 56	×274

3.6
PROBLEM SET:
ANALYSIS OF THE MULTIPLI-
CATION ALGORITHM FOR
WHOLE NUMBERS

Overview: Included are problems concerning the three multiplication algorithms in base ten, uses of multiplication pieces and chip computer in base ten, a comparison of the advantages of each algorithm and of each embodiment, analysis of the shift rules, the use of the distributive property in multiplication, identifying uses of large multiplication problems in the classroom, and eight different historical multiplication algorithms.

11

a.	b.	c.
36	437	356
×45	× ₁56	× ₁274
₁ 226	₁ 3272	₁₁670
1700	26330	132020
2126	31622	73400
		127310

3.6.1 **a.** If the unit for base-ten multiplication pieces is $\frac{1}{4} \times \frac{1}{4}$ inch, what size are the rest of the base-ten multiplication pieces?[12]

Long   Square   Thin long   Fat long   Huge

b. What are the trade rules for base-*ten* multiplication pieces?[13]

c. For each base-*ten* picture below, tell the multiplication problem, write the copy algorithm steps (recording from the picture), mentally trade to get the answer, and record the answer.[14]

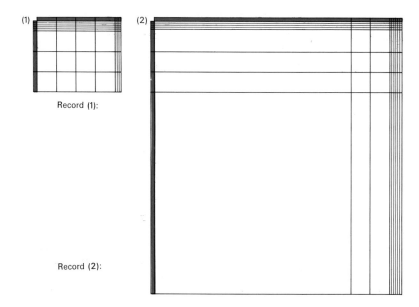

(1)

Record (1):

(2)

Record (2):

d. Use base-ten multiplication pieces (or draw sketches; graph paper

---

[12] Actually, in real life, errors in cutting build up. Ten units put together really are about $2\frac{5}{8}$ inches long. This measurement can be used to make the rest of the pieces:

Long	Square	Thin long	Fat long	Huge
$\frac{1}{4} \times \frac{5}{8}$	$2\frac{5}{8} \times 2\frac{5}{8}$	$\frac{1}{4} \times 25$	$2\frac{5}{8} \times 25$	25×25

This is a basic rule of thumb when making embodiments: Make the smallest pieces first and then see how large the next largest piece actually is, using several different combinations of the small pieces you cut. Continue this process for larger pieces.

[13] See Appendix I, Part B, for measurements of a smaller set of base ten pieces. Ten units = ten longs, ten longs = 1 square or 1 thin long, ten squares or ten thin longs = 1 fat long, ten fat longs = 1 huge.

with small squares is helpful) and the copy algorithm to do these base-ten multiplication problems.

(1) 45
$\times 32$

(2) 214
$\times \ 63$

(3) 114
$\times 123$

3.6.2 **a.** To be sure that you have the three multiplication algorithms clear in your own mind, do the following base-*ten* problem in all three ways.[15]

746 *Copy*   *Place-Value*   *Place-Value*
$\times 352$ *Intermediate Form*   *Compact Form*

---

[14]

(1) 43	(2) 126
× 35	× 134
43	126
43	126
43	126
43	126
43	1260
430	1260
430	1260
430	12600
1505	16884

[15]

Copy	*Place-Value Intermediate Form*	*Place-Value Compact Form*
746	746	1
× 352	× 352	13
746	12	21
746	80	746
7460	1400	× 352
7460	300	1492
7460	2000	37300
7460	35000	223800
7460	1800	262592
74600	12000	
74600	210000	
74600	262592	
262592		

b. For each base-*ten* chip computer below, give the multiplication problem and the algorithm used to do the problem, write out the symbolic steps for that problem (recording from the picture), trade mentally to get the answer, and record the answer. Problem (3) is a bit of a puzzle; try hard.[16]

c. Do these problems using a base-*ten* chip computer and the specified algorithm.

(1) Copy algorithm
352
×143

(2) Intermediate place-value algorithm
426
× 35

(3) Compact place-value algorithm
936
× 84

d. Describe some advantages and disadvantages of each of the three algorithms. Indicate in what order you would teach them and why. Compare your responses with those of your colleagues. (See also the discussion in section 3.7.)

[16]

Place-Value Intermediate Form		Copy		Place Value Compact Form	
(1)	214	(2)	41	(3)	34
	× 63		× 35		34
	12		41		346
	30		41		×708
	600		41		2768
	240		41		242200
	1600		12 41		244968
	12000		410		
	13482		410		
			410		
			1435		

3.6.3 There are many mathematical concepts involved in the multiplication algorithms. We used two different embodiments for the algorithms. Each was probably better in showing certain of these concepts. For each concept below, decide which model was better and give reasons for your choice. Discuss your choices and your reasons with your colleagues.

  a. $23 = 20 + 3$
  b. $(20 + 3) \times 14 = (20 \times 14) + (3 \times 14)$
  c. $20 = 10 + 10$
  d. $10 \times 24 = 240$ (small shift rules)
  e. $2 \times 3 = 6$
  f. $30 \times 40 = 1200$
  g. $100000 \times 437 = 43700000$ (large shift rules)
  h. A feeling for a rough approximation of 234×46
  i. Understanding of the repetitive nature of the place-value algorithm (i.e. that the same process continues on and on for larger numbers.)

3.6.4 All the multiplication algorithms depend on the fact that multiplication of whole numbers is *distributive* over addition of whole numbers. The multiplication pieces show this property quite clearly. Look at the sketch of base-ten multiplication pieces. In the copy algorithm, the number being multiplied (32) is viewed as a complete entity: a row of pieces. The multiplier splits up into its separate places (40 and 5). The distributive property is what lets the 45 split up:

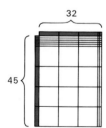

$$45 \times 32 = (40 + 5) \times 32 = (40 \times 32) + (5 \times 32)$$

In the place-value algorithm, the multiplied number is also separated into its separate places (30 and 2) as each place is multiplied separately. The place-value algorithm uses the distributive property over both numbers:

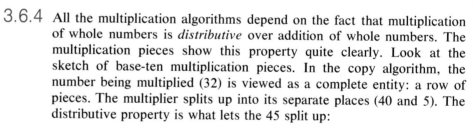

$$45 \times 32 = (40 + 5) \times (30 + 2)$$
$$= [(40 + 5) \times 30] + [(40 + 5) \times 2]$$
$$= (40 \times 30) + (5 \times 30) + (40 \times 2) + (5 \times 2)$$
$$\quad\ \ \text{(A)} \qquad \text{(B)} \qquad \text{(C)} \qquad \text{(D)}$$

Study the sketch and identify the pieces for (A), (B), (C), and (D).
  Write out 352×746 showing all the distributive steps as above. (Omit parentheses if you find them confusing.) Also do the problem with base-ten multiplication pieces or sketch the pieces. Check your final step with the place-value intermediate form you did in section 3.6.2, problem a. (That was the same problem.) Your final step using the distributive prop-

erty should contain all the simple products shown in the rows of the intermediate form. Identify each simple product in your pieces or in your sketch (i.e., find where the pieces show each simple product).

Write out 68 × 29 showing all the distributive steps.

3.6.5 Let's look again at the shift rules used for multiplication.

a. The shift rules for base-*ten* multiplication pieces are developed in exactly the same way that the shift rules are developed in base eight. Review sections 3.2.2 and 3.2.3, imagining that all of the sketches are of base-ten pieces. (There are no trades involved in any of these problems; trading is the only respect in which the base-eight and base-ten pieces differ.) Using base-ten multiplication pieces results in exactly the same shift rules as those for base eight.

b. 10 (one-oh) on a base-ten chip computer is ten chips. So multiplying by 10 (one-oh) in base ten means making ten copies of a number. Use this method to find these products:

$$\begin{array}{r} 14 \\ \times 10 \\ \hline \end{array} \qquad \begin{array}{r} 23 \\ \times 10 \\ \hline \end{array} \qquad \begin{array}{r} 302 \\ \times\ 10 \\ \hline \end{array}$$

The results are 140, 230, and 3020. This means that multiplying by 10 *shifts* a number *one* place to the *left*.

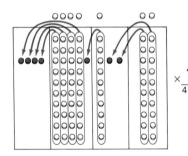

$$\begin{array}{r} 412 \\ \times\ \ 10 \\ \hline 4120 \end{array}$$

A sort of general "proof" of this shift rule is similar to that used in section 3.3.3 for base eight: a chip-by-chip trade. You have to make ten copies of each chip, but ten chips trade for one chip in the column to the left. Therefore, multiplying by 10 just makes a stack (or a column) of chips for each chip, and each stack is just the right size to be traded to the next column to the left.

The 100, 1000, 10000, etc. shift rules follow from the 10 shift rule just as they did in section 3.3.3. You may wish to review that section.

c. Shift rules change multiplication problems from those we do not know how to do (multiply by 10, 100, 1000, etc.) to those we do know how to do: Multiply by units by making multiple copies of a number.

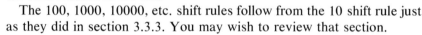

$$\begin{array}{r} 475 \\ \times\ 10 \\ \hline \end{array} \text{becomes} \begin{array}{r} 4750 \\ \times\ \ \ \ 1 \\ \hline \end{array} \qquad \begin{array}{r} 238 \\ \times\ 50 \\ \hline \end{array} \text{becomes} \begin{array}{r} 2380 \\ \times\ \ \ \ 5 \\ \hline \end{array}$$

$$\begin{array}{r} 482 \\ \times 300 \\ \hline \end{array} \text{becomes} \begin{array}{r} 48200 \\ \times\ \ \ \ \ 3 \\ \hline \end{array} \qquad \begin{array}{r} 294 \\ \times 6000 \\ \hline \end{array} \text{becomes} \begin{array}{r} 294000 \\ \times\ \ \ \ \ \ \ 6 \\ \hline \end{array}$$

d. The shift rules were used mentally when doing a problem and were not reflected in the way we wrote any algorithm. Look at the example below. How does this method better reflect the shift rules we use?

(1)	(2)	(3)

$$
\begin{array}{r}
1 \\
746 \\
\times 352 \\
\hline
1492 = 2 \times 746
\end{array}
\qquad
\begin{array}{r}
23 \\
1 \\
7460 \\
\times 352 \\
\hline
1492 \\
37300 = 5 \times 7460
\end{array}
\qquad
\begin{array}{r}
11 \\
23 \\
1 \\
74600 \\
\times_1 352 \\
\hline
_1 1492 \\
_1 37300 \\
\underline{223800} = 3 \times 74600 \\
262592
\end{array}
$$

This symbolic method was invented by an elementary school teacher after using a base-ten poker chip computer for multiplication. It makes the "carries" always lie in the correct column.

With sticks used as counters a multiplication process similar to the one above was used by the Chinese on counting boards. These counting boards were in use before Christ was born. The Japanese used them as late as the late eighteenth century. When multiplying by a multiple of 10, the Chinese would move the number being multiplied one place to the left (equivalent to adding a zero at the right). When multiplying by a multiple of 100, the number being multiplied was moved two places to the left. These number sticks gave rise to a system of numeration, described in section 7.3.3 (System 6).

3.6.6 Quick and accurate multiplication reflexes ($5 \times 7 = 35$, known automatically without thought) are essential in doing the compact form of the place-value algorithm efficiently. There are many possibilities for error with this algorithm.

a. As you work the problem below by the compact place-value algorithm, use a tally system to record each time you use one of the reflexes listed at the right.

$$
\begin{array}{r}
946 \\
\times 357
\end{array}
$$

requires

_____ multiplication reflexes
_____ correct application of shift rules
_____ trades after multiplying
_____ addition reflexes (Remember, add only two numbers at a time.)
_____ trades for addition

Total: _____ possibilities of error[17]

[17] Roughly: 9, 3 or 9 (depending on your interpretation), 9, 19, 3; total 43 (or 49).

b. What does this tell you about the common practice of marking student problems either right or wrong?

c. What might be a more helpful way to mark multiplication problems?

d. Analysis of the patterns in a base-ten multiplication table can be helpful in learning the basic multiplication facts ("reflexes"). Make a base-ten multiplication table and look for patterns. Compare the patterns you find with patterns your colleagues find. Also see Part C, 4.1.2, for a discussion of patterns in the base-ten multiplication table and for a description of finger multiplication.

Students can make errors resulting from lack of understanding or from carelessness. Make up base-ten multiplication problems that contain errors in each of the 5 areas listed in problem *a*, above. Trade your problems with those of a colleague and see if you can detect each other's errors.

3.6.7 All the work on learning how to do multiplication with large whole numbers will be wasted unless students know when to use this process. To learn this, they must practice identifying real situations that require the use of multiplication of at least two-place whole numbers. List three nonmathematical situations or projects (art, history, reading, etc.) requiring the multiplication of at least two-place whole numbers.

List three mathematical situations requiring the multiplication of at least two-place whole numbers.

List three situations in which adults would need to multiply two-place or larger whole numbers.

*3.6.8 For practice and in order to examine some of the characteristics of the place-value algorithm, try working it in some different ways. Similar inquiries might be interesting activities for good students in sixth, seventh, and eighth grades.

a. Let the bottom number be the size of the set and multiply by the top number. This method was used in ancient Greece.

$$\begin{array}{r} 35 \\ \times 74 \\ \hline \end{array} \qquad \begin{array}{r} 482 \\ \times 375 \\ \hline \end{array}$$

What are the advantages and disadvantages of this method?

b. Let the top number be the size of the set. Start multiplying by the bottom number on the left, instead of on the right. This is the algorithm commonly used in Europe, and it was also used in ancient Greece.

$$
\begin{array}{r}
39 \\
\times 62 \\
\hline
2340 \\
78 \\
\hline
2418
\end{array}
\qquad
\text{Try:}
\begin{array}{r}
47 \\
\times 35 \\
\hline
\end{array}
\qquad
\begin{array}{r}
358 \\
\times 427 \\
\hline
\end{array}
\qquad
\begin{array}{r}
225 \\
\times 638 \\
\hline
\end{array}
$$

What are the advantages and disadvantages of this method? (Do you get an approximate answer more quickly? Might this be advantageous? Could you use this method for multiplying by numbers like 0.3333 . . . or 0. 142857142857 . . . ?)

3.6.9 Throughout history, there have been many ways to do large multiplication problems. Some of these methods have been symbolic, and some have used calculating devices (abacus, medieval "reckoning on the lines,"[1] Napier's rods). Several of these methods are outlined below. As you try these methods, consider how each one handles shift rules, multiplication reflexes, and addition of partial products. Decide whether each one uses the distributive property or some other mathematical property or relationship.

a. Lancelot Hogben reports in *The Wonderful World of Mathematics*[2] that many clay tablets containing tables of simple addition and multiplication facts and tables of squares of numbers have been unearthed in a temple library near the Euphrates River. He conjectures that the Babylonians used these tables for multiplication of large numbers in the following way:

For x, y whole numbers:

$$
xy = \left(\frac{x+y}{2}\right)^2 - \left(\frac{x-y}{2}\right)^2
$$

That is, the product of two numbers is always equal to the difference

[1] Karl Menninger, *Number Words and Number Symbols,* MIT Press, Cambridge, Mass., 1972, pp. 360–361.
[2] Doubleday, Garden City, N. Y., 1955, p. 23.

between the square of half their sum and the square of half their difference.

Try finding 14×22 by this method. If you wish, multiply 47×135, using the above process. Remember that you would have tables available for many of the steps. Identify which steps would be done with a table and which steps in your head (or in some other way). Remember that an addition table will work for subtraction and a multiplication table gives you division facts.

b. The ancient Egyptians used doubling, halving, multiplying by ten, and addition in their multiplication process.[3] The basic process was to make a table of successive doublings of the number that was being multiplied (see the table for twelve, below). From the left column of the table, you would choose numbers that would sum to the desired multiplier. The numbers to the right of these chosen entries would then be added.

Table for Twelve		To multiply 10×12, choose the rows 2 and 8 $(2 + 8 = 10)$:		
1	12	2	24	
2	24	8	96	
4	48	10	120	(That is, 10 twelves are 120.)
8	96	To multiply 23×12, choose the rows 1, 2, 4, and 16		
16	192	$(1 + 2 + 4 + 16 = 23)$:		
		1	12	
		2	24	
		4	48	
		16	192	
		23	276	(That is, 23 twelves are 276.)

Sometimes the table would include products of ten and of five (half of the ten value). These products of ten were not simple shift rules, however, because the Egyptians did not use a base, place-value system (see section 7.3.2, system 3, for a description of a Greek system similar to that used by the Egyptians.) These tables were often ad hoc affairs, containing entries that would probably be used, rather than always progressing regularly as in the table for twelve. The literal translation for the Egyptian expression meaning "multiply 80" is "add beginning with 80," thus recognizing the structure of their multiplication process.

Do the problems below, using the Egyptian approach. Then try to decide whether a table for twelve, if carried far enough, would give an answer to any problem.

$18 \times 25 \qquad 27 \times 32 \qquad 74 \times 86 \qquad 175 \times 147$

---

[3] B. L. van der Waerden, *Science Awakening,* Cambridge University Press, London, 1960, pp. 18–19.

27×38

27	38
54	19
108	9
216	4
432	2
864	1

1026

c. Variations of Egyptian multiplication were used for centuries. The Egyptian influence can be seen in the independent operations "duplation" (doubling) and "mediatio" (halving) that were taught in the Middle Ages. One widely known variation of this method is the "Russian peasants" method.[4] It works as follows: Write each number at the head of a column. In one column, multiply by 2 each time. In the other column, divide successively by 2, discarding any remainder, and stopping when the quotient is 1. Cross out in the doubled column any entry which corresponds to an even entry in the halved column. Add the numbers in the doubled column which have not been crossed out.

Try the following problems by this method:

$43 \times 57 \qquad 31 \times 74 \qquad 135 \times 151$

Why does this method work: (Hint: Consider the doubling as 27 times various powers of 2 and the halving as leaving a chip in a column of a base-two chip computer only when the halving was odd. A complete explanation is given in the footnote.)[18]

d. *Multiplicare per corcetta* (multiplication by the cross) was the method normally used in Venice in the 1400s. This method had long been familiar in India. It was taught in computation textbooks as far as 2 four-place factors. As one German textbook author, Adam Riese, remarked "It takes much skill."[5]

13×42:

```
4   2
 \ /
 / \
1   3
5   4 6
```

[4] Helen A. Merrill, *Mathematical Excursions*, Dover, New York, 1964, pp. 24–25.

[5] Menninger, op. cit. pp. 441–442.

[18] The halved column gives a binary (base-two) representation of 38: Think of 38 chips piled on the ones column of a base-two chip computer. Make all right-to-left trades. The results are shown in shorthand form on the computer on the right. In base two, 38 is 100110 (this means $32 + 4 + 2$, because those are the values of those places).

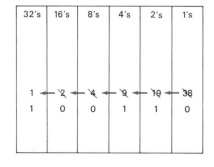

32's	16's	8's	4's	2's	1's
1 ←	2 ←	4 ←	9 ←	19 ←	38
1	0	0	1	1	0

Notice that if the number of chips in a column is odd, when those chips are halved, one chip will remain in that column. Thus the odd columns give the columns with ones in the base-two representation. Odd columns correspond to odd entries in the table. You can read the base-two representation of 38 from the table (read from the bottom up) using odd and even: 38 = odd-even-even-odd-odd-even = 100110.

The doubled half of the table contains one 27, two 27's, four 27's, etc. The base-two representation of 38 tells which of these products to select for a total of 38 27's:

$38 = 32 + 4 + 2$

Therefore,

$38 \times 27 = (32 \times 27) + (4 \times 27) + (2 \times 27)$

As shown in the above example, the "units column" digits were mentally multiplied and the units resulting were recorded ($3 \times 2 = 6$). The sum of "tens over the cross" were then calculated $[(3 \times 4) + (1 \times 2) = 12 + 2 = 14]$. Of this sum the tens part (4) was recorded and the hundred (1) was remembered. The digits in the tens columns were then multiplied and the unrecorded hundred was added in $[(1 \times 4) + 1 = 5]$.

Try this method for a couple of two-place factors; it is actually a handy method to use once you "get the hang of it." Then see if you can figure out the procedure for three-place factors. If you feel really adventurous, you might try four-place factors.

*(Ask yourself what this method has to do with the multiplication of algebraic equations.)

e. Another Italian method was "multiplication by factors."[6] With this method a number was multiplied by the factors of a number, not by the number itself. Each factor multiplies the previous product, building up the total product.

42×16:

	16 · 42
2	32
3	96
7	672

Try some problems using this method. This is a multiplication algorithm that uses division. How?[19]

What property of multiplication guarantees that this method will work?[20]

f. The following method was widely used in India and all over Western Europe. It was done both symbolically and with a special calculating device—Napier's rods (or Napier's bones). John Napier, a Scottish nobleman, invented his rods in 1617. They quickly became popular all over Western Europe, and were used as late as the nineteenth cen-

---

6 Ibid., p. 442.

---

19 Division is used in the factoring. If you know 2 is a factor of 42, then $42 \div 2$ gives you the product of the other factors.

20 Associativity: $42 \times 16 = (7 \times 3 \times 2) \times 16 = (7 \times 3) \times (2 \times 16) = (7 \times 3) \times 32 = 7 \times (3 \times 32) = 7 \times 96 = 672$.

tury. Chinese versions of the rods appeared in Japanese textbooks as late as the nineteenth century.

There are minor variations, but the basic idea is as follows: Vertical strips (or rods) are made for each number from 1 to 9. Each strip contains the multiplication products for its number in ascending order of size. The strips for 3, 7, and 6 appear in the example. A special strip containing the numbers 1 through 9 is used for the multiplier.

Example: 4 × 376

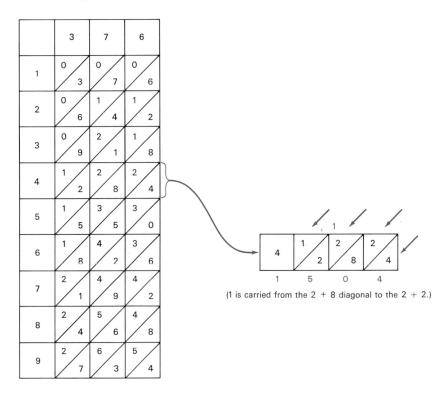

(1 is carried from the 2 + 8 diagonal to the 2 + 2.)

To multiply with the strips, you select strips and make one of the factors (here 376). The special multiplier rod is placed next to these rods. To multiply 376 by 4, read the horizontal row of numbers touched by four, adding numbers diagonally.

In order to multiply by larger numbers, simply record the horizontal sum for the number in each place of this larger number (remembering to add in each of the diagonals). You must know and use the shift rules in order to put these recorded numbers in the correct places.

Example:

452 × 376

Record from 2 row: 752
Record from 5 row: 1880
Record from 4 row: 1504
Then using the fact that the "5" is actually 50 and the "4" is actually 400, find this sum:

$$150400$$
$$18800$$
$$\underline{752}$$
$$169952$$

Make a set of Napier's rods. (Use tongue depressors, cardboard or posterboard strips, or pieces of wood. You will need a couple of rods for each number. Why?) Try some multiplication problems with them. What part of the work do these rods do and what part do you still have to do?

g. The symbolic counterpart to Napier's rods is lattice (or "gelosia") multiplication. This method was used in India and all Arabic nations, and in Western Europe with minor variations (the diagonals run in the opposite direction in Arabic manuscripts). A rectangle divided into horizontal and vertical strips is drawn. The multiplied number is placed at the top, and the multiplier is placed vertically on the right. Each small square in the rectangle is divided in half diagonally, and the product of the numbers in the row and column determining that square are entered in the square. *All* the numbers in each diagonal are summed and entered at the bottom of the diagonal. The answer is then read from the upper left down and around to the bottom right. Look at the example on the left.

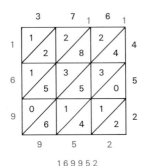

169952

Try some problems using this method. Why don't you need shift rules for this method? What do you need to know for this method that you do not need to know for the rods?

h. See section 7.5.2, problem 5.d for multiplication using other systems of numeration.

*3.6.10 Show that the same shift rules for multiplication of a number by 10, 100, 1000, etc. work in any base. (Hint: See section 3.6.5.)

*3.6.11 In Part A, Units 2 and 4, addition and subtraction slide rules were made using lengths. How might a multiplication slide rule be made? (Hint: A way to change multiplication to addition is needed. See Part C, section 3.8, for a suggestion.)

3.7 PEDAGOGICAL REMARKS

Developing the ability to estimate answers is very important for multiplication of large whole numbers. There are so many possibilities for error in a single multiplication problem (see section 3.6.6) that being able to tell at a glance whether an answer is reasonable is quite valuable.

The ability to estimate answers probably comes from at least three sources. The first is a good intuition about the size of numbers. This intuition probably comes from experience with real world embodiments of large numbers. The second source of the ability to estimate answers is useful symbolic "rules of thumb" for obtaining rough estimates including manipulation of powers of ten (see section 5.5.4). The third source is a kind of symbolic intuition about answers that would come from doing many problems and observing the nature of the answers. (For a more detailed discussion of these points, see section 5.6.)

Another check on the reasonableness of an answer is to look at the situation in which the problem arises and ask whether the answer is a reasonable one for the situation. Because most multiplication problems in school are not done in the context of real situations, this kind of check is rarely performed. Therefore many people do a problem in real life and never even think to check the answer with the problem situation to see if it is reasonable. Children need practice in this type of answer estimation.

Having children do multiplication problems that arise from real situations is also a way to help them strengthen their ability to translate from the real world to the mathematical world of symbols. Even if children understand and can do the multiplication algorithm, they may not be able to recognize when it should be used. They need practice in deciding which real world situations require the mathematical model of multiplication of large whole numbers. Correctly making the links between the real world and the world of mathematics takes practice.

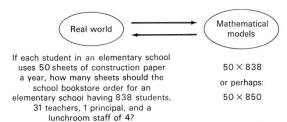

If each student in an elementary school uses 50 sheets of construction paper a year, how many sheets should the school bookstore order for an elementary school having 838 students, 31 teachers, 1 principal, and a lunchroom staff of 4?

50×838

or perhaps:

50×850

Each of the multiplication algorithms in this unit has certain advantages and disadvantages. The copy algorithm is intuitively obvious, and requires only shift rules and addition facts. But if the multiplier contains large digits (6, 7, 8, or 9 for base ten), this algorithm gets tedious. The place-value algorithm is much more efficient, but it requires good multiplication reflexes and a better understanding of the distributive property (see section 3.6.4).

The compact place-value algorithm is the most efficient algorithm, but it is by far the most complex. Students are likely to get lost in its format or to use it without understanding the reasons underlying its success. The intermediate form may help students understand the compact form. Some students can move fairly quickly from the intermediate to the compact form, while others may need to stay with the intermediate form for some time. If the intermediate form is used by everyone first, students who are proficient in symbolic mathematics might be asked to discover shorter methods of recording. Such students may also want to investigate other algorithms for multiplication, such as some of those in sections 3.6.5.d, 3.6.8, and 3.6.9.

The needs and abilities of particular students must be assessed in order to decide what experiences are best for them. An optimum program for many might be to begin with the copy algorithm and move to the place-value intermediate form as soon as students really understand the copy algorithm. Students with poor multiplication reflexes can use a base-ten multiplication table (and an addition table, if necessary); these students should also have experiences with manipulative materials and with symbolic pattern-finding that would help them improve their multiplication reflexes.

For older students who know only the place-value algorithm, a development of the shift rules and a brief look at the copy algorithm would probably be helpful. With these students, the intermediate-form place-value algorithm might be a useful check of their understanding of the compact form.

Each embodiment has its advantages and disadvantages. The multiplication pieces show quite clearly the shift rules for multiplying by 1, 10, and 100; the relative size of the units, tens, hundreds, thousands, and ten thousands; the copies of the multipied number in the copy algorithm; and the distributivity of both factors (e.g., you can see from the pieces that $243 \times \square = 200 \times \square + 40 \times \square + 3 \times \square$; and also that $\triangle \times 365 = \triangle \times 300 + \triangle \times 60 + \triangle \times 5$). But the pieces can be cumbersome to work with, and the multiplier is limited to three places. With the chip computer, the relative size of places (units, tens, etc.) is not shown; the shift rules for 100, 1000, etc., must be derived from that for 10; and distributivity must be assumed rather than being embodied (e.g., multiplying by 357 must be assumed to mean $300 \times \square + 50 \times \square + 7 \times \square$). But the chip computer can deal with much larger numbers than can the multiplication pieces. Therefore a general pattern for the shift rules can be established, and four-place or larger multipliers can be used if desired. Also the layout of chips on the computer more closely parallels the symbols in the place-value algorithm than does work with the pieces.

For these reasons, a plausible sequence might be to begin the shift rules with the multiplication pieces, and then, when a general pattern for shift rules for larger numbers is needed, to find such a pattern with the chip computer. With the copy algorithm, the pieces might be used for the initial introduction. The chip computer is perhaps best suited to the place-value algorithm. A plausible order of activities with the place-value algorithm is as follows: intermediate form using the chip computer, intermediate form without the chip computer (students with weak multiplication reflexes will need a multiplication table at this point), compact form on the chip computer, compact form without the chip computer. A quick look at the compact form with the multiplication pieces might be helpful to some students.

Although, ultimately, students probably would profit from learning with both embodiments, if there is time pressure, sustained work on one embodiment might be preferable to a hasty view of two. The best way to make such decisions is by analysis of your experience with these embodiments in your own teaching. Work on the multiplication algorithms will probably be spread over 2 to 3 years.

It is assumed that all of the experiences described above will be in base ten. There is certainly no need for students who are appoaching multiplication algorithms for the first time to work in base eight. It is an open question whether such work with base eight embodiments might be useful for seventh- or eighth-grade students who have little understanding of multiplication but who have some memorized reflexes and habits which might interfere with a reexamination of the algorithms in base ten. This approach seems to work fairly well with adults, but at present the results with young students are not known.

After students have developed a fairly good understanding of the compact form, it would probably be interesting and helpful to discuss the role of distributivity in the multiplication algorithms. The multiplication pieces would be helpful in such a discussion.

Comprehension of the shift rules and of how the multiplication algorithms work often greatly increases teachers' understanding of the base-ten numeration system. These multiplication algorithms use the special properties of a base, place-value system and thus illustrate these properties. Therefore, learning how and why multiplication algorithms work not only enables you to multiply large numbers, but also enables you to understand better the structure of our system of numeration.

unit 4

algorithms for the division of whole numbers

4.1

INTRODUCTION

As with the other three operations on whole numbers, we want you to start afresh with the division algorithm. Try to forget (for the moment) all that you have learned about the division algorithm. To aid in this, you will do the two division algorithms in base eight first. This will force you to think about what you are doing instead of just dividing mechanically in base ten.

We will use the same two embodiments—multiplication pieces and chip computer—that were used for multiplication in Unit 3. The shift rules for multiplying by 10, 100, 1000, etc., are also needed; review sections 3.2 and 3.3 if the shift rules are not fresh in your memory.

4.1.1

Uses of Division

For each problem below, give a mathematical model for finding a solution. Find the solution if you wish.

1. The Northern Illinois Gas Company had a cutback in supply of 77 billion cubic feet of gas in 1974. This represents enough fuel to serve 385,000 Illinois families. Using these figures, what is the average amount of gas used by one such family?

Mathematical model:

2. In 1973 the United States paid $35,700,000 to Turkish farmers to compensate them for not raising poppies (the source of heroin). About 100,000 families grew poppy crops in 1972. What was the average amount received by a Turkish family for not growing poppies?
Mathematical model:

3. United States oil companies shipped 5,136,726 gallons of gasoline to other countries in January 1974. This would have provided 5 gallons each to how many United States motorists? United States oil companies exported only 798,000 gallons in January 1973. How many times this figure did they ship in 1974?
Mathematical models:

4. If the United States fertility rate for 1973 was 69 births per 1,000 women in the age group fifteen to forty-four, and there were 3,141,000 births in 1973, how many women of childbearing age were there?
Mathematical model:

5. If in 1970 there were 37,100,000 children enrolled in elementary schools and if the elementary pupil-teacher ratio was about 24 to 1, how many elementary teachers were there in that year?
Mathematical model:

6. Amtrak reported an increase of 314,110 passengers in January 1974, over the figure of 1,109,078 rides in January 1973. It also reported 230,000 reservations for the next few months as against a normal reservation rate of 80,000 advance bookings. As compared with the increase in January, do you predict a greater increase of riders later in the year, about the same increase, or a smaller increase?
Mathematical models:

7. Cut out three newspaper or magazine articles that involve division of large whole numbers. Share your clippings with your colleagues. Write your mathematical models.
Mathematical models:

Overview: A copy division algorithm is performed with base-eight multiplication pieces and with the base-eight chip computer, and a place-value division algorithm is done with the base-eight chip computer.

Materials needed: For each group of four or five—a set of base-eight multiplication pieces.

For each individual—a base-eight chip computer (chips and a calculating sheet).

4.2.1
**The Copy Division
Algorithm with Base-Eight
Multiplication Pieces**

When *multiplying* with the base-eight multiplication pieces, the numbers being multiplied were embodied by two adjacent sides of a rectangle. The product (the answer) was embodied by the pieces in the rectangle. For *division*, we know the pieces in the rectangle and the pieces for one of the sides. We must find the pieces for the other side of the rectangle.

$$375 \leftarrow \text{Side}$$
$$\times \underline{128} \leftarrow \text{Side}$$

$$48000 \leftarrow \text{Rectangle}$$

$$375 \leftarrow \text{Side}$$
$$128\overline{)\,48000} \leftarrow \text{Rectangle}$$
$$\text{Side}$$

Remember that the number dividing is the *divisor* (128 in the example above) and the number being divided is the *dividend* (or "total"; 4800 in the example). The answer is the *quotient.*

Dividing with the multiplication pieces is like doing a puzzle:

Step 1. Count out enough pieces to represent the dividend (these pieces will be used to build the rectangle).

Step 2. Count out thins (units, longs, or thin longs) to represent the divisor and put them in a horizontal row.

Step 3. Use the pieces from the dividend to make a rectangle below the divisor. Use the largest pieces first. Record after each copy of the divisor is made.

For the copy division algorithm, one copy (it may be a 100, 10, or a 1 copy) of the divisor is made at a time and recorded. Like the copy multiplication algorithm, no multiplication is needed. Copies of the divisor are successively taken from the dividend until it is all gone (or until it is less than the divisor). The number of copies made is the answer (the quotient).

Note that there are two sizes of 100 pieces. You do not know in ad-

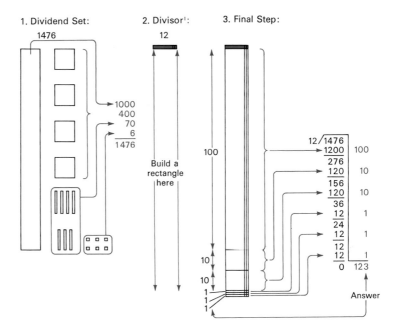

vance which kind will be needed. Use either size for the dividend, knowing that you may need to trade square 100s for long thin 100s or vice versa. In the example above 2 square and 2 thin long 100s were needed.

The example above does not show the middle steps, but after each copy is made, the remainder in the symbolic problem is the same as the number of pieces in the dividend set. For example, after making the first 100 copy, the pieces below would have remained in the dividend set:

2 100s + 7 10s + 6 1s = 276

The remainder in the symbolic problem after the first step is 276.

Try the problems below with your pieces. Do only *one* row at a time and *record* your results *immediately*. You may need to trade pieces in your dividend set to get pieces the right size to make rows (e.g., trade a 10 for eight 1's or trade a square 100 for a long 100).[1]

---

[1] As with multiplication, it is less confusing if the sides of the rectangle (here, the divisor) are of a different color from the pieces in the rectangle.

---

[1] a. 12, b. 23, c. 153 R1, d. 21, e. 23.

a. $6\overline{)74}$ **b.** $12\overline{)276}$ **c.** $4\overline{)655}$

d.[2] $213\overline{)4473}$ **e.** $246\overline{)6122}$

*4.2.2
**The Copy
Algorithm on the Base-Eight
Chip Computer**

See section 3.3.1 for a description of the base-eight chip computer. To divide on the chip computer:

1. Put chips for the divisor just above the calculating sheet.
2. Put chips for the dividend at the top of the calculating sheet (draw a line under this area, or color it.)
3. *Use chips from the dividend* to make copies of the divisor. Make large copies first and record after each copy.

Steps 1 and 2: Set up.   Step 3: Final step.

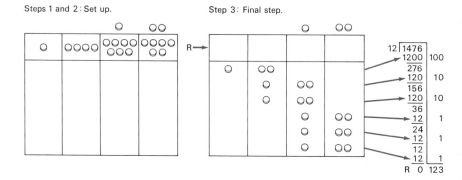

Work the example above on your chip computer. To tie the symbolic work closely to the embodiment, be sure to record *after making each copy.* The remainder in the symbolic problem at each step is the same as the number of chips remaining in the dividend, so check the chips with your remainder at each step. Remember that trades are in base eight (one for eight). Because the division algorithms sometimes require many trades, it is helpful to make five or six piles of eight chips off to the side somewhere so that trades can be made quickly and without counting.

Do the following problems using your chip computer and the copy algorithm.[2]

[2] Remember to use thin longs to make the divisor.

[2] **a. 124, b. 34, c. 241 R2, d. 124 R3.**

a. $5\overline{)\,644}$ **b.** $12\overline{)\,404}$ **c.** $25\overline{)\,6467}$ **d.** $273\overline{)\,36537}$

4.2.3
The Division
Place-Value Algorithm on the
Base-Eight Chip Computer
In the division place-value algorithm, trial copies (several copies at a time) are *estimated* as in the usual symbolic algorithm. To simulate these trial copies, extra chips are used and then compared with the chips remaining in the dividend. If the estimate was too high, the "trial" chips can be removed and another estimate made. If the estimate was not too high, chips equal to the extra chips used are removed from the dividend.

The trial copy is the product of multiplying the divisor place-by-place by the estimated number of trial copies. This product can be found in three ways:

1) by using chips to make the required number of copies of the divisor and then trading if necessary;
2) by using a multiplication table and recording the answers for each place with chips;
3) by knowing the products symbolically and recording these answers in chips.

In Step 1 of the example below, 40×23 could be found by

1) making 4 piles of 230 and trading;
2) by using a base-eight table to find $4 \times 3 = 14$, recording it with chips in the proper column, looking up $4 \times 2 = 10$, and recording that with chips;
3) by knowing the products and recording them in chips.

Chips can be used at the bottom of the calculating sheet to record the number of trial copies made. Thus the answer accumulates at the bottom of the sheet.

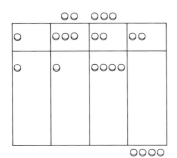

$23\overline{)\,1322}$

Step 1 *Estimate:* Can make a 40 copy of 23. Multiply 40×23 place by place:

40×3, trade to get 140
40×20, trade to get 100

Therefore, $40 \times 23 = 1140$

Since the estimated "trial" chips do not exceed the dividend, subtract from the dividend a number of chips equal to that of the "trial" chips: Subtract 1140 from the dividend chips (trade in the dividend to get 4 chips to subtract).

Record the copies made (40), and the trial chips (1140), and the chips remaining in the dividend (162).

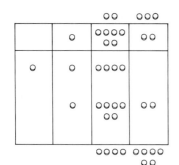

$$23\overline{)1322}$$
$$1140 \quad 40$$
$$\overline{162}$$

Step 2 Estimate: Can make 6 copies of 23 from 162. Multiply 6 × 23 place by place:

6 × 3, trade to get 22

6 × 20, trade to get 140

Therefore, 6 × 23 = 162

Since the estimated "trial" chips do not exceed the dividend, subtract from the dividend a number of chips equal to that of the trial chips: Subtract 162 chips from the dividend chips.

Record the copies made (6), the trial chips (162), and the remaining dividend (0).

$$23\overline{)1322}$$
$$1140 \quad 40$$
$$\overline{162}$$
$$162 \quad\; 6$$
$$\overline{0} \quad\; 46$$

Try the following problems using your chip computer. Remember to record as you go. Don't worry about inefficient trial estimates. You have had very little opportunity to develop base-eight intuitions of sizes. Many children are in just this position with respect to intuition in base ten, and so your experiences may help you to understand their feelings better.

If you have several small guesses using the same shift rule (that means the answers are all in the same place), your problem is not "wrong." You are just taking longer to find the answer.[3]

a. $3 \overline{) 163}$ **b.** $32 \overline{) 11110}$ **c.** $23 \overline{) 15641}$ **d.** $124 \overline{) 36537}$

4.3
ACTIVITY:
DIVISION ALGORITHMS
FOR BASE-TEN
WHOLE NUMBERS

Several approaches may be used to this section. If you are confident about the various kinds of base-eight division, you probably need only to do one example in each set in order to be sure that base ten is clear to you. In this case, try the last example of each kind. The symbolic answer and a picture of the final stage of the multiplication pieces or of the base-ten chip computer for the problems are at the end of the section.

If your understanding of base-eight division is still hazy, additional practice in base ten will help clarify things for you. The base-ten shift rules and division processes are identical to those in base eight; only the trade rules differ. As you do the exercises remember that the trades are ten for one and one for ten. Do as many problems as necessary to clarify each process.

Overview: **A copy division algorithm is done with the base-ten multiplication pieces and the base-ten chip computer, and a place-value division algorithm is done with the base-ten chip computer.**

Materials needed: **Each group needs a box of poker chips and a computing sheet (the one you used for base eight will do). One set of base-ten multiplication pieces can be rotated from group to group for working the problems in section 4.3.1, each group can have one set, or the problems can be sketched (graph paper with tiny squares helps).**

4.3.1
The Copy Division
Algorithm with Base-Ten
Multiplication Pieces

The copy division algorithm is done with base-ten multiplication pieces exactly as it was done with base-eight pieces. Pieces for the divisor form one side of a rectangle, and pieces for the dividend are used to make a rectangle having that side. The quotient (answer) is the side of the

[3] a. 46 R1, b. 264, c. 564 R5, d. 273 R3.

rectangle adjacent to the divisor side. Remember that base-ten pieces trade ten for one and one for ten. Do the following problems.[4]

a. $5\overline{)65}$ **b.** $24\overline{)768}$ **c.** $43\overline{)1034}$ **d.** $52\overline{)12012}$

*4.3.2
**The Copy
Division Algorithm on the
Base-Ten Chip Computer**

Make single copies of the divisor on the chip computer, using the shift rules to make large copies first. Make the copies of the divisor using chips from the dividend chips until the remaining dividend is smaller than the divisor. Do the following problems.[5]

[4] a. 13, b. 32, c. 24 R2.

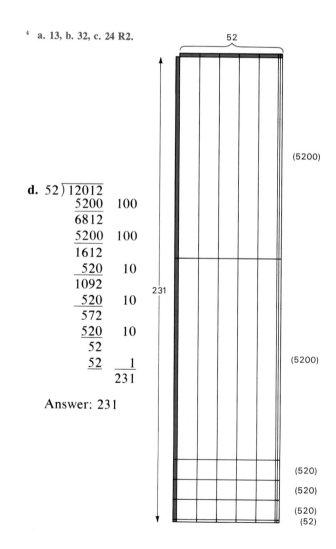

d. $52\overline{)12012}$

$$\begin{array}{r} 5200 \quad 100 \\ \hline 6812 \\ 5200 \quad 100 \\ \hline 1612 \\ 520 \quad 10 \\ \hline 1092 \\ 520 \quad 10 \\ \hline 572 \\ 520 \quad 10 \\ \hline 52 \\ 52 \quad 1 \\ \hline 231 \end{array}$$

Answer: 231

a. $7\overline{)91}$ **b.** $34\overline{)1428}$ **c.** $213\overline{)7255}$ **d.** $314\overline{)72534}$

4.3.3
The Place-Value Division Algorithm on the Base-Ten Chip Computer

By using extra chips, make trial copies of the divisor (several copies at a time: 40 or 6 or 300, etc.). Compare the trial chips with the dividend and subtract a number of chips equal to the trial chips from the dividend. Continue until the dividend is less than the divisor. Do the following problems.[6]

a. $8\overline{)5859}$ **b.** $12\overline{)4380}$ **c.** $37\overline{)2072}$ **d.** $232\overline{)62521}$

---

[5] **a. 13, b. 42, c. 34 R13.**

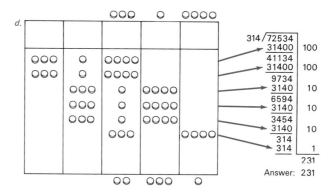

[6] **a. 732 R3, b. 365, c. 56.**

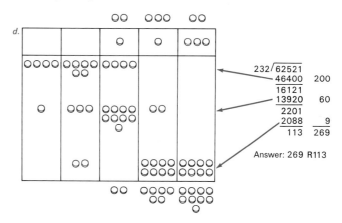

4.4
PROBLEM
SET: ANALYSIS OF THE
DIVISION ALGORITHMS
FOR WHOLE NUMBERS

All the following problems, except part of section 4.4.4, are in base ten.

Overview: This section includes problems concerning assessment of the advantages and disadvantages of the two embodiments and of the two division algorithms, estimation, the inverse relationship between multiplication and division, use of tables in doing division, uses of division, student errors, and historical methods of division.

4.4.1 These questions are discussed in section 4.5, but you should think about them before reading that section.

a. What aspects of the copy division algorithm do the multiplication pieces show most clearly? What aspects does the chip computer show most clearly? Which would you do first with students and why?

b. Could you do the place-value division algorithm with the multiplication pieces? Describe how.

c. What are the differences between the copy division algorithm and the place-value division algorithm? (What reflexes and understandings does one require that the other does not?)

d. What are the similarities of the copy division algorithm and the place-value division algorithm? (What reflexes and understandings do both division algorithms require?)

4.4.2 The place-value algorithm requires guessing how many copies of a particular size will fit into the dividend. This guessing is frequently the most difficult part of the division algorithm, for at least three reasons.

a. Reasonable guessing requires good intuition about the numbers involved. Schools have rarely spent time helping children develop their mathematical intuition. Learning by rote or learning at a purely symbolic level is not likely to aid the development of such intuition. What can help to develop good intuition are considerable use of manipulative materials in the classroom (especially if these materials are varied) and activities that involve estimating and subsequent verification of the answers to various kinds of problems.

Estimating (which is really sensible guessing) should be a part of every activity in the mathematics classroom. Habits of predicting what will happen, verifying what did happen, and comparing the prediction with the result for improved understanding of what is occurring can be developing in students at all times. Students can be learning to learn from their experiences. In this rapidly changing world, learning to learn would seem to be a paramount goal.

However, estimating a reasonable answer to a problem (or estimating a reasonable range into which an answer should fall) should be seen as an activity useful in real life uses of mathematics, not just as an additional step which the teacher requires in doing a problem. Using estimates in doing various activities in the classroom can make estimating real. List below three situations in which estimation of a division answer could play a useful role in a classroom (the situations might well be in subject areas other than mathematics).

(1)

(2)

(3)

b. There are certain "rules of thumb" that can make guessing the number of copies of the divisor more efficient. Most of these involve rounding off the divisor in some way. Share with your colleagues the rules of thumb you use. Record them here:

Most of them involve rounding off, and they work only part of the time. They work particularly well when the second number is 0,1,8, or 9, and fairly poorly when the second number is 4, 5, or 6. Why?

Therefore these rules of thumb are only somewhat helpful in making good guesses.

c. Many children (and adults) have psychological difficulties with guessing. They have learned that guessing is bad, or that only dumb people have to guess, or that guessing has very little chance of arriving at the right answer. Because *the answer* is the *only* goal in many mathematics classrooms, guessing seems not only not worth doing, but is often punished. Thus fear sometimes prevents children and adults from making a guess in long division—they are afraid their guess will be wrong.

A way to avoid this difficulty is to encourage a person to *use* his guess, no matter what the guess is. The following approach is only a minor adaptation of the place-value algorithm. It is of particular value with children who have trouble guessing. Of course, the ultimate goal is reasonable and even efficient guessing, but intuition and reflexes for that kind of estimation of divisors do not develop overnight. Meanwhile, the following approach can be used.

Look at the following examples. Can you see the mind of the child working? What questions might you ask the child to enable him to *use* the guesses he has made to make improved guesses? Role-play these examples with your colleagues if you wish.

```
3) 165              23) 13641
   3    1              230      10
 162                 13411
   3    1           -23000-   -1000-
 159                  2300      100
   6    2            11111
 153                  6900      300
  30   10             4211
 123                -4600-    -200-
  60   20             2300      100
  43                  1911
   6    2              230       10
  37                  1681
  30   10              690       30
   7                   991
   6    2              690       30
   1   48              301
                        92        4
                       209
                       115        5
                        94
                        92        4
                       R2       593
```

Why does the above process work? We are viewing division as *repeated subtraction* and taking away bunches of copies of the divisor until we have subtracted all we can subtract. That is, for the first example, $3\overline{)\,165}$, we subtracted 1 copy of 3, then 1 copy of 3, then 2 copies of 3, then 10 copies of 3, then 20 copies of 3, then 2 copies of 3, then 10 copies of 3, then 2 copies of 3. We could then subtract no more 3s, and so we added up the copies we had made to find out how many 3s there were in 165.

Try the following problems, deliberately making some very low guesses so that you are sure you understand how the above process works.

$$34\overline{)2145} \qquad\qquad\qquad 46\overline{)29597}$$

4.4.3 To do either division algorithm, we use the fact that division is an inverse operation of multiplication in several ways:

a. $23\overline{)2745}$ $\qquad$ $\square \;\times\; 23 \;=\; 2745$ $\qquad$ We ask *how many* copies

$\qquad\qquad\qquad\qquad$ Number $\quad$ Size $\qquad\qquad$ of 23 are in 2745.

$\qquad\qquad\qquad\qquad$ of $\qquad\qquad$ of

$\qquad\qquad\qquad\qquad$ sets $\qquad\quad$ sets

b. We use *multiplication shift rules* to make large copies

c. We use *multiplication reflexes* when we multiply the divisor by a guess to find how large a number to subtract from the dividend.

d. We use the *same embodiments* for the division algorithms as we used for the multiplication algorithms. For multiplication, the two factors are embodied first and the product is found. For division, a factor and the product is embodied first, and the missing factor is found.

To make sure that you clearly understand the procedure, show how each of the three numbers in a multiplication and in a division problem are embodied in the two embodiments used earlier.

$\qquad\qquad\qquad$ **Multiplication** $\qquad\qquad$ **(A) Division**

$\qquad\qquad\qquad\qquad\qquad\qquad\qquad\qquad\qquad\;\;\triangle$

$\qquad\qquad\qquad 45 \times 29 = \square \qquad 29\overline{)1305}$ $\;$ or $\;$ $1305 \div 29 = \triangle$

$\qquad\qquad\qquad$ (A) (B) (C) $\qquad$ (B) (C) $\qquad\quad$ (C) (B) (A)

Multiplication pieces:

$\quad$ (A) vertical column of pieces $\qquad$ (A)

$\quad$ (B) $\qquad\qquad\qquad\qquad\qquad\qquad$ (B)

$\quad$ (C) $\qquad\qquad\qquad\qquad\qquad\qquad$ (C)

Poker chip computer:

$\quad$ (A) $\qquad\qquad\qquad\qquad\qquad\qquad$ (A)

$\quad$ (B) $\qquad\qquad\qquad\qquad\qquad\qquad$ (B)

$\quad$ (C) $\qquad\qquad\qquad\qquad\qquad\qquad$ (C)

e. A multiplication table can be used to find division facts. Find the divisor in the left column, find the dividend in the divisor's row, and follow the dividend's column up to the top to find the quotient. (Try it with the base-eight table in section 4.4.4.)

f. The place-value division algorithm is just the place-value multiplication algorithm upside down. In the multiplication algorithm, large copies of a number are added up to make the product. In the division algorithm, large copies of the number are subtracted from this product (called the *dividend* now) until it is all gone. That is, the division algorithm *undoes* the multiplication algorithm.

```
              18            18⟌846
            ×47            ↗720  40 (×18)
 7 × 18:   126↖            126
40 × 18:   720↙          ↗126   7  (×18)
           846
```

The analogy is even clearer if the multiplication by the bottom number moves from left to right, as is done in Europe:

```
               426            426⟌161028
             ×378           →127800  300 (×426)
300 × 426: 127800←            33228
 70 × 426:  29820←          →29820   70 (×426)
  8 × 426:   3408←            3408
           161028          →3408    8  (×426)
```

Work another example for yourself to demonstrate this inverse relationship.

Now do an example to demonstrate the inverse relationship of the copy multiplication algorithm and the copy division algorithm.

4.4.4 Each division problem requires the use of many reflexes. Look at the following division problem. Tell how many of each listed reflex or concept must be used for this problem. Remember that an operation takes *two* numbers and assigns to them a unique third number.

```
246⟌14268
   12300  50
    1968
    1968   8
       0  58
```

This problem involves:[7]

a. _____ addition operations (Remember to include trades.)

b. _____ subtraction operations (Remember to include trades.)

[7] a. 7, b. 10, c. 6, d. 6 (or 2, depending on your interpretation).

    c. _____ multiplication operations (This is the place-value algorithm.)

    d. _____ shift rules

You can see that there are many possibilities for error. For a child with weak reflexes, the probability of getting the right answer is fairly low.

One solution to this problem is the same one proposed for addition, subtraction, and multiplication: Give students with poor reflexes tables containing the required facts. Let them use the tables to work on the problem at hand, while also at different times giving these students experiences to help them improve their reflexes.

The copy division algorithm requires addition and subtraction reflexes; therefore, an addition table is necessary. The place-value division algorithm requires addition, subtraction, and multiplication reflexes; both an addition and a multiplication table is needed for this algorithm.

In order to put you in the same position as a student with poor reflexes, use tables to do problems in _base eight_. This will enable you to decide what skills and understandings are necessary to do the place-value division algorithm even if basic reflexes are provided. To add or multiply with the tables, find the addends (or factors) in the left column and top row; the sum (or product) is in the intersection of that row and column. To subtract, find the smaller number in the left column of the addition table, follow that row over until you find the larger number, and read that column up at the top to find the difference. Use the tables and the place value algorithm to do the problems below.[8]

Base-Eight Addition Table

+	0	1	2	3	4	5	6	7
0	0	1	2	3	4	5	6	7
1	1	2	3	4	5	6	7	10
2	2	3	4	5	6	7	10	11
3	3	4	5	6	7	10	11	12
4	4	5	6	7	10	11	12	13
5	5	6	7	10	11	12	13	14
6	6	7	10	11	12	13	14	15
7	7	10	11	12	13	14	15	16

Base-Eight Multiplication Table

×	0	1	2	3	4	5	6	7
0	0	0	0	0	0	0	0	0
1	0	1	2	3	4	5	6	7
2	0	2	4	6	10	12	14	16
3	0	3	6	11	14	17	22	25
4	0	4	10	14	20	24	30	34
5	0	5	12	17	24	31	36	43
6	0	6	14	22	30	36	44	52
7	0	7	16	25	34	43	52	61

[8] e. 43 R1, f. 54 R5, g. 205 R21, h. 232 R35.

e. $6\overline{)323}$ f. $52\overline{)3475}$ g. $36\overline{)7647}$ h. $47\overline{)13623}$

If you wish, make base-ten addition and multiplication tables and use them to do several base-ten division problems.

What skills and understandings are necessary to do the place-value division algorithm using addition and multiplication tables?

4.4.5 As with the algorithms for the other operations, all the time and energy spent on learning and understanding the division algorithms is useless if children do not know how or when to use them. Practice with real world situations that require the division of large whole numbers is absolutely necessary. List three such situations below (they may arise outside the area of mathematics). Share your situations with your colleagues.

4.4.6 For each student's problem below, describe the mistake that was made, the concept that is not understood, and what experiences you would provide to help the student acquire the necessary understanding. Also for each problem, estimate the answer and decide if estimation would have revealed the presence of an error.

a. $28\overline{)1473}$
      $\underline{820}$ 40
      653
      $\underline{460}$ 20
      193
      $\underline{100}$ 5
      93
      $\underline{64}$ 3
      29
      $\underline{28}$ $\underline{\ 1}$
       1 69

b. $28\overline{)1473}$
      $\underline{1040}$ 50
      433
      $\underline{280}$ 10
      153
      $\underline{140}$ $\underline{\ 5}$
      13 65

c. $39\overline{)2346}$
      $\underline{1950}$ 50
      1616
      $\underline{1560}$ 40
      156
      $\underline{156}$ $\underline{\ 4}$
        94

d. $60\overline{)40000}$
      $\underline{36000}$ 6000
      4000
      $\underline{3600}$ 600
      400
      $\underline{360}$ $\underline{60}$
      40 6660

e. $18\overline{)846}$
      $\underline{720}$ 40
      126
      $\underline{118}$ $\underline{\ 7}$
       8 47

f. $5\overline{)1535}$ (quotient $3\ 7$)
      $\underline{15}$
      35
      $\underline{35}$

g. $7\overline{)2940}$ (quotient 42)
      $\underline{28}$
      14
      $\underline{14}$
       0

Do problems **f** and **g** writing the quotient out at the side. Are the errors that were made in **f** and **g** as likely to be made when done in this form?

4.4.7 Over the years the number of ways to do division has not developed as extensively as has the number of ways to do multiplication. This may have been because division was used less often or because it is a more difficult operation. Several methods have been popular, however, and four of these are described below.

a. Ancient Egyptian:[3] (Before attempting this, review section 3.6.9, problem *b*, concerning ancient Egyptian multiplication by doubling.)

The Egyptians regarded division as an inverse operation to multiplication. The operations were done identically, except that in multiplication the sum of the *number* of doublings, the multiplier, was *known* and the sum of the *doublings* themselves, the product, was *unknown*. In division the sum of the *doublings* themselves was *known*, and you had to find *how many* doublings of a given number gave that sum (the dividend). The procedures looked identical.

For example, No. 69 in the Rhind papyrus says: "Multiply 80 (or literally: add beginning with 80) until you get 1120" (1120 ÷ 80).

(1) 1	80		(2) 1	80
2	160		10	800
4	320	sum = 1120	2	160
8	640		4	320

(1) sum = 1120
So there are 2 + 4 + 8 = 14
80's in 1120

(2) sum = 1120
So there are 10 + 4 = 14
80's in 1120

(Sometimes, as in the second example, the tables of doublings included products of ten as a shortcut. But because the Egyptians did not have a place-value system, new symbols were used for larger numbers. We have instead used our usual shift rule with our numerals.)

Try some problems using first a simple doubling table and then a table that includes products of ten.

b. Babylonian[4] Division was done by multiplying the dividend by the reciprocal of the divisor: $x \div y = x \times \dfrac{1}{y}$. For ease of calculation, the $\dfrac{1}{y}$ was changed to an equivalent fraction with a denominator of 60. Be-

---

[3] B. L. van der Waerden, *Science Awakening,* Cambridge University Press, London, 1960, p. 19.

[4] Carl Boyer, *A History of Mathematics,* John Wiley and Sons, Inc., New York, 1968, p. 32.

cause the Babylonian system was a place-value, base-sixty system, it was only necessary to multiply by the top number in the fraction and shift the decimal point one place to the left (the result of dividing by 60).

In our base-ten system, an equivalent process is as follows:

$$27 \div 5 = 27 \times \frac{1}{5} = 27 \times \frac{2}{10} = \frac{27 \times 2}{10} = \frac{54}{10} = 5.4$$

Briefly, $2 \times 27 = 54$ and shift the decimal point: 5.4. To divide a number by 2, you can multiply by 5 and shift the decimal point one place to the left. The Babylonians had tables that would enable them to go from the first step to the third step (see the blue arrow above) directly for some numbers.

Because ten has only divisors 1, 2, 5, and 10, the above process is not too helpful to us. But 60 is divisible by 1, 2, 3, 4, 5, 6, 10, 12, 15, 20, 30, and 60. The reciprocal of each of those numbers can be expressed in terms of an equivalent fraction with a denominator of 60 and a numerator of the number's factor-mate (e.g. 2 and 30, 6 and 10, 15 and 4 are factor-mates). Therefore, division by each of these numbers is a simple procedure: Multiply by its factor-mate and move the decimal point.

For simplicity, use our numerals with a bar drawn over each place to represent Babylonian numbers. The value of the first three places in the Babylonian system is:

3600 60 1 e.g. $\overline{3}\ \overline{12} = 3 \times 60 + 12 = 192$

Do these problems using the Babylonian method.[9]

(1) $\overline{2}\ \overline{0} \div \overline{15}$ (2) $\overline{5}\ \overline{24} \div \overline{12}$ (3) $\overline{3}\ \overline{4}\ \overline{18} \div \overline{6}$

c. "Strike-out", "scratch", or "galley" division[5]: This method of long division is similar to ours except that subtraction is done from left to right and the pattern of writing out the numbers is different. As numbers are used, they are crossed out (hence the first two names). The third name arose because the finished form looked like a galley or boat. This method became widespread in Europe in the fifteenth century. It is

[5] Ibid., pp. 239–240; Menninger, op. cit., pp. 330–331.

[9] (1) $\overline{8}$, (2) $\overline{27}$, (3) $\overline{30}\ \overline{43}$.

thought to be derived from a similar Indian "erasure" operation on a sand table.

In the example below, multiplications are written below the dividend and the subtractions are written above (subtract from left to right).

1.

       232 62521 2
       464

Multiply by 2

2.
      1
      261
  232 62521 2
      464

Subtract

3.
      1
      261
  232 62521 26
      4642
      139

Multiply by 6

4.
      2
      132
      261
  232 62521 26
      4642
      139

Subtract

5.
      2
      132
      261
  232 62521 269
      46428
      1398
      2

Multiply by 9

6.
      21
      1321
      26123
  232 62521 269
      46428
      1398
      2

Subtract

Answer:
269
R 113

Try doing a few division problems using this method (perhaps select problems from section 4.3 so you can compare processes). What concepts does this method use? Would you call this a rote method or an understanding method?

d. "Iron division" was a method of division used on the medieval counting board. It was so named because it was "so extraordinarily difficult that its hardness surpasses that of iron."[6] We will do the procedure with our numerals. (See Menninger for details of how the counting board procedure worked.)

For any problem, the divisor is first increased to the next higher multiple (in the example below, 32 to 40); the amount of increase (8) is called the *supplement*. Multiples of this supplemented number are subtracted from the dividend, with the same multiple of the supplement added back in each time.

6 Menninger, op. cit., pp. 327–329.

$$14624 \div 32 \ (=40 - 8)$$

(40×300)	$-$	$\underline{12000}$	300
		2624	
(8×300)	$+$	$\underline{2400}$	
		5024	
(40×100)	$-$	$\underline{4000}$	100
		1024	
(8×100)	$+$	$\underline{\ 800}$	
		1824	
(40×40)	$-$	$\underline{1600}$	40
		224	
(8×40)	$+$	$\underline{\ 320}$	
		544	
(40×10)	$-$	$\underline{\ 400}$	10
		144	
(8×10)	$+$	$\underline{\ \ 80}$	
		224	
(40×5)	$-$	$\underline{\ 200}$	5
		24	
(8×5)	$+$	$\underline{\ \ 40}$	
		64	
(40×1)	$-$	$\underline{\ \ 40}$	1
		24	
(8×1)	$+$	$\underline{\ \ \ 8}$	
		32	
		$\underline{32}$	$\underline{\ \ 1}$
			457

Work some division problems using this method. Is it faster when the units place is 7, 8, 9 or when it is 1, 2, or 3? What similarities are there to the methods used in class?

4.5
PEDAGOGICAL REMARKS
Division of large whole numbers is a difficult process. Part of the reason it is difficult is that it requires successful use of addition, subtraction, and multiplication. Any student who has difficulty with any of these processes will also have difficulty with division. The cumulative nature of much of mathematics is clearly illustrated by this aspect of division. Consequently, many errors made in division of large whole numbers are not errors in division per se; they are errors in addition, subtraction, or multiplication (see section 4.4.6 for examples).

The division process is also difficult because you must keep several different kinds of steps clear in order to understand the process. This is one reason that embodiments are so helpful for division. Embodiments make these different steps visual in different ways, so that the pattern of repetitive steps is clearer than when the steps are done symbolically. For example, it is not obvious that every second line in a division algorithm is the constantly shrinking dividend, and that the interspersed lines are the copies of the divisor being successively subtracted from the dividend. These roles are quite clear with the multiplication pieces, for visible copies are made using pieces from the dividend.

Several things are necessary for the division algorithm to be understood. Embodiments can help clarify some of these. The multiplication pieces and the copy algorithm provide a basic view of what the division process is about: the successive subtraction of copies of the divisor from the dividend, with multiplication shift rules being used for making large ($\times 10$, $\times 100$, $\times 1000$, etc.) copies of the divisor. With the multiplication pieces, the shift rule effects on the size of the copies of the divisor, the using up of the dividend to make these copies, and the inverse relationship of the multiplication and division algorithms (both copy and place value; see section 4.4.3, problem f) are quite clear. The base-ten chip computer using the copy algorithm is a bit more abstract on the first and third points above, but it is closer to the symbolic form of the algorithm. If desired, it can be used as a bridge between the multiplication pieces and the symbolic algorithm done without any embodiments.

As with all of the other operation algorithms, the ultimate goal in division is an efficient symbolic process. The place-value algorithm is more difficult, but much more efficient than the copy algorithm. The copy division algorithm requires addition, subtraction, and simple multiplication shift rules. The place-value algorithm requires those, and also multiplication and estimation of multipliers (the subtraction involved is also usually more difficult).

Quotient above the Dividend	Quotient Out at the Side	
$\begin{array}{r} 251 \\ 14\overline{)3514} \\ 28 \\ \hline 71 \\ 70 \\ \hline 14 \\ 14 \\ \hline \end{array}$	$\begin{array}{r} 14\overline{)3514} \\ 2800 \\ \hline 714 \\ 700 \\ \hline 14 \\ 14 \\ \hline \end{array}$	$\begin{array}{r} \\ 200 \\ \\ 50 \\ \\ 1 \\ \hline 251 \end{array}$

If the place-value algorithm is done in the usual way by writing the quotient above the dividend instead of out at the side (as done in the activities), understanding of the process involved can be rendered more difficult. With the quotient written above, you write and seem to multiply by a 2 instead of by a 200 (which is actually the case) or by a 5 instead of a 50, etc. With the quotient-above method, it is also more difficult to get a sense of the decreasing dividend, because the whole products (2800, 700) are not written out and subtracted from the dividend. Finally, with the quotient-above method the answer is "magically" present at the end of the division process rather than consisting of the sum of the copies of the divisor that were made. The algorithm with the quotient written above the dividend is a faster method and can be used efficiently by many people. But the quotient-at-the-side method is probably a more effective and more meaningful introduction to the place-value algorithm.

The multiplication pieces can be used for the place-value algorithm, but because trades have to be made in each place before recording, the rectangle is not left intact. Therefore the chip computer is probably preferable for doing the place-value algorithm. The advantages of the chip computer are: its layout is identical to that in the symbolic algorithm; the fact that multiple copies of the divisor are being made and then subtracted from the dividend has an exact parallel in the chips; and the subtraction process is quite clear (if a trade must be made in the dividend chips, the symbolic algorithm will involve a "borrowing").

As described in section 4.4.4, students who have poor addition, subtraction, and multiplication reflexes can still learn to do the place-value division algorithm if they are allowed to use base-ten addition and multiplication tables. To do the place-value division algorithm with tables requires that you know how to use the tables directly (for addition and multiplication) and inversely (for subtraction and division), that you be able to use multiplication shift rules, and that you understand the basic process of subtracting large copies of the divisor from the dividend. With tables you no longer need either to know automatically the addition, subtraction, or multiplication facts or to estimate the number of copies of the divisor to make. Now you merely look up in the multiplication table the divisor and the dividend-at-any-stage, and find the largest number in the divisor row that is smaller than the dividend; the number at the top of that column is the number of copies to make. Of course, because the goal is still to enable all students to do the algorithm without tables, students should have other experiences to help them learn the basic addition, subtraction, and multiplication reflexes.

Estimation skills are required in order to do the place-value division algorithm. Estimation skills will also help detect many division errors. Estimation skills can be improved by practice in estimating answers in real world situations. This requires that estimating an answer before doing a division problem become a standard procedure in the classroom. Occasionally such estimates can be discussed in order to focus attention on improved methods. Another kind of practice is of a symbolic sort. Estimation of the answers to a whole group of division problems can be done and the estimates compared with the exact answers (provided by the teacher). Experience itself will also improve estimation skills, and discussion of tactics used and discoveries made can contribute to an improvement.

As with the other algorithms for large whole numbers, the time and energy spent on learning the division algorithms is wasted if students do not know when to use them. This can be learned only by confronting real problems that require division of large numbers. Planning so that such problems arise is difficult at first, but with practice it becomes easier. Sharing situations with colleagues is a good way to increase the number of division situations each teacher is able to use with students.

Learning to understand the multiplication and division algorithms means learning to understand some basic characteristics of our place-value, base-ten numeration system. Multiplication and division are frequently quite difficult operations to perform in many numeration systems. It is with these operations that the advantages of our system of numeration are quite evident. (See section 7.5.2 for details.)

unit 5

decimals: basic operations, algorithms, and the metric system

5.1
INTRODUCTION Decimal fractions are numbers written in a base-ten place-value notation using places to the right of the ones place. These places are reached from the ones place by successive one-for-ten (left-to-right) trades.

| Ones | Trade: One for Ten. | Trade: One for Ten. | Trade: One for Ten. | Trade: One for Ten. | Trade: One for Ten. | Trade: One for Ten. | . . . |

A period, called the *decimal point* (a comma in some European countries) separates the ones place and the first decimal fraction place—the tenths place.

The set of decimal numbers includes all numbers that can be written in a base-ten place-value system using places both to the right and to the left of the ones place. This includes the set of whole numbers (all places to the left of the decimal point), the set of rational numbers (many of the numbers written using places to the right of the decimal point), and some new numbers called *real numbers*. The relationship between the set of rational numbers and the set of decimal fractions is discussed in Unit 6. Real numbers are discussed in Unit 6.

This unit begins with historical information about decimals and continues with uses of decimal fractions. Section 5.2 contains activities on the metric system of measurement. The metric system uses one-for-ten trades for all exchanges within a given type of measurement. Therefore it is both an embodiment of the decimals and a user of decimal symbolic notation. Section 5.3 examines the basic meaning of operations on small (three-place) decimal fractions. Section 5.4 extends the patterns to decimal fractions of many places, thus developing algorithms for addition, subtraction, multiplication, and division of decimal fractions. A problem set containing a variety of symbolic explorations of decimals, including decimals in exponential form, scientific notation, and approximations using powers of ten follows. Pedagogic remarks about the teaching of decimals conclude the unit.

5.1.1 Historical Background of Decimals[1]

Numbers written in a place-value notation using the places to the right of the ones place were used by the ancient Babylonians. The trades between places in this system were one for sixty, and so these numbers can be called *sexagesimal* (base-sixty) fractions. (See section 7.3.1, system 2, for more details of sexagesimal fractions.) These numbers were used by the Greeks, Arabs, and others in astronomy because they were easier to calculate with than ordinary fractions. Sexagesimal fractions were still being used in Europe for astronomical purposes when decimal fractions began to become popular in 1585.

Decimal fractions gradually displaced sexagesimal fractions because operations with decimal fractions could be performed in the same way operations with whole numbers were done; a number no longer needed to have its whole number part separated from its fractional part in order for computations to be done.

Decimal fractions were used in ancient China, in medieval Arabia, and in Renaissance Europe.[2] No one really knows how they came about. At least two possibilities seem reasonable. Someone who was aware of both the base-ten system for whole numbers and the sexagesimal fractions might have seen that base-ten fractions could be made analogous to the sexagesimal fractions. In calculating, these new decimal fractions would be dealt with as decimal whole numbers were. Decimal fractions might also have arisen from the use of an abacus or calculating board. At

[1] You may wish to review the history of whole numbers in section 7.2.

[2] Carl B. Boyer, *A History of Mathematics,* John Wiley & Sons, Inc., New York, 1968, p. 348, and D. J. Struik, ed., *A Source Book in Mathematics, 1200–1800,* Harvard University Press, Cambridge, Mass., 1969, p. 7.

some time someone might have carried the larger-for-smaller trades past the ones place. The Greek abacus and the medieval European counting board had fractional places to the right of the ones place, but these places were fourths or other fractions different from tens. That is, a base-ten system was used on these devices for whole numbers, but was abandoned for fractions. Someone might have seen how easy it would be to keep consistent one-for-ten trade rules in the fractional parts of a number. These one-for-ten trades would have produced decimal fractions.

By the late sixteenth century some mathematicians in Western Europe were acquainted with decimal fractions, but decimal fractions were not commonly used in applied mathematics or in commerce. In 1579 Francois Viete, the outstanding French mathematician of the time, advocated using decimal fractions instead of sexagesimal ones. But it was the publication in 1585 of Simon Stevin's *De Thiende* (The Tenth) that began the common use of decimal fractions in Western Europe.

Stevin used the following notation for decimal fractions: .3759 was 3①7②5③9④. He called this 3 primes, 7 seconds, 5 thirds, and 9 fourths. In calculations, the circled numbers were placed at the top of columns. Here is a subtraction example from Stevin[3]:

```
    ⓪ ① ② ③
2  3  7  5  7  8
   5  9  7  3  9
―――――――――――――
1  7  7  8  3  9
```

Stevin treated the decimal fractions as whole numbers and simply gave rules for operating with them. In his demonstration of each problem, Stevin would show the same problem worked in fractions and get the same answer he had gotten with the decimal fractions. Because people did not have to understand decimal fractions in order to use them and found them easier to use than ordinary fractions, decimal fractions soon became widely used in science, engineering, and commerce. Here are three problems appearing in early European arithmetics[4] before decimal fractions became popular. Imagine how much easier such problems were if decimal fractions were used.

1521, Italian: A man bought a number of bales of wool in London, each bale weighing 200 pounds, English measure, and each bale cost him 24 fl. He sent the wool to Florence and paid carriage duties, and other expenses,

[3] Struik, op cit, p. 9.
[4] Howard Eves, *An Introduction to the History of Mathematics,* Holt, Rinehart & Winston, Inc., New York, 1964, p. 234.

319 DECIMALS:
BASIC
OPERATIONS,
ALGORITHMS,
AND THE
METRIC
SYSTEM

amounting to 10 fl. a bale. He wishes to sell the wool in Florence at such a price as to make 20 percent on his investment. How much should he charge a hundredweight if 100 London pounds are equivalent to 133 Florence pounds?

1202, Italian: A certain man puts one denarius at interest at such a rate that in five years he has two denarii, and in five years thereafter the money doubles. I ask how many denarii he would gain from this one denarius in 100 years.

1556, Italian: A merchant gave a university 2814 ducats on the understanding that he was to be paid back 618 ducats a year for nine years, at the end of which the 2814 ducats should be considered as paid. What compound interest was he getting on his money?

Many different kinds of notation were used for decimal fractions. Some of these appear below:

$$123 \overset{456}{} \qquad 123|456 \qquad 123(456 \qquad 123{:}4\ 5\ 6$$

$$\qquad\qquad\qquad\qquad\qquad\qquad\qquad\qquad (1)\ (2)\ (3)$$

$$123|\underline{456} \qquad \mathbf{123} \qquad 456 \qquad 123 \cdot\ 4\ \ 5\ \ 6$$

John Napier[5] in various publications in 1616, 1617, and 1619 proposed the use of a point as the separator of the units and tenths places. The "decimal point" became standard in England from that time, but many other European countries gradually came to use a comma instead.

Simon Stevin also suggested that a decimal system of weights and measures be adopted, but no country adopted his proposal until 1799. After the French Revolution, a committee of outstanding mathematicians established the metric system in France. This system became compulsory in France in 1837 and gradually spread to all of non-English-speaking Europe. England has recently started to convert to the metric system. The United States is the only remaining large, modern country that does not use the metric system.

5.1.2
Uses of
Decimal Fractions

Decimal fractions have several advantages over ordinary fractions. Decimal fractions make it quite easy to write and to calculate with small numbers. Comparison of the size of decimal fractions is trivial. With the addition of a few more shift rules about the placement of the decimal point, the algorithms for the four basic operations on whole numbers

---

[5] He was the inventor of Napier's rods for multiplying large numbers (see section 3.6.9, problem *f*, for details) and co-inventor of logarithms.

work for decimal fractions. The algorithms for calculating with decimal fractions are repetitive, and so they can easily be programmed on a computer. Problems involving mixed numbers ($34.768 \times 125,000.26$) can be done in a single step, instead of doing the whole number and fractional parts separately, as must be done with ordinary fractions.

For these reasons, decimal fractions have many uses. The following list of uses[6] of decimal fractions indicates the great range of uses. After working section 5.2, you may want to reread some of these uses. The sizes in the examples may be more meaningful to you then.

Uses

1. The school tax in a certain district is 25 mills (= $.025) of the assessed value of a house. The assessed value is 30% of the current market value. How much school tax do the new purchasers of a $40,000. house pay in the year following their purchase?

2. In modern miniature cameras using 35 mm film, the opening through which a picture is taken takes less than .02 seconds to travel across the picture area. Thus the image of a fast moving object, say a racing car which takes about .2 seconds to traverse the picture area, would undergo a distortion of about 10%.

3. Tree trunks have a very complex structure. Individual glucose molecules are synthesized in leaves. These form chain molecules containing 6,000–8,000 glucose monomers. 100 chain monomers form a crystallite filament .000006–.000008 millimeters thick. 10–100 filaments make a microfibril .00002–.00008 millimeters thick. 10–100 microfibrils make a fibril, which is just visible under an ordinary microscope.

4. A sparkplug gap is 0.025–0.03 inches (0.6–0.7 millimeters).

5. If a is one edge of a tetrahedron, the total surface area of the tetrahedron is $1.73205a^2$ and the volume is $0.11785a^3$.

6. Because of the wave character of light, it is possible to distinguish details of a size down to the approximate wavelength of light: .0004 to .0007 millimeters (.000016 to .000028 inches). Thus the limit of useful magnification using a light microscope is 2000x. An electron microscope improves on this.

7. An installment charge of 1.5% a month on a revolving charge account is equivalent to 18% a year.

8. The chemical element mercury has an atomic weight of 200.61; a density of 13.546; a melting point of $-38.87°C$; a boiling point of 356.58°C.

---

[6] The data for the technical uses come from *The Way Things Work*. Simon & Schuster, New York, 1967. This book contains simple and understandable explanations of how many products of modern technology work.

321 DECIMALS:
BASIC
OPERATIONS,
ALGORITHMS,
AND THE
METRIC
SYSTEM

9. The major foreign constituents in sea water (in grams per kilogram):

chlorine	19.0	potassium	0.38
sodium	10.6	bicarbonate	0.14
sulfate	2.65	bromine	0.065
magnesium	1.27	boric acid	0.026
calcium	0.40	strontium	0.013

10. The approximate wavelengths used for various purposes are:

radio, television, communications	1,000 km to 1 cm
infrared	0.03 to 0.000076 cm
visible light	0.000076 to 0.000040 cm
ultraviolet	0.000040 to 0.0000013 cm
X rays	0.000001 to 0.000000001 cm
Gamma rays	0.00000001 to 0.00000000005 cm

11. Cloud droplets are about 0.002 cm (centimeters) in diameter and in concentrations of a few hundred per cubic centimeter. Drizzle drops have a diameter of about 0.2 millimeter. The largest raindrops are about 5 millimeters in diameter (.5 cm).

12. The First National Bank pays 5% interest compounded daily.

13. An electron has a charge of 0.00000000000000001602 Coulombs, a rest mass of 0.00000000000000000000009108 grams, and a radius of 0.0000000000282 centimeters.

14. The gas used in homes contains 50% hydrogen, 20–30% methane, 7–17% carbon monoxide, 3% carbon dioxide, 8% nitrogen, and 2% hydrocarbons.

15. Sin 27° = .454

16. High precision pendulum clocks are accurate to within 0.0000001 (that means an inaccuracy of 3 seconds a year). Quartz clocks have accuracies to within 0.000000001 to 0.0000000001. Atomic clocks have an accuracy ten times greater and are used to check quartz clocks. Atomic clocks use gaseous ammonia, which acquires vibrations of 24,000,000,000 cycles per second. This high frequency energy remains very accurately constant.

17. Some data about the planets in our solar system:

Name:	Miles from Sun:	Astronomical Units from Sun	Surface Gravity (Earth = 1):
Mercury	35,950,000	0.3871	0.37
Venus	67,180,000	0.7233	0.89
Earth	92,880,000	1.0000	1.00
Mars	141,520,000	1.5237	0.39
Jupiter	483,320,000	5.2037	2.54
Saturn	889,880,000	9.5809	1.06
Uranus	1,775,600,000	19.1168	1.09
Neptune	2,797,200,000	30.1157	1.41
Pluto	3,651,000,000	39.3133	?

18. Tungsten wire 0.01 millimeters (0.0004 inches) in diameter is used to make filaments for lightbulbs. Nearly 200 miles of such wire can be made from one pound of tungsten. The filaments are doubly coiled to allow a greater length of wire in a filament. The total length of filament wire in a 15-watt bulb is 0.75 meters (= 30 inches). The first coil has 3,000 turns; this is then coiled in 100 larger turns. The overall length of the completed filament is 3 cm (= 1.25 inches).

19. Tape recorders for amateur use have speeds of $7\frac{1}{2}$ in., $3\frac{3}{4}$ in., and $1\frac{7}{8}$ inches per second. The widths of tape for recording each oscillation of an overtone of 5000 cycles per second are 0.0015 in., 0.00075 in., and 0.000375 inches respectively.

20. Masers and lasers can detect power outputs as low as 0.00000000000000000000000001 Watts.

21. π equals approximately 3.14159.

22. A photo-electric cell consists of an iron plate provided with a thin coating of silenium. The silenium is covered with a coating of platinum 0.00001 millimeters thick.

23. A diffraction grating breaks the visible spectrum of light into 100,000 colors. A diffraction grating is a thick and slightly concave mirror about 6 inches long. A diamond needle cuts 30,000 equidistant lines to the inch. These lines are thus 0.0000333 . . . inches apart. This is equivalent to cutting 100 lines on the *edge* of a thin page of paper. The wavelengths of the six major colors are:

violet	0.000040–0.000042 cm.
blue	0.000042–0.000049 cm.
green	0.000049–0.000057 cm.
yellow	0.000057–0.000059 cm.
orange	0.000059–0.000065 cm.
red	0.000065–0.000076 cm.

323 DECIMALS:
BASIC
OPERATIONS,
ALGORITHMS,
AND THE
METRIC
SYSTEM

24. A surveyor's description of a lot might read: Beginning at the Northwest corner of Lot 237; thence North 235.17 feet; thence East 79.37 feet; thence South 235.17 feet; thence West 79.37 feet to the place of beginning containing 0.423 acres.

25. Amounts of various kinds of matter in sewage is measured in milligrams per liter (or parts per million). Ordinary sewage going into a sewage treatment plant has 250 mg/1 (or .000250 of the total) of solids and 2 to 3 mg/1 (or .000002 of the total) of phosphates. Treatment reduces these amounts to 50 mg/1 (.000050 of the total) of solids and .5 mg/1 (.0000005 of the total) of phosphates.

26. A small town needs to build a new water tower. The engineer plans to make it the shape drawn at the left. He has to answer questions like these: a) If the tank has a 40 foot diameter and a hemispherical bottom, and if it is to hold 150,000 gallons of water, what should the dimensions of the water tank be? (7.48 gallons in a cubic foot of water). b) If the water level in the tank is 150 feet above the water lines in the ground and a column of water one foot high has a pressure of 0.4335 lbs/sq in, what will the pressure of the water coming from the tank be? Is this enough to make the water flow in the pipes all over town?

27. The highest lifetime batting average is .367. It belongs to Ty Cobb.

You have read a variety of scientific and economic uses of decimal fractions. Although you have probably been unaware of many of the uses, they do affect your daily life. Now collect some uses of decimal fractions that more obviously affect you. Compare your responses to the assignments below with those of your colleagues.

1. Keep a diary for three days of all uses you make of decimal fractions.
2. Record some interesting uses of decimal fractions you have made in the last six months.
3. Clip five articles concerning decimal fractions from a newspaper or magazine. Try to find a variety of uses.

5.2
ACTIVITY AND PROBLEM SET: THE METRIC SYSTEM

This section has three goals. The first is to help develop a sense of the approximate size of metric measures for length, area, volume, liquid capacity, and weight. The second is to establish relationships between the types of metric measures. The third is to indicate the relationships between the English (our usual) and the metric system of measurement. Because the metric system is so regular, the first two goals are fairly easy.

Overview: Activities with metric length, area, volume, liquid capacity, and weight will be done. A problem set that compares the ease of conversions within the metric system with the ease of conversions within the English system follows. A final section deals with metric-English equivalents. (See each section for the materials needed. Sources are in Appendix I.)

5.2.1
Language for the Metric System

Each type of metric measure has one main measurer. All other measurers of that type are multiples or fractional parts of the one main measurer. These multiples and fractional parts are related in a very simple way: They are all positive or negative powers of ten. Standard names are used for all the multiples and fractional parts. The names are prefixes that are added to the main measurer. The most common prefixes are:

Mega-   1000000 × main measurer
Kilo-   1000 × main measurer
Hecto-   100 × main measurer
Deka-   10 × main measurer
Deci-   0.1 × main measurer
Centi-   0.01 × main measurer
Milli-   0.001 × main measurer
Micro-   0.000001 × main measurer

The prefixes for multiples greater than one are Greek in origin. Prefixes for parts smaller than one come from Latin. There are other prefixes, but these are the most common ones.

The Main Measurers

	Length	Area	Volume	Liquid Capacity	Weight
Main Measurer:	Meter	Square meter	Cubic meter	Liter	Gram
Abbreviation:	m	sq m	cu m	l	gr

Some examples of the use of prefixes:

1000 meters = 1 kilometer (km)
0.1 meter = 1 decimeter
0.01 meter = 1 centimeter (cm)
1000 grams = 1 kilogram (kg)

1000 liters = 1 kiloliter (kl)
10 liters = 1 dekaliter
0.001 liters = 1 milliliter (ml)
0.001 grams = 1 milligram (mg)

5.2.2
The Metric Measures

Materials needed: **White and orange rods, meter sticks (some unmarked, one divided into tenths), string, paper or chalkboard. Optional: Stop-watch or second hand on a watch.**

1. Metric Length

a. How many orange rods = 1 meter? _____ Therefore an orange rod is a _____ meter.[1]

How many white rods = 1 meter? _____ (Did you do this directly or use a short cut? Which would be more convincing to children?) Therefore a white rod is a _____ meter.[2]

Make a string 10 meters long. Can you stretch out this string in your classroom? What is the metric measure of this string? One _____.[3] How many such strings would it take to make a kilometer (pronounced ki-lóm-i-ter)? _____[4]

b. Use rods, sticks, string, or whatever and answer some of the following questions.

How long is the chalkboard in your room? _____

How tall are you ? _____

How long is this page? _____

Pick two people. How much taller is one than the other? _____

What is the circumference of your head? _____

How far can you jump? _____

How high can you jump? _____

How long is your skirt (pants) from the waist to hem? _____

What is the circumference of your ring finger? _____

How thick is a piece of your hair? _____

How thick is your thumbnail? _____

c. For each of the following lengths, first draw a line segment using no measuring instruments, i.e., draw your best guess; then check your guess. Record whether your guess was bigger or smaller than the actual measurement and approximately how much bigger or smaller it was. Draw on paper or on the chalkboard. (See table on page 326.)

***d.** Working with a small group, have everyone draw a line segment. Then everyone guesses how long each line segment is. Record all the guesses and then measure the line segments.

***e.** Make a pendulum 1 meter long. (Hang a weight—anything heavy

[1] Decimeter.

[2] Centimeter.

[3] Dekameter.

[4] 100.

Length	My Guess Was (Smaller or Larger):	My Guess Differed from the Correct Length by Approximately:
4 centimeters	_____	_____
5 millimeters	_____	_____
36 centimeters	_____	_____
2 meters	_____	_____
126 centimeters	_____	_____
7 decimeters	_____	_____
1.8 meters	_____	_____
7.5 centimeters	_____	_____

and small—from a piece of string and tie the string where it can swing freely.) How much time does it take for one left-to-right swing? (You may want to time five swings and find the average.) _____ [7]

2. Metric Area   *Materials needed:* **many white rods, some orange rods, two meter sticks, some 10 × 10 cm squares (squares cut from centimeter graph paper or from orange cardboard are nice), some square meters from newspaper, tagboard, or posterboard, some centimeter graph paper.**

a. Look at the top of a table, or a desk, or a notebook. The top surface is two-dimensional. It has area. To measure such a surface, we need a measurer that can cover the surface. One-dimensional measurers such as were used to measure length can never cover a surface, because line segments have no width. For area, a measurer with two dimensions is needed. Any two-dimensional shape will do, though some are more difficult to use than others. Equilateral triangles, regular hexagons, trapezoids made of three equilateral triangles   , rectangles, and squares cover surfaces nicely. Because right angles are used so frequently in our world, the simplest figure with right angles, the *square,* is usually used to measure area.

[7] The French commission that invented the metric system in the 1790s almost used this property to define the meter. But because the earth had recently been measured quite accurately, they chose to define 1 meter as one ten-millionth of the distance from the earth's equator to the North Pole. The meter defined in this way in 1799 and recorded as the distance between two parallel lines scratched on a platinum-iridium bar maintained at the temperature of melting ice turned out to be greater than one ten-millionth of a later, more accurate measure of the earth. But this inaccuracy only makes a difference in the fourth decimal place. In 1960 the meter was defined as 1,650,763.73 wavelengths of orange-red light emitted by krypton 86. This definition is accurate to one part in 100 million.

In the metric system, the square measurers have sides of metric length:

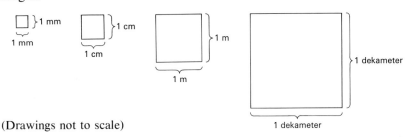

(Drawings not to scale)

b. Use the measurers to answer some of the following:

What is the area of this page? _____

What is the area of one wall of this classroom? _____

What is the area of the paper money with you in class? _____

What is the area of the back of your shirt (blouse, skirt)? _____

What is the area of this dot? · _____

What is the area of the bottom of your hand? _____

What is the area of your left thumbnail? _____

What is the area of your notebook? _____

What feminine article of clothing would one square meter make?

_____

What is the area of your watchband? _____

What is the area of the eraser on your pencil? _____

What is the area of the change in your pocket (purse)? _____

c. For all the questions below, use the materials or draw a picture to help you answer.[5]

(1) How many square decimeters in 1 square meter? _____

(2) How many square centimeters are in 1 square decimeter? _____

(3) How many square centimeters are in 1 square meter? _____

(4) How many square millimeters in 1 square centimeter? _____

(5) How many square millimeters in 1 square meter? _____

(6) How many square meters in 1 square kilometer? _____

For area, the usual relationships according to the prefixes do not work. The relationships instead are of the usual ones squared.

$10000 (= 100^2)$ square centimeters = 1 square meter

$100 (= 10^2)$ square decimeters = 1 square meter

d. Draw 4 square centimeters. Draw 4 centimeters square. What is the difference?

[5] (1) **100,** (2) **100,** (3) **10,000,** (4) **100,** (5) **1,000,000,** (6) **1,000,000.**

Draw approximations of the following areas and then check your approximations. Record whether your guess was larger or smaller than the actual measurement and approximately how much larger or smaller it was. Discuss problems (1), (4), and (9) with your colleagues. More than one rectangular shape is correct for these. See if you can figure out what arithmetic procedure leads to these different rectangular shapes.

Area	My Guess Was (Smaller or Larger):	My Guess Differed from the Correct Area by Approximately:
(1) 12 square centimeters	_____	_____
(2) 7 square centimeters	_____	_____
(3) 3 centimeters square	_____	_____
(4) 24 square centimeters	_____	_____
(5) 2 square meters	_____	_____
(6) 0.5 square meters	_____	_____
(7) 0.5 meters square	_____	_____
(8) 50 centimeters square	_____	_____
(9) 18 square decimeters	_____	_____

3. Metric Volume *Materials needed:* **many white rods, some orange rods, three meter sticks, some cubic decimeters from cardboard (preferably orange), centimeter graph paper, cardboard, scissors, tape.**
Optional: **centicubes (See Appendix I).**

a. Think of an empty milk carton. It has three dimensions—length, width, and height. To measure this type of shape, a measurer that can fill the space is needed. An area measurer can cover the bottom, but such measurers have no height. To cover or fill the milk carton, the measurer must have height. So a volume measurer must have three dimensions. As with area, the simplest shape that has right angles—the *cube*—is usually used to measure volume. The cubic metric measurers have sides of metric length.

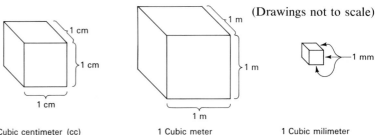

(Drawings not to scale)

1 Cubic centimeter (cc)   1 Cubic meter   1 Cubic milimeter

329 DECIMALS:
BASIC
OPERATIONS,
ALGORITHMS,
AND THE
METRIC
SYSTEM

b. Use the measurers to answer some of the following questions and problems.

What is the volume of this book? _____
What is the volume of your thumb? _____
What is the volume of your shoe? _____
Use the cardboard, scissors, and tape to make a box without a top that can be measured by filling it with white rods. Trade boxes with someone and find the volume of each other's boxes.
Using the white rods, make a "building" 3 rods wide, 5 rods long, and 2 rods high. What is the volume of this building?
Using white rods, how many different buildings that have a volume of 24 cubic centimeters can you make?
How many people fit into a cubic meter?
Cut a shape out of centimeter graph paper and fold it up to make an open box (see example). What is the volume of your box?

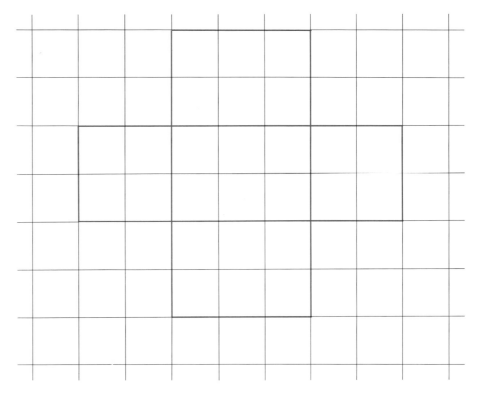

c. Use the measurers or draw pictures to answer the following questions.[6]

[6] (1) 1000, (2) 1000, (3) 1,000,000, (4) 1000.

(1) How many cubic centimeters are in a cubic decimeter? _____
(2) How many cubic decimeters are in a cubic meter? _____
(3) How many cubic centimeters are in a cubic meter? _____
(4) How many cubic millimeters are in a cubic centimeter? _____
For volume, the usual relationships according to the prefixes do not work. The relationships instead are of the usual ones cubed.

$$1000 (= 10^3) \text{ cubic decimeters } = 1 \text{ cubic meter}$$
$$1000000 (= 100^3) \text{ cubic centimeters} = 1 \text{ cubic meter}$$

---

4. Metric Liquid Capacity *Materials needed:* **open cubic decimeter (lined with a plastic bag if made out of cardboard); liter containers, graduated liter containers (perhaps borrowed from the chemistry department); milliliter droppers (from vitamin or medical bottles); some containers labeled A, B, C, D, E, F; water; paper towels.**

The measurer for metric liquid capacity is derived from the measurer for metric volume:

1 liter = 1 cubic decimeter = 1000 cubic centimeters (cc's)

A milliliter is the only multiple of a liter commonly used. A milliliter is one-thousandth of a liter, or 0.001 of 1000 cubic centimeters = 1 cubic centimeter.

1 milliliter (ml) = 1 cubic centimeter

Cubic centimeters are used to measure vitamins and medicine. Milliliters are used in much scientific work involving small amounts of liquid.

a. Fill the cubic decimeter with water. You now have a _____[7] of water. If you could fill a white rod with water, you would have a _____[8] of water.

b. Guess approximately how much each container A through F will hold. Record your guess. Check your guess and record the real approximate capacity.

Container	Guessed Capacity	Measured Capacity	Container	Guessed Capacity	Measured Capacity
A	_____	_____	D	_____	_____
B	_____	_____	E	_____	_____
C	_____	_____	F	_____	_____

---

[7] Liter.

[8] Milliliter.

331 DECIMALS:
BASIC
OPERATIONS,
ALGORITHMS,
AND THE
METRIC
SYSTEM

Measure a cup from a soft drink or coffee machine. How many milliliters do you drink a day? A week?

c. Tell whether each of the containers with the following dimensions holds more than 1 liter, less than 1 liter, or 1 liter.[9]

(1) $10 \times 11 \times 9$ cm: _____

(2) $5 \times 25 \times 8$ cm: _____

(3) $20 \times 4 \times 11$ cm: _____

(4) $10 \times 5 \times 20$ cm: _____

---

5. Metric Weight[8] *Materials needed:* **A liter and a milliliter measure and some water; things to weigh (ranging in weight from a few grams to a couple of kilograms) labeled A, B, C, D, E, F; gram weights (centicubes, some kinds of paper clips, and a new nickel $\cong$ 5 grams, chemistry weights), kilogram weights; equal-arm balance. (See Appendix I.)**

---

a. Metric *weight* is related to metric *volume* and therefore also to metric *liquid capacity:*

1 cubic centimeter of water at 4°C weighs 1 gram.

1 milliliter of water (= 1 cc) weighs 1 gram.

1 liter (= 1000 cc) weighs 1000 grams = 1 kilogram).[9]

b. Use the milliliter dropper to drop a milliliter of water on your hand. Is a gram heavy or light?

c. Use the equal-arm balance and either water or gram and kilogram weights to measure the weight of objects A through F. First guess the weight and record your guess. Then check your guess and record the real weight.

Object	Guessed Weight	Measured Weight	Object	Guessed Weight	Measured Weight
A	_____	_____	D	_____	_____
B	_____	_____	E	_____	_____
C	_____	_____	F	_____	_____

[8] Grams are actually the unit of metric *mass*, which is a measure of a body's inertia or its gravitational effect. *Weight* is the gravitational pull or force exerted by Earth on a physical body. Because weight is proportional to mass at any given point, weight may be measured in units of mass (and vice versa) when ·n object is not moving (e.g., in commerce). In the English system, the pound is a unit of weight and the slug is a unit of mass.

[9] Nearly a century ago a standard kilogram was made in France. In 1927 a liter of water was measured very accurately and found to weigh only 0.999972 of the standard kilogram.

---

[9] (1) <, (2) =, (3) <, (4) =.

Is a milligram heavy, light, or very light? What things might be measured in milligrams?[10]

At home, lift some cans of food. Guess how much they weigh and then check the labels. (Most food cans are now labeled in grams.)

5.2.3
Summary of the Metric System
1. Within-Type Metric Trade Rules

Within a given type of measure (e.g., length, weight), all trade rules from one measurer to another involve only multiples of ten. To change an answer in one measurer to one using another measurer, you need only use the shift rules for multiplying by 10, 100, 1000, etc., or those for dividing by 10, 100, 1000, etc. (these rules move numbers in the opposite direction from multiplication shift rules).

6 meters = 600 centimeters $\quad$ ($100 \times 6 = 600$; the 6 shifts 2 places to the left)

4000 milliliters = 4 liters $\quad$ ($4000 \div 1000 = 4$; the 4 shifts 3 places to the right)

To change the measurer in the English system requires much more difficult arithmetic because the trade rules for the English system are much more complicated.

12 inches = 1 foot $\quad$ 3 feet = 1 yard

$5\frac{1}{8}$ yards = 1 rod $\quad$ 5,280 feet = 1 mile

16 ounces = 1 pound $\quad$ 4 quarts = 1 gallon

To illustrate the comparative simplicity of measure changes in the metric system, some changes are posed below. For each metric and English measure, write in the blank the arithmetic that must be performed to make the change. You need not work the arithmetic.[11]

Thus because of the inaccuracy in the original standard kilogram, a liter of water weighs very close to 1 kilogram, but not exactly that.

---

[10] **Nutritional contents of vitamins, chemical solutions, medicines.**

[11]

Metric System	English System
$25 \div 100$	$25 \div 12$
$17 \div 10$	$17 \div 3$
$4735 \div 1000$	$4735 \div 5280$
0.053×1000	$0.053 \times (16 \times 36)$
0.780×100	0.78×36
$475 \div (100)^2$	$475 \div 144$
$68 \div 10^2$	$68 \div 9$
0.0035×100^2	$0.0035 \times (36 \times 36)$
$987 \div 100^3$	$987 \div (12 \times 12 \times 12)$

333 DECIMALS:
BASIC
OPERATIONS,
ALGORITHMS,
AND THE
METRIC
SYSTEM

Metric System		English System	
25 cm = _____	**m**	25 in. = _____	ft
17 decim = _____	**m**	17 ft = _____	yd
4735 m = _____	km	4735 ft = _____	miles
0.053 m = _____	mm	0.053 yd _____	$\frac{1}{16}$ in.
0.780 m = _____	cm	0.780 yd = _____	in.
(Be careful on the next six.)			
475 sq cm = _____	sq m	475 sq in. = _____	sq ft
68 sq decim = _____	sq m	68 sq ft = _____	sq yds
0.0035 sq m = _____	sq cm	0.0035 sq yd = _____	sq in
987 cc = _____	cu m	987 cu in. = _____	cu ft
50000 cc = _____	cu m	50000 cu in. = _____	cu yd
0.097 cc = _____	cu mm	0.097 cu in. = _____	cu $\frac{1}{16}$ in.
275 ml = _____	liters	275 tsp = _____	qts
0.87 liter = _____	centil	0.87 gal = _____	qts
450 g = _____	kg	450 oz = _____	lbs
0.72 kg = _____	grams	0.72 lb = _____	oz

2. Between-Type Metric Trade Rules The trade rules between types of metric measures are simple. Two main trade rules relate small measures (g, cc, and ml) and large measures (kg, cu dm, 1):

> 1 cc = 1 ml = 1 gm   (with respect to water)
> 1 cu dm = 1 liter = 1 kg   (with respect to water)

The only comparative trade rule for the English system is the little known, but very useful:

A pint's a pound
The world around.

That is, a pint of water weighs about a pound. (Optional: Find a rule that will relate English volume to English liquid capacity and weight.)

To illustrate the difference between the metric and English systems with respect to intermeasure conversions, fill in the blanks below. For

Metric System	English System
$50000 \div 100^3$	$50000 \div (36 \times 36 \times 36)$
0.097×10^3	$0.097 \times (16 \times 16 \times 16)$
$275 \div 1000$	$275 \div (3 \times 16 \times 4)$
0.87×100	0.87×4
$450 \div 1000$	$450 \div 16$
0.72×1000	0.72×16

the English system just give the measurers that would be involved.[12]

Metric System	Types of Measures Compared	English System
1 cc = 1 g	volume, weight	cu in, oz
1 liter = 1000 _____	_____, volume	____, ____
1 kg = 1 _____	_____, liquid capacity	____, ____
1 ml = 1 _____	_____, weight	____, ____
1 gram = 1 _____	_____, volume	____, ____
1000 cc = 1 _____	_____, weight	____, ____

Conversion between different types of metric measure is very simple, while conversion between different types of English measure is quite difficult.

5.2.4
English-Metric Conversions

From your work with metric measurers you should have a fairly good idea of the approximate size of these measurers. The activities below attempt to link these metric measurers to their approximate equivalents in English measures.

Materials needed: **Length—inches, yardsticks; white rods, metersticks. Area—the above plus square inches, square feet, square yard, square meter.**
Volume—the above plus inch cubes.
Liquid capacity—cup, pint, quart, gallon, graduated liter.
Weight—ounces, pounds, grams, kilograms, equal arm balance (see Appendix I).

1. Length

a. Compare a yardstick and a meter stick. Which is longer? _____ How much longer? _____
Compare an inch and a centimeter. Which is longer? _____ Approximately how many centimeters are in an inch? _____

[12]
Metric System	Types of Measures Compared	English System
1 cc = 1 g	volume, weight	cu in., oz
1 liter = 1000 cc	liquid capacity, volume	quart, cu in.
1 kg = 1 liter	weight, liquid capacity	lb, qt
1 ml = 1 g	liquid capacity, weight	qt, lb
1 gram = 1 cc	weight, volume	oz, cu in.
1000 cc = 1 kg	volume, weight	cu ft, lb

335 DECIMALS:
BASIC
OPERATIONS,
ALGORITHMS,
AND THE
METRIC
SYSTEM

Summary: $2\frac{1}{2}$ centimeters = 1 inch

1 meter = a bit more than a yard (this bit is about 0.1 yard, and so 1 meter = about 1.1 yards)

Use the 1.1 figure to find the relationship between a mile and kilometer.[13]

b. John and Mary live 4 miles from school. How many kilometers will they have to ride their bikes to get to school? _____

How many meters long is a $4\frac{1}{2}$ yard piece of fabric? _____

How many meters tall are you? _____

How many inches wide is an 8-cm-wide ribbon? _____

What is the fastest legal driving speed in kilometers in your state? _____

How many meters of material would you need to buy for a pattern requiring 4 yards of material? _____

How would you buy a 30-inch belt in metric measures? _____

Instead of the present 34 inches, $25\frac{1}{2}$ inches, 36 inches, a ladies size-12 dress pattern would read: _____

How many meters high is a standard room ceiling (8 feet)? _____

2. Area Use materials or draw pictures to help solve these problems.

a. Approximately how many square centimeters in a square inch? _____[14]

Approximately how many square yards in a square meter? _____[15]

Approximately how many square feet in a square meter? _____[16]

b. Give approximate answers for the following:

How many square meters in a 9×12-foot rug? _____

Suppose you had to paint a room that had 540 square feet of paintable surface, and you had to give it two coats of paint. How many cans of paint would you buy if each can would paint 40 square meters?

How many square centimeters does a sheet of $8\frac{1}{2} \times 11$-inch paper contain?

3. Liquid Capacity **a.** A quart of milk measures 7 by 7 by 20 centimeters.[10] Is a quart greater than or less than a liter? _____

---

[10] Paper cartons are not quite this tall; the bowing out of the sides allows them to contain more than their measurements indicate.

---

[13] 1 mile = $\frac{5280}{3}$ = 1760 yards. Decrease this by .1 to get meters: $.1 \times 1760 = 176$. $1760 - 176 =$ about 1600 meters = 1.6 kilometers.

[14] **6.25**

[15] **1.2.**

[16] **11.**

Are they close to each other? _____
Use the containers to check this.
Using your knowledge above, first predict your answer in liters for the English measurers below and then check using water.

1 pint = _____ liters   1 gallon = _____ liters

b. Give approximate answers for these questions.
A car that will hold 15 gallons of gas will hold how many liters of gasoline? _____
If a gallon of gas costs 50 cents, how much will a liter of gas cost? _____
If a half-gallon of milk costs 70 cents, how much will a liter of milk cost? _____
How many liters in a giant (48-ounce) bottle of Coke? _____
If a baby drinks four 8-ounce bottles of milk a day, how many liters of milk do the parents have to buy in a week? _____
A bottle of wine labeled 75 centiliters contains how many quarts? _____

4. Weight **a.** Now that you know that a quart is about the same as a liter, use "A pint's a pound" to figure out the relationship between a pound and a kilogram (a liter weighs about a kilogram).[17] Now check this using the pound and kilogram weights.
   Use the gram and ounce weights to find the relationship between these measures. _____ grams = 1 ounce.[18]

b. Give approximate answers for these questions.
How much do you weigh in kilograms? _____
How many kilograms does a 5-pound bag of flour weigh? _____
Would you graph the weight gain of a mouse in grams or kilograms? _____

Approximately how many kilograms does a gallon of milk weigh (assume milk weighs the same as water)? _____

5. Summary of English-Metric
Equivalents
(*The symbol* ≅ *means "is approximately equal to."*)

1 meter ≅ 1.1 yards   1 inch ≅ 2.5 centimeters
1 square meter ≅ 11 square feet
1 liter ≅ 1 quart   1 kilogram ≅ 2.2 pounds

[17] A pint's a pound means that a quart is about 2 pounds. 2 pounds = 1 quart = 1 liter = 1 kilogram. Therefore a kilogram is about 2 pounds. (Actually the kilogram is about 2.2 pounds.)
[18] A bit more than 28.

337 DECIMALS:
BASIC
OPERATIONS,
ALGORITHMS,
AND THE
METRIC
SYSTEM

As a reference, a table of more exact metric-English equivalents is given below.

Table of Metric-English Equivalent

Length:
    1 centimeter = 0.39 inches   1 inch = 2.54 centimeters
    1 meter = 1.09 yards   1 yard = 0.91 meters

Area:
    1 square centimeter =   1 square inch =
        0.155 sq in.   6.25 square centimeters
    1 square meter =   1 square yard =
        1.196 square yards   0.836 square meters

Liquid Capacity:
    1 liter = 1.06 quarts   1 quart = 0.946 liters

Weight:
    1 kilogram = 2.2 pounds   1 pound = 0.45 kilogram
    1 gram = 0.035 ounces   1 ounce = 28.35 grams

**5.2.5
Developing
Continuing Awareness of
the Metric System**

For two weeks collect examples of situations where metric measures might be used. Specify which metric measurer you would use in the situation.

Compare your list with the lists of your colleagues.

**5.3
ACTIVITY:
THE MEANING OF ADDITION,
SUBTRACTION, MULTIPLICA-
TION, AND DIVISION
OF DECIMALS**

As in some of the units in Part A, we will begin here with a new set of numbers, the decimals, and examine relations and operations on this set of numbers.

The set of decimals includes all numbers written filling in any [11] of the blanks below with symbols 0, 1, 2, 3, 4, 5, 6, 7, 8, 9:

. . . _ _ _ _ _ _ _ . _ _ _ _ _ _ . . .

For example, 47.0032 and 2705 and 0.008 are decimals.

The relationship between any adjacent places is that a one in the place on the left is worth ten times as much as a one in the place on the right. A decimal may be as large or as small as you wish.

[11] Because all positions are determined with respect to the decimal point, zeros must be included in all positions between a given symbol and the decimal point.

Overview: The relations $<$, $=$, and $>$ and the operations addition, subtraction, multiplication, and division will be examined with two embodiments of decimals. In this section, only decimals between 1 and 0.001 will be used. Algorithms for larger and smaller decimals will be discussed in section 5.4.

Materials needed: For each group—one set of base-ten blocks, one set of play money, 5 sheets of paper or a flat table, masking tape (or calculating sheets from Part B, Unit 1).

5.3.1
How the Embodiments for Decimals Work

Embodiments that show the different sizes of each decimal place are most valuable for the initial exposure to decimals. We will use two such embodiments here—the base-ten blocks and money (dollars, dimes, pennies, and green stamps; see Appendix I for different ways to make the money). The different size of the decimal places is embodied in the different size of the blocks; with the money, the different size is really embodied by the experience of each person with money and with the comparative worth of dollars, dimes, pennies, and green stamps (one-tenth of a penny). In elementary school, this money embodiment will only work with students who have already had enough experience with money to understand these relationships.

1. For the Blocks

Today, suppose the cube (the biggest block) is one (1). Then write in decimal form what each of the following would be:[19] (a) one flat: _____. (b) one long: _____ (c) one small cube: _____.

Either make calculating sheets from four pieces of 8½″ by 11″ paper as pictured below, or use the calculating sheets you made for algorithms for operations on whole numbers.

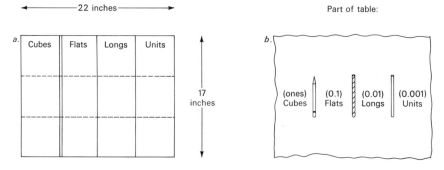

Another approach would be to divide four spaces on a table using

---

[19] (a) **0.1**, (b) **0.01**, (c) **0.001**.

pencils, straws, or whatever. The decimal point should be somehow specified.

2. For the Money Make a calculating sheet as pictured below:

b. Or use the calculating sheet for the blocks.

c. Or use part of a table as pictured in *b* above.

a.

← 11 inches →			
Dollars	Dimes	Pennies	Green stamps

$8\frac{1}{2}$ inches

3. For Both Embodiments To symbolize a number:

1. Make all possible right-to-left trades. (Why?)
2. Count the number of pieces in a column and record that number in the place for that column.
3. Place a period after the ones place.
4. Include zeros in empty places between the decimal point and non-empty places farther to the right. (Why?)

Symbolize each of the following situations[20]:

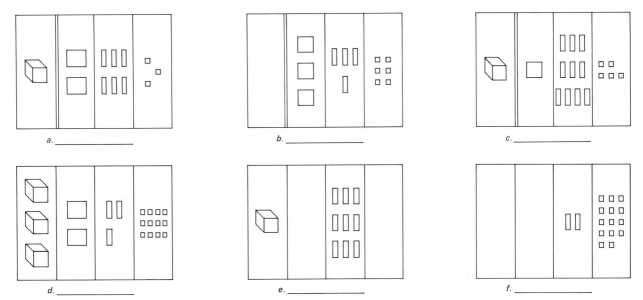

a. _____

b. _____

c. _____

d. _____

e. _____

f. _____

[20] a. 1.263, b. 0.346, c. 1.205, d. 3.242, e. 1.09, f. 0.034.

The embodiments in this section are limited in the number of places they can embody. Look for patterns in this section, and in section 5.4 these patterns will be extended to an arbitrary number of places using a chip computer for decimals.

* Some people find a rod computer to be helpful with decimals. Review sections 1.2.6 and 2.2.3 to recall how a rod computer works. For decimals, you must add columns to the right of one. The one-for-ten (left-to-right) trade rules continue for these new places to the right of one.

If you use the rod computer, try some of the problems in each section that follows. No special instructions are necessary.

All four operations are done on the rod computer as they were done in Part A, except that the trains are vertical instead of horizontal and trading between columns is sometimes necessary to get a large enough or small enough number.

***5.3.2**

Relations for Decimals

Use your embodiments to complete the blanks below with >, =, or <. Try to figure out a general way to tell which of two numbers is larger.

a. 0.56 ＿ 0.65 **b.** 0.04 ＿ 0.004 **c.** 0.285 ＿ 0.235

d. 0.3021 ＿ 0.297 **e.** 1.964 ＿ 2.011 **f.** 0.027 ＿ 0.072

g. Which of the above problems are likely to be difficult for children and why?

h. Describe your method of deciding which of two decimal numbers is larger.

i. Compare your method with those of some of your colleagues. Did any of you say that a number is larger if you can make the other number out of it and still have pieces left over?

Example: For *a.* 0.56 ＿ 0.65: If you trade one flat from the 0.65 you get five flats and fifteen longs. With this you can make 0.56 (five flats and six longs) and have nine longs left over.

This is the method usually used to define <: $\triangle < \square$ if $\triangle + \bigcirc = \square$ Try a couple of the problems above using this definition of <.

5.3.3

Addition of Decimals

First estimate an answer and then give a mathematical model for each problem.[21]

---

[21] **a.** $1.3 + 1.8 = \square$, **b.** $0.016 + 0.017 = \square$, **c.** $1.58 + 1.73 = \square$.

341 DECIMALS:
BASIC
OPERATIONS,
ALGORITHMS,
AND THE
METRIC
SYSTEM

a. Jack drove 1.3 miles to the grocery store. He drove 1.8 miles to get back because he drove over to the cleaner's on his way home. How far did he go on this round trip?
Estimate: _____ *Mathematical model:* _____

b. First-grade students at the King Elementary School found that the bean they had planted grew 0.016 meter in the first week and 0.017 meter in the second week. How tall was it at the end of the second week?
Estimate: _____ *Mathematical model:* _____

c. Carolyn has $1.58 and George has $1.73. Do they have enough money together to buy a truck that costs $3.25?
Estimate: _____ *Mathematical model:* _____

Here is how addition of decimals is done with the two approximate size embodiments:

To Add Place pieces representing the first number in the top row of the calculating sheet. Place pieces representing the second number in the second row. Beginning at the right-hand column which contains pieces, push all pieces into the bottom row. Make all possible trades. Record the answer. Continue in this manner for each column, moving to the left.

Do the problems below with your embodiments. By the end, be sure you can do problems with both embodiments.[22]

d. $1.8 + 0.5 =$ ___ **e.** $0.016 + 0.017 =$ ___ **f.** $1.4 + 0.73 =$ ___
g. $2 + 0.05 =$ ___ **h.** $0.048 + 0.75 =$ ___ **i.** $1.486 + 0.97 =$ ___

Make up other problems and try them if you are not fully confident about both of the embodiments.

j. Give three real life situations where addition of decimals is necessary (make at least one of them require thousandths).

**5.3.4
Subtraction
of Decimals** First estimate an answer and then give a mathematical model for each problem below and on page 342.[23]

a. First-grade students at King Elementary School found that their plant that had been fed enriched plant food grew 0.042 meters in the first three weeks while the plant not fed the enriched plant food grew only

---

[22] d. 2.3, e. 0.033, f. 2.13, g. 2.05, h. 0.798, i. 2.456.
[23] a. $0.042 - 0.027 = \square$, b. $0.72 - 0.55 = \square$, c. $6.2 - 3.7 = \square$.

0.027 meters. How much taller was the enriched plant food plant?
Estimate: _____ *Mathematical model:* _____

b. Billie Jean spent $.55 of her $.72 lunch money for a Halloween mask. How much can she spend for lunch that day?
Estimate: _____ *Mathematical model:* _____

c. Becky noticed that her new bicycle odometer read 3.7 when she left home and 6.2 when she got to her friend's house. How far had she ridden?
Estimate: _____ *Mathematical model:* _____

To Subtract Put pieces representing the larger number in the top row. Put pieces representing the smaller number in the second row. Then ask yourself one of the following questions:

(1) The number in the second row *plus how many more* equals the number in the top row?

(2) The number in the top row *minus* the number in the second row equals how many?

Place the number of pieces in the answer to your question in the bottom row. Record this number of pieces. Continue in this manner for each column, moving to the left.[12]

Do the problems below with your embodiments. Before you reach the end of this section, be sure you can subtract with both embodiments.[24]

d. $1.7 - 0.32 =$ _____ **e.** $2.3 - 0.14 =$ _____ **f.** $0.24 - 0.078 =$ _____
g. $0.042 - 0.027 =$ _____ **h.** $.502 - 0.43 =$ _____
i. $1.3 - 0.002 =$ _____

Do other problems if you need the experience.

j. If you write subtraction problems vertically instead of horizontally, what must you be careful to do? Why?

---

[12] You can also subtract using a *take-away* approach: put the larger number on the sheet. Take off pieces for the second number. Answer is the pieces remaining on the sheet.
  You can also use a *comparison* approach; you want to split the larger number into two sets, one of which is the size of the number being subtracted. Put the larger number in the top row, the smaller in the bottom row. Using pieces from the top row, make in the second row a set equal to the bottom row. Answer is the pieces remaining in the top row.

---

[24] d. 1.38, e. 2.16, f. 0.162, g. 0.015, h. 0.072, i. 1.298.

k. Give three real life situations where subtraction of decimals is necessary (Make at least one involve thousandths, probably by using the metric system).

5.3.5
Multiplication of Decimals

First give an estimate and then write a mathematical model for each of these problems.[25]

a. Julie rode her bicycle 0.4 mile to school every day. How far did she ride to school and back in one week?
Estimate: _____ *Mathematical model:* _____

b. A mother has some ribbon 0.007 meters wide. At the bottom of a dress she puts three rows of ribbon, leaving between each row a space the same width as the ribbon. How wide is this decorative band? Is this a reasonable size of decoration for the hemline border of a 5-year-old child's dress?
Estimate: _____ *Mathematical model:* _____

c. A grocery store is having a special: 20 percent off on all brand X fruits. How much would you save on a jar of applesauce costing $.30?
Estimate: _____ *Mathematical model:* _____

d. The store in the third-grade classroom had a 3 percent sales tax. How much tax is there on a purchase of $.67?
Estimate: _____ *Mathematical model:* _____

Most people think of multiplying decimals as involving moving the decimal point around. In reality it is the digits themselves which move to different columns (or places) and not the decimal point which moves. As you do the following activities, think of the numbers as lying on a stationary calculating sheet: The numbers shift around, but the columns (and the decimal point) do not.

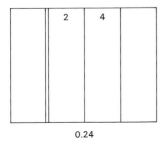

0.24

may shift to:

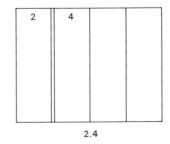

2.4

or

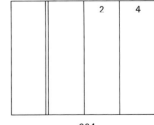

.024

[25] a. $10 \times 0.4 = \square$, b. $5 \times 0.007 = \square$, c. $0.2 \times 0.3 = \square$, d. $0.03 \times 0.67 = \square$.

In the activities that follow, *do only as many problems of each kind* as is necessary for you to see the shift rule involved.

To multiply decimals, some *shift rules* are necessary. First, the *old* whole number shift rules for 1, 10, 100, etc., need to be checked to see if they work for the new places to the right of the decimal point. Then *new* shift rules for multiplying by 0.1, 0.01, 0.001, etc., will be found.

1. Whole Number Shift Rules Applied to the New Decimal Places

a. *Shift Rule for 1:* The multiplicative identity for whole numbers is 1. This means that 1 just makes a single copy of any whole number. Is 1 the multiplicative identity for decimals to the right of the decimal point? Try the problems below with your embodiments.

$$1 \times 2.452 = \text{\_\_\_\_\_} \qquad 1 \times .004 = \text{\_\_\_\_\_} \qquad 1 \times 0.36 = \text{\_\_\_\_\_}$$

Is 1 the multiplicative identity for all decimals?[26]

b. *Shift Rule for 10:* With embodiments for whole numbers, multiplying by 10 meant for every piece, select a piece one size larger (or a piece one piece to the left). Symbolically, this had the effect of shifting the number one place to the left (that is, $10 \times 147 = 1470$).

Remember that you can approach the shift rules either by keeping the multiplied number an unseparated whole (that is, 10×0.4: make ten piles of 0.4, trade to get 4.0) or by multiplying each piece in a place:

Ten flats = one cube
$10 \times 0.1 = 1.0$
Do this for each piece:
each flat trades for a cube
$10 \times 0.4 = 4$ Cubes $= 4.0$

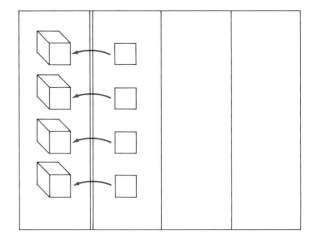

The latter approach is probably more helpful for decimal fractions.

Try the following problems with embodiments and decide if the same shift rule works for places to the right of the decimal point.

[26] **Yes.**

345 DECIMALS:
BASIC
OPERATIONS,
ALGORITHMS,
AND THE
METRIC
SYSTEM

$10 \times 0.4 =$ _____ $10 \times 0.05 =$ _____ $10 \times 0.002 =$ _____

$10 \times 0.43 =$ _____ $10 \times 0.027 =$ _____ $10 \times 0.364 =$ _____

Does the shift rule for multiplying whole numbers by 10 work for places to the right of the decimal point?[27]

c. *Shift Rule for 100:* The symbolic shift rule for multiplying whole numbers by 100 was to shift the number two places to the left and multiply by 1. Work the problems below with your embodiments and decide if the same shift rule works for places to the right of the decimal point. (Multiplying *one piece at a time* by 100 is probably the easiest way.)

$100 \times 0.3 =$ _____ $100 \times 0.06 =$ _____ $100 \times 0.004 =$ _____

$100 \times 0.72 =$ _____ $100 \times 0.053 =$ _____ $100 \times 0.241 =$ _____

Does the shift rule for multiplying whole numbers by 100 work for numbers using places to the right of the decimal point?[28]

Conclusion: The shift rules for multiplying by 1, 10, and 100 *do* work for all decimals.

In 5.4.3 the shift rules for multiplying by 1000, 10000, etc., will be checked.

2. New Shift Rules for Multiplying by 0.1, 0.01, and 0.001 Look for a general pattern in the shift rules below. By the end see if you can predict what the shift rule for multiplying by 0.001 and 0.0001 will be.

a. *Shift Rule for 0.1*

2×3 can mean 2 sets *of* 3.

$0.1 \times \square$ can mean 0.1 *of* $\square$, so for each piece in the embodiment, take the piece that is 0.1 (one-tenth) of that piece (or, for each ten, take one).

0.1×0.3: find one-tenth of 3 tenths (of 3 flats); a long is one-tenth of a flat, so take a long for each flat.
Answer: 3 longs $= 0.03$

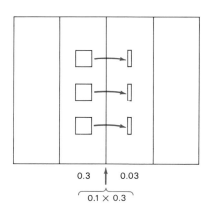

0.3   0.03

0.1×0.3

[27] **Yes.**

[28] **Yes.**

0.1 × 0.02: find one-tenth of 2 hundredths (of 2 longs); a unit is one-tenth of a long, so take a unit for each long.
Answer: 2 units = 0.002

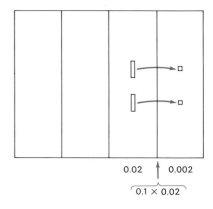

Do these problems with the embodiments.

0.1 × 3 = _____   0.1 × 0.5 = _____   0.1 × 0.06 = _____
0.1 × 2.3 = _____   0.1 × 0.42 = _____   0.1 × 0.125 = _____

Generalization for multiplying by 0.1: The effect with the embodiments of multiplying by 0.1 is that each piece gets traded for a piece in the column to the right. Symbolically, each number gets shifted _____ place to the _____[29] and multiplied by 1 (that is, 0.1 × 0.3 becomes 1 × 0.03 = 0.03).

b. *Shift Rule for 0.01*

0.01 × □ means 0.01 of □, so for each piece in the embodiment, take the piece that is 0.01 (one-hundredth) of that piece (or, for each hundred, take one).

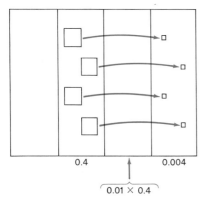

0.01 × 0.4: find one-hundredth of 4 tenths (4 flats); a unit is one-hundredth of a flat, so take a unit for each flat.
Answer: 4 Units = .004.

Do these problems with the embodiments.

0.1 × 4 = _____   0.01 × 0.7 = _____   0.01 × 0.04 = _____
0.01 × 2.5 = _____   0.01 × 0.15 = _____   0.01 × 1.32 = _____

Generalization for multiplying by .01: With the embodiments, each piece gets traded for a piece _____ places to the _____. Symbolically, this

---

[29] One, right.

347 DECIMALS:
BASIC
OPERATIONS,
ALGORITHMS,
AND THE
METRIC
SYSTEM

has the effect of shifting each number _____ places to the _____[30] and multiplying by one (that is, 0.01×4 becomes $1 \times 0.04 = 0.04$).

c. *Shift Rule for 0.001*

$0.001 \times \square$ means 0.001 of $\square$, so for each piece in the embodiment, take the piece that is 0.001 (one-thousandth) of that piece (or, for each thousand, take one).

There are only four places in these embodiments, and so you can only really do one case for 0.001s. Draw pictures or imagine the size of new pieces needed to do some of the following problems.

$0.001 \times 2 =$ _____ $0.001 \times 0.3 =$ _____
$0.001 \times 0.04 =$ _____ $0.001 \times 0.51 =$ _____

Generalization for multiplying by .001: With the embodiments, each piece gets traded for a piece _____ places to the _____. Symbolically, this has the effect of shifting each number _____ places to the _____[31] and multiplying by one (that is, 0.001×0.3 becomes $1 \times 0.0003 = 0.0003$).

d. *Multiplying by multiples of 0.1, 0.01, and 0.001*

$0.2 \times \square = 2 \times 0.1 \times \square = 2 \times$ (use 0.1 shift rule on $\square$)
$0.05 \times \square = 5 \times 0.01 \times \square = 5 \times$ (use 0.01 shift rule on $\square$)
$0.007 \times \square = 7 \times 0.001 \times \square = 7 \times$ (use 0.001 shift rule on $\square$)

In each case, multiplying by a multiple of 0.1, 0.01, or 0.001 is the same as first multiplying by 0.1 (or 0.01 or 0.001) and then multiplying by the whole number multiple.

Do these problems. First give an approximate answer (guess). Then find the answer by using the proper shift rule and multiplying (remember that 0.35 is hundredths, 0.249 is thousandths).[32]

(1) $0.4 \times 2.3 =$ _____   **(2)** $0.05 \times 0.61 =$ _____
    Guess: _____ *Answer:* _____   *Guess:* _____ *Answer:* _____
(3) $0.008 \times 4.1 =$ _____   **(4)** $0.12 \times 7.3 =$ _____
    Guess: _____ *Answer:* _____   *Guess:* _____ *Answer:* _____

[30] **Two, right.**

[31] **Three, right.**

[32] **Answers: (1) 0.92, (2) 0.0305, (3) 0.0328, (4) 0.876, (5) 0.00128, (6) 1.675.**

(5) $0.002 \times 0.64 =$ _____

    Guess: _____   *Answer:* _____

(6) $6.7 \times 0.25 =$ _____

    Guess: _____   *Answer:* _____

Each of the shift rules changes a multiplication problem we do not know how to do (multiply by 10, by 100, by 0.1, by 0.01, etc.) to a problem we do know how to do: multiply by 1. The problem is changed by shifting both the number being multiplied and the multiplying number. The multiplying number always shifts to the units place.

For example: 0.1×0.3 becomes $1 \times 0.03 = 0.03$

                  0.01×0.4 becomes $1 \times 0.004 = 0.004$

This is another reason for the results above: Each decimal fraction multiplier is changed by the appropriate shift rule to a whole number (ones place) multiplier. For example, 0.5×0.03 becomes 5×0.003 and 0.275×15.72 becomes 275×0.01572.

For the link between the decimal shift rules and the usual rule ("Count the number of places and add") for multiplying decimals, see the end of section 5.4.3.

e. *Predict a General Shift Rule for Multiplying by Decimal Fractions*

Look back over the shift rules for multiplying by 0.1, 0.01, and 0.001. Try to find a pattern. Use this pattern to predict the shift rule for multiplying a number by 0.0001:

Predict a shift rule for multiplying a number by 0.00001:

Predict a general shift rule for multiplying by N decimal places

$$\overbrace{0.000 \ldots 001:}$$

Such shift rules will be examined in section 5.4.3.

5.3.6
**Division
of Decimals**
For each problem below, first estimate an answer and then give a mathematical model. (Intuitions about division of decimals are often weak, and so it may be difficult to make an estimate. Don't spend much time on this; make a rough approximation.)[33]

a. A string of licorice 0.5 meters long is divided equally among four girls. How long a piece did each girl get?

Estimate: _____   *Mathematical model:* _____

[33] a. $0.5 \div 4 = \square$, b. $1 \div 3 = \square$, c. $3 \div 0.2 = \square$, d. $0.6 \div 0.04 = \square$.

349 DECIMALS:
BASIC
OPERATIONS,
ALGORITHMS,
AND THE
METRIC
SYSTEM

b. The oldest child in a family with three children was given $1. He was to split this money evenly at the toy store. How much money did each child have to spend?

Estimate: _____ *Mathematical model:* _____

c. Sarah and Joe each get a dime a day for feeding the neighbor's cat while the neighbors are away. They want to buy a game that costs $3. How many days will it take them to get the money?

Estimate: _____ *Mathematical model:* _____

d. Christopher notices that his savings account paid $.60 interest this year. The bank pays 4 percent interest rate. How much money did he have in the bank?

Estimate: _____ *Mathematical model:* _____

In order to divide by decimal fractions, some *division shift rules* will be needed. Actually there are at least three ways to approach division of decimal fractions. The other two ways involve using the multiplicative identity (1) in useful forms and using the fact that division is the inverse operation to multiplication. These other two methods are described in section 5.5.1.

1. Shift Rule for Dividing by 0.1 The most difficult part of division by decimal fractions is deciding what this division *means*. A whole number example can help:

$6 \div 2$: the 2 can be the *size* of the set or the *number* of sets; the former is easier for decimal fractions.

$6 \div 2$ means "How many 2s in 6?"

Therefore,

$1 \div 0.1$ means "How many 0.1s in 1?"
or "How many flats in one cube?"
or "How many dimes in one dollar?"
Answer: 10

$0.5 \div 0.1$ means "How many 0.1s in 0.5?"
or "How many flats in five flats?"
or "How many dimes in five dimes?"
Answer: 5

$0.01 \div 0.1$ means "How many 0.1s in 0.01?"
or "How many flats in one long?"
or "How many dimes in one penny?"
Answer: one-tenth or 0.1

Try the following problems with the embodiments.[34]

                                                   Answer

e. $2 \div 0.1$ means "How many flats (dimes) in 2 cubes (dollars)?"   _____

f. $0.4 \div 0.1$ means _____ _____

g. $1.6 \div 0.1$ means _____ _____

h. $0.02 \div 0.1$ means _____ _____

i. $0.45 \div 0.1$ means _____ _____

j. $0.008 \div 0.1$ means _____ _____

k. $0.234 \div 0.1$ means _____ _____

Generalization for dividing by 0.1: With the embodiments, the effect is to trade each piece for a piece _____ place to the _____. Symbolically, this has the effect of shifting each number _____ place to the _____[35] and dividing by 1 (that is, $2 \div 0.1$, becomes $20 \div 1 = 20$).

2. Shift Rule for Dividing by 0.01 $2 \div 0.01$ means "How many 0.01s in 2?"
                or "How many longs in two cubes?"
                or "How many pennies in two dollars?"
                Answer: 200
    $0.3 \div 0.01$ means "How many 0.01s in 0.3?"
                or "How many longs in three flats?"
                or "How many pennies in three dimes?"
                Answer: 30

Try these problems with the embodiments.[36]

                                                   Answer

a. $1 \div 0.01$ means "How many longs (pennies) in one Cube ($1)?"   _____

b. $0.8 \div 0.01$ means _____ _____

[34] e. 20, f. 4, g. 16.

    h. There is not a whole flat in 2 longs. What part of a flat is in 2 longs? (Think of trading the flat for ten longs.) Answer: 0.2

    i. 4.5.

    j. There is not a whole flat (dime) in 8 units (green stamps). What part of a flat is in 8 units? (Think of trading the flat in for 100 Units.) Answer: 0.08.

    k. 2.34.

[35] **One, left.**

[36] **a. 100, b. 80, c. 4, d. 0.1, e. 62, f. 270.**

351 DECIMALS:
BASIC
OPERATIONS,
ALGORITHMS,
AND THE
METRIC
SYSTEM

c. $0.04 \div 0.01$ means _____ _____

d. $0.001 \div 0.01$ means _____ _____

e. $0.62 \div 0.01$ means _____ _____

f. $2.7 \div 0.01$ means _____ _____

Generalization for dividing by 0.01: With the embodiments, the effect is to trade each piece for a piece _____ places to the _____. Symbolically, this has the effect of shifting each number _____ places to the _____[37] and dividing by 1 (that is, $0.8 \div .01$ becomes $80 \div 1 = 80$)

3. Shift Rule for Dividing by 0.001

$1 \div 0.001$ means "How many 0.001s in 1?"
  or "How many units in one cube?"
  or "How many green stamps in one dollar?"
  (Think of trading a cube to get _____ units or of trading one dollar to get _____ green stamps.)
  Answer: 1000

$0.04 \div 0.001$ means "How many 0.001s in 0.04?"
  or "How many units in four longs?"
  or "How many green stamps in four pennies?"
  Answer: 40

Try these problems with the embodiments.[38]

Answer:

a. $3 \div 0.001$ means "How many units (green stamps) in 3 cubes ($3)?" _____

b. $0.2 \div 0.001$ means _____ _____

c. $0.06 \div 0.001$ means _____ _____

d. $0.009 \div 0.001$ means _____ _____

e. $1.5 \div 0.001$ means _____ _____

f. $0.47 \div 0.001$ means _____ _____

g. $0.358 \div 0.001$ means _____ _____

Generalization for dividing by 0.001: With the embodiments, the effect is to trade each piece for a piece _____ places to the _____. Symbolically, this has the effect of shifting each number _____ places to the _____[39] and dividing by 1 (that is, $0.2 \div .001$ becomes $200 \div 1 = 200$).

[37] Two, left.

[38] a. 3000, b. 200, c. 60, d. 9, e. 1500, f. 470, g. 358.

[39] Three, left.

4. Dividing by Multiples of 0.1, 0.01, 0.001

The multiplication shift rules for decimals changed problems with non-unit multipliers to problems with unit (ones place) multipliers. The division shift rules do the same thing: they change problems to new problems having unit divisors.

$0.2 \div 0.1$ becomes $2 \div 1 = 2$ (by the use of the 0.1 shift rule)
$0.5 \div 0.01$ becomes $50 \div 1 = 50$ (by the use of the 0.01 shift rule)

The same thing will happen when the divisor is a multiple of 0.1, 0.01, or 0.001:

$0.6 \div 0.2$ becomes $6 \div 2 = 3$ (using 0.1 shift rule, 0.6 moves one place to the left: 6)
$0.9 \div 0.03$ becomes $90 \div 3 = 30$ (using 0.01 shift rule, 0.9 moves two places to the left: 90)

A division problem can be checked in two ways. The first is from the meaning of the division problem: "How many △'s in □?" The second is by using multiplication.

"Problem Means" Check:
$0.6 \div 0.2$: How many 0.2s in 0.6? __3__
$0.9 \div 0.03$: How many 0.03s in 0.9? __30__

Multiplication Check:
$3 \times 0.2 = 0.6$
$30 \times 0.03 = 0.9$

Try these problems using the proper shift rule. Check your answers using both checks as in the examples. Use your embodiments if you wish (especially for the first check).[40]

		Answer	Problem Means	Answer	Multiplication Check
a.	$0.6 \div 0.03$	20	How many 0.03s in 0.6?	20	$20 \times 0.03 = 0.6$
b.	$0.7 \div 0.2$				
c.	$1.6 \div 0.04$				
d.	$0.01 \div 0.005$				
e.	$0.2 \div 0.5$				
f.	$0.48 \div 0.6$				
g.	$0.042 \div 0.07$				

These problems come out even (terminate). Many division problems do not (for example, $0.1 \div 0.3$). The number of places required in the answer is usually indicated by the problem situation.

[40] b. 3.5, c. 40, d. 2, e. 0.4, f. 0.8, g. 0.6.

353 DECIMALS:
BASIC
OPERATIONS,
ALGORITHMS,
AND THE
METRIC
SYSTEM

5. Predict a General Shift Rule for Dividing by Decimal Fractions

Look back over the shift rules for dividing by 0.1, 0.01, 0.001. Try to find a pattern. Use the pattern to predict the shift rules for dividing a number by 0.0001:

Predict a shift rule for dividing a number by 0.00001:

Predict a general shift rule for multiplying by N decimal places
$$\overbrace{0.000 \ldots 01}:$$

Such shift rules will be examined in section 5.4.4.

5.4

ACTIVITY: ALGORITHMS FOR ADDITION, SUBTRACTION, MULTIPLICATION, AND DIVISION OF DECIMALS

In section 5.3 the basic meaning of addition, subtraction, multiplication, and division of decimals was examined. The embodiments in that section involved four places: 1.0, 0.1, 0.01, and 0.001. These places were enough to indicate a pattern of what would happen with other places. In this section a chip computer will be used to decide whether the patterns you noticed in section 5.3 do apply to other decimal places. These patterns will enable general repetitive procedures (algorithms) to be established for each of the four operations. In each case, the algorithm for decimals is only a minor adaptation of the algorithm for whole numbers.

Overview: **A chip computer will be used to extend the patterns noticed in section 5.3 to more places to the right and to the left of the decimal point. These patterns will be used to establish algorithms for addition, subtraction, multiplication, and division of decimals.**
Materials needed: **For each person: fifty chips, three sheets of paper.**

5.4.1

The Chip Computer for Decimals

Make a calculating sheet as pictured at the left from two sheets of paper.
   The A, B, C, D columns are a base-ten chip computer. That is, the rules for trading chips are:
   One chip trades for ten chips in the column to the right.
   Ten chips trade for one chip in the column to the left.
Now extend the same trade rules to the columns to the right of one. The names of columns (a), (b), (c), and (d) need to be decided.

D	C	B	A	(a)	(b)	(c)	(d)

a. One chip in A trades for ten chips in (a). Therefore one chip in (a) is one-tenth of an A chip. Each A chip is 1. Therefore each (a) chip is 0.1

b. One chip in A trades for ten chips in (a). *Each* of those ten (a) chips trades for ten (b) chips. So a 1 chip from A makes _____[41] chips in (b). Therefore each (b) chip is worth _____.[42]

c. One chip in A trades for ten chips in (a). *Each* of those ten (a) chips trades for ten (b) chips. *Each* of those hundred (b) chips trades for ten (c) chips. So a 1 chip from A makes _____[43] chips in (c). Therefore each (c) chip is worth _____.[44]

d. Explain the value of a (d) chip[45]:

Put another sheet to the right of your calculating sheet. Divide it into four columns. Call them (e), (f), (g), (h). What is the value of each column?[46] Could you put another sheet to the right of that sheet? What would be the size of its four columns?[47] Could you put another sheet to the right of that sheet? How long could you keep putting new sheets out to the right?[13]

We saw with the whole numbers that you could also keep adding places out to the left indefinitely. Therefore we can make numbers as large as we wish (add places to the left) or as small as we wish (add places to the right).

There are many labels that could be given to each column in a chip computer. Fill in the blanks below. If you find any of these labels helpful, put them on your chip computer.

Labels (c) and (d) come from the shift rules.

Are the labels in (e) symmetric about the decimal point or about the ones place?

Because whole numbers are recorded by counting chips in a column and recording them in order, it seems natural to do the same for these new columns. Because some way is needed to tell from which columns we are recording, a period is placed after the chips from the ones col-

---

[13] You probably answered forever, or infinitely. Or course, you really could only put out a finite number of sheets. But this illustrates a process by which any decimal place can be reached. Also the process of adding sheets very quickly reaches any numbers we actually use. How long does it take to get to 60 decimal places if you add a new sheet every 4 seconds? Find out the very largest numbers (astronomy?) and the very smallest numbers that are really used. How long would it take you to make a computer that showed these numbers?

---

[41] 100.

[42] One-hundredth or 0.01.

[43] 1000.

[44] One-thousandth or 0.001.

[45] 1 A chip = 10000 (d) chips, and so 1 (d) chip is worth 0.0001.

[46] 0.00001, 0.000001, 0.0000001, 0.00000001.

[47] 0.000000001, 0.0000000001, 0.00000000001, 0.000000000001.

	D	C	B	A	a	b	c	d
(a)	_____	_____	Tens	Ones	Tenths	_____	_____	_____
(b)	_____	_____	10	1	0.1	_____	_____	_____
(c)	_____	_____	$\frac{1}{10} \times 100$	$\frac{1}{10} \times 10$	$\frac{1}{10} \times 1$	_____	_____	_____
(d)	_____	_____	10×1	10×0.1	10×0.01	_____	_____	_____
(e)	_____	10×10	10	1	$\frac{1}{10}$	$\frac{1}{10} \times \frac{1}{10}$	_____	_____

umn. A 0 is used to indicate empty columns between any filled columns and the period.

Give symbols for each of these situations[48]:

a. _____   b. _____

5.4.2

Addition and Subtraction Algorithms for Decimals

In sections 5.3.3 and 5.3.4 you discovered that only pieces from the same places could be added or subtracted. That is, flats could only be added to or subtracted from flats, longs to or from longs, units to or from units, dimes to or from dimes, etc. Trying to add unlike pieces, say 3 flats and 5 longs, results only in 3 flats and 5 longs.

The above point is made most clearly with the blocks and money. After it has been made, the chip computer can be used to add and subtract with larger and smaller numbers. For either addition or subtraction,

[48] a. 6231.5029, b. 207.013.

begin in the column on the right and *record trades and answers after doing each column*. This relates the symbolic algorithm very closely to the operations on the chips.

Try some of the problems below to see how the algorithms arise from work with the chip computer.[49]

a. $3118.7654 + 239.932 = $ _____   **b.** $3645.7 + 82.853 = $ _____

c. $7.605 + 48.0284 = $ _____   **d.** $37.46 - 5.786 = $ _____

e. $1234.56 - 987.6543 = $ _____   **f.** $1111.002 - 978.35 = $ _____

5.4.3
The Multiplication Algorithm for Decimals

In section 5.3.5, Part 1, you discovered that the shift rules for multiplying by 10, 100, 1000, etc., worked for the new places to the right of the decimal point. Using embodiments in section 5.3.5, Part 2, you established shift rules for multiplying by 0.1, 0.01, and 0.001. These rules were as follows:

0.1: To multiply a number by 0.1, shift the number one place to the right and multiply by 1.

0.01: To multiply a number by 0.01, shift the number two places to the right and multiply by 1.

0.001: To multiply a number by 0.001, shift the number three places to the right and multiply by 1.

What is your prediction for the shift rule for multiplying by 0.0001?

On the chip computer, multiplying by 0.0001 (0.0001 *of* a number) means that each chip must be traded until there are 10,000 chips in some column; then *one* of those 10,000 chips is taken (0.0001 × □: one ten-thousandths of □). If any chip is traded four columns to the right, ten-thousand chips will result.

One of the blue 10,000 chips above is 0.0001. Therefore, to take 0.0001 of a number: For each chip, take a chip four columns to the right. Symbolically, this has the effect of shifting the whole number four places to the right.

What is your prediction for the shift rule for multiplying by 0.00001?

Explain your prediction using the chip computer.

Now try to make a generalization of the above cases:

General Shift Rule for Multiplying a Number by 0.000 . . . 01: To multi-

[49]   a. 3358.6974, b. 3728.553, c. 55.6334, d. 31.674, e. 246.9057, f. 132.652.

DECIMALS:
BASIC
OPERATIONS,
ALGORITHMS,
AND THE
METRIC
SYSTEM

Any column				● = a stack of ten chips	● = a stack of 100 chips

| 1 chip | → | 10 chips | → | 100 chips | → | 1000 chips | → | 10,000 chips |

ply a number by 0.000 . . . 01 (where n is the number of places in 0.000 . . . 01), shift the number _____ [50] and multiply by 1.

There really is no new algorithm for multiplication by decimal fractions. Instead we change a problem involving multiplying by decimal fractions to an equivalent problem we already know how to do: multiplying by a whole number. The shift rules are what enable us to change a problem with a *decimal fraction multiplier* to a problem with a *whole number multiplier.*

2.57
×0.43
The shift rule for multiplying by 0.01 changes this problem to:
0.0257
× 43

14.056
× .247
The shift rule for multiplying by 0.001 changes this problem to:
0.014056
× 247

0.0005
× 0.7
The shift rule for multiplying by 0.1 changes this problem to:
0.00005
× 7

[50] *n* places to the right.

2685	The shift rule for multiplying by 0.01 changes	26.85
× 4.59	this problem to:	× 459

To make sure that you understand how these shift rules work on problems, for each problem below write the shift rule needed and the new problem created by this shift rule.[51]

Problem	Shift Rule Needed	New Problem
a. 29.53		
× 0.46	_____	_____
b. 0.268		
× 0.06	_____	_____
c. 57.29		
× 12.8	_____	_____
d. 0.0068		
× 0.003	_____	_____
e. 7892.98		
× 0.045	_____	_____
f. 389.2		
×346.5	_____	_____
g. 265.87		
×0.0472	_____	_____

Try two of the problems above on your chip computer, if you wish.
Most people use the following rule to find the decimal point in the answer of a problem with a decimal fraction multiplier. This rule says:

[51] **a.** 0.01 shift rule
0.2953
× 46

b. 0.01 shift rule
0.00268
× 6

c. 0.1 shift rule
5.729
× 128

d. 0.001 shift rule
0.0000069
× 3

e. 0.001 shift rule
7.89298
× 45

f. 0.1 shift rule
38.92
× 3465

g. 0.0001 shift rule
0.026587
× 472

359 DECIMALS:
BASIC
OPERATIONS,
ALGORITHMS,
AND THE
METRIC
SYSTEM

Count the decimal places in the top and bottom numbers, add them together, and the sum gives the number of places in the product.

This rule was used at least as long ago as the Middle Ages for placing the decimal point in the final answer of calculations done on the European counting board. This rule is very efficient, but difficult to understand. How do the shift rules explain this rule?[52] (Look at the examples on page 358.)

Of course, once you understand how this rule works, it is fine to continue to use it. Using the shift rules to create a workable problem from an unworkable problem is a slower process. Once understanding has been reached, the faster "count and add" method can be used.

5.4.4
A Division Algorithm for Decimals

There are at least three approaches to division by decimal fractions. Two are described in section 5.5.1. The third, the approach used here, comes from the basic meaning of division by a decimal. Shift rules established in section 5.3.6 for division by 0.1, 0.01, and 0.001 were as follows:

  0.1: To divide a number by 0.1, shift that number one place to the left and divide by 1.
  0.01: To divide a number by 0.01, shift that number two places to the left and divide by 1.
  0.001: To divide a number by 0.001, shift that number three places to the left and divide by 1.

What is your prediction for the shift rule for dividing by 0.0001?

Try to find the shift rule for dividing by 0.0001 by using your chip computer. $1 \div 0.0001$ means "How many 0.0001 chips in 1?" (Think about trading a 1 chip for a certain number of chips. How many 0.0001 chips do you get?). Answer: _____ [53]

$$0.02 \div 0.0001 = \text{_____} \quad [54] \quad 300 \div .0001 = \text{_____} \quad [55]$$

---

[52] The shift rules shift the top number to the left the number of decimal places that are in the bottom number. Thus the new top number has the number of decimal places that were in the original top number *plus* the number of decimal places that were in the original bottom number. Because multiplying by a whole number does not change the number of decimal places, the answer will have as many decimal places as the new top number has.

[53] **10,000**

[54] **200**

[55] **3,000,000**

How many places did each of the above numbers shift? _____[56] What is your prediction for the shift rule for dividing by 0.00001?[57]

Check your prediction using your chip computer. Look at the above cases and formulate a generalization:

General Shift Rule for Dividing a Number by 0.000 . . . 01: To divide a number by 0.000 . . . 01 (where n is the number of places in 0.000 . . . 01), shift the number _____ [58] and divide by 1.

As with the multiplication shift rules, division shift rules change a problem with a decimal fraction divisor to an equivalent problem with a whole number divisor.

$1.5 \div 0.03$	The shift rule for dividing by 0.01 changes this to:	$150 \div 3$
$0.021 \div 0.7$	The shift rule for dividing by 0.1 changes this to:	$0.21 \div 7$
$5.23 \div 0.0045$	The shift rule for dividing by 0.0001 changes this to:	$52300 \div 45$

For each problem below, record what shift rule would be used to change the problems to those with a whole number divisor (remember that 0.45 is hundredths, 0.0076 is ten-thousandths, 37.8 is tenths, etc.). Write the new problem created by the use of the shift rule. (Remember that a division problem can be written three ways:

$$20 \div 5 \quad \text{or} \quad 5\overline{)20} \quad \text{or} \quad {}^{20}/_5$$

The problems below are written in all three ways.)[59]

Problem	Shift Rule Needed	New Problem
a. $4.5 \div 0.09$	_____	_____
b. $\dfrac{23.4}{0.78}$	_____	_____
c. $14.73\overline{)275.}$	_____	_____
d. $\dfrac{0.007}{0.3}$	_____	_____
e. $0.045\overline{)278.5}$	_____	_____
f. $0.029 \div 0.0036$	_____	_____
g. $2.65\overline{)0.0153}$	_____	_____

[56] four

361 DECIMALS:
BASIC
OPERATIONS,
ALGORITHMS,
AND THE
METRIC
SYSTEM

The rule most often used for placing the decimal point in the answer of a division problem with a decimal fraction divisor is as follows:

> Move the decimal point in the divisor to the right of the last place in the divisor. Then move the decimal point in the number being divided the same number of places to the right. Make a caret and place the decimal point in the answer above the caret.

Explain this rule by the shift rules for dividing by a decimal fraction.[60] As with multiplication, once you understand why this rule works, it makes sense to use it. It is much faster than rewriting the whole new problem each time.

5.5
PROBLEM SET:
ANALYSIS OF DECIMALS

Overview: **This problem set contains problems concerning other motivations for the multiplication and division algorithm for decimals, decimals expressed in exponential form, a brief look at logarithms, scientific notation, and analysis of errors in decimal problems.**

5.5.1 Part *a* below outlines how the division shift rules can be derived from the multiplication shift rules and points out the relationship between the multiplication and division shift rules for decimals. Part *b* demonstrates how to change a problem with a decimal divisor to an equivalent problem with a whole number divisor by using the multiplicative identity.

a. Assume you do not know how to divide by a decimal, but that you do know how to multiply by a decimal. Division and multiplication are inverse operations. Use your multiplication knowledge to answer division problems.

$3 \div 0.1 = \square$ is equivalent to $3 = 0.1 \times \square$
$3 = 0.1 \times \boxed{30}$ and so $3 \div 0.1 = \boxed{30}$

$0.5 \div 0.1 = \square$ is equivalent to $0.5 = 0.1 \times \square$

---

[57] Dividing by .00001 shifts a number five places to the left.

[58] *n* places to the left.

[59] a. 0.01 shift rule, $450 \div 9$ b. 0.01 shift rule, $2340/78$. c. 0.01 shift rule, $1473\overline{)27500.}$ d. 0.1 shift rule, $0.07/3$. e. 0.001 shift rule, $45\overline{)278500.}$ f. 0.0001 shift rule, $290 \div 36$. g. 0.01 shift rule, $265\overline{)1.53.}$

[60] Shifting a number *n* places to the left is the same as moving the decimal point *n* places to the right.

$0.5 = 0.1 \times \boxed{5}$ and so $0.5 \div 0.1 = \boxed{5}$

$7 \div 0.01 = \square$ is equivalent to $7 = 0.01 \times \square$

$7 = 0.01 \times \boxed{700}$ and so $7 \div .01 = \boxed{700}$

You can continue to get answers to individual division problems by using multiplication, but you can also use this inverse relationship of multiplication and division to derive the division shift rules from those for multiplication.

1. Shift Rule for Dividing by 0.1 The shift rule for multiplying by 0.1 is: Shift the number one place to the right. But $\square \times 0.1 \div 0.1 = \square$. That is, if you multiply any number by 0.1 and then divide that answer by 0.1, you get back your original number.

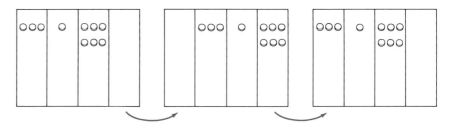

$\times 0.1$ shifts the number one place to the *right*   and so $\div.1$ must shift the number one place to the *left* to get it back where it started.

2. Shift Rule for Dividing by 0.01 $\square \times 0.01 \div 0.01 = \square$

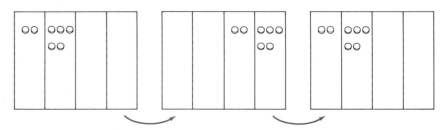

$\times 0.01$ shifts the number two places to the *right*   and so $\div 0.01$ must shift the number two places to the *left* to get it back where it started.

3. Shift Rule for Dividing by 0.001 $\square \times 0.001 \div 0.001 = \square$

363 DECIMALS:
BASIC
OPERATIONS,
ALGORITHMS,
AND THE
METRIC
SYSTEM

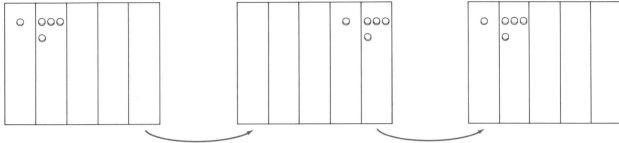

$\times 0.001$ shifts the number three   and so $\div 0.001$ must shift the number
places to the *right*   three places to the *left* to get
                                                 it back where it started.

The above process could be continued for more division shift rules. In general, the inverse relationship of multiplication and division means that:

The multiplication and division shift rules shift numbers in *opposite* directions.

Once the division shift rules are known, the algorithm for dividing by a decimal fraction is obtained in the same way it was done in section 5.4.4: the shift rules change the problem to a new problem with a whole number divisor.

b. A division problem can be written at least three ways:

$$0.6 \div 0.2 \quad \text{or} \quad 0.2\overline{)0.6} \quad \text{or} \quad {}^{0.6}\!/_{0.2}$$

We will use the last form for this method of division. Our goal is to use the identity for multiplication of decimals, 1, to change a number with a decimal fraction divisor to one with a whole number divisor. We do this by putting 1 in a form useful for a specific problem.

$\dfrac{0.6}{0.2}$ $0.2 \times 10 =$ a whole number. But if only 0.2 is multiplied by 10, the problem will be changed. So write 1 as $^{10}/_{10}$ and multiply by it.

$$\frac{0.6}{0.2} = 1 \times \frac{0.6}{0.2} = \frac{10}{10} \times \frac{0.6}{0.2} = \frac{10 \times 0.6}{10 \times 0.2} = \frac{6}{2} = 3$$

$\dfrac{0.09}{0.03}$ $0.03 \times 100 =$ a whole number. So use $\boxed{1 = \dfrac{100}{100}}$

$$\frac{0.09}{0.03} = 1 \times \frac{0.09}{0.03} = \frac{100}{100} \times \frac{0.09}{0.03} = \frac{100 \times 0.09}{100 \times 0.03} = \frac{9}{3} = 3$$

$$\frac{0.08}{0.4} \qquad 0.4 \times 10 = \text{a whole number. So use} \boxed{1 = \frac{10}{10}}$$

$$\frac{0.08}{0.4} = 1 \times \frac{0.08}{0.4} = \frac{10}{10} \times \frac{0.08}{0.4} = \frac{10 \times 0.08}{10 \times 0.4} = \frac{0.8}{4} = 0.2$$

$$\frac{24.6}{0.003} \qquad 0.003 \times 1000 = \text{a whole number. Use} \boxed{1 = \frac{1000}{1000}}$$

$$\frac{24.6}{0.003} = 1 \times \frac{24.6}{0.003} = \frac{1000}{1000} \times \frac{24.6}{0.003} = \frac{1000 \times 24.6}{1000 \times 0.003} = \frac{24600}{3} = 8200$$

Do the problems below using the above procedure. First tell what form of 1 you will have to use and then write out as many steps of the process as you need to in order to understand the process (write out all steps for at least three problems).[61]

Problem	Form of 1 Used	Steps
a. $\dfrac{4.5}{0.3}$	$\dfrac{10}{10}$	$1 \times \dfrac{4.5}{0.3} = \dfrac{10}{10} \times \dfrac{4.5}{.3} = \dfrac{10 \times 4.5}{10 \times 0.3} =$
b. $\dfrac{1.5}{0.05}$		
c. $\dfrac{0.027}{0.9}$		
d. $\dfrac{4870.}{0.005}$		
e. $\dfrac{42.28}{0.14}$		

Once you understand how the above method works, it is easy to apply it to division problems written in the more usual form.

This is another way to understand the usual "count and caret" method.

$0.25\,\overline{)\,16.738}$ *Think:* I must multiply 0.25 by 100 to make it a whole number, and so I must also multiply 16.738 by 100: $25\,\overline{)\,1673.8}$

$0.047\,\overline{)\,64.}$ *Think:* I must multiply 0.047 by 1000 to make it a whole number, and so I must also multiply 64 by 1000: $47\,\overline{)\,64000.}$

[61] a. $^{10}/_{10}$, b. $^{100}/_{100}$, c. $^{10}/_{10}$, d. $^{1000}/_{1000}$, e. $^{100}/_{100}$.

365 DECIMALS:
BASIC
OPERATIONS,
ALGORITHMS,
AND THE
METRIC
SYSTEM

5.5.2 **a.** Look at the following labels for columns in the base-ten chip com-
Exponential puter:
Notation

10000	1000	100	10	1	0.1	0.01	0.001	0.0001	0.00001
$10 \times 10 \times 10 \times 10$	$10 \times 10 \times 10$	10×10	10	1	$\frac{1}{10}$	$\frac{1}{10} \times \frac{1}{10}$	$\frac{1}{10} \times \frac{1}{10} \times \frac{1}{10}$	$\frac{1}{10} \times \frac{1}{10} \times \frac{1}{10} \times \frac{1}{10}$	$\frac{1}{10} \times \frac{1}{10} \times \frac{1}{10} \times \frac{1}{10} \times \frac{1}{10}$
10^4	10^3	10^2	10^1	$10^{\square}$	$10^{\square}$	$10^{\square}$	$10^{\square}$	$10^{\square}$	$10^{\square}$

The labels in the third row use exponents. An *exponent* tells how
many times the base number is multiplied times itself. For example,

$$10^5 = 10 \times 10 \times 10 \times 10 \times 10 \qquad 10^2 = 10 \times 10$$

Fill in the boxes in the third row with exponents for 1, 0.1, 0.01, etc.
Check your answers by reading the sections below.

1. Exponents for Decimal (1) $\dfrac{10^a}{10^b} = 10^{a-b}$ for $a > b$. For example,
Fractions

$$\frac{10^5}{10^3} = \frac{10 \times 10 \times 10 \times 10 \times 10}{10 \times 10 \times 10} = 10 \times 10 = 10^2 = 10^{5-3}$$

(Notice that canceling just uses $1 = {}^{10}\!/_{10}$.)

What happens with $a < b$?

$$\boxed{\frac{10^3}{10^5}} = \frac{10 \times 10 \times 10}{10 \times 10 \times 10 \times 10 \times 10} = \frac{1}{10 \times 10} = \boxed{\frac{1}{10^2}}$$

(2) If $\dfrac{10^a}{10^b} = 10^{a-b}$, also holds for $a < b$, $\boxed{\dfrac{10^3}{10^5}} = 10^{3-5} = \boxed{10^{-2}}$

(3) Combining the blue boxes from (1) and (2),

$$\frac{1}{10^2} = 10^{-2}$$

In general,

$$\frac{1}{10^n} = 10^{-n}$$

Therefore the columns to the right of 1 on the chip computer should have been labeled 10^{-1}, 10^{-2}, 10^{-3}, 10^{-4}, etc.

2. Expressing 1 as a Power of Ten

If $\dfrac{10^a}{10^b} = 10^{a-b}$ also applies when $a = b$, then

$$1 = \frac{10^4}{10^4} = 10^{4-4} = 10^0$$

In general,

$$1 = \frac{10^n}{10^n} = 10^{n-n} = 10^0$$

3. Expressing All Decimal Places as Powers of Ten

The simplified means of expressing every decimal place can now be used:

$$\cdots 10^5 \ 10^4 \ 10^3 \ 10^2 \ 10^1 \ 10^0 \ . \ 10^{-1} \ 10^{-2} \ 10^{-3} \ 10^{-4} \ 10^{-5} \cdots$$

Notice that the base-ten system is symmetric about the units place, 10^0, and not about the decimal point. The system would actually reflect its many symmetries better if we placed the decimal point *under* the units place instead of to the right of that place.

*b. $10^a \times 10^b = 10^{a+b}$ is a basic relationship of exponents. Illustrate this relationship with two examples:

Use this relationship to show why decimal fractions are written with negative exponents. [62]

Use this relationship to show why $1 = 10^0$ [63]

c. Use exponents to show why the multiplication shift rules work[64]:

Shift rule for multiplying by 0.1:

Shift rule for multiplying by 0.01:

Shift rule for multiplying by 0.001:

---

[62] For example, $(10 \times 10) \times \frac{1}{10} = 10 \Rightarrow 10^2 \times 10 = 10^1 \Rightarrow 2 + \square = 1 \Rightarrow \square = -1 \Rightarrow \frac{1}{10} = 10^{-1}$

[63] Try $10^2 \times 10^{-2}$.

[64] $0.1 \times 10^n = 10^{-1} \times 10^n = 10^{n-1}$, i.e., any place (100, 10, 1, 0.1, 0.01, etc.) multiplied by 0.1 has its exponent decreased by 1, or the numerals in that place shift one place to the right.

367 DECIMALS:
BASIC
OPERATIONS,
ALGORITHMS,
AND THE
METRIC
SYSTEM

General shift rule for multiplying by 10^{-n}:

d. Use exponents to show why the division shift rules work[65]: Shift rule for dividing by 0.1:

General shift rule for dividing by 10^{-n}:

5.5.3 Scientific notation is a method of writing in a standard form using expo-
Scientific nents of ten any number expressed in decimal form. The standard form
Notation is:

$$a.bcdef \ldots \times 10^n$$

That is, one numeral is in the units place and all other numerals are in places to the right of one; the n tells how many places and in what direction the number was shifted to get it to the units place. ($a,b,c,d,e,f,$ and n are integers.)

Scientific notation is helpful for very large and for very small numbers. For example,

Example	Number in Scientific Notation
Pluto is 3,651,000,000 miles from the sun.	3.651×10^9
Masers and lasers can detect power outputs as low as 0.0000000000000000000000000001 watts.	1.0×10^{-28}
An electron has a charge of 0.00000000000000001602 Coulombs	1.602×10^{-17}
Gaseous ammonia acquires vibrations of 24,000,000,000 cycles per second.	2.4×10^{10}

Notice that to find the exponent, you count the number of *shifts* needed to move the left-most numeral into the ones place (or the number of shifts to move the numeral in the ones place back to where it was). Small numbers have negative exponents, large numbers have positive exponents.

---

[65] $\dfrac{10^n}{0.1} = \dfrac{10^n}{10^{-1}} = 10^{n-(-1)} = 10^{n+1}$; thus the numerals in any place shift one place to the left.

Example	Number in Scientific Notation
(1) Venus is 67,180,000 miles from the sun.	_____
(2) An electron has a radius of 0.0000000000282 centimeters.	_____
(3) The wavelengths of violet light range from 0.000040 to 0.000042 centimeters	_____

Example	Number in Scientific Notation
(4) A midyear population estimate for the continent of Asia in 1971 is 2,104,000,000 people.	_____
(5) In 1969 there were approximately _____ _____ students in elementary school in the United States	3.1955×10^7
(6) Ultraviolet rays have wavelengths that range from _____ to ___ _____ centimeters.	4.0×10^{-5} 1.3×10^{-6}
(7) An electron at rest has a mass of _____ _____ grams.	9.108×10^{-24}
(8) A *B. pneumosinter* bacteria has a length of 1×10^{-7}	_____

a. Fill in the blank for each example below.[66]

b. When can you add and subtract with numbers in scientific notation?[67]

c. How would you multiply with numbers in scientific notation?[68]

d. How would you divide with numbers in scientific notation?[69]

5.5.4
Approximations Using Powers of Ten

When multiplying or dividing very large numbers, intuition often fails us. Scientific notation can help get quick approximate answers.

Example: In 1970 there were about 80,427,000 cars in use in the United

[66] (1) 6.718×10^7, (2) 2.82×10^{-11}, (3) 4.0×10^5, to 4.2×10^5, (4) 2.104×10^9, (5) 31,955,000, (6) 0.000040 to 0.0000013, (7) 0.0000000000000000000009108, (8) 0.0000001.

[67] You can only add or subtract numbers in scientific notation if they have the same exponent. Otherwise you are adding or subtracting unlike places.

[68] See problem 4.

[69] See problem 4.

369 DECIMALS:
BASIC
OPERATIONS,
ALGORITHMS,
AND THE
METRIC
SYSTEM

States. These cars used about 62,448,000,000 gallons of gasoline. What was the average number of gallons used per car?

$$\frac{6.2 \times 10^{10}}{8.0 \times 10^{7}} = \frac{6.2}{8.0} \times \frac{10^{10}}{10^{7}} = 0.8 \times 10^{3} = 800 \text{ gallons}$$

Notice that only the first two digits were kept in writing each number in scientific notation because only an approximation was desired.

Use scientific notation and the relationships:

$$\frac{10^{a}}{10^{b}} = 10^{a-b} \qquad \text{and} \qquad 10^{a} \times 10^{b} = 10^{a+b}$$

to find approximate answers for the problems below.

a. Black-controlled banks grew from 11 institutions in 1963 to 53 banks in 1973. The aggregate assets grew from $77,000,000 to $1,000,000,000. What is the percent increase in aggregate assets? Is this greater or less than the percent increase in the number of banks? (To put these figures in context, the total assets of all these banks is less than half the assets of the fiftieth largest commercial bank in the nation.)

b. The chairman of the New York Stock Exchange says that over the next ten years, American corporations will need $2,000,000,000,000 in new capital. If the population of the United States is approximately 200,000,000, how many dollars is that per person?

c. More than $61,000,000,000 in United States savings bonds are now outstanding. More than 24,500,000 families own savings bonds. What is the average dollar amount of savings bonds each of these families holds?

d. U.S. Commerce Department figures show that consumers paid an extra $17,000,000,000 in 1973 to buy food. If the population of the United States is approximately 200,000,000, how many extra dollars did each person on the average pay for food?

e. Of the extra money paid by consumers, $6,000,000,000 ended up going to the owners of large farms (having more than $40,000 in annual cash receipts). If there are 297,000,000 large farms in the United States, how much of this extra money did each large farmer get?

f. In 1972 each large farm received an average of $5,100 in cash payments from the federal government. If there were about 297,000,000 large farms, how much did this cost?

g. If there were 50,293,000,000 pieces of first-class and air-mail letters in 1972, and the population of the United States was approximately 200,000,000, how many letters on the average did each person send?

h. In 1969 the Chicago public schools enrolled 558,000 pupils. If the cost of running these schools was $516,000,000, what was the average per pupil cost?

5.5.5
Orders of Magnitude
"An order of magnitude larger" often means larger by a factor of ten. Changes in an order of magnitude often are not merely changes in the quantity of some aspect of a situation; they often change the quality of a situation.

a. Consider the population of a town. For each population given below, respond concerning these aspects and any others you wish to consider:

What part of the town would you know well?
What part of the town would you know by sight?
Could you walk anywhere in fifteen minutes?
Could you drive anywhere in fifteen minutes?
How many grocery stores will there be?
How many doctors will there be?
How many schools will there be?
How many movie theaters will there be?
How many stories will the tallest buildings have?

Populations:

2   20   200   2,000   20,000   200,000   2,000,000

b. A person can walk about 5 miles per hour, a car can go about 50 miles per hour, and a jet can fly about 500 miles per hour. Record some changes in your own life that these different orders of magnitude would make: if people could only walk (if there were no cars, planes, or animals), if people had cars but no planes, and finally, if you could fly on a plane.

c. What kind of changes would occur if the cost of gasoline decreased by a factor of ten, to 5 cents a gallon (cost of airplane tickets, etc.)? What if the cost increased by a factor of ten, to $5 a gallon?

d. Mass production and improved technology often decrease the cost of products. The cost of hand calculators is decreasing rapidly and soon will have decreased by almost a factor of ten. What are the different effects of calculators that cost $400 and those that cost $40? What are the different effects of having calculators that weigh 2 pounds instead of 20 pounds?

e. The speed of large electronic computers has increased by at least a factor of 1000 and the cost has decreased by a factor of 1000. This has meant that they can now be used for entirely new problems, e.g., interest can now be compounded daily instead of quarterly. What other new things can be done by computers that were impossible to do without them?

f. Describe a situation where order of magnitude changes the quality of the situation. Share the situation with your colleagues.

5.5.6
**A Brief
Look at Logarithms** In problem 2, integers were used as exponents for the base ten. *Logarithms* are just exponents that are decimal fractions. Common logarithms use the base ten.

$$10^{0.6990} = 5, \qquad 0.6990 \text{ is the logarithm}$$

$1 = 10^0$	$10 = 10^1$	$100 = 10^2$
$3 = 10^{.4771}$	$30 = 10^{1.4771}$	$300 = 10^{2.4771}$
$5 = 10^{.6990}$	$50 = 10^{1.6990}$	$500 = 10^{2.6990}$
$7 = 10^{.8451}$	$70 = 10^{1.8451}$	$700 = 10^{2.8451}$
$9 = 10^{.9542}$	$90 = 10^{1.9542}$	$900 = 10^{2.9542}$
$1000 = 10^3$	$10000 = 10^4$	$100000 = 10^5$
$3000 = 10^{3.4771}$	$30000 = 10^{4.4771}$	$300000 = 10^{5.4771}$
$7000 = 10^{3.8451}$	$70000 = 10^{4.8451}$	

The examples above illustrate that you can write any number as 10 to some exponent if you are allowed to use decimal exponents.[14] Notice that the decimal fraction part of the exponent is the same for 3, for 30, for 300, for 3000, and for 30,000. The whole number part of the exponent tells the place (ones, tens, etc.) in which the 3 is. Numbers like 472, 5.17, 5002.5 also have decimal exponents; these are all included in a common logarithm table (found in most second year algebra high school textbooks). Because the whole number part of the exponent just tells how far to the left or to the right a number is placed, a single table of logarithms using only decimal fraction exponents can be used for all numbers.

Sometimes the values of the decimal exponents are a bit of a puzzle. For example, if $10^0 = 1$ and $10^1 = 10$, then $10^{0.5}$, which is halfway between 10^0 and 10^1, would seem to be halfway between 1 and 10. But what is $10^{0.5}$?

$$10^{\square} \times 10^{\square} = 10^1, \text{ and so } \square + \square = 1, \text{ or } \boxed{0.5} + \boxed{0.5} = 1$$

Therefore $10^{0.5}$ is that number which when multiplied times itself gives 10 (that is, $10^{0.5} \times 10^{0.5} = 10^1 = 10$):

$3 \times 3 = 9$ and $4 \times 4 = 16$

and so that number must be a bit bigger than 3 and less than 4 (actually $3.162 \times 3.162 \cong 10$, and so $10^{.5} \cong 3.162$).

One of the main uses of logarithms is the following:

The equations $10^a \times 10^b = 10^{a+b}$ and $\dfrac{10^a}{10^b} = 10^{a-b}$

can be used to reduce multiplication and division problems to addition and subtraction (vastly easier arithmetic operations).

For example, 4178×59873

Write each number in logarithmic form:
$4178 = 10^{3.6210}$ $5987 = 10^{4.7771}$

Then

$$4178 \times 59873 = 10^{3.6210} \times 10^{4.7771}$$
$$= 10^{3.6210 + 4.7771} = 10^{8.3981} = 250660000.$$

(10^{3981} was looked up in the table of logarithms to see of what number it was the exponent; the 8 tells in what position to place the 2.)

*Find a table of logarithms and use them to do some multiplication and division problems.

---

[14] In most cases, the decimal fractions do not terminate; they go on and on without any pattern. The examples use only the first four places of these decimal fractions.

373 DECIMALS:
BASIC
OPERATIONS,
ALGORITHMS,
AND THE
METRIC
SYSTEM

*Logarithms can be used to make a multiplication and division slide rule. See Part C, section 3.8, for details.

5.5.7
Error Analysis of Decimal Problems

For each problem below, describe the error that was made and the mathematical concept not understood by the person making the error. Then tell which embodiment(s) you would use in clarifying this concept and why.

Addition
a. $2.405 + 3.312 = 5.762$
b. $1.06 + 0.23 = 3.36$
c. $16.48 + 5.73 = 11.11$
d. $2.7 + 3.6 = 5.13$
e. $0.42 + 1.5 = 0.67$
f. $0.3 + 0.2 = 0.05$

Subtraction
a. $6.42 - 3.36 = 3.16$
b. $14.3 - 11.27 = 3.17$
c. $5.6 - 0.43 = 0.13$
d. $0.59 - 0.3 = 2.9$
e. $88.62 - 6.431 = 24.31$
f. $88.62 - 6.431 = 82.191$

Multiplication

a.
$$\begin{array}{r} 0.2 \\ \times 0.3 \\ \hline 0.6 \end{array}$$

b.
$$\begin{array}{r} 0.04 \\ \times\ 0.3 \\ \hline 0.12 \end{array}$$

c.
$$\begin{array}{r} 0.16 \\ \times\ 0.4 \\ \hline 0.424 \end{array}$$

d.
$$\begin{array}{r} 3.06 \\ \times 0.02 \\ \hline 0.6120 \end{array}$$

e.
$$\begin{array}{r} 13.43 \\ \times\ 0.2 \\ \hline 268.6 \end{array}$$

Division
a. $0.6 \div 0.2 = 0.03$
b. $0.14 \div 0.07 = 0.02$
e. $\dfrac{0.1}{0.2} = 2.$
c. $2.412 \div 0.4 = 6.3$
d. $4.6\overline{)0.23}\,\overset{\textstyle 2.}{}$

5.6
PEDAGOGICAL REMARKS

A good way to motivate the existence of places to the right of the units place is by division of whole numbers. 100 could be placed on a base-ten chip computer. Students could be asked to divide 100 by 3. This would involve making sets of three or three sets (in this case they look the same) in each column, trading any left-over chips.

Sometimes students will voluntarily suggest that the leftover chip could be traded for ten chips in a column to the right of the sheet. If no student suggests doing this, the teacher could ask if it is necessary to stop trading, or if another calculating sheet could be added. This process could continue, and one could make sets of 3 and trade the extra chip as long as one wished. After it is clear that these new places could exist,

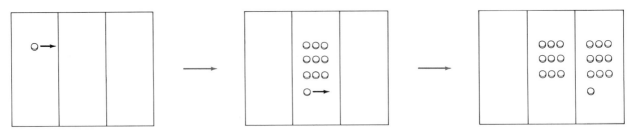

then the names (values) of the places need to be determined. Using an embodiment with different sizes in different places (such as blocks) and discussing cutting the units piece might help in this naming.

The existence of decimals can also be motivated by real situations involving decimals: money, car odometer, etc. Older children can do projects finding out where decimals are used in business and science. The metric system of measurement is an invaluable aid both to understanding decimals and to seeing them in use. The metric system provides embodiments of the decimal system using length, weight, and liquid capacity. Working with length, weight, and liquid capacity metric measurers will aid students in seeing the relationships involved in the decimal system, and explicit work with and discussion of the decimal system will help illuminate the relationships in the metric system. Thus the metric system will not be just an additional teaching burden. It will be an aid in teaching the decimal system of numeration.

The decimals have several characteristics that need to be understood. These characteristics include the ten-for-one (or one-for-ten) trades that occur between each pair of adjacent columns, the symmetry about the *units* place (*not* about the decimal point), the repeated use of the same 0 to 9 numerals in each place, and the fact that the places go on and on in either direction (getting smaller and getting larger). Embodiments can help these characteristics of decimals gain meaning. Some of these characteristics will acquire additional meaning when experience has been gained with numeration systems lacking these characteristics. (See section 7.3 for examples of such systems.)

The ten-for-one trades are essential for getting decimals started. Embodiments that show the relative sizes of different places make the trades seem less artificial and enable students to discover the trades themselves. Some such embodiments are:

Base-ten blocks
Bundled toothpicks (the largest bundle is 1)
A length embodiment (string 10 meters long = 1, meter sticks = 0.1, orange rod = 0.01, white rod = 0.001)
A weight embodiment (kilogram = 1, hectogram = 0.1, dekagram = 0.01, gram = 0.001)

375 DECIMALS:
BASIC
OPERATIONS,
ALGORITHMS,
AND THE
METRIC
SYSTEM

These embodiments also are best for addition and subtraction. With them it is quite clear that $0.4 + 0.03$ is *not* 0.7 or 0.07: for example, 4 flats (0.4) added to 3 longs (0.03) is only 0.4 plus 0.03. Unlike places *cannot* be combined.

Embodiments in which the pieces for all the places are the same size indicate more clearly the repeated use of the same 0 to 9 numerals in every place (e.g., every column in a chip computer *looks* the same as every other column). Because these embodiments do not get smaller or larger, they can have any (reasonable) number of places. Thus they show the fact that one can go on adding places either on the right or left. These embodiments thus can also show the repetitive nature of the algorithms for operations on decimals.

As mentioned above, the most important point for addition and subtraction of decimals is that only like places can be combined. The embodiments with different sizes for different places establish this point most clearly. Embodiments that can have many places, such as the chip computer, can be used to add or subtract decimals with many places.

One error in subtraction of decimal fractions is made so frequently that it deserves particular mention. In problems like:

$$\begin{array}{r} 5.30 \\ -2.16 \\ \hline \end{array}$$

a student often thinks something like the following: "I can't subtract 6 from 0, so I bring down the 6." This results in an answer of 3.26 (the correct answer of course is 3.14). These students obviously cannot visualize what the 0 means, that it means 0 hundredths and thus they had better get some more hundredths from somewhere if they are to subtract 6 of them. Watch out for language like "bring down the 6." It is often an indication of manipulation of symbols without understanding.

The chief difficulty with multiplication and division of decimal fractions, as with common fractions, is that the answers are contrary to intuition (which is largely based on whole number results). That is, multiplication usually makes things larger and division makes things smaller. This is not always so with decimal fractions, which act in just the opposite way. The embodiments in which the different places are different sizes can help to build intuitions that are congruent with the operations of multiplication and division of decimal fractions. Considerable work with embodiments of decimals can make more natural the fact that multiplying by a number using only places to the right of 1 results in a smaller number, and division by such a decimal results in a larger number. Multiplication and division problems that arise in real situations can also be helpful in aiding students to understand the increase (division) or decrease (multiplication) of the original number when decimal fractions are involved.

In division, you might select one of the three routes described in sections 5.4.4 and 5.5.1. After this route has been thoroughly explored, the others might be offered to, but not demanded of, students. Each may seem clear to some students.

Developing the ability to estimate answers is particularly important for operations with decimals. One source of this ability to estimate answers is good intuitions about the size of large numbers. Embodiments can help develop this intuition. The base blocks used in units 1 and 2 and the multiplication pieces used in Units 3 and 4 can be used. Children can make a 10,000 piece, a 100,000 piece, and a 1,000,000 piece[15] for each type of embodiment.

Other embodiments of large numbers can also help children develop their intuitions about large numbers. Long-term projects like collecting a million bottle caps, or a million dots on paper, or a million toothpicks would give time, area, volume and cost aspects to a million:

Examples:

How long does it take the whole school to collect a million bottlecaps?
How much storage space does it take for a million bottlecaps?
How much do 1,000,000 toothpicks cost?

Some of these could be problems to solve rather than real collections. Such a problem might be:

Problem:

We could afford, and would have time to collect, and would have storage space for a million _____.

Suggestions with supporting data pro and con could be kept in a display. In the upper grades, answering similar questions about a billion might help to give some meaning to that word.

And finally, another check on the reasonableness of an answer is to look at the situation in which the problem arose and ask whether the answer is a reasonable one for the situation. Unfortunately with very large or very small numbers, intuition sometimes fails us. In this case, making approximations using powers of ten (see section 5.5.4) is probably most helpful.

---

[15] Think about how big each of these is. (Hint: How many cubic centimeters—white rods—are in a cubic meter?) The blocks would probably need to be empty and perhaps made out of tagboard if they were to be moved.

unit 6

extension of the rational numbers to the real numbers

Overview: Fractions and decimals are reviewed. Questions are raised that indicate that the rational number system should be extended to a new number system.

This unit will review and tie together rational numbers expressed in either of two ways: as fractions and as decimals. With rational numbers in those two forms, most of the measuring and computing that comes up in the practical work of the world can be accomplished. In spite of that still another extension of the number system is needed.

The first part of this unit (6.1.1 to 6.1.6) raises some questions that *could* suggest the need for further extension of our number system, depending on the answers to the questions. These are the same sorts of questions that led us to extend the whole numbers to the integers and the integers to rational numbers. You are not necessarily expected to know the answers to these questions but you should convince yourself that they are legitimate and worthwhile questions to ask.

377

6.1.1
**The
Basic Definition of
Rational Numbers**

A rational number is any number that *can be* written as $\frac{a}{b}$, where a is any integer and b is any nonzero integer. Can *all* numbers be so expressed? If not, then some nonrational numbers exist and we should extend our number system to include them.

6.1.2
**The
Number
Line**

Between *any two points* named by rational numbers on the number line there are an infinite number of other points named by rational numbers. We call this the "density" property of rational numbers (see Part A., section 7.6.10). It means that infinities of infinities of points are named by rational numbers. Is it nevertheless possible that there are points on the number line *not* named by rational numbers?[1]

6.1.3
**Terminating
and Repeating Decimals**

Decimals were treated in considerable detail in the last unit, with an emphasis on calculations involving finite, terminating, decimals. But in some division problems you can keep getting "remainders" and keep on dividing. This happens, for example, in dividing one by three:

$$
\begin{array}{r}
.33333\ \ldots \\
3\,)\overline{1.00000\ \ldots} \\
\underline{9} \\
10 \\
\underline{9} \\
10 \\
\underline{9} \\
10 \\
\underline{9} \\
10 \\
\underline{9} \\
1\ \ldots
\end{array}
$$

A remainder of 1 keeps coming up, we keep adding zeros to the decimal part of 1.0000 . . . , and the process would never end. Yet we know that $1 \div 3 = \frac{1}{3}$ and so even though this is an infinite decimal it represents a rational number.[2] Do all rational fractions have such predictable

---

[1]   Remember that these are questions to think about; you are not expected to answer them at this point.

[2]   When there is a repeating cycle this is shown by putting a bar over the repeating part. Thus, 0.333333 . . . is written simply as $0.\overline{3}$. It is obvious that $0.\overline{3}$ is *not* the same as 0.3 without the bar, since $0.\overline{3}$ names $\frac{1}{3}$ and 0.3 names $\frac{3}{10}$. Similarly, 12.34797979 . . . would be written 12.34$\overline{79}$, with the bar only over the repeating pair of digits, and 0.123412341234 . . . would be written as $0.\overline{1234}$.

379 EXTENSION
OF THE
RATIONAL
NUMBERS
TO THE
REAL NUMBERS

repeating patterns when changed to decimal form? On the other hand, can all repeating decimals be written as rational fractions? Are there any decimals that do not eventually settle into such predictable repetition?

6.1.4
Closure of Operations

One of a number of reasons for extending the whole numbers to the integers is so that subtraction will always have answers; that is, so that subtraction will be "closed." Similarly, one of the reasons for extending the integers to the rationals is so that division will be "closed" (except for the essential exclusion of division by zero). As soon as we have (positive and negative) rational numbers, addition, subtraction, multiplication, and division are all closed. Are there operations *not* closed even with the rational numbers available?

6.1.5
Applications of Mathematics to the Common World

We have stressed throughout this book the need to forge links between mathematics and the common world. Are there aspects of our common world that are not adequately described by rational numbers that could be described if the rational number system were extended in some suitable way?

6.1.6
Summary

As it happens, resolution of each of the issues raised above is in a direction that would suggest that the number system should be extended. The sections that follow will first tie together the fraction and decimal forms of rational numbers, then extend those numbers still further to the real number system.

6.2
CHANGING RATIONAL FRACTIONS TO DECIMALS AND VICE VERSA

Overview: **There are two equivalent ways to define rational numbers: as fractions or as repeating decimals. How to convert from one to the other and back again will be explored.**

6.2.1
Changing a Rational Fraction to a Repeating Decimal

The fact that one of the interpretations of the fraction notation is

$$\frac{a}{b} = a \div b$$

suggests how fractions are changed to decimals: Do the division and carry it out as far into decimals as is appropriate.

1. When the division is carried out for some fractions it terminates rather quickly; for others it takes longer but it does terminate. Convert each of the fractions below to terminating decimals as indicated by the first example.

a. $3/8 = 0.375$

b. $1/2 =$

c. $3/16 =$

d. $9/10 =$

e. $3/4 =$

f. $7/20 =$

g. $90/80 =$

$$
\begin{array}{r}
0.375 \\
8{\overline{\smash{\big)}\,3.000}} \\
2\,4 \\
\hline
60 \\
56 \\
\hline
40 \\
40 \\
\hline
0
\end{array}
$$

2. In changing some fractions to decimals, the decimals do not terminate. An example is $1/3 = 0.3333$ . . . . Do the decimal division for each of the following either until a repeating pattern sets itself up or until you get tired of the problem.[1]

a. $2/6$ d. $4/9$

b. $2/3$ e. $1/33$

c. $1/7$

*3. Observe which fractions in problems 1 and 2 above terminate and which do not, and try to make some statement about how they are different. Regard this as a conjecture about when a given fraction will or will not result in a terminating decimal. Test your conjecture. If it seems true to you, see if you can formulate general argument about why it ought to be true. Discuss these matters with colleagues and see if you have the same conjectures.[2]

---

[1] a. $0.\overline{3}$, b. $0.\overline{6}$, c. $0.\overline{142857}$, d. $0.\overline{4}$, e. $0.\overline{03}$.

[2] If denominators of fractions that result in terminating decimals are factored into prime factors, all these factors are 2s or 5s. As to a general argument, it might well hinge on the fact that the prime factorization of 10 is 2×5.

381 EXTENSION
OF THE
RATIONAL
NUMBERS
TO THE
REAL NUMBERS

*4. How would you do conversions from fractions to decimals on a base-ten chip computer?[3]

6.2.2
Why *Must* the Decimal Form of a Rational Fraction be a Repeating Decimal?

In Part A, Unit 5, we remarked that any division $a \div b$ results in both a quotient q and a remainder r *less than the divisor,* such that $a = b \times q + r$. In the usual long division algorithm, this takes the form of partial quotients that give remainders at each point that are in some sense less than the divisor.[3] The long division that converts $1/7$ to a decimal is shown in the example. Observe that at each point the (intermediate) "remainder" is less than 7 (the divisor).

```
       0.14285714 . . .
     _____
  7) 1.00000000 . . .
     7
    ____
   →30
    28
    ____
    20
    14
    ____
    60
    56
    ____
    40
    35
    ____
    50
    49
    ____
    10
     7
    ____
   →30
    28
    ____
     2 . . .
```

1. If we require that each intermediate remainder in the long division algorithm be less than the divisor, then what are the possible intermediate remainders for division by 7? For division by 2? For division by 13? For division by 723? Write an expression for the *maximum* number of different, nonzero, remainders for division by n.[4]

2. Eventually the business of continuing the division process to more decimal places comes down to adding more zeros and "bringing the zero down" to be combined with the last remainder for yet another division step. Do you see why this coupled with the results of the previous problem would mean that eventually more division would just lead to the same divisions over and over again in the same pattern? Look at the divisions that led to repeating decimals in problem 2 of section 6.2.1 above and observe when that begins to happen for each of those.

3. Note that if there is a zero remainder after a certain point, then all subsequent remainders are also zero. You can say either that such a fraction "terminates" or that the repeating part of it is zero repeated; for example, $1/4 = 0.250000000$ . . . or, in other words, $0.25\overline{0}$.

---

[3] Strictly speaking, the interim remainder in the partly worked example below is *not* less than 7 because the partial quotient is really 40, the product 280, and the remainder 20. But this does not affect the reasoning above.

```
          4
    7) 300
       28
       ___
        2
```

---

[3] For $3/8$, for example, put 3 chips on the ones place and then divide by 8 by making piles of eight in each place. You will have to trade to the right beyond the decimal point to get enough chips. Keep trading.

[4] There are at most $n - 1$ different nonzero remainders.

Usually we don't bother with the zeros, but if we want to say that all rational fractions become repeating decimals, those that actually "terminate" can be regarded as "repeating."

4. Try your hand here at a general statement of what *must* happen as a rational fraction $\frac{a}{b}$ is converted to a decimal: Compare your statement with statements of colleagues and refine it as much as you can.[5]

*5. In converting $\frac{1}{7}$ to a decimal all possible remainders except zero appeared (first 3, then 2, then 6, then 4, then 5, then 1, then 3 again and so on). Hence the "period" of the repeating part of this decimal is six digits long. Find another fraction $\frac{a}{b}$ whose period has exactly $b - 1$ digits.

6.2.3
Changing Repeating Decimals to Fractions

1. A terminating decimal can often be written as a fraction in just the way its verbal reading indicates. For example, 0.7, which we read as "seven-tenths" can be written as $\frac{7}{10}$; similarly, 0.025 is read as "twenty-five thousandths" and written as $\frac{25}{1000}$. A mixed number is a bit more complicated; here we use the actual digits in the number for numerator, and the name of the decimal part of the number as denominator. For example, $83.2 = \frac{832}{10}$ and $25.44 = \frac{2544}{100}$. Complete this table:

Decimal Form	Fraction Form
a. 0.0082	
b.	$\frac{495}{100}$
c. 22	
d.	$\frac{3728}{10,000,000}$
e. 28.28	

2. Changing repeating decimals to fractions requires an algebraic procedure that is easy to understand once you see it, but that few people would think of on their own. It uses the fact that multiplication by 10

[5] One of many possible versions would be this one: "If a rational fraction $\frac{a}{b}$ is changed to decimal form, the decimal will be a repeating decimal (sometimes with zero repeated) and the maximum number of digits *in the repeated part* of the decimal will be $b - 1$."

383 EXTENSION
OF THE
RATIONAL
NUMBERS
TO THE
REAL NUMBERS

shifts the decimal by one place; multiplication by 100 by two places; by 1000, three places, and so on. This procedure also requires a firm conviction that repeating decimals repeat forever—that there is always more "out there" to use. The procedure is best conveyed by example, so study these two examples:

Example 1:

$$\text{Let } x = 0.3333 \ldots$$
$$\text{Then } 10x = 3.3333 \ldots$$
$$\text{and } 10x - x = 3.0000 \ldots$$
$$\text{Hence } 9x = 3$$
$$\text{and } x = \frac{3}{9} = \frac{1}{3}$$

Example 2:[4]

$$\text{Let } x = \quad 2.52222 \ldots$$
$$\text{Then } 10x = \quad 25.22222 \ldots$$
$$\text{and } 100x = 252.22222 \ldots$$
$$100x - 10x = 227.00000 \ldots$$
$$90x = 227$$
$$x = \frac{227}{90} = 2\frac{47}{90}$$

Clearly it is always *possible* to do such algebra with infinite repeating decimals. Try it with several of the examples below and as many more as you like. (The second example gives a rather surprising result; if you find it puzzling, talk it over with colleagues or with your professor.) Remember that for these conversions to work you must believe what your intuition will never tell you, namely that these decimals go on forever without end.[6]

a. $0.111 \ldots$

b. $0.999 \ldots$

c. $0.\overline{25}$

d. $0.\overline{123}$

e. $0.2252525 \ldots$

6.2.4
Two
Equivalent Ways to Define
"Rational Number"

Definition 1: A number is a rational number if and only if it can be expressed as a fraction $\frac{a}{b}$, with a an integer and b a nonzero integer.

Definition 2: A number is a rational number if and only if it can be expressed as an infinite repeating decimal. For this purpose such a ter-

---

[4] In this example, you have to multiply the number first so that the repeating part begins in the tenths place. Then you do another multiplication so that subtraction will yield a whole number.

[6] a. ¹/₉, b. 1, c. ²⁵/₉₉, d. ¹²³/₉₉₉, e. ²²³/₉₉₀.

minating decimal as 0.25 is considered to have repeated zeros
(0.250000 . . . or 0.25$\overline{0}$) to make it a repeating decimal.

Since we have shown that either sort of representation can be converted to the other, the definitions are indeed equivalent. If we now hunt for numbers that are *not* rational we have the choice of looking either for numbers that cannot be expressed as fractions as specified in Definition 1, or for decimals that never settle into a repeating cycle. In this connection, recall the table of 4,000 digits of the number π given in Part A, Unit 7. Nowhere within those 4,000 digits does a repeated cycle get established, but that is not conclusive proof that π is not rational because it could conceivably begin to set up such a cycle at some point beyond the 4,000th digit. (It doesn't, but it could.)

6.3
PROBLEM SET: DO NONRATIONAL NUMBERS EXIST?

Overview: **The existence of nonrational numbers will be approached by several ways of looking for a number** x **such that** $x \cdot x = 2$; **or, in other words, such that** $x^2 = 2$.

Are there points on the number line not named by rationals? Are there essential operations in arithmetic that are not closed for the rational numbers? Are all numbers expressible as rational fractions? Are there common life applications that involve nonrational numbers? As it turns out, all these questions can be investigated by looking at a single question in a number of different ways: What number multiplied by itself gives 2 as the product?

6.3.1
The Square Root Operation

1. To "square a number" is to multiply the number by itself. Fill in the blanks in the table of squares below:

x	x^2	x	x^2
0	0	7	___
1	1	8	___
2	4	9	___
3	9	10	___
4	___	11	___
5	___	12	___
6	___	13	___
		14	___
		15	___

385 EXTENSION
OF THE
RATIONAL
NUMBERS
TO THE
REAL NUMBERS

2. Now think of reversing this operation by asking of some non-negative numbers, "What number was squared in order to get this number?" If you can answer the question, you will have provided a "square root" of the number. The symbol for the non-negative number that is the square root of x is $\sqrt{x}$.

a. Why is this question asked only of non-negative numbers?

b. By simply reversing yourself in the table you completed in problem 1 above, you can fill in some of the entries in the table below. Do that for as many as you can find easily and leave the others blank.

x	$\sqrt{x}$	x	$\sqrt{x}$
0	0	64	—
1	1	75	—
2	—	81	—
3	—	100	—
4	2	120	—
9	—	121	—
10	—	*9/4	—
25	—	*2.25	—

3. Probably the first blank you did not fill in was for $\sqrt{2}$. It is clear that the answer is somewhere between 1 and 2 because $1^2 = 1$ and $2^2 = 4$. You should verify that, of numbers to one decimal place, 1.4 is too small (since $1.4^2 < 2$) and 1.5 too big (since $1.5^2 > 2$). By trial and error, or however you like, find out which of 1.41, 1.42, . . . , 1.49, is too small to be the square root of 2 and which is too big. Then find what is too small and too big to the third decimal place, and then perhaps to the fourth decimal place. (The labor of calculation is considerable; share it out among the group, or work with a calculator.) That is, fill in the following table as far as indicated:

a. $\quad 1 < \sqrt{2} < 2$

b. $\quad 1.4 < \sqrt{2} < 1.5$ $\qquad$ (To one decimal place)

c. $\quad 1.14- < \sqrt{2} < 1.4-$ $\qquad$ (To two decimal places)

d. $\quad 1.4-- < \sqrt{2} < 1.4--$ $\qquad$ (To three decimal places)

*e. $1.4--- < \sqrt{2} < 1.4---$ $\qquad$ (To four decimal places)

If you were to continue this process you would eventually find that (to ten decimal places):

$$1.4142135623 < \sqrt{2} < 1.4142135624$$

Clearly, if $\sqrt{2}$ is really a repeating decimal, it doesn't begin the repeating cycle very soon.

The process begun above squeezes $\sqrt{2}$ into smaller and smaller intervals on the number line. That is, $\sqrt{2}$ is always trapped between two numbers, and these come closer and closer to the true value of $\sqrt{2}$. If we could imagine magnifying the interval between 1 and 2 to see where $\sqrt{2}$ is, then magnifying the interval between 1.4 and 1.5, and then the interval between 1.41 and 1.42, and so on, we could see the successively smaller *nested intervals* that squeeze in on $\sqrt{2}$. ("Nested" because each falls entirely within the previous interval.)

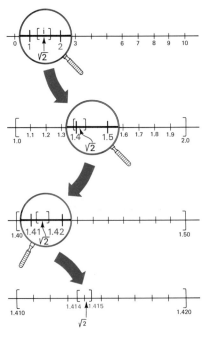

6.3.2

$\sqrt{2}$ **As the**
Length of a Segment

1. Fill in the blanks in the following commentary, which refers to the diagram: The length of the side of the large square $ABCD$ is 2, so its area is $2^2 =$ _____. Each of the small squares has an area $1^2 = 1$ and is cut in half by a diagonal. (For example, the upper left square $ALQK$ is cut in half by the diagonal $\overline{KL}$.) Hence the total area of the inscribed square $KLMN$ is just half that of the larger square. Hence the area of $KLMN$ is _____.

If the length of one side of $KLMN$ is a, then the area is a^2. Hence, $a^2 = 2$. Hence a must be the number $\sqrt{}$.

2. As in problem 1, fill in the blanks in this additional commentary about the diagram: As already noted, each of the sides of $KLMN$ is also a diagonal of a unit square (such as ALQK) with area = _____. Hence the diagonal of any unit square has length $a = \sqrt{}$.

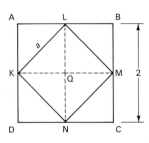

387 EXTENSION
OF THE
RATIONAL
NUMBERS
TO THE
REAL NUMBERS

From these two examples (in problems 1 and 2 on page 386) we see that $\sqrt{2}$ as a length might occur in common situations.

6.3.3
$\sqrt{2}$ **on the**
Number Line

It is possible to construct a unit square with one side on a number line. If you then draw the diagonal of the square, and transfer the length of the diagonal down onto the number line, you locate a definite point on the number line. Because the length of the diagonal is $\sqrt{2}$, the point is named by the number $\sqrt{2}$.

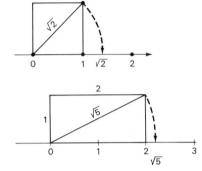

*1. You may recall from school geometry that for any *right* triangle, lengths of the hypotenuse and sides of the right triangle are related by the theorem of Pythagoras: $a^2 + b^2 = c^2$. This lets you mark many other square root points on the number line; for example, $\sqrt{5}$ is marked as indicated in the diagram. (Since $1^2 + 2^2 = (\sqrt{5})^2$.)[5]

In a similar way, find these lengths and mark them on the number lines:

a. $\sqrt{13}$

b. $\sqrt{10}$

6.3.4
At Least
One Nonrational
Number Exists

You cannot fail to have detected from all this buildup that $\sqrt{2}$ is probably *not* a rational number. This would not be proved for sure even if a million decimal digits of $\sqrt{2}$ were computed without finding a repeating cycle, because the repeating pattern could begin even later. Yet there is a simple proof that $\sqrt{2}$ cannot be rational, provided you are willing to believe certain other things *for sure* and say that $\sqrt{2}$ can't be rational if its being rational would violate those things. (Mathematical "proof" generally means showing things consistent or inconsistent with "axioms," which are things that we "agree to agree" must be accepted no matter what the consequences. This simply means that what you can prove depends on what your rock-bottom axioms are—a point that could profitably be better understood by those who argue with each other about this or that.)

1. To build up to the proof, consider these exercises.

a. As indicated in Part C, Unit 5, a prime number p is a positive whole number greater than one that has only itself and one as factors.

---

[5] $1^2 + 2^2 = 1 + 4 = 5$; also $1^2 + 2^2 = c^2$; hence $c^2 = 5$ and $c = \sqrt{5}$.

Circle the prime numbers in this list[6]:

2,   3,   4,   5,   6,   7,   8,   9,   10,   11,   12,   13

b. The main "unshakable belief" that would be violated if $\sqrt{2}$ could be written as a rational fraction is this statement: "Every whole number greater than 1 is either a prime number or can be written as a product of primes in one and only one way, except for the order in which the primes appear."

Factor the numbers below into prime factors. Write "prime" by any that are already prime numbers. The first two are done for you. The easy way to do this is first to divide by 2 as many times as possible, then divide the quotient by 3, if possible, then by 5, and so on.

(1) $12 = 2 \times 2 \times 3$ **(5)** 17

(2) 13 (prime)   **(6)** 34

(3) 77   **(7)** 36

(4) 39

The phrase "except for the order of the factors" means that, for example, $2 \times 2 \times 3$, $2 \times 3 \times 2$, and $3 \times 2 \times 2$ are not considered different ways of factoring 12 into prime factors. If factoring into primes could lead to different factors for the same number, arithmetic would be messy and unpredictable, which may be why this statement is called "the fundamental theorem of arithmetic."

c. If a number a were factored into five prime factors (so that $a = p_1 p_2 p_3 p_4 p_5$), how many prime factors would a^2 have, and what would they be? In general, if a whole number x has n prime factors, how many does x^2 have?[7]

---

[6] If you have any doubts about prime numbers or want to act this out, count out the appropriate number of chips and see if you can form a rectangular array with more than one row using the chips. Those numbers that make only one-row arrays are prime numbers. The number "1" is excluded from the primes for several reasons, but mainly because as multiplicative identity it is a factor of *everything* and can be used twice or hundreds of times as a factor without changing anything.

---

[7] Ten prime factors, because each of the prime factors of a would be used twice in a^2. The factorization would be $a^2 = (p_1 p_2 p_3 p_4 p_5)(p_1 p_2 p_3 p_4 p_5) = p_1 p_1 p_2 p_2 p_3 p_3 p_4 p_4 p_5 p_5$. If a number has n prime factors, then the number squared has $2n$ prime factors—which means that the square of any whole number has an even number of prime factors.

389 EXTENSION
OF THE
RATIONAL
NUMBERS
TO THE
REAL NUMBERS

d. Convince yourself that each of the following statements is true for any appropriate replacement for a, b, or c:

(1) If $a = b$, then $a^2 = b^2$.

(2) For any $a \geqslant 0$, $(\sqrt{a})^2 = a$.

(3) If $x = \dfrac{a^2}{b^2}$, then $xb^2 = a^2$.

(4) If $\sqrt{p} = \dfrac{a}{b}$, then $p = \left(\dfrac{a}{b}\right)^2 = \dfrac{a^2}{b^2}$.

2. Proof that $\sqrt{2}$ is irrational

Essentially all the steps in the proof given below have been dealt with in the exercises above. The proof uses one other standard mathematical maneuver sometimes called "proof by contradiction." In such a proof you work with a statement *as if* it were true (even though you suspect it is false), to see where it leads. If valid reasoning leads to something that is in conflict with one of your basic axioms, then you must either scrap that axiom or assume that the statement you started with is false. Remember that an axiom is something we "agree to agree" is true without any question, so there should be no contest; the initial statement has to be counted false, not the axiom.

Now the proof:

a. Assume for the moment that $\sqrt{2}$ *is* rational and see where that gets us. That is, assume that $\sqrt{2} = \dfrac{a}{b}$ where in this case a and b are whole numbers.

b. Squaring, we get $2 = \dfrac{a^2}{b^2}$ and this in turn leads us to $2b^2 = a^2$.

c. Now suppose that $a = \underbrace{p_1 p_2 p_3 \, \cdots \, p_n}_{n \text{ factors}}$ and $b = \underbrace{q_1 q_2 q_3 \, \cdots \, q_m}_{m \text{ factors}}$ are the prime factorizations of a and b. Then $a^2 = p_1 p_1 p_2 p_2 p_3 p_3 \, \cdots \, p_n p_n$ and $b^2 = q_1 q_1 q_2 q_2 q_3 q_3 \, \cdots \, q_m q_m$ are the prime factorizations of a^2 and b^2.

d. Substituting these prime factorizations into $2b^2 = a^2$, we get this equation:

$$\overbrace{2\ q_1q_1q_2q_2q_3q_3 \ \cdot \ \cdot \ \cdot \ q_mq_m}^{2m\ \text{factors}} = \overbrace{p_1p_1p_2p_2p_3p_3 \ \cdot \ \cdot \ \cdot \ p_np_n}^{2n\ \text{factors}}$$

$$\underbrace{}_{2m + 1\ \text{factors}}$$

But this is impossible because it violates our conviction (really our agreement) that "Any whole number greater than one is either prime or can be factored into primes in one and only one way except for the order of the prime factors." Do you see why this is violated? Talk it over with colleagues.[8]

Hence our initial assumption that $\sqrt{2}$ can be written as a rational fraction has led us to an impossible situation. We therefore reject it; that is, we declare that $\sqrt{2}$ cannot be rational after all.

3. Notice that there is nothing special about 2 in the above proof; that is, 3 or 5 or any other prime number would have played exactly the same role in the proof as did 2. So what are some more numbers that we know for sure are not rational?

4. In what other ways could this result be extended and still preserve the contradiction of having an even versus an odd number of prime factors in the proof?

5. Why would this particular proof *not* be conclusive with respect to showing $\sqrt{6}$ not rational, even though in fact $\sqrt{6}$ isn't rational?

*6.3.5
**Some Other
Nonrational Numbers**

First, the usual vocabulary for "nonrational numbers" is to say instead *irrational numbers*. If the set of rational numbers (which includes the whole numbers and integers) is extended by including the set of irrational numbers, the entire set is called the set of *real numbers*.

Next, it must be remarked that the extension of rational numbers to real numbers is a large and important step in mathematics that can be and is treated in entire books, while we have discussed it only for a few

---

[8] It doesn't matter about the *p*'s and *q*'s because various *p*'s could be the same as various *q*'s and one of the *p*'s could be 2 to take care of the 2 on the left. The key thing is that there is an odd number of prime factors on the left side of the "equation" and an even number on the right, and so the prime factorizations cannot possibly be the same.

391 EXTENSION
OF THE
RATIONAL
NUMBERS
TO THE
REAL NUMBERS

pages. One such book that is accessible and readable and a goldmine of information for teachers is *Numbers: Rational and Irrational,* by Ivan Niven.[7]

It is clear that square roots of many numbers are irrational. It is also the case that many, but not all, cube roots, fourth roots, fifth roots, and so on are irrational, where, for example, the fifth root of 8 (written $\sqrt[5]{8}$) is that number which raised to the fifth power gives 8. Every such root r which is marked on the positive side of the number line corresponds to some negative number $-r$, and so the number line on both sides of zero has many new irrational points named. These roots now give solutions to such equations as $x^2 - 2 = 0$ (namely $\sqrt{2}$ and $-\sqrt{2}$) and many other *polynomial equations* with integer coefficients. These roots and solutions of certain polynomials constitute a subset within the set of irrational numbers; they are called "algebraic numbers."[8]

It would be wrong, however, to leave the impression that these are the only irrational numbers. Below are some other irrational numbers that play a role in everyday affairs but are not roots of numbers nor solutions to polynomial equations with integer coefficients. Such numbers, by the way, are called "transcendental numbers" and any irrational number that is not an algebraic number is a transcendental number.

1. The number π comes up in an astonishing number of places, but most prominently in schoolwork in connection with circles. One definition of π is as the ratio of the circumference of a circle to the diameter of a circle. As indicated by the table of 4,000 digits of π in Part A, Unit 7, this is not a rational number even though it is a ratio because the circumference and diameter of a circle have no common measuring unit that would make one a rational multiple of the other. This means that in some theoretical sense the full power of ratios is only available when we have the entire set of real numbers and not merely the rational numbers. Incidentally, it was only proved in 1882 that π is a transcendental number—which isn't so very long ago.

   For practical purposes, however, rational approximations for π are used. A rounded-off decimal approximation is 3.1416, or as many more places as you'd like to take from the table for π. A surprisingly accurate fraction approximation is $^{22}/_7$. Take a few minutes now to change $^{22}/_7$ to a decimal, say to five decimal places, and see how it compares with the "actual" value of π.

---

[7] Random House, New York, 1961.

[8] Any solution of a polynomial equation with integer coefficients is an algebraic number, but such equations often have no real number solutions at all. A simple example is $x^2 + 1 = 0$; there is no real number that you can square and add to 1 to get zero as the sum.

2. The physical constant denoted as *e* is a transcendental number whose decimal begins $e = 2.7182$. It is something like π in that it appears as an important number in an astonishing number of descriptions of scientific and other phenomena from common life. Two examples will be cited but not developed in detail. First, suppose you were able to find a generous bank that was willing to give you interest on your savings at the rate of 100 percent per year, and also willing to compound this interest not merely semiannually or quarterly or daily but every instant of every day. Would you be rich within a year or so? The answer is that you would be rich only if you started rich, for it can be proved by the methods of the calculus that at the end of a year under such a generous arrangement you would have *e* times as much money as you started with; that is, about 2.7 times as much. Nice, but you aren't all that much more wealthy.

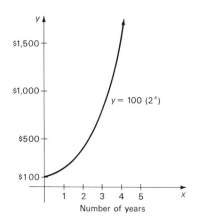

Of course, if you could leave your money in the bank so that it would more than double every year for a few years you would soon be very rich indeed, as you might want to verify by seeing what happens if you start with $100 and it doubles every year for, say, 10 years. We can draw a graph showing such a bank account that is $100 at the start, $200 at the end of the first year, $400 at the end of the second year, and so on; doubling each year. You can see that after a while the amount begins to climb very steeply.[9]

The doubling of money graph leads us to a second example of the use of the number *e* that has to do with the rate at which populations grow. Such populations as bacteria, insects, and so on follow the same sort of curve as shown above if they are allowed to reproduce without restraint. (In practice there always are such restraints; limited food supply, for example.) The base for such a function that often fits the common life facts is not 2 but the number *e*. The curve that is a picture of $y = e^x$ is shown here and variations on it are common as mathematical models of population growth. The curve has the very interesting mathematical feature that the slope (steepness) of a line drawn tangent to it at any point is exactly equal to the *y* coordinate of that point. That is, for a point on the curve one unit above the horizontal axis, the steepness (ratio of rise to run) is 1 and for a point on the curve 10 units above the horizontal axis the steepness ratio is 10 to 1. Or in other words, the higher the curve goes, the steeper it gets. As a model of population growth, this says roughly that the bigger a population gets, the faster it grows, which may account for why a lot of people worry about the possibility of overpopulation, a population explosion, and so on. This isn't necessarily to suggest that *you* must

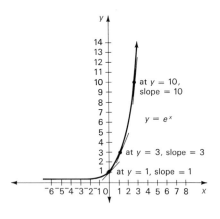

---

[9] Such graphs come up again in Part C, section 3.7.

393 EXTENSION
OF THE
RATIONAL
NUMBERS
TO THE
REAL NUMBERS

worry about such matters or that there is a "mathematical" and hence "correct" way to say for sure what the problems are. The assumptions you make alter considerably the conclusions that can be drawn. But you should at least be aware of a basis in mathematical models for believing there might be a problem worth thinking about.[10]

3. Trigonometry is taken by many high school juniors and seniors, and tables in school books give decimal approximations of sines or cosines for various angles. Most sine and cosine values, however, are actually irrational numbers.

4. Logarithms of numbers are mentioned briefly in section 5.5.6. Again, although we use rational decimal approximations for logarithms, they are usually irrational, transcendental numbers.

6.4
PROPERTIES OF THE REAL NUMBERS

One way to define the real numbers is to say that they consist of *all* infinite decimals, whether repeating decimals or not. This includes such rational numbers as -13, 0.5, $-1/7$, $-13.\overline{0}$, $0.5\overline{0}$, and $-0.\overline{142857}$; such algebraic numbers as $\sqrt{2}$, $\sqrt{3}$, and $\sqrt{8}$; and such transcendental numbers as π, e, $\log 2$, and $2^{\sqrt{2}}$.[11]

As to the properties of real numbers, they are precisely the same, up to a point, as the properties of rational numbers. Any genuine extension of the number system, however, leads to at least one brand-new property. In the case of the extension of rational numbers to the real numbers, the new property essentially guarantees that all points on the number line now have names; there are no "holes" left and there is no further need for extension of the number system in order to account for all number line points. Stated informally, this new property says that every real number corresponds to some point on the number line and every point on the number line is named by some real number. One of the many versions of a more formal statement of this property relies on setting up a system of *nested intervals* for each number, as we did on page 386 for $\sqrt{2}$. A formal statement of the continuity property then looks like this:

Cantor's principle of continuity: For every nested system of intervals

---

[10] An old but elegant and readily accessible warning about the possible problems of population growth versus food supply is by Thomas Malthus (1766–1834), "Mathematics of Population and Food," reprinted in J. R. Newman, *The World of Mathematics,* V. II, Simon and Shuster, New York, 1956.

[11] It has only been known for sure since 1934 that $\log 2$ and $2^{\sqrt{2}}$ are transcendental. (See Niven, op. cit., p. 71.) Many new mathematical results have been discovered in modern times, and this growth in mathematics continues unabated at present.

$[a_n, b_n]$ there exists one and only one real number r that belongs to each of these intervals.

This describes what happens when we take sequences of closer and closer rational approximations to a number with the number remaining within each smaller and smaller interval. Since every real number is an infinite decimal, there is no limit on how far we can take this approximation process.[12]

6.5 RATIOS AND PROPORTIONS AGAIN

Overview: Ratios and proportions are reviewed and extended.

With completion of the real number system, the numbers and operations needed for many common life applications of mathematics are available. In particular, ratios and proportions are used many times in such applications, as already indicated in Part A, section 7.2.2. Ratios sometimes involve irrational numbers, but even when that is true we use rational approximations to the irrational numbers, usually expressed as finite decimals, for any actual calculations.

Some of the most frequent uses of ratios are as percents, which merely standardize whatever ratio is being talked about on a "per hundred" basis. A survey of nearly any issue of a large city newspaper or a weekly news magazine will turn up examples of informations given as percents. You should verify this and at the same time try to find other uses of ratios in such sources of information.

It is possible to discuss at length the teaching of ratios, proportions, and percents, but we will not do so here. A proportion is simply a statement that two ratios are equal. For children who have developed good intuition about ratios, skill in handling equivalent fractions, and common sense about keeping track of the relationships in a situation, proportions need present little difficulty.

In addition to use in common life situations, proportions become "important" to many people because there are frequently many proportion problems on tests of (supposed) mathematical ability, achievement tests, civil service and other job placement tests, and so on. Listed below are some examples of the use of percents, ratios, and proportions from common life situations or adapted from achievement tests. You should work through these and discuss them with colleagues. You should also try to sort out what some important pedagogical concerns might be in making youngsters good at exploiting ratios and proportions.

---

[12] In the case of "terminating" decimals, such as $0.25\overline{0}$, the successive approximations soon get the same result, with no improvement needed or possible.

395 EXTENSION
OF THE
RATIONAL
NUMBERS
TO THE
REAL NUMBERS

6.5.1
**Examples of
Ratios, Proportions, and
Percents from Common
Life Situations**

1. The *New York Times* of March 17, 1974, reported that 70 percent of the 33,412 students who enrolled on the various campuses of the City University of New York when an open admissions policy took effect in 1970 were still enrolled four semesters later. How many of these students were still enrolled?

2. The same issue of the *New York Times* reported that in the 1961–1971 period the United States inflation rate averaged 3.1 percent per year, while in Europe the average was 3.7 percent. How much more should a person who earned $10,000 in 1961 in the United States have been making in 1971 just to keep up with inflation? (The same article reports that the increase in consumer prices in the United States in 1973 was 9.6 percent and in Europe 11 percent.)

3. The *Chicago Sun-Times* of March 15, 1974, printed a letter from a woman to her apartment house management who had announced "modest" rent increases. Here is an excerpt: ". . . I presented the letter pointing to the 4% to 6% increase, and then, laughingly, to my 13-plus-percent increase. My incredulous ears heard him say, 'There's no mistake. . . . The 4% to 6% is for one year. . . . Since you have a two-year lease, the increase becomes 8% to 12%. . . .'" Is the manager right and if not, what is wrong with his reasoning?

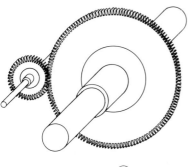

4. The *New York Times* on March 24, 1974, reported that in 1934 the United States highway fatality rate was 16.75 deaths per 100 million vehicle miles, while in 1973 the rate was 4.3 deaths per 100 million vehicle miles. Given that the number of United States highway deaths in 1973 was about 55,600, about how many vehicle miles does this represent? If the death rate were still as high as in 1934, about how many traffic deaths might there have been in 1973?

5. Gear arrangements are often used in machinery either to control speed or control amount of power delivered. For example, in the gears illustrated, the shaft attached to the 15 tooth gear will turn twice as fast as the one attached to the 30 tooth gear. More generally, this proportion governs the relationships:

$$\frac{T}{t} = \frac{r}{R}$$

where T and t are the number of teeth and R and r are the number of revolutions in a given time for the larger and smaller gears respectively.

If you want to reduce the speed from 100 to 25 revolutions per second, and start with one gear having 50 teeth, as shown in the diagram, how many teeth should the other gear have? (As the speed is reduced, the power is increased by about the same amount. Does this give you some notion about how your automobile operates, with lower transmission gear ratios for slow speed but high power?)

6. The conversion of power (or energy) from one form to another is usually notoriously inefficient. An electric motor producing ¼ horsepower might use about 300 watts of electrical power, while if there were no losses 1 horsepower would be equivalent to 746 watts. By computing the ratio of power that goes out of the motor to power put into the motor, attach a "percent efficiency" rating to this motor. (If the motor runs for a while it feels warm to the touch, which accounts for much of the power loss.)

7. The book *Mapping* by David Greenhood[13] tells us that ratios are also used in defining standards of accuracy for surveying. "First order of accuracy" is one unit error allowed in 25,000 units; "second order of accuracy" is one unit in 10,000 units; "third order of accuracy" is one unit in 5,000 units. What would be the allowable error in miles for each of these three standards of accuracy for a direct line coast-to-coast survey for the United States (about 3,000 miles)? The same source tells of a satellite tracking task at Cape Kennedy for which the U.S. Coast and Geodetic Survey delivered one unit in one million accuracy. With that sort of accuracy, how many feet of error might there be in a coast-to-coast survey of the United States?

6.5.2
**Some Examples
Typical of Those Found
on School Mathematics
Achievement Tests**

1. What is the value of x if $\dfrac{2}{x} = \dfrac{x}{8}$?

2. What percent of 300 is 12?

3. If 6 of 30 squares are shaded, how many of 100 squares must be shaded to maintain the same proportion?

[13] University of Chicago Press, Chicago, 1961.

397 EXTENSION
OF THE
RATIONAL
NUMBERS
TO THE
REAL NUMBERS

4. A graph not more than 4 inches wide must display values of 0 to 3600. Which of these scales should you use?

    a. $1'' = 500$ **b.** $\frac{1}{2}'' = 500$ **c.** $1'' = 1000$ **d.** $\frac{1}{4}'' = 100$

5. A suit marked down 30 percent is now $75. What was the original price?

Other problems on such tests involve finding lengths in right triangles with trigonometry, consumer and tax problems, mixtures such as antifreeze and water, sports averages, average speed or gasoline mileage for a trip, and geometry problems using ratios. On one widely used test 14 out of fewer than 40 questions involved the use of ratios, proportions, or percents in some way.

6.6
PEDAGOGICAL REMARKS

Extension of the number system to include irrational numbers is a very important step, mathematically speaking. Until this is done, for example, there are not numbers to go with every point on the number line, and these "gaps" pose possible difficulties in a variety of processes, especially those that use calculus. Having the entire set of real numbers also opens up interesting questions in set theory; for example, is the set of real numbers larger (more infinite, so to speak) than the set of whole numbers, or the set of rational numbers?[14]

The question of how best to make the extension from rational to real numbers has been handled in various ways by excellent mathematicians and has led to the invention (or discovery) of some fine mathematics. Yet most of the issues here are clearly beyond what is appropriate for elementary school children, though some groundwork can be laid for the extension of rational numbers to real numbers.

Real numbers play a role in many ways in applications of mathematics to common life. Such constants as π and e, most square roots, most values of trigonometric functions, and most results from the use of logarithm and exponential functions are irrational. Such numbers are used in a great many applications, including some that come up in work at the elementary school level (e.g., intuitive approaches to π, to square roots, and to trigonometric functions in indirect measure). Hence in one sense the real numbers are very important in common life situations. But in

---

[14] The answer is "yes." If you are interested in pursuing why this is so, ask your instructor for a reference.

another sense, the fact that many such numbers are irrational is nearly irrelevant. This is so because in practice we invariably use decimal approximations to irrational numbers, with as many decimal places as are appropriate in a given situation. It is clearly impossible to do computations with decimals infinite in length, and in any case we never need that sort of precision. An oversimplified summary would be that the irrational numbers are an important theoretical concern, but rational versions of them are all that are needed for common life. This *is* an oversimplification, however, because development of the theoretical side of mathematics not infrequently leads to elegant and profound consequences for application of mathematics in common life.

The subject of approximations is an important one and the use of finite decimal approximations to infinite decimals is one aspect of this. Also, "sneaking up on" an answer by getting better and better decimal approximations is an important idea worth developing whenever children work with decimals. Good judgment about how accurate an answer is possible or appropriate in a given situation needs to be developed. For example, if you are measuring something with a ruler accurate to tenths, then it is silly to keep answers to thousandths or ten-thousandths when you multiply or divide such measures. Few school books handle "rounding off" or "significant figures" well, and common sense is probably a better guide than most of the elaborate rules that sometimes appear in books. But such common sense needs to be developed. Rounding off can be described as using "close but easier numbers." A rough guide to how many significant figures or decimal places to keep from a calculation is that the answer cannot be better than the weakest bit of input information.

We have stressed the importance of ratios and proportions a number of times in this book, and the extension to real numbers extends the applicability of these. In spite of this importance, the sort of attention given ratios and proportions in school books is sometimes less than helpful. Many books focus on cases, problem types, fixed recipes for setting up and solving proportions, and so on. We believe that schools should over a long time period aim to build genuine gut-level intuition about how ratios operate and about exploiting fraction notation. A proportion is simply a statement that two ratios are equal, and for children with skill in dealing with equivalent fractions and a good sense of what is going on in a given situation, proportions need present few difficulties. Similar remarks apply to percents, which are in very common use in our world. We don't wish to minimize the complications or difficulties in these matters but only to suggest that broad experience and soundly built intuition will serve children better than narrow rules and procedures, no matter how "efficient" such rules may seem to be for particular kinds of problems.

unit 7

analysis of different systems of numeration

7.1
INTRODUCTION Throughout history the need for numbers has been varied. Such needs have ranged from simple number words ("one," "two," "many") to complex systems of numeration, and from no calculation with numbers to calculations requiring the aid of elaborate machinery. These varied needs, words, symbols, and means of calculation are discussed in section 7.2.

There are many different ways to build up symbols for larger and larger numbers. Some ways that have been used in different cultures at different times are outlined in section 7.3. Two Babylonian systems of numeration, three Greek systems, and two Chinese systems are described. Each system has some feature that the others lack, but each also has some features in common with other systems. Considered as a whole, these systems illustrate the most important characteristics that systems of numeration can possess.

Characteristics of the seven systems outlined in section 7.3 and of our decimal system of numeration are explored in section 7.4. Advantages and disadvantages of these systems and of the decimal system are discussed in section 7.5.

In the first four units of Part B, base four and base eight were used. These experiences are summarized in Section 7.6 along with a more general discussion of base, place-value systems.

The unit closes with pedagogical remarks about problems connected with teaching the decimal system of numeration and remarks about teaching numeration in general.

399

7.2
READING AND ACTIVITY: A BRIEF HISTORY OF NUMBER WORDS AND NUMBER SYMBOLS, OF MEANS OF RECORD-KEEPING, AND OF CALCULATION WITH NUMBERS

The history of the development of numeration systems is a complex subject that cannot be covered thoroughly in this book. (Several whole books attempt this; they are listed in Appendix II.) Certain aspects of this development are common to most cultures, however, and will be described in some detail in this section.

First, numbers arise from the needs of people. Different needs give rise to different systems. The simplest systems consist only of number words; they have no number symbols. More complex needs and perhaps the presence of certain facilitators ("writing materials," etc.) result in symbols for numbers. These symbols are recorded in some fashion.

The keeping of records is a need that often has resulted in number symbols, but occasionally has instead resulted in inventive means of record keeping that do *not* require symbols. Calculation with numbers also has sometimes been done for number systems with symbols and sometimes for number systems without symbols. Almost without exception, this calculation was done with objects rather than with symbols before the advent of our base-ten, place-value system of numeration.

Each of the general areas in the development of systems of numeration is described in this section. Important similarities and differences in these areas for different cultures are noted.

7.2.1
The Needs for Numbers

Overview: **The need for counting objects in primitive cultures has been overestimated, and the need for measuring has been underestimated. Some needs for numbers for five kinds of primitive cultures are indicated, and you are asked to think of other needs. Number needs for more advanced cultures are then discussed.**

The need for counting objects in primitive cultures has commonly been overestimated in mathematics books and in popular literature, and the need for measuring uses of numbers in such cultures has been underestimated. The answer to the question "Why did man need numbers?" is usually: "He used numbers to count his possessions—his sheep or cows, his warriors, his children, etc."

This answer ignores the fact that primitive cultures are not affluent cultures, and primitive people are quite close to the few possessions they do have. If a sheep or llama or cow is missing, the owner knows not only that one is missing, but also which one is missing (e.g., the smallish female who had twins two springs ago and who has the jagged scar on her left flank). Animals, pots, baskets, children, clothes, pipes, and other possessions are individuals, one of a kind, and are remembered as individual things. Only when individual characteristics of things have no meaning or significance or when the number of things grows so large that a list of individual objects is too long to be practical does it become reasonable to count things. Neither of these circumstances usually arises in primitive cultures.

A partial reason that counting uses of numbers are overestimated is that the wrong question was asked. A more accurate and more helpful question is: "Why did people (men, women, and children) need numbers?" This question focuses more fully on all aspects of daily life in primitive cultures. Suddenly more measure needs for numbers appear. Some examples of questions involving measure needs for numbers that might arise in primitive cultures are given below:

Do I have enough water in the pot to mix with this much powdered corn?
Do I have enough wood to make a fire that will burn three nights?
How much salt can I use each day if I am to make this pile of salt last until the next trading expedition?
How much dried meat do I need to carry for a journey of 15 days?
Do I have enough extra rice to trade to the pot maker for a new pot?
Is this piece of cloth large enough to make a cloak for the oldest son?
Do I have enough shells to make a double row on this dress?
Where can I find trees at least this tall to make the posts for my house?
Do I have a long enough thong to tie heads on ten arrows?
Do we have enough baskets of grain to eat all winter and still have grain to plant in the spring?

Of course counting uses appear, too. "Are there enough bananas for everyone to have two?" is the counterpart to a child's question, "Will I get two bananas?"

For each of the five kinds of primitive cultures[1] listed below, list several examples where a need for numbers, either in counting or measuring, might arise.

1. *Food browsers*—wandering from place to place and eating whatever they find; no storing of food.
2. *Food gatherers*—wandering, eating, and collecting as they wander; wandering perhaps systematic and seasonal; storage of gathered food.
3. *Hunters*—hunting animals for food; probably accompanied by gathering or farming; may be nomadic or settled.
4. *Farmers*—planting, tending, and reaping plant food; perhaps accompanied by gathering, hunting, or herding.

---

[1] Our own classification.

5. *Herders* — tending of domesticated animals which are used for food (milk, blood, meat), beasts of burden, clothing, shelter, or fuel; perhaps accompanied by gathering or farming.

Trading between tribes must have led to new needs for numbers. Measurement of length, area, volume, and weight would be increasingly necessary. In many cultures, standard measures of certain often-used commodities arose. Lengths of cloth, quantities of rice, weights of certain metals would be measured by a single, agreed-upon standard. Although much trade was by means of barter, various highly prized or rare objects became generally accepted means of exchange, i.e., money. Shells, certain types of stones, and precious metals were common forms of money.

Kingdoms or empires also created new needs for numbers. Both conditions for counting objects were now satisfied: The individual characteristics of booty won would not matter to the ruler and there would certainly be too many possessions to be listed separately. Animals, drinking vessels, slaves, etc., would each be counted; only the number of each type of possession would matter. Rulers would want records of exploits and captured materials kept, so symbols or some means of record keeping would be needed. Subjugated people would probably have to pay taxes to support the administration and subsequent expeditions of the ruler. What other new needs for numbers might arise in empire cultures?

In more sophisticated urban cultures, economic, mathematical, and religious needs for numbers arose. More than 4,000 years ago the Chaldean cities of Ur, Nippur, and Babylon developed a culture in which "weights and measures, bills, receipts, legal contracts, promissory notes, interest (simple and compound) were commonplace."[2] In the area of less applied mathematics, quadratic equations were solved; arithmetic tables were constructed for the use of the accountant, the statistician, and the algebrist (including tables of logarithms); and geometry was used in engineering and architecture.[3] Astronomy was developed as a religious, as well as a scientific, endeavor.

Many of the above areas now use numbers in more sophisticated ways, but the same general needs are still operating. Can you think of new needs for numbers that now exist and are missing from the above list (disregarding mathematical and scientific uses of number for the moment)? List some below and compare your list with those of your colleagues.

[2] Edna E. Kramer, *The Nature and Growth of Modern Mathematics,* Hawthorn Books, New York, 1970, p. 3.

[3] Ibid., p. 3.

Mathematical uses of numbers have greatly expanded. Part C of this book gives some indications of the new kinds of uses of numbers in mathematics. Scientific uses of numbers have also increased enormously. Glance through section 5.1 to get some indication of the wide range of scientific uses of numbers. List below other new scientific uses of numbers that occur to you.

7.2.2
Number Words

Overview: **Common sources of number words are described. Examples are given of three common ways of forming larger number words from smaller number words; these methods are additive, subtractive, and multiplicative.**

Now that we have briefly examined some of the needs for numbers, let us turn to the number words themselves. We think of numbers as being completely abstracted from objects. "Three" has a meaning without any reference to specified objects. But originally number words were much more closely tied to the objects they described. For example, a tribe of Indians in British Columbia has different words for counting animate things, round things, long things, and days. "Two men" are "*maalok* men" and "two days" are "*matlp'enequls* days."[4] The Fiji Islanders call ten boats *bola,* ten coconuts *koro,* and 1000 coconuts *saloro.*[5] We see this intertwining of number and object in English in various forms of two: twins (two babies), duet (two musical performers), yoke (two oxen), brace (two partridges), and pair (two, usually matching, objects).

Many number words have been taken from names for real things. Parts of the body are perhaps the most common source of number words. People in all parts of the world have taken number words from their words for parts of the body. A tribe on the island of Papua has taken this to extremes. They count beginning on the right side of the body and naming the following parts of the body: little finger, ring finger, middle finger, index finger, thumb, wrist, elbow, shoulder, ear, eye, eye, nose, mouth, ear, and so on backwards through the sequence down the left side of the body.[6] Because the words they use for these parts of the body do not distinguish left and right, their words for one and twenty-two, two and twenty-one, three and twenty, etc., are the same. (What is the highest number for which these people have a word?)

Many number words come from finger gestures, rather than from

---

[4] Karl Menninger, *Number Words and Number Symbols,* Massachusetts Institute of Technology Press, Cambridge, Mass., 1969, p. 30.

[5] Ibid., p. 11.

[6] Ibid., p. 35.

names for the fingers. In British New Guinea, 99 is: "four men die (80), two hands come to an end (10), one foot ends (5), and 4",[7] The African Sotho construction for the same number (99) is: "tens which bend one finger which have units which bend one finger,"[8] The finger gestures for numbers of many African tribes are so distinctive that ethnologists use these finger gestures (and sometimes the derived number words) to trace historical roots of tribes.

Traces of the influence of finger gestures are visible in the West. In English, we call units "digits," which comes from the Latin for fingers. The Roman phrase *numerare per digitos* meant to count with the fingers, and *novi digitos tuos* meant literally "I know your fingers" but was an idiom for "I recognize your skill in calculation."

New words can be made for each new number. But eventually this results in a list too long to remember. Therefore most peoples have formed larger numbers by combining words for smaller numbers. New words are then added only for certain large numbers.

Larger number words are formed from smaller number words in three general ways: additive, subtractive, and multiplicative. Examples of each follow.[9] Notice that some peoples form larger words by more than one method.

Many of the number systems below had only number words, and no number symbols. In all cases our usual symbols are used to tell the meaning of the number word or to explain the formation of number words. Sometimes the actual number words used were not available; in this case only the method of formation of the number word is given.

Table 7.1 Additive Ways of Making Larger Number Words

Igbo of Nigeria:

11	*iri na otu*	10 and 1		30	*ohu na iri*	20 and 10
12	*iri na abuo*	10 and 2		31	*ohu na iri na otu*	20 and 10 and 1
21	*ohu na otu*	20 and 1				

Hausa of Northern Nigeria:

13	12 + 1		16	12 + 4
14	12 + 2		17	12 + 5
15	12 + 3		18	12 + 6

Huku of Central Africa:

$7 = 6 + 1$ $13 = 12 + 1$

---

[7] Ibid., p. 36.

[8] Claudia Zaslavsky, *Africa Counts,* Prindle, Weber & Schmidt, Boston, 1973, p. 38.

[9] African examples are from ibid. and the other examples are from Menninger, op. cit.

Table 7.1 (*Continued*)

Ekoi of Cameroon:

3	*esa*	6	*esaresa* (*esa* and *esa*, $3 + 3$)
4	*eni*	7	*eniresa* (*eni* and *esa*, $4 + 3$)
5	*elon*	8	*enireni* (*eni* and *eni*, $4 + 4$)
		9	*eloneni* (*elon* and *eni*, $5 + 4$)

Because their number words are based on finger gestures, many African tribes form their words in the following way:

6	$5 + 1$	11	$10 + 1$	16	$10 + 5 + 1$
7	$5 + 2$	12	$10 + 2$	17	$10 + 5 + 2$
8	$5 + 3$	13	$10 + 3$	18	$10 + 5 + 3$
9	$5 + 4$	14	$10 + 4$	19	$10 + 5 + 4$
10	$5 + 5$ or a new word	15	$10 + 5$	20	$10 + 10$ or "whole man"

English:

13	thirteen (three and ten)	21	twenty-one (twenty and one)
14	fourteen (four and ten)	35	thirty-five (thirty and five)

Which numbers have been used by various peoples as "building blocks" for making larger numbers?

Can you think of reasons why these particular numbers might have been chosen?

Table 7.2 **Subtractive Ways of Making Larger Number Words**

Sotho (Africa):

9   units which bend one finger $(10 - 1)$

Babylonian (2000 B.C.):

19	𒌋𒌋𒐎	$(20 - 1)$	37	𒌋𒌋𒌋𒌋𒐈	$10 + 10 + 10 + 10 - 3$

Late Roman:

4	IV ($5 - 1$)	40	XL ($50 - 10$)
9	IX ($10 - 1$)	90	XC ($100 - 10$)

Ancient Greek:

58   *dyoîn deóntes hexēkonta*   2 lacking from 60

Latin:

19	*un-de-viginti*	1 from 20
58	*duo-de-sexaginta*	2 from 60

Anglo Saxon:

19   *anes wona twentig*   1 less than 20

Table 7.2 (*Continued*)

Old Norse:

| 54 men | *man midr en halfr setti tögr* | 1 man less than half six tens |

Sanskrit:

19	*(ek-) una-vimsati*	(1) lacking (from) 20	similarly for all tens
39	*una-čatvarimsat*	(1) lacking 40	

Ainu (Northern Japan):

6	*i-wan*	4 from 10
7	*ar-wan*	3 from 10
8	*tu-pesan*	2 steps down
9	*shine-pesan*	1 step down
10	*wan*	

Finnish:

8	*kahdeksa*	2 from 10
9	*yh-deksan*	1 from 10

Sicilian:

| 85 | *cente me quinci* | $100 - 15$ |

Bantu:

7	*mufungate*	"bind three fingers" $= 10 - 3$
9	*kenda*	"take 1" $= 10 - 1$

Examples of the subtractive method of forming larger number words are fairly rare. Few languages use the subtractive method consistently (the Yorabu system in Table 7.4 is one of the few exceptions). Isolated cases seem to exist in a wide variety of languages, however.

Look at the subtractive example above. Can you think of how some of the various examples might have occurred?

Table 7.3 **Multiplicative Ways of Making Larger Number Words**

British New Guinea:

| 80 | "four men die" | 4×20 | 10 | "two hands come to an end" | 2×5 |

Huku of Central Africa:

8	2×4	16	$(2 \times 4) \times 2$	20	2×10
9	$2 \times 4 + 1$	17	$(2 \times 4) \times 2 + 1$		

Igbo of Nigeria:

40	*ohu abuo*	20×2
60	*ohu ato*	20×3
200	*ohu iri*	20×10
300	*ohu iri noohu ise*	$(20 \times 10) + (20 \times 5)$
400	*nnu*	
160000	*nnu khuru nnu*	"400 meets 400" $= 400 \times 400$

Table 7.3 (*Continued*)

Enggana (south of Sumatra):
100	*ariba ekaha*	"hand man" = 5 × 20
400	*kahaii edudodoka*	"one our body" = one man times our body = 20 × 20

English (in Lincoln's time):
87	"four score and seven years ago"	(4 × 20) + 7

English (present time):
20	twen-ty	["twin(?)-ty"] two tens	2 × 10
30	thir-ty	three tens	3 × 10
40	for-ty	four tens	4 × 10
50	fif-ty	five tens	5 × 10
100	hundred	from Gothic meaning "tenned from tens"	

French:
80	quatrevingt	four twenties	4 × 20

What are the "building blocks" for making larger numbers in the examples above?

How do you suppose these particular numbers were chosen? (Don't ignore the Huku.)

The Yorabu number system is an interesting combination of all three methods of forming larger number words from smaller number words. Look at the examples given, and specify for each number greater than ten whether it is a new number word or by which of the three methods (additive, subtractive, or multiplicative) it is formed from smaller number words.

If you wish, you might then describe how to make some of the numbers that are missing. You might even try to figure out what the new number word would be.

The additive and multiplicative means for making larger number words are used in most languages. The subtractive method is used much less frequently.

*Activity Look up the number words for a non-English language. List some examples where additive, multiplicative, and subtractive (if they occur) methods are used to form words for large numbers.

Table 7.4 **Number Words of the Yorabu of Nigeria[10]**

1	*ookan*	
2	*eeji*	
3	*eeta*	
4	*eerin*	
5	*aarun*	
10	*eewaa*	
11	*ookan laa* (*laa* from *le ewa* = in addition to ten)	$1 + 10$
12	*eeji laa* (2 in addition to 10)	
13	*eeta laa* (3 in addition to 10)	
14	*eerin laa* (4 in addition to 10)	
15	*eedogun* (from *arun din ogun* = "five reduces twenty")	$20 - 5$
16	*eerin din logun* (4 reduces 20)	$20 - 4$
17	*eeta din logun* (3 reduces 20)	$20 - 3$
18	*eeji din logun* (2 reduces 20)	$20 - 2$
19	*ookan din logun* (1 reduces 20)	$20 - 1$
20	*ogun*	
21	*ookan le logun* (1 on 20)	$20 + 1$
25	*eedoogbon* (5 reduces 30)	$30 - 5$
30	*ogbon*	
35	*aarun din logoji* ("five less than two twenties")	$(20 \times 2) - 5$
40	*ogoji* ("twenty twos")	
45		$(20 \times 3) - 10 - 5$
50	*aadota*	$20 \times 3 - 10$
60	*ogota* ("twenty in three ways")	3×20
100	*ogorun* = *orun*	20×5
105	*aarun din laadofa*	$(20 \times 6) - 10 - 5$
106		$(20 \times 6) - 10 - 4$
200	*igba*	
300	*oodunrun* = *oodun*	$20 \times (20 - 5)$
315	*orin din nirinwo odin marun*	$400 - (20 \times 4) - 5$
400	*irinwo*	
525		$(200 \times 3) - (20 \times 4) + 5$
2000	*egbewa*	200×10
4000	*egbaaji*	2×2000

[10] Zaslavsky, op. cit.

Compare your list with that of someone who investigated a different language.

7.2.3 Number Symbols *Overview:* Number symbols have had their source in tally systems, in alphabets, in ideographs, and in calculating devices. Our numerals originated in India in the second or third century B.C. and entered Western

Europe about the tenth century via the Arab world. These numerals and the decimal system of numeration did not become widely used in Western Europe until the sixteenth century. Roman numerals were used prior to that time in most of Western Europe.

Many cultures have number words but have no symbols for numbers. Some of the sources of number symbols will be briefly examined below. Analysis of number symbols used to build systems of numeration in several different cultures is made in sections 7.3 and 7.4.

One common source of number symbols is the tally, or stroke. Many peoples "kept score" of some aspect of their lives by marking short line segments on sand, wood, or whatever. These strokes, or tallies, grew more sophisticated as the need for larger numbers arose. The strokes became grouped in various ways, resulting in primitive number systems. Roman numerals, Mayan numerals, and Chinese rod numerals perhaps show such a tally influence.

Tally system

I II III IIII IIIII IIIIII IIIIIII IIIIIIII IIIIIIIII IIIIIIIIII

Mayan numerals

Grouped tally system

I II III IIII ͰͰͰ ͰͰͰ I ͰͰͰ II ͰͰͰ III ͰͰͰ IIII ͰͰͰ ͰͰͰ

Chinese rod numerals

I II III IIII IIIII ⊤ ⊤⊤ ⊤⊤⊤ ⊤⊤⊤⊤ —

Roman numerals[11]

I II III IV V VI VII VIII IX X

The alphabet was another source of number symbols. Either the letters themselves were ordered in some fashion and then used as numbers (for example, A: 1, B: 2, C: 3, D: 4) or the first letter of the number word was used to symbolize the number (for example, O: one, T: 2, Th: 3. This method obviously has difficulties if the number words reuse any of the same letters). The Greeks and Hebrews used the former method, and the Greeks in an earlier period used the latter method.

Greek: First Letter as Number Symbol

Number word	ΔΕΚΑ	ΗΕΚΑΤΟΝ	ΧΙΛΙΟΙ	ΜΥΡΙΟΙ
Number symbol	Δ	Η	Χ	Μ
Value	10	100	1000	10000

[11] These subtractive Roman numerals developed comparatively late. Earlier numerals used IIII and VIIII.

Greek Alphabetical Numerals [12]

1	2	3	4	5	6	7	8	9	10
α	β	γ	δ	ϵ	ς	ζ	η	ϑ	ι

20	30	40	50	60	70	80	90	100	200
κ	λ	μ	γ	ξ	o	π	?	ρ	σ

300	400	500	600	700	800	900	1000	. . .
τ	υ	φ	χ	ψ	ω	ɱ	$, \alpha$	

An ideograph of some object related to a number was sometimes used. The ancient Egyptians used ideographs. See below. Some people have suggested that the Roman numerals are ideographs.

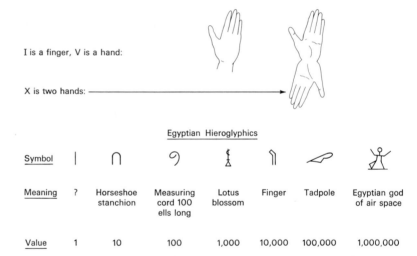

I is a finger, V is a hand:

X is two hands: ——————————————→

Egyptian Hieroglyphics

Symbol	|	∩	⌒		⌁	⌐	𓀭
Meaning	?	Horseshoe stanchion	Measuring cord 100 ells long	Lotus blossom	Finger	Tadpole	Egyptian god of air space
Value	1	10	100	1,000	10,000	100,000	1,000,000

At least one set of numerals came from a calculating instrument. The ancient Chinese used a set of short rods for calculating. The rods were laid out in configurations for different numbers. (See the last example in the tally system chart above.) These configurations were later adopted as numerals, which were used in Japan as late as the eighteenth century. (See section 7.3.3, System 6, for more details of this system.)

The numerals we use had their origins in India. Some were seen as early as the second or third century B.C. These numerals came through the Arab world into Spain, and from there into Western Europe where they appeared in monastic manuscripts as early as the tenth century. However, they were not widely used in Western Europe until the late

[12] The letters for 700, 800, and 900 are Semitic. The Greek alphabet contained only 27 letters.

sixteenth century when books that popularized calculation with the decimal system began to appear. Even then the use of Roman numerals continued into the eighteenth century.

The family tree of the Indian numerals. Reprinted from p. 419 of *Number Words and Number Symbols* by Karl Menninger by permission of the M.I.T. Press, Cambridge, Massachusetts.

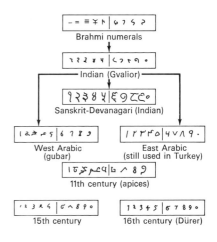

Brahmi numerals

Indian (Gvalior)

Sanskrit-Devanagari (Indian)

West Arabic (gubar)

East Arabic (still used in Turkey)

11th century (apices)

15th century

16th century (Dürer)

7.2.4
Recordkeeping

Overview: **Concrete materials of various kinds have been used by people whose culture lacked number symbols or by individuals who did not know the symbols. Tally sticks, knots on rope, pebbles, pegs, and cowrie shells are examples of such use.**

Tally sticks have been used to keep records by peoples all over the world.[13] Tally sticks are wood sticks that have notches cut into them. The notches may be simple ones (one notch standing for one object) or they may be grouped for easier reading. They may also involve different kinds of notches representing different sizes of numbers.

Tally sticks were used all over Western Europe for hundreds of years to keep many kinds of records. Innkeepers recorded debts on tally sticks. Idioms arising from this practice exist in many European languages (In Dutch: *De kerfstock loopt to hoog:* "The bill (tally stick) is getting too high.") In Switzerland tallies were kept of milk outputs from cattle grazing in the high summer common range. Water rights for cattle were also recorded on tallies. The Finns kept records of work done on tally sticks, and the snow removal men in Vienna did likewise. Some double or triple tally sticks (sticks split lengthwise and then held side by side when the tallies were cut so that forgeries could not be made) had the force of legal documents as late as 1804.

[13] Menninger, op. cit., pp. 223–240. Many of the following examples in section 7.2.4 are from these pages.

Tally sticks were so commonly used in Western Europe that they appeared as metaphors. For example, Martin Luther, in beginning a letter to a friend to whom he had not written in a long time, said, "I must cut off the tally stick [cancel my debt], for I have not answered your letter for a long time."

Russian tax records were cut onto wooden rods which were then bound into "tax books." Repeated scoring and cutting off of the paid taxes made the tax rods very thin. Fiji Islanders cut notches on their warclubs for the number of enemies they had killed, as did some American Indians on their tomahawks and American cowboys on their guns. Wooden number sticks from the time of the Han dynasty, 2,000 years ago, have been found on the Great Wall of China.

The Royal British Treasury used tally sticks for keeping records as late as the 1920s. A sheriff would do his calculations on a counting board, record his answers on a tally stick, and send the stick to the Treasury. The word *check* (*cheque*, in Britain) comes from the use of tallies. The Royal Treasury issued double tally sticks. A person could take such a tally to the Treasury and it would pay out money for the amount recorded on the tally. Tally sticks could be exchanged between individuals, and thus were a kind of currency. The tally sticks later became a written certificate, or "check."

Words for the verbs "to number" or "to count" in many languages come from tally sticks. The English word *score* (to "keep score") is from the Old Saxon *sceran* meaning "to shear, cut." The Serbian word *broj,* "number," comes from *britj,* "to cut." The Bantu *vala* means both "to notch" and "to reckon, to count." The Latin *putare* means "to cut in, to indent." "To cut a notch for someone" (*imputare*) meant to assign a debt, while *deputare* meant "to cut away," to cancel a debt. The Chinese character for "contract" consists of three characters which mean "large tally stick." The Chinese character for "law" is a bundle of tally sticks lying on a table. Some people also think that the vertical column writing of the Chinese comes from writing on vertical tally sticks.

Knots on ropes were used by several peoples as a tally system. The Incans, who controlled a vast empire in western South America, kept detailed and sophisticated records on "quipu" by using different kinds of knots for different sizes of numbers. On the Ryukyu Islands (between Japan and Taiwan) workmen braid straw and reeds with different fringes to indicate wages they have earned. The ancient Chinese (fifth century B.C.) used knots in cords for numbers and for some writing.

Various African cultures have used pebbles, pegs, and cowrie shells (sea-shells) for keeping records.[14] In nineteenth century Buganda, records of available warriors were kept by white, black, and red pegs on

---

[14] All this information is from Zaslavsky, op. cit.

a pegboard (the colors represented 10, 100, and 1,000, respectively). When the king handed a certain number of pegs to a chief, that meant the chief was expected to supply that number of warriors. In nineteenth century Dahomey, statistics on births, deaths, amounts of vegetable produce, etc., were kept by means of boxes of pebbles. Strings of cowrie shells were money. The terms for this shell money were: 40 = 1 string, 2,000 = 1 head, 20,000 = 1 bag.[15] In a battle with the Yoruba, the King of Dahomey was beaten and sustained a loss of "2 heads, twenty strings, and twenty" (or 4,820) warriors.

7.2.5
Calculation

Overview: **Throughout history, most calculations have been made with the aid of concrete objects. Writing materials have been too scarce or numeration systems too cumbersome to use symbols for making calculations. Loose objects grouped in various ways, objects used on some background layout, or objects fixed in some way have all been used as calculating devices. The prevalence of these devices is reflected in the words for calculating in many languages.**

Throughout history, very few people have used their number symbols to make calculations. Until machine-made wood pulp paper became available in the middle of the nineteenth century, writing materials were very expensive. The raw materials were often difficult to obtain in quantity, and the process of preparing the writing material was often quite laborious. Papyrus made from reeds was widely used in the Mediterranean countries 2,000 to 4,000 years ago. Parchment from the skins of sheep and lambs and vellum from calves' skin was used in Western Europe in the Middle Ages. Rag paper was hand-made in China 2,000 years ago and was made in Europe beginning about the twelveth century.

In addition, many numeral systems did not facilitate easy computing, especially of multiplication and division.

Most peoples have calculated with the help of objects. These objects might be grouped in various ways. The pebbles or cowrie shells widely used for calculation in Western Africa are sometimes grouped in twenties, sometimes in sixes, and sometimes in groups of other sizes.

Calculating objects might be used on a background, such as a board or cloth with lines drawn to distinguish columns (or rows) of different value. The Incas of South America calculated with kernels of wheat on a board divided into spaces. The Greeks and Romans used tables or boards made of wood or marble for calculations. The Romans called

---

[15] In the 1860s the value of cowrie shells in British money was 1 string = 1 pence (penny), 1 head = 3–6 pence, 1 bag = 14–16 shillings. A slave cost 2 bags.

Merchant using medieval counting board. Adapted from woodcut on p. 363 of Menninger, op. cit.

such a calculating table an "*abacus.*" Medieval Europeans used calculating tables, boards, and marked cloths that were put on tables when in use. Counters of various kinds were used on these counting boards. These counters were quite fancy and valuable between 1500 and 1700 and were often stamped in metal with commemorative motifs. Records of these counters are present in many wills of the time, as they were handed down to later generations. The Chinese, and subsequently the Japanese, used a board divided into columns as a background to their calculations with their reckoning stocks (See section 7.3.3, System 6 for details.).

Sometimes the counters were permanently fixed to the counting board and arranged in rows or columns to represent different values. The Romans used a forerunner of such an arrangement. This consisted of grooves on which sat round balls. Short grooves at the top of each column held a ball representing five, and a longer groove in each column held as many as four balls. This type of calculator was not used by any cultural descendants of the Romans, and it disappeared. In the twelfth century, the *suan pan* (literally, "reckoning board") appeared in China. Whether it came from the Roman grooved arrangement, no one knows. It consisted of beads fixed on wires. Each wire represented a different power of ten. Two beads at the top were used to represent five, and each of five beads in the lower portion of each column represented one. The Japanese *soroban* came from China in the sixteenth century. It has only one "five" bead at the top of each column. The Russian *ščët* is another form of a fixed counter calculator. It has ten beads on each wire arranged horizontally. The fifth and sixth beads are dark in order to aid the counting. The latter three calculators are still in use today.

These calculating devices live on in many languages.

Language	Word	Original Meaning[16]
Greek	*Pséphizein*	To move pebbles
Latin	*Calculos ponere*	To place stones
Medieval Latin	*Calculare*	To move pebbles
French	*Jeter, compter, calculer*	To throw
English	*To cast, to count*	To throw
English	*To calculate*	(Via Latin) to move pebbles
Chinese	*Suan* (to compute)	A character showing calculating sticks

[16] Menninger, op. cit., pp. 373, 368.

Commercial terms often come from these calculating instruments. The Greek and Latin words for a reckoner, be he merchant or moneychanger, were *trapezitēs* and *mensarius,* i.e., tabler, a worker on a table. The English word *banker* derives from the medieval "counting bank" or table. *Exchequer* derives from the checkered cloth used to cover a table on which calculations of royal receipts were made.

Mechanical calculators began to appear in the seventeenth century. Blaise Pascal, a French mathematician, invented in 1642 a calculator that used geared wheels. This calculator was used on the estate of Pascal's father to help with the records.

Mechanical calculators gradually became faster and capable of more difficult arithmetic operations. Finally, in the late 1940s electronic calculators using vacuum tubes were built. The later development and use of miniaturized components greatly reduced the size and increased the reliability of such machines and enabled machines of much greater capacity to be built. Technical advances and improvements in the programming languages used in the machines decreased the time of operation of a sample program from one hour to a few seconds. In spite of inflation, the cost of using computers has likewise decreased greatly. In 1950 a dollar would pay for processing about 35,000 single operations on a computer, while in 1968, a dollar would pay for 35 million such operations. Computing machines have revolutionized business and science. Problems formerly beyond the realm of the possible are now solved routinely.

Activity List some areas of business and of science in which work would be impossible without computers. (See Appendix II for some sources of this information.)

7.3
ACTIVITY:
SOME SYSTEMS OF
NUMERATION

Section 7.2 provided much information about number words and number symbols, but did not indicate very clearly how systems of number symbols can be organized. This section indicates various possibilities for constructing symbolic numeration systems.

Numeration systems have at least six possible characteristics. Systems with various mixtures of these characteristics (two Babylonian, three Greek, and two Chinese systems) were chosen for inclusion in this section. These choices indicate not only the range of possibilities, but also some of the changes that numeration systems undergo over time.

Overview: **In this section you will gain experience with seven different numeration systems either by reading about them or by practicing writing numbers in them. Your experiences with these numeration systems will be used in the following two sections, where general characteristics of the** systems and relative advantages and disadvantages of the systems will be analyzed. One of the systems is the same as our usual system of numeration, except that different symbols are used.

7.3.1 Babylonian Numeration Systems

The numeration systems described below are a simplification of two fairly late Babylonian numeration systems. The history of Babylonian numeration is very complex and contains many gaps and unanswered questions. At different times the Babylonians used two different styluses (a cylindrical one early and a wedge-shaped one later) to make marks in wet clay. Each kind resulted in different numerical symbols. But each set of symbols evolved through time also, resulting in at least four different systems of Babylonian numeration. We will describe here the later, wedge-shaped symbols and the two systems of numerals written with these symbols.[17]

1	10	60	600	3600	36000	216000

System 1: Middle Babylonian

Examine the examples that are given to discover how the above symbols were used. If you wish, try covering some of our numerals and see if you can tell what the Babylonian number is. Notice that the symbol for 60 is larger than the symbol for 1.

1	29	106
2	30	
3	40	109
4	50	
5	60	110
6	61	
7	62	120
10	63	130
11	65	
12	70	170

[17] Ibid., pp. 162–168.

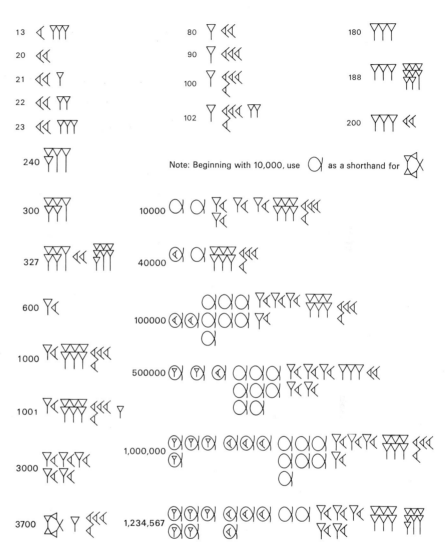

System 2: Late Babylonian Later the size difference between 1 (Υ) and 60 (Υ) disappeared, and 60 was indicated only by its position to the left of 1. The symbols greater than 60 were also abandoned, and the symbols for 1 and 10 were used in positions further to the left of 60 to indicate 3600 and 216000.

Υ	$\triangleleft$	Υ	$\triangleleft$	Υ	$\triangleleft$	Υ
1	10	60	600	3600	36000	216000
			(10 × 6)	(60 × 60)	(10 × 3600)	(60 × 3600)

Numbers were written with symbols for the largest numbers on the left.

For hundreds of years this system was used without a zero. Therefore:

Ⓨ   could mean 1 or 60 or 3600 or 216000.

◁   could mean 10 or 600 or 36000.

◁ Ⓨ   might be 11 or 601 or 36001 or 36060 or 39600 (36000 + 3600).

The meaning of the symbols could sometimes, but not always, be told from the context in which it was used. Finally in the sixth century B.C. a sign for a missing gap appeared, and about 300 years later, a sign for zero appeared at the end of a number. We will use the notation that the Greek astronomer Ptolemy used in 150 A.D.[18] Ptolemy placed a bar over the symbols in a given place and used a 0 (Greek *oudein,* "nothing") for a missing place.

$\overline{◁}\,\overline{Ⓨ}$ = 11 $\overline{◁}\ \overline{Ⓨ}$ = 601 $\overline{◁}\ \overline{○}\ \overline{Ⓨ}$ = 36001 $\overline{◁}\ \overline{Ⓨ}\ \overline{○}$ = 36060 $\overline{◁}\ \overline{Ⓨ}\ \overline{○}\ \overline{○}$ = 39600

Use of Symbols: Examine the examples that are given to discover how the above symbols were used. Compare how some numbers are written in late Babylonian with how they were written in middle Babylonian. What are the differences?

The numbers up through 59 in this system are identical to those of System 1 except that a bar would be drawn over all symbols. Therefore 60 will be the first number given.

| 60 | 61 | 62 | 65 | 80 | 90 | 100 | 102 | 120 | 130 | 170 | 180 | 200 | 240 | 300 | 327 |

18   The Babylonian sexagesimal place-value system was used for centuries by astronomers, though the Greek alphabetical numerals (see System 4) were usually substituted for the Babylonian symbols. This sexagesimal (60) notation is the source of the divisions of both the hour and the circle into minutes and seconds (60′ = 1°, 60″ = 1′; and 60 minutes = 1 hour, 60 seconds = 1 minute). These divisions are actually sexagesimal fractions (cf. our decimal fractions).

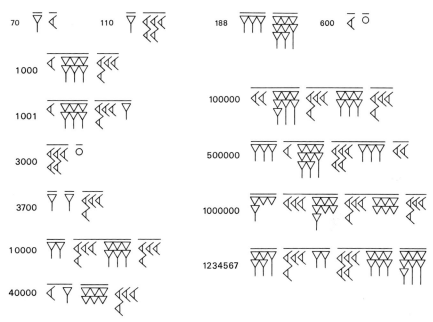

The Babylonians actually used sexagesimal fractions, i.e., they used symbols to the right of one as well as to the left. The trade rule (left to right: one for sixty) remained constant for the places to the right. Therefore these new places had value:

$$\frac{1}{60} \qquad \frac{1}{60} \times \frac{1}{60} = \frac{1}{3600} \qquad \frac{1}{60} \times \frac{1}{60} \times \frac{1}{60} = \frac{1}{216000} \qquad \text{etc.}$$

For example:

$$60 + 12 + \frac{1}{60} + \frac{23}{3600}$$

$$= 72\,\frac{60 + 23}{3600} = 72\,\frac{83}{3600}$$

$$600 + 60 + 6 + \frac{11}{60} + \frac{6}{3600} = 666 + \frac{660}{3600} + \frac{6}{3600}$$

$$= 666 + \frac{666}{3600}$$

These sexagesimal fractions were used by astronomers, other scientists, and mathematicians in Europe, Northern Africa, and the Middle East for hundreds of years. Gradually mathematicians began to realize that similar fractions could be made with the Indian-Arabic base-ten, place-value system. Not until the 1600s did these new decimal fractions begin to see fairly wide use.

7.3.2 Greek Numeration Systems

Three numeration systems used by the Greeks[19] at different times are described below.

[19] The three Greek systems are taken from Menninger, op. cit., pp. 268–274.

System 3: Greek Repeated Symbolic

The Athenian Greeks used these numerals from the middle of the fifth century B.C. well through the first century B.C. The symbols (except the symbol for one) were the initial letters of the number words.

Number word		ΔΕΚΑ	ΗΕΚΑΤΟΝ	ΧΙΛΙΟΙ	ΜΥΡΙΟΙ
Number symbol	1	△	H	X	M
Value	1	10	100	1000	10000

These symbols could be grouped together into five of any symbol by using Γ(ΓΕΝΤΕ, five).

$\lceil = 5 \qquad \lceil△ = 5·△ = 50 \qquad \lceil H = 500 \qquad \lceil X = 5000 \qquad \lceil M = 50000$

Examine the examples to discover how the symbols were used. Fill in the blanks.[1]

1 |	24	100	327
2 ||	25	H||	HHHH△△△|||
3 |||	26	H|||	600
4 ||||	△△⌐||||	106	⌐HHHH
5 Γ	△△△	109	1000
6 Γ |	40	110	1001
7 Γ||	⌐	120	1232
10 △	60 ⌐△	H△△△	XXX
11 △|	61	H⌐△△	3700
12	62	180	
13	63	188	10000
20 △△		200	13016
21 △△|	⌐△Γ	HH||	40000
22	⌐△△	240	
23	⌐△△△	300	
	90		

[1]
12 △||	70	202
13 △|||	80	240 HH△△△△
22 △△||	90 ⌐△△△△	300 HHH
23 △△|||	100 H	327 HHH△△⌐||
24 △△||||	102	433
25 △△Γ	103	600 ⌐H
26 △△Γ|	106 H Γ|	900
29	109 H Γ||||	1000 X
30	110 H△	1001 X|
40 △△△△	120 H△△	1232 XHH△△||
50	130	3000
61 ⌐△|	170	3700 XXX ⌐HH
62 ⌐△||	180 H⌐ △△△	10000 M
63 ⌐△|||	188 H⌐ △△△ Γ|||	13016 MXXX△Γ|
65	200 HH	40000 MMMM

For numbers greater than 99,999 new symbols would be needed. (For numbers this large Athenians usually used System 4.) Suppose $Y = 100,000$ and $Z = 1,000,000$. Then fill in the blanks below.[2]

$100,000 = $ _____   _____ $= \lceil^\rceil$ $1234567 = $ _____

$300,000 = $ _____ $1,000,000 = $ _____

System 4: Greek Multi-enciphered Greek alphabetical numerals appeared as early as the fifth century B.C. but did not become the official system of numeration in Athens until the first century B.C. For these numerals, the Greeks used the 24 letters of their alphabet and three Semitic letters. For simplicity, we will use the English alphabet and the symbol $\triangle$.

A	B	C	D	E	F	G	H	I		J	K	L	M	N	O	P	Q	R
1	2	3	4	5	6	7	8	9		10	20	30	40	50	60	70	80	90

S	T	U	V	W	X	Y	Z	$\triangle$		,A	,B	,C	,D	,E	,F	,G	,H	,I
100		300		500		700		900		1000		3000		5000		7000		9000
	200		400		600		800				2000		4000		6000		8000	

For numbers 10,000 and larger, three methods were used at various times. The method of Diophantus of Alexandria, a famous mathematician in the third century B.C., is used below. This method is to use the symbols above and to place a dot after the *myrioi*, or ten-thousands.

F. $= 6 \times 10,000 = 60,000$
SLE.$\triangle$Q $= 135 \times 10000 + 980 = 1350980$

Use of Symbols: Examine the examples to discover how the above symbols are used. Fill in the blanks.[3]

[2] 100000 Y
300000 YYY
500000
1000000 Z
1234567:
  ZYYMMMXXXX ⊓⊓ △ ⌈||

[3]									
4	D	50	N	103		240		3700	
5	E	60	O	106	SF	300		4219	,DTJI
6	F	61	OA	109	SI	327		10000	A.
7	G	62	OB	120	SK	434	VLD	13016	
13	JC	63	OC	130		600	X	40000	D.
23	KC	65	OE	170		900		100000	J.
24	KD	70	P	180	SQ	1000	,A	300000	L.
25	KE	80		188	SQH	1001	,AA	500000	N.
29	KI	90		200	T	1232	,ATLB	1000000	S.
40	M	100		202	TB	3000		1234567	SKC.,DWOG

1 A	21 KA	63		SL	1000	
2 B	22 KB	65		SQ	1001	
3 C	23	70	180		1232	
4	24	QQ	188			,C
5	25	RR	200			,CY
6	29	SS	202		4219	
7	30 L	102 SB		TM	10000	
10 J	40	SC		U		A.,CJF
11 JA	50	106		UKG	40000	
12 JB	60	109	434	\	100000	
13	61	110 SJ	600		300000	
20 K	62	120		△	500000	
1000000:		1234567:				

Can you think of a way to simplify this system? (Hint: Eliminate either the comma or the dot.)

Why do you suppose this system developed using both the comma and the dot?

System 5: Greek Place-value In the fifteenth century, a third Greek system began to appear. It showed the influence of the Indian-Arabic place-value, base-ten system that was beginning to become established in Western Europe. The alphabetical numerals A to I were used for 1 to 9, and a dot (according to the Eastern Arabic fashion) was used for zero. Examine the examples below to discover how the system works. Fill in the blanks.[4]

[4] 4 D	60 F.	106 A.F	240		3700	
5 E	62 FB	109 A.I	300		4219 DBAI	
6 F	63 FC	120 AB.	327		10000 A....	
7 G	64 FD	130	434 DCD		13016 AC.AF	
24 BD	65 FE	170	600 F..		40000 D....	
25 BE	70 G.	180	900 I..		100000 A.....	
26 BF	80 H.	188 SHH	1001 A..A		300000 C.....	
29 BI	90 I.	200 B..	1232 ABCB		500000 E.....	
50 E.	103 A.C	202 B.B	3000 C...		1000000 A......	
					1234567 ABCDEFG	

1	A	21	BA	62		120		I..
2	B	22	BB	63			AC.	1000 A...
3	C	23	BC	65			AG.	1001
4		24		70			AH.	1232
5		25		80		188		3000
6		26		90		200		CG..
7		29		100	A..	202		4219
10	A.	30	C.	102	A.B		BD.	10000
11	AA	40	D.	103			C..	13016
12	AB	50		106			CBG	40000
13	AC	60		109		434		100000
20	B.	61	FA	110	AA.	600		300000
500000:		1000000:				1234567:		

7.3.3 Chinese Numeration Systems

Until modern times, the Chinese did not have separate words and symbols for numbers. Their number symbols were characters for the respective number words. In English, this would be as if we had no numerals (0, 1, 2, 3, 4, etc.) and always wrote out the words (e.g., five hundred thirty-seven).

At least four sets of indigenous Chinese numerals with long histories are still in use today—the basic, official, commercial, and stick numerals. The first three are similar systems, but the characters for each differ in complexity; the commercial is the simplest, and the official is very elaborate in order to avoid forgery. Some documents contain all of the first three kinds of numerals. For example, a bank draft might use the commercial characters for the check number, the official characters for the amount of the check, and basic numerals for the date. Since 1955, Indian numerals (i.e., our numerals) have become the officially approved system of numeration, but the indigenous systems are still used.

The stick numerals and a system like the basic, official, and commercial systems are Systems 6 and 7.[20]

System 6: Chinese Stick Numerals

Two thousand years ago the Chinese began to use little bamboo or wooden sticks as calculating pieces (*chou*) on a reckoning board. In 600 A.D. the Japanese adopted this system, and they used it into the 1800s. Earlier versions of the reckoning board had unmarked columns in which sticks were placed. Later versions were divided into squares to aid the vertical and horizontal placement of sticks. Columns to the right of 1 represented 1/10, 1/100, 1/1000, etc. With the arrival in the thir-

[20] The Chinese numeration systems are from Menninger, op. cit., pp. 368–371, 450–467.

teenth century of the zero from India, the sticks could be recorded as symbols. They then formed a written numeration system as well as a physical calculating system.

The sticks were vertical in the units place and horizontal in the tens place. This alternation of orientation continued in all further places (hundreds vertical, thousands horizontal, ten-thousands vertical, hundred-thousands horizontal, etc.). Because the symbols were often written touching each other, this alternation made them easier to read. The alternation probably originated on the old unmarked reckoning boards as a way of aiding the distinguishing of columns.

A small circle, o, was used for zero (*ling*, "gap, vacancy").

	|| ||| |||| ||||| ⊤ ⊤ ⊤ ⊤	— = ≡ ≣ ≣ ⊥ ⊥ ⊥ ⊥
1 2 3 4 5 6 7 8 9	10 20 30 40 50 60 70 80 90

Use of symbols: Examine the examples to discover how the above symbols were used. Fill in all blanks.[5]

1	|	25		103		900
2	||	26			|o⊤	1000
3		29	≣|||	109		1001 —oo|
4		30		110		1232
5		40			⊢o	≡ooo
6		50			⊢o	≣⊤oo
7	⊤	60			⊢o	4219
10		61	⊣	180		10000
11	⊣	62		188		13016
12	⊣|	63		200		40000
13	⊣||		⊣||||	202		—ooooo
20			⊥		|≣o	300000
21	≣|		≐	300		≣ooooo
22	≣||	90		327		1000000
23		100	|oo		|||⊟|||	1234567
24		102	|o||	600		

[5]

3	|||	62	⊣|	300	|||oo	100000	
4	||||	63	⊣||	327	||⊢⊤	300000	≡ooooo
5	|||||	90	≐o	434		500000	
6	⊤	103	|o|||	600	⊤oo	1000000	|oooooo
10	—o	106		900	⊤⊤⊤o	1234567	⊢|≣|||⊣⊤
20	=o	109	|o||||	1000	—ooo		
23	≣||	110	⊢o	1232	—⊣⊟		
24	≣|||	120		3000			
25	≣||||	130		3700			

System 7: Chinese Named-place Numerals

The Chinese basic, official, and commercial numeration systems use related but different symbols. They are all organized in the same manner. They each have characters for the digits one through nine and also for the places ten, hundred, thousand, ten-thousand, hundred-thousand, million, etc. Each place beyond the units place is named both by the character for the digit in that place (1 to 9) and by a character for the size of the place (tens, hundreds, etc.). As with all Chinese writing, the numbers are written from top to bottom with the larger places at the top, and from right to left across the page.

Because the Chinese characters are difficult to write, English abbreviations of our English number words are used here for the names of places. As a reminder that the Chinese had no number symbols separate from their number words, the following abbreviations of our number *words* will be used instead of our *numerals:*

O	W	R	F	V	X	S	E	N
1	2	3	4	5	6	7	8	9

T	H	Th	TTh	HTh	M
10	100	1000	10000	100000	1000000

As before, fill in the blanks in the examples on page 426.[6]

5

26 ⊐丁	170	4219 ≡⊢⫿
30 ≡○	180 ⊨○	10000 |○○○○
40 ≣○	188 ⩜丁	13016 ⊨○⊤
50 ≣○	200 ||○○	40000 ||||○○○○
60 ⊥○	202 ||○||	
	240	

6

			63	62	60	50		29	26	25	24	13	6	5
80	70	65	X	X	X	V	40	W	W	W	W	O	X	V
			T	T	T	T		T	T	T	T	T		
			R	W				N	X	V	F	R		

327	300			200	188	180			120	109	106	103
R	R	240	202	W	O	O	170	130	O	O	O	O
H	H			H	H	H			H	H	H	H
W					E	E			W	N	X	R
T					T	T			T			
S					E							

300000	40000	13016	4219	3700	3000	1232			600	434
R	F	O	F	R	R	O	1001	900	X	F
HTh	TTh	TTh	Th	Th	Th	Th			H	H
		R	W	S		W				R
		Th	H	H		H				T
		O	O			R				F
		T	T			T				
		X	N			W				

25	24	23	22	21	20	13	12	11	10	7	6	5	4	3	2	1
	W	W	W	W			O	O	O	S			F	R	W	O
		T	T	T			T	T	T							
		R	W				W									

103	102	100	90	63	62	61	60	50	30	29	26
O	O	N	E	X		X			F	R	
H	H	T	T	T		T			T	T	
W				V		O					

327	300	200	188	180	120	110	109	106
	W	W			O	O	O	
	H	H			H	H	H	
	F	W			S	R	O	
	T				T	T	O	
							T	

10000	4219	3700	3000	1232	1000	600	434
O					O	O	N
TTh					Th	Th	H
					O		

1234567	1000000	500000	300000	100000	40000	13016
				O		
				HTh		

7.4 PROBLEM SET: ANALYSIS OF CHARACTERISTICS OF NUMERATION SYSTEMS

Overview: In section 7.4.1 six common characteristics of numeration systems are described. In section 7.4.2 you are asked to decide which of the characteristics apply to each of the numeration systems outlined in section 7.3. Disparities between our number words and our number symbols are discussed in section 7.4.3.

[6] 1234567	1000000	500000
O	O	V
M	M	HTh
W		
HTh		
R		
TTh		
F		
Th		
V		
H		
X		
T		
S		

7.4.1
**Six Characteristics
of Numeration Systems**

The characteristics are phrased in terms of questions. An affirmative answer means that the system in question does possess the characteristic. In the section following this one you will be asked to answer these questions about the numeration systems in 7.3. Now just read through the questions.

1. Does the system use *additive* ways of making larger numbers? (See section 7.2.2, Table 7.1, for a reminder of what "additive" means.)
2. Does the system use *multiplicative* ways of making larger numbers? (See section 7.2.2, Table 7.3, for a reminder of "multiplicative.") If the answer is yes, does the system use *explicit* symbols for this multiplication (e.g., four *hundred*), or is the multiplication *implicit* (400)?
3. Is the system *positional*? That is, are larger numbers made by assuming that a symbol in one place has a value different from its value in another place? If the system is not positional, is the *size* of a numeral *contained within any given symbol* (e.g., △ or H) or is the size of a symbol *named by an extra, "size" symbol*?
4. Is ten the *main base* that is used to make larger numbers? If not, what is the main base?
5. Is a *sub-base* to a larger base used? For example, the Roman numeral system uses a main base of ten and a sub-base of five.
6. Does the system use *repeated* symbols (for example, △△△|| or TTTOO for thirty-two) or *enciphered* symbols (for example, 32 for thirty-two)?

7.4.2
**Characteristics of
Various Numeration Systems**

Focus in turn on each of the six characteristics above. Decide whether our decimal numeration system and each of the seven numeration systems in section 7.3 possesses each of the characteristics. (Call our decimal system System 8).

1. Which of the eight systems use additive means to make larger numbers?

2. Which systems use multiplicative means to make larger numbers?

For which systems is this multiplication explicit (i.e., named)?

For which systems is this multiplication implicit (i.e., not named)?

Which systems do not use multiplicative means to make larger numbers?

3. Which systems use purely positional means to tell the size of a numeral?

Which systems use nonpositional means to tell the size of a given numeral?

4. Which systems use ten as the main base?

Which systems use a base other than ten as the main base, and what is this base?

5. Which systems use a sub-base to a larger base and what sub-base is used?

Which systems do not use a sub-base to the main base?

6. Which systems use repeated symbols (like Roman numerals: III is three)?

Which systems use enciphered symbols (all the symbols for the first nine numbers are different)?

Compare your description of the characteristics of numeration systems with the following description. Resolve any discrepancies by discussing them with your colleagues.

1. Does the system use additive means to make larger numbers? The answer is *yes* for every system. Numeration systems always use additive means to combine smaller numbers to make a larger one. Often this addition is of various multiples of the base (e.g., thousands plus hundreds plus tens plus units or ones plus sixties plus thirty-six hundreds). It is difficult to think of a numeration system that does not use additive means. Can you make up such a system?

2. Does the system use multiplicative means to make larger numbers? Is the multiplication explicit or implicit?

Systems 1, 3, and 4 do not use multiplicative means to make larger numbers. In these systems, larger numbers have their own new symbols. (In system 3 the use of Γ, five, as a shorthand is a multiplicative means, but the major formation of numerals does not use multiplication.)

System 7 explicitly uses multiplication to make larger numbers. It has a basic set of numerals for one through nine, and the multiplication of these small numerals by a larger one is specifically described (four hundred, $\begin{smallmatrix}F\\H\end{smallmatrix}$; one thousand fifty six, O Th V T X (horizontal instead of vertical)).

In systems 2, 5, 6, and 8 the multiplication is implicit. These systems also have a certain basic set of numerals for small numbers, but they have no additional numerals that tell the size of larger numbers. The size of any numeral is indicated by its position. That is, the position of a numeral is what tells whether it is multiplied by ten, a hundred, thirty-six hundred, or whatever.

3. Is the system a positional one or not?

Systems 2, 5, 6, and 8 are positional. That is, you can tell the size of a given numeral only by looking at its position within a given number.

Although the other systems do follow a general order from larger to smaller in writing a number, the size of a given numeral can be told by the nature of the symbol used (Systems 1, 3, and 4) or by the name following a numeral (System 7).

4. Is ten the main base that is used to make larger numbers? If not, what is the main base?

Systems 3, 4, 5, 6, 7, and 8 use ten as the main base. Systems 1 and 2 use sixty as the main base.

5. Is a sub-base to a larger base used?

Systems 4, 5, 7, and 8 use no sub-base to the main base ten. Systems 1 and 2 use a sub-base ten to the main base sixty, and systems 3 and 6 use a sub-base five to the main base ten.

6. Does the system use repeated symbols or enciphered symbols?

Systems 1, 2, 3, and 6 use repeated symbols (e.g., forty is ⫷⫷

(a & b), △△△△(c), ≡ (f)). Systems 4, 5, 7, and 8 use enciphered symbols (1 to 9 have different symbols).

System 3 carries encipherment to an extreme, with new symbols for ten, twenty, two hundred, etc., instead of using the symbols for 1 to 9 over again.

**7.4.3
Disparities
between Our Number Words
and Our Number Symbols**

Our number words form a different system of numeration from our number symbols. Our number words name the values of each numeral:

4702 is four thousand seven hundred two
530 is five hundred thirty
3,508,691 is three million five hundred eight thousand six hundred ninety one

Our number symbols do not name the values of each numeral:

4702 is just four seven zero two
530 is just five three zero
3,508,691 is just three five zero eight six nine one

Both our number words and our number symbols use additive and multiplicative ways of making larger numbers, they both have a main base of ten, and they are both enciphered. Both also have a sort of "supra" base of a thousand, reflected in the words by the reading of each of thousands, million, billions, etc., all together (e.g., 475,000 is four hundred seventy-five thousand, not four hundred thousand, seventy ten-thousand, five thousand) and in the symbols by the placing of commas after the thousands, the millions, the billions, etc.

But the words and the symbols are different in two important characteristics.

1. Is the multiplication in our number words implicit or explicit? In our number symbols?[7]
2. Are our number words positional or named-value? Our number symbols?[8]

Thus our number words are similar to the Chinese named-value system and our number symbols are similar to the Greek place-value system.

These differences between our number words and our number symbols may account for some confusion in the early grades. It certainly is responsible for a lessening of understanding of the power of our number symbols. As will be discussed in the next section, the efficiency of our numeration symbols for calculation and for writing any real numbers at all (small or large) derives from the fact that it is not a named-value system, that the value of its symbols are *understood* by their positions. As long as 47802 is thought of as forty-seven thousand eight hundred two instead of as four seven eight zero two, the power and even the nature of the implicit positional values of the places is not fully understood.

The other main difference between our number words and our number symbols is in the words for the new places: ten, hundred, thousand, etc. Ten sounds like a new single digit numeral, just like 0, 1, 2, 3, 4, 5, 6, 7, 8, and 9. But it is 10: "one-zero" or "one-oh"—one digit in the new place. Similarly for one hundred ("one-zero-zero", or "one-oh-oh"), one thousand ("one-oh-oh-oh"), etc. They sound like a new numeral instead of a positional reuse of old numerals.

---

[7] Multiplication is explicit in our number words; it is implicit in our number symbols.

[8] Our number words are a named-value system; our number symbols are positional.

7.5
PROBLEM SET:
ADVANTAGES OF VARIOUS
NUMERATION SYSTEMS

Overview: Advantages and disadvantages of the seven numeration systems in section 7.3 and of our decimal system of numeration will be discussed.

7.5.1
A Comparison of
the Systems from Section 7.3

Some criteria for deciding advantages and disadvantages of numeration systems are listed below. Answer the questions for the seven systems described in section 7.3 (Babylonian, Greek, and Chinese).

1. Which systems have few symbols to learn?

Which systems have many symbols to learn?

2. Which systems use a small space for writing large numbers?

Which systems use a large space for writing large numbers?

3. Which systems can you read immediately by knowing only the meaning of the symbols?

Which systems can you not read if you know only the symbols?

Which type ("read immediately" or "not read immediately") would be easier to teach to someone who did not know it?

4. With which systems can you write any number, no matter how large, without inventing new symbols?

Which systems could be extended to numbers less than one without inventing any new symbols (or words)?

With which systems can you write any number, no matter how small, without inventing new symbols?

*5. Consider addition and subtraction in the systems. For which systems would the basic facts for 1 to 9 be easy to write? Why?

For which systems would the basic facts be less obvious? Why?

For which systems are the values of the trades ("borrowing" and "carrying") obvious? Why?

For which systems are the trades not obvious? Why?

*6. Consider multiplication in the systems. Which systems require only one basic multiplication table to do problems with numbers no matter how large?

Which systems require new multiplication tables for every new value (think about multiplying 3 million $\times$ 8 million)?

*7. Consider division in the systems. In which systems would it be easy to estimate trial quotients? Why?

For which systems would it be more difficult to estimate trial quotients? Why?

*8. Consider operations $(+, -, \times, \div)$ with numbers less than one. For which systems can addition and subtraction of numbers less than one be done without learning any new addition facts?

For which systems can multiplication by numbers less than one be done without learning any new multiplication tables?

For which systems can division by numbers less than one be done without learning any new division facts?

9. What other advantages and disadvantages can you think of for numeration systems? How do the various systems come out on these other criteria?

10. In the light of criteria 1 to 4 and 9, which of Systems 1 to 7 is the best numeration system? Why?

*11. Individually or with a group make up a numeration system that is superior to some of the systems 1 through 7.

12. Which of systems 1 to 7 is identical in structure (different symbols are used) to our usual decimal system of numeration?[9] How does the decimal system come out with respect to the advantages described in 1 through 4? in 5 through 8?

7.5.2

Advantages and Disadvantages of the Decimal System of Numeration

1. The decimal system uses additive and multiplicative ways of building up larger numbers. The multiplication is implicit: it is *understood* that 40 means 4×10, 700 means 7×100, and 0.003 means 3×0.001.

The implicit nature of the multiplication means that the decimal system is more difficult to learn initially. It also makes the writing of numbers quite concise, because you do not have to name the value of any numeral. Thus numbers can be written quickly and easily. This conciseness is particularly helpful in calculation, because there it is necessary to write many numbers.

2. The decimal system is positional: The value of a given numeral is *understood* from its position (i.e., the value is implicit in the position):

472.89 is understood to mean 4 100s, 7 10s, 2 1s, 8 0.1s, and 9 0.01s

The positional aspect of the decimal system makes it initially more difficult to learn, both because the values are implicit and because position, unlike a symbol, involves relations, not just attributes. That is, a given position only has meaning *in relation to* the positions around it. The units position is the only position that has independent meaning. All other positions derive their meaning from their relationship to the units

---

[9] System 5—the Greek place-value system.

place (two places to the left of the units place, three places to the right of the units place, etc.).

The positional nature of the decimal system also makes it tremendously efficient. All algorithms for addition, subtraction, multiplication, and division of decimal numbers (both to the right and to the left of the ones place) use the position of the numerals. In addition and subtraction you line up like places with like places (this is a much more meaningful statement than saying "Line up the decimal points"; why should I line up the decimal points?) and then you can merrily add or subtract, knowing that the positional system will keep everything straight. In multiplication and division the positions are used to decide where to write products (in division you subtract products of the divisor successively until the dividend is too small to permit any more copies of the divisor to be subtracted). In all the algorithms, the positions work so efficiently to keep answers straight that someone can use them without really understanding what is happening. This is a disadvantage for mathematics education, but perhaps an advantage for real life uses of our decimal system.

3. The decimal system has a main base of ten and no sub-base. Mathematically, ten is not a particularly good choice for a base. See section 7.6.5 for a discussion of advantages of other bases.

4. The decimal system is an enciphered system. Each of its nine basic numbers (one, two, three, four, five, six, seven, eight, nine) has a different symbol.

Again this probably makes the decimal system initially difficult to learn. You first have to learn all the symbols 0 through 9. But once these symbols are learned, the decimal system is quite efficient. An enciphered system takes less time and space to write a number than does a repeated symbolic system.

The enciphered nature of the decimal system probably makes basic addition and subtraction facts more difficult to remember in symbolic form. With a repeated symbolic system, the symbols themselves are so representational of real objects that you can just add with the symbols.

Even when the sum involves some regrouping, such regrouping can be done mentally from the symbols.

Compare these examples with $3 + 2 = 5$, $51 + 53 = 104$, $40 + 70 = 110$.

5. A combination of the positional and enciphered natures of the decimal system are responsible for the following advantages and disadvantages.

a. With the decimal system it is not obvious why you add and subtract like places only. (Why should $12 + 4$ not equal 52?) With a repeated symbolic system, it is obvious that $\triangle || + |||| = \triangle ||||||$ and not $\triangle\triangle\triangle\triangle\triangle ||$. With a named-value system, it is also clearer that 3 tens + 4 hundreds do not equal 7 tens or 7 hundreds, but simply 3 tens and 4 hundreds.

b. Trading ("borrowing" and "carrying") is not as obvious in the decimal system as in repeated symbolic or named-value systems. For repeated symbolic systems the values of the trades are in the symbols (ten $\triangle$'s obviously equal one H). Similarly for named-value systems, you are always aware whether you are dealing with tens, hundreds, etc. In the decimal system, however, the values of the numerals are not named and are only implicit in the places.

c. Because no new symbols or words are needed to make larger and larger numbers, the decimal system can be used to write numbers as large as one wishes. This is not true for repeated symbolic or named-value systems. For example, what is a trillion $\times$ a trillion $\times$ a trillion $\times$ a trillion? It is easy to write using decimal notation: 1 followed by 48 zeros. But you run out of words and symbols for such large numbers if you need new words or new symbols for each place.

d. The decimal system requires only one multiplication table for the products of all combinations of 0 through 9. With the table and a general shift rule for multiplying by powers of ten (10, 100, 1000, etc.), multiplication of any two whole numbers can be performed. Named-value systems need two multiplication tables: one for the products of combinations of 0 through 9 and one for the products of names of places (e.g., ten $\times$ hundred, ten $\times$ thousand, hundred $\times$ hundred, etc.). Each new symbol for a place requires a new row in this second multiplication table. Since there are always new places, and thus new names, this second multiplication table can never be completed.

The situation for repeated symbolic systems is much worse. First, tables are needed for combinations of each symbol because II $\times$ III = VI looks different from XX $\times$ XXX = LX. Then tables are needed for all possible combinations of different symbols (units times tens, units times hundreds, etc., tens times hundreds, tens times thousands, etc., hundreds times thousands, etc.). Because each new large number requires a new symbol, new entries would constantly have to be made. None of the tables could ever be finished.

e. Because division uses multiplication, the decimal system can do division of arbitrarily large numbers, while repeated symbolic and named-value systems cannot.

6. The most advantageous aspect of the decimal system has not really been described as yet, because it arises from several characteristics of the system. This advantage is that the same basic set of numerals can be used in positions to the right of the ones place. These positions are

defined by the same one-for-ten trade rule that applies to all other positions. This creates a symmetric system that can be used to write any real number, no matter how large or how small. The symmetry is about the ones place, not about the decimal point. This would be clearer if we put the decimal point under the ones place instead of to the right of it.

Because the same set of numerals are used over in each place and because the relationship between places is constant (one-for-ten trades for all places), the algorithmic procedures for calculation with whole numbers expressed in decimal notation will generalize easily to the new positions to the right of the ones place. No change of the algorithms is necessary for addition or subtraction, and only shift rules for multiplying by places to the right of one (by 0.1, 0.01, etc.) need to be known in order to multiply and divide with all decimal places by using the old procedures for the places to the left of one. This is the real power of the decimal system of numeration. The decimal system makes it simple to write any real number or nonterminating decimal to as many places as we wish, and with only minor adaptations, the algorithmic procedures for adding, subtracting, multiplying, and dividing can be used for all new numbers to the right of the ones place. Compare this situation with the problem created by the set of fractions, for example.

7. A summary of the above points might be: The decimal system creates many difficulties for primary and middle grade teachers, but makes life simple for junior high, secondary, and university teachers. That is, many aspects of the decimal system are difficult to teach initially, mainly because there are so many implicit facets to this system. But once these properties of the decimal system have been learned by the students, the system is an efficient and powerful tool.

7.6 NON-TEN NUMBER BASES

Overview: **Non-ten number bases are summarized, and advantages of some different bases are described.**

There have been at least three historical positional systems of numeration: Babylonian (base sixty), Mayan (base twenty), and Chinese rod numerals (base ten). These are all repeated symbolic systems.

68 in these systems:

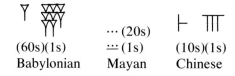

(60s)(1s)   ···(1s)   (10s)(1s)
Babylonian   Mayan   Chinese

Our decimal system of numeration is a positional system, but it is enciphered. By varying the main base of ten used in the decimal system but keeping all its other characteristics, you can get many enciphered "number-base systems" (base two, base four, base twelve, etc.). These systems are like the decimal system except they have different trade rules (base two trades one for two, base four trades one for four, base twelve trades one for twelve, etc.).

As a means of drawing together the experiences with base four in Units 1 and 2 and with base eight in Units 3 and 4, some number bases will be briefly described. A discussion comparing advantages of different bases follows. See especially section 1.2.2 for base four and section 3.2.1 for base eight if you have not had experience with embodiments for other bases.

7.6.1 Look at the sketches to remind yourself of the base-four embodiments.
Base Four

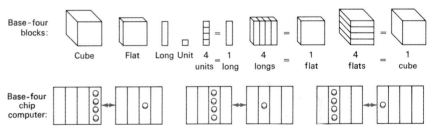

Base-four symbols: 1, 2, 3, 0 or A, B, C, 0 or □, △, ⧄, ○ or · · ·

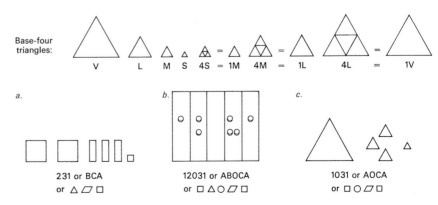

Base-four trade rules: One for four (left to right)
Four for one (right to left)

Trade a trades 4 ones for 1 A: A $= 4^1$
Trade b trades 4 A $=$ 1 B: 1 B $= 4 \times 4 = 4^2$
Trade c trades 4 B $=$ 1 C: 1 C $- 4 \times (4 \times 4) = 4^3$
Trade d trades 4 C $=$ 1 D: 1 D $= 4 \times (4 \times 4 \times 4) = 4^4$
Trade e trades 4 D $=$ 1 E: 1 E $= 4 \times (4 \times 4 \times 4 \times 4) = 4^5$
Trade f trades 1 one $=$ 4 F: 1 F $= 1/4 = 4^{-1}$
Trade g trades 1 F $=$ 4 G: 1 G $= 1/4 \times 4 = 4^{-2}$
Trade h trades 1 G $=$ 4 H: 1 H $= 1/4 \times (4 \times 4) = 4^{-3}$
Trade i trades 1 H $=$ 4 I: 1 I $= 1/4 \times (4 \times 4 \times 4) = 4^{-4}$

You can more succinctly write base four using exponential notation as follows:

$$\cdots 4^5 \quad 4^4 \quad 4^3 \quad 4^2 \quad 4^1 \quad 4^0.4^{-1} \quad 4^{-2} \quad 4^{-3} \quad 4^{-4} \cdots$$

Obviously the trades could continue indefinitely in either direction. Thus any real number can be written using only the symbols 0, 1, 2, and 3 and the understood trade rules described above.

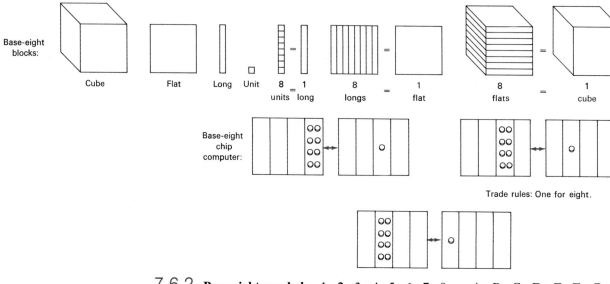

7.6.2
Base Eight

Base-eight symbols: 1, 2, 3, 4, 5, 6, 7, 0 or A, B, C, D, E, F, G, 0 or . . .

Base-eight trade rules: One for eight (left to right).
Eight for one (right to left).

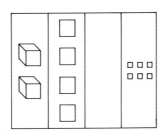

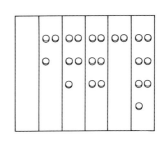

2406 means:
$(2 \times 8^3) + (4 \times 8^2) + (6 \times 8^0)$

35627 means:
$(3 \times 8^4) + (5 \times 8^3) + (6 \times 8^2)$
$+ (2 \times 8^1) + (7 \times 8^0)$

. . . E D C B A ones . F G H I . . .

Use the trade rules to figure out the size of each place above. Express your answers in term of multiples of eight and also in powers of eight (e.g., 8^3).

1 A = _____   I F = _____
1 B = _____   1 G = _____
1 C = _____   1 H = _____
1 D = _____   1 I = _____
1 E = _____

Express each place below using exponents with a base of eight.

. . . — — — — — — . — — — — — . . .

7.6.3 Draw base-five blocks and show the trades between the different blocks.
Base Five

Show the trades on a base-five chip computer:

Base-five Symbols: Give a set of symbols for base five:
Give the trade rules for base five:

. . . E D C B A ones . F G H I . . .

Use the trade rules to figure out the size of each place. Express your answers in term of multiples of five and also in powers of five.

1 A = _____   1 F = _____
1 B = _____   1 G = _____
1 C = _____   1 H = _____
1 D = _____   1 I = _____
1 E = __ _____

7.6.4   **Base-twelve Symbols:** Give a set of symbols for base twelve:
Base Twelve

Base-twelve Trade Rules: Give the trade rules for base twelve:

Fill in each place below in terms of a power of T (for twelve)

. . . — — — — —t— — — — — . . .

Notice the small t above instead of a decimal point. Some numbers using places to the right of one ("duodecimals") will be written next, and the t is to remind us that they are not decimal fractions.
    Write $\frac{1}{3}$ in base twelve using places to the right of the one place. (Think of putting one chip in the ones place on a base-twelve computer and then making piles of three from it; of course you will have to make a one-for-twelve trade before you can do this.)[10]

What is $\frac{1}{4}$ in base twelve? (Put one chip on the ones place and try to make piles of four from it; trade first, of course.)[11]

What is $\frac{1}{6}$ in base twelve?[12] What is $\frac{1}{2}$ in base twelve?[13]

Many people have advocated that we change from a base ten to a base twelve system. Does the above give you one idea why base twelve might have advantages?[14]

7.6.5 Give a set of symbols, the trade rules, and the values of the places below
Base n expressed in powers of the base for base n.

[10] $\frac{1}{3} = 0_t4$ (Trade a chip in the ones place for twelve chips in the place to the right. Make *four* piles of three.)
[11] $_t3$
[12] $_t2$
[13] $_t6$
[14] See section 7.6.6.

Base-*n* Symbols:

Base-*n* Trade Rules:

$$\cdots \text{—}\text{—}\text{—}\text{—}\text{—}\,n\,\text{—}\text{—}\text{—}\text{—}\text{—}\cdots$$

7.6.6
**Advantages of
Different Bases**

Many arguments have been made through the ages (and particularly in the last 100 years) about the comparative advantages of different main bases. Base two has the obvious advantage of requiring only two symbols: 0 and 1 (or A and B, or on and off). This characteristic is actually used in computers. A given circuit can be either on or off. Therefore a series of circuits can give a number in base two:

> On-on-off-off-on is 11001 (or $2^4 + 2^3 + 2^0 = 16 + 8 + 1 = 25$)

The disadvantage of base two, as you can see from the example, is that it takes many more places than does base ten to represent a number. This does not matter for an electronic computer, which has millions of circuits, but it does matter for people who have to write out large numbers. Imagine making out the Federal budget in base two, or even your own family budget. (How many places would you need to represent $10,000?)

Base eight is a sort of short-cut version of base two and is therefore used in some computer languages. One place in base eight is three places in base two ($2^3 = 8$).

$$101110001111_{two} = 5617_{eight}$$

$$101 = 4 + 1 = 5 \qquad 110 = 4 + 2 = 6 \qquad 001 = 1 \qquad 111 = 4 + 2 + 1 = 7$$

Base twelve has had many advocates. Its chief advantage would derive from the fact that it has divisors 1, 2, 3, 4, 6, and 12. Therefore fractions with any of these numbers as denominator would be expressible in base twelve using only the first place to the right of one. (See section 7.6.4 for details of why this works.)

$$\frac{1}{2} = {}_t6 \qquad \frac{1}{3} = {}_t4 \qquad \frac{1}{4} = {}_t3 \qquad \frac{1}{6} = {}_t2 \qquad \frac{1}{12} = {}_t1$$

(The symbol t is used instead of a decimal point to remind us that these are not decimal fractions.) Because the fractions involved with base twelve are the most commonly used, base twelve would make calculations with fractions much less frequent. You would use instead their "twelvimal" (or "duodecimal") representations.

$$\frac{1}{3} + \frac{1}{4} = {}_t4 + {}_t3 = {}_t7 = \frac{7}{12}$$

Ten has only divisors 2 and 5, and so only fractions with denominators of 2 and 5 can be expressed as decimals of one place.

$$\frac{1}{3} + \frac{1}{4} = 0.333 \cdots + 0.25 = 0.58333 \cdots = ?$$

Such problems are easier to do with fractions than with base-ten decimals. (Who wants to multiply by $\frac{1}{6} = 0.1666 \ldots$?, whereas multiplying by $_t2$ would be simple.)

7.7 PEDAGOGICAL REMARKS

The summary given in section 7.5.2 of the advantages and disadvantages of our decimal system of numeration described the implications of our system for teachers as follows: "The decimal system creates many difficulties for primary and middle grade teachers, but makes life simple for junior high, secondary, and university teachers." In the early grades there is a great deal to learn about the decimal system, chiefly because there are so many implicit facets to the system. These implicit facets include additive and multiplicative ways of making larger numbers and the use of position to tell the value of a numeral.

Embodiments can help to make explicit the implicit characteristics. Embodiments having different sized pieces for different places (e.g., base-ten blocks, meter length embodiment (cm, dm, m, dekameter), weight embodiment (gram, dg, hg, kg), toothpick or coffee stirrer bundles) can easily illustrate the additive and multiplicative means for making larger numbers. Position involves the one-for-ten trade rules and the use of zero for empty places. Size embodiments are quite clear on these points also.

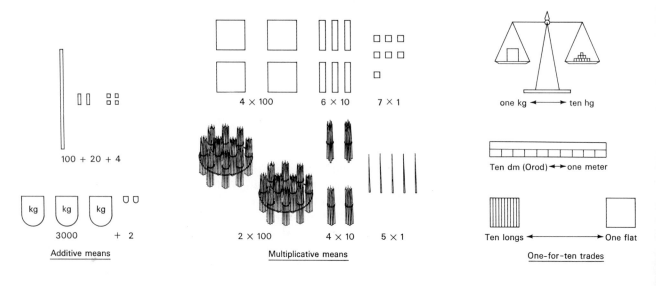

100 + 20 + 4

3000 + 2

Additive means

4 × 100   6 × 10   7 × 1

2 × 100   4 × 10   5 × 1

Multiplicative means

one kg ⟷ ten hg

Ten dm (Orod) ⟷ one meter

Ten longs ⟷ One flat

One-for-ten trades

Of course, only if the size embodiments are used on calculating sheets or on some other background that imposes left-to-right positions do they show position. Size embodiments do not need to have positions to show the value of numbers:

Therefore embodiments that do not have different sizes for different valued pieces are required to show the aspects of the positional system. A chip computer, a rod computer, and a bead abacus must have trade rules provided, but they clearly show that a chip, a rod, or a bead has a different value depending upon which column it is in. Chips, rods, or beads used without a *known* relationship to the ones place have no meaning:

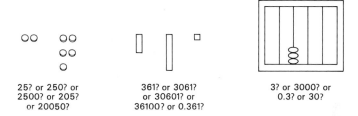

25? or 250? or 2500? or 205? or 20050?   361? or 3061? or 30601? or 36100? or 0.361?   3? or 3000? or 0.3? or 30?

The meaning of zero is particularly clear with these embodiments. Each of the situations below is obviously a different situation, but they cannot be symbolized differently without a zero.

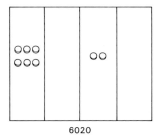

6020

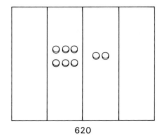

620

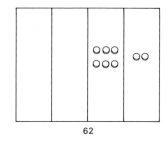

62

With respect to the enciphered nature of the decimal system, it is not too difficult for children to learn the basic ciphers, the symbols for one through nine ("Sesame Street" will have done the job already for many children entering school). What is more difficult is using these ciphers for addition and subtraction and even for basic multiplication and division.

There is nothing about 2, 7, or 8 that shows their two-ness, seven-ness, or eight-ness.

For children who seem to be having difficulty with writing the basic facts using our numerals, a symbol system midway between objects (embodiments) and numerals might be introduced.

enciphered symbols ↔ pictorial symbols ↔ objects

Students could first record their operations with embodiments by using a repeated symbolic system. Any such system could be used, but a version of the tally system might be most familiar. Small sums, differences, and products could probably be found with this system symbolically without supporting manipulatives more quickly than with our usual symbols. Then students would need to have experience in double recording, that is, recording in this tally system and then immediately recording in our usual symbols. In this way links would be built up between the tally pictorial symbols and our usual symbols and would also continue to be built up directly between the embodiments and our usual symbols.

I	II	III	IIII	�				
I	II	III	IIII	ℍℍ	ℍℍ I	ℍℍ II	ℍℍ III	ℍℍ IIII
1	2	3	4	5	6	7	8	9

T	TT	TTT	TTTT	etc.	H	HH	HHH	HHHH	etc.
10	20	30	40		100	200	300	400	

Two aspects of our number *words* differ from our system of number *symbols* and further complicate the early teaching of the decimal system. The first of these is the word *ten*. We count "one, two, three, four, five, six, seven, eight, nine, ten." *Ten* sounds like just another number, with nothing special to distinguish it from the previous numbers. There is certainly nothing about the word that implies that two symbols (1 and 0) are used to represent it. We do not say "one-oh" (or better perhaps, "one-no," for no units). A special word that distinguished ten as the first number using symbols in the second column would be much more helpful and less misleading than the usual word *ten*. Perhaps a "New Name for Ten" contest could be run in a classroom to help get this point across. This same problem occurs with one hundred (one-oh-oh), one thousand (one-oh-oh-oh), etc.

The other difficulty with our number words is that they form a named-place system while our number symbols do not. We say "five *thousand* four *hundred* six*ty*-eight" for 5468 instead of saying five-four-six-eight (place-value words). That is, we explicitly *name* the value of each place. Because the naming is done explicitly, this system of words is easy to understand. In the system of symbols, the value of each numeral is *un-*

derstood by its position rather than being explicitly named. If this disparity between our number words and number symbols is not pointed out, confusion may result. It might help some children if they occasionally read aloud our symbols in a place-value way (e.g., 4239 is just four-two-three-nine). Reading in the place-value way is much simpler, too, and children are able to do it much earlier.

Our decimal system of numeration begins to show its advantages when algorithms are begun. Because the same symbols are used in every place and because the relationships between adjacent positions are the same for all positions (one-for-ten trades), simple recurring patterns can be used over and over again in every place. These result in algorithms for addition, subtraction, multiplication, and division.

The pedagogical implications for the other main advantage of our decimal system of numeration, the ability to write and calculate with numbers less than one, are discussed in section 5.6.

The positional nature of the decimal system is the basis for all the algorithms for operations with decimals. People can learn the nature of the decimal positional system in two ways. The first is by memorizing the names (values) of each of the places (ones, tens, hundreds, thousands, etc.) and thus turning the system into a named-place system (479 becomes four *hundred* seven*ty* nine). This named-place view of our system is emphasized by the named-place method we use to read our numerals. This is probably advantageous for addition and subtraction of decimal numbers (see the discussion in section 7.5.2 for more on this), but if this view is not later replaced by a more sophisticated view of the pattern of trading, flexibility for thinking in multiplication, division, algebra, and higher mathematics is lost.

The more sophisticated view of the nature of the decimal positional system is one that focuses on the relationships between positions (the trades) rather than just on the value of the places. This view sees the whole system in terms of the one-for-ten trades that define the relationships between all adjacent positions. The value of any position can be determined by using these trades.

The difference between the above approach and the approach of memorizing the values of the places is that, with the above approach, you can *understand* why each position has the value it does have, and you can find *by yourself* the value of *any* position (what happens to the memorizer when he comes to a new place?). You also have a valuable tool (the one-for-ten trades between adjacent positions) for understanding the trades ("borrowing" and "carrying") in addition and subtraction, the development of decimal places to the right of the units place, the shift rules in multiplication (i.e., multiplying by 10, 100, 1000, etc., or by 0.1, 0.01, 0.001, etc.), exponential notation, scientific notation, and other ideas.

This is not to suggest that a person should not know that the second place on the left (of the decimal point) is the tens place, the third place is the hundreds place, etc. It is rather to stress the importance of continuing on to this second very powerful means of understanding the meaning of the positions in our decimal system of numeration. Embodiments like base-ten blocks, the base-ten chip computer, and the other embodiments described in Unit 5 can aid in the development of this second kind of understanding of the value of the positions.

A few remarks about the teaching of numeration systems in general follow. A basic aspect of every numeration system is trading: a certain number of smaller units are traded for one larger unit.

Babylonian   Early Greek   Decimal system   Base-five blocks

Base blocks, toys, and food provide opportunities for playing trading games. Bases smaller than ten have more trades to represent a given number than does base ten, and it would probably be easier to count without error the pieces for trading in small bases (base three, base four, etc.). Many games can be invented which will provide experience with trading. Dice with dots or symbols, a spinner, or drawing cards from a bag could be used to give the number of pieces received on each turn.

A base-five blocks game: spin for units; the first to get a flat wins.

For place-value systems, the position of a symbol is important. The idea that position matters, that being in a certain position has greater value than being in other positions, can be conveyed and practiced in many ways. In addition to games with embodiments, games can be played in which the position of *students* matters (if you are here, you get one piece of cereal; if you are there, you get five pieces of cereal; etc.).

In the middle and upper grades, some study of the history of our numeration system and of other numeration systems is probably valuable. More understanding probably results, however, if the other numeration systems are selected to illustrate as many differences as possible. The systems most commonly studied are the Roman and the Egyptian systems. These are structurally identical except for the minor point that the Roman has a sub-base of five and the Egyptian system does not. One of those systems plus the Greek multi-enciphered (System 4) and the Chinese named-value system (System 7) would indicate the range of possibilities for numeration systems much better. A system much like ours (the Greek place-value, System 5, or the Chinese rod system, System 6) might give a student a different feeling for the characteristics of our numeration system.

A look at other bases through the use of embodiments might give students a broader understanding of base systems of numeration. Work that is entirely symbolic is likely to add only confusion. Work entirely within a given system will give a good feeling for how that particular system works. Translation back and forth between bases provides arithmetic practice but very little idea of how another base really works; such translation is therefore not recommended. Because the greatest difficulty with other bases is the use of our familiar number symbols to mean new numbers (e.g., 13 in base four is one four and three ones, or seven, not thirteen), when doing non-ten bases you might consider using a tally system, alphabetical symbols, or other symbols. You would eventually need to introduce the standard symbols, but meanwhile considerable confusion might have been avoided.

part c
underlying mathematical concepts and structures

unit 1
sets and logic

1.1
INTRODUCTION
Manipulating sets of objects, using logical connectives (e.g., "if . . . then . . . ," "and," "or"), and using logical quantifiers (e.g., some, all, none) are familiar activities to everyone. In fact, such activities are so common that they are typically used without even being noticed. However, like many things that become overused, they are often *misused* without being noticed. This unit will present activities that should help you reexamine some basic ideas from logic and from set theory, and help you sort out some errors and difficulties that often go unnoticed during everyday activities.

1.2
NUMBER
CONCEPTS AND BASIC
IDEAS ABOUT SETS
Overview: **This section will illustrate some ways that elementary number concepts are related to basic ideas about sets; and it will illustrate how children's difficulties with operations on sets are sometimes reflected in their misunderstanding of certain number concepts.**

The well-known child psychologist Jean Piaget has gathered a great deal of evidence indicating that a surprising number of mathematical ideas evolve from basic set concepts during the normal intellectual development of children. Important misunderstandings that children commonly develop concerning many mathematical concepts sometimes stem from their failure to have mastered the basic set-theoretic notions that are related to the concepts. For a brief summary of Piaget's descrip-

451

tion of the development of classification skills and logical thinking in children, read chapter 3 in *How Children Learn Mathematics* by Richard Copeland.[1]

1.2.1 Piaget's Number Conservation Task

Piaget's famous "number conservation" tasks have shown that kindergarten and first-grade children frequently do not realize that the number of objects in a set is independent of the arrangement of the objects. For instance, if a row of white poker chips is placed in front of a kindergarten child with the instruction, "Place the same number here," he will usually respond correctly by pairing his chips in a one-to-one fashion with the model row.

However, if one of the rows is then pushed together, many children will not recognize that the two rows still have the same number of poker chips. Children who give incorrect responses usually believe that the longer row contains "more," even though no poker chips were added to or removed from either row.

Similar tasks have also shown that young children may refuse to accept facts like $4 + 3 = 7$, if one of the two rows of circles is separated into two sets. Even children who seem to have learned their "basic facts" frequently deny these facts in concrete situations.

Problem: Imagine that a well-educated spaceman from a faraway planet showed up at one of your classes, and it was your job to explain to him the correct answer for the number conservation task described above. What explanation would you give? Do you think that your explanation would be convincing to a kindergartner? What problems might a kindergartner have?

1.2.2 One-to-One Correspondence

Adults realize that whenever the elements in one set can be paired in a one-to-one fashion with the elements in another set, the two sets have the same number of elements. Consequently, they often find it difficult to understand why children would fail to realize that the number of elements in a set does not depend upon the arrangement of the elements. In order to understand some of the difficulties that children are experiencing, consider the following "rational number" problem.

Imagine the set of counting numbers distributed on a number line.

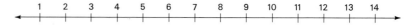

[1] Richard W. Copeland, *How Children Learn Mathematics*. Macmillan Publishing Co., Inc., New York, 1974, Chap. 3.

Of course, no one would have time to write the entire set (since it is infinite), but you can imagine that it continues in the same fashion. Now imagine the set of rational numbers distributed on a number line. For instance, here are some of the rational numbers that are between 1 and 2.

Can you think of a way to make a one-to-one correspondence between the set of counting numbers and the set of positive rational numbers?[1]

After you have determined a way to make a one-to-one correspondence between the counting numbers (1, 2, 3, 4, . . .) and the positive rational numbers, remember that on a number line there are many (in fact, infinitely many) rational numbers between any two counting numbers.

[1] Here is a method that can be used to imagine the set of positive rational numbers:

$1/1$ $1/2$ $1/3$ $1/4$ $1/5$ $1/6$ $1/7$ etc.
$2/1$ $2/2$ $2/3$ $2/4$ $2/5$ $2/6$ etc.
$3/1$ $3/2$ $3/3$ $3/4$ $3/5$ etc.
$4/1$ $4/2$ $4/3$ $4/4$ etc.
$5/1$ $5/2$ $5/3$ etc.
etc.

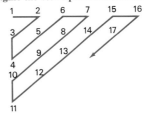

Looking at the bent number line, can you find a counting number to correspond to every rational number? Can you find a rational number to correspond to every counting number?

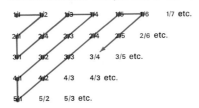

To convince yourself that the counting numbers can be matched one-to-one with the positive rational numbers, notice that the bent number line can be superimposed onto the entire set of positive rational numbers.

Question: Are there the same number of positive rational numbers as there are counting numbers?

1. How is this "rational number-counting number" problem similar to Piaget's number conservation tasks? How is it different?

2. If an adult finds it difficult to believe that there are really just as many counting numbers as there are positive rational numbers, it is probably because the adult has simply not had enough experiences working with infinite sets. Similarly, if a child responds incorrectly to one of Piaget's number conservation tasks, one reason could be because the child has not had enough experiences working with finite sets. What kind of experiences might be helpful to a child who responded incorrectly to the conservation task described in section 1.2.1?

3. If you still find that it is somewhat unbelievable that there are just as many counting numbers as there are rational numbers, think about the following "counting number–even number" problem. It also involves infinite sets.

  Think of a way to convince a friend that there are just as many even numbers (2, 4, 6, 8, 10, . . .) as there are counting numbers (1, 2, 3, 4, 5, 6, . . .). (Hint: Remember that two sets have the same number of elements if their elements can be paired in a one-to-one fashion.)

4. Use this diagram to convince a friend that there are just as many natural numbers (0, 1, 2, 3, 4, . . .) as there are integers.

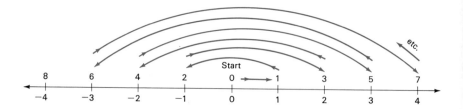

The point of this section has been that even a seemingly simple idea such as "two sets have the same number of elements if their elements can be paired one-to-one" can be confusing in certain contexts (e.g., using infinite sets). However, if infinite sets sometimes seem confusing to adults, it is important to realize that finite sets are sometimes no less confusing to children. A kindergartner who has watched a one-to-one pairing being made between a short row of circles and a long row of circles may be no more convinced that the two sets really contain the same number of elements than an adult who has watched a one-to-one pairing being made between the set of counting numbers and the set of positive rational numbers.

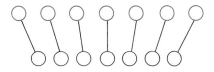

Sections 1.2.3 to 1.2.7 will focus on some of the problems that are involved in determining the number of elements in *finite* sets. Section 1.3 will give some activities which can help overcome some of these difficulties.

Several infinite sets have been discussed throughout this book. They include the set of natural numbers, the set of integers, the set of rational numbers, and the set of real numbers. Some of the properties of these sets of numbers have also been investigated. However, a general study of infinite sets will have to be left for another course in which a more thorough treatment can be given. In the meantime, the "poker chip paradox" below shows how some interesting issues about infinite sets can stem from basic and seemingly simple ideas about sets.

5. *The Poker Chip Paradox*

Imagine that a poker chip is placed on each of the counting numbers on a number line. Label the first poker chip "1," the second poker chip "2," and so forth. At 1 minute before midnight, put the first ten poker chips from the number line into a paper bag, and then return poker chip 1 to its original position on the number line. At $\frac{1}{2}$ minute before midnight, put the next ten poker chips into the paper bag and then return poker chip 2 to its original position on the number line. At $\frac{1}{3}$ minute before midnight, put the next ten poker chips into the paper bag, and then return poker chip 3 to its original position on the number line. If you continue the process, how many poker chips will be in the bag at midnight? Would all the poker chips be back on the number line? [2]

---

[2] If you thought that there would be infinitely many poker chips in the bag at midnight, ask yourself which poker chips would still be remaining in the bag. Would the 350th poker chip still be in the bag? No, it would have been removed at $\frac{1}{350}$ minute until midnight. What about the 1,000,350th poker chip? Try to name one poker chip that *would* remain in the bag at midnight. (For more about this problem, see chap. 11 of Martin Gardner's book *New Mathematical Diversions from Scientific American*, Simon & Schuster, New York, 1966.)

1.2.3
**An Area
Problem**

1. Make two identical loops of string, and put both loops in the shape of a square. Then, change one of the loops into a rectangular shape.

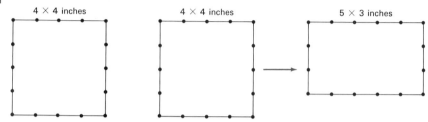

4 × 4 inches   4 × 4 inches   5 × 3 inches

a. Is the area inside the square the same as the area inside the rectangle? (After you have answered this question, read the footnote at the bottom of this page.)[3]

b. How is this area problem similar to a Piagetian number conservation problem? How is it different?

c. What is wrong with the explanation that the area inside the square did not change because the string was only rearranged, and because it could be put back into its original position?

2. If a child does not realize that the number of objects in a set is invariant under simple displacements, is it enough to explain that the objects were only rearranged and that they can be returned to their original positions? Consider problem 1c and then read the footnote.[4]

[3] If the square was 4 × 4 inches, then it is 16 inches around, and it has an area of 16 square inches. If the rectangle is 3 × 5 inches, then it is 16 inches around, just like the square. But, the rectangle only has an area of 15 square inches. Therefore the area inside the rectangle is less. In fact, as the rectangle gets thinner and thinner, its area gets progressively smaller, and finally disappears entirely.

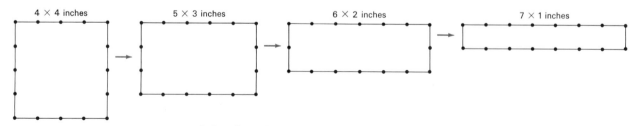

4 × 4 inches   5 × 3 inches   6 × 2 inches   7 × 1 inches

[4] In order to determine whether or not the area of a figure changes when something is done to the figure, it is important to know what a unit of area is. Then, whether or not the area of the figure changes depends upon what is done to the figure. Some changes in the figure will

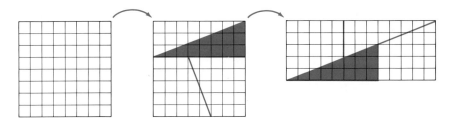

1.2.4
A "Number-Area" Problem

It is important to realize that although "number" is invariant under simple displacements, it is not invariant under all transformations. For example, a checkerboard can be divided into four pieces (as shown). The four pieces can then be reassembled to form either a rectangle or a square. How many spaces are in the rectangle? How many are in the square? What happened?[6]

The point of this problem is that to measure an object (or to count a set of objects), the object (or set) must be partitioned into units; and, the units must be equal with regard to the property that is being measured. Then, the process of making a one-to-one correspondence will be meaningful.

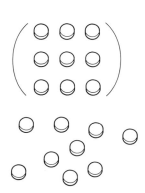

Measuring an object may seem to be very different from counting a set of objects, but in fact the two processes are very similar. An adult may feel that he can simply look at a 3×3 array of poker chips and see "nine" without doing anything to the set. But, he may feel less confident about seeing "nine" if the set is not already organized for him. (See chips at left.) The sensation of feeling as though we perceived "nine" in a 3×3 array is somewhat similar to the feeling that people usually get when they finally see the disguised figure in a hidden picture puzzle. Once the picture is recognized, it is difficult to realize how it had ever been disguised. In the same way that a hidden picture puzzle needs to be

---

change its area and some will not. But, just because it is possible to undo what has been done to the figure does not guarantee that the area does not change. Similarly, whether or not two sets contain the same number of elements depends entirely upon whether their elements can be paired one-to-one. To make this pairing, it is important to realize that each element in the set (whether it is an elephant or an ant) must be considered to be a unit equivalent to the other elements in the set.

[5] This example shows that the number of spaces is not invariant under a transformation that divides and reassembles spaces. But, in order for the number of spaces to have changed, the size (i.e., area) of some of the spaces must have changed; and this is exactly what happened. In the rectangle, some of the reassembled spaces are slightly smaller than the spaces that were in the square.

[6] For a discussion of this point, see James A. McLellan and John Dewey, *Psychology of Number,* D. Appleton and Company, New York, 1895.

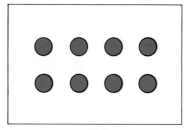

red balls

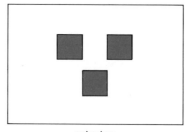

red cubes

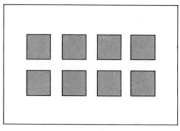

green cubes

mentally organized in order for the picture to be seen, the set of circles also has to be organized in order for "nineness" to be seen. But what rules of organization does a child need to master in order to recognize the "number" property that should be associated with a set of objects?

Piaget and Inhelder have argued that many of the misunderstandings that children have regarding number concepts stem from difficulties that they are having with set concepts and operations on sets. To illustrate some of these difficulties, several more problem situations will be described in sections 1.2.5, 1.2.6, and 1.2.7.[2]

1.2.5
A
Problem about
Subsets

A first grader can be given three clear plastic boxes containing 8 red balls, 3 red cubes, and 8 green cubes respectively. If he is then asked, "Are there more red things or more balls?" the response is often "More balls."

[2] Jean Piaget, *The Child's Conception of Number*. W. W. Norton and Company, Inc., 1965. Barbel Inhelder and Jean Piaget, *The Early Growth of Logic in the Child*. W. W. Norton and Company, Inc., New York, 1964.

The picture "My Wife and My Mother-in-law," by cartoonist W. E. Hill was originally published in Puck in 1915. Can you find the wife? Can you find the mother-in-law?

According to Piagetians, the difficulty is not that young children misunderstand the intent of the question. The difficulty seems to be that when the child's attention is drawn to the set of balls, the subsuming set of red things is cognitively destroyed. Therefore, the child usually compares the set of balls with the set of red cubes. Similarly, psychologists have devised other tasks that indicate that when attention is directed toward subsuming sets, its subsets are often confused and overlapping. Children have difficulties coordinating part-whole relationships within sets.

Until a child has organized his classification skills to an extent that enables him to give a correct response to the above task, he tends to have several cognitive characteristics that affect his understanding of number concepts. Two of these characteristics are "nonanalytic thinking" and "centering." Tasks that illustrate these characteristics are given in the following two sections.

1.2.6 Nonanalytic Thinking

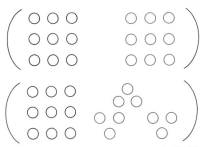

Children who are able to copy a 3 × 3 array of circles and who have stated that each of the two arrays contain nine circles, are often convinced that the two arrays no longer contain the same number of circles after one of the two arrays has been partitioned into three clusters. (See chips at left) When attention is drawn to a numerical whole, the parts (or units) are cognitively neglected. When attention is directed toward component parts, the whole is often cognitively destroyed. Such children tend to view sets of objects as a global unanalyzed whole, rather than analytically.

1.2.7 Centering

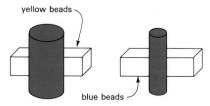

yellow beads

blue beads

Two cylindrical glasses of different diameters can be placed in front of identical boxes, each of which contain 30 half-inch beads. A first grader can then be directed to take a blue bead in one hand, a yellow bead in the other, and to put the beads into the two cylindrical glasses at exactly the same time. After ten beads have been put into each of the two glasses, young children often believe that there are more beads in the glass where the beads reach a higher level.

Children who respond incorrectly tend to center (i.e., to focus their attention) on only the most obvious perceptual features of an object or set of objects. For example, they may notice height, but neglect thickness or other relevant variables.

1.3

ATTRIBUTE GAMES

Overview: **This section will give several types of games that can be used to practice your use of words like** *and, or, not, same,* **and** *different.* **Modified versions of these games can be used to help children overcome some of their "part-whole" classification difficulties and their tendency to center on only the most obvious properties of objects.**

Materials needed: A set of attribute blocks will be used in this section and in several other sections of this unit. However, if a set of attribute blocks is not available, each of the games in this section can still be played by drawing pictures as shown below. [3]

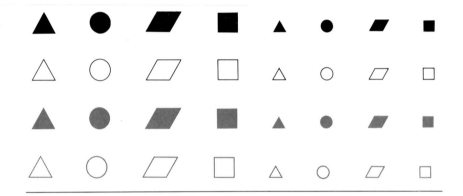

As you work through the activities in this section, look for instances in which you are forced to consider several properties of an object or set of objects simultaneously. Watch for instances in which you are forced to switch back and forth between considering individual objects within a set and considering a whole set. In other words, look for instances in which you are forced to decenter and to examine objects and sets of objects analytically.

Pay particular attention to your use of words and phrases like *and, or, not; if . . . then, same, different; some, none,* and *every.* The use of these words will be examined in other sections of this unit.

---

[3] It is easy to make a set of attribute blocks by cutting shapes out of colored sponges or out of colored poster board. The set of attribute blocks that will be considered in this section will include four different colors (red, yellow, green and blue), four different shapes (circles, triangles, squares and rhombuses), and two different sizes (large and small). The *entire* set contains 32 blocks. Larger sets of blocks can be made if "thickness" is included as one of the variables. Commercially made sets of attribute blocks can be purchased from several publishing companies or school supply companies. Activity cards that are appropriate for elementary school children accompany some of these sets of materials.

**1.3.1
One-
Difference
Sequence**

Here is the beginning of a one-difference sequence:

Each block differs from the block on its immediate left by exactly one attribute.

1. Make a one-difference sequence that contains all 32 blocks. (Note: If you are drawing the blocks, remember that each block can be used only once.)

2. Starting with the large red circle, make a one-difference sequence that contains exactly five blocks. How many different responses could you have given to this problem if you were allowed to use only the following eight blocks:

$$\boxed{R} \quad \textcircled{R} \quad \boxed{\boxed{R}} \quad \textcircled{\textcircled{R}} \quad \boxed{Y} \quad \textcircled{Y} \quad \boxed{\boxed{Y}} \quad \textcircled{\textcircled{Y}} \, .$$

3. Using any of the 32 blocks, build a circular, one-difference sequence that contains exactly five blocks. Make sure that the fifth block differs from the first block by exactly one attribute. Can you build a circular, one-difference sequence that contains exactly three blocks? If you were allowed to use only the eight blocks in problem 2, could you make a circular, one-difference sequence that contains exactly five blocks?

4. What logical or mathematical ideas did you use in problems 1, 2, and 3 above? (Hint: Think about the words you used in each problem.)

5. Could any of these activities be helpful to a child who responds incorrectly to Piagetian conservation tasks?

**1.3.2
Two-
Difference
Sequences**

1. Make a sequence in which each block differs from the block on its left by *exactly* two attributes. Can you use all 32 blocks? Can you make your sequence circular?

2. Beginning with the large blue circle, make a two-difference sequence that contains exactly five blocks. How many responses could you have given to this problem if you were allowed to use only the following eight blocks:

R Ⓡ ⊡R Ⓡ Y Ⓨ ⊡Y Ⓨ

3. Build a circular, two-difference sequence that contains exactly five blocks. Are there any circular two-difference sequences that are impossible to make?

4. Did you conclude that blocks that differ by exactly two attributes are the same as blocks that have exactly one similarity? Did you make any other logical observations or inferences?

1.3.3
One-Difference Matrices

1. Here is a one-difference matrix that has been partially filled in for you. Notice that blocks that are adjacent horizontally differ by *exactly* one attribute. Blocks that are adjacent vertically also differ by *exactly* one attribute. Complete the matrix. Can you use several different arrangements?

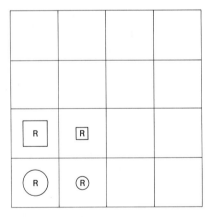

2. Did you use "if . . . then" statements more often in this activity than in the previous two activities?

1.3.4
Two-Difference Matrices

1. Arrange 16 blocks on a 4 × 4 matrix so that blocks adjacent horizontally differ by *exactly* two attributes, and blocks adjacent vertically differ by *exactly* two attributes. Can you use several different arrangements?

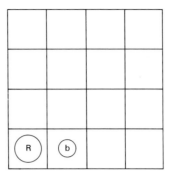

2. Were "if . . . then" statements important in this activity? What about words like *no, not,* and *none*?

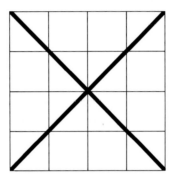

1.3.5
Graeco-
Latin Squares

1. Make a Graeco-Latin square by arranging sixteen large blocks on a 4×4 matrix so that no two blocks of the same shape or the same color are in any row and so that no two blocks of the same shape or the same color are in any column.

2. Make another 4×4 Graeco-Latin square using only the small attribute blocks. Add one new stipulation. No two blocks of the same shape or the same color should be on either of the diagonals.

3. Use the small attribute blocks to make a Graeco-Latin square on top of the Graeco-Latin square that you made using the large blocks. But make sure that no two blocks of the same shape or the same color are on the same square of the matrix. For instance, a small blue block should never be on top of a large blue block, and a small triangle should never be on top of a large triangle.

4. Using these four blocks, □ ○ ■●, is it possible to make a 2×2

Graeco-Latin square? Using these nine blocks □ ○ △ ■ ● ▲ □ ○ △, is it possible to make a 3 × 3 Graeco-Latin square?[4]

1.3.6 Guess the Block

This game should be played with a small group of people. To begin the game, the entire set of 32 attribute blocks is placed in a paper bag. One person in the group (the leader) removes a block without showing it to anyone else in the group. The group's task is to guess which block was selected. Clues are given by removing other blocks from the box. Each time a block is removed, the leader tells how many attributes are different from the hidden block. The first person to guess the hidden block is the new leader. Rules may be devised to punish wrong guesses. What logical observations and logical influences are needed to play this game? What ideas about sets are involved?

1.4 THE WORDS SAME AND DIFFERENT

Overview: **Whenever mathematics is used, it is important to be able to determine exactly what elements are in each set that is being discussed. This section will point out the close relationship that exists between the formation of sets and the use of the words *same*, and *different*. It will also show that the process of deciding whether two things are "the same" can change depending on the situation.**

Sets can be collections of objects, pictures, symbols, or words. Examples of sets include a *set* of crayons, a *group* of students, a *deck* of cards, a *collection* of stamps, or a *herd* of cows. Therefore the word *set* can be used in place of many other words like *group, herd,* or *pile.* Can you think of some other words that can sometimes be replaced by the word *set*? Name some sets that do not consist of concrete objects.

By working with sets of abstract symbols instead of with sets of concrete objects, mathematical ideas can be applied to many types of concrete situations. But symbols can also create certain difficulties that are easier to avoid when sets of concrete objects are used.

To illustrate some of the differences between sets of objects and sets of symbols, imagine a kindergarten class that is reading a story about Snow White and the Seven Dwarfs. One page of the book might show a picture of a table with chairs around it that belonged to each of the

---

[4] A 6 × 6 Graeco-Latin square is impossible to make; and until 1959, it was thought many other Graeco-Latin squares might be impossible to make. For an interesting account of how this guess was proved to be wrong, read chap. 14 of Martin Gardner's *New Mathematical Diversions from Scientific American.* Simon & Schuster, New York, 1966. In fact, 2 × 2 and 6 × 6 are now known to be the only two impossible Graeco-Latin squares.

dwarfs. Looking at the picture, the children might say that there are seven "chairs" on the page. Of course, they would realize that the pictures of chairs were not real chairs. A picture of a chair is just a symbol that stands for a chair. Nonetheless, the teacher could talk about a set of "chairs" in the picture without confusing the children. Everyone would realize that the pictures were temporarily being treated as though they were "the same" as real chairs. After the book about Snow White had been put back on the bookshelf, the children could be asked to count the chairs in their classroom. Probably no one would decide to count the seven "pictures of chairs" that were shown in the Snow White book.

It does not make sense to ask questions like, "How many chairs are in the classroom?" if no decision has been made about what kinds of things are going to be called "chairs." In some situations, toy chairs and pictures of chairs may be considered to be the same as "real" chairs, and in other situations they may not. In some situations, two pictures of Grumpy's chair may be considered to be the same, and in other situations they may not. Realizing that such decisions must be made is an important part of understanding how to use mathematics in real situations.

*1.4.1 Some Issues to Consider

1. Objects that Are "the Same"

Use of the word *same* can become amazingly complicated because no two distinct things are ever *exactly* identical. For example, when a student goes to his closet to find a pair of shoes, he would probably say that he is looking for two shoes that are "the same." But when the student sits down to put on the shoes, he would probably refer to them as being "different." Whenever people agree to say that two things are the same, they always have to agree to ignore certain differences. List below five more examples where the decision about whether two things are "the same" can change depending on the situation.

2. Sets of Symbols

Symbols always have the property of representing something and yet remaining distinct from the thing that is represented. Furthermore, the thing that a symbol represents can change depending on the situation. Determine how many different elements are in each of these sets of symbols. Can you justify several different answers that could be given?

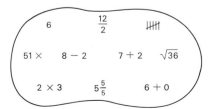

3. Numbers and Numerals Some mathematics educators believe that children should be made aware of the distinction that exists between *numbers* and *numerals*. These educators have emphasized that *number* is an abstract property that is associated with *sets* of object, and that a *numeral* is a symbol that associated with the property of numerousness. For example, the *number* three is the abstract property that is associated with all sets whose elements can be paired in a one-to-one fashion with a set that consists of an apple, a pear, and a banana; on the other hand, the *numeral* 3 is the symbol that is assigned to all sets that have the property of "three-ness."

Other educators have argued that even though the number-numeral distinction is important, young children may only be confused if it is explicity pointed out. Rather than risk overemphasizing a potentially confusing idea, some educators would prefer to avoid drawing attention to the distinction between numbers and numerals.

Keeping in mind the distinction between a "real" chair and a "picture" of a chair, write a brief statement of your opinion about the importance of emphasizing the number-numeral distinction with a class of first-grade children.

4. Sets of Straight Lines There is a close relationship between the formation of sets and the use of the word *same*. Whenever two elements are the same in some way, their property of sameness can be used to define a set; and whenever a set contains two elements, the two elements can be considered to be the same in a certain respect: they are both in the same set. But since the decision about whether two things are "the same" can change depending on the situation, the elements included in a set may also have to change

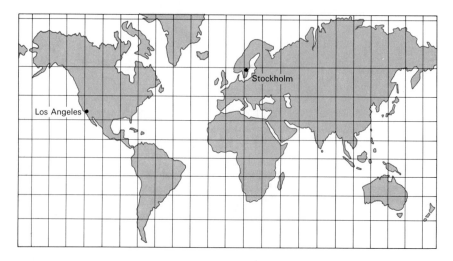

depending on the situation in which the set is intended to be used.

On each of the following three maps draw a "straight line" from Los Angeles to Stockholm. Do the elements that you include in "the set of straight lines" change depending on the situation in which the set is used? Can you think of other examples where this happens?

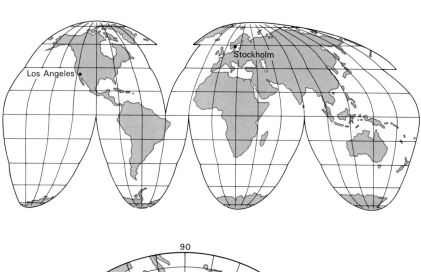

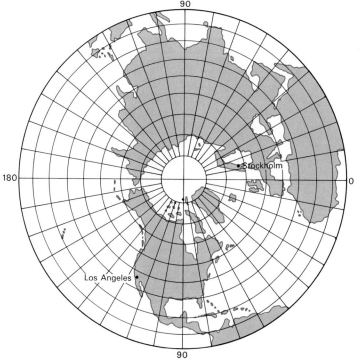

What would a straight line look like using a globe?

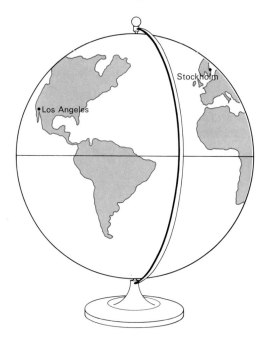

5. Definitions People are able to learn about many things without being given a definition. For instance, the simplest way to teach a young child to recognize bears may not be to give a definition. If you say that a bear is a large, furry animal that growls, he may point to a St. Bernard and say "bear." On the other hand, if you give him a more accurate verbal definition, he may not understand the words. The best way to teach a child to recognize bears may be to actually show and identify some bears and some animals that are not bears, without giving a formal definition. As soon as his universe of experience becomes larger, the set of bears may have to be redefined by adding some new members. Or, it may later become appropriate to give a precise description of the elements in the set using a definition.

Give a definition of the word *triangle*. What method would you use to teach a preschool child to recognize triangles?

1.5
SETS:
A DISCUSSION SESSION
Overview: This section will give two ways to define sets: (1) by giving a *precise description* of the properties of elements in the set and (2) by listing the elements of the set in *tabular form. Well-defined sets, one-element sets,*

empty sets, and *universal sets* will be discussed, and the meaning of the words *and* and *or* will be discussed.

This section may be conducted as an in-class discussion session or it may be read independently. If you choose to have a discussion session, it is *not* necessary to read the section beforehand. In fact, the material consists of class notes recorded by another student. These notes may be used as a discussion guide in your class and should be reviewed after class to add points you believe are important.

Class Discussion on Sets

Set Notation.

A shorthand method that can be used to say that "B is the set of people who are male" is to write $B = \{$people who are male$\}$.

Problem: Using this notation, give some more sets that can be formed using students in the class as elements.

Possible responses

$B = \{$people who are male$\}$
$G = \{$people who are female$\}$
$P = \{$people wearing pants$\}$
$C = \{$people wearing blue$\}$
$S = \{$people who are sophomores$\}$
$F = \{$people who are freshmen$\}$
$J = \{$people who are juniors$\}$

$H = \{$blond-haired people$\}$
$R = \{$people wearing rings$\}$
$W = \{$people with beards$\}$
$T = \left\{ \begin{array}{l} \text{people who are at} \\ \text{least 6 feet tall} \end{array} \right\}$
$M = \{$people with brothers$\}$
$N = \{$people with sisters$\}$

One-element Sets:

Problem: Is W a set, if $W = \{$Harvey Matthews$\}$?

Response: Yes. In mathematics, it is permissible for a set to have only one element.

Comment: The word *set* is sometimes used interchangeably with the words *group, pile,* and *collection.* Since one person is not called a "group," some people may wonder why mathematicians have decided to refer to one person as a set. The answer is that in order to reduce the number of words that must be used, the word *set* is used to refer to all kinds of collections of elements — even collections that have only one element.

Empty Sets:

Question: Is O a set if $O = \{$green-haired students$\}$?

Response: Since this set does not have any elements, it is an *empty set*. But in mathematics it is permissible for sets to be empty.

Question: What are some other ways to describe the empty set?

Universal Set:

Problem: What is another way to describe the set of people who have noses?

Response: Since this set includes everyone in the class, the set could be described in a variety of ways. But, in mathematics, the term *universal set* is used to refer to the set that includes all of the elements that are being considered.

Well-Defined Collections:

Mathematicians use the word *set* in a way that is slightly different from the way nonmathematicians use the word. Not only do they use it in the place of words like *group* and *collection*, but they also use it to refer to empty sets and sets that have only one element. However, not every collection of objects deserves the honor of being called a "set." Only *well-defined* collections are called "sets"; and a collection is not well-defined unless it is possible to determine exactly which elements are in the collection and which elements are not in the collection.

Question: Is the set $H = \{$blond-haired people$\}$ well-defined? What about the other suggested sets that were given at the start of the discussion?

Response: From the descriptions that were given, it was not clear exactly which students were in some of the sets. This uncertainty became clear when students were asked to raise their hands if they were in the set $H = \{$blond-haired people$\}$. There are many different shades of blond hair. Some blonds are nearly brownettes, and others are almost redheads. But when should a person be called a brunette instead of a blond? What about the people who have partly brown hair and partly blond hair? What about the people with bleached hair (perhaps only their hairdressers know for sure)? More stipulations have to be made to form several of the suggested sets into well-defined sets.

Tabular Form:

Sometimes it is difficult to make a set well-defined by giving a precise description of the properties that the elements in the set are supposed to have. In order to make it clear which elements are in a set, it is sometimes easier to define a set by listing its elements in *tabular form*. For instance, the set of people wearing blue could be written in tabular form as shown below.

$C = \{$Alfred, Betty, Carl, Debby, Elmo, Fran$\}$

Problem: For any of the suggested sets that are not yet well-defined, give a definition by listing their elements in tabular form.

Tabular Form versus Precise Descriptions:

Two different methods can be used to define sets. One way is to list the elements of the set in tabular form; the other way is to give a precise description of the properties that elements of the set are supposed to have.

Each of these methods has certain advantages and disadvantages.

Problem: Form a set by randomly selecting five people from the class. Then, try to define the set by giving a precise description of the elements that are in the set. (Make sure that the description excludes everyone in the class except the five students and that the description is not just a disguised form of a tabular list.)

Comment: The above problems illustrate that many sets that are awkward to define by giving precise descriptions are quite easy to define by listing their elements in tabular form. On the other hand, however, some sets that are easy to describe are difficult or impossible to write in tabular form. For example, the set of even counting numbers cannot be written in tabular form because it has an infinite number of elements. If a slight cheat is allowed, then it is possible to write {2, 4, 6, 8, 10, 14, . . .} to stand for the set of even counting numbers. But this method is really not the same thing as listing the elements in tabular form. What this method does is to list only enough elements so that it is possible to detect the rule that describes the rest of the elements in the set. The ellipses (three dots) at the end of the set mean that the same pattern continues.

Problem: Give five more examples of sets that are easy to write in tabular form but difficult to describe. Give five more examples of sets that are easy to describe but difficult or impossible to write in tabular form. (Use the three-dot notation wherever it is appropriate.)

Using the Word And:

Problem: "If G = {girls} and N = {people with sisters}, then all students who are in "the set of elements that are in G *and* in N," raise your hands."

Problem: "If W = {people with beards}, then all students who are in G *and* in W, raise your hands."

Response: No one raised a hand. This was an empty set.

Question: Using the word *and* and the sets that were given at the beginning of this discussion, what are some other ways to describe the empty set?

Using the word Or:

Problem: "If G = {girls} and N = {people with sisters}, then all students who are in the set of elements that are in G or in N, raise your hands."

Response: To be "in G or in N" means:

1. To be in G but not in N (e.g., girls who do not have sisters.)

2. To be in G and in N (e.g., girls who have sisters.)

3. To be in N but not in G (e.g., boys who have sisters.)

Comment: The word *or* has a slightly different meaning in set theory than it often has in everyday language. For instance, when a young man asks his date whether she wants to go to a dance or to a movie, he would probably be surprised if her answer was, "Yes, I'd like to go to a dance *and* to a movie." But, if the young man's date knew set theory, then she would realize that the set of elements that are "in the set of movies *or* in the set of dances" includes the elements that are in *both* sets.

In everyday language, the phrase "to be in X or in Y" often means:

1. To be in X
2. Or to be in Y
3. But not to be in both X and Y

But, in set theory, the phrase "to be in X or in Y" means

1. To be in X
2. Or to be in Y
3. Or to be in both X and Y

Problem: Give some examples to illustrate the difference between the everyday or and the set theory or. In everyday situations notice that the word or is often used to describe events which must occur one after the other (i.e., never simultaneously).

---

*1.6 Materials needed: A deck of playing cards.
PROBLEMS

1. Complements of sets

Look at the 12 face cards from a deck of playing cards.

K ♣   K ♠   K ♡   K ◇
Q ♣   Q ♠   Q ♡   Q ◇
J ♣   J ♠   J ♡   J ◇

Rewrite each of the following sets by describing the properties of the elements.

$A = \{$K♣, Q♣, J♣, K♠, Q♠, J♠, K♡, Q♡, J♡, K◇, Q◇$\}$
$B = \{$K♣, Q♣, J♣, K♠, Q♠, J♠, K◇, Q◇, J◇$\}$
$C = \{$K♣, Q♣, K♠, Q♠, K♡, Q♡, K◇, Q◇$\}$

After you have described sets A, B, and C, read the footnote.[5]

2. Power Sets

Using three playing cards, how many different sets can be formed?

[5] The sets A, B, and C can be described as follows. $A = \{$not the jack of diamonds$\}$, $B = \{$not hearts$\}$, $C = \{$not jacks$\}$. These are *negative* descriptions since they describe properties that elements in the set do *not* have. For instance, the set $B = \{$not hearts$\}$ includes everything in the universal set (in this case the universal set consisted of all of the face cards) except the elements that are in the set $H = \{$hearts$\}$. To emphasize this fact, the set B can be called the *complement* of the set H with respect to the universal set $U = \{$all face cards$\}$.

Could A, B, and C be described in the same way if the universal set had been the entire deck of playing cards (rather than just the face cards)?

Fill out the following table to find out how many different sets can be formed using all 12 face cards from a deck of playing cards. (Start at the beginning of the table and try to discover a pattern.)

Number of cards	1	2	3	4	5	6	7	8	9	10	11	12
Number of sets		4										

Using two cards (for example, J♣, K♠), four different sets can be formed. They are: {the empty set}, {J♠}, {K♠}, {J♠, K♠}. Have you discovered a rule that tells how many different sets could be formed using all 52 cards from the deck? Does your rule predict that you should be able to form 1,024 different sets using 10 cards? If not, recheck your answers in the table and try to think of a new rule. Then read the footnote.[7]

3. Sets of Sets:

In the previous problem, the "elements" in the power set were not individual playing cards. The "elements" in the power set were "sets of playing cards." Therefore the power set is a *set of sets* because it consists of sets that were taken from the original collection.

For any collection of objects, there are many more sets of sets than there are sets of objects. For instance, using a deck of playing cards, one set of sets that can be discussed is the set of all "poker hands" (or the set of all five element sets). Other smaller sets of sets would be the set of "flushes," "straights" or "full houses." It would also be possible to talk about the set of all two-element sets, or the set of all pairs of cards where both cards are of the same suit. Think of three more "sets of sets" that can be formed using a deck of cards. The set of football teams in the National Football League is an example of a set of sets. Think of five more sets of sets that can be formed using people as elements in the original collection.

1.7
OPERATIONS
ON SETS AND
RELATIONS BETWEEN
SETS

Overview: **This section will present activities to investigate the following operations on sets: (1) finding the *intersection* ($\cap$) of two sets, (2) finding the *union* ($\cup$) of two sets, and (3) finding the *complement* (') of a set. *Venn diagrams* will be used to illustrate these operations.**

Two different relations between sets will also be investigated; they are: set *equality* (=), and "is a *subset* of" ($\subset$).

---

7   **If you begin with a collection of 12 elements, 2^{12} different sets can be formed. Or, if you begin with a collection of 52 elements, 2^{52} different sets can be formed. These "two to the 52nd power" sets can be considered to be "elements" of a new set that is called the "power set" of the original collection.**

Some of the problems will illustrate laws concerning how sets can be combined using intersections, unions, and complements. The laws about identity elements and inverse elements, and the properties of associativity, commutativity, and distributivity are similar to laws about the basic arithmetic operations (+, −, ×, ÷). However, the objective is not so much to study the algebra of combining sets as it is to practice the three basic set operations, and to show how these operations can be interpreted differently using different types of materials and different kinds of sets.

Materials needed: Three 36-inch loops of colored yarn. A set of attribute blocks with three colors (red, yellow, and green), three shapes (squares, triangles, and circles), and two sizes (large and small). One deck of playing cards (preferably an old deck that you do not mind cutting up).

Using attribute blocks and playing cards, four different sets of materials will be used in this section: *face cards, small cards, computer cards, and attribute blocks.* Groups of four people may work together on the activities in this section. One person in each group may serve as the "expert" on each set of materials.

Preliminary Instructions

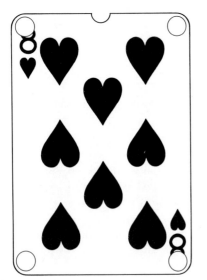

The four sets of materials which will be used are:

1. *Attribute Blocks:* The set of attribute blocks that will be used in this section includes three colors (red, yellow, blue), three shapes (circle, triangle, square) two sizes (large, small) and three loops of colored yarn.
2. *Face Cards:* The set of face cards consists of the jacks, queens, and kings in all four suits.
3. *Small Cards:* The set of small cards consists of the aces, twos, threes, and fours in all four suits.
*4. *Computer Cards:* The set of computer cards can be made using the sevens, eights, nines, and tens in all four suits. (Directions for making computer cards are on p. 475.)

If you work with three other people, one person should work with computer cards, one should work with face cards, one should work with small cards, and one should work with attribute blocks. Although each person will be working with different sets of materials, the problems that you will be doing will be the same.

Use a paper punch to punch holes in the four corners of each card. Then put a notch in the "top" of each card. Make sure that the holes in each card are punched in *exactly* the same places. To do this, begin punching holes in a single card (e.g., the eight of hearts as shown on p.

474), and then use this card as a guide to punch holes in the other 15 cards.

Next:

a. Cut the upper-right-hand corners off all of the red cards (hearts and diamonds).

b. Cut the upper-left-hand corners off all of the odd cards (the sevens and nines).

c. Cut the lower-right-hand corners off all of the diamonds, hearts, and clubs.

d. Cut the lower-left-hand corners off all of the sevens and nines and tens.

The eight of hearts should still have holes in the upper left hand corner and in the lower left hand corner.

As soon as all the computer cards have been punched and cut, they should be put together into a deck, facing the same direction, with the notched sides up (as shown in the illustration). A paper clip can be used to select cards that are in a particular set. For instance, in order to select cards that have a hole in the upper right hand corner, just insert the paper clip and pull.

1.7.1
Operations
on Sets
Ordinary sentences are sometimes not well suited to describe operations on sets. For example, imagine that you were in a classroom where these three sets had been defined.

G = {people who are female}
M = {people with brothers} N = {people with sisters}

1. a. Do you think that some confusion might occur if all of the students who were "in G, and in M or in N" were asked to raise their hands?

b. Are the following sets the same? "The set of students who are in G, and in M or N" and "the set of students who are in G and in M, or in N."

2. Is "the set of students who are not in G or in M" the same as:

a. The set of students who are not in G or not in M.

b. The set of students who are not in G, or in M.

c. The set of students who are not in G and not in M.

The above questions involve (1) finding the *intersection* (∩) of two sets; (2) finding the *union* (∪) of two sets; and (3) finding the *comple-*

ment (') of a set. To describe these three operations, *Venn diagrams* can be used.

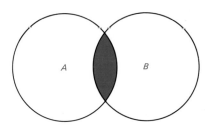

For instance, using a set of attribute blocks and two loops of yarn, let *A* be the set of circles and let *B* be the set of blue blocks. To find the intersection of the sets *A* and *B* (to find $A \cap B$) use the yarn to make two overlapping loops (as shown above). Put all the circles inside the *A* loop and put all the blue blocks inside the *B* loop. $A \cap B$ will consist of the blocks that are inside the *A* loop *and also* inside the *B* loop (in the shaded part of the diagram above). $A \cap B$ will be the set of blue circles.

1.7.2 Intersections

For the problems in the remainder of section 1.7, the sets *A*, *B*, *C* and *D* are defined as follows for each set of materials.

Attribute blocks:
A is the set of circles.
B is the set of blue blocks.
C is the set of large blocks.
D is the set of blue blocks.

Face cards:
A is the set of queens (hearts, diamonds, clubs, spades).
B is the set of black cards (spades and clubs).
C is the set of male cards (kings and jacks).
D is the set of one-eyed cards (jack of clubs, jack of hearts, and king of diamonds).

Small cards:
A is the set of deuces (that is, 2s).
B is the set of cards in the suit of spades.
C is the set of even-numbered cards.
D is the set of black cards (spades and clubs).

Computer cards:
A is the set of cards with holes in the upper-right-hand corner.
B is the set of cards with holes in the upper-left-hand corner.
C is the set of cards with holes in the lower-right-hand corner.
D is the set of cards with the holes in the lower-left-hand corner.

1. Using each set of materials, find $A \cap B$.

2. a. Using each set of materials, find $B \cap D$.

   b. Which of the following Venn diagrams is like each set of materials?

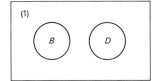
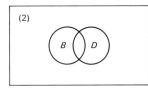
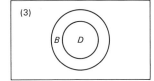
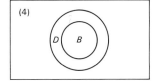

   c. Shade in $B \cap D$ for each of the above Venn diagrams.

3. Using each set of materials, find $C \cap D$.

1.7.3 Unions

In each of the following diagrams, $A \cup C$ has been shaded.

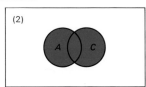
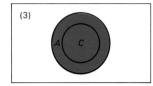

1. a. Use loops of yarn on attribute blocks to illustrate $A \cup C$. Notice that $A \cup C$ consists of three different types of blocks: (1) blocks which are just in A (small circles); (2) blocks which are in A and in C (large circles); and (3) blocks which are just in C (large triangles and squares).

   b. Find $A \cup C$ for the other three sets of material.

   c. Which of the Venn diagrams above is like each set of materials?

2. Using each set of materials, find $C \cup D$.

3. Using each set of materials, find $B \cup D$.

1.7.4 Complements

Using a set of attribute blocks, A is the set of circles. The complement of A (written A') is the set of attribute blocks that are not circles. The shaded part of the Venn diagram to the left shows A'.

Notice that A' consists of all the elements in the universal (entire) set that are not elements of A. Therefore the complement of the universal set is the empty set; and the complement of the empty set is the universal set.

1. Find A' for each set of materials.

2. For each set of materials, find $A' \cap C$. Find $A' \cup C$. Draw Venn diagrams to illustrate these problems.[8]

3. For each set of materials, find $A \cap D'$. Find $A \cup D'$. Draw Venn diagrams to illustrate these problems.

4. For each set of materials, find $A \cap C$. Then find $(A \cap C)'$. [Hint: $(A \cap C)'$ consists of all elements in the universal set that are not elements in $A \cap C$.]

5. For each set of materials, find $(A \cup C)'$. [Hint: $(A \cup C)'$ consists of all of the elements in the universal set that are not elements in $A \cup C$.]

**1.7.5
Relations
between Sets**

Two sets are equal if they consist of exactly the same elements.

1. For which set of materials is it true that $A' = C$?

2. If W is the universal set, for which sets of materials is it true that $A \cup C = W$?

Set A is a subset of a set B if every element in A is also in B. This means that the set A is contained in the set B, or written symbolically $A \subset B$. If some element in A is not in B, then the set A is not a subset of the set B. In the Venn diagram of $A \subset B$, the set A is not contained in the set B because the element a is not in B.

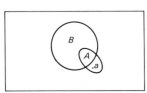

$A \not\subset B$

3. For which sets of materials is it true that $A \subset C$?

4. For which sets of materials is it true that $C \subset A$?

5. For which sets of materials is it true that $D \subset A'$?

$A \subset B$

6. For which sets of materials is it true that the empty set is a subset of every set?[9]

7. For which sets of materials is it true that $A \cap D \subset D$?

8. For which sets of materials is it true that $(A \cap B)' = A' \cup B'$?

8 $A' = C$ and $C \cap C = C$, and so $A' \cap C = C$.

9 The empty set is always a subset of every other set because every element (there are none) is in every other set.

9. For which sets of materials is it true that $C \cap (A \cup B) = (C \cap A) \cup (C \cap B)$? (Hint: Look at the sequence of Venn diagrams below.)

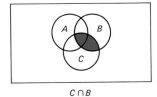 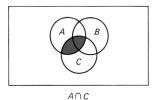 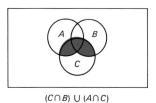

$C \cap B$ $A \cap C$ $(C \cap B) \cup (A \cap C)$

*1.7.6
Some
Laws about Sets

1. Using attribute blocks, computer cards, small cards, and face cards, give examples to illustrate the meaning of each of the following laws about sets.

Identity Laws: If W is the universal set, $\emptyset$ is the empty set, and X is any set:

a. $W \cap X = X$ **c.** $X \cap O = O$
b. $W \cup X = W$ **d.** $x \cup \emptyset = X$

Commutative Laws: If X and Y are any two sets:

e. $X \cap Y = Y \cap X$ **f.** $X \cup Y = Y \cup X$

Associative Laws: If X, Y, and Z are any three sets:

g. $(X \cap Y) \cap Z = X \cap (Y \cap Z)$
h. $(X \cup Y) \cup Z = X \cup (Y \cup Z)$

Distributive Laws: If X, Y, and Z are any three sets:

i. $X \cap (Y \cup Z) = (X \cap Y) \cup (X \cap Z)$
j. $X \cup (Y \cap Z) = (X \cup Y) \cap (X \cup Z)$

DeMorgan's Laws: If X and Y are any two sets:

k. $(X \cup Y)' = X' \cap Y'$ **l.** $(X \cap Y)' = X' \cup Y'$

2. a. At the beginning of section 1.7, you were given three sets G, M, and N and were asked if there is a difference between (1) the set of elements that are "in G, and in M or in N" and (2) the set of elements that are "in G and in M, or in N." This is equivalent to asking whether it is true that $G \cap (M \cup N) = (G \cap M) \cup N$. What is the answer?

b. You were also asked whether "the set of elements that are "not in G or in M" is the same as (1) the set of elements that are not in G or not in M, (2) the set of elements that are not in G, or in M, (3) the set of elements that are not in G and not in M. This is equivalent to asking whether $(G \cup M)$ is equal to (1) $G' \cup M'$, (2) $G' \cup M$, (3) $G' \cap M'$. What is the answer?

1.8 LOGIC AND ELECTRICAL CIRCUITS

Overview: **Compound sentences are built up in a manner that is similar to the way complex electrical switches are formed using simple electrical switches. This section will show how the words *and* and *or* can be used to describe circuits consisting of switches that are connected "in series" or "in parallel," and it will show how some complex electrical switches can be simplified using laws about sets.**

Circuit charts will be given for several different kinds of complex circuits. Circuit charts are similar to truth tables which can be used to investigate the truth or falsity of compound sentences.

The words *and*, *or*, and *not* can be used to describe the intersections ($\cap$), unions ($\cup$), and complements ($'$) of sets. However, logical language can be used for purposes other than to organize and combine sets of objects. For instance, words like *and, or,* and *not* can also be used to build up compound sentences out of simple sentences.

An element is either in the set or not in the set; there are no other possibilities. Similarly, a simple electrical switch is either "on" or "off."

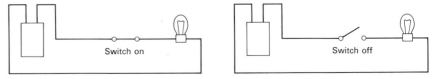

| Switch on | Switch off |

1.8.1 Parallel and Series Circuits

More complicated circuits may involve more than one switch. For example, two switches A and B can be connected "in series" or "in parallel."

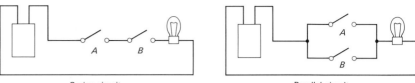

Series circuit   Parallel circuit

1. $A \wedge B$ is a shorthand way of writing "the circuit consisting of switch A connected in series with switch B." When will the light be on for the series circuit $A \wedge B$? Fill out the circuit chart below.

Series Circuit Chart

A	B	Light
On	On	
On	Off	
Off	Off	
Off	On	

Notice:

   a. The symbol $\wedge$ looks very similar to the intersection symbol $\cap$.
   b. An element is in the set $A \cap B$ if it is in the set A *and* in the set B.
   c. The series circuit $A \wedge B$ is on if the switch A is on *and* the switch B is on.

2. $A \vee B$ is a shorthand way of writing "the circuit consisting of a switch A connected in parallel with a switch B. When will the light be on for the parallel circuit $A \vee B$? Fill out the circuit chart below.

Parallel Circuit Chart

A	B	Light
On	On	
On	Off	
Off	Off	
Off	On	

Notice:

   a. The symbol $\vee$ looks very similar to the union symbol $\cup$.

b. $A \cup B$ is the set of elements that satisfy one of the following conditions: (1) in A and not in B, (2) in A and in B, (3) in B and not in A.

c. The parallel circuit $A \vee B$ is on if one of the following conditions hold: (1) the switch A is on and the switch B is not on, (2) the switch A is on and the switch B is on, (3) the switch B is on and the switch A is not on.

1.8.2
More
Complicated
Circuits

1. From the above two types of basic circuits, many more complicated circuits can be constructed. For example, these diagrams show the circuit $A \wedge (B \vee C)$ and the circuit $A \vee (B \wedge C)$.

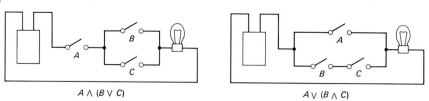

$A \wedge (B \vee C)$ $A \vee (B \wedge C)$

Fill out the circuit charts below for $A \wedge (B \vee C)$ and $A \vee (B \wedge C)$.

$A \wedge (B \vee C)$

A	B	C	Light
On	On	On	
On	On	Off	
On	Off	On	
Off	On	On	
On	Off	Off	
Off	On	Off	
Off	Off	On	
Off	Off	Off	

$A \vee (B \wedge C)$

A	B	C	Light
On	On	On	
On	On	Off	
On	Off	On	
Off	On	On	
On	Off	Off	
Off	On	Off	
Off	Off	On	
Off	Off	Off	

2. So far, all the circuits have consisted of switches that act independently. But, circuits can also be constructed where two or more switches open and close simultaneously. For example, in the circuit $(A \wedge B) \vee (A \wedge V)$, both A switches open and close simultaneously.

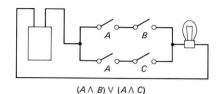

(A ∧ B) ∨ (A ∧ C)

Finish filling out the circuit chart for $(A \wedge B) \wedge (A \wedge C)$.

(A ∧ B) ∨ (A ∧ C)

A	B	C	Light
On	On	On	
On	On	Off	
On	Off	On	
Off	On	On	
On	Off	Off	
Off	On	Off	
Off	Off	On	
Off	Off	Off	

3. Earlier in this unit you learned that $(A \cap B) \cup (A \cap C) = A \cap (B \cup C)$. Look at the circuit chart for $(A \wedge B) \vee (A \wedge C)$. Then look at the circuit chart for $A \wedge (B \vee C)$. What do you notice?

4. Two circuits are equivalent if their circuit charts are identical (as they were for the two circuits in exercise 2 above).
   a. Draw a diagram of a circuit that you think may be equivalent to $A \vee (B \wedge C)$. [Hint: Think of another way to describe the set $A \cup (B \cap C)$.]

   b. Fill out the circuit chart on page 484 for the circuit you drew in problem a. If your circuit is equivalent to $A \vee (B \wedge C)$, then its circuit chart should be identical to the circuit chart for $A \vee (B \wedge C)$. Check to see whether this is true.

   c. Which of the two circuits is simpler? (Which has fewer switches?)

5. Not only can circuits be constructed in which two or more switches

$A \vee (B \wedge C)$

A	B	C	Light
On	On	On	On
On	On	Off	On
On	Off	On	On
Off	On	On	On
On	Off	Off	On
Off	On	Off	Off
Off	Off	On	Off
Off	Off	Off	Off

A	B	C	Light
On	On	On	
On	On	Off	
On	Off	On	
Off	On	On	
On	Off	Off	
Off	On	Off	
Off	Off	On	
Off	Off	Off	

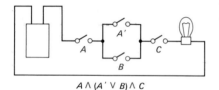

$A \wedge (A' \vee B) \wedge C$

open and close simultaneously, but circuits can also be constructed in which opening one switch will automatically close another (or vice versa). For example, in the diagram at the left when switch A is on, switch A' is off; and whenever switch A is off, switch A' is on.

Can you think of a way to simplify the circuit $A \wedge (A' \vee B) \wedge C$? Fill out the circuit chart below to justify your answer. (Hint: To find an equivalent circuit which has fewer switches, think of an equivalent way to describe the set $A \cap (A' \cup B) \cap C$.)

$A \wedge (A' \vee B) \wedge C$

A	B	C	A'	Light
On	On	On	On	
On	On	Off	On	
On	Off	On	Off	
Off	On	On	On	
On	Off	Off	Off	
Off	On	Off	On	
Off	Off	On	On	
Off	Off	Off	On	

**1.9
LOGIC**

Overview: **This section will reemphasize some relationships between logic and basic set ideas. Topics that will be considered include:** *compound and/or sentences, truth tables,* **and the quantifiers** *all, some,* **and** *none.* **The distinction between truth and validity will also be pointed out. The section ends with some problems from recreational logic.**

Underlying all of mathematics is a method of thinking, called "logic," which has its roots in common sense and everyday experience, but which is more formal and rigorous. However, because reliable information about real world situations is often not available, the rules that rigorous logical arguments must obey are sometimes too restrictive to be used to solve everyday problems. Consequently, common sense may be better adapted to the solution of some everyday problems since it is able to deal intuitively with ambiguous situations or problems in which some relevant information may be missing. Nonetheless, a brief review of several ideas from logic may allow certain mistakes to be avoided, and may enable common sense to be used more effectively in everyday problems.

**1.9.1
A Brain
Teaser**

An event is described on the last page of this unit. The event has not yet taken place, but it either will or will not occur. Without knowing the event that is described, your job is to guess whether or not the event will take place. Use the box below to record your prediction. Write "Yes" in the box if you think the event will happen. Write "No" in the box if you think that it will not happen.

Write your
prediction
here. ⟶

You do not know the event that has been described. Your instructor does not know whether you will write "Yes" or "No." If you guess correctly, he will probably be willing to give you an A for your work in this unit.

**1.9.2
Compound
Sentences and
Truth Tables**

Previous sections pointed out that the word *or* can be used to describe the elements in the union (∪) of two sets, and that it can also be used to describe electrical switches that are connected "in parallel" (∨) Similarly, the word *and* can be used to describe the elements in the intersection (∩) of two sets, and it can also be used to describe electrical switches that are connected "in series" (∧). But the words *and* and *or* can be used for other purposes besides describing electrical circuits or combining sets of objects; they can also link together simple sentences to form compound sentences.

For instance, the sentence "John is playing his guitar" can be combined with the sentence "John is in his tree house" to form either of two compound sentences: (1) "John is playing his guitar, *and* John is in his tree house," and (2) "John is playing his guitar, *or* John is in his tree house."

A truth table can be used to show how the truth of a compound sentence depends on the truth or falsity of the sentences that are combined. Two examples of truth tables are given below. The sentence A can be thought of as being "John is playing his guitar," and the sentence B can be thought of as "John is in his tree house."

A	B	A **and** B	A	B	A **or** B
T	T	T	T	T	
T	F	F	T	F	
F	T	F	F	T	
F	F	F	F	F	

1. The first truth table shows that the compound sentence "A and B" is only true when *both* A and B are true. Compare this truth table with the circuit chart for two switches that are connected "in series." Notice that the truth or falsity of the sentence A (or B) corresponds to the on-off positions of the switch A (or B). Also, notice that the truth or falsity of the sentence "A and B" under various conditions corresponds to whether or not the light is on under similar conditions for the circuit $A \wedge B$. For this reason $A \wedge B$ is sometimes used as a shorthand way of writing the compound sentence "A and B."

2. Finish filling out the second truth table and compare your answers with the circuit chart for two switches that are connected "in parallel." Explain how these two situations are similar. Notice that the logical "or" in the sentence "A or B" is used in the same way that it was used to describe the union of two sets. Review the distinction between the logical "or" and the everyday "or" in section 1.5.

$A \vee B$ is sometimes used as a shorthand way of writing the compound sentence "A or B".

1.9.3 **Conditional Sentences** Another important kind of compound sentence can be formed using the words *if . . . then*. For instance, the two sentences "Astronauts eat peanut butter," and "Astronauts get stomachaches" can be combined into the *conditional* sentence "If astronauts eat peanut butter, then they get stomachaches."

1. What can you conclude about the truth or falsity of the sentence "If astronauts eat peanut butter, then they get stomachaches" under each of the following circumstances?

    a. You know an astronaut who did not eat peanut butter, and then did not get a stomachache. Could the "if . . . then" sentence be true?

    b. You know an astronaut who did not eat peanut butter, but got a stomachache. Could the "if . . . then" sentence still be true?

    c. You know an astronaut who ate peanut butter, and then got a stomachache. Could the "if . . . then" sentence still be true?

    d. You know an astronaut who ate peanut butter, and did not get a stomachache. Could the "if . . . then" sentence still be true?

2. The following truth table for "if . . . then" sentences shows how the truth or falsity of a conditional sentence depends on the truth of the sentences that are combined. Explain how the four rows of the truth table are related to the four situations in exercise 1.

A	B	If A, then B	
T	T	T	(situation *c*)
T	F	F	(situation *d*)
F	T	T	(situation *b*)
F	F	T	(situation *a*)

    In order to fill out the above truth table, notice that you must determine whether the sentence "If A, then B" could be true under four different circumstances. You are *not* trying to determine whether B is true under the four circumstances, or whether A is true under the four circumstances. This distinction is somewhat tricky in the third and fourth lines of the truth table (situations *b* and *a*).

3. Just as compound ("and," "or") sentences are related to the set operations ∩ and ∪, conditional ("if . . . then") sentences are related to the subset relation ⊂. $A \subset B$ means that if an element is in A, *then* it will also be in B.

    What can you conclude about the truth or falsity of the sentence "A is contained in B" under each of the following circumstances:

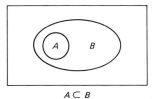

$A \subset B$

a. You have found an element that is not in A and not in B. Could it be true that $A \subset B$?

b. You have found an element that is not in A but is in B. Could it be true that $A \subset B$?

c. You have found an element that is in A and in B. Could it be true that $A \subset B$?

d. You have found an element that is in A, but is not in B. Could it be true that $A \subset B$?

Compare the above four situations to the four situations in exercise 1. Explain how the above four situations are related to the truth table in problem 2.

4. Throughout this section, the symbols used have emphasized correspondence between logic and set theory. In logic:

a. $A \wedge B$ is the compound sentence "A and B."
b. $A \vee B$ is the compound sentence "A or B."
c. $A \rightarrow B$ is the conditional sentence if A then B.

In set theory:

a. $A \cap B$ is the set "A intersect B."
b. $A \cup B$ is the set "A union B."
c. $A \subset B$ is the set relation "A is contained in B."

The set relation $A \cap B \subset B$ corresponds to the logical statement "If A and B, then B." What fact about sets corresponds to the logical statement "If B, then A or B"? What logical statement corresponds to the set relation $A \cap B \subset A \cup B$?

1.9.4 Logical Precision

In an attempt to determine the truth of the sentence, "If astronauts eat peanut butter, then they get stomachaches," some questions may arise. For instance: "When should a person be considered to be an astronaut?" "Should a person only be considered to be an astronaut when he is actually flying through space in a rocket ship?" "When should a person be considered to have a stomachache (instead of 'heartburn,' 'constipation,' 'the flu,' or some other illness)?" In order to answer these questions, some rather artificial restrictions may have to be made. Consequently, the rules that logic must obey can sometimes impose artificial or unrealistically stringent restrictions on the type of decisions that can be made in everyday situations. Nonetheless, some practice in logical reasoning may enable common sense to be used more effectively in everyday situations. For instance, logical reasoning certainly calls for the precise use of language; without the careful use of syntax and semantics even the simplest idea may become confused. For example, statements like the ones below sometimes appear as advertisements in newspapers.

For Sale: Chevrolet wagon by little old lady too large for her garage.

Apartment Wanted: Elderly lady desires two room apartment where she can cook herself.

For Sale: Walnut dining room table, seats eight people with spirally turned legs.

Headline: Computer goes berserk, charges hundreds of people.

Announcement: Church picnic 2 p.m. August 6. Raindate August 2.

Another hindrance to the precise use of language is the ability of a word to convey a variety of meanings. Explain why the following arguments seem to involve correct reasoning but lead to false conclusions.

1. A stupid person is a dope. A dope is a drug. Therefore, a stupid person is a drug.

2. The plane taking off cannot get smaller. But what I see as it takes off grows smaller. Therefore, what I see is not an airplane.

3. The Bible is the Word of God. The Bible is written in English. Therefore, English is the language of God.

4. Improbable events happen every day. Events which happen every day are probable events. Therefore, improbable events are probable events.

In order to avoid problems that can occur when a word has been defined ambiguously or when it has more than one meaning, a logician may redefine the word or stipulate that the word is to be used in only one way. We repeat that such definitions and restrictions may sometimes be somewhat artificial.

1.9.5
The Quantifier
All, Some, and *None*

You can fool all of the people some of the time, and you can fool some of the people all of the time, but you can't fool all of the people all of the time.

Abraham Lincoln

Some of Farmer Jones's horses are brown.

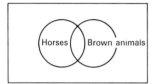

The words *all, some,* and *none* (or *no*) are *quantifiers* since they tell "how many." *All* and *none* refer to every member of a set, while *some* means "at least one," but allows for the possibility of "all." For instance, the statement "Some of Farmer Jones's horses are brown" tells that there is at least one brown horse, but it does not tell whether or not all the horses are brown. If all the horses were brown, which section of the diagram at the left would be empty?

1. Use Venn diagrams to illustrate the errors in the following arguments.

   a. All students who study will pass. Alfred never studies. Alfred will not pass.

   b. No animals without wings can fly. All birds have wings. All birds can fly.

   c. No interesting speakers are bores. Some college professors are interesting speakers. Therefore, some college professors are bores.

2. Illustrate problems *a* and *b* below with Venn diagrams, and then answer these questions about each problem:

   (1) Is it true that some rectangles are squares?

   (2) Is it true that some trapezoids are rhombuses?

   (3) Is it true that no parallelograms are squares?

   a. All squares are rectangles. All rhombuses are parallelograms. All rectangles are parallelograms.

   b. All parallelograms are quadrilaterals. All trapezoids are quadrilaterals. No trapezoids are parallelograms.

*3. Only those requests that were accompanied by a stamped self-addressed envelope were returned. My request was accompanied by a stamped self-addressed envelope. Therefore, my request should have been returned. But it wasn't! Where was my logic wrong?

1.9.6
Validity versus Truth
Because Albert Einstein was an applied mathematician, he once said to a friend who was a pure mathematician, "My job is harder than yours. My results must not only be correct, they must also be true." Einstein was referring to the fact that validity (correctness or reasoning) is separate from the truth of a statement. If the chain of reasoning leading to a conclusion is completely correct, the conclusion is valid. If, in addition, the assumptions on which the conclusion was based are true, then the conclusion is true. The difference between the validity and the truth of a conclusion is apparent when an argument is considered in which the assumptions have no meaning and therefore cannot be true.

> Assumptions: All dings are dongs.
> All dongs are dills.
> Valid conclusion: All dings are dills.

Validity, then, is determined, not by the *meanings* of the sentences concerned, but by *how* the sentences are linked together to form a logical argument.

State whether you think the conclusions of the following are valid, true, both, or neither. Compare your answers with those of your colleagues.

1. All vehicles have four wheels. A bicycle is a vehicle. Therefore, a bicycle has four wheels.

2. If the butler was the murderer, he had to be at the scene of the crime. The butler was at the scene of the crime. Therefore, the butler did it.

3. Animals that talk are human beings. A parrot is an animal that talks. Therefore, a parrot is a human being.

4. Every time the rooster crows, the sun comes up. Therefore, the crow of a rooster makes the sun rise.

5. An artist is a man. Therefore, a good artist is a good man.

6. "Were it crime, I should feel remorse. Where there is no remorse, crime cannot exist. I am not sorry; therefore I am innocent." Thackeray

7. Tigers are disappearing. This animal is a tiger. This animal must be disappearing.

8. In the space of 176 years the Lower Mississippi has shortened itself 242 miles. This is an average of a trifle over one mile and a third per year. Therefore, any calm person, who is not blind or idiotic, can see that in the old Silurian Period, just a million years ago next November, the River was upward of 1,300,000 miles long, and stuck out over the Gulf of Mexico like a fishing rod. And by the same token, any person can see that 742 years from now the Lower Mississippi will be only a mile and three-quarters long, and Cairo and New Orleans will have joined their streets together. . . .

Mark Twain, *Life on the Mississippi*

Any reasoning that contains a flaw in its logic is called a "fallacy." Many fallacies are difficult to detect, but it is important to be on the lookout for these roadblocks to clear thinking. Advertisers, politicians, editorial writers, and other people who would like to sway peoples' thinking often try to use carefully worded, but misleading, arguments to support their points of view.

Before your next class meeting, find an example of a logical fallacy that has been comitted by a magazine, a newspaper, a television commentator, the author of a letter to the editor, a football coach (in locker-room slogans), a politician, a professor (during lectures), or someone else. Quote the example, and then be prepared to explain why it is a fallacy.

*1.9.7
Logic
Problem for Fun

1. Mr. White, Mr. Brown, and Mr. Green were having coffee together. Mr. Brown said, "Isn't it interesting that our names are White, Brown, and Green, and that one of us is wearing a white tie, one is wearing a brown tie, and one is wearing a green tie?" The man with the green tie replied, "Yes, and none of us has a tie that matches his name." What color is each man's tie? (Hint: Use the diagram below to eliminate the impossible combinations.)

	Mr. White	Mr. Brown	Mr. Green
White tie			
Brown tie			
Green tie			

2. Eight coins are similar except that one is underweight and therefore is counterfeit. Describe the process for finding the counterfeit coin by using only two weighings on a balance scale. (Hint: Try a simple problem first. For instance, can you solve the problem for three coins? For four coins? For five coins?)

3. A phonograph record has a total diameter of 12 inches. The recording itself leaves an outer margin of ½ inch; the diameter of the unused center of the record is 4½ inches. There are an average of 90 grooves to the inch. How far does the needle travel when the record is played? (Hint: Eliminate all the irrelevant information.)

4. A farmer delivering milk in a village has only three pails. One holds 8 quarts, one holds 5 quarts, and one holds 3 quarts. There are no markings on the pails. How can he measure out 4 quarts of milk to a customer?

5. Steve and Sally Sanders are home this evening with their two children, Sue Ellen and Peter, and their dog Andy.

   a. If Steve is watching television, so is his wife.
   b. Either Andy or Sue, or both of them, are watching television.
   c. Either Sally or Peter, but not both, is watching television.
   d. Andy or Peter are either both watching, or both not watching.
   e. If Sue Ellen is watching television, then Steve and Andy are also watching.

   Who is watching TV?

6. On the island of Wayout, the population consists of Dogooders, who never lie, Dissemblers, who always lie, and Diplomats, who alternately lie and tell the truth. If you meet a native of Wayout, how, with just two questions, can you determine to which group he belongs?

7. Starting from an addition problem, a different letter of the alphabet was assigned to each digit from 0 through 9. The resulting problem is shown below. What was the original problem?

```
  F O R T Y
  + T E N
  + T E N
  ---------
  S I X T Y
```

8. Three men who are sharing a room in a motel pay $10 each, or $30 in all. Later, the proprietor feels that he charged too much. He gives the bellboy $5 to return to them. The bellboy decides that since there is

no way to divide the $5 evenly among the three men, he will give each man $1, and keep the other $2 for himself. That makes the room cost each man $9, or $27 in all. The $27 paid for the room plus $2 that the bellboy kept makes $29. But the men paid $30 originally. What happened to the other dollar?

9. The final results of an intramural soccer tournament are as follows:

School	No. of Games	Won	Lost	Tied	Goals for	Goals Against
North	3	2	1	0	2	1
South	3	0	2	1	1	4
East	3	2	0	1	4	1
West	3	0	1	2	0	1

Because each school played one match against each of the other three, it is possible to reconstruct the individual results of the six matches. Try!

1.10 PEDGODICAL REMARKS

Modern mathematicians have made it possible for a large quantity of diverse mathematical ideas to be "built up" out of basic set-theoretic notions. A brief look through the mathematics section of a college bookstore will indicate that the topic of sets is often one of the first chapters in a variety of different kinds of books—algebra books, geometry books, probability books, statistics books, and sometimes even calculus and analysis books. Because many different types of mathematical concepts can be introduced by beginning with ideas from set theory, sets are sometimes used to furnish a unifying theme in college mathematics. By showing that modern mathematics is not just a series of unconnected topics, university textbook writers have hoped to emphasize the underlying structure of mathematics. And by using set language and symbolism, a reduction has sometimes been able to be made in the number of words and symbols that students must learn when they move from one mathematics subject area to another.

In an attempt to reflect the spirit and content of modern mathematics, some authors also include "sets" as one of the topics that is covered in elementary school textbooks. A look at some "scope and sequence charts" showing outlines of the topics that are covered in various textbook series will reveal that some set concepts are often introduced as early as kindergarten. However, "the structure of mathematics" has proved to be an illusive notion to try to convey to elementary school children. Also, sets have seldom been used effectively to furnish a unifying theme in elementary school mathematics. In fact, rather than helping to reduce the words and symbols that students must learn, sets have frequently become only another isolated cluster of words and symbols to be learned. Nonetheless, if children's use of words like *and, or, all, some,* and *none* is gradually refined by using them in concrete situations, then the topic of sets can serve a positive function in the elementary school. Learning to organize information and to communicate in a clear, precise manner is an important part of mathematics, and organizing objects and information is a part of everyday life.

Some of the activities in this unit (the attribute games, the Venn diagram activities) are analogous to activities that can be used with children. However, it would almost certainly be hazardous to use these lessons and work sheets with children without considerable elaboration and adaptation. The aim of this unit was not to discuss how sets and logic should be taught to children. The aim was to make you sufficiently at home with the ideas, and sufficiently aware of the difficulties, so that you will be able to make appropriate pedagogical judgments when working with children.

Answer to section 1.9.1

For those students who were trying to predict whether or not the "brain teaser" event would occur, the event that you were trying to predict is given below.

Event: You (the reader) will write "No" in the box.

Question: Did you correctly predict whether the event would occur? Is it possible that anyone in your class predicted the event correctly? Explain.[6]

---

[6] For a brief explanation of this paradox and several others, see W. U. Quine's article "Paradox" in the April 1962 issue of *Scientific American*.

unit 2
relations

There are many examples of relations in mathematics, in the world around us, and in the elementary school. Here are some relations that frequently occur in the everyday experience of most people. Read the list below and then add five more examples that you think might be relations.

"Is taller than"   "Is the telephone number of"
"Is a friend of"   "Is the social security number of"
"Is the same age as"   "Is the algebra final exam grade of"
"Is the hometown of"   "Is the author of"

Relations do not have to refer to people. Here are some relations that occur frequently in mathematics. Study them and list five more examples which you think might be relations.

"Is greater than"   "Is 1 greater than"
"Is equal to"   "Is congruent to"
"Is similar to"   "Is parallel to"
"Is a divisor of"   "Is a multiple of"
"Is the square root of"   "Is the area of"
"Is 2 more than 3 times the square root of"

In this unit many different kinds of relations will be given. The examples will illustrate some properties that relations can have and will point out some uses that these properties can serve in mathematics and in everyday situations.

2.2
FAMILY
RELATIONSHIPS

Overview: **Sometimes words in mathematics have meanings similar to the meanings that they have in everyday language. For instance, if you were asked to name some people who are related to you, you might name your father, your mother, your sister, and your uncle. The relations involved in these examples are: "is the father of," "is the mother of," "is a sister of," and "is an uncle of." In order to introduce some properties of mathematical relations, this section will give several examples of relationships that can exist within a family.**

The Jones family was having a family picnic when the picture below was taken. Your job is to figure out who is who in the picture. As soon as you have identified a person write his name next to his picture. In order to help you identify the people at the picnic, diagrams of certain relations are given. The following is a diagram of the relation "is the father of." By using this diagram and the Jones family tree (see page 498), you should be able to identify some of the people in the picture of the family picnic.

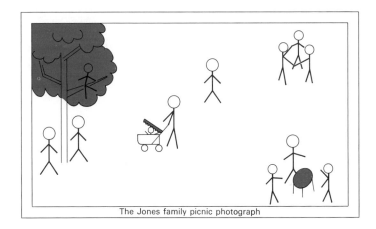

The Jones family picnic photograph

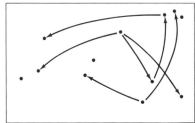

"Is the father of"

1. Using the family tree and the diagram of the relation "is the father of" can you identify the men at the picnic? Who are the women? Are there any people about whom you are not sure?

How many more people can you identify after studying the diagram for the relation "is the mother of"?

The Jones Family Tree

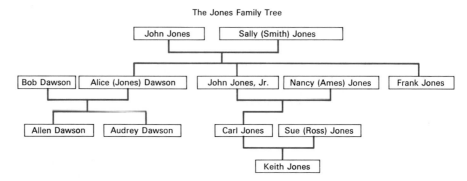

2. Using the information that you have gained from the previous two diagrams, fill in the missing lines in the diagram showing the relation "is married to."

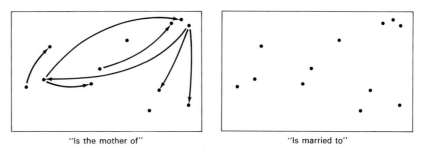

"Is the mother of"   "Is married to"

3. The diagrams for "is a brother of" and "is a sister of" should give you enough new information to discover the names of everyone in the family photo. Write the names in the appropriate places in the family photo.

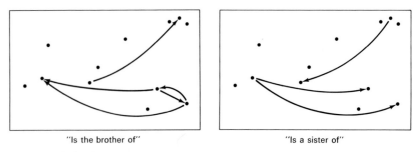

"Is the brother of"   "Is a sister of"

4. The relations "is a sister of" and "is a brother of" could have been combined into one relation "is a sibling of." Fill in the missing lines in

the diagram for "is a sibling of." Could this relation have replaced the other two and given you the same information? Did you need both "is a sister of" and "is a brother of" or would one of them alone have furnished all the information that you needed?

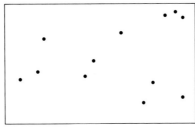

"Is a sibling of"

2.3 ORDERED PAIRS

Overview: **In the last section, relations were described in two ways: (1) a short phrase was given to describe the relationship and (2) an arrow diagram was drawn to illustrate the relationship. In this section, a third method will be given. The third method is to list the pair elements that are related. This method will be used to give a concise definition of what it means to be a "relation."**

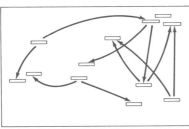

"Is a son of"

The relation "is a son of" could have been given using the diagram at the left. The relation "is a son of" could also have been given as shown below.

John Jones	John Jones
Sally (Smith) Jones	Sally (Smith) Jones
Bob Dawson	Bob Dawson
Alice (Jones) Dawson	Alice (Jones) Dawson
John Jones, Jr.	John Jones, Jr.
Nancy (Ames) Jones	Nancy (Ames) Jones
Frank Jones	Frank Jones
Allen Dawson	Allen Dawson
Audrey Dawson	Audrey Dawson
Carl Jones	Carl Jones
Sue (Ross) Jones	Sue (Ross) Jones
Keith Jones	Keith Jones

Another way to give the relation "is a son of" is to list the pairs that are related. Using this method, the relation "is a son of" includes the following pairs:

(John Jones, Jr., John Jones)   (Allen Dawson, Alice Dawson)
(John Jones, Jr., Sally Jones)   (Carl Jones, John Jones, Jr.)
(Frank Jones, John Jones)   (Carl Jones, Nancy Jones)
(Frank Jones, Sally Jones)   (Keith Jones, Carl Jones)
(Allen Dawson, Bob Dawson)   (Keith Jones, Sue Jones)

1. Consider the relation "is a daughter of." Is the pair (Audrey Dawson, Alice Dawson) included in this relation? Is the pair (Alice Dawson, Audrey Dawson) included in this relation? Why wasn't (John Jones, Frank Jones) included in the relation "is a son of"?

   So far, all the relations that have been given have consisted of pairs of elements from the same set. This does not always have to be the case; for instance, the relation "is the birth month of" relates months of the year to members of the Jones family.

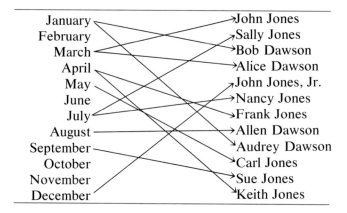

2. Two of the following pairs are not included in the relation "is the birth month of": (January, Bob Dawson), (January, Audrey Dawson), (Frank Jones; April), (July, Alice Dawson). Which pairs are they?

3. Each of the examples below gives pairs that are included in some relation. Give a rule or phrase that describes each relation and list two more pairs that could be included in each relation.

   a. (Springfield, Illinois), (Montgomery, Alabama), (Denver, Colorado), (Juneau, Alaska),

   b. (A, a), (B, b), (C, c), (D, d),

   c. (Ford, Rockefeller), (Johnson, Humphrey), (Kennedy, Johnson), (Eisenhower, Nixon),

   d. $(32°, 0°)$, $(212°, 100°)$, $(0°, -17.778°)$, $(98.6°, 37°)$, $(-40°, -40°)$,

e. (1 inch, 2.54 cm.), (1 yard, .91 meter), (1 mile, 1.6 kilometers), (1 quart, .95 liter), 1 ounce, 28.35 grams), (1 pound, .45 kilogram),

f. (1, 1), (2, 4), (3, 9), (4, 16),

g. (3 pencils, 10¢), (12 pencils, 40¢),

Why shouldn't (Arizona, Phoenix) be included in the relation that is given in example *a*?

Definition of a Relation: If *D* and *R* are two sets, then a *relation* that associates elements in *D* to elements in *R* is a set of *ordered pairs (d, r)* where *d* is an element from the set *D* and *r* is an element from the set *R*.

The term *ordered pairs* is used because the order in which the elements are listed is important. The elements in the set *D* that are related to something in *R* are called the "domain of the relation," and the elements in *R* to which elements in the domain are assigned are called the "range of the relation."

4. What is the domain and range of each of the relations given in examples *a* to *g* in exercise 3? List three examples in which the domain and range are elements of the same set.

5. a. In alphabetical order, list the names of all of the people in your class. Instruct everyone to point to the person whose name immediately follows his own in the list. One person in the class will not point to anyone. Who is it? Will everyone in the class have someone pointing to him?

b. A diagram of the relation "is listed (alphabetically) immediately before" could be made by drawing arrows between people who are alphabetically related. Ask all the people who are in the domain of the relation to raise their hands. Who is not in the domain? Who is not in the range?

c. Write out another relation that can be defined using people in your class as both the domain and range.

6. a. In problem 5 above, the relation "is listed (alphabetically) immediately before" is easy to describe, and this relation is also easy to define by listing pairs of people who are related by the relation. However, it is sometimes very difficult to describe relations that are quite easy to define by listing pairs of elements. For some examples, ask each person in your class to write his or her name on a slip of paper and to put the paper into a box. A relation can be defined by drawing out pairs of names at random. For instance, if the pair (Bob White, Jean Cox) is selected, then Bob White will be considered to be related to Jean Cox. After 10 pairs have been drawn, try to think of a way to describe the relation.

b. Think of another relation that is difficult to describe but is easy to define by listing pairs of elements. Define the relation.

c. Think of a relation that is easy to describe but difficult (or impossible) to define by listing pairs of elements. Describe the relation.

d. Is it possible to list all the pairs of elements that are in the relation "is the star whose distance from the earth is"?

2.4 STRUCTURAL PROPERTIES OF RELATIONS

Overview: **This section will discuss three properties which are used to describe and distinguish between different types of relations. These properties are the *reflexive property*, the *symmetric property*, and the *transitive property*. The relations that will be considered in this section will have the same set as both the domain and range.**

In the first two sections of this chapter, you considered six different relations that exist between members of the Jones family: "is the father of," "is the mother of," "is a brother of," "is a sister of," "is a sibling of," and "is a son of." Think of five more examples that could have been given, and list them.

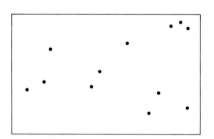
"Has the same last name as"

1. Fill in the arrows in the diagram to illustrate the relation "has the same last name as." Don't forget to include the fact that each person has the same last name as himself.

The Reflexive Property: Whenever each member of the domain is related to itself, the relation satisfies the reflexive property.

2. The relation "is the husband of" is not reflexive because Bob Dawson is not the husband of Bob Dawson. Is the relation "has the same last name as" reflexive?

The Symmetric Property: A relation is symmetric if whenever *a* is related to *b*, it is also true that *b* is related to *a*.

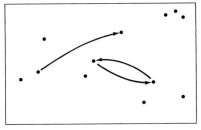

The R relation

The relation "is a brother of" is not symmetric since Allen "is the brother of" Audrey, but Audrey is not the brother of Allen.

3. Another relation, R, that could have been given is shown in the diagram at the left. Without even knowing what the relation is, it is possible to tell whether R is symmetric by just looking at the diagram. Is R symmetric? How do you know? Is the relation "has the same last name as" symmetric?

The Transitive Property: A relation is transitive if whenever a "is related to" b and b "is related to" c, it is always true that a "is related to" c.

The relation "is the father of" is not transitive because even though John Jones, Jr., "is the father of" Carl Jones, and Carl Jones "is the father of" Keith Jones, it is *not* true that John Jones, Jr., "is the father of" Keith Jones.

4. Two other relations that could have been given are shown in the diagrams below. Explain why each of the relations is not transitive.

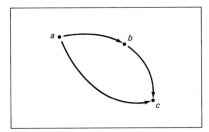

A transitive relation

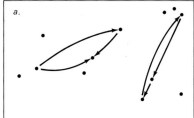
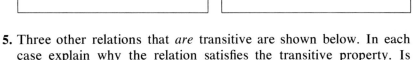

5. Three other relations that *are* transitive are shown below. In each case explain why the relation satisfies the transitive property. Is the relation "has the same last name as" transitive?

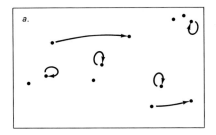
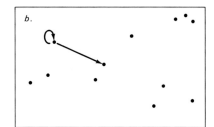
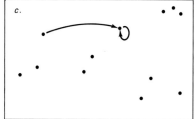

6. In the table on p. 504, the relations that are given refer to the Jones family. For each relation, record whether the relation satisfies

the reflexive property, the symmetric property, and the transitive property. The relation "has the same last name as" has been completed for you. The correct answers are given in exercise 7.)

	Reflexive	Symmetric	Transitive
a. "Has the same last name as"	Yes	Yes	Yes
b. "Was born less than a year apart from"			
c. "Is not older than"			
d. "Is not named Jones, and neither is"[1]			
e. "Is younger than the mother of"			
f. "Is a brother or sister of"			
g. "Is older than"			
h. "Is the father of"			

7. In the table below, each of the relations that is given refers to a pair of integers. Remember that the integers include the positive and negative counting numbers and zero. Use the table below to record whether each relation satisfies the reflexive property, the symmetric property, and the transitive property. The correct answers correspond to the answers in exercise 6. Notice that examples have been given of relations satisfying every possible combination of these three properties.

	Reflexive	Symmetric	Transitive
a. $y = x$			
b. $\|y - x\| < 5$			
c. $y \geqslant x$			
d. $x \times y = 0$			
e. $y - x < 5$			
f. $y \neq x$			
g. $y > x$			
h. $y = x + 1$			

*8. A relation that can be defined on a set of colored rods is "is the same color as." "Is the same color as" is reflexive, symmetric, and transitive. In the table on p. 505, give appropriate examples that can be

[1] Notice that for a relation to be reflexive each and every member of the domain must be related to itself.

defined on a set of colored rods. For example, on line 2 of the table you should list a relation that is reflexive and symmetric but not transitive. For some hints, look at the tables in exercises 6 and 7.

	Reflexive	Symmetric	Transitive
a. "Is the same color as"	Yes	Yes	Yes
b.	Yes	Yes	No
c.	Yes	No	Yes
d.	No	Yes	Yes
e.	Yes	No	No
f.	No	Yes	No
g.	No	No	Yes
h.	No	No	No

2.5
INVERSES

***Overview:* This section will investigate the properties of some pairs of *inverse relations*.**

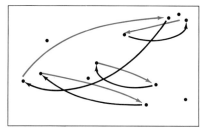

In the diagram to the left, the black arrows show the relation "is the husband of" and the blue arrows show the relation "is the wife of." The relation "is the husband of" is the *inverse* of the relation "is the wife of" because whenever a person *x* is related to a person *y* by the relation "is the wife of," *y* is related to *x* by the relation "is the husband of." The inverse relationship between these two relations is obvious from the diagram since the blue arrows connect the same pairs as the black arrows (but the blue arrows point in the opposite direction).

1. In the Jones family is the relation "is a sister of" the inverse of the relation "is a brother of?"

In the diagram to the left the black arrows show the relation "is a brother of." The blue arrows show the relation "is a sister of." If a black arrow goes from some point p_1 to another point p_2, is there always a blue arrow going from p_2 back to p_1?

2. Explain why "is the father of" and "is a son of" are not inverses.

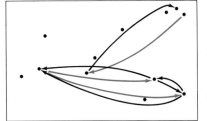

3. Are the relations "is a factor of" and "is a multiple of" inverse relations? Why or why not?

4. Use the set of positive integers as the domain, and determine whether the relations "is the square root of" and "is the square of" are inverses. What happens if the domain includes all the integers?

5. Is it possible for a relation to be its own inverse? "Is parallel to" and "is the same age as" are two examples. Name three others.

6. Will a symmetric relation always be its own inverse?

7. What is the inverse of "is older than?" What is the inverse of "is the author of?"

8. What is the inverse of each of the following relations?[2]

Relation	Inverse Relation
a. $y = x + 1$	$x = y - 1$
b. $y > x$	
c. $y \geqslant x$	
d. $y = x$	
e. $y \neq x$	
f. $x \times y \neq 0$	
g. $|y - x| < 5$	
h. $y < 5 + x$	

2.6
REVIEWING
SOME PROPERTIES

Overview: In the previous sections of this unit the focus was on relations between people and relations between objects. This section will emphasize mathematical relations and will review some of the properties of relations which were presented in sections 2.4 and 2.5.

2.6.1
"Is a
divisor of"

a. Use this figure to draw an arrow diagram of the relation D, "is a divisor of." Is D reflexive? If so, don't forget to indicate this fact in your arrow diagram. Is D symmetric? Is D transitive?

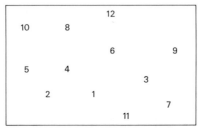

"Is a divisor of"

---

[2] **a.** $x = y - 1$, **b.** $x < y$, **c.** $x \leqslant y$, **d.** $x = y$, **e.** $x \neq y$, **f.** $x \times y \neq 0$, **g.** $|y - x| < 5$, **h.** $x > y - 5$.

b. Use this figure to draw an arrow diagram of the relation M, "is a multiple of." Is M reflexive? Symmetric? Transitive? What relationship exists between the relation D and the relation M?

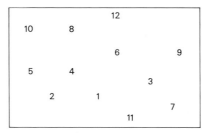

"Is a multiple of"

2.6.2

"Is a subset of"

Using a deck of playing cards, identify each of the sets in this figure. Draw in the arrows to illustrate the relation C, "is a subset of." Don't forget to include these facts:

a. Every set is a subset of itself.

b. Every set is a subset of the universal set. (The universal set is the whole deck of playing cards.)

c. The empty set is a subset of every other set.

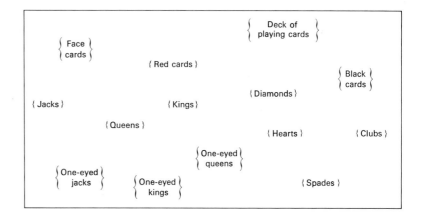

Is C symmetric? Is it transitive? What is the inverse of C?

2.6.3

"Is relatively prime to"

a. Consider the relation P, "is relatively prime to," as it relates to the set $\{0, 1, 2, 3, 4, 5, 6\}$. Remember that a number m "is relatively prime to" a number n if m has no common factors (except 1) with n. Is the relation P reflexive? Symmetric? Transitive? What relation is inverse to P?

b. In which of these fractions are the numerator and denominator relatively prime?

(1) $\frac{2}{3}$ (2) $\frac{15}{18}$ (3) $\frac{3}{24}$ (4) $\frac{10}{11}$ (5) $\frac{10}{26}$

c. Which of the above fractions are reduced to lowest terms? What does the relation "is relatively prime to" have to do with reducing fractions to lowest terms?

2.7
EQUIVALENCE
RELATIONS

Overview: The notion of equivalence is more general than the idea of equality (in the sense of two things being *exactly* the same, or identical). This section will present several examples of *equivalence relations* in mathematics, and will introduce the notion of *equivalence classes.*

In order to travel from your home to a grocery store there are many possible paths to take; and in a certain sense, all these paths are equivalent because they all start and end at the same point. However, the paths are not all *exactly* the same. Some paths are much longer; some are not as convenient to use in certain situations.

The most obvious example of an equivalence relation is "is equal to," but several other equivalence relations have been mentioned throughout this book. For example:

a. If their elements can be paired in a one-to-one fashion, a set of bowling balls may be considered to be equivalent to a set of watermelons even though the two sets are by no means identical.

b. In order to calculate $274 - 127 = \square$, it is useful to know that $(2 \times 100) + (7 \times 10) + 4$ is equivalent to $(2 \times 100) + (6 \times 10) + 14$. Why?

Notice that the equals sign in the equation $(2 \times 100) + (7 \times 10) + 4 = 274$ is used in a slightly different sense than the equal sign in the equation $(2 \times 100) + (7 \times 10) + 4 = (2 \times 100) + (6 \times 10) + 14$. Also notice that the expression $(2 \times 100) + (7 \times 10) + 4$ and the expression $(2 \times 100) + (6 \times 10) + 14$ are each convenient to use in different situations. How is this situation similar to the example at the beginning of this section about "equivalent" paths from your home to a grocery store?

c. In order to calculate $\frac{1}{2} + \frac{1}{6} = \square$, it is useful to know that $\frac{1}{2}$ and $\frac{3}{6}$ are equivalent ways to express the same fraction. Why?

Notice that even though 1 is equivalent to $\frac{6}{6}$, one whole puzzle may be quite different from 6 sixths of a puzzle. Can you think of some other examples like this?

d. In order to use a Hassler-Whitney minicomputer to calculate $43 + 28$, the following equivalences are used:

$$3 + 8 = 2 + 9 = 1 + 10 = 0 + 11$$
$$40 + 20 + 10 = 50 + 20 + 0 = 60 + 10 + 0 = 70 + 0 + 0$$

See Part B, section 1.4.12, for an explanation of the minicomputer. Subtraction problems on the minicomputer also depend on equivalence relations. Use the computer to calculate $43 - 28$, and then describe why the computer calculations worked (see Part B, section 2.4.8).

Examples a, b, and c above illustrate that the notion of equivalence is a more general idea than the idea of equality. A general definition of equivalence is given below.

Equivalence Relation: If a relation is reflexive, symmetric, and transitive, then it is an *equivalence* relation.

Using the above definition, some other examples of equivalence relations are: "is congruent to," "has the same area as," "has the same last name as," and (from the unit about operations) "is isomorphic to." Think of three other examples.

2.7.1
Equivalence Classes

1. What equivalence relation describes all of the numbers connected by blue arrows in this diagram?

When an equivalence relation is defined on a set, the relation divides the set into smaller "equivalence classes" of related elements. For instance, in the above example the complicated sounding equivalence relation "is a multiple of 2 different from" divides the counting numbers into two equivalence classes: the odd numbers and the even numbers. However, as this example shows, it is sometimes easier to describe the equivalence classes which are formed than it is to describe the relation. Some other examples in which this occurs will be given.

The number lines a to l below focus on the rational numbers between 0 and 1. Number line b has been divided in half, number line c has been divided into three equal parts, and number line *d* has been divided into four equal parts.

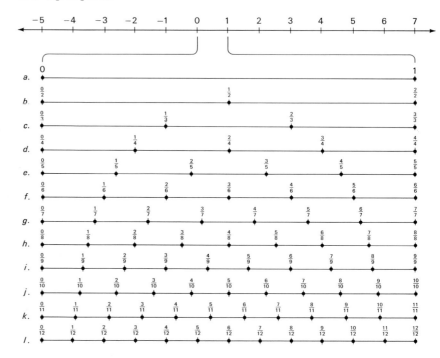

2. a. Let *E* be the relation "represents the same point on the number line as." In exercise 1, for instance, ²/₄ represents the same point on the number line as 1/2. Looking at the number lines in exercise 1, list some other numbers that are *E*-related to ²/₆, to ⁶/₈, and to ⁵/₇.

Without simply saying "equivalent fractions," can you think of another way to describe the relation "represents the same point of the number line as"? (One answer can be found in the footnote.[3])

b. Is *E* reflexive? Symmetric? Transitive?

3. a. List some numbers that are *E*-related to ³/₇. List some numbers that are *E*-related to ⁹/₂₁. Compare your two lists. What can you conclude?

b. If a number is *E*-related to ²/₃, is it always *E*-related to ⁶/₉? Why?

---

[3] *a/b* "is equivalent to" *c/d* whenever $a \times d = b \times c$.

c. Could you ever find a number that is E-related to both $\frac{4}{7}$ and $\frac{5}{9}$? How do you know for sure?

Since E is an equivalence relation, all the numbers that are E-related to a particular number form a set that is called the "equivalence class of that number under the relation E." For instance, the equivalence class of $\frac{1}{2}$ (under the relation E) is:

$$\frac{1}{2} = \{\frac{1}{2}, \frac{2}{4}, \frac{3}{6}, \frac{4}{8}, \frac{5}{10}, \frac{6}{12}, \ldots\}$$

Exercise 3 illustrates that (1) when two numbers are E-related, their equivalence classes are exactly the same and (2) when two numbers are not E-related, their equivalence classes do not intersect. In fact, *every* equivalence relation (every relation that is reflexive, symmetric, and transitive) divides its domain into equivalence classes that do not intersect.

4. List three more equivalence relations and name the equivalence classes that are formed using each relation. [Hint: Look at some of the relations that have been given in this unit (e.g., relations between people, between sets, between numbers, between algebraic expressions).]

*2.7.2
Activity

1. From the members of your mathematics class, designate one person as the leader. The leader should think of an equivalence relation, and divide the class into groups of people who are related (for example, is wearing the same color shirt as). The first person in the class to guess the relation becomes the new leader.

2. Randomly divide the class into five groups. These five groups are equivalence classes for some relation. What is the relation?[4]

2.8
FUNCTIONS

Overview: In the previous sections, some relations have had their domain and range in the same set, and others have described connections between elements in two different sets.

A *function* is a special kind of relation in which *every* element in the domain is assigned to *something* in the range, and in which *every* element in the domain is assigned to *only one* element in the range.

[4] "Is in the same group as."

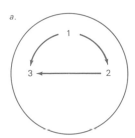

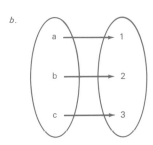

In order to introduce the idea of functions, the section will begin by classifying relations according to whether they are *one-to-one, one-to-many, many-to-one,* or *many-to-many.*

2.8.1
One-to-one,
one-to-many, many-to-one,
and many-to-many relations

1. Draw arrows to illustrate each of the following four relations.

(1) "Is a divisor of"		(2) "Is one more than"		(3) "Is a number whose last digit is"		(4) "Is the number of digits of"[a]	
12	12	12	12	12	12	12	12
11	11	11	11	11	11	11	11
10	10	10	10	10	10	10	10
9	9	9	9	9	9	9	9
8	8	8	8	8	8	8	8
7	7	7	7	7	7	7	7
6	6	6	6	6	6	6	6
5	5	5	5	5	5	5	5
4	4	4	4	4	4	4	4
3	3	3	3	3	3	3	3
2	2	2	2	2	2	2	2
1	1	1	1	1	1	1	1

[a] Note: The domain of this relation only includes two elements.

One of the above relations is one-to-one, one is one-to-many, one is many-to-many, and one is many-to-one. Which is which? After you answer this question, read the footnote.[5]

2. Using the diagram on p. 513, draw arrows to illustrate the relation "is the square root of." Is this relation one-to-one, one-to-many, many-to-many, or many-to-one?

---

[5] The examples below illustrate four different types of relations between elements in the set {a,

"Is the square root of"	
5	5
4	4
3	3
2	2
1	1
0	0
−1	−1
−2	−2
−3	−3
−4	−4
−5	−5

3. Write down a relation about the Jones family that is one-to-one. Write down a relation that is one-to-many, another that is many-to-one, and another that is many-to-many.

4. One-to-one relations are sometimes called one-to-one correspondences. Counting involves making a one-to-one correspondence between a set of objects and a set of counting numbers. Write three more *mathematical* relations that are one-to-one.

5. Look at the pairs of numbers below, and then list some more pairs of numbers that should be included in the relation "is the area of the circle whose radius is."

(3.14, 1)   (12.56, 2)   (28.63, 3)

6. If the domain is the set of students at a given university, and the range is the set of seats in the football stadium, season tickets to football games can assign students to seats according to a relation that is one-to-one, many-to-one, or many-to-many. Think of a method for assigning seats to illustrate each of these three types of relations, and write down descriptions of the three methods.

b, c, d} and elements in the set {1, 2, 3, 4}. What is the domain and range of each relation?

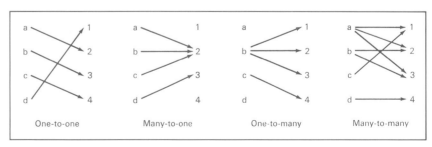

7. In order to enable people to find books in libraries, a relation has been established between a set of reference cards and the location of the books in the library. In your library is this relation one-to-one, one-to-many, many-to-many, or many-to-one? Can you think of libraries where each of these situations could occur?

2.8.2
Functions

In some situations, it is important for every element in the domain to be assigned to some element in the range. For example, every book must be assigned to at least one author by the relation "is the book written by." Think of three more examples of relations in which every element of the domain is assigned to at least one element of the range, and write them down.

In addition to the stipulation that every element in the domain should be assigned to at least one element in the range, it is sometimes important that *only one* element in the range should be assigned to each element in the domain. Three examples are given.

1. "Lives at the address"

Mary Moore ⟶ 12 Maple Street
David Moore ⟶
Cindy Moore ⟶
Alice Johnson ⟶ 13 Maple Street
Sandy Sacks ⟶
Bob Sacks ⟶ 14 Maple Street

2. "Rounds off to"

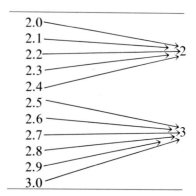

2.0
2.1
2.2 ⟶ 2
2.3
2.4
2.5
2.6
2.7 ⟶ 3
2.8
2.9
3.0

3. "Is the social security number of"

1234-12-8401 $\longrightarrow$ R. Singer
1234-12-8402 $\longrightarrow$ A. Mitchell
1234-12-8403 $\longrightarrow$ W. Sanders
1234-12-8404 $\longrightarrow$ L. Cascino
1234-12-8405 $\longrightarrow$ R. Rodger

Give three examples of relations where it is important that only one element from the range be assigned to each element of the domain.

2.8.3
Function
Machines

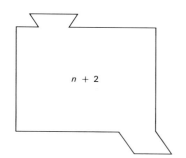

1. Imagine that you are operating an "$n + 2$" machine. When five pieces of paper are put in, seven come out. What will a "$3n$" machine do to an input of four pieces of paper? What will an "n^2" machine do to an input of four pieces of paper?

2. What kind of machine could give each of the following sets of "input-output" pairs?

a. $\{(3, 24), (6, 48), (1, 8), (0, 0), (14, 112)\}$

b. $\{(5, -1), (10, 4), (3, -3), (100, 94)\}$

c. $\{(2, 5), (7, 50), (5, 26), (1, 2)\}$

d. $\{(1, 1), (5, 120), (2, 2), (4, 24), (3, 36)\}$

Definition of a function: A *function* is a relation in which *each* element of the domain is paired with one, and only one, element of the range.

3. Can a one-to-many relation be a function? How about a many-to-one relation? One-to-one? Many-to-many?

4. Below are five examples of relations between the set $\{a, b, c, d\}$ and the set $\{1, 2, 3, 4, 5\}$. Which of the examples are functions? (Draw an arrow diagram if it helps.)

a. (a, 1), (a, 2), (b, 3), (c, 4), (d, 5)
b. (a, 1), (b, 3), (c, 4), (d, 2)
c. (a, 2), (b, 2), (c, 3), (d, 3)
d. (a, 1), (d, 5)
e. (a, 1), (b, 3), (c, 5), (c, 3), (d, 1), (d, 4), (d, 5)

5. Not all machines must have a unique output for every element that is processed. For instance, here are some machines that are not function machines. What will each of these machines do to an input of twelve sheets of paper? Is there more than one possible output?

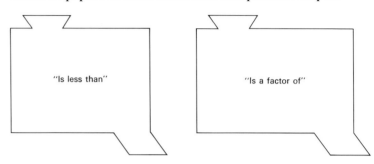

In order for a machine to be a *function* machine, two things must be true:

a. Every input should result in *some* output.
b. Every input should result in only *one* output.

2.8.4
A Function Machine Game The following game can be played by a group of three to five people. One person should be selected as the machine operator. Other members of the group should try to guess the relation that the machine is using. Clues are given as indicated below.

1. When the input is 1, the output is 1.
2. When the input is 2, the output is 2.
3. When the input is 3, the output is 3.
4. When the input is 4, the output is 5.

As soon as someone in the group can guess the relation, he or she becomes the new machine operator. People who make incorrect guesses are eliminated for the round.

For the above relation, the input-output pairs continued as follows:

5. When the input is 5, the output is 7.
6. When the input is 6, the output is 11.
7. When the input is 7, the output is 13.

Can you guess the relation?

To start the game, some suggested relations are given in the table below. Make a copy of the table, and cut the relations into individual strips. Individual strips can be drawn from a hat by the machine operator. After the group has played several rounds, the machine operators can be allowed to make up their own relations. To add another dimension, the group can be allowed to call out the input for each clue.

$y = 5 - x$	1	2	3	4	5	6		
	↓	↓	↓	↓	↓	↓		
	4	3	2	1	0	−1		

$y = x^2$	1	2	3	4	5	6		
	↓	↓	↓	↓	↓	↓		
	1	4	9	16	25	36		

$n!$	1	2	3	4	5	6		
	↓	↓	↓	↓	↓	↓		
	1	2	6	24	120	720		

Evens $y = 2x$	1	2	3	4				
	↓	↓	↓	↓				
	2	4	6	8				

Odds $y = 2x - 1$	1	2	3	4				
	↓	↓	↓	↓				
	1	3	5	7				

$y = \dfrac{x(x-1)}{2}$	1	2	3	4	5	6		
	↓	↓	↓	↓	↓	↓		
	0	1	3	6	10	15		

$y = 7x + 1$	1	2	3	4	5			
	↓	↓	↓	↓	↓			
	8	15	22	29	36			

Primes	1	2	3	4	5	6	7	8
	↓	↓	↓	↓	↓	↓	↓	↓
	1	2	3	5	7	11	13	17

Primes squared	1	2	3	4	5	6	7	
	↓	↓	↓	↓	↓	↓	↓	
	1	4	9	25	49	121	169	

$y = x^3$	1	2	3	4	5			
	↓	↓	↓	↓	↓			
	1	8	27	64	125			

$y = x^2 + 1$	1	2	3	4				
	↓	↓	↓	↓				
	2	5	10	17				

*2.8.5

Problems

1. A boy says, "I have as many brothers as sisters." His sister says, "I have twice as many brothers as sisters." How many brothers and sisters are in the family?

2. An equation-guessing trick: Ask a friend to make up a secret equation of the type $y = ax^2 + bx + c$ by choosing numbers for a, b, and c. The numbers can be positive, negative, or zero, but you should not be allowed to see them. After the numbers have been chosen, you can guess the equation if your friend tells you just three things: what the equation equals when $x = 0$, when $x = 1$, and when $x = 2$. Be sure you get the answers in that order.

For example, if the secret equation is $y = 2x^2 - 10x + 15$, your friend will answer 15, 7, and 3.

To guess the secret equation, write down (in a row) the three numbers 15, 7, and 3. Then find the differences between adjacent pairs of numbers. For example:

Next, find the difference between the two numbers in the second row. The numbers a, b, and c can be found using the circled numbers in the following diagram.

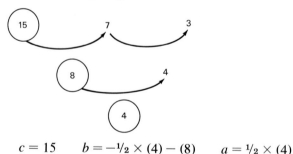

$$c = 15 \qquad b = -\tfrac{1}{2} \times (4) - (8) \qquad a = \tfrac{1}{2} \times (4)$$

Try the guessing game several times.

A similar method can be used to guess equations of the form $y = ax^3 + bx^2 + cx + d$. See if you can find a way to guess third-degree equations.

2.9

FROM RELATIONS TO COORDINATE GRAPHS

Overview: **In this unit, relations have been defined by listing ordered pairs of related elements, and relations have been described using arrow diagrams. This section will show how arrow diagrams and ordered pairs can be converted into rectangular coordinate graphs.**

Here is a relation between elements in the set {0, 1, 2, 3, 4, 5, 6, 7, 8, 9}.

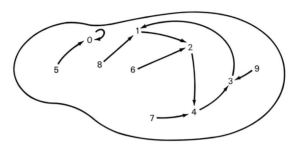

Writing the situation in two parallel lines, this relation can be represented as shown below.

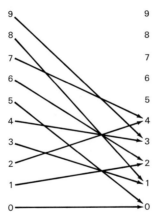

Another way to draw the arrow diagram is to use one vertical row and one horizontal row.

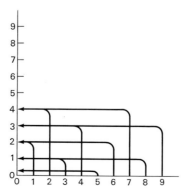

To make the diagram easier to read, the arrows can be omitted so that
only the turning points remain.

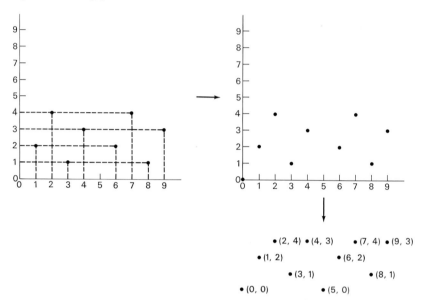

The graph on the right (above) is very similar to listing the pairs of elements that are related.

1. a. Use the graph below to plot the relation that includes the following
pairs of numbers: (0, 5), (1, 4), (2, 3), (3, 2), (4, 1), (5, 0), (6, 1), (7,
2), (8, 3), (9, 4), (1, 6), (2, 7), (3, 8), (4, 9).

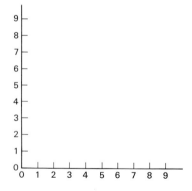

b. Is this relation reflexive? Can you tell just by looking at the graph?

c. Is this relation symmetric? Can you tell just by looking at the
graph?

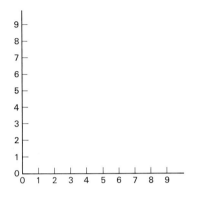

d. Is this relation transitive?

e. Is it one-to-one, one-to-many, many-to-one, or many-to-many?

2. Here are some clues about another relation.

    a. The relation is reflexive.
    b. The relation includes the pairs (4, 1) and (1, 3).
    c. The relation is symmetric.
    d. The relation is transitive.

If you only plot points that are necessary in order to satisfy the above conditions, what does the graph of the relation look like?

3. Sketch a graph of the inverse of each of the relations given below. Remember that if 4 is related to 3 under a given relation, then 3 must be related to 4 under its inverse. Therefore, if (4, 3) is included in a given operation, then (3, 4) must be included in its inverse.

a.
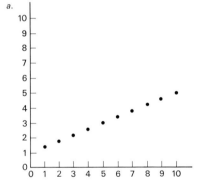

b.
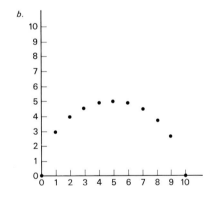

c.
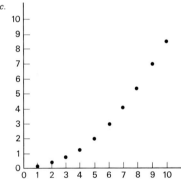

a.
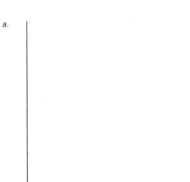

b.

c.

4. Graphs have the advantage of being able to illustrate more pairs of numbers than it would be possible to list. For example, consider the following three relations.

a.

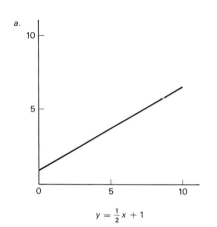

$$y = \frac{1}{2}x + 1$$

b.

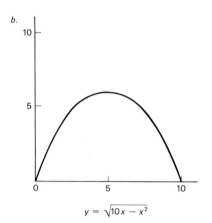

$$y = \sqrt{10x - x^2}$$

c.

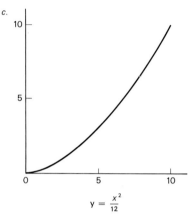

$$y = \frac{x^2}{12}$$

List five pairs of numbers that are included in each of the above three relations.

Plot a graph of the inverse of each of the above relations.

a.

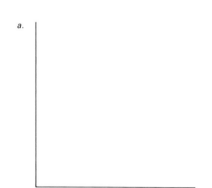

b.

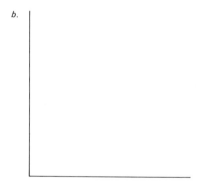

c.

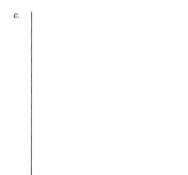

Plot a graph of the inverse of the four relations given below. For each of the four relations, determine whether the relation is reflexive, symmetric, transitive, one-to-one, one-to-many, many-to-one, or many-to-many. Which of the relations are functions? Are any of the relations equivalence relations?

The subject of coordinate graphs will occur again in the unit dealing with graphing (Unit 3). The emphasis of the graphing unit will be on the graphs themselves rather than on the relations illustrated in the graphs. However, the graphing unit should reemphasize the many different types

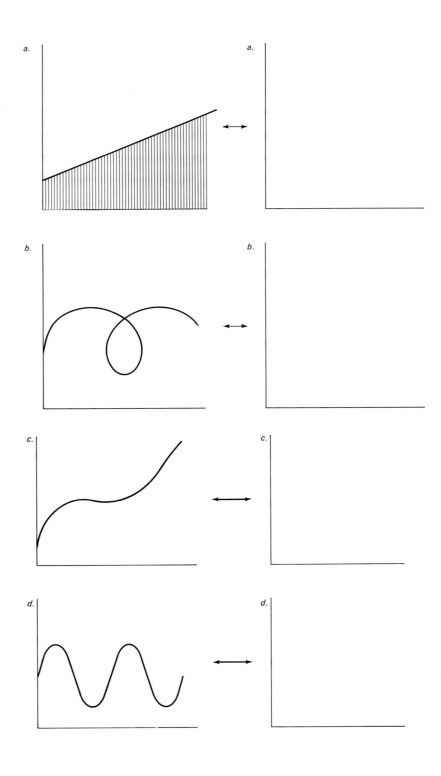

of relations that occur in elementary school mathematics and in everyday situations.

2.10 PEDAGOGICAL REMARKS

Algebraic systems are created by taking a set of elements, together with some operations and relations defined on the set, and adding some rules that tell how the operations and relations work. Consequently, relations are fundamental building blocks for modern mathematics. In fact, even operations can be considered to be special types of relations. For instance, addition can be considered to be a relation that associates a number (i.e., the sum) with any pair of numbers that are given (i.e., the addends). Nonetheless, many elementary school textbooks attempt to deemphasize relations. This deemphasis results from the fact that children can be taught to work with equals ($=$), less than ($<$), and other mathematical relations without explicitly dealing with these concepts as relations. However, many other people believe that relations are very helpful in introducing a wide variety of mathematical topics.

Georges Papy and Frederique Papy have developed a number of fascinating techniques in which arrow diagrams (somewhat like the ones about the Jones family earlier in this unit) and other concrete relations can be used to introduce mathematical ideas to young children. One of the keys to the Papy approach is to lead children gradually from concrete situations involving common objects and familiar ideas to progressively more abstract ideas. Two books filled with specific classroom examples (including accounts of children's responses to questions) of teaching techniques using manipulative materials and colored graphs are *Mathematics and the Child* by Dr. Frederique Papy,[1] and *Graphs and the Child* by Frederique Papy and Georges Papy.[2]

[1] Algonquin Publishing, Inc., Montreal, 1971.
[2] Algonquin Publishing, Inc., Montreal, 1970.

unit 3
displaying information with graphs

3.1
INTRODUCTION
Graphs have been used throughout this book. For instance, in Unit 2, each of the following three types of graphs were used. In Unit 2 the emphasis was on *using* graphs to study other topics. In this unit, graphs will be studied for their own sake.

The Relation "Is a Divisor Of"

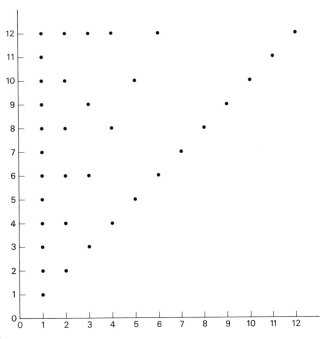

The Relation "Is a Divisor Of"

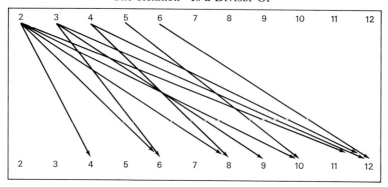 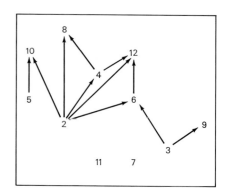

Because the word *graph* is used in so many different ways, it is difficult to describe what kinds of things should be called graphs. For example, a teacher may find the following types of graphs in school books.

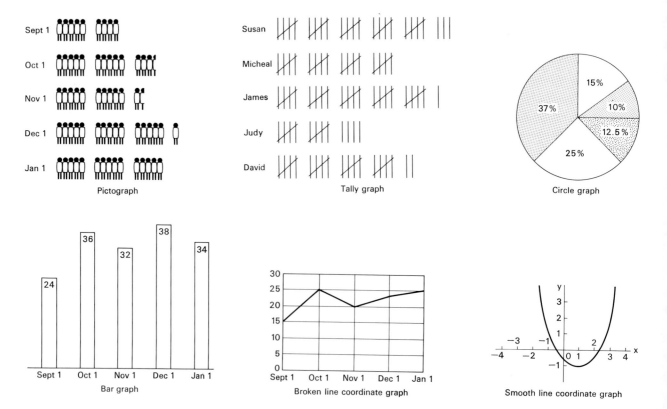

Because graphs can simply and concisely organize quantities of information that might otherwise have been unmanageable, they emphasize important relationships and provide an efficient means of helping people analyze data and form generalizations. In elementary school, for instance, graphs can be used to help children see important number relationships, and can provide useful intermediate links between mathematical ideas and the real world.

Number Relationships

"Plus 2"

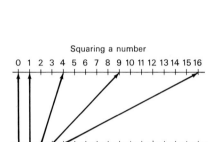

Squaring a number

"Multiplied by 2"

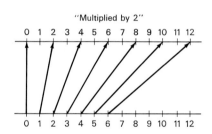

Adding to make 10

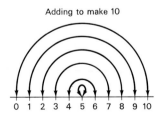

The Prime Numbers

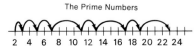

Links between Mathematical Ideas and the Real World

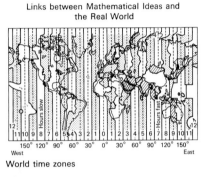

World time zones

Hours of Daylight

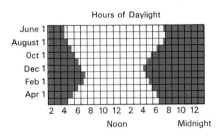

Noon   Midnight

The changing pyramid of income distribution

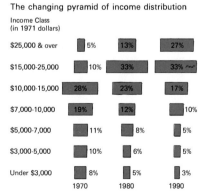

Knitting directions

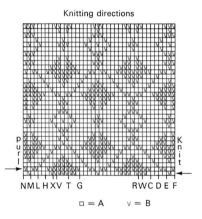

□ = A   v = B

The normal electrocardiogram.

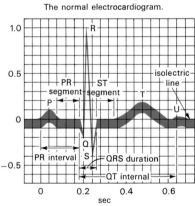

Crouch & McClintic;
Source: Human Anatomy & Physiology

Graphs are used in newspapers, in magazines, and on television. Though they are most often used to communicate information in a clear and simple way, they can also be misleading. For this reason it is important for the educated citizen to learn to analyze and interpret graphs critically.

Study the pairs of graphs shown below. In each case determine how the two graphs are similar and how they are different. Decide whether one or both of the graphs may be misleading.

Graphs of unemployment figures.

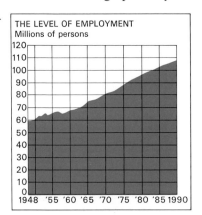

Advertisement for chewing gum.

The number of children with birthdays during school vacations.

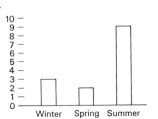

The number of packages of notebook paper sold in our school store in one week.

Heights of players on the eighth grade basketball team.

f. Percent of students who stay for after school activities.

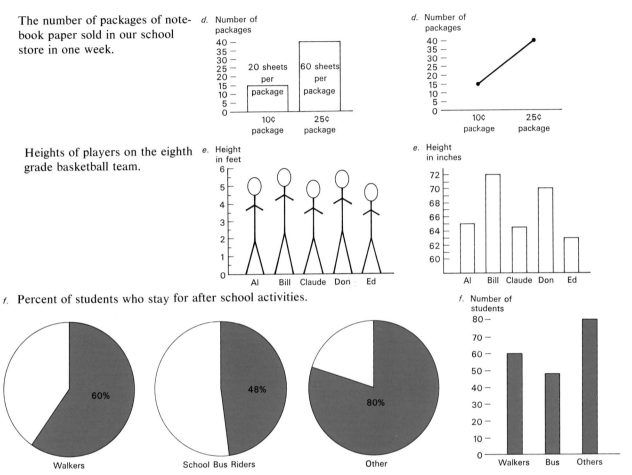

In this unit, you will investigate some properties of several different kinds of graphs. You will evaluate some misleading graphs, make predictions based on information given in graphs, and select and draw graphs appropriate for various types of information. At the end of the unit, several kinds of coordinate graphs will be considered.

Research Assignment: During the next three days, collect at least ten graphs from newspapers, magazines, or television. (Make sketches of the television graphs.) The graphs you collect can be used for class discussion. Try to collect different types of graphs, and pay particular attention to graphs that you believe may be misleading. Advertisements and political literature are especially good sources of misleading graphs. Do you think some of their graphs are biased? If so, try to find an example.

3.2
ORGANIZING
AND SIMPLIFYING
INFORMATION

Overview: **This section will give an example of a situation in which graphs can be useful to illustrate information that is given in a table of data.**

Even though a table of data may be filled with facts, it may not be the best way to communicate the information. Sometimes the quantity of data is too unmanageable to be useful, or the reader may have difficulty in distinguishing relevant from irrelevant information concerning a given issue. Organizing and simplifying data sometimes means that extraneous information must be omitted in order to focus on trends or relationships that might otherwise have been ignored.

3.2.1
Interpreting
Achievement Test Scores

1. Imagine that you are the freshman counselor at a high school, and that you have been given the achievement test scores in Table 3.1. Your school offers three tracks of math courses (track I, track II, and track III, which is an accelerated sequence). From looking at the information in Table 3.1, which of the youngsters would you recommend for each track? (Don't be surprised if you find this table of data confusing and not very helpful in answering the question. Do the best you can and as you continue with this section, you will find suggestions about how to simplify your work.)

In your school system, achievement tests are given each year in mathematics and in language arts. The scores are given in terms of grade level of achievement. For instance, in third grade Adam was

Table 3.1 **Math and Reading Achievement Test Scores (Recorded as grade level of achievement)**

	Third Grade		Fourth Grade		Fifth Grade		Sixth Grade		Seventh Grade		Eighth Grade	
	Math	Read-ing	Math	Read-ing	Math	Read-ing	Math	Read-ing	Math	Read-ing	Math	Read-ing
Adam	2.1	3.0	2.9	3.5	3.3	5.0	3.6	6.2	5.9	7.8	8.6	8.2
Bob	3.5	3.1	3.8	3.1	4.5	4.8	4.8	5.5	5.9	6.1	6.2	6.1
Carl	4.8	5.0	5.7	6.2	6.8	7.2	7.6	8.0	8.8	9.1	10.8	9.2
David	4.8	4.9	5.0	5.8	5.5	7.8	6.1	9.6	7.5	10.8	8.8	12.6
Edith	5.0	5.9	6.8	7.1	8.0	8.8	10.2	11.0	10.8	12.1	11.0	12.2
Fran	5.0	5.3	5.8	5.9	6.6	6.6	7.2	7.3	7.5	7.8	8.0	8.1
George	1.5	2.3	2.6	3.5	4.2	4.5	4.8	5.0	7.0	7.5	8.5	8.8
Hank							2.3	1.5	5.8	6.0	9.3	8.8
Ida	3.3	3.1	4.5	4.8	5.6	5.5	6.8	6.9	7.8	8.1	8.9	9.2
Jerry	5.6	5.1	7.9	7.0	9.0	7.5	9.6	8.0	10.8	8.3	9.1	7.8

Table 3.2 **Math Achievement Test Scores Compared to Grade Level of Student**

	Third Grade	**Fourth Grade**	**Fifth Grade**	**Sixth Grade**	**Seventh Grade**	**Eighth Grade**
Adam	−0.9	−1.1	−1.7	−2.4	−1.1	+0.6
Bob	+0.5	−0.2	−0.5	−1.2	−1.6	−1.8
Carl	+1.8	+1.7	+1.8	+1.6	+1.8	+2.8
David	+1.8	+1	+0.5	+0.1	+0.5	+0.8
Edith	+2	+2.8	+3	+4.2	+3.8	+3
Fran	+2	+1.8	+1.6	+1.2	+0.5	0
George	−1.5	−1.4	−0.8	−1.2	0	−0.5
Hank				−3.7	−1.2	+1.3
Ida	+0.3	+0.5	+0.6	+0.8	+0.8	−0.9
Jerry	+2.6	+3.9	+4	+3.6	+3.8	+1.1

doing mathematics at the second-grade level and reading at the third-grade level. Hank did not move into your school district until he was in the sixth grade, and so third-, fourth-, and fifth-grade achievement test scores are not available for him.

2. Because you are primarily interested in mathematics achievement scores, you might decide to make a new table (Table 3.2) that omits the reading scores for each student. To make Table 3.2 easier to read, you might decide to convert achievement grade level scores into scores that show the difference between actual grade level and achievement level. For example, if a student were in the fifth grade and his achievement grade level score were 6.8, then his new score would be +1.8.

Use the information in Table 3.2 to decide which youngsters you would recommend for each of the three tracks. Did you choose a cut-off point for placement in each track? Where did you place Hank and Jerry?

Who would you have recommended for each track if the only information available was the eighth-grade achievement test scores? Would any of your decisions have been different?

Who would you have recommended for each track if the only achievement test scores that were available were the seventh- and eighth-grade ones?

3. In order to further simplify the information in Table 3.2, a fellow counselor decided to plot a graph (Graph 3.1) showing the average differences between actual grade level and achievement level score for each youngster. For example, since Adam's scores were −0.9, −1.1, −1.7, −2.4, −1.1, and +0.6, his average score would be −1.1.

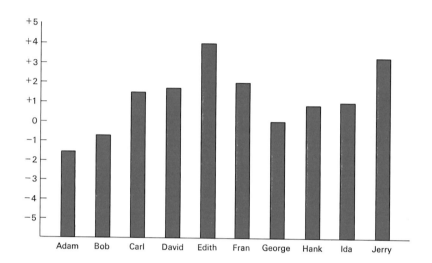

Graph 3.1

Using the information in Graph 3.1, which youngsters would you recommend for each of the three tracks? Did you change your mind concerning any of the students?

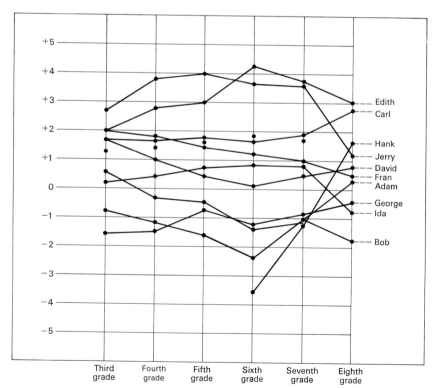

Graph 3.2

Perhaps you think that Graph 3.1 "lumped together" too much information; or perhaps you think that too much information was eliminated. What kind of graph would you have drawn?

Using the information in Table 3.1 or 3.2, draw a graph that might be helpful in selecting students for the three mathematics tracks.

4. Compare Graph 3.2 with the graph you drew in exercise 3. Would Graph 3.2 have led you to consider different information from that in your graph? What is your final decision concerning the placement of youngsters in the three mathematics tracks? Is there additional information that you would like to request before making your final recommendations?

3.3
SOME
COMMON GRAPHS AND
THEIR PROPERTIES

Overview: **Different types of graphs are best suited to describe certain kinds of information. In selecting an appropriate type of graph for emphasizing a particular trend or relationship, some factors to be considered are: how much, how accurately, how simply, and how effectively the information is communicated.**

In this section, you will investigate some properties of graphs that are commonly used to describe everyday situations.

---

1. How I Spend My Day

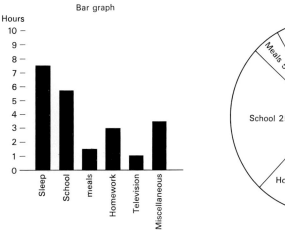
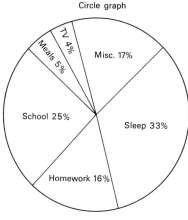

a. What is the single most noticeable fact in each graph? (This is sometimes the only fact that people notice when they read a graph.)

b. What similarities and differences do you see between the bar graph and the circle graph? What are the advantages and disadvantages of using each type of graph?

c. The circle graph emphasizes the relationship between parts and the whole. What does the bar graph emphasize?

2. Age Distribution of United States Population, 1900–1980

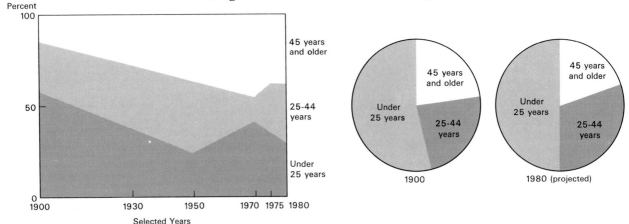

a. What general impressions are given by each of the two graphs above?

b. The purpose of some graphs is to show trends so that gaps in the data can be "filled in" or so that predictions can be made from the given information. What are the advantages and disadvantages of each of the two types of graphs above?

3. Number of Books Checked out from School Library by Each Child

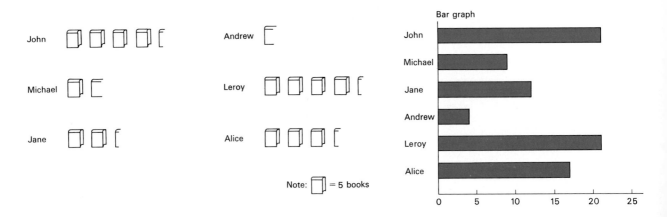

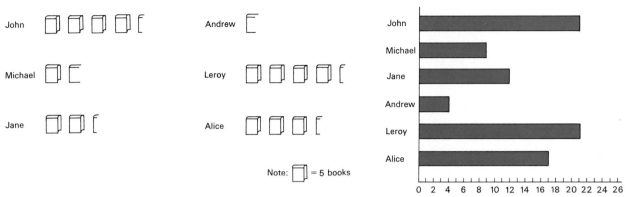

Note: ⬜ = 5 books

a. Sometimes the simplest graph is the best graph. Which of the above three graphs would be easiest for a child to read? Which would be easiest for a child to make?

b. Sometimes it is important to be able to read a graph accurately. Looking at the pictograph, try to determine how many books Jane checked out.

c. Do you think that it is always possible to convert a bar graph to a pictograph? If not, give an example. Do you think that it is always possible to convert a pictograph to a bar graph? If not, give an example.

4. Number of Items Sold by Junior Achievement Clubs

Pictograph   Bar graph

Number of Items Sold

Club

A ⬜⬜⬜⬜⬜

B ⬜⬜⬜⬜

C ⏣⏣⏣

D ⚙⚙⚙⚙⚙⚙⚙

E ▱▱▱▱▱

Key:

⬜ = 100 pints of fruit drink.

⏣ = 10 warning lights.

⚙ = 1 pound of cookies.

▱ = 1 box of candy bars. (24 pieces)

a. Try to convert the pictograph into a bar graph in the space provided. What difficulties arise?

b. Can you think of another type of graph that could be used to illustrate the information in the pictograph?

Notice that the meaning of the pictograph would change considerably if the symbols were interpreted differently. For example: ⬜ = 1000 pints, 🔆 = 5 warning lights. How might a nonreader interpret the pictograph?

5. Number of Experiments Finished by Members of a Science Class

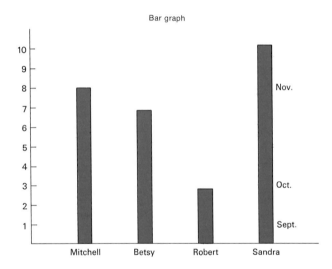

Bar graph

Pictograph

a. Try to convert the bar graph into a pictograph in the space provided. What difficulties arise?

b. Can you think of another type of graph that could be used to illustrate the information in the bar graph?

6. Hourly Temperatures on May 16 (See graphs on page 537)

a. What similarities and differences do you see between the bar graph and the broken line graph? Which graph do you think is most appropriate? Why? Would a pictograph have been appropriate?

b. What would you guess the temperature was at 9 P.M.? Which graph is

most helpful in answering the question? (After you answer these
questions, read the footnote.[1])

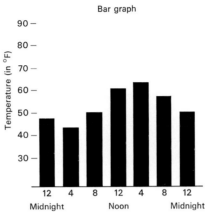

Bar graph

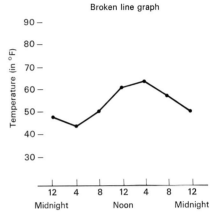

Broken line graph

7. Test Scores

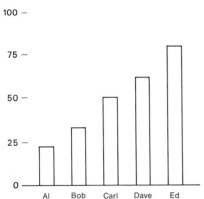

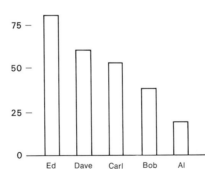

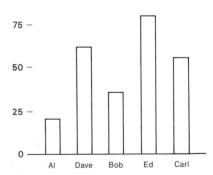

a. How might the order in which the data are listed affect the impression
given by the graph?

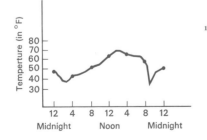

[1] Real situations do not always change gradually or continuously. Sometimes abrupt changes
occur. For instance, look at the smooth line graph of the temperature on May 16. What was
the actual temperature at 9 P.M.? (The sudden change in temperature occurred because
it rained from 8:00 to 8:30.)

Can you think of a situation in which a broken line graph would be appropriate, but a
smooth line graph would not? Can you think of a situation in which a smooth line graph
would be appropriate, but a broken line graph would not? Watch for situations like these in
the problems in the rest of this section.

b. Which of the previous three graphs would you prefer to display the test grades for a class you were teaching?

c. Would a broken line graph have been appropriate?

d. Would it make sense to reorder the columns of the bar graph in problem 6?

8. Number of Textbooks in the Classroom

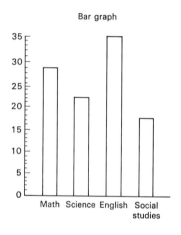

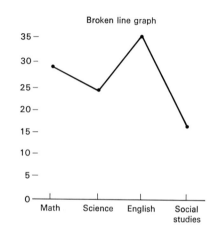

a. Which of the two graphs above do you think is most appropriate? Why?

b. Would a smooth line graph have been appropriate? Why, or why not?

c. Could the columns of the bar graph have been put in the following order: "Social Studies, Science, Math, English"?

d. How would the broken line graph be altered if the columns were reordered?

9. Attendance at Six School Basketball Games

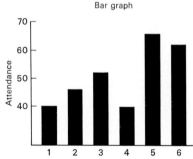

a. Which graph do you think is most appropriate, the bar graph or the broken line graph?

b. Would a smooth line graph have been appropriate?

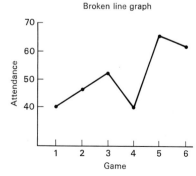

c. Does either of the two graphs give any clues to predict the approximate attendance at the ninth game?

10. Review: Go over the examples given in this section, and write some generalizations about the kind of circumstances in which each of the following types of graphs is most appropriate: circle graph, pictograph, bar graph, broken line graph, smooth line graph.

Compare your generalizations with the conclusions of a colleague. Modify your list of generalizations if your discussions indicate a point that you did not consider.

Which type of graph would you prefer to use to illustrate each of the following situations?

a. History—lengths of wars in which the United States has been engaged.

b. Economics—this year's federal budget, showing how a single budget dollar is divided up.

c. Health—rising cost of health services.

d. Shop—number and kind of tools, inventory of an industrial arts room.

e. Home economics—balanced daily diet makeup for each day.

f. Current events—population of each of the members of the United Nations.

g. Sports—number of baskets made by each player on the team during season.

h. Astronomy and space—flight times of manned space flights.

11. Description
Write a paragraph story to fit each of the following four graphs.

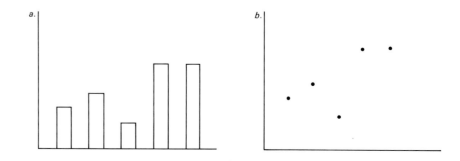

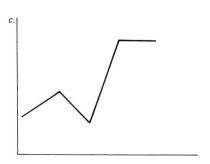 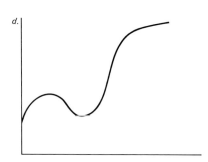

a.

b.

c.

d.

**3.4
SELECTING
AND DRAWING APPROPRIATE
GRAPHS**

Overview: In this section, you will be asked to draw graphs that are appropriate for different kinds of situations. The problems will focus on *selecting an appropriate type of graph, choosing appropriate scales, making comparisons between sets of data, making estimations and predictions, and supporting a position.*

**3.4.1
Selecting an
Appropriate Graph**

1. Assume that you are an elementary school teacher trying to help your students learn the multiplication facts. Each week you give a test of 30 products. Some weeks you eliminate from the test the items that everyone has learned and add new ones. Ask the children to keep track of their progress with a graph showing the number of products they get right. How would you suggest that they do it? How would you suggest that they mark the points where new facts were added to the test so that if their number of correct facts dropped they would understand why?

2. Check the stock market in today's paper and choose three stocks to buy. Pretend that you buy 100 shares of one stock, and 50 shares each of the other two stocks. For the next week, keep a graph (or several graphs) showing your total earnings (or losses), and how each stock has done individually. Talk to some other people to decide upon the best type of graph to use. Together, decide how to make a graph showing the general market performance to compare with the performance of your three stocks. At the end of the week, decide whether your graphs suggest that you should hold on to the stock, or should sell some or all of it.

3. To be legally acceptable, car brakes should have the following stopping distances:

Stopping Distances on Dry, Hard Surfaces

Speed (in miles per hour)	Distance Traveled after Braking (in feet)
10	6
20	21
30	46
40	82
50	128
60	217

Draw a graph of the above facts, and then estimate the stopping distances for 15, 25, 45, and 65 mph.

4. Draw a graph comparing the areas of the oceans of the world.

Ocean	Area (in millions of square miles)
Pacific	70.8
Atlantic	41.2
Indian	28.5
Antarctic	7.6
Arctic	4.8

5. Draw a graph to illustrate the information in the table below.

Wind Speed (in miles per hour)	Thermometer Temperatures (in °F)													
	35	30	25	20	15	10	5	0	−5	−10	−15	−20	−25	−30
	Equivalent wind-chill temperatures													
5	33	27	21	16	12	7	1	−6	−11	−15	−20	−26	−31	−35
10	21	16	9	2	−2	−9	−15	−22	−27	−31	−38	−45	−52	−58
15	16	11	1	−6	−11	−18	−25	−33	−40	−45	−51	−60	−65	−70
20	12	3	−4	−9	−17	−24	−32	−40	−46	−52	−60	−68	−76	−81
25	7	0	−7	−15	−22	−29	−37	−45	−52	−58	−67	−75	−83	−89
30	5	−2	−11	−18	−26	−33	−41	−49	−56	−63	−70	−78	−87	−94
35	3	−4	−13	−20	−27	−35	−43	−52	−60	−67	−72	−83	−90	−98
40	1	−4	−15	−22	−29	−36	−45	−54	−62	−69	−76	−87	−94	−101
45	1	−6	−17	−24	−31	−38	−46	−54	−63	−70	−78	−87	−94	−101
50	0	−7	−17	−24	−31	−38	−47	−56	−63	−70	−79	−88	−96	−103

3.4.2

Choosing Appropriate Scales

1. Use graphs *b* and *c* to regraph the information in graph *a*. Which differences in values become obscured, and which ones get overemphasized by making the scale small? By making the scale large?

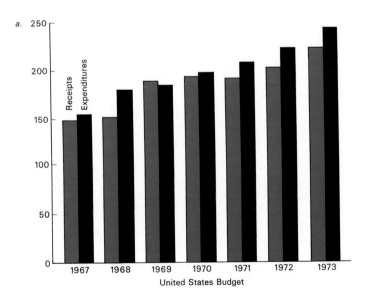

a.

United States Budget

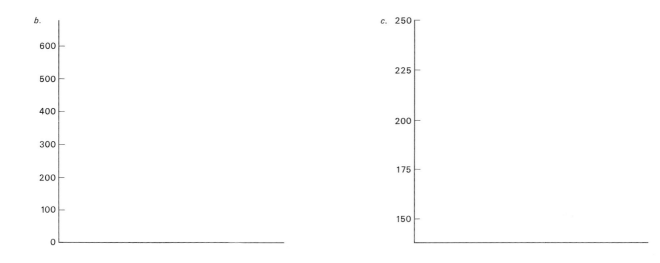

b.

600
500
400
300
200
100
0

c. 250
225
200
175
150

2. Make a graph to illustrate the information in the table below. Compare expenditures and receipts as above, *or* provide the same comparison by graphing the surplus deficit numbers, *or* use the gross debts at the end of each year. Each set of numbers is based on the same underlying data. Defend your choice of scales and describe what effect a different choice would have had on the total impact of your graph.

The United States Budget and the Gross Federal Debt[a,b]

Fiscal Year	U.S. Budget Receipts	U.S. Budget Expenditures	Surplus (+) or Deficit (−)	Gross Debt at End of Year	Fiscal Year	U.S. Budget Receipts	U.S. Budget Expenditures	Surplus (+) or Deficit (−)	Gross Debt at End of Year
1789–1849	$ 1,160	$ 1,090	+70	$ 63	1952	$ 68,011	$ 67,962	+49	$258,834
1850–1900	14,462	15,453	−991	2,700	1954	69,920	71,138	−1,218	270,808
1905	544	567	−23	1,132	1955	65,462	68,503	−3,041	274,339
1910	676	694	−18	1,147	1956	74,581	70,461	+4,121	272,721
1915	683	746	−63	1,191	1957	79,958	76,748	+3,210	272,289
1920	6,649	6,357	+291	24,299	1958	79,621	82,575	−2,954	279,147
1925	3,598	2,881	+717	20,516	1959	79,179	92,111	−12,932	287,739
1930	4,058	3,320	+738	16,185	1960	92,492	92,223	+269	290,862
1935	3,706	6,497	−2,791	32,824	1961	94,389	97,795	−3,406	292,895
1936	3,997	8,422	−4,425	38,497	1962	99,676	106,813	−7,137	303,291
1937	4,956	7,733	−2,777	41,089	1963	106,560	111,311	−4,751	310,807
1938	5,588	6,765	−1,177	42,018	1964	112,662	118,584	−5,922	316,763
1939	4,979	8,841	−3,862	45,890	1965	116,833	118,430	−1,596	323,154
1940	6,879	9,589	−2,710	48,497	1966	130,856	134,652	−3,796	329,474
1941	9,202	13,980	−4,778	55,332	1967	149,552	158,254	−8,702	341,348

(Table continues on page 544)

Fiscal Year	U.S. Budget Receipts	U.S. Budget Expend- itures	Surplus (+) or Deficit (−)	Gross Debt at End of Year	Fiscal Year	U.S. Budget Receipts	U.S. Budget Expend- itures	Surplus (+) or Deficit (−)	Gross Debt at End of Year
1942	15,104	34,500	−19,396	76,991	1968	153,671	178,833	−25,161	369,769
1943	25,097	78,909	−53,812	140,796	1969	187,784	184,548	+3,236	367,144
1944	47,818	93,956	−46,138	202,626	1970	193,743	196,583	−2,845	382,603
1945	50,162	95,184	−45,022	259,115	1971	188,392	211,425	−23,033	409,467
1946	43,537	61,738	−18,201	269,898	1972	208,649	231,876	−23,227	437,329
1948	45,357	36,493	+8,864	252,366	1973	232,192	246,603	−14,412	468,426
1950	40,940	43,147	−2,207	256,853	1974 (est.)[c]	268,700	266,000	−2,700	490,500

[a] Figures are given in $ millions.

[b] Based on unified budget concept for 1954–74, on consolidated cash statement for 1940–53, and on administrative budget for 1789–1939.

[c] Mid-Session Review of 1974 Budget on June 1, 1973.

SOURCE: Office of Management and Budget.

3.4.3
Making
Comparisons between
Sets of Data

Comparisons between sets of information can be done on a bar graph by juxtaposing the bars of the separate data.

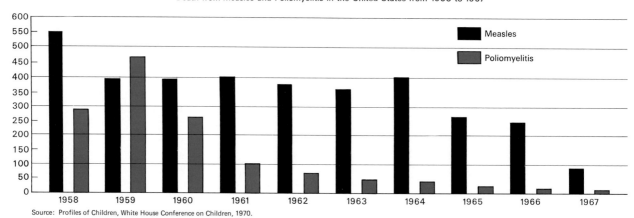

Death from Measles and Poliomyelitis in the United States from 1958 to 1967

Source: Profiles of Children, White House Conference on Children, 1970.

Such comparisons may also be made by using more than one line on a broken line graph.

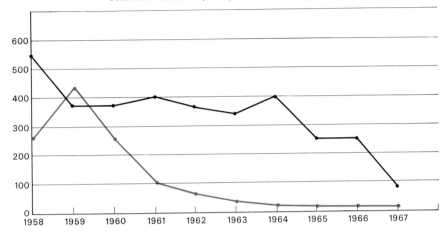

Death from measles and poliomyelitis in U.S. from 1958 to 1967.

Using two other colors, add the following information to each of the graphs above.

Cause of death	1958	1959	1960	1961	1962	1963	1964	1965	1966	1967
Diphtheria	74	72	69	68	41	45	42	18	20	32
Pertussis (whooping cough)	177	269	118	76	83	115	93	55	49	37

SOURCE: *Profiles of Children*, White House Conference on Children, 1970.

Comparing the bar and broken line graphs above, which do you find is less confusing; which is easier to read; which shows trends the best?

3.4.4
**Making
Estimations and
Predictions**

1. In the United States, the first census was taken in 1790. The population was found to be 3,929,000.[1] By 1860, the same source reports that the population had grown to 31,513,000. On the basis of this information, President Lincoln predicted that by 1930 the population would reach 250,689,914. How do you suppose he arrived at this number? Use the information in the table at top of page 546 to make your own prediction about the population in 1930. Compare your prediction with those of your classmates (it may be helpful to make a graph).

What factors would you guess might have led to the discrepancies between the two lists?[2] How accurately do you think a census can be

[1] *Historical Statistics of the U.S. Colonial Times to 1957.*

[2] For example, territories (later to become states), minority groups not considered citizens, and armed forces overseas have not been included in some counts.

Census Year	Population	Population
1790	3,929,214	3,929,000
1800	5,308,483	5,297,000
1810	7,239,881	7,224,000
1820	9,638,453	9,618,000
1830	12,866,020	12,901,000
1840	17,069,453	17,120,000
1850	23,191,876	23,261,000
1860	31,444,321	31,513,000

SOURCES: *Statistical Abstract of U.S., 1972; Historical Statistics of the U.S. Colonial Times.*

taken? Would you say that the population would be the same in January as in June of the same year? When would it make sense to give an exact number for the population of the United States? How accurately do you think it might be possible to determine the exact population of Chicago at any given moment? What kinds of problems would be involved in finding an accurate estimation?

The table below gives the population of the United States from 1870 to 1970. How closely were you able to estimate the 1930 population?

Using the information in both the tables given in this exercise, estimate the population of the United States in the year 2000. Compare your estimate with those of your colleagues.[3]

Census Year	Population
1870	39,818,449
1880	50,155,783
1890	62,947,714
1900	75,994,575
1910	91,972,266
1920	105,710,620
1930	122,775,046
1940	131,669,275
1950	151,325,798[1]
1960	179,323,175[1]
1970	203,211,926[1]

[1] See text footnote 3.
SOURCE: *Statistical Abstract of U.S. 1972.*

[3] Includes Alaska and Hawaii. How much would you guess these inclusions influence the total population? 1 percent? 5 percent? 10 percent?

2. How do you think drawing a graph of the data helped to make predictions for the future growth of population?

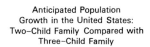

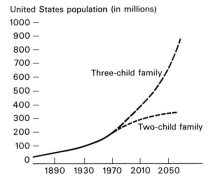

Anticipated Population
Growth in the United States:
Two–Child Family Compared with
Three–Child Family

3. Real life occurrences don't usually form perfect lines on graphs, and therefore estimations and predictions need to be made from the line of best fit. For example, a group of students decided to check the cost of a hamburger sold in various neighborhood restaurants and compare it with the average number of hamburgers sold per day.

Restaurant	Cost	Number Sold
Mac's	$ .39	200
Cozy Corner	1.65	80
Peter Pan	.69	125
Cindy's	1.25	100
The Hangout	.50	180
Diner	.75	150
Drive Inn	.69	180
Sad Sack's	.99	100
The Fireside	1.75	60
Malt Shop	.50	160
Frank's	1.50	90
The Hut	1.39	85

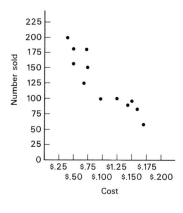

Place a pencil (or other straight object) on the graph so that it "fits" the points. The line represented by your pencil is called the "line of best fit." The graph showing all the points is called a "scattergram."

4. The scattergram on page 548 shows the heights and ages of a group of children. Where will the line of best fit fall for age six?

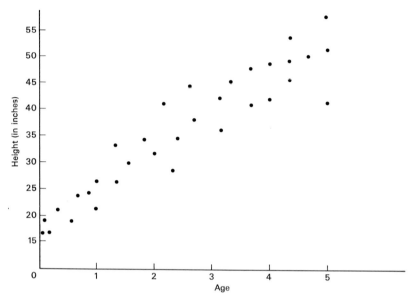

5. The IQ scores and mathematics achievement test scores for a ninth-grade class are shown in this table.

Student	Table Scores	Achievement
a	93	7.0
b	101	10.4
c	86	7.0
d	87	6.2
e	103	8.0
f	95	8.2
g	101	8.9
h	101	9.2
i	91	6.7
j	84	7.8
k	113	9.2
l	107	12.2
m	90	7.2
n	88	6.2
o	113	8.9
p	112	11.4
q	108	12.1
r	102	7.6
s	99	9.6
t	107	8.9
u	114	9.6

Compare the scores on the two tests by recording the information in a scattergram. Give a brief justification for the scales that you use for the horizontal and vertical axes. Compare your graph with the ones that other students have made. Notice that a small scale tends to obscure differences between scores, whereas a large scale accentuates differences.

6. The Hare and the Lynx

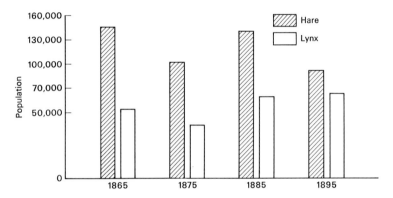

What would you estimate the population of hares and lynx was in 1868? Did you consider the possibility that there could be more lynx than hares at any point during this period?

Examine carefully the graph below, which was based on the pelts handled by the Hudson's Bay Company. Answer the questions that follow.

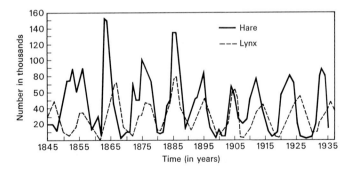

What information does the second graph give that the first one does not? Is there a difference in the impression given by each graph? Is it possible that the pelt count is not an adequate estimator of the actual populations of the hare and lynx?

What must you know before you can make an estimation between two points on a graph? What must you know before you can make a prediction about a point that is past the last data given for the graph? On what would the accuracy of your estimations and predictions depend? How can you increase this accuracy? Did any of the graphs you found for your research assignment (in section 3.1) have points that were listed as estimations or predictions?

3.4.5
Supporting a Position
Assume that you want to make the point that space programs are getting little money. Choose the information from the table below that would best fit your case and graph it in the best manner for your case. Compare your graph with those of all your classmates, and then decide which is the most convincing.

A look at space spending in relation to social action spending

* In 1969, the government spent $65.2 billion on social action programs and 4.2 billion on space.

* In 1970, $75.4 billion on social action programs and $3.7 billion on space.

* In 1972, the federal budget calls for social action spending in the amount of $100 billion while the space budget falls to a low of $3.2 billion.

1972 Federal Budget Estimate

Social action programs	Percent of total budget	Expenditures in billions of dollars
Income security	26.5	$ 60.7
Health	7.0	16.0
Veterans benefits and services	4.6	10.6
Education and manpower	3.8	8.8
Community development and housing	2.0	4.5
Total	43.9	$100.6
Space research and technology, Total	1.4	$3.2

SOURCE: General Electric, *For the Benefit of All Mankind,* 1970, p. 8.

To avoid being misled by statistics given in tables or graphs, it is important to ask, "Does that make sense?" or "How could they have known that?" For instance, would it make sense to say that in the year 2000 the exact population of the United States will be 602,788,201?

1. The U.S. Bureau of Economic Analysis reports that the average income of United States citizens in 1972 was $3,920. But the 1974

World Almanac indicated it was $3,943. How do you account for these conflicting reports? What is the point of giving such exact figures?

2. Compare the graphs of two opinion polls on any current issue or election. If their results differ, try to determine from whom they got their opinions, how many people they polled, how wide a diversity they tried to achieve as to location, economic level, and other factors, and any other information that might have affected their results.

3. Read Darrell Huff's book, *How to Lie with Statistics.*[4]

3.5
PICTURING
LOCATIONS

Overview: **Throughout this unit, the word** *graph* **has been assumed to include all sorts of pictures and diagrams used to communicate information. In sections 3.1 through 3.4 the emphasis was on picturing** *data***. In this section, the emphasis will be on picturing** *locations***.**

There are at least two reasons to focus on picturing locations. First, many problems that are involved in picturing the relative positions of objects are analogous to problems that are involved in picturing data, and therefore an examination of some of these problems can contribute to a better understanding of graphing processes in general. A second reason to focus on picturing locations is that, by visualizing numbers (or number relations) as positions on a line (or positions on a graph), algebraic problems can sometimes be converted into geometric problems or geometric problems can be converted into algebraic problems according to whichever kind is easier to solve. The second point will be considered in section 3.7, which deals with some problems involved in *map making***.**

An old saying is, "One picture is worth a thousand words." For instance, nearly everyone has experienced the difficulty of trying to give travel directions over a telephone when a map is not available. An itinerary that would be simple to show on a map can often become amazingly complex to describe.

History provides many other examples in which songs or stories were memorized to help travelers remember complicated travel routes in situations where maps were not available. For example, around the time of the Civil War, the American folk song "Follow the Drinkin' Gourd" (or "The Muddy Road to Freedom") gave directions to escaping slaves following the underground railroad out of the South. Runaway slaves and sympathizers sang the directions: "Keep your eyes pinned to the skies,

---

4 W. W. Norton, Inc., New York, 1954.

and when the clouds cover the stars, then follow the river. Sleep by day
. . . travel under the cover of darkness. . . ." It was a song of hope and
encouragement, but mostly it was a road map that could be memorized
and transferred without detection. The most important of its many directives was to follow the big dipper (i.e., the "drinkin' gourd").

1. One of the functions that a graph can perform is to organize and
simplify large quantities of information. However, in order to clarify
some information, other information may have to be omitted or distorted. For example, these maps illustrate some of the problems that
are involved in making flat maps of a three-dimensional world. In each
case, some information was distorted in order to focus on other relationships. Discuss the advantages and disadvantages of each of these
maps, and indicate the areas where the greatest amount of *distortion*
occurs.

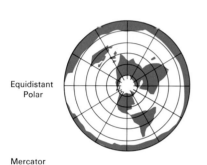

Equidistant
Polar

Mercator

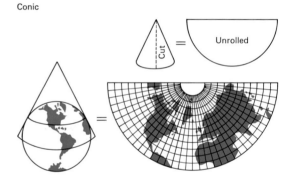

Conic

Homolographic

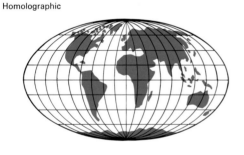

Interrupted Homolosine

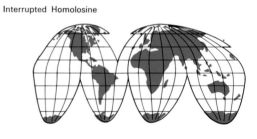

2. a. Imagine that you and a few friends were transported back through
time to the fourteenth century, and that it was your job to make a
map of the world. As a group, decide how you would proceed. Who
could furnish reliable *information*?

b. How would you make an original map of your hometown if airplane photographs were not allowed? What information-gathering process would you use to minimize errors?

3. How are the two map-making problems above analogous to problems that are involved in graphing data?

3.6
Coordinates

Overview: **There are several ways that numbers can be used to describe position on maps. The *coordinate systems* presented in this section will lead to the introduction of several basic ideas in preparation for analytic geometry in section 3.7.**

*3.6.1
A Geoboard
Tournament

Materials needed: One geoboard per person (or at least eight geoboards for a class), several rubber bands of different colors.

Since a major function of graphs is to communicate information, this activity will focus on communication between pairs of people. To begin the tournament, the class should be divided into two-man teams. Pairs of people who are on the same team should sit back to back with their geoboards in front of them (see Figure 3.1). Competing teams should sit next to one another. For instance, in Figure 3.1, players 1 and 2 are a team, and players 3 and 4 are their opponents.

To begin a game, one of the partners on each team should construct a geoboard picture using three rubber bands (see Figure 3.2 for an example). As soon as each picture has been constructed, it should be turned face down and handed to one of the players on the opposing team. When the instructor signals "go," the geoboards should be turned

```
Team 1 ─┐
        ├─── Winner ─┐
Team 2 ─┘            ├── Champion
Team 3 ─┐            │
        ├─── Winner ─┘
Team 4 ─┘
```

Figure 3.1

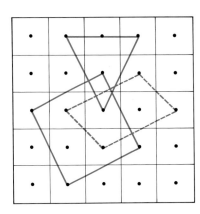

Figure 3.2

over. For each team, the object is for the partner who was given the picture to tell his teammate how to construct a picture identical to the one he was given. Directions must be given while the teammates remain back to back. The first team to complete a correct duplicate wins.[5]

As the tournament proceeds, winning communication strategies should become apparent. When a tournament winner has been established, a brief discussion should be conducted to determine the "best" communication strategy.

3.6.2 Using Numbers to Describe Positions

Many familiar examples can be given in which numbers are used to specify the locations of objects. Street addresses, zip codes, apartment numbers, and library book reference numbers are just a few examples.

1. Notice the addresses on the houses of a street near your home. What would you guess about the relative locations of the houses whose addresses were: 1311 East Main Street, 1313 East Main Street, 1314 East Main Street, 1214 East Main Street, 1214 East Maple Street, 1214 West Maple Street, and 1214 South Washington Avenue?

   Notice that the number 1311 really conceals a pair of numbers: 13 and 11. What information is given by each of these coordinates?

2. If a new house is built in a vacant lot near your home, how is the new address assigned? How is a telephone number assigned to the residents of the house? What is similar about the way the telephone number is assigned and the way the house number is assigned? What is different?[6]

3. If a youngster asked you to locate his room in a large hotel, how would you advise him to proceed if his room number was 1213? Under what different kinds of circumstances might four-digit room numbers be used? Can you think of any circumstances in which three separate coordinates would be needed to specify the location of a room?

---

[5] The game can be made more difficult depending on the type of pictures that are allowed. To finish, the geoboard pictures must be *identical*. That is, the same shapes and the same colored rubber bands must be put in exactly the same positions.

[6] Not all countries assign addresses in the way that is typical in the United States. In Tokyo, Japan, for instance, addresses are assigned in a manner that is closer to the way telephone numbers are assigned in the United States. That is, in Tokyo, addresses within a given area are assigned according to when the building was constructed. For instance, on a given block the first house built would be assigned the smallest number regardless of its location on the block. Needless to say, Tokyo is a very confusing place in which to find a house with a particular address — even for taxi drivers.

4. How would you describe the location of the two seats that are circled? How many coordinates did you use? Can you think of a better method of numbering the seats? Why do you suppose this particular numbering system was used?

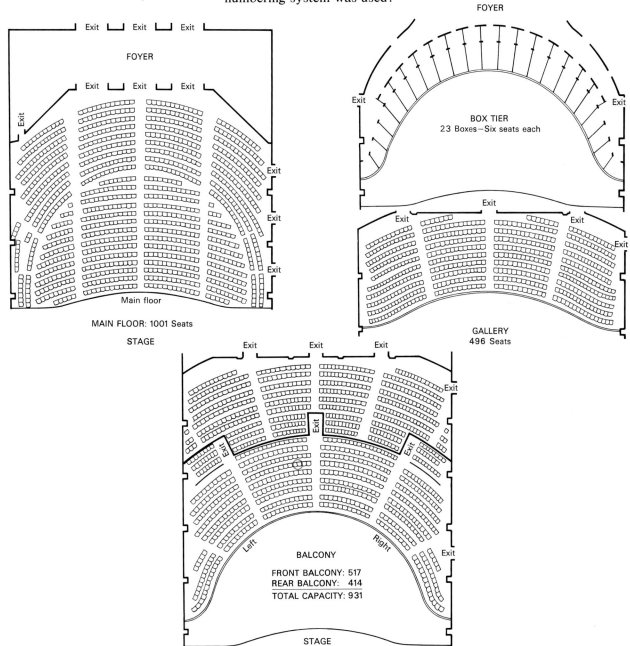

Seating Diagram
Orchestra Hall, Chicago

5. On the map of Chicago, the coordinates of the University of Chicago are (5.6, 3.6). Find the coordinates of O'Hare Airport.

   Some of the maps at the beginning of this section used lines of longitude and latitude to locate positions on the earth. Using these lines as frames of reference, it is possible to describe locations by giving pairs of coordinates. For instance, Chicago is located at 87° 37 minutes West longitude and 41° 50 minutes North latitude. Check a globe to find the coordinates of your hometown.

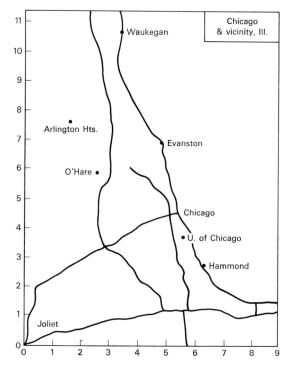

3.6.3 Rectangular Coordinates

Using a coordinate system, section 2.9 of the relations unit showed how pairs of numbers could be used to describe the positions of points in a plane. For some practice plotting points on a rectangular coordinate graph, do exercises 1 and 2 below.

1. In Figure 3.3, form a picture by drawing lines to connect the points below. As is customary, the first number in each pair refers to the horizontal axis, and the second number refers to the vertical axis. Connect the dots as you go along. If a point is repeated, draw a line returning to that point.

   (7, 16), (4, 14), (4, 11), (5, 9), (3, 4), (5, 0), (8, 0), (11, 3), (13, 3),

Figure 3.3

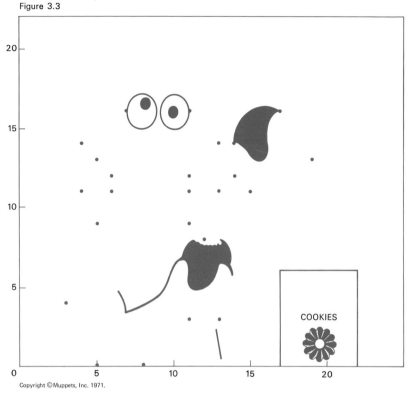

(19, 13), (17, 16), (14, 14), (14, 12), (15, 11), (12, 8), (11, 9), (3, 11), (13, 14), (11, 11), (6, 11), (5, 13), (6, 12), (11, 12), (13, 14), (11, 16)

2. Use a large sheet of graph paper to make a poster of Big Bird. How could you use coordinates to enlarge the picture into a 12×16 foot billboard?

3.7
**SOME
INTRODUCTORY IDEAS IN
ANALYTIC GEOMETRY**

Although the idea of using number coordinates to locate positions was used by the ancient Egyptians, Greeks, and Romans for surveying and for map making, the merger of arithmetic, algebra, and geometry did not occur until *analytic geometry* was devised by René Descartes (1596–1650) and Pierre de Fermat (1601–1665). Using a Cartesian coordinate graph (named after Descartes), the techniques provided by analytic geometry allow algebraic equations to be interpreted as geometric shapes, and allow geometric shapes to be described using algebraic equations. Because analytic geometry unifies arithmetic, algebra, and geometry, it has become one of the cornerstones of modern mathematics, and it has provided a powerful tool in many applied sciences. In fact, many people agree that the conception of analytic geometry was one of the greatest single steps ever made in the progress of the exact sciences.

3.7.1 *Overview:* **The problems in this section will illustrate some basic techniques from analytic geometry.**

a. Mark 25 points anywhere on Grid 1.

b. Circle all the points whose coordinates add up to less than 2.

c. Put a cross (X) on all of the points whose coordinates add up to exactly 2.

d. Mark ten more points and circle and cross the points as above.

e. If fewer than five points are crossed, find others whose coordinates add up to exactly 2. What pattern do you see?

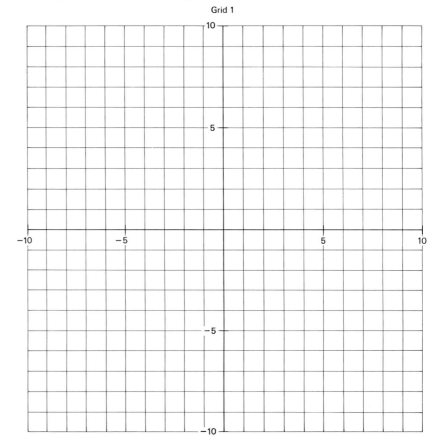

Grid 1

3.7.2 **a.** Fill out the following table, showing pairs that satisfy the equation $\triangle = \square - 3$.

$\square$	0	1																
$\triangle$	-3	-2																

On Grid 2, mark at least 20 points whose coordinates ($\square$, $\triangle$) satisfy the equation $\triangle = \square - 3$. What pattern do you see?

Grid 2

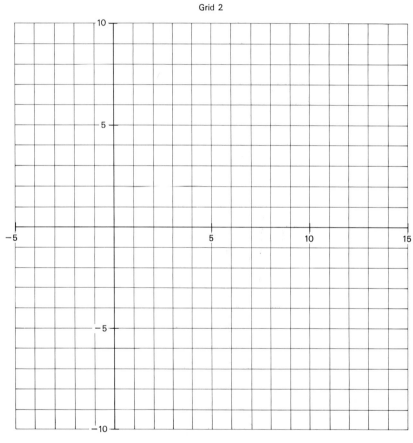

Use Grid 2 to mark at least 20 points whose coordinates ($\square$, $\triangle$) satisfy the equation $\triangle = \frac{1}{2} \square$.

b. Find a point on the graph whose coordinates satisfy the equation $\triangle = \frac{1}{2} \square$, and at the same time also satisfy the equation $\triangle = \square - 3$. Use Grid 2 to mark at least 10 points whose coordinates ($\square$, $\triangle$) satisfy the equation $\triangle = 3 \square - 3$.

c. Find a point whose coordinates satisfy the equation $\triangle = 3 \square - 3$ and at the same time also satisfy the equation $\triangle = \square - 3$.

d. Find a point whose coordinates satisfy the equation $\triangle = 3 \square - 3$, and at the same time also satisfy the equation $\triangle = \frac{1}{2} \square$.[7]

3.7.3 Find an equation that describes the coordinates of the points lying on the blue line in Grid 3. (Hint: It may be helpful to fill out the table below, showing the coordinates of some of the points on the line. Look for a pattern in the table.)

3.7.4 On Grid 4, the points that lie on the blue circle have coordinates satisfying the equation $\square^2 + \triangle^2 = 25$. Notice that, to indicate all of the points whose coordinates satisfy this equation, a smooth line graph was used.

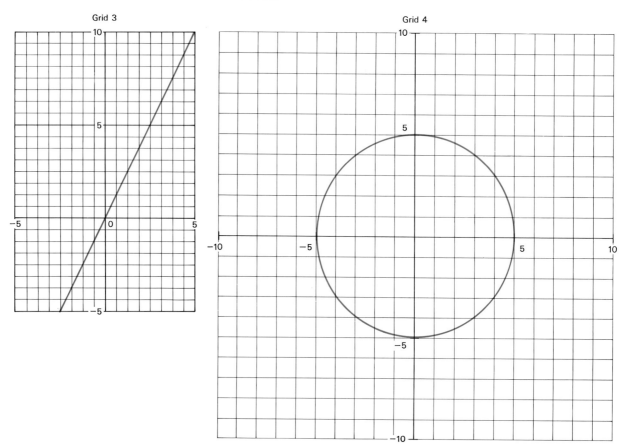

Grid 3

Grid 4

[7] Equations of the form $\triangle = m\square + n$ are called "linear equations."

a. Using Grid 4, make a smooth line graph showing the points where coordinates satisfy the equation $\square + \triangle = 7$.

b. Find two different points on the graph whose coordinates satisfy the equation $\square + \triangle = 7$, and at the same time also satisfy the equation $\square^2 + \triangle^2 = 25$.

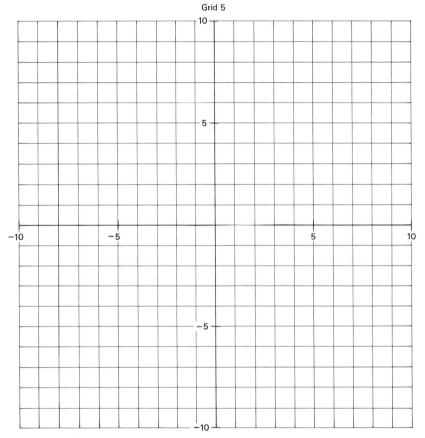

Grid 5

3.7.5 Use Grid 5 to make a graph of the points whose coordinates satisfy the equation $\triangle = 1/\square$. (Remember that $1/\square$ is not defined when $\square = 0$.) You will find that the graph consists of two separate parts.

3.7.6 **a.** Grid 6*a* shows the graph of the equation $\triangle = \square^2$. The blue arrow in Grid 6*a* shows that $\sqrt{30}$ is approximately equal to 5.5 (or $5\frac{1}{2}$). To see whether 5.5 is slightly too large, slightly too small, or just right, check this: $(5.5)^2 = \triangle$.

b. Use Grid 6*a* to find a rational number (which can be in decimal form) that is approximately equal to $\sqrt{70}$.

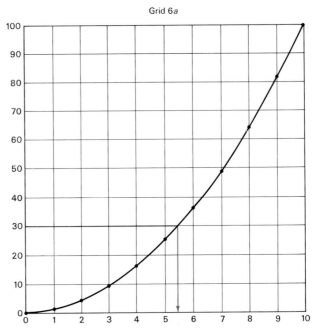

Grid 6a

c. Use Grid 6b to make a graph of the equation $\triangle = \sqrt{\square}$. (Hint: It will be helpful to use information from Grid 6a.)

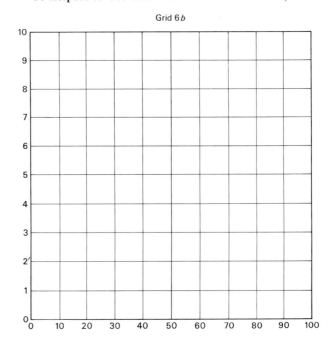

Grid 6b

a. You know that $2^3 = 2 \times 2 \times 2 = 8$; and you probably remember that $2^1 = 2$; but you may have forgotten that $2^0 = 1$ (This fact will be explained in section 4.10). Complete the table below for the equation $\triangle = 2^\square$.

$\square$	0	1	2	3	4	5	6	7	8	9	10
$\triangle$	1	2		8							

*b. Starting with 2, and using an electric hand calculator, how many times do you have to multiply by 2 in order to exceed the capacity of the calculator? Notice that $2^\square$ gets very large very fast.

c. Grid 7 shows the graph of the equation $\triangle = 2^\square$ when $\square$ is between 0 and 4. Notice that every number between 1 and 16 (and in fact any positive real number) can be expressed as a power of 2. For instance, the arrows show that 3 is approximately $2^{1.6}$, and that 10 is approximately equal to $2^{3.3}$. These facts have been indicated in the blue ruler beneath Grid 7.

   Use the Graph (Grid 7) to find approximate solutions to each of the following equations: $5 = 2^\square$, $6 = 2^\square$, $7 = 2^\square$, $9 = 2^\square$. Record your answers on the blue ruler beneath Grid 7.

   The ruler that you constructed in problem *c* is, in fact, part of a simple "slide rule." Section 3.8 will show how your slide rule can be used to multiply numbers.

   Throughout section 3.7, it has been shown that by representing pairs of numbers by points on a rectangular coordinate grid, some algebraic equations can be illustrated using geometric shapes. (1) Some geometric shapes (e.g., lines, circles) can be described using algebraic equations. (2) Pairs of equations (for example, $\triangle = 3 \square - 3$ and $\triangle = \frac{1}{2} \square$) can be solved simultaneously using graphs. (3) Graphs can sometimes be helpful to use to 'undo' (i.e., find the inverse of) certain functions. For example, by looking at the graph of the equation $\triangle = \square^2$, you were able to find the square root of certain numbers.

   The fact that analytic geometry merges geometry, algebra, and arithmetic means that it is able to furnish some very valuable mathematical tools. One of the most valuable procedures that is used in mathematics is to take a problem that is difficult to solve in one situation (e.g., in algebra) and to transform the problem to another situation (e.g., in geometry) where it is easier to solve. Examples of this problem-solving procedure were given throughout section 3.7.

Grid 7

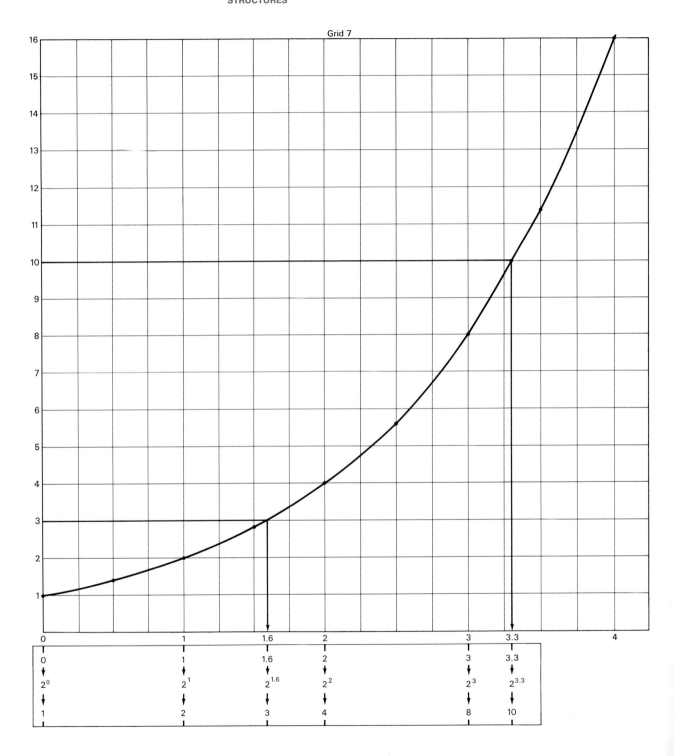

	0	1	1.6	2	3	3.3
	↓	↓	↓	↓	↓	↓
	2^0	2^1	$2^{1.6}$	2^2	2^3	$2^{3.3}$
	↓	↓	↓	↓	↓	↓
	1	2	3	4	8	10

*3.8 In section 3.7.7 you constructed part of a simple slide rule by graphing
SLIDE RULES the equation $\triangle = 2^{\square}$. The slide rule scale should have looked like this:

3.8.1
The
Multiplicative
Slide Rule

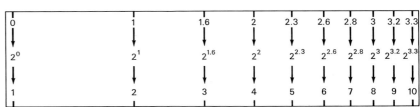

Notice that the numbers at the top of the ruler are exponents and that
the numbers at the bottom of the ruler are the values of $\triangle$ obtained
when the exponents are "plugged into" the equation $\triangle = 2^{\square}$. The slide
rule automatically converts back and forth between $\triangle$ and $\square$ in the
equation $\triangle = 2^{\square}$.

The top edge of the slide rule also makes it easy to add exponents. For
example, the illustration below shows that $1.6 + 1.6 = 3.2$.

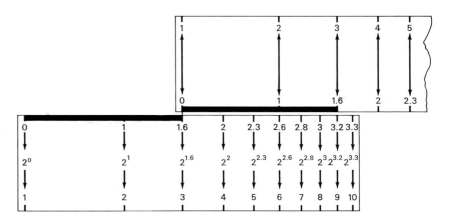

However, this fact is not particularly exciting except when you notice
that the other edge of the slide rule automatically turns the above addition equation into the multiplication equation $3 \times 3 = 9$.

Starting with a multiplication problem $m \times n = \square$, a slide rule works
because: If m and n are positive real numbers, then they can be expressed in exponential form; for example, $m = 2^a$ and $n = 2^b$. (See section 3.7.7 for a justification of this fact.)

To understand how the slide rule works, it is helpful to have a better

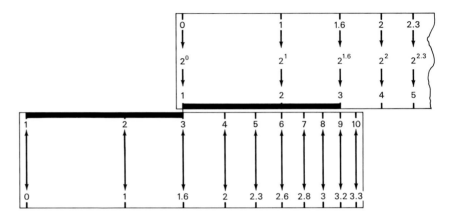

slide rule. This can be made by pasting two strips of logarithmic graph paper[8] to pieces of cardboard.

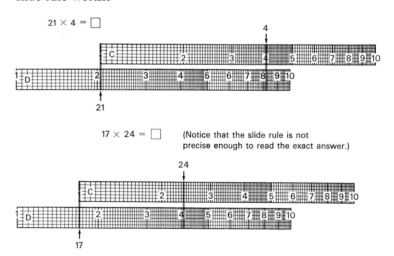

Notice that the "log paper" slide rule is just a more refined version of your homemade slide rule. A few examples should illustrate how the slide rule works.

$21 \times 4 = \square$

$17 \times 24 = \square$ (Notice that the slide rule is not precise enough to read the exact answer.)

1. Try these problems using your slide rule. (Approximate answers are acceptable.)

---

[8] Logarithmic graph paper can be purchased in most office or school supply stores.

a. $25 \times 28 = \square$ **c.** $31 \times 31 = \square$
b. $19 \times 42 = \square$ **d.** $16 \times 4 = \square$

2. Now try this problem. $51 \times 3 = \square$. What happens?

3. Look at the example below, and then try exercise 2 again.

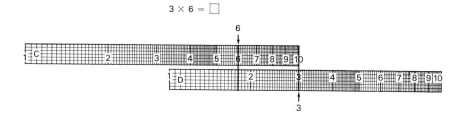

$3 \times 6 = \square$

4. Try these problems on your slide rule.
     a. $9 \times 17 = \square$ **c.** $16 \times 82 = \square$
     b. $16 \times 19 = \square$ **d.** $50 \times 62 = \square$

3.8.2
**The
Additive Slide
Rule** To make the multiplicative slide rule seem less mysterious, try a few problems on an additive slide rule. An additive slide rule can be made out of rectangular graph paper.

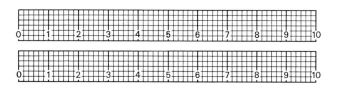

The following examples illustrate how the additive slide rule works.

$4 + 3 = \square$

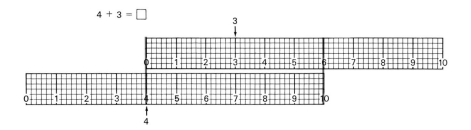

$8 + 7 = \square$

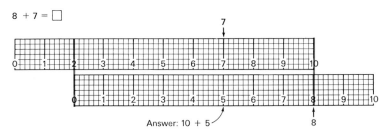

Answer: 10 + 5

1. Try these problems on an additive slide rule.

a. $42 + 27 = \square$ **c.** $68 + 9 = \square$

b. $51 + 34 = \square$ **d.** $68 + 91 = \square$

*2. Explain why the additive slide rule works.

3.9
PEDAGOGICAL REMARKS

The fact that graphs are often used to sell products and ideas demonstrates the power of picturing information. Graphs can simplify information, emphasize relationships, and provide an efficient means of helping people analyze data and form generalizations. However, graphs can also be used to mislead. Consequently, it is important for the educated citizen to learn to analyze and interpret graphs critically.

Even though the study of graphs is important in its own right, graphs are slighted in many elementary school textbook series. In elementary schools, graphs are more often used as "tools" to help "sell" mathematical ideas, and to help children notice mathematical relationships and form mathematical generalizations. Nuffield mathematics materials (British elementary school materials) make particularly heavy use of graphs. Several examples of children's graphs, and mathematical graphs that are appropriate for children, have been given throughout this unit and Unit 2. For other examples, see these sources:

1. *Graphs and the Child* by Frederique and Papy.[9]

2. *Notes on Mathematics in Primary Schools* by members of the Association of Teachers of Mathematics.[9]

3. *School Mathematics Project* (SMP) Materials Books A-H.[11]

[9] Algonquin Publ., Montreal, 1970.

[10] Cambridge Univ. Press, Cambridge, England, 1967.

[11] Cambridge University Press, Cambridge, England, 1969.

unit 4
operations

Within the experience of most adults, many situations occur that are worth thinking about in a mathematical way and a substantial portion of these situations are not restricted to exercises in counting, measuring, adding, subtracting, multiplying, and dividing.

Throughout this book, colored rods, poker chips, and other concrete objects have been used to illustrate the properties of various number systems. However, mathematics is more than learning how to solve equations and calculate with numbers; it can also involve systems of operations and relations defined on other kinds of sets. This unit will investigate some operations defined on sets of concrete objects (e.g., rods, chips), and on sets of movements (e.g., rotations on a cube), as well as on sets of numbers. By studying several different kinds of simple algebraic systems, some old familiar properties (e.g., the commutative property, the associative property) of operations will be reexamined. For each property, a simple algebraic system will be given in which the property does not hold.

Even though words like *commutativity, associativity,* and *distributivity* have been used to describe number systems, in other parts of this book these words represent general algebraic properties that can be applied to many different types of systems. One of the goals of this unit is to show how these properties can be used to describe a variety of concrete situations, and to show how rods, counters, and other concrete objects can be used to illustrate different types of algebraic systems.

569

However, since the objective of this unit is to take a general look at basic ideas that have been used in specific contexts throughout this book, the unit will differ from others in that there will be fewer direct analogies between the material presented and material included in the elementary school curriculum.

4.1.1
Refreshing Your Memory about Some Basic Facts

1. What does the *associative property* have to do with the problem $7 \times 8 \times 3 = \square$? How many basic multiplication facts would there be if people had to memorize them for triples of numbers in the same way that they memorize them for pairs of numbers?

2. Imagine that you suddenly became ill with "multiplication amnesia" and that you forgot the 100 basic multiplication facts. In order to relearn the combinations in a multiplication table, it would be helpful to remember the *commutative property* of multiplication. Since $n \times m = m \times n$ for any two numbers, the number of facts that you would have to remember would be reduced to 55; explain why, using Table 4.1.

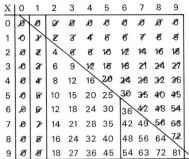

Table 4.1

3. It is easy to remember that $n \times 0 = 0$ for any number; and if you remember that 1 is the *identity element* for multiplication, then you will automatically know that $n \times 1 = n$ for any number. After crossing out these easy facts, how many facts remain to be memorized in Table 4.1? How many of the remaining facts do you think are "easy" to remember? What makes them easy?

4. Most people think that multiplication by 2, 3, 4 and 5 is easy. The difficult facts are the ones in which both of the factors are bigger than 5. Fortunately, however, after the "easy" facts are crossed out, there are only ten difficult facts left to remember in the "terrible triangle" in the lower right hand corner of the multiplication table (see Table 4.1). Using the *distributive law*, addition facts, and multiplication facts from other parts of the table, find a way to figure out each of the products in the terrible triangle.

   a. $6 \times 6 = ($_____ $\times$ _____$) + $ _____
   b. $7 \times 6 = ($_____ $\times$ _____$) + $ _____
   c. $8 \times 6 = ($_____ $\times$ _____$) + $ _____
   d. $9 \times 6 = ($_____ $\times$ _____$) + $ _____
   e. $7 \times 7 = ($_____ $\times$ _____$) + ($_____ $\times$ _____$)$
   f. $8 \times 8 = ($_____ $\times$ _____$) + ($_____ $\times$ _____$)$
   g. $9 \times 9 = ($_____ $\times$ _____$) + ($_____ $\times$ _____$)$

h. $7 \times 8 = (\underline{\hspace{1cm}} \times \underline{\hspace{1cm}}) + (\underline{\hspace{1cm}} \times \underline{\hspace{1cm}})$
i. $7 \times 9 = (\underline{\hspace{1cm}} \times \underline{\hspace{1cm}}) + (\underline{\hspace{1cm}} \times \underline{\hspace{1cm}})$
j. $8 \times 9 = (\underline{\hspace{1cm}} \times \underline{\hspace{1cm}}) + (\underline{\hspace{1cm}} \times \underline{\hspace{1cm}})$

*4.1.2
"Finger
Multiplication" and the
"Basic Facts"

Here is another way that you can use simple addition and multiplication facts to find products in the terrible triangle. The method is called "finger multiplication." To illustrate how it works, follow the steps in the example problem below.

Example: To begin, number your fingers (on each hand) from 6 to 10. Then, in order to multiply 7×8, follow these steps:

Step 1. Touch the 7 finger on your left hand to the 8 finger on your right hand. Then, bend the fingers that are below the touching fingers.

Step 2. Count 10 for each straight finger. In this case, five fingers are straight, and so the answer is 50.

Step 3. Multiply the number of bent fingers on your left hand times the number of bent fingers on your right hand. In this case, the answer is 2×3 (or 6).

Step 4. Add the answer from step 2 to the answer from step 3. The final answer is $50 + 6$ (or 56).

1. Work each of these problems using finger multiplication.

a. $\begin{array}{r} 9 \\ \times 8 \\ \hline \end{array}$
b. $\begin{array}{r} 7 \\ \times 6 \\ \hline \end{array}$
c. $\begin{array}{r} 6 \\ \times 9 \\ \hline \end{array}$

2. Can you explain why finger multiplication works?

4.2
**BINARY
OPERATIONS**

Addition, subtraction, multiplication, division, and exponentiation are all examples of *binary operations*. The word *binary* means that these operations work on *pairs* of numbers. In other words, binary operations are like "two-input" machines in which *two* things are put in, and *one* thing comes out.

Overview: For a two-input machine to work properly, three properties must be satisfied: (1) Whenever two things are put in, *something* must come out. (2) Whenever two things are put in, *only one thing* comes out. (3) For two situations where the inputs are identical, the outputs must also be the same.

The examples in this section will draw attention to three properties that binary operations must satisfy. The three properties are similar to properties that "two-input" machines must satisfy in order to work properly.

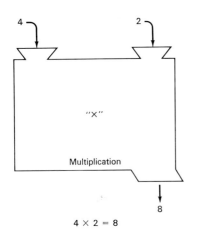

4 × 2 = 8

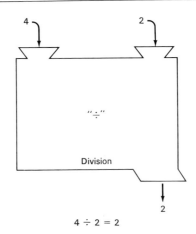

4 ÷ 2 = 2

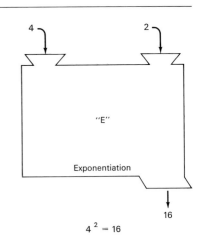

$4^2 = 16$

4.2.1
Operating on Colored Rods

Many different binary operations can be performed on a set of colored rods. Later in this unit a method is given that can be used to "add" and "multiply" the rods. A simpler operation used with a set of rods is the operation that selects the longer of two rods given. For example, when a red rod and a green rod are operated on, the result is a green rod because the green rod is longer. So, if the operation is denoted by the symbol "o", then r o $g = g$.

1. Does "o" satisfy the three properties described in the overview to this section? What about two rods of the same length? Can you think of a simple way to modify the rule to take care of the exceptional case?

2. Make up a rule for assigning pairs of people in your mathematics class to other persons in the class. Be sure every pair of people is assigned to some person, and also be sure that the rule clearly and unambiguously assigns only one person to each pair. If these two conditions are not satisfied, your rule will not qualify as describing a binary operation.

4.2.2
Adding
Rows of Numbers

Operations can be defined to operate on whole rows of numbers. For instance, consider the following four rows of numbers.

Red row: 1,   5,   9,   13, 17, 21, 25, . . .
Purple row: 2,   6,   10, 14, 18, 22, 26, . . .
Green row: 3,   7,   11, 15, 19, 23, 27, . . .
White row: 4,   8,   12, 16, 20, 24, 28, . . .

The names that were given to each row were chosen to make it easier to compare the system with systems that will be given later in the unit. To "add" the red row and the green row, follow these steps:

Operation Table 4.1

$\oplus$	r	p	g	w
r		g		
p				
g		r		g
w	r			

Step 1. Pick any number in the red row.
Step 2. Pick any number in the green row.
Step 3. Add the two numbers, and find the row that contains the answer.

In this case, the sum of the two numbers is in the white row. Therefore:

$$r \oplus g = w$$

1. Does it matter which numbers you pick from the rows that are being combined? Is the answer always in the same row? Try it. Pick any number from the red row; pick any number from the green row; and add. Is the answer always in the white row?

2. Use the method described above to "fill in the box" for the following four equations.

a. $w \oplus r = \square$ **c.** $g \oplus w = \square$
b. $r \oplus p = \square$ **d.** $g \oplus p = \square$

3. Operation Table 4.1 shows that the correct answers to the problems are: (a) w, (b) g, (c) g, and (d) r. Finish filling out Table 4.1.

Operation Table 4.2

$\otimes$	r	p	g	w
r				
p				
g				
w				

4.2.3
Multiplying
Rows of Numbers

By looking at the "addition" operation given in the previous section, make up a rule that can be used to "multiply" the four rows of numbers. Use Operation Table 4.2 to record the result of combining pairs of rows using your "multiplication" operation.

Make sure that the result of operating on two rows does not have several alternative answers. For instance, if $w \otimes g = g$, then it should not also be true that $w \otimes g = r$. If several alternative answers are possible, then your rule does not qualify as being a binary operation.

4.2.4
**Turning
a Square**
Operations defined on whole rows of numbers can be used to describe cyclic (or repeating) systems. Many examples of cyclic systems can be found in everyday situations. For instance, the seasons of the year follow each other in a repeating cycle (i.e., fall, winter, spring, summer, fall, winter, spring, etc.), and so do the minutes in an hour, the hours in a day, and the months in a year. Each of these systems is related to cyclic occurrences in astronomy. Other examples of cyclic systems can be found in music, chemistry, physics, sociology, and other sciences.

More examples of cyclic systems will be given later in the unit. However, to show how operations on rows of numbers can be used to describe cyclic systems, a simple example involving turns on a square can be used. The turns that will be used are described below. The names given to each turn were chosen to make it easier to compare this system with systems that will be given later in the unit.

Red turn *R*: Move the square ¼ turn clockwise (i.e., so that whatever corner is in the red position of the frame moves to the white position).

Purple turn *P*: Move the square ½ turn clockwise (i.e., so that whatever corner is in the purple position of the frame moves to the white position).

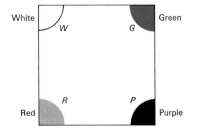

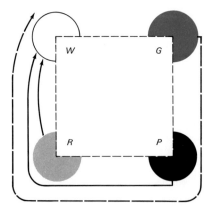

To keep track of combinations of turns, it is helpful to color the corners of the square. The colored square can then be cut out and put into a frame.

In each series of turns, the white corner of the square should start in the white position of the frame.

Green turn *G*: Move the square ¾ turn clockwise (i.e., so that whatever corner is in the green position of the frame moves to the white position).

White turn *W*: Move the square one full turn.

An operation that can be performed on these four turns is to follow one turn by another. For example, a green turn (that is, a ¾ turn) followed by a purple turn (that is, a ½ turn) is equivalent to a red turn (that is, a ¼ turn). Therefore, $G \circ P = R$.

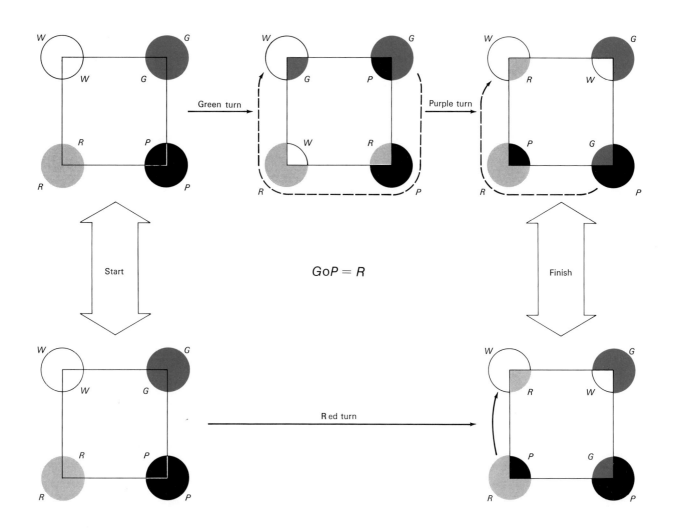

$GoP = R$

Operation Table 4.3

	R	P	G	W
R			W	R
P	G			
G	W	R		
W		P	G	

Notice that at the start of each series of operations, the square and the frame must match.

1. Using a colored square and a frame, complete Operation Table 4.3 for the operation "followed by."

2. Compare Operation Table 4.3 with Operation Table 4.1. How are the two systems similar? Section 4.2.5 will show how it is possible to describe the turns on a square by referring to numbers or to rows of numbers.

4.2.5
Mod
Four Addition
To see how rows of numbers can be used to describe the above four turns of a square, number the corners of the square 1, 2, 3, and 4, respectively. Then (treating the edge of the square as though it were a loop of string), change the square to make it look like a circular number line that repeats itself after four steps.

$\{4, 8, 12, 16, 20, 24, \cdots\}$ = white row.

Green row = $\{3, 7, 11, 15, 19, 23, \cdots\}$

$\{1, 5, 9, 13, 17, 21, \cdots\}$ = red row.

Purple row = $\{2, 6, 10, 14, 18, 22, \cdots\}$

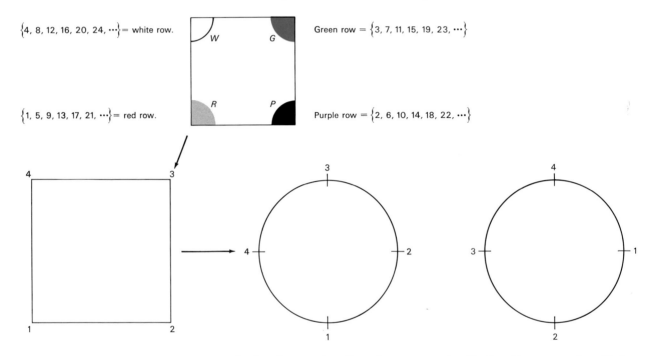

A circular number line that repeats itself after four steps is called a "mod four" number line. Notice that the positions on the circular number line can really be considered to stand for whole sets of numbers. For instance, "1" stands for $\{1, 5, 9, 13, 17, 21, \ldots\}$.

Mod four addition is similar to addition on a regular number line, except that the numbers repeat. For instance, to add 3 and 2 on a mod four number line, take 2 steps from 3; you land on 1; therefore $3 + 2 = 1$ (mod four).

Operation Table 4.4

+ (Mod four)	1	2	3	4
1			4	1
2		4		
3	4	1		3
4				4

1. Fill in Operation Table 4.4 for addition mod four. To make sure that you are performing the operation correctly, check some of the answers that have been filled in for you.

2. Compare Operation Table 4.4 with Operation Tables 4.3 and 4.1. What do you notice?

Using the information in Operation Table 4.4, can you predict the result of a "red turn followed by a white turn followed by a blue turn followed by a green turn"?

In some respects, the three systems considered in this section are very similar, but in other respects they are different. For instance, in the case of addition mod four, numbers (representing positions on a circular number line) were combined using a special addition operation. In the case of turns on a square, the elements were movements (not objects), and the movements were combined by following one movement by another. In the case of addition of rows of numbers, the elements were whole rows of numbers.

One of the goals of this unit is to show how a simple mathematical model can be used to describe a variety of different types of systems. As you proceed through the unit, do not expect elements always to be things (for example, sometimes they may be movements), and do not expect actions (or movements) always to be operations.

4.3 THE CLOSURE PROPERTY

1. a. If two counting numbers (that is, 1, 2, 3, 4, . . .) are added, is the sum always some other counting number?

b. If two counting numbers are multiplied, is the product always some other counting number?

2. a. Give an example where the result of subtracting a counting number from a counting number is not a counting number.

b. Give an example where the result of dividing a counting number by a counting number is not a counting number.

The above two types of situations can be described by saying that the counting numbers are *closed* under addition and multiplication, and that the counting numbers are *not closed* under subtraction or division.

3. a. Give some examples to show that the set of integers is closed under subtraction, but not closed under division.

b. What set of numbers is closed under division, but not closed under subtraction?

c. What set of numbers is closed under both division and subtraction?

Overview: In the first section of this chapter, the operations described took pairs of objects from a set, and gave back some other object that was in the same set. In this section, two algebraic systems studied do not satisfy the closure property. The two nonclosed systems will be changed into closed systems using two different methods: (1) The set will remain the same, but the operation will be modified. (2) The operation will remain the same, but some new elements will be added to the set.

Materials needed: Colored rods.

4.3.1
Adding Colored Rods
Two colored rods can be "added" by putting them end to end, and then finding a single rod equal in length to the two that were given. For example, the red rod r, plus the yellow rod y, equals the black rod k.

r	y

k

1. Is a set of colored rods closed under addition? If it is, the sum of any two rods should be equal to some other single rod! Check to see whether this is true.

2. Is it possible to answer the following four addition problems? Remember that the answer must be a single rod.
   a. $n + r = \square$ **c.** $e + p = \square$
   b. $k + w = \square$ **d.** $n + y = \square$

4.3.2
Addition Mod Orange
Using the "addition" operation from the previous section, there was no single rod that was equal to the blue rod plus the purple rod. Consequently, a set of colored rods is not closed under the "addition" operation that puts rods end to end. One way to make a set of rods closed under addition would be to add some new rods to the set. However, this procedure makes for difficulties. How many new rods would have to be added?

Another way to make a set of rods closed under "addition" is to modify the way the "addition" rule works. For example, "addition mod orange" is a new way to "add" rods so that the answer will always be some other rod. The addition mod orange rule consists of two parts.

Part A. If the two rods together *are not* longer than the orange rod, then the addition rule described in the preceding section can be used.

p	y
b	

$p + y = b$ (mod orange)

Part B. If the two rods together *are* longer than the orange rod, then the sum will be found as illustrated below.

Brown	Yellow

Orange	Green

$b + y = g$ (mod orange)

1. Finish filling out the operation table for addition mod orange. Save time by noticing patterns in the table. When the table is finished, look for patterns that might have been helpful in completing the table.

2. a. By looking at Operation Table 4.5, how is it possible to tell that a set of colored rods is closed under addition mod orange?

Operation Table 4.5

+ (Mod orange)	w	r	g	p	y	d	k	n	e	o
w	r	g	p	y	d	k	n	e	o	w
r	p									
g	y									
p	d									
y	k									
d	n									
k	e									
n	o									
e	w									
o	r									

b. What would have happened if the system were not closed?

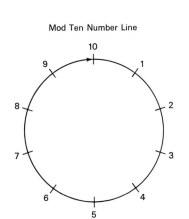

Mod Ten Number Line

Using a regular number line, $7 + 5 = 12$; but a mod ten number line is circular, so $7 + 5 = 2$ (mod ten)

4.3.3
The
"Mod Ten"
Number Line

1. To get a better understanding of addition mod orange, do a few addition problems on a "mod ten" number line. Explain how mod ten addition is like addition mod orange.

2. Try other addition problems on the mod ten number line.

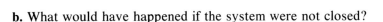

$6 + 2 = \square$ (mod ten) $\quad 4 + 5 = \square$ (mod ten) $\quad 8 + 3 = \square$ (mod ten)
$6 + 8 = \square$ (mod ten) $\quad 7 + 9 = \square$ (mod ten) $\quad 0 + 4 = \square$ (mod ten)

How is mod ten addition like addition mod orange?

4.3.4
The
"Different-From"
Operation

Another operation that can be performed on a set of colored rods is the "different-from" operation. Some examples should illustrate how the operation works.

Example 1 A red rod is "different-from" a green rod by a white rod. Therefore r o $g = w$.

w	g
	p

Example 2 A purple rod is "different-from" a white rod by a green rod. Therefore p o $w = g$.

r	w
g	

Is a set of colored rods closed under the "different-from" operation? If so, then the difference between any two rods should be another rod. Is this true? After answering this question, read the footnote.[1]

4.4
THE
ASSOCIATIVE
PROPERTY

Imagine that an operation "o" is defined on a set S. The operation "o" will satisfy the associative property if the equation $(m$ o $n)$ o $q = m$ o $(n$ o $q)$ is true for any three elements m, n, q, in the set.

1. If S is the set of integers, does addition satisfy the associative property? Does multiplication? Does subtraction? Be careful! Convince a friend that your answers are correct.

Overview: It is often difficult to determine whether or not a system is associative. In this section you will investigate whether the associative property holds for the "different-from" operation described in section 4.3.

In the previous section, it was determined that a set of colored rods is not closed under the "different-from" operation. One way to create a new set of rods that will be closed under the "different-from" operation is to invent a new rod that will represent the difference between a red rod and a red rod. A small square of clear plastic acetate can easily be

[1] The difference between a red rod and a red rod is not a rod. Consequently, a set of colored rods is not closed under the "different-from" operation. Can you add some new rods to the set so that the new set *will* be closed under the "different-from" operation? Can you think of a way to modify the operation slightly so that it will be closed on a set of colored rods?

imagined to be a rod with absolutely no length. Therefore, it can be denoted by c (for the clear rod). This rod can be the rod that is the difference between a red rod and a red rod (or a green rod and a green rod, etc.). Therefore, r o $r = c$, g o $g = c$, p o $p = c$.

2. An operation table for the "different-from" operation is given in Operation Table 4.6. Using a set of colored rods plus the clear rod, does the "different-from" operation satisfy the associative property?[2]

Operation Table 4.6

o	c	w	r	g	p	y	d	k	n	e	o
c	c	w	r	g	p	y	d	k	n	e	o
w	w	c	w	r	g	p	y	d	k	n	e
r	r	w	c	w	r	g	p	y	d	k	n
g	g	r	w	c	w	r	g	p	y	d	k
p	p	g	r	w	c	w	r	g	p	y	d
y	y	p	g	r	w	c	w	r	g	p	y
d	d	y	p	g	r	w	c	w	r	g	p
k	k	d	y	p	g	r	w	c	w	r	g
n	n	k	d	y	p	g	r	w	c	w	r
e	e	n	k	d	y	p	g	r	w	c	w
o	o	e	n	k	d	y	p	g	r	w	c

4.5

THE
COMMUTATIVE
PROPERTY

Overview: **To save time and avoid confusion, pairs of people may want to work together in this section. One person in each pair can investigate the system entitled "Invariance Moves on a Triangle" (section 4.5.1), and the other person can investigate the system entitled "Permutations on Poker Chips" (section 4.5.2). One partner will be the "expert" on each system. The task will be to compare the two systems, to determine how they are similar and how they are different, and to determine whether or not each satisfies the commutative property.**

Materials needed: poker chips, red and blue colored pencils.

When some people read the equation $3 \times 4 = 12$, they say "3 times 4

---

[2] It is true that $(d$ o $c)$ o $f = d$ o $(c$ o $f)$; but in order for the associative property hold for a system, the equation $(m$ o $g)$ o $g = m$ o $(g$ o $g)$ must be true for *any* three elements that are selected. Therefore, if just one example can be found where the equation is not true, then the associative property is not satisfied. Notice that $(w$ o $r)$ o $g \neq w$ o $(r$ o $g)$. Find at least three more examples where the associative property does not hold.

equals 12." Other people say "3 multiplied by 4 equals 12" (or just "3 by 4 equals 12"). Yet, for many people, the phrase "3 times 4" has a slightly different meaning than "3 multiplied by 4." To become aware of the distinction, look at these two illustrations.

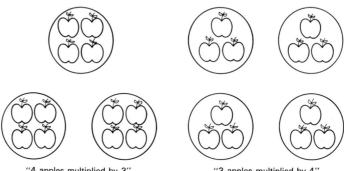

"4 apples multiplied by 3"   "3 apples multiplied by 4"

Which of the above two illustrations would you associate with the phrase "3 times 4"? Many people think "three times four" is like "four multiplied by three." Do you agree?

Even though it makes sense to talk about "3 apples multiplied by 4," it does not make sense to talk about "4 multiplied by 3 apples." Nonetheless, using arrays of circles, it is easy to give a convincing argument that $3 \times 4 = 4 \times 3$.

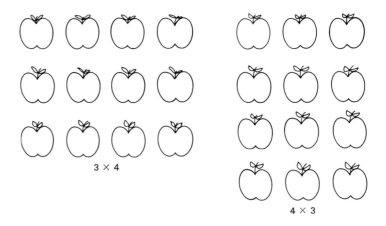

3×4

4×3

The fact that $3 \times 4 = 4 \times 3$ seems somewhat more surprising if a number line is used. For instance, if a "three-jumping frog" jumps 4 times, it may not be completely obvious why he should end up in the same place as a "four-jumper" who jumps 3 times. Furthermore, the situation can become even more confusing when fractions are involved. For instance, the meaning of a "one-half-jumper" jumping 3 times is clear, but a "three-jumper" jumping ½ time is not as clear.

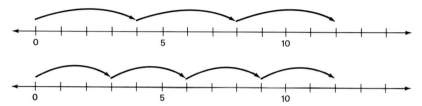

The commutative property of multiplication says that $n \times m = m \times n$ for any two numbers m and n; but, for this fact to be useful, other units have emphasized that you must be able to interpret its meaning in real life situations. It is not sufficient simply to memorize the rule that "When two numbers are multiplied, order is not important," because order is very important for some other number operations, such as subtraction and division. The question is, "What is special about multiplication and addition, so that the commutative property holds?"

4.5.1 Invariance Moves on a Triangle

There are several ways that an equilateral triangle can be moved so that it will look the same (except for the color of the vertices) after the move has been made. Such moves are called "invariance moves."

In order to describe the invariance moves on an equilateral triangle, it is helpful to color the three corners of the triangle red, white, and blue, respectively (Figure 4.1). The triangle should be colored on both sides (e.g., the red corner should be red on both sides and similarly for the blue and white corners.)

The colored triangle can be put into a frame (Figure 4.2) so that the

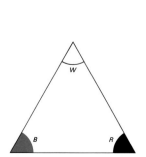

Figure 4.1

Figure 4.2

white corner is in the white position, the red corner is in the red position, and the blue corner is in the blue position.

1. Three invariance moves on the triangle are illustrated. Use a colored frame and triangle to determine whether there are any other invariance moves.

    • *B* flips the corner from the blue position of the frame to the white position.

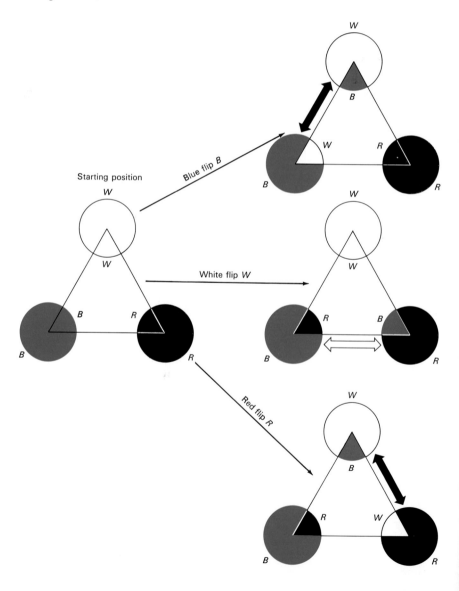

• *W* flips the triangle, but the corner in the white position of the frame remains in the white position.
• *R* flips the corner in the red position of the frame to the white position.

The operation "followed by" can be applied to the three invariance moves *W*, *B*, and *R*. For instance, a blue flip *B* followed by a white flip *W* results in a move that rotates the triangle one-third turn clockwise. Since one-third turn clockwise rotates whatever was in the blue position of the frame to the white position, it is convenient to write *B* o *W* = *b*, and to call *b* a blue turn.

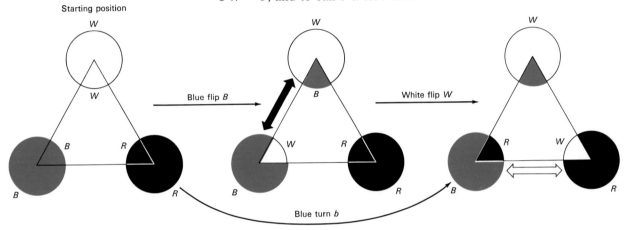

Starting position

Blue flip *B*

White flip *W*

Blue turn *b*

2. a. What invariance move is equivalent to a red flip *R* followed by a white flip *W*? Call this move a *w* move.

b. What invariance move is equivalent to a white flip *W* followed by a white flip *W*? Call this move a *w* move.

c. Figure 4.3 can be used as a frame to show the six invariance moves

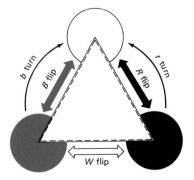

Figure 4.3

W, B, R, w, b, and *r.* Use the frame to investigate whether there are any more invariance moves on an equilateral triangle.

Operation Table 4.7

o	w	b	r	W	B	R
w		b			B	
b					R	
r					W	
W		R	B	w		b
B					w	r
R		B		r		

3. To determine whether the six invariance moves *w, b, r, W, B,* and *R* are closed under the operation "followed by," complete Operation Table 4.7. Notice that the elements in this system are not the corners of the triangle. The elements are *movements* (i.e., the invariance moves on a triangle).

4. Does the system in Operation Table 4.7 satisfy the commutative property?[3]

5. Compare Operation Table 4.7 with Operation Table 4.8, and with the help of your partner, explain how the two systems are similar. If your partner has not yet completed this section, investigate whether the associative property seems to be satisfied by the system in Operation Table 4.7. Your partner will be able to give you some help when he completes his section.

4.5.2
Permutations
on Poker Chips[1]

Three poker chips (white, blue, and red) can be put in order in six different ways. Are there any other possibilities?

By beginning with the order "white, red, blue," it is possible to arrive

---

[1] Some braiding games that are similar to permutations on poker chips are given in chap. 2 of Martin Gardner's book *New Mathematical Diversions from Scientific American,* Simon and Schuster, New York, 1966.

[3] *W* o *R* ≠ *R* o *W.* Find some other examples in which the commutative property is not satisfied.

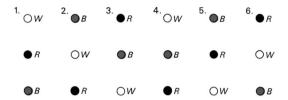

at the six orderings by using the following moves (or permutations).

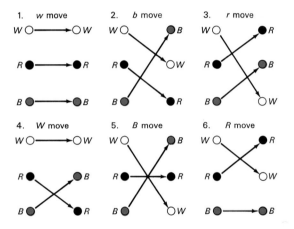

The names of the moves were chosen to make it easier to compare this system with the system given in section 4.5.1. Notice that both *w* and *W* move the white chip to the white position; both *b* and *B* move the blue chip to the white position; and both *r* and *R* move the red chip to the white position. Also notice that each of the "capital letter" moves interchanges two chips while leaving the third chip in the position where it started. The "smaller letter" moves either do not move any chips or else they move all three chips.

Pairs of permutations can be combined by performing one move "followed by" the second move. For instance, this figure shows that an *r* move followed by a *B* move is equivalent to a *W* move. Therefore $r \circ b = W$. Notice that the elements in this system are not the poker chips; the elements are permutations (i.e., movements).

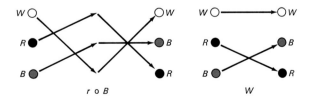

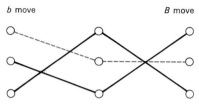

Figure 4.4   Figure 4.5

Note on Embodiments A geoboard (or a pegboard) is often useful in order to investigate the operation "followed by" when it is applied to permutations. For example, in order to demonstrate "*b* followed by *B*," three rubber bands can be used as illustrated in Figure 4.4. In order to combine the two operations using a geoboard, the rubber bands are simply removed from the middle pegs (Figure 4.5). Therefore a "*b* move followed by a *B* move" is equivalent to an *R* move.

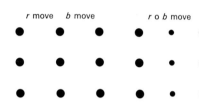

If a geoboard or pegboard is not available, then you will probably find it helpful to begin each operation by drawing dots on a piece of paper as in the diagram at the left.

1. Complete Operation Table 4.8 for "followed by."
   a. What patterns do you see?

   b. What do you think might have caused these patterns to occur?

   c. Does "followed by" satisfy the commutative property?

2. Compare Operation Table 4.8 with Operation Table 4.7. What do you notice? With the help of your partner, explain how the two systems are similar.

Operation Table 4.8

o	*w*	*b*	*r*	*W*	*B*	*R*
w			*r*			
b		*r*	*w*		*R*	
r		*w*			*W*	
W			*B*	*w*	*r*	
B		*W*		*b*		
R			*W*		*b*	

4.5.3
Checking
for Properties

1. Try a few examples to investigate whether the equation (*m* o *n*) o *g* = *m* o (*n* o *g*) seems to be true for any three elements from Operation Table 4.8. Remember that if you can find just one example where this equation is not true, then the system will fail to satisfy the associative property.

2. Imagine that you had just verified that (*m* o *n*) o *g* = *m* o (*n* o *g*) was true for 25 cases. How many more cases would you have to check to *prove* that the associativity property was satisfied for all cases?

3. Sometimes there is an easier way to demonstrate that a property holds than to try to verify the property for all cases. Sometimes the nature of the system allows you to know immediately that a given property will be satisfied in all cases. For example, this diagram shows that the series of moves "*W* followed by *b* followed by *B*" can be accomplished in two different ways corresponding to the two sides of the equation (*W* o *b*) o *B* = *W* o (*b* o *B*).

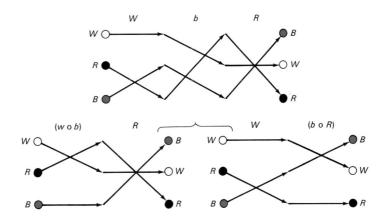

a. What single move is equivalent to *W* o (*r* o *R*)?

b. What single move is equivalent to (*W* o *r*) o *R*?

c. Draw a diagram to show that (*r* o *B*) o *b* = *r* o (*B* o *b*). Then, looking at the illustration you sketch, explain why the operation "followed by" satisfies the associative property for any three permutations that are given.[4]

4. From exercise 3 you know that the operation "followed by" is as-

---

[4] Hint: If a pegboard and rubber bands are used to illustrate that *r* o *B* = *W*, then to combine the two permutations, the middle pegs are simply removed.

sociative when it is applied to permutations on poker chips. You also know that the system in Operation Table 4.8 is the same as the system in Operation Table 4.7. From these facts, can you conclude that the operation "followed by" is associative when it is applied to the invariance moves on a triangle?

5. Review the operation tables in this unit. By looking at the tables, it is possible to know immediately whether or not each operation is commutative. How can this be done?

**4.6
IDENTITY
ELEMENTS**

If an algebraic system has an identity element, then whenever the identity element is combined with any other element in the system, the result is equal to the other element. For instance, zero is the identity element for addition because $n + 0 = n$ for any number n.

1. a. What is the identity element for multiplication?

b. Is there an identity element for subtraction?

c. Is there an identity element for division?

2. a. Look at Operation Table 4.5, and find the identity element for addition mod orange.

b. What is the identity element in Operation Table 4.2? Operation Table 4.3? Operation Table 4.6?

Overview: **Some algebraic systems do not have an identity element. This section will present an unfamiliar algebraic system. The task will be to determine whether or not the system has an identity element.**

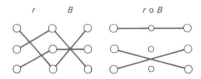

r B $r \text{ o } B$

To illustrate that $(r \text{ o } B) \text{ o } b = r \text{ o } (B \text{ o } b)$, you essentially have to demonstrate that it does not matter in which order you remove the middle pegs.

*4.6.1 Use the letters *a, b, c,* and *d* to label the four corners of a square. A
The thumb tack should be put in the center of the square so that it can be ro-
"Turned-To" tated. The *a* corner should be put in the "start" position. The "turned-
Operation to" operation can be performed as described below.

b o *c* is read "*b* turned to *c*." This means that the square should be rotated so that the *b* corner moves to the position that had been occupied
by the *c* corner. The result is that the *d* corner is in the "start" position.
Therefore *b* o *c* = *d*.

Similarly, *d* o *b* = *c*, because when the *d* corner is turned to the position that had been occupied by the *b* corner, the *c* corner is in the "start"
position.

Each time that the "turned-to" operation is performed, the *a* corner of
the square should be returned to the "start" position.

1. Complete Operation Table 4.9 for "turned-to."
2. Does the operation "turned-to" have an identity element?[5]

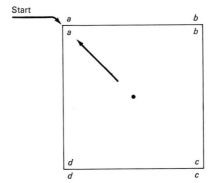

Operation Table 4.9

o	a	b	c	d
a	a			b
b			d	
c		b	a	
d	d	c		

4.7 Imagine that you were given an algebraic system involving a set *S* and
INVERSE an operation "o," and that the identity element for the system was *i*. If *a*
ELEMENTS and *b* were two elements from *S* that satisfied the equation *a* o *b* = *i*,
then *b* would be the *right inverse* of *a*, and *a* would be the *left inverse* of
b. If it were also true that *b* o *a* = *i*, then *b* would be called the inverse
(meaning both left and right) of *a*, and *a* would be the inverse of *b*. Notice that if a system does not have a right (left) identity element, then it
does not make sense to talk about right (left) inverse elements.

[5] Notice that *a* o *a* = *a*, *b* o *a* = *b*, *c* o *a* = *c*, and *d* o *a* = *d*; therefore *a* is a *right identity element* for this system. However, *a* o *b* = *d* and *a* o *d* = *b*; therefore *a* is not a *left identity element*. Therefore *a* is not an identity element (i.e., both left and right) for the system.

1. What is the right inverse of 7 under multiplication? What is the left inverse?

2. What is the right inverse of 7 under addition? What is the left inverse?

3. What is the right inverse of 7 under subtraction? Explain why it does not make sense to talk about a left inverse of 7 under subtraction.

4. What is the right inverse of 7 under division? Does it make sense to talk about a left inverse of 7 under division?

Overview: **This section will reconsider two systems that were presented earlier in the chapter. In each case, the goal will be to determine whether or not every element in the system has an inverse.**

4.7.1 Mod Ten Addition

An operation table for addition on a mod ten number line is shown below. (See section 4.2 for an explanation of mod ten addition.)

1. What is the identity element for mod ten addition?

2. The inverse (under mod ten addition) of 4 is 6 because $4 + 6 = 0$ (mod ten).

3. What is the inverse (under mod ten addition) of 7? Of 3? Of 9?

4. How can Operation Table 4.10 be used to help answer the above questions?

Mod Ten Number Line

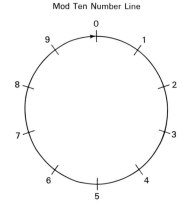

Operation Table 4.10

+(Mod ten)	0	1	2	3	4	5	6	7	8	9
0	0	1	2	3	4	5	6	7	8	9
1	1	2	3	4	5	6	7	8	9	0
2	2	3	4	5	6	7	8	9	0	1
3	3	4	5	6	7	8	9	0	1	2
4	4	5	6	7	8	9	0	1	2	3
5	5	6	7	8	9	0	1	2	3	4
6	6	7	8	9	0	1	2	3	4	5
7	7	8	9	0	1	2	3	4	5	6
8	8	9	0	1	2	3	4	5	6	7
9	9	0	1	2	3	4	5	6	7	8

4.7.2
Mod Ten
Multiplication

Operation Table 4.11 is an operation table for mod ten multiplication.

Operation Table 4.11

×(Mod ten)	0	1	2	3	4	5	6	7	8	9
0	0	0	0	0	0	0	0	0	0	0
1	0	1	2	3	4	5	6	7	8	9
2	0	2	4	6	8	0	2	4	6	8
3	0	3	6	9	2	5	8	1	4	7
4	0	4	8	2	6	0	4	8	2	6
5	0	5	0	5	0	5	0	5	0	5
6	0	6	2	8	4	0	6	2	8	4
7	0	7	4	1	8	5	2	9	6	3
8	0	8	6	4	2	0	8	6	4	2
9	0	9	8	7	6	5	4	3	2	1

1. Use a mod ten number line to explain why $6 \times 8 = 8$ (mod ten). Also, explain why $3 \times 9 = 7$ (mod ten).

2. What is the identity element for mod ten multiplication?

3. What is the inverse (under mod ten multiplication) of 3? Of 9? Of 7?

4. Does 2 have an inverse under mod ten multiplication?

5. Use the operation table to find three numbers that do not have inverses under mod ten multiplication.

6. Does mod ten multiplication satisfy the commutative property?

7. Although it is tedious to verify, and not so easy to prove, mod ten multiplication does satisfy the associative property. Check a few examples to illustrate this fact.

4.8
GROUPS

If a binary operation is defined on a set, then the resulting algebraic system is called a "group" whenever the following four properties are satisfied:

Property 1. The system is *closed*. (See section 4.3.)

Property 2. The operation satisfies the *associative property*. (See section 4.4.)

Property 3. The system has an *identity element*. (See section 4.6.)

Property 4. Every element in the set has an *inverse element*. (See section 4.7.)

If the operation also satisfies the *commutative property* (see section 4.5), then the system is called a "commutative group."

1. Groups are among the most basic and fundamental systems that occur in mathematics. Several examples of groups have been given in this chapter. For instance, only one of the following systems is not a group. Which one is it?

   a. Rotations on a square (section 4.2)
   b. Addition mod orange (section 4.3)
   c. Mod ten addition (section 4.7)
   d. Mod ten multiplication (section 4.7)
   e. Invariance moves on a triangle (section 4.5)

2. Each of the systems in exercise 1 involved sets that included only a finite number of elements. But groups can also involve infinite sets. For instance, which of the following systems are groups?

   a. The set of integers together with the operation "addition"
   b. The set of integers together with the operation "subtraction"
   c. The nonzero rational numbers together with the operation "multiplication"

   Since groups can be used to describe a variety of different kinds of concrete situations, they are useful in many sciences. In physical chemistry, for instance, Pierre Curie used finite groups to analyze and classify crystals; in psychology, Jean Piaget has used finite groups to describe the thought processes of elementary school children; and in more applied sciences, group theory has been used to form a basis for the formulation of coded messages in order to develop better communications systems.[2]

[2] For some other applications of group theory, read Hans Freudenthal's article "What Groups Mean in Mathematics and What They Should Mean in Mathematics Education," *Proceedings of the 1972 International Congress on Mathematical Education (Developments in Mathematical Education,* edited by A. G. Howson), Cambridge: Cambridge University Press, 1973, and W. W. Sawyer's article, "Algebra," *Scientific American,* September 1964, p. 102.

Throughout this book, many examples have been given of situations which can be described using counting numbers, integers, or rational numbers. However, in each case where a system of symbols was used to describe a concrete situation, it was important to become aware of similarities and differences between the system of symbols being used and the concrete system being described. But, to become skillful at detecting similarities and differences between algebraic systems, it is useful to practice by comparing simple finite systems that involve concrete materials. Consequently, the objective of this section will be to help you establish *isomorphisms* between several different finite systems.

Isomorphic systems are systems whose operations and relations behave in exactly the same way. In section 4.3 "addition mod orange" was isomorphic to "mod ten addition"; and in section 4.5, the system associated with the "invariance moves on a triangle" was isomorphic to the system that was associated with "permutations on poker chips."

Overview: **A mathematician named Cayley proved (although he did not state it in this way) that every finite group is *isomorphic* to a group involving permutations on poker chips. Consequently, every real world system that satisfies the properties of a finite group can be described using a system of poker chips as a model.**

This section will begin by showing how a system involving the multiplication of colored rods can be converted into a system involving permutations on poker chips. The system of permutations on poker chips will then be converted into a system involving invariance moves on geometric figures. Finally, the section will show how some invariance moves on geometric figures can be described using numbers and number operations. The entire sequence of exercises should illustrate what it means to say that two systems are *isomorphic,* and should furnish practice in detecting similarities and differences between algebraic systems.

Materials needed: Colored rods, poker chips, colored pencils.

Preparation Activity Several of the systems described in this section involve permutations on poker chips. For this reason, it is important to be familiar with permutations, and to be able to determine how many different permutations are possible using a given number of chips.

In section 4.5.2, you saw that there are six possible ways that three chips can be put in order.

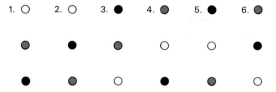

Each of the above six orderings can be obtained using a permutation (or reordering) of the order "white, red, blue." Consequently, there are six possible permutations that can be performed on a row of three chips.

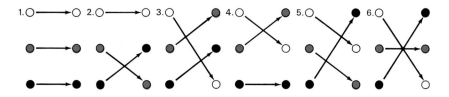

How many different permutations can be performed on a row of four chips? (Notice that a permutation is a *movement*, not a row of poker chips.)

4.9.1
Multiplication
Mod Yellow

Multiplication mod yellow is an operation that can be defined on the first four colored rods (white, red, green, purple). The only reason for restricting the operation to the first four rods is to reduce the amount of tedious computation that must be done. The example below illustrates how "multiplication mod yellow" works.

To multiply the green rod and the purple rod, follow these five steps.

Step 1. Stand the green rod on end next to the purple rod.

Step 2. Stack up more purple rods until they form a wall as high as the green rod.

Step 3. Put the purple rods in a row, end to end.

p	p	p

Step 4. Place as many yellow rods as possible on top of the row of purple rods.

y	y	
p	p	p

Step 5. The answer is the rod that is needed in order to make the yellow row as long as the purple row. In this case, the answer is the red rod.

y	y	r
p	p	p

Therefore $g \times p = r$ (mod yellow).

1. Check the answers that have been given in Operation Table 4.12. Complete the table.

Operation Table 4.12

× (Mod yellow)	w	r	g	p
w	w			p
r	r			
g				r
p				w

2. Are the four group properties satisfied? Is the commutative property satisfied?

4.9.2 Permutations on Poker Chips

In section 4.9.1 the elements were rods and the operation was multiplication mod yellow. In this section, the elements will be movements (permutations) and the operation will be "followed by."

The diagram (p. 598) shows how different permutations on poker chips can be derived from the columns of the operation table for "multiplication mod yellow." Using four chips (white, red, green, purple), the four permutations can be called the "W move," the "R move," and "G move," and the "P move."

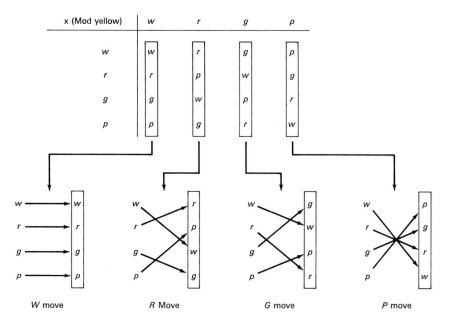

x (Mod yellow)	w	r	g	p

W move   R Move   G move   P move

In the same way as in section 4.5, permutations can be combined using the "followed by" operation. For instance, this diagram shows that an *R* move followed by a *P* move is equal to a *G* move.

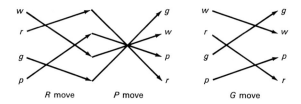

R move   P move   G move

1. A partially completed operation table for "followed by" (as it applies to the four permutations *W*, *R*, *G*, and *P*) is given in Operation Table 4.13. Complete the table.

2. Notice that *W*, *R*, *G*, and *P* are only four out of the 24 possible permutations on four chips. Is the set {*W*, *R*, *G*, *P*} closed under the operation "followed by"?

3. Compare Operation Table 4.13 with Operation Table 4.12. Do the operations behave in the same way?

Using the procedure illustrated above, Cayley's theorem says that any finite group can be converted into an isomorphic system involving permutations on poker chips. Section 4.9.3 will show how many permuta-

Operation Table 4.15

o	W	R	G	P
W	W		G	
R			W	G
G			P	
P		G	R	W

tion systems can be converted into systems that involve invariance moves on geometric figures.

4.9.3
Turning a Square

Another way to look at the four permutations given in the previous section is to put the four poker chips in a square arrangement.

The *R* move took the red chip to the position that had been occupied by the white chip, the white chip to the position that had been occupied by the green chip, the green chip to the position occupied by the purple chip, and the purple chip to the red position. Thus, an *R* move is just like turning a square ¼ turn.

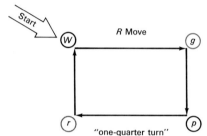

1. Sketch some more diagrams (like the one shown) to demonstrate that the four permutations *W, R, G,* and *P* are just like the four turns on a square — one-quarter turn, one-half turn, three-quarter turn, and full turn.

2. In section 4.2, Operation Table 4.4 summarized the results of applying the operation "followed by" to the rotations of a square. Compare Operation Table 4.14 with Operation Table 4.12 and 4.13. What do you notice?

3. **a.** If Operation Tables 4.14 and 4.13 do not seem to represent isomorphic systems, then translate the answers in Operation Table 4.14 to Operation Table 4.15

   b. Compare Operation Table 4.15 with Operation Table 4.13, and notice that the operations in these two tables behave in exactly the same way.

Operation Table 4.14

o	R	P	G	W
R	P	G	W	R
P	G	W	R	P
G	W	R	P	G
W	R	P	G	W

4.9.4
Comparing Several Systems

The facts below summarize the information that has been established so far in section 4.9:

a. The system "multiplication mod yellow" (Operation Table 4.12) was isomorphic to the system of permutations on poker chips given in Operation Table 4.13.
b. The system of permutations on poker chips (Operation Table 4.13) was isomorphic to the system of rotations on a square.

However, the system of rotations on a square was isomorphic to addition mod four (Operation Table 4.14). Therefore, operations in each of the above four systems behave in exactly the same way.

Operation Table 4.13

o	W	R	G	P
W				
R				
G				
P				

Addition Mod-Four

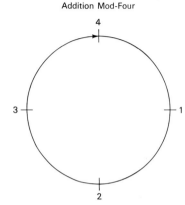

Operation Table 4.16

×(Mod yellow)	w	r	g	p
w	w	r	g	p
r	r	p	w	g
g	g	w	p	r
p	p	g	r	w

Operation Table 4.17

+(Mod four)	1	2	3	4
1	2	3	4	1
2	3	4	1	2
3	4	1	2	3
4	1	2	3	4

To convince yourself that multiplication mod yellow behaves in the same way as addition mod four, the rules below can be used to translate the problems in one system to problems in the other system.

$$\times \text{(Mod yellow)} \xleftrightarrow{\text{corresponds to}} + \text{(mod 4)}$$
$$w \xleftrightarrow{\text{corresponds to}} 4$$
$$r \xleftrightarrow{\text{corresponds to}} 1$$
$$g \xleftrightarrow{\text{corresponds to}} 3$$
$$p \xleftrightarrow{\text{corresponds to}} 2$$

1. Use Operation Tables 4.16 and 4.17 to do the following pairs of problems.

a. $r \times g = \square$ (mod yellow)
$\updownarrow \quad \updownarrow \quad \updownarrow$
$1 + 3 = \square$ (mod 4)

b. $w \times p = \square$ (mod yellow)
$\updownarrow \quad \updownarrow \quad \updownarrow$
$4 + 2 = \square$ (mod 4)

c. $g \times p = \square$ (mod yellow)
$\updownarrow \quad \updownarrow \quad \updownarrow$
$3 + 2 = \square$ (mod 4)

d. $g \times g = \square$ (mod yellow)
$\updownarrow \quad \updownarrow \quad \updownarrow$
$3 + 3 = \square$ (mod 4)

2. Make up other pairs of problems like the ones above. Do the answers always correspond? How are the two systems similar? How are they different?[6]

Four isomorphic systems have been mentioned in this section: multiplication mod yellow (Operation Table 4.16) permutations on poker chips (Operation Table 4.13), turns on a square (Operation Table 4.15), and addition mod four (Operation Table 4.17). However, even though each of these systems involved operations on four element sets, the elements that were in the sets were different.

Operation Table	Elements	Operation
4.12	Colored rods	Multiplication mod yellow
4.13	Movements (permutations on chips)	Followed by
4.15	Movements (turns on a square)	Followed by
4.17	Numbers	Addition mod four

[6] For two systems to be isomorphic, the operations and relations in the two systems must

One of the goals of this unit is to show how a single mathematical system can often be used to describe a variety of seemingly different concrete situations. For instance, each of the above four systems was characterized by the same four-element group.

3. To verify that the above four systems satisfy the four properties of a group: *a.* Verify that each system is closed. *b.* Find the identity element for each system. *c.* Verify that each element (in each system) has an inverse. *d.* Verify that the associative property is satisfied for one of the systems. (Hint: Review section 4.5.3.)

4.9.5 A Mystery Number System

The previous section could have given the impression that all four-element groups are isomorphic. The example below shows that this is not true.

Imagine that an archeologist has unearthed some ancient documents that contain information about a mysterious number system. The four symbols in the system are: ○ ⊖ ① ⊕; and the operation that was used is shown in Operation Table 4.8.5.

Operation Table 4.18

∘	○	⊖	①	⊕
○	○	⊖	①	⊕
⊖	⊖	○	⊕	①
①	①	⊕	○	⊖
⊕	⊕	①	⊖	○

1. Although the associativity property is tedious to verify, it is easy to check the other group properties.

   a. How do you know that the system is closed?

   b. What is the identity element?

   c. What is the inverse of each element?

In Operation Table 4.18, each element is its own inverse, and this was not true for any of the systems in section 4.9.4. Consequently, the mystery number system is not isomorphic to any of the systems that were mentioned in section 4.9.4. The mystery number system is

---

behave in exactly the same way. However, in this unit, relations between elements in the sets have been ignored. For instance, multiplication mod yellow (defined on the first four colored rods) and addition mod four can only be considered to be isomorphic systems if the order of the elements in the two sets is ignored.

isomorphic to the system that results when the operation "followed by" is applied to the following four flips on a square.

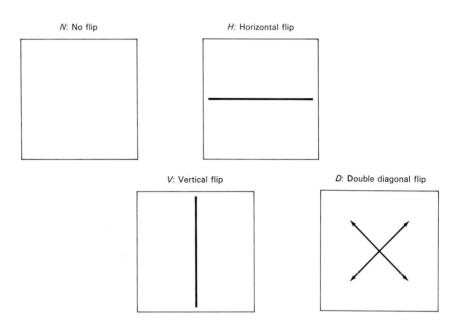

N: No flip

H: Horizontal flip

V: Vertical flip

D: Double diagonal flip

*4.9.6 The four projects in this section may not be easy.

Projects

1. a. Can you think of a number that satisfies the equation $n^2 = -1$? In order to create numbers that would be the square root of negative numbers, "imaginary" numbers were invented. For example, the imaginary number $i = \sqrt{-1}$ was invented to satisfy the equation $n^2 = -1$; and similarly, $2i$ satisfies the equation $n^2 = -4$.

b. A simple system can be created by applying the operation $\times$ (multiplication) to the four numbers $1, -1, i$ and $-i$. Complete Operation Table 4.19 to determine whether this system is a group.

c. Find some other system that is isomorphic to the system above. (Hint: Several such systems have already been given, but you may have to reorganize Operation Table 4.19 in order to find them. For instance, the numbers $1, -1, i$, and $-i$ do not have to come in any particular order, and so their order can be changed.)

Operation Table 4.19

$\times$	1	-1	i	$-i$
1	1	-1	i	$-i$
-1		1		
i			-1	
$-i$				-1

2. Invariance Moves on a Square

Eight different invariance moves can be performed on a square.

White turn

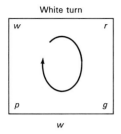

w   r

p   g

w

Red turn

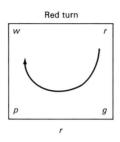

w   r

p   g

r

Green turn

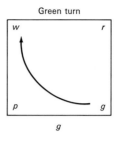

w   r

p   g

g

Purple turn

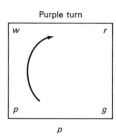

w   r

p   g

p

White flip

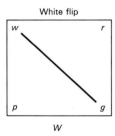

w   r

p   g

W

Red flip

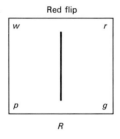

w   r

p   g

R

Green flip

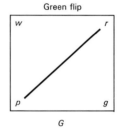

w   r

p   g

G

Purple flip

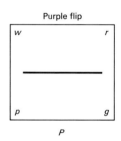

w   r

p   g

P

a. Describe these eight invariance moves using permutations on poker chips.

b. What properties are satisfied by the operation "followed by" when it is applied to the invariance moves on a square. (Hint: You can answer this question without filling out an operation table.)

c. The system described in section 4.9.3 was a *subsystem* of the above system. Can you think of any other examples of subsystems that occurred in this unit?

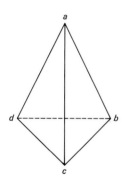

3. Invariance Moves on a Tetrahedron

Investigate the properties of the system that is formed when the operation "followed by" is applied to the 12 invariance moves of a tetrahedron.

+ (mod 4) $\xleftrightarrow{\text{corresponds to}}$ × (mod 5)

1 $\xleftrightarrow{\text{corresponds to}}$?

2 $\xleftrightarrow{\text{corresponds to}}$?

3 $\xleftrightarrow{\text{corresponds to}}$?

4 $\xleftrightarrow{\text{corresponds to}}$?

4. Use the diagram to the left to describe the rules that can be used to translate addition mod 4 problems into multiplication mod 5 problems. Then use the diagram to make up some new pairs of problems. Make sure that the answers always correspond.

Notice that even though addition mod 4 is very similar to multiplication mod 5, two important things change when mod 4 numbers are translated into mod 5 numbers. For one thing, no number on the mod 4 number line corresponds to the number 5 on the mod 5 number line. And, since 1 goes to 4, 2 goes to 2, 3 goes to 1, and 4 goes to 3, the order of the elements gets changed when mod 4 numbers are translated into mod 5 numbers. Consequently, even though the two systems are alike in some ways, they are not isomorphic. In order for systems must be alike. Even though different symbols can be used in the two systems, their operations and relations must behave in exactly the same way.

4.10
THE
DISTRIBUTIVE
PROPERTY

Sometimes more than one operation is defined on a set. For instance, addition and multiplication are both defined on the counting numbers. When two operations are defined on the same set, there is sometimes a rule that relates the two operations to each other. For instance, *a distributive property for addition over multiplication* says that $p \times (m + n) = (p \times m) + (p \times n)$ for any numbers p, m, and n.

Overview: **This section will investigate whether a distributing property is satisfied in several different two-operation systems.**

Materials needed: Colored rods.

4.10.1
Counting
Numbers

1. An array of counters can be used to illustrate the fact that $3 \times (2 + 3) = (3 \times 2) + (3 \times 3)$. Show how colored rods can be used to illustrate the same fact.

$(3 \times 2) + (3 \times 3)$

○ ○ ● ● ●
○ ○ ● ● ●
○ ○ ● ● ●

$3 \times (2 + 3)$

2. Use the number line to illustrate that $3 \times (2 + 3) = (3 \times 2) + (3 \times 3)$. Do you think counters, colored rods, or number lines most clearly explain the distributive property?

3. Show that $3 + (2 \times 3) \neq (3 + 2) \times (3 + 3)$.

4.10.2 Three operations that can be defined on the first four rods are addition
Colored mod purple, multiplication mod yellow, and multiplication mod purple.
Rods Tables for these three operations are shown below.

Addition Mod Purple

+(Mod purple)	w	r	g	p
w	r	g	p	w
r	g	p	w	r
g	p	w	r	g
p	w	r	g	p

Multiplication Mod Yellow

×(Mod yellow)	w	r	g	p
w	w	r	g	p
r	r	p	w	g
g	g	w	p	r
p	p	g	r	w

Multiplication Mod Purple

×(Mod purple)	w	r	g	p
w	w	r	g	p
r	r	p	r	p
g	g	r	w	p
p	p	p	p	p

Determine whether the equation $x \text{ o } (y \square z) = (x \text{ o } y) \square (x \text{ o } z)$ is satisfied in each of the following situations:

a. o is addition mod purple, and $\square$ is multiplication mod yellow.

b. o is multiplication mod yellow, and $\square$ is multiplication mod purple.

c. o is addition mod purple, and $\square$ is multiplication mod purple.

4.10.3 Is a distributive property satisfied for mod ten addition and mod ten mul-
The tiplication?
Mod Ten Number
Line

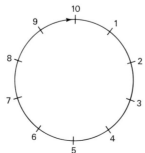

4.11

EXPONENTIATION

Overview: In the introduction to this unit, exponentiation was given as an example of a binary operation. However, in this unit and in other units of this book, exponentiation has been slighted in order to focus on addition, subtraction, multiplication, and division.

This section will investigate some of the properties of exponentiation. Throughout the section, the exponentiation operation will be considered to be operating on pairs of real numbers (i.e., numbers on the real number line).

Sometimes multiplication can be interpreted as repeated addition.

$$2 \times 3 = \overbrace{2 + 2 + 2}^{3 \text{ times}}$$

But, sometimes it is awkward to think of multiplication as repeated addition.

$$\tfrac{1}{2} \times \tfrac{1}{3} = \square$$

In the same way, exponentiation can sometimes be interpreted as repeated multiplication.

$$2 \text{ E } 3 = \overbrace{2 \times 2 \times 2}^{3 \text{ times}}$$

But, sometimes it is awkward to think of exponentiation as repeated multiplication.

$$\tfrac{1}{2} \text{ E } \tfrac{1}{3} = \square$$

Notice that $2 \times 2 \times 2$ is being written as $2 \text{ E } 3$ rather than as 2^3 (which is the more typical notation) in order to emphasize that exponentiation can be considered to be a binary operation much like addition, subtraction, multiplication, and division. This somewhat unusual notation will make it easier to pose questions about the properties of the exponentiation operation.

4.11.1

Some Properties of Exponentiation

1. Convert each of the following exponentiation problems to repeated multiplication problems, and solve:

Example: 2 times

3 E 2 = ☐ becomes $\overbrace{3 \times 3}$ = 9

a. 5 E 3 = ☐   **c.** 2 E 4 = ☐

b. 3 E 5 = ☐   **d.** 4 E 2 = ☐

2. Is exponentiation commutative? 3 E 2 = 2 E 3

3. Does exponentiation have an identity element? (Hint: Do the problems below.)[7]
a. $7^1 = 7$ **d.** 1 E 7 = ☐
b. $5^1 = $ ☐   **e.** 1 E 5 = ☐
c. $101^1 = $ ☐   **f.** 1 E 101 = ☐

4. Does exponentiation satisfy the associative property?[8]

(2 E 3) E 2 = 2 E (3 E 2)

5. Does exponentiation satisfy a distributive property with respect to multiplication?[9]
a. 2 E (3 + 2) = (2 E 3) + (2 E 2)
b. 2 E (3 × 2) = (2 E 3) × (2 E 2)
c. 2 × (3 E 2) = (2 × 3) E (2 × 2)
d. 2 + (3 E 2) = (2 + 3) E (2 + 2)

6. Notice that 2 E (3 + 2) = (2 E 3) × (2 E 2), because:

(2 E 3) × (2 E 2) = (2 × 2 × 2) × (2 × 2)
= (2 × 2 × 2 × 2 × 2) = 2 E (3 + 2)

a. Show that: n E (3 + 2) = (n E 3) × (n E 2) for any number n.

[7] 1 is a right identity element for exponentiation, but exponentiation does not have a left identity element.
Therefore the associative property is not satisfied.

[8]   (2 E 3) = (2 × 2 × 2) E 2 = 8 E 2 = 8 × 8 = 64

but

2 E (3 E 2) = 2 E (3 × 3) 2 E 9 = 2 × 2 × 2 × 2 × 2 × 2 × 2 × 2 × 2 = 512

[9] **a.** 2 E (3 + 2) = 2 E 5 = 32 but (2 E 3) + (2 E 2) = 8 + 4 = 12.
b. 2 E (3 × 2) = 2 E 6 = 64 but (2 E 3) × (2 E 2) = 8 × 4 = 32.
c. 2 × (3 E 2) = 2 × 9 = 18 but (2 × 3) E (2 × 2) = 8 E 4 = 4096.
d. 2 + (3 E 2) = 2 + 9 = 11 but (2 + 3) E (2 + 2) = 5 E 4 = 625.
The distributive property is not satisfied.

b. Would it also be true that: n E$(101 + 102) = (n$ E $101 \times (n$ E $102)$?

7. Even though exponentiation does not satisfy a distributivity property with respect to addition, subtraction, multiplication, or division, it does satisfy a property that looks somewhat like distributivity. The property states that: a E $(b + c) = (a$ E $b) \times (a$ E $c)$.
   Use this rule to complete the following equations.
   a. 5 E $(7 + 11) = ($_____ E _____$) \times ($_____ E _____$)$
   b. _____ E $($_____ $+$ _____$) = (2$ E $5) \times (2$ E $7)$
   c. _____ E _____ $= (2$ E $3) \times (2$ E $5)$
   d. 2 E $(5 + 0) = ($_____ E _____$) \times ($_____ E _____$)$

8. What is 2 E 0? For example, 2 E $0 = \square$.
   First Hint:
   2 E $3 = 2$ E $(3 + 0) = ($_____ E _____$) \times ($_____ E _____$)$
   Therefore $8 = 8 \times (2$ E $0)$
   Second Hint: Solve this equation: $8 = 8 \times \square$
   Answer[10]: _____

9. **a.** 1 was the right identity element for exponentiation. What is the right inverse of 5? For example, 5 E $\square = 1$

   b. What is the right inverse of 101?

   c. What is the right inverse of n where n is any nonzero real number?

   d. Does it make sense to talk about left inverses under exponentiation?[11]

10. What is 2 E (-3)? For example, 2 E $(-3) = \square$.
    First Hint:
    2 E $0 = 2$ E $(-3 + 3) = ($_____ E _____$) \times ($_____ E _____$)$
    Therefore $1 = [2$ E $(-3)] \times (2$ E $3)$
    Second Hint: $1 = \square \times (2$ E $3)$
    Answer[12]: _____

11. Is exponentiation defined for any pair of real numbers?[13]

---

[10] 2 E $0 = 1$.

[11] The right inverse of any nonzero real number is 0, because n E $0 = 1$ if $n \neq 0$. Zero does not have a right inverse because 0 E 0 is not defined. To see one reason why 0 E 0 is not defined, guess what should "fill in the blanks" in the following two sequences.
a. 0 E $4 = 0 \to 0$ E $3 = 0 \to 0$ E $2 = 0 \to 0$ E $1 = 0 \to$
b. 4 E $0 = 1 \to 3$ E $0 = 1 \to 2$ E $0 = 1 \to 1$ E $0 = 1 \to$
For sequence a, you probably guessed that 0 E $0 = 0$; but in sequence b, you probably guessed that 0 E $0 = 1$. To eliminate this troublesome situation, 0 E 0 is not defined. (For an analogous situation, remember that division by zero is also not defined.)

12. a. What is 2 E ½? For example, 2 E ½ = □.
First Hint: (2 E ½) × (2 E ½) = _____ E (_____ + _____) = 2 E 1 = 2
Second Hint: □ × □ = 2
Answer[14]: _____

b. 13 E ½ = □

c. n E ½ = □

13. a. Is there a real number which satisfies the equation (−1) E ½ = □?

b. Is the set of real numbers closed under exponentiation?[15]

4.11.2

Summarizing the Properties of Exponentiation

In section 4.11.1, you found that:

a. The set of real numbers is *not closed* under exponentiation. That is, if a and b are real numbers, a^b is not always a real number. (See section 4.11.1, exercise 13.)

b. Exponentiation is *not associative*. That is, it is not always true that $(a^b)^c = a^{(b^c)}$. (See section 4.11.1, exercise 4.)

c. Exponentiation is *not commutative*. That is, it is not always true that $a^b = b^a$. (See section 4.11.1, exercise 2.)

d. Exponentiation has *no left identity* element, but its *right identity element* is 1. That is, $a^1 = a$ for every real number a. (See section 4.11.1, exercise 3.)

e. Zero is the *right inverse* of every number except zero (zero has no right inverse). That is, $a^0 = 1$ for every number $a \neq 0$. (See section 4.11.1, exercise 1.)

f. Exponentiation is *not defined* for every pair of real numbers. That is, 0^{-1} amounts to division by zero, which is not defined. 0^0 is not defined. (See section 4.11.1, exercise 11.)

g. Exponentiation does *not* satisfy a *distributive property* with respect to addition, subtraction, multiplication, or division (See section 4.11.1, exercise 5.)

h. If a, b, and c are any three real numbers, then $a^{b+c} = a^b \times a^c$.

---

[12] 2 E (−3) = ½ E 3 = ⅛

[13] 0 E 0 is not defined. (See footnote 11.) 0 E (−1) is not defined, because division by zero is not defined. For what other pairs of numbers do you think exponentiation is not defined?

[14] 2 E ½ = $\sqrt{2}$

[15] The set of real numbers is not closed under exponentiation, because (−1) E ½ = $\sqrt{-1}$, and because $\sqrt{-1}$ is an imaginary number. Imaginary numbers are part of the system of complex numbers.

4.12
SUMMARY
OF PROPERTIES OF
OPERATIONS

In Part A of this book, it was pointed out that the set of counting numbers is included in the set of integers, which is included in the set of rational numbers, which is in turn included in the set of real numbers. The real numbers are also included in a larger set of numbers called the "complex numbers."

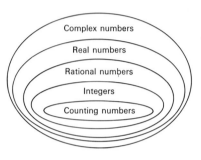

Starting with the counting numbers, two kinds of reasons were usually given to justify studying progressively larger systems of numbers:

1. To be able to describe other types of real world situations.
2. To tie up some mathematical loose ends. Here are some examples of tying up mathematical loose ends:

a. The natural numbers were not closed under subtraction and so the integers were introduced.

b. The integers were not closed under division and so the rational numbers were introduced.

c. The rational numbers were not closed under exponentiation and so the real numbers were introduced.

d. The real numbers were still not closed under exponentiation and so the complex numbers were introduced.

A summary of these facts and others are given in the table below. Give an example to illustrate what goes wrong in all of the blocks of the table that are not checked.

Although words and phrases like *commutativity, associativity, distributivity, identity elements,* and *inverse elements* have been used in other units, the objective of this unit was to take a general look at basic algebraic ideas that have been used in specific contexts throughout the book, and to focus on these recurring ideas.

The table shows the properties of $+, \times, -, \div$, and E when these operations are acting on pairs of real numbers. Give specific examples to illustrate what goes wrong in all of the cells of the table that are not checked.

In both of the tables on page 611, addition and multiplication satisfy exactly the same properties. The distributive property is the one that distinguishes addition from multiplication, because $a \times (b + c) = (a \times b) + (a \times c)$, but $a + (b \times c) \neq (a + b) \times (a + c)$.

	Closed under Addition	Closed under Multiplication	Closed under Subtraction	Closed under Division	Closed under Exponentiation
Natural Numbers	✔	✔			✔
Integers	✔	✔	✔		
Rational Numbers	✔	✔	✔	✔	
Real Numbers	✔	✔	✔	✔	
Complex Numbers	✔	✔	✔	✔	✔

Properties of Addition, Multiplication, Subtraction, Division, and Exponentiation on the Set of Real Numbers.

	Addition (+)	Multiplication (×)	Subtraction (−)	Division (÷)	Exponentiation (E)
Closed on the real numbers	✔	✔	✔	✔	
Defined on all pairs of real numbers	✔	✔	✔		
Identity element	✔	✔	Right identity only	Right identity only	Right identity only
Inverse elements	✔	✔	Right inverses only	0 has no right inverse	0 has no right inverse
Associative	✔	✔			
Commutative	✔	✔			

One of the goals of this unit was to show how several general algebraic properties can be used to describe a variety of different types of concrete situations, and to give examples of simple algebraic systems in which each of these properties does not hold.

As the tables above indicate, for each of the properties discussed in this unit a number system could have been used as an example of a system in which the property does not hold. However, number systems are almost too familiar to use for this purpose. Sometimes it is difficult to recognize a general concept in things that have become very familiar. By using simple but unfamiliar contexts to deal with ideas like commutativity and associativity, many people are able to reach a better understanding of the meaning of these concepts.

4.13 PEDAGOGICAL REMARKS

One of the most important pedagogical benefits teachers can expect to learn from experiences like those in this unit is that they may become better able to recognize a variety of mathematical possibilities when they deal with a set of colored rods, a square, or poker chips. One of the most useful skills a teacher can acquire is the ability to use familiar objects in a variety of ways to illustrate many different mathematical ideas. Nonetheless, because this unit focused on general algebraic ideas and on counterexamples, it differs from other units in this book in that there are fewer direct analogies between the material presented and material included in the elementary school curriculum.

Examples have been given throughout this book to illustrate how ideas like commutativity, associativity, and inverses must be used to solve basic arithmetic problems. Furthermore, section 4.1 of this unit showed how an intuitive understanding of some of these general algebraic properties can help children remember basic facts or figure out forgotten facts. It is not necessary for children to become formally aware of words like *associativity* in order to use such ideas in specific situations. Just as children typically learn to use perfectly correct rules of grammar long before they become explicitly aware of these rules, they also use general algebraic ideas to solve specific types of arithmetic problems without being forced to learn these ideas formally. Therefore, even though these ideas are important, it is not necessary for them to be learned formally by children.

unit 5

problem solving in number theory

5.1 INTRODUCTION

5.1
INTRODUCTION

Number theory has to do with the most familiar of all numbers, the counting numbers: one, two, three, four, five, etc. Since the study of counting numbers frequently does not require a large quantity of prerequisite mathematical training, it has been a favorite area for amateur mathematicians who want to participate in the process of creating mathematics.[1]

Number theory has been a popular pastime for amateur mathematicians partly because some seemingly simple problems have proved to be difficult (or even impossible) to solve. Mathematics is not just concerned with answering questions. What is also important in mathematics is to learn to ask questions and to form reasonable guesses (i.e., hypotheses) about possible solutions. Even in the case of problems that have remained unsolved, the search for a solution has frequently been rewarding. It is useful to gain some intuition about what kind of problems are reasonable to attempt to answer, and to learn to "break up" complex problems into simpler problems that can provide stepping-stones to the more complex problems. Forming hypotheses, gathering and organizing information, looking for patterns, and verifying hypotheses can provide experiences with techniques that can be used in all kinds of situations. Furthermore, attempts to formulate simpler problems have sometimes

[1] See C. Stanley Ogilvy, *Unsolved Problems for the Amateur: Tomorrow's Math,* Oxford University Press, New York, 1972.

613

resulted in spin-off results which have been even more interesting than the original problems that were posed.[2]

Perhaps it is true that many of the problems in number theory may never have any really important real world application. On the other hand, amateur mathematicians have devised problems that have had both practical and theoretical importance. However, even when no apparent applications seem available, finding unsuspected number patterns can be enjoyable experiences, even for people who think they do not like mathematics. Finding unsuspected relationships between seemingly unrelated situations can be suprisingly enjoyable. This is why relationships between numbers underlie so many games, tricks, puzzles, and problems in recreational mathematics. This accounts for the fact that many teachers use number theory problems to entice children to think about problems and to practice mathematical skills that might otherwise have been looked upon as drudgery.

The study of "Graeco-Latin squares" (see section 1.3.5) is an example of a seemingly frivolous topic that has led to a variety of interesting mathematical problems and to some important applications.[3] For example, Graeco-Latin squares are now widely used in designing statistical experiments in agriculture, biology, medicine, sociology, and economics.

Another example of a topic that was begun as a recreational pastime is Samuel Golomb's invention of the study of "polyominos" in 1954 while he was a student at Harvard. The study of polyominos has led to applications in the area of biology dealing with cell growth. One type of polyomino problem is illustrated below.

Notice that five different shapes can be made using four sugar cubes. Try to determine how many shapes can be made with *n* sugar cubes (where *n* is some large number). A formula has never been found that solves this problem for all cases.

By considering several different types of problems from number theory, this unit will focus on some basic number relationships and on some important problem-solving strategies. To emphasize the open-ended nature of mathematical inquiry, some sections will pose situations

[2] In an article in *Scientific American,* Paul Halmos states, "Everyone who has tried to prove Fervat's conjecture has failed, but some of the efforts have produced the most fruitful concepts in modern algebra and in number theory." "Innovation in Mathematics," September 1958, p. 6.

Paul Horwitz gives another example in the July 1951 issue of *Scientific American.* According to Horwitz, Gauss began the study of "congruences" in order to deal with diophantine equations. Although diophantine equations are often introduced in courses about elementary number theory, there is little doubt that the study of "congruences" has turned out to be a far more important idea. "The Theory of Numbers," p. 52.

[3] See chapter 14 of Martin Gardener's book, *New Mathematical Diversions from Scientific American,* Simon and Schuster, New York, 1966.

in which you will be asked to formulate the questions. The goal will be to encourage you to get *actively* involved in the process of *doing* mathematics.

5.2
**FIGURATE
NUMBERS**

***Overview:* In this section, several different kinds of sequences of numbers will be investigated. Here is an example: 1, 2, 3, 5, 7, 11, 13, ... Can you guess the next five numbers in this sequence?**

Looking for patterns in sequences of numbers can emphasize some important number relationships. Furthermore, the technique of looking for patterns in simple problems is often a powerful method to use in solving complex problems. For instance, this technique will be used in section 5.2.2 to find the sum of the first 100 counting numbers.

Materials needed: Poker chips.

Small groups of about four people should work together on this section. Some topics within the section have been labeled A and B. Half of each group should work on the A parts and half should work on the B parts. Sometimes problems in the A sections can be solved by getting hints from information in the B sections, and vice versa. Although people within each group may focus on different problems, it will be helpful to talk to one another.

Nine poker chips can be put in a square configuration (a 3 × 3 array), but eight poker chips cannot. For this reason, nine can be called a "square number."

If "one" is considered to be a square number, list (in order) the first ten square numbers. What is the 101st square number? What is the difference between the first square number and the second square number? The second square number and the third square number? The third square number and the fourth square number? Continue this process. Do you see a pattern? What would be the difference between the 100th and the 101st square numbers?

In the problems below, half of the group should work on problem A and half should work on problem B.

5.2.1
Pyramid
Numbers

A. A pyramid shape can be made using fourteen poker chips. For this reason, fourteen can be called a "pyramid number." If "one" is considered to be a pyramid number, list (in order) the first ten pyramid numbers.

B. There are fourteen different squares on a 3 × 3 grid. Find them.

How many different squares can be found on an 8 × 8 chess board? (Hint: Look for a pattern in some easier problems. For example, how many squares can be found in a 2 × 2 grid? A 3 × 3 grid? A 4 × 4 grid?)

 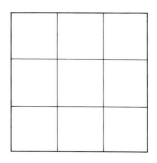

*Problem What square number is also a pyramid number?

5.2.2 Half of the group should work on part A and half on part B.
Triangle
Numbers **A.1.** A triangle can be made with three poker chips or with six poker chips. Therefore, three and six can be called "triangle numbers." If "one" is considered to be a triangle number, list the first ten triangle numbers. What is the 101st triangle number?

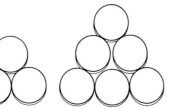

A.2. What is the sum of the first 100 counting numbers? (Hint: $1 + 2 = \square$, $1 + 2 + 3 = \square$, $1 + 2 + 3 + 4 = \square$. Can you find a pattern?)

B.1. The first four *oblong numbers* are shown below. What are the next six oblong numbers?

    2   6   12   20

What is the 101st oblong number?

How are oblong numbers related to triangle numbers? (Hint: Look at the diagram and talk with the members of your group who are working on the A problems.

B.2. What is the sum of the first 100 even numbers? (Hint: look at the diagram.)

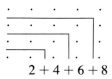

$$2 + 4 + 6 + 8$$

*Problem **1.** What triangle number is also a square number?

2. How are triangle numbers related to square numbers? Can you think of an equation to express this relationship?

```
•   •   •   •   •
•   •   •   •   •
•   •   •   •   •
•   •   •   •   •
•   •   •   •   •
```

5.2.3
Finding
Patterns

A.1. Cutting a Pizza. With three straight cuts, a circular pizza can be cut into at most seven pieces. Draw a sketch to show how this can be done. (No pieces can be moved until all the cuts have been made.)

How many pieces can be made with ten straight cuts? (To solve this problem, look for patterns as you fill out the table below.)

Table 5.1

Number of cuts	0	1	2	3	4	5	6	7	8	9	10
Number of pieces (maximum)				7							

A.2. Cutting a Block of Cheese. With three straight cuts, a block of cheese can be cut into at most eight pieces. Explain how this can be done. (No pieces can be moved until all of the cuts have been made.)

How many pieces can be made with ten straight cuts? (This may not be easy to determine, but make a good guess.)

Table 5.2

Number of cuts	0	1	2	3	4	5	6	7	8	9	10
Number of pieces (maximum)				8							

B.1. Connecting Points on a Circle. Mark four points on the edge of a circular pizza. Then make straight cuts to connect each pair of points. Six different cuts will have to be made, and the pizza will be divided into eight pieces. How many cuts will have to be made to connect ten points on the edge of a pizza?

How many pieces will result when straight cuts are made to connect each of the ten points? To solve these problems, look for patterns as you fill out the table below.

Table 5.3

Number of points	1	2	3	4	5	6	7	8	9	10
Number of cuts				6						
Number of pieces				8						

5.2.4 Investigating Differences The technique of solving complicated problems by looking for patterns in easier problems can be very useful. But, it can also lead to incorrect conclusions if you do not investigate why the patterns occur. For instance, consider the following examples.

A.1. What would you guess to be the next few numbers in the sequence 1, 2, 4, 8? In the previous section, the table showing the number of pieces of cheese that can be formed from ten cuts should have looked like this:

Table 5.4

Number of cuts	0	1	2	3	4	5	6	7	8	9	10
Number of pieces	1	2	4	8	15	26	42	64	93	130	176

Did you fill out the table correctly? How many pieces of cheese did you think could be made with ten cuts?

If you guessed that ten cuts would make 1,024 pieces of cheese, think about what led you to this incorrect conclusion.

A.2. Look at the differences between successive numbers in the sequence: 1, 2, 4, 8, 15, 26, 42, 64, ... Do you see a pattern in the differences?

A.3. The table showing the number of pieces of pizza that can be formed from ten cuts should have looked like this:

Table 5.5

Number of cuts	0	1	2	3	4	5	6	7	8	9	10
Number of pieces	1	2	4	7	11	16	22	29	37	46	56

Investigate the differences between the numbers in the above sequence. Can you explain why this pattern occurred?

A.4. What is the connection among 1, 2, 3 above?

B.1. Table 5.6 shows the number of cuts and pieces that are formed when straight cuts are made between points on the edge of a pizza.
a. Did you fill out the table correctly? If not, try to determine what led you to an incorrect sequence.

Table 5.6

Number of points	1	2	3	4	5	6	7	8	9	10
Numbes of cuts	0	1	3	6	10	15	21	28	36	45
Number of pieces	1	2	4	8	16	31	57	99	163	256

b. Investigate the differences between successive numbers in the sequence 1, 2, 4, 8, 16, 31, 57, 99, 163, 256. Can you find the pattern in the sequence of differences? Where have you seen this pattern before?

c. Investigate the differences between successive numbers in the sequence: 0, 1, 3, 6, 10, 15, 21, 28, 36, 45. Where have you seen this sequence before? How is this sequence related to the sequence in Table 5.1?

d. The first diagram shows that six cuts will have to be made to connect four points on the edge of a pizza. The second diagram shows that when another point is added, four new cuts will have to be made. How many new cuts will have to be made if a sixth point is added? Use diagrams like these to explain the occurrence of the sequence 0, 1, 3, 6, 10, 15, . . . , in Table 5.6.

*5.2.5
Problems

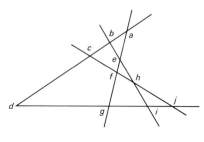

1. Five straight lines can be used to form at most ten triangles. For instance, if the points of intersection are labeled as shown, then one of the triangles is △*acf*. Find the other nine triangles. How many points of intersection can be formed using ten straight lines? How many triangles can be formed using ten straight lines?

2. Each of 1,000 politicians shake hands once with each of the other 999. How many handshakes occur altogether?

3. In a school corridor, 1,000 little boys walked past a row of 1,000 lockers. The first little boy opened all the doors. The second closed the lockers numbered 2, 4, 6, 8, 10, ... The third boy changed the lockers that were numbered 3, 6, 9, 12, 15, . . . ; if the door was open, he closed it, and if it was closed, he opened it. The fourth little boy changed the lockers that were numbered 4, 8, 12, 16, 20, ... This process continued until each of the 1,000 boys had walked past the row of lockers. Which doors were left open and which ones were closed? Was the 1,000th door open or closed?

5.2.6
**Problems
Posed by Students**

The examples below are problems that were posed by elementary education majors. Look over the problems; do not attempt to solve them unless you are really interested. Instead, as you proceed through this chapter, make up a problem situation of your own, and then try to find a solution to your own problem. Remember that mathematics is not just concerned with answering questions; learning to ask questions and to form reasonable guesses (i.e., hypotheses) about possible solutions is also important. It is useful to gain some intuition about what kinds of problems are reasonable to attempt to answer, and to learn to "break up" complex problems into simpler problems.

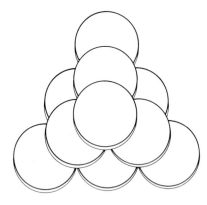

1. Tetrahedral Numbers

After working on the problems about triangle numbers, square numbers, and pyramid numbers, one student posed some problems about tetrahedral numbers.

a. "Ten" is a tetrahedral number because ten poker chips can be put in the shape of a tetrahedren. If 1 is considered to be a tetrahedral number, list in order the first ten tetrahedral numbers.

b. What is the 100th tetrahedral number? (This problem is not easy.)

c. What is the relationship between pentagon numbers and tetrahedral numbers?

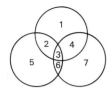

2. Interesting Circles

After working on the problem about the maximum number of triangles that can be formed using ten straight lines, one student posed the following "circle" problems:

a. Three circles can enclose at most seven regions. How many regions can be enclosed using ten circles?

b. How many points of intersection can be obtained by intersecting ten circles?

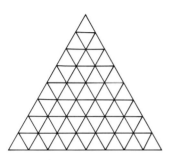

3. Triangles

After trying to find the number of squares on an 8 × 8 checkerboard, one student tried to find the number of triangles in an 8-unit base triangle. The solution to her problem was not easy, but it led to several interesting relationships between an 8-unit base triangle and an 8 × 8 square. For instance, count the number of small squares in an 8 × 8 checkerboard and then count the number of small triangles in an 8-unit base triangle.

4. Triominos

After hearing about polyominos, one student made up a "triominos" problem. The problem was, "How many different shapes can be made with 100 equilateral triangles?" (This problem was not easy.)

5.3
PRIME AND
COMPOSITE NUMBERS

Overview: Many questions have never been answered about *prime numbers*. It is known that they form an infinite set; but there is no known formula that describes all the primes. Consequently, when a particular number is given (say, **792, 439, 717**) there may be no easy way to determine whether or not it is prime. Nonetheless, certain "short-cut" techniques that work in some instances have been devised, and a "sieve of Eratosthenes" can be used to find some of the smaller primes.

The ability to express a number as the product of its prime *factors* is a useful skill. For instance, adding fractions can involve finding a *least common multiple* of two numbers, and the least common multiple can be found by expressing each number as a product of its prime factors. Similarly, in order to *reduce a fraction to lowest terms,* it is helpful to be able to find the *greatest common factor* of the numerator and the denominator. This can involve finding the prime factors of the numbers.

Materials needed: Poker chips.

5.3.1
Line and Rectangle Numbers

A rectangular shape can be made using 15 poker chips. Therefore, 15 can be called a "rectangle number." But a rectangular array cannot be made using 11 poker chips. Numbers that are not rectangle numbers can be called "line numbers."

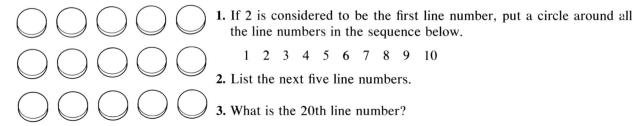

1. If 2 is considered to be the first line number, put a circle around all the line numbers in the sequence below.

1 2 3 4 5 6 7 8 9 10

2. List the next five line numbers.

3. What is the 20th line number?

5.3.2
The Sieve of Eratosthenes

In section 5.3.1, you noticed that the line numbers were prime numbers, and that the rectangle numbers were composite numbers. A prime number is a positive whole number with exactly two whole number factors, namely itself and 1. All other counting numbers (except 1) have more than two factors and are called "composite numbers." Because 1 is the only counting number that has only one factor, it is not considered to be either a prime number or a composite number.

In the last problem of section 5.3.1, you were asked to find the 20th prime number. Although it is relatively easy to determine whether small numbers are prime, larger numbers present more difficulties. In fact, no rule has ever been devised for finding the nth prime number when n is a large number.

The "sieve of Eratosthenes" is a method that can be used to find some of the smaller prime numbers. However, it is too time-consuming (even for a computer) to use this method to find very large primes. Here is how the sieve works.

1	2	3	4	5	6	7	8	9	10
11	12	13	14	15	16	17	18	19	20
21	22	23	24	25	26	27	28	29	30
31	32	33	34	35	36	37	38	39	40
41	42	43	44	45	46	47	48	49	50
51	52	53	54	55	56	57	58	59	60
61	62	63	64	65	66	67	68	69	70
71	72	73	74	75	76	77	78	79	80
81	82	83	84	85	86	87	88	89	90
91	92	93	94	95	96	97	98	99	100

In the diagram above, all multiples of 2 will be composite numbers, so they can be crossed out. Circle 2 and draw a *vertical* line through all the multiples of 2. The multiples of 2 should form a pattern. Why did this particular pattern occur?

After the multiples of 2 have been crossed out, 3 is the next number that is not circled or crossed out. Three is a prime number, and so it should be circled. But all the multiples of 3 are composite numbers. Therefore, draw a *horizontal* line through all of the multiples of 3. Do the multiples of 3 form a pattern?

Which numbers have been crossed out by both a vertical line and a horizontal line? Do these numbers form a pattern?

Has 4 and its multiples already been crossed out? Do the multiples of 4 form a pattern?

After the multiples of 2 and 3 have been crossed out, what is the smallest number that has not been circled or crossed out? Should it be crossed out or circled? Put an X over all of its multiples. Do the X's form a pattern?

Now what is the smallest number that has not been circled or crossed out? Should it be crossed out or circled? Cross out all its multiples.

Put circles around all of the numbers that have not been crossed out. Are any of the circled numbers composite? Are there any prime numbers in the diagram that were crossed out? Why did this happen? What is the first prime counting number that is not included in the table?

If you continue the process that was used above, how far would you have to go in order to find all the prime numbers less than 500?

In the diagram below, circle all the prime numbers. What pattern do you see? Will this pattern continue if the diagram is extended to include more numbers?

1	2	3	4	5	6
7	8	9	10	11	12
13	14	15	16	17	18
19	20	21	22	23	24
25	26	27	28	29	30
31	32	33	34	35	36

(Diagram continues on p. 624)

37	38	39	40	41	42
43	44	45	46	47	48
49	50	51	52	53	54
55	56	57	58	59	60
61	62	63	64	65	66
67	68	69	70	71	72
73	74	75	76	77	78
79	80	81	82	83	84
85	86	87	88	89	90

Are there more primes between 101 and 200 or between 1101 and 1200? Why do you think so?

Pairs of prime numbers like (3, 5), (11, 13), (17, 19), (59, 61), are called "twin primes." Find three more pairs of twin primes.

It is believed that there are infinitely many twin primes, but no one has ever been able to prove whether this is really true.

Another famous unproven conjecture is known as "Goldbach's conjecture." In 1742, Christian Goldbach asked Leonard Euler whether he could prove that every even number can be written as the sum of two primes. Although the conjecture has never been proven or disproven, the search has led to several interesting and important mathematical facts. If you could prove it, you would be famous.

*Problem Write 16, 20, 24, 48, and 60 as the sum of two odd primes in as many ways as possible. Write these numbers as the sum of three primes in as many ways as possible.

5.3.3

Factorization

1. Using 24 poker chips, make as many different rectangular arrays as possible. (Each rectangle must use all 24 chips.) Use these arrays to show that 2, 3, 4, 6, and 8 are all factors of 24.

2. Using 42 poker chips, it is possible to make a 6 × 7 array, and so 6 and 7 are factors of 42. But using 6 poker chips, it is possible to make a 2 × 3 array, so you can automatically conclude that 2 and 3 are also factors of 42. Explain why, using some poker chips and the tree diagram to the left.

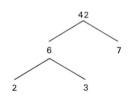

3. The following figure shows three different factor trees for 60.

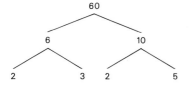 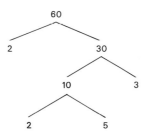 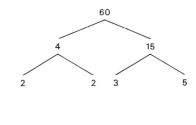

Make two more factor trees for 60. Notice that branches can continue separating until all the numbers on the bottom branches are prime numbers. These numbers are called the prime factors of 60. No matter how the branches separate, will the numbers on the ends of the branches end up being 2, 2, 3, and 5?

4. Find the prime factors of 2310 by making a factor tree. By looking at the prime factors, determine how many different rectangles could be made using 2310 poker chips.

5. Find the prime factors of 1260. How many different rectangles can be made using 1260 poker chips?

5.3.4
Least
Common Multiple

In order to add fractions, it is sometimes helpful to be able to find the least common multiple of two numbers.

Examples:

a. $\frac{1}{2} + \frac{1}{3} = \frac{3}{6} + \frac{2}{6} = \frac{5}{6}$ and 6 is the least common multiple of 2 and 3.

b. $\frac{1}{6} + \frac{1}{4} = \frac{2}{12} + \frac{3}{12} = \frac{5}{12}$ and 12 is the least common multiple of 6 and 4.

1. Each of the numbers below has been written as a product of its prime factors. Determine whether each number is a multiple of $84 = 2 \times 2 \times 3 \times 7$.

a. $924 = 2 \times 2 \times 3 \times 7 \times 11$

b. $180 = 2 \times 2 \times 3 \times 3 \times 5$

c. $210 = 2 \times 3 \times 5 \times 7$

   d. $6930 = 2 \times 3 \times 3 \times 5 \times 7 \times 11$

   e. $84084 = 13 \times 7 \times 11 \times 2 \times 3 \times 2 \times 7$

   f. $300300 = 5 \times 13 \times 2 \times 11 \times 5 \times 3 \times 7 \times 2$

   g. $420 = 2 \times 3 \times 5 \times 7 \times 2$

   h. $882 = 2 \times 3 \times 3 \times 7 \times 7$

2. Are any of the above numbers multiples of $30 = 2 \times 3 \times 5$?

3. Numbers that are multiples of both 84 and 30 are called "common multiples" of 84 and 30. Which of the numbers above were common multiples of 84 and 30?

4. Among the common multiples of 84 and 30, the smallest positive multiple is called the "least common multiple" of 84 and 30. What is the least common multiple of 84 and 30?

5. Find the least common multiple of each of the following pairs of numbers:

    42 and 15   45 and 175   8 and 27

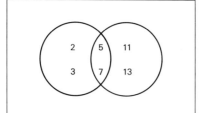

6. How is finding the least common multiple of 210 and 5005 like finding the union of the two sets of numbers that are shown in the diagram to the left?

5.3.5
Greatest
Common Factor

In order to reduce fractions to lowest terms, it is useful to find the *greatest common factor* of the numerator and the denominator. For instance, in order to reduce 36/42 to lowest terms, divide the numerator and the denominator by 6 (because 6 is the greatest common factor of 36 and 42).

$$\frac{36}{42} = \frac{6 \times 6}{7 \times 6} = \frac{6}{7}$$

1. Each of the numbers below has been written as a product of its prime factors. Determine whether each number is a factor of $1260 = 2 \times 2 \times 3 \times 3 \times 5 \times 7$.

   a. $18 = 2 \times 3 \times 3$ **c.** $105 = 3 \times 5 \times 7$

   b. $8 = 2 \times 2 \times 2$ **d.** $33 = 3 \times 11$

e. $98 = 2 \times 7 \times 7$ **g.** $75 = 3 \times 5 \times 5$

f. 3   **h.** $70 = 2 \times 5 \times 7$

2. Which of the above numbers are factors of $7350 = 2 \times 3 \times 5 \times 5 \times 7 \times 7$?

3. Numbers that are factors of both 1260 and 7350 are called "common factors" of 1260 and 7350. Which of the numbers above were common factors of 1260 and 7350?

4. Among the common factors of 1260 and 7350, the largest positive factor is called the "greatest common factor" of 1260 and 7350. What is the greatest common factor of 1260 and 7350? Is it included among the eight numbers that were given above?

5. Find the greatest common factor of 462 and 525 ($462 = 2 \times 3 \times 7 \times 11$ and $525 = 3 \times 5 \times 5 \times 7$).

6. Find the greatest common factor of 3822 and 3990.

7. Reduce each of these fractions to lowest terms:
   a. $36/90$
   b. $45/105$
   c. $48/84$

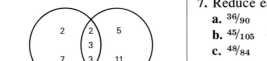

8. Use the Venn diagram to the left to describe how to find the greatest common factor of 252 and 990. ($252 = 2 \times 2 \times 3 \times 3 \times 7$ and $990 = 2 \times 3 \times 3 \times 5 \times 11$)

*5.3.6
Divisibility Rules

1. Without actually carrying out the division, determine which of the following numbers have 2 as a factor: 497,436; 267,423; 27,950; 3,764,578; 465,781. What rule can be used to decide whether a number is divisible by 2?

2. Determine which of the following numbers have 5 as a factor: 467,590; 6,427,545; 7,327,544; 484,396. What rule can be used to determine whether a number is divisible by 5?

3. What rule can be used to determine whether a number is divisible by 9? (Hint: Look at the sequence of numbers that are the multiples of 9: 9, 18, 27, 36, 45, 54, 63, 72, 81. Do you see a pattern?) Try out your rule on a few large numbers to make sure that it works.

4. The divisibility rule for 3 is similar to the divisibility rule for 9. Use this hint to find a rule to determine whether a number is divisible by 3. Find two large numbers that have 3 as a factor, but not 9.

5. If a number is divisible by 2 and by 3, then it is divisible by 6. Find a divisibility rule for 4 and for 8.

6. Divisibility rules for 7, 11, and 13 are more complicated. An example that illustrates the divisibility rule for 11 is given below. To determine whether 90,766,159 is divisible by 11, follow these steps.

a. Add the alternate digits: 9 0, 7 6 6, 1 5 9 →27

b. Add the remaining digits: 9 0, 7 6 6, 1 5 9 →16

c. Find the difference between the two sums: $27 - 16 = 11$

d. If the difference is divisible by 11, then the number is divisible by 11. Use this rule to determine whether each of the following numbers is divisible by 11:

   6,432,198   4,041,653   8,418,564

1. Remainders

a. If n is some counting number, then what are the possible remainders when n is divided by 2? By 3? By 5? By 9?

b. What is the remainder when 2769 is divided by 10? By 5? By 2? By 9? By 7?

c. A group of less than 100 people stood in a line. When they counted off by 2s, the remainder was 1. When they counted off by 3s, the remainder was 2. And when they counted off by 5s, the remainder was 4. How many people were in the line?

2. Casting Out Nines

a. When the sum of the digits of a counting number is divided by 9, the remainder is the same as when the number itself is divided by 9. Check this fact for the following numbers.

   4721   2347   8136

b. Carry out each of the calculations. Do you see a pattern?

$$\frac{54321 - 12345}{9} = \qquad \frac{89543 - 34589}{9} = \qquad \frac{6743 - 3476}{9} =$$

   c. Write down any counting number. Form a new number by reordering the digits of the original number. Find the difference between the original number and the new number, and divide the difference by nine. What is the remainder?

3. Perfect Numbers

   Numbers have always played an important role in magic, sorcery, astrology, and in the casting of horoscopes. Some numbers that have frequently been given mystical significance are known as "perfect numbers." A number is perfect if it is the sum of 1 plus its prime divisors. For instance, 6 is a perfect number since $6 = 1 \times 2 \times 3$ and $6 = 1 + 2 + 3$. Fewer than thirty perfect numbers are known, but there is another perfect number less than 100. Can you find it? (The number 1 is not considered a perfect number.)

5.4
FINDING
NUMBER PATTERNS

Overview: **Many number patterns occur in a hundreds chart, a multiplication table, or an addition table. Investigating some of these patterns can lead to a better understanding of numbers and number operations.**

   In this section, you will be looking for number patterns in several different kinds of number tables and number diagrams.

Groups of two or four people should work together in this section. After a few short introductory problems, the section is divided into two problem situations, one labeled A, the other labeled B. Half the members in each group should work on part A, and the other half should work on part B.

1. Take five minutes to list as many number patterns as you can find in the three number charts below.

Hundreds Chart

1	2	3	4	5	6	7	8	9	10
11	12	13	14	15	16	17	18	19	20
21	22	23	24	25	26	27	28	29	30
31	32	33	34	35	36	37	38	39	40
41	42	43	44	45	46	47	48	49	50
51	52	53	54	55	56	57	58	59	60
61	62	63	64	65	66	67	68	69	70
71	72	73	74	75	76	77	78	79	80
81	82	83	84	85	86	87	88	89	90
91	92	93	94	95	96	97	98	99	100

Addition Table

+	0	1	2	3	4	5	6	7	8	9
0	0	1	2	3	4	5	6	7	8	9
1	1	2	3	4	5	6	7	8	9	10
2	2	3	4	5	6	7	8	9	10	11
3	3	4	5	6	7	8	9	10	11	12
4	4	5	6	7	8	9	10	11	12	13
5	5	6	7	8	9	10	11	12	13	14
6	6	7	8	9	10	11	12	13	14	15
7	7	8	9	10	11	12	13	14	15	16
8	8	9	10	11	12	13	14	15	16	17
9	9	10	11	12	13	14	15	16	17	18

Multiplication Table

×	0	1	2	3	4	5	6	7	8	9
0	0	0	0	0	0	0	0	0	0	0
1	0	1	2	3	4	5	6	7	8	9
2	0	2	4	6	8	10	12	14	16	18
3	0	3	6	9	12	15	18	21	24	27
4	0	4	8	12	16	20	24	28	32	36
5	0	5	10	15	20	25	30	35	40	45
6	0	6	12	18	24	30	36	42	48	54
7	0	7	14	21	28	35	42	49	56	63
8	0	8	16	24	32	40	48	56	64	72
9	0	9	18	27	36	45	54	63	72	81

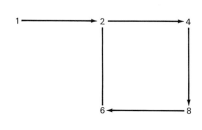

2. Begin with the number "1" and start doubling.

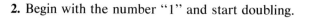

$$\underline{1} \xrightarrow{\times 2} \underline{2} \xrightarrow{\times 2} \underline{4} \xrightarrow{\times 2} \underline{8} \xrightarrow{\times 2} 1\underline{6} \xrightarrow{\times 2} 3\underline{2} \xrightarrow{\times 2} 6\underline{4} \xrightarrow{\times 2} 12\underline{8} \xrightarrow{\times 2}$$

If you only look at the last digit in each of the products in the above sequence, the sequence looks like the diagram at the left.

3. Now begin with the number 2 and start doubling. What sequence of numbers do you get as the last digit in each product? What sequence do you get when you begin with 4? With 6? With 8?

4. Begin with the number 3 and start doubling. What sequence do you get? What sequence do you get when you begin with 7? With 9? Use the diagram at the bottom of p. 630 to illustrate these facts.

5. Make another diagram, only multiply by 8 instead of doubling. How does this diagram compare with the doubling diagram?

*Problem Make a diagram for tripling, and then make one for multiples of 7. How are these two diagrams related? Can you find another pair of numbers that are related in this way?

5.4.1
Two
Tables of
Numbers

A.1. Finish filling out the table below.

1	2	3	4	5	6	7	8	9
2	4	6	8	0	2	4	6	8
3	6	9	2	5	8	1	4	7
4	8	2						
5								
6								
7								
8								
9								

A.2. What number patterns do you see in the table? Can you explain what caused them to occur? Which rows contain all of the numbers from 1 to 9? Can you explain why it only happened in these rows?

A.3. Compare the second row with the eighth row. How are they related? What other pairs of rows are related in this way? Why do the numbers repeat in the rows that contain zeros?

A.4. Draw diagonals on the table in exercise A.1. Compare the numbers on both sides of the diagonals. What do you notice?

A.5. Point out the patterns in your table to the members of your group who are working on part B. Wherever you can, explain why the patterns occurred.

A.6. Now can you find some more patterns in the hundreds chart, multiplication table, or addition table?

B.1. Finish filling out the table below.

1	1	1	1	1	1	1	1
2	4	8	6	2	4	8	6
3	9	7	1	3	9	7	1
4	6	4	6				
5	5	5					
6							
7							
8							
9							

B.2. What number patterns do you see in the table? Can you explain what caused them to occur?

B.3. Which columns contain all of the numbers from 1 through 9? Look at the sequence of numbers in the second column. What do you notice? What other columns have this property? Notice the relationship between the second column and the sixth column. What other pairs of columns are related in this way?

B.4. How is the second row related to the eighth row? What other pair of rows is related in this way?

B.5. Point out the patterns in your table to the members of your group who are working on part A. Explain why the patterns occurred if you can.

B.6. Can you find more patterns in the hundreds chart, multiplication table, or addition table?

5.5
PASCAL'S
TRIANGLE
Overview: **Many number patterns occur in a hundreds chart, or in a multiplication or addition table. Pascal's triangle is an array of numbers that is also filled with interesting number patterns. The first half of this section will give several concrete situations that can be described using Pascal's triangle; the last half of the section will investigate some of the patterns that occur in the triangle.**

Materials needed: Poker chips, attribute blocks, and colored rods.

Groups of about four people should work together in this section.

Think of a situation that would explain the positions of the numbers that are given in the diagram below.

20	10	4	1	4	10	20
10	6	3	1	3	6	10
4	3	2	1	2	3	4
1	1	1	■	1	1	1
4	3	2	1	2	3	4
10	6	3	1	3	6	10
20	10	4	1	4	10	20

Look for a pattern in the table below, and then finish filling out the chart.

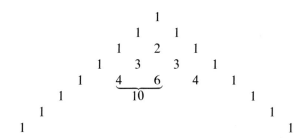

5.5.1
**Situations Related
to Pascal's Triangle**
Since the A and B problems give examples of different kinds of situations that can be described using Pascal's triangle, and since a goal of the section is to become familiar with a variety of situations involving Pascal's triangle, members of the group who work on the A problems should compare their work with the work of people who are working on the B problems, and vice versa.

A.1. Using white poker chips and blue poker chips, it is possible to make eight different three-poker chip rows. One of the rows will contain three white poker chips; three rows will contain two white poker chips; three rows will contain one white poker chip; and one row will contain no white poker chips. This information is in Table 5.7. Finish filling out the table. (Look for a pattern.)

Table 5.7 **Number of White Poker Chips in the Row**

Number of chips in the row	0	1	2	3	4	5	6	7
1								
2								
3	1	3	3	1				
4								
5								
6								
7								

A.2. Fill in the blanks in each of the following equations.

$(a+b)^1 = \underline{\quad} a + \underline{\quad} b$

$(a+b)^2 = \underline{\quad} a^2 + \underline{\quad} ab + \underline{\quad} b^2$

$(a+b)^3 = \underline{\quad} a^3 + \underline{\quad} a^2b + \underline{\quad} ab^2 + \underline{\quad} b^3$

$(a+b)^4 = \underline{\quad} a^4 + \underline{\quad} a^3b + \underline{\quad} a^2b^2 +$

$\underline{\quad} ab^3 + \underline{\quad} b^4$

$(a+b)^5 = \underline{\quad} a^5 + \underline{\quad} a^4b + \underline{\quad} a^3b^2 +$

$\underline{\quad} a^2b^3 + \underline{\quad} ab^4 + \underline{\quad} b^5$

$(a+b)^{10} = \underline{\hspace{5cm}}$

*A.3. a. There are four different ways to add together colored rods to make a train that is three units long. One way uses three rods, two ways use two rods, and one way uses only one rod. In how many different ways can you make a train that is 10 units long? Specifically, in how many ways can you do it using 1 rod? Using 2 rods? Using 3 rods? Using larger numbers of rods?

b. If order does not count, then there are only three different ways to make a train three units long. If order does not count, how many different ways can you make a train 10 units long? In how many ways can you do it using 1 rod? Using 2 rods? Using 3 rods? Using larger numbers of rods?

B.1. Using three attribute blocks, eight different sets can be formed. One set can contain all the objects; three different sets can contain two objects; three sets can contain only one object; and the other set is the empty set. This information is recorded in Table 5.8. Finish filling out the table. (Look for a pattern.)

$$\{\bigcirc, \square, \triangle\} \quad \{\bigcirc, \square\} \quad \{\triangle\} \quad \{\ \ \}$$

$$\{\bigcirc, \triangle\} \quad \{\bigcirc\}$$

$$\{\square, \triangle\} \quad \{\square\}$$

Table 5.8 **Number of Elements in the Set**

Number of attribute blocks being used	0	1	2	3	4	5	6	7
1								
2								
3	1	3	3	1				
4								
5								
6								
7								

B.2. Carry out each of the following calculations.

$11^1 =$ _____

$11^2 =$ _____

$11^3 =$ _____

$11^4 =$ _____

$11^5 =$ _____

*B.3. If 128 balls were dropped into a pinball machine like the one shown below, and each ball took a different path, how many balls would end up in each slot?

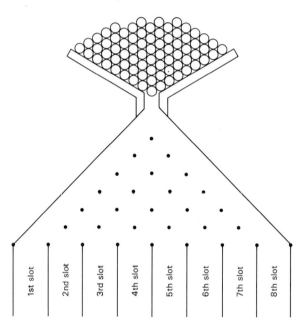

1st slot 2nd slot 3rd slot 4th slot 5th slot 6th slot 7th slot 8th slot

5.5.2
Patterns in Pascal's Triangle

1. Two different versions of Pascal's triangle are given below. Find at least four different number patterns that occur in these arrays of numbers.

```
                              1
                           1     1
                        1     2     1
                     1     3     3     1
                  1     4     6     4     1
               1     5    10    10     5     1
            1     6    15    20    15     6     1
         1     7    21    35    35    21     7     1
      1     8    28    56    70    56    28     8     1
   1     9    36    84   126   126    84    36     9     1
1    10    45   120   210   252   210   120    45    10     1
1   11    55   165   330   462   462   330   165    55    11    1
1   12   66   220   495   792   924   792   495   220   66   12   1
```

1	1	1	1	1	1	1	1	1
1	2	3	4	5	6	7	8	9
1	3	6	10	15	21	28	36	45
1	4	10	20	35	56	84	120	165
1	5	15	35	70	126	210	330	490
1	6	21	56	126	252	462	792	1282
1	7	28	84	210	462	924	1716	2998
1	8	36	120	330	792	1716	3432	6430
1	9	45	165	495	1282	2998	6430	12860

2. What pattern occurs when you circle all the even numbers in Pascal's triangle? What pattern occurs when you circle the multiples of 3? The multiples of 5? The multiples of 7?

3. Can you find the *triangle numbers* in Pascal's triangle? What about the *tetrahedral numbers*?

4. In the triangular version of Pascal's triangle, 7 divides every number in its row (except for the number 1). For what other numbers is this true? Do you see a pattern?

5. Three more sequences of numbers that can be derived from Pascal's triangle are shown below. Where have you seen each of these sequences before?

a.

```
  1  ←——————————————1
  2  ←—————————————1    1
  4  ←————————————1    2    1
  8  ←———————————1    3    3    1
 16  ←——————————1    4    6    4    1
 32  ←—————————1    5   10   10    5    1
 64  ←————————1    6   15   20   15    6    1
128  ←———1    7   21   35   35   21    7    1
```

b.

```
  1  ←——————————————1
  2  ←—————————————1    1
  4  ←————————————1    2    1
  8  ←———————————1    3    3    1
 16  ←——————————1    4    6    4    1
 31  ←—————————1    5   10   10    5    1
 57  ←————————1    6   15   20   15    6    1
 99  ←———1    7   21   35   35   21    7    1
```

c.
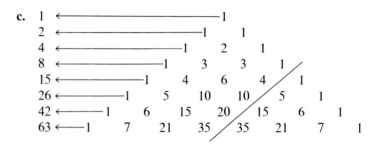

5.6
THE
FIBONACCI
SEQUENCE

Overview: **The Fibonacci sequence is one of the most interesting sequences that occur in mathematics. It has been found to have so many interesting properties and so many diverse applications that a magazine called the** *Fibonacci Quarterly* **(published since 1963) is entirely devoted to the remarkable properties of the sequence. Several of these properties will be investigated in this section.**

Look for a pattern in the sequence of numbers below, and then guess the next five numbers in the sequence.

1   1   2   3   5   8   13   21   34

This sequence of numbers arose in connection with a problem that was formulated in 1202 by Leonardo de Pisa (nicknamed "Fibonacci"). The problem was: "What is the number of pairs of rabbits at the beginning of each month if a single pair of newly born rabbits is put into an enclosure at the beginning of a month, and if each pair breeds a new pair at the beginning of the second month following birth, and an additional pair at the beginning of each month thereafter?"

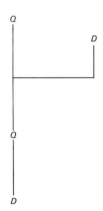

A problem that is similar to Fibonacci's rabbit problem concerns the family tree of a male bee (drone). A drone bee has only one parent, the queen. But, a queen has two parents, a queen and a drone. The figure at the left shows the family tree of a drone bee back to his grandparents. Continue the family tree back five more generations. Assuming no intermarriages, how many ancestors are in each generation?

*Problem   If you are allowed to go upstairs one or two steps at a time, then there are five different ways to get to the fourth step. In how many different ways can you reach the twentieth step?

5.6.1
The
Divine Proportion

If you take the ratio of successive numbers in the Fibonacci sequence, the ratio comes closer and closer to the "divine proportion."

$$1/_1 = 1 \rightarrow 2/_1 = 2 \rightarrow 3/_2 = 1.5 \rightarrow 5/_3 = 1.66 \rightarrow 8/_5 = 1.60 \rightarrow 13/_8 = 1.625$$

$$89/_{55} = 1.6182 \leftarrow 55/_{34} = 1.6176 \rightarrow 34/_{21} = 1.6190 \leftarrow 21/_{13} = 1.6154$$

The "divine proportion" is the ratio between the sides of a "golden rectangle." An example of a golden rectangle is shown at the left. Its sides are in the ratio 1 to 1.6154. The golden rectangle was believed by the ancient Greeks to be the most beautiful four-sided figure. Consequently, many examples of "golden rectangles" can be found in Greek art and architecture (e.g., the Parthenon; see Figure 5.1). Think of at least five different everyday examples of things that are approximately the shape of a golden rectangle (e.g., postcards, notebook paper, blackboards, etc.); measure their sides; and, find the ratio of the short sides to the long sides. Are any of the examples golden rectangles?

Figure 5.1 (left)

Figure 5.2 (right)

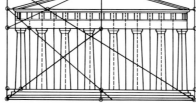 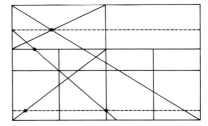

If a square is removed from a golden rectangle, as shown in Figure 5.3, then the remaining rectangle (which is shown in blue) will also be a golden rectangle. Furthermore, if you continue this "square-removing" process, and if you connect the cut-off points as shown in Figure 5.4, then a logarithmic spiral is obtained. The logarithmic spiral is the only spiral that does not change shape as it grows. This fact helps explain why it occurs so often in nature. Think of several examples of such spirals occurring in nature.

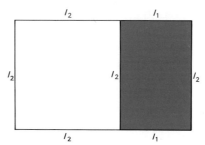

Figure 5.3

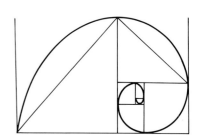

Figure 5.4

Try this square-removing process with a piece of notebook paper to test whether it is a golden rectangle. Does it work? If the remaining square is the same shape as the original notebook paper, then the notebook paper is a golden rectangle. Otherwise, it is not.

In the above figure, if the sides of the small golden rectangle are of length l_1, and l_2, then the sides of the square are of length l_2, and the sides of the large golden rectangle are of length l_2 and $l_1 + l_2$. Therefore, because the small golden rectangle and the large golden rectangles are similar figures, their dimensions are proportional. That is:

$$\frac{l_2}{l_1} = \frac{l_1 + l_2}{l_2}$$

The above equation gives another way to describe the golden ratio (or the divine proportion). For example, a line segment is said to be divided according to the divine proportion if the ratio of the short segment to the longer segment is the same as the ratio of the longer segment to the whole segment. Measure the line segments below, and determine which ones most closely satisfy the equation

$$\frac{l_2}{l_1} = \frac{l_1 + l_2}{l_2}.$$

1. $\vdash\!\!\!\!\!\!\frac{\qquad l_2 \qquad}{}\!\!+\!\!\frac{\quad l_1 \quad}{}\!\!\dashv$

2. $\vdash\!\!\!\!\!\!\frac{\qquad l_2 \qquad}{}\!\!+\!\!\frac{\quad l_1 \quad}{}\!\!\dashv$

3. $\vdash\!\!\!\!\!\!\frac{\qquad l_2 \qquad}{}\!\!+\!\!\frac{\quad l_1 \quad}{}\!\!\dashv$

5.6.2 Human Anatomy

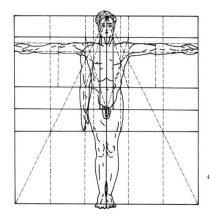

Several books[4] have been written that support the Greek point of view that the divine proportion is the most artistically pleasing of all proportions. For instance, some students may be interested to learn that (according to Zwising) in order for a woman to have a perfect figure, the ratio of the height of her navel to her overall height should be "the divine proportion" (approximately 1.618).

At the beginning of the Renaissance, Luca Pacioli's book *Divina Proportione* (1509) emphasized the role of proportion in the human body and living shapes in general. These two illustrations by Leonardo da Vinci appeared in Pacioli's book. Notice the many examples of golden rectangles and of line segments that are divided according to the divine proportion.

---

[4] Adolf Zwising, *Der Goldene Schnitt*, Teubner, Leipzig and Berlin, 1884; Samuel Colman, *Nature's Harmonic Unity*, G. P. Putnam's Sons, New York, 1913; Sir Theodore Cook, *The Curves of Life*, H. Holt and Company, New York, 1914.

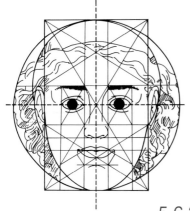

1. Measure the length of your hand (the tip of your longest finger to your wrist) and your forearm. Find the ratio.

2. Measure the three bones of your middle finger. Is the longest bone equal to the sum of the other two?

3. Mark your height on the blackboard and then mark the tip of your middle finger when your arm is extended naturally downwards (e.g., look at the right arm of the figure in the Leonardo drawing). Does the tip of your finger divide your total height according to the divine proportion?

5.6.3
Fibonacci Numbers in Biology

The phenomenon called "phyllotaxis" refers to the leaf arrangement of plants. For instance, the leaves of some trees, such as basswood, occur alternately on opposite sides of a twig. This arrangement is called "$1/2$ phyllotaxis." In other trees, such as beech and hazel, the passage from one leaf to the next involves a $2/3$ rotation. Still other trees involve a $3/5$ rotation, such as an oak, or an $8/13$ rotation, such as a willow. How are these rotations related to the Fibonacci sequence?

Other examples of phyllotaxis occur in the spiral arrangement of seeds in a sunflower, scales on a pine cone, and the bristles on a pineapple. For a more thorough discussion of phyllotaxis as it relates to the Fibonacci sequence, see M. Ghyka's book *The Geometry of Art and Life*.[5]

5.6.4
Fibonacci Numbers in Music

Not only is the "Fibonacci sequence" related to the "divine proportion," but the "divine proportion" (which divides a segment with one point) is in turn related to "harmonic progression" (which divides a segment with two points). In geometry, four points (a, b, c, d) on a line form a harmonic progression if: $\dfrac{(b-o)}{(c-o)} = \dfrac{(d-o)}{(b-o)}$ (where o is halfway between a and b).

As the word "harmonic" suggests, harmonic progressions have applications in music. For example, select a string on a guitar and pluck it. Decrease the length of the string to half its original length by holding your finger on the midpoint; pluck the string. What is the relationship between the two notes?

Strings of length 12, 9, 8 and 6 units will give the notes "do," "fa," "sol," and "do" respectively. Do these numbers form a harmonic progression?

For a specific example in which Fibonacci numbers can be seen to occur in music, look at a piano keyboard. The 13 keys shown in the illustration form one octave of the "chromatic" scale. The number 8 corresponds to the number of white keys in an octave, called the notes of a "major" scale. The number 5 corresponds to the number of black keys in an octave, called the notes of the "pentatonic" scale.

For students interested in other connections between mathematics and music, Georges Cuisenaire was a musician. Cuisenaire noticed that many musical patterns that children mastered with ease were identical to the mathematical patterns and relationships that caused them difficulties. So, Cuisenaire invented his colored rods to help "concretize" the mathematics that his children were supposed to be learning.

5.6.5 Patterns in the Fibonacci Sequence

Just as many events in nature are related to the Fibonacci sequence, the sequence is also related to other topics in mathematics. For instance, the diagram at the left shows a relationship between the Fibonacci sequence and Pascal's triangle.

Just as many interesting patterns occur in Pascal's triangle, many patterns also occur in the Fibonacci sequence. A few examples are given in the problems below.

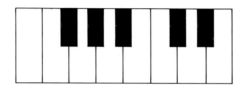

1. The first 30 numbers in the Fibonacci sequence are shown below. What is the 31st number? Draw a line under the numbers that are divisible by 2. Is there a pattern? Circle the numbers that are divisible by 3. Is there a pattern? Is there a pattern for numbers that are divisible by 4? What about 5, 6, or 7?

1	1	2	3	5
8	13	21	34	55
89	144	233	377	610
987	1597	2584	4181	6765
10946	17711	28657	46368	75025
121393	196418	317811	514229	832040

2. The sum of the first two numbers is equal to the fourth number minus 1. The sum of the first three numbers is the fifth number minus 1. The sum of the first four numbers is the sixth number minus 1. Does this pattern continue?

3. Determine whether the following statement is true: If n is bigger than 2, then the nth Fibonacci number is prime if n is prime.

---

*5.7

PROBLEMS

Overview: The problems in this section arise from several topics introduced throughout this unit. Some problems are easy, some are not so easy, and some may be solved in a variety of ways. The problems involve organizing information, looking for patterns, forming hypotheses, testing hypotheses, and all of the other problem solving skills introduced throughout the unit.

Materials needed: Colored rods, scissors, and paper.

---

1. Square Roots

This diagram illustrates that n^2 is equal to the sum of the first n odd integers. This fact can be used to find the square root of a number. For instance, in order to find the square root of 36, subtract successively larger odd numbers (starting with one). The square root will be equal to the number of odd numbers that are subtracted before reaching zero.

$$1^2 = 1 \qquad 2^2 = 1 + 3 \qquad 3^2 = 1 + 3 + 5 \qquad 4^2 = 1 + 3 + 5 + 7$$

```
       36
     −  1
       35     Since six odd numbers were subtracted,
     −  3        the square root of 36 is 6.
       32
     −  5
       27
     −  7
       20
     −  9
       11
     − 11
        0
```

Use this method to estimate the square root of 20.

Use the same method to estimate the square root of 2,000. Does your answer suggest a better estimation for the square root of 20?

2. Colored Rod Equations

Use colored rods to illustrate the fact that $(n + 1)^2 = n^2 + 2n + 1$. Hint: Look at diagram *a*. What equations are suggested by diagrams *b* and *c*? Illustrate another equation using a pattern that you make up yourself.

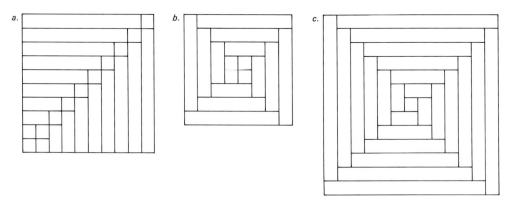

Use rods to illustrate that $n^2 = [(n + 1) \times (n - 1)] + 1$.

3. Beads in a Jar

Two glass jars were sitting on a table. One contained 1,000 blue beads, and the other contained 500 yellow beads. A teacher took 20 beads out of the blue bead jar, and put them into the yellow bead jar. Then she shook the yellow bead jar until the blue beads were thoroughly mixed. Next, she randomly selected 20 beads from the yellow bead jar and put them into the blue bead jar.

Are there more blue beads in the yellow bead jar than there are yellow beads in the blue bead jar? (Hint: Eliminate all irrelevant information.)

4. A Strategy Game for Two Players

    a. The first player calls a number from 1 to 10.

    b. The second player calls a number that is the first number plus any number from 1 to 10. (For instance, if the first player called 7, then the second player could call any number from 8 to 17.)

    c. The first player calls a number that is the second number plus any number from 1 to 10.

d. This process continues. The player who calls 100 wins. What strategy guarantees a victory for the first player?

5. Combining Digits

Here is a problem that was posed by an elementary education major during a course entitled "Algebra for Teachers."

Step 1: Write any number.

Step 2: Add successive digits two at a time. For example, three different ways to do this are shown here.

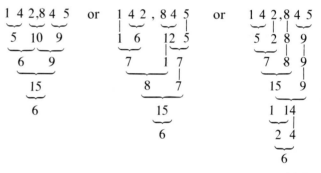

Question: Do you always get the same result no matter which way you combine the digits?

6. Cutting Paper

Take five sheets of paper. Cut some of them into five pieces, and then cut some of these pieces into five pieces. Continue the process for a few more times, and then count the pieces. Could the total ever be 1973?

7. Products

If you took the product of the first 100 counting numbers, how many zeros would be in the answer?

8. Integers

Imagine that all the integers are written in order, with 1 in the first place, 2 in the second place, 3 in the third place, and so forth (1, 2, 3, 4, 5, 6, 7, 8, 9, 10, 11, 12, 13, . . .). What digit is in the 206,788th place?

9. The Tower of Hanoi

The "Tower of Hanoi" problem involves three tower sites. A "tower" (consisting of a stack of colored rods arranged in descending order) is placed on one of the sites. The problem is to move the tower to one of the other sites, but only one rod can be moved at a time, and a larger rod can never be placed on a smaller rod. What is the minimum number of moves needed to move all ten rods to another site?

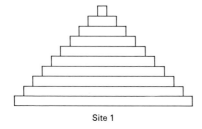

Site 1   Site 2   Site 3

10. A Ruler Problem

Find the minimum number of marks needed on a 10-inch stick, so that each of the 10 lengths from 1 to 10 is represented as the distance between two of the marks.

Hint: A 3-inch stick requires 3 marks.

0   1   3

Ten marks are required for a 36-inch stick. Can you find a way to do it? (This problem is not easy.)

5.8
PEDAGOGICAL
REMARKS

Some of the problem situations in this unit could be presented to elementary school children. However, as you probably discovered, many seemingly simple questions soon escalate into difficult problems. Nonetheless, part of the beauty of number theory is that many problems are easy to present in concrete situations. Students can be allowed to attack the problem at a level of sophistication appropriate for them. For instance, problems about figurate numbers can often be investigated either by using "fancy" equations or by counting and organizing handfuls of poker chips, and looking for patterns.

Teachers seem to use number theory problems for two quite different reasons. Number theory problems often lead to fascinating projects for advanced students. Such projects can emphasize the open-ended nature of mathematical inquiry by allowing children to be "question askers" as well as "answer givers." Number theory problems can also be used with children who are experiencing difficulties by enticing them to notice number relationships and to practice skills that otherwise have been looked upon as drudgery. Looking for patterns in addition and multiplication tables can help children learn their basic facts and can lead to important insights about the four basic operations $(+ -, \times, \div)$.

The study of odd and even numbers is an example of a number theory topic that would be appropriate for many elementary school children. Some questions might be

1. Using double-row arrays of colored circles, how do the shapes representing odd numbers differ from the shapes representing even numbers?

Odd	o	o o	o o o	o o o o	o o o o o
		o	o o	o o o	o o o o

Even	o	o o	o o o	o o o o	o o o o o
	o	o o	o o o	o o o o	o o o o o

2. When you add an even number to an even number, what kind of number is the sum? What about an odd added to an odd, or an odd added to an even?

Hint:
$5 + 3$ $4 + 3$
o o ● ●   o o ● ●
o o o ●   o o ●

3. If the sum of two numbers is odd, what do you know about the numbers?

4. Without actually performing the following calculation, figure out whether the answer is odd or even.

$$2 + 3 + 5 + 7 + 9 + 4 + 6 + 1 + 8 = \square$$

5. When you multiply an odd number by an even number, what kind of number is the sum? What about an odd by an even, or an even by an even?

3×5 o o ● o o ● o o
                 o ● ● o ● ● o

6. Fill out the following tables for the addition and multiplication of odd and even numbers:

7. Johnny cannot remember whether 7×8 is 56 or 65; can you help him if you know about odd and even numbers?

One of the benefits to be derived from questions like these is simply to encourage children to ask themselves "Is that reasonable?" when they give the answer to a question.

+	Even	Odd
Even		
Odd		

×	Even	Odd
Even		
Odd		

appendix 1

how to get the laboratory materials for this book

It is unusual for college mathematics classes to use "laboratory equipment." Hence it will often take some extra effort to assemble the materials necessary to teach this course for the first time. This appendix is intended to simplify the initial process as much as possible by giving specific suggestions on ordering from commercial distributors or on making the necessary materials.

Only a minimum set of materials available to each student is needed for most sections in the book. This consists of a set of rods and a set of chips and access to rulers, paper, marking pens, scissors, and glue. We usually ask each student to provide himself with rods and chips, perhaps through campus bookstores. Alternatively, classroom sets of rods and chips can be loaned to the students.

At the beginning of each exercise the materials needed in that exercise are listed. When these go beyond the basic materials noted above, directions are given for making or obtaining the additional materials. This appendix supplies specific ordering information and more detailed directions for making materials.[1]

Instructors who are unaccustomed to the use of laboratory materials will find rather quickly that the pedagogical values and the positive effects on motivation,

---

[1] Suggestions for a class "making day" are included in this appendix, Part B.

649

attitude, and learning make the effort of getting started in this way more than worthwhile.

Specific order numbers and distributors are sometimes mentioned in this appendix, but only to make the initial ordering of materials easier. That is, listing of a particular distributor does *not* suggest any preference for that source over many other distributors. In a few cases we mention prices, but only to give you a general idea of what to expect. Prices change often, and current information must be obtained from distributors, who are very willing to supply catalogs.

To make things easier for you, the addresses of distributors mentioned in this appendix are listed below. There are many other reliable sources of materials and you can sometimes save money by comparing prices from several sources.

Creative Publications
P.O. Box 10328
Palo Alto, Calif. 94303

Cuisenaire Company of America
12 Church Street
New Rochelle, N.Y. 10805

A. Daigger and Company
Educational Teaching Aids Division
159 W. Kinzie Street
Chicago, Ill. 60610

Dick Blick
P.O. Box 1267
Galesburg, Ill. 61401

Ideal School Supply Co.
11000 S. Lavergne Avenue
Oak Lawn, Ill. 60453

Math Shop
5 Bridge Street
Watertown, Mass. 02172

Selective Educational Equipment, Inc.
3 Bridge Street
Newton, Mass. 02195

MATERIALS NEEDED IN PART A Rods and chips plus such basic supplies as rulers, paper, glue, marking pens, and posterboard suffice as a minimum for all the lessons in this part of the book. Here is an indication of what you should plan to have for each unit:

Unit 1: Decks of playing cards, rods, chips.

Unit 2: Rods, chips, rulers (with centimeters), paper, poster board, glue.

Unit 3: Same as Unit 2 plus graph paper or dot paper. (Dot paper is marked with a rectangular array of dots, say with 0.5-centimeter spacing; or a stencil can be made on a typewriter by typing periods with spaces between them.)

Unit 4: Same as Unit 2.

Unit 5: Same as Unit 3, plus string or ribbon.

Unit 6: Chips colored white on one side and blue on the other, rods, marking pens in several colors.

Unit 7: Same as Unit 2 plus, for each student, about 20 paper strips about 1.5 cm wide and exactly 24 cm long. (The strips are easily produced with a paper cutter; cut up several sheets at once.)

By "rods," we mean, of course, colored sticks graduated in lengths from 1 to 10 centimeters. These were first marketed as *Cuisenaire rods* (Cuisenaire is a registered trademark) but similar rods are now part of the line of nearly every distributor of mathematics laboratory equipment. The original Cuisenaire colors have a long tradition, and hence many work cards and exercises in commercially published materials refer to them. However, sets are marketed in various color schemes. In this book we have either avoided mentioning color or, when that would have been awkward, have used the traditional Cuisenaire color scheme. If rods with other colors are used, it should be easy to make the appropriate adjustments.

As far as we can tell, the sets of rods of the various distributors are pretty much equivalent both in utility and price, with $4 or less a typical price of a serviceable set of individual rods. If rods are ordered in classroom sets, bonus books as well as cheaper prices sometimes result.

Although our general point of view is that most equipment used in mathematics laboratories is best "homemade" (both to save money and because the making itself is frequently a useful learning experience), we have found it impractical to make and color the rods. We do make special rods for special purposes. For example in Unit 7 the exercise of constructing equivalent fraction lengths with rods on a number line suggests using a few rods that are 12 centimeters long (in order to mark $0/2$, $1/2$, $2/2$ with a "unit" 24 centimeters long). These can be sawed out of wood ($3/8$-inch cabinet stock is handy since $3/8$ inch is close to 1 centimeter) or cut out of cardboard. Similarly, though they are not used in this book, it is sometimes useful to have rods 100 centimeters long; either they can be made with a table saw, or wooden dowels or sticks cut to the correct length can be substituted.

At this writing we know of one quite cheap substitute for the rods. The Addison Wesley Publishing Company distributes sets of cardboard centimeter strips graduated in lengths from 1 to 10 centimeters and printed in the traditional colors (order number 1264; about $2 for ten sets).

As to chips, we use ordinary gaming chips (poker chips) in our classes. These are widely available in variety and department stores and are not very expensive. A set of 100 chips is plenty for two people working together. But any convenient counter can be substituted for the chips; for example, steel washers or nuts, squares or discs cut from tagboard, even beans. It is sometimes helpful to have chips of two or three colors.

In Unit 6 one of the embodiments of positive and negative integers uses chips that are white on one side and blue on the other. As explained at the beginning of section 6.2.1, there are a variety of ways of getting such chips. For our classes we simply spray one side of either blue or white chips with aerosol spray paint of the opposite color. Dots of sticky label paper could be put on one side of the chips. If tagboard discs or squares are used, construction paper or self-stick shelf paper of another color than the tagboard can be glued on one side before the counters are cut out; or counters already made for the other units can be marked on one side with marking pens or crayons of another color.

In Unit 1 decks of playing cards are used to generate various sets, and it is suggested that good drill on number facts and the like can be generated by various uses of playing cards. Again, these are widely available. If ordered in wholesale lots, both chips and cards can be obtained fairly reasonably from Arrco Playing Card Company, 310 South Racine Avenue, Chicago, Ill. 60607, and no doubt from other places as well.

MATERIALS NEEDED IN PART B In Part B the following materials and embodiments are used. One set is needed for each group of three to six students.

> Units 1 and 2: Base-four blocks, chips, base-ten blocks, colored rods (optional).
> Units 3 and 4: Base-eight pieces, Base-ten pieces[2] (optional), chips.
> Unit 5: Base-ten blocks, play money, a rather large collection of things for the metric system (see section 3).
> Unit 6: No materials needed.
> Unit 7: No materials needed.

Except when dealing with the metric system, the only uncommon materials needed are base-four blocks, base-ten blocks, and either base-eight or base-ten pieces. Base-four blocks and base-ten blocks can be ordered cut at a lumberyard or can be cut from foam. Base-eight or base-ten pieces are cut from tagboard. Students can cut the pieces and the foam blocks either outside of class or in a special class "making day" described below. The procedures for making the blocks and pieces are described below.

1. What to Make for Units 1 through 4 Base Four Blocks and Base Ten Blocks

One set of base-four blocks serves as many as six students and includes:

12 units: ▱   12 longs: ▭

---

[2] Usually students need experience with pieces in only one base. Experience with base eight leads to a more generalized understanding of the multiplication and division algorithms. If base eight is used, it is helpful for students to see several problems done with base-ten pieces so that the extension to base ten is clear. Only one set of base-ten pieces for the whole class is really necessary in this unit.

10 flats: 4 cubes:

One set of base-ten blocks serves as many as six students and includes:

30 units: 28 longs:

24 flats: 4 cubes:

Option 1: Have the lumberyard do the work. Have a lumberyard cut ³⁄₈-inch plywood into squares.
   For each base-four set: 26 squares each 4 by 4 centimeters.
   For each base-ten set: 64 squares each 10 by 10 centimeters.
   Since ³⁄₈ inch is approximately 1 centimeter, the Cuisenaire (or other) rods can be used for units and longs as follows:

Base-four blocks: Units— white (unit) rods.
                   Longs—purple (4-centimeter) rods.
                   Flats— the 4- by 4-centimeter wood squares above.
                   Cubes—four 4- by 4-centimeter wood squares fastened together with a rubber band (or, since 4 cm ≅ 1¹⁄₂ inches, just 4- by 4- by 4-centimeter solid blocks).
Base-ten blocks: Units— white (unit) rods.
                   Longs— orange (10-centimeter) rods.[3]
                   Flats— the 10- by 10-centimeter wood squares above.
                   Cubes—ten 10- by 10-centimeter wood squares fastened together with a rubber band.

If your lumberyard charges too much for cutting the squares, try building and grounds departments of a university, the woodshop at local schools, friends with a table saw. A 4- by 4-foot sheet of plywood will yield about 144 base-ten flats. Thus, from three such sheets, you can get five sets of base-ten flats and cubes, and five sets of base-four flats and cubes.
   These base-ten blocks can also be used for metric measurement.
   The ³⁄₈-inch plywood is sometimes slightly less than 1 centimeter thick. A sheet of tagboard (in the appropriate color) glued on the top of the plywood will make the flats almost exactly 1 centimeter thick. This is especially important for the base-ten cube, which needs this treatment so that you can make a cube 10 centimeters high by piling up 10 flats.

Option 2: Have the students do the work. Order foam from Sears (or another mail-order company) or obtain the foam from a local source. Use ¹⁄₂-inch-thick foam for the units, longs, and flats of both bases, use 2-inch-thick foam for the base-four cubes, and use 5-inch-thick foam for the base-ten cubes.

[3] Extra 10-centimeter rods can be purchased inexpensively from the Cuisenaire Company of America (order no. 70120), or from other suppliers.

Dimensions:
  Base-four blocks:
      Unit—$\frac{1}{2} \times \frac{1}{2} \times \frac{1}{2}$ inch   Long—$\frac{1}{2} \times \frac{1}{2} \times 2$ inch
      Flat—$\frac{1}{2} \times 2 \times 2$ inch   Cube—$2 \times 2 \times 2$ inch
  Base-ten blocks:
      Unit—$\frac{1}{2} \times \frac{1}{2} \times \frac{1}{2}$ inch   Long—$\frac{1}{2} \times \frac{1}{2} \times 5\frac{1}{4}$ inch[4]
      Flat—$\frac{1}{2} \times 5\frac{1}{4} \times 5\frac{1}{4}$ inch   Cube—$5 \times 5\frac{1}{4} \times 5\frac{1}{4}$ inch
      $\frac{1}{2}$-inch-thick foam—18 inches wide (e.g., Sears catalog no. 24B87519)
      2-inch-thick foam—18 inches wide (e.g., Sears catalog no. 24B86835P)
      5-inch-thick foam—18 inches wide (e.g., Sears catalog no. 24B87845P)

Cut the $\frac{1}{2}$-inch foam with scissors. Squeeze the 2-inch foam together along the cutting line and use scissors or a knife. Use an electric knife or a bread knife (the former makes smoother cuts) for the 5-inch foam.

Option 3: Purchase some pieces to use with the colored rods. Use colored rods for the units and longs and purchase flats and cubes from A. Daigger or another supplier. This set can be used in metric measurement.

Option 4: Purchase the original Dienes blocks or equivalent. Purchase the wooden blocks originally made for Zoltan Dienes, or an equivalent set. They are wooden, have a unit less than a centimeter, and are grooved in units. Classroom sets cost about $75 to $100 from various suppliers.

Option 5: Have students make tagboard pieces
This embodiment is inferior to the first four options and should only be used if the others are impossible to obtain.

  Base-four blocks: Units— unit rods
                     Longs— 4-centimeter rods
                     Flats— 4- by 4-cm squares cut from tagboard in a color that matches the longs
                     Cubes— 4- by 4- by 4-cm cubes made from tagboard
  Base-ten blocks: Units— unit rods
                     Longs— 10-centimeter rods[5]
                     Flats— 10- by 10-cm squares cut from tagboard to match the longs
                     Cubes— 10- by 10- by 10-cm cubes made from tagboard

The problem with this embodiment is that 10 such tagboard "flats" will not stack up to make a cube. It would, of course, be possible to make 10- by 10- by 1-centimeter tagboard boxes as flats, but it would be pretty tedious to do so. However, making one such piece of each set would probably be helpful, just to give the idea.

[4] The $5\frac{1}{4}$-inch size of the base-ten blocks is due to small errors in the units which add up when 10 of them are used to make a long.

[5] See footnote 2 about purchasing extra 10-centimeter rods.

Base Eight Multiplication Pieces and Base Ten Multiplication Pieces

A set of pieces (either base) for use by as many as six students consists of the following number of pieces:

24 units: ☐

24 longs: ▭

15 squares: ☐

8 thin longs: ▭

10 fat longs: ▭

1 huge: ☐

(Sketches not to scale)

All pieces are cut from tagboard (colored cardboard) using a paper cutter. If a cutting sheet with marks showing how far to move the tagboard for each cut is made and taped to the paper cutter, no pieces need to be drawn on the tagboard sheets. Making such a sheet is a good non-trivial problem. Different colors might be used for each size piece, but the squares and the thin longs should be the same color (because they represent the same number).

It is quite helpful if in addition to the pieces above, 8 units, 8 longs, and 4 thin longs are cut for each set from a color not used for the regular set (blue is used in the book illustrations). These pieces are used for making the sides of the multiplication rectangle to differentiate them from the pieces used in the interior of the rectangle.

Base-Eight Multiplication Pieces[6]

Name of piece:	Unit	Long	Square	Thin long	Fat long	Huge
Dimension in inches:	$\frac{1}{4} \times \frac{1}{4}$	$\frac{1}{4} \times 2\frac{1}{8}$	$2\frac{1}{8} \times 2\frac{1}{8}$	$\frac{1}{4} \times 17$	$2\frac{1}{8} \times 17$	17×17

Base-Ten Multiplication Pieces[6]

Name of piece:	Unit	Long	Square	Thin long	Fat long	Huge
Size 1: Dimension in inches	$\frac{1}{4} \times \frac{1}{4}$	$\frac{1}{4} \times 2\frac{5}{8}$	$2\frac{5}{8} \times 2\frac{5}{8}$	$\frac{1}{4} \times 26\frac{1}{4}$	$2\frac{5}{8} \times 26\frac{1}{4}$	$26\frac{1}{4} \times 26\frac{1}{4}$
Size 2: Dimension in millimeters	5×5	5×52	52×52	5×520	52×520	520×520

Size 2 for the base-ten pieces has been preferred by most of the teachers using the pieces. There is not really much difference in the ability to handle the units in size 1 and size 2, and in size 2 the larger pieces are more compact. Thus size 2 requires less table space and problems can better be seen in their entirety.

[6] Small errors in the units add up when 8 or 10 of them are put together to make a long. Because it is important that 8 (or 10) units do actually make 1 long, the longs are made slightly larger than is mathematically correct to allow for this error.

2. How to Make Embodiments for Units 1 through 4

Choice 1: "Making Day." One or two class periods (about two hours) can be set aside as a materials-making session. Advance preparation for such a session is vital and consists of the following:

A. The instructor may decide which of the options for making blocks and pieces he wishes to use and how many sets of each embodiment are needed.

B. Option 1: The instructor may figure out how much raw material of each kind (wood, foam, tagboard) is needed.

Option 2: The instructor may describe the embodiments to the students and they may figure out how much raw material of each kind is needed.

This is an excellent and nontrivial real world mathematics problem. If minimal use of raw materials is desired, students need to examine different layouts of pieces, etc. Trying to minimize labor time introduces another set of variables and may change the approach (e.g., a cutting sheet with lines telling how much to move the tagboard sheets may be taped on a paper cutter, eliminating the step of drawing pieces on the tagboard). Making embodiments is also a problem that students will encounter in teaching, and they will therefore be able to recognize its relevance.

The problems will need to be described well in advance of the making day in order for students to have enough time to work on them and also to give lead time to order the materials. The class may, for example, be divided into a base-four block group, a base-ten block group, and a multiplication pieces group. Each group may be asked to submit a minimum materials and a minimum time proposal. This assignment is probably worth doing even for classes that already have the embodiments available. New solutions will undoubtedly arise and will lead to interesting mathematical discussions. The groups might also wish to study the various proposals for making each embodiment and make a recommendation. This again is an excellent and relevant mathematics problem.

C. The instructor (or a secretary) may order the raw materials. Tagboard can usually be obtained immediately. Mail-ordered foam usually takes about a week to arrive. Lumberyards may require some lead time if they are cutting the squares, as may building and grounds departments, school woodshops, and other places that might cut the wood.

D. The instructor may divide students into groups to work on the different embodiments. Either the instructor or the students should make sure that the necessary tools are brought on the making day. The necessary tools are listed below.

Base-Four Blocks Group:

Option 1: Nothing is needed unless you choose to cover the flats with tagboard, in which case you will need tagboard, a paper cutter or several scissors, two meter sticks, and glue.

Option 2: Felt-tip pens (they mark well on foam), yardsticks, scissors.

Option 3 and 4: Nothing is needed.

Option 5: Tagboard, Scotch tape, meter sticks, scissors or paper cutter.
Base-Ten Blocks Group:

Same as base-four blocks group except that a different color of tagboard is needed for Options 1 and 5, and Option 2 requires an electric knife or a bread knife for cutting the 5-inch-thick foam.

Base-Eight or Base-Ten Multiplication Pieces Group:

A paper cutter greatly simplifies this work, and two or three would speed the task. Check to see whether the cutters will cut the tagboard and whether they will cut entire or only partial sheets. This group should make advance plans on how they will do the cutting based on the restrictions of their paper cutters. For example, the larger pieces may need to be drawn and cut with scissors or a sharp knife, while the smaller pieces may be cut using a master sheet taped on the paper cutter. Scissors can be used if there is no paper cutter available. Sometimes students have access to school paper cutters, and each student might then be assigned a particular size of piece to make outside of class.

The number of students in each group varies according to the tools available and the options chosen. The base-ten blocks group needs to be about three times as large as the base-four blocks group. Shift people among groups as needed during the making day. If everything is not finished, the remaining tasks can be divided among the students, who can then finish making things outside of class.

Choice 2: "Students make the embodiments outside of class." The steps for "making day" above are followed, but the various tasks are parceled out to the students individually or in groups, and they make the embodiments outside of class.

Choice 3: "Instructor, secretary, lab assistants, paper grader, spouse, children, etc., make the embodiments." The steps for "making day" are followed, but the above individuals or others make the embodiments. If this option is chosen, bear in mind the inverse relationship between the number of people and the amount of time each puts into the making.

3. Embodiments for Unit 5, Decimals and the Metric System

Base-ten blocks are discussed in section 1 above. To make play money, make "one dollar" bills on a duplicating machine (use green ditto paper if possible), buy small washers to use for dimes, use real pennies for pennies, and use real trading stamps or small green rectangles cut out of construction paper for green stamps.

Gathering and ordering materials for the metric system takes time and money. The following list is the shortest list that includes adequate materials. All purchased items are the least expensive available in mid-1974. These materials only have to be gathered or purchased once, but it is a time-consuming process. When the instructor sees the difference in students' understanding of the metric system after having really seen and used metric measurers, however, the effort seems worthwhile. It should also be borne in mind that if the metric system is taught to teachers merely as a vocabulary and set of memorized relationships, then it is very likely that these teachers will teach the metric system in this way to their elementary school students.

Schools (especially high schools) and university chemistry departments might be sources from which some of the metric equipment could be borrowed.

Commonly available materials required for the metric section are not listed below. Check Part B, section 5.2.2 for the complete list. Students may be assigned to collect the easily obtainable materials.

Metric Length

Meter sticks: Buy ³/₈-inch wood stock 4 or 8 feet long and cut off meter lengths, or buy any flat sticks and cut them off at meter lengths. (Unmarked sticks are actually better at first than sticks with many marks on them.) Alternatively, purchase marked meter sticks from any of many sources.

Stopwatch (optional): The second hand on a watch will do, but a stopwatch is nicer. They cost about $10 from Selective Educational Equipment, Inc., or other sources.

Centimeter graph paper, for example:
  a. Fifty sheets, order no. 38714, Creative Publications.
  b. Five pads of 100 sheets, order no. 30060, Cuisenaire Company of America.

Metric Volume

Centicubes: Plastic 1-centimeter cubes weighing 1 gram. They come in five colors, but the white ones are more accurate in weight (to within 0.5 percent). They are available from several distributors (e.g., Daigger, SEE, Creative Publications) for something like $20 for 500 cubes.

Metric Liquid Capacity

Liter: Plastic liter graduated in 50 milliliters (for example, no. 5181, Math Shop).
  Graduated liter cube (a cubic decimeter) (for example, no. 5183, Math Shop).

Metric Weight

Gram weights: Centicubes (each weighs 1 gram; above); ¹/₂-inch washers, each weighing approximately one gram (for example, 100 for less than $1 from Creative Publications); twenty 5-gram, twenty 10-gram, and ten 20-gram weights (for example about $6 for order no. 88089, Dick Blick); kilogram weight (for example, order no. 88078, Dick Blick).

Equal-arm balance: (For example, order no. SEEBAL from Selective Educational Equipment for about $6); or make from a yardstick and pieces of wood and bottoms of 2 large plastic containers.

English Measurers (needed for section 5.2.4)

Inches, yardsticks: Cut them from ³/₈-inch wood stock or from any flat wood sticks.

Square inches, feet: Make them from tagboard.

Square yard, square meter: Make them from newspaper so they will fold up to store.

Inch cubes: Twenty-seven cubes of six colors (order no. 3605, Ideal School Supply Co.); or make some cubes from paper tagboard. (This is a good geometry assignment; e.g., "How many different ways can you make a cube from a flat piece of paper?")

Cup, pint, quart, gallon: Use a measuring cup to mark empty cardboard containers correctly (milk, cream, half and half, school milk containers).

Ounces, pounds: Fishing weights from Sears are accurate 1-ounce weights. Make 1-pound weights out of sand (or rice) and a plastic bag; or, for example, A. Daigger and Company distributes iron weights in pounds (order no. 4246A) and ounces (order no. 4238A).

MATERIALS NEEDED IN PART C

In Part C each group of four people will need the following materials:

Unit 1: Attribute blocks—one individual set for each group (description given below).

Playing cards—one deck for each group (an old deck will do).

Unit 2: Colored rods—one individual set (6 to 10 rods of each color) for each group.

Unit 3: Rectangular graph paper—one sheet per person.

Log graph paper—one sheet per person.

Geoboard (optional)—two per group (description given below).

Unit 4: Colored rods—one individual set per group.

Poker chips or counters—preferably four colors (e.g., 4 red, 4 white, 4 blue, and 4 green/yellow).

Crayons or colored pencils—to correspond to the colors of the counters.

Unit 5: Poker chips, coins, or counters—at least fifty per group.

All materials except the attribute blocks and geoboards are described in Parts A and B of this appendix.

Attribute blocks: One individual set of attribute blocks is shown. The blocks involve four different colors (red, yellow, green, blue), four shapes (triangle, square, rhombus, circle), and two sizes (small, large). The *entire* set contains 32 blocks. Larger sets can be made by including three sizes (small, medium, and large) or by including "thickness" as one of the variables.

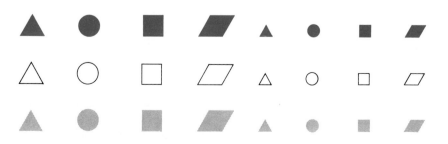

It is not difficult to make a set of attribute blocks by cutting shapes out of colored sponges, poster board, or plywood. However, commercially made sets of attribute blocks can be purchased from several publishing companies or school supply companies. Prices usually range between $4 and $8 per set. Activity cards that are appropriate for elementary school children can be bought for some of these sets of materials.

Some Sources	Order No.
Creative Publications	30412
Math Shop, Inc.	5006
Selective Educational Equipment (SEE)	DESK48
Webster Division, McGraw-Hill	07-018481-x
Herder and Herder, Inc.	Z80007

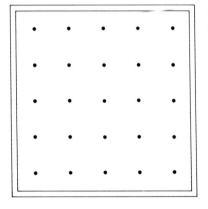

Geoboards: An entire classroom set of geoboards can be made for about 40 cents per student. Because a geoboard is a useful and versatile teaching device, many students may want to make their own geoboards as a class project.

Most lumber yards will be willing to cut 7½-inch squares out of ¾-inch pine boards. Small screws or ¾-inch brass escutcheon pins can be used to make the geoboard pegs. Escutcheon pins (available from upholsterers) work better than nails because nails are often so thin that they cut the rubber bands and the pointed heads of the nails can be painful. The pegs should be equally spaced as shown in the diagram above. If students are making their own geoboards, it is helpful to make a paper "nail guide" that can be taped onto the board to show where the pegs should be placed. A 25-peg geoboard can be made by dividing the board into twenty-five 1½-inch squares and putting a nail in the center of each of the small squares. Such geoboards can be placed next to one another to build up larger geoboards.

Commercially made sets of geoboards can be purchased from several publishing companies or school supply companies. Prices usually range between 60 cents and $2. Activity cards that are appropriate for elementary school children accompany some of these geoboard sets.

Some Sources	Order No.
Creative Publications	34010 or 34020
Cuisenaire Company	20100

Although commercially made geoboards are fairly inexpensive, the project of making their own geoboards can be a very worthwhile experience for students. Measuring and purchasing lumber, locating the positions for pegs, estimating the amount of paint that will be needed, dividing up the cost, and keeping records of payments that are involved; all these activities can be interesting and useful mathematical experiences. However, if a teacher has never participated in such a class project and has never seen how important mathematical skills can be emphasized during such experiences, it is unlikely that the teacher will be able to effectively manage similar projects for children.

Colored Counters A set of 200 counting chips, in eight different colors, can be purchased from Creative Publications (order no. 38400, approximate price: $2.50).

appendix II
bibliography and references

The books that are listed here are those referred to in the text plus others that we believe should be available as a minimum library for elementary school teachers. You should at least "thumb through" as many of these books as are available in your library or department. Many of them contain practical ideas about mathematical experiences, problems, and projects that are appropriate for children, or provide interesting background material for teachers to use to enrich and supplement the material they teach to youngsters. Other references are on the psychology of learning mathematical concepts, on problems involved in implementing a mathematics laboratory, or simply material on mathematics and its uses that you might enjoy.

In addition to the books that are listed here, prospective teachers should also look through at least one current elementary mathematics textbook series, as well as the teachers' guides and scope and sequence charts that accompany such textbooks. Your library or department may be able to provide some of these kinds of materials, or you may look at them in a nearby school.

A. BOOKS FOR ADULTS ABOUT MATHEMATICS

Bell, M. S.: *Mathematical Uses and Models in Our Everyday World: Studies in Mathematics,* vol. 20, School Mathematics Study Group, Stanford, Calif., 1972. (Distributor: Vromans, Inc., 2085 E. Foothill Blvd., Pasadena, Calif. 91109.)

Berganini, D.: *Mathematics: Life Science Library,* Silver Burdett Company, Morristown, N.J., 1963.

662

Butts, T.: *Problem Solving in Mathematics,* Scott, Foresman and Company, Glenview, Ill., 1973. Butts focuses on problem-solving situations in elementary number theory and arithmetic.

Boyer, Carl B.: *A History of Mathematics,* John Wiley & Sons, Inc., New York, 1968.

Eves, Howard: *An Introduction to the History of Mathematics.* Holt, Rinehart, and Winston, Inc., New York, 1964.

Fitzgerald, W., D. Bellamy, P. Boonstra, J. Jones, and W. Oosse: *Laboratory Manual for Elementary Mathematics,* Prindle, Weber & Schmidt, Incorporated, Boston, 1973. This laboratory manual contains mathematics laboratory activities for adults using a variety of concrete materials.

Gardner, M.: *New Mathematical Diversions from Scientific American,* Simon & Schuster, Inc., New York, 1966. This book is one of a series of books by Gardner, each of which contain interesting games, puzzles, problems, and tricks in recreational mathematics.

Greenes, C. E., R. E. Willcutt, and M. A. Spikell: *Problem Solving in the Mathematics Laboratory,* Prindle, Weber & Schmidt, Incorporated, Boston, 1972. *Problem Solving* contains mathematics laboratory activities for adults, using colored rods, attribute blocks, geoboards, and multibase blocks.

Huff, D.: *How to Lie with Statistics,* W. W. Norton & Company, New York; 1954.

Jacobs, H. R.: *Mathematics: A Human Endeavor,* W. H. Freeman and Company, San Francisco, 1970. This is an enjoyable, easy-to-read book for adults, dealing with a variety of mathematical topics from logic to statistics.

Klein, G.: *Analytical Arithmetic Problem Books—Fractions,* 1973. Min Math Materials, 11 N. LaSalle Street, Chicago.

Kramer, Edna: *The Nature and Growth of Modern Mathematics,* Hawthorn Books, Inc., New York, 1970.

Lipton, J.: *An Exaltation of Larks,* Grossman Publishers, Inc., New York, 1968. A charming book full of names of sets; e.g., "pride of lions," "skulk of foxes," "bevy of beauties."

Menninger, Karl: *Number Words and Number Symbols,* The MIT Press, Cambridge, Mass., 1972.

Newman, J. K. (ed.): *The World of Mathematics,* vols. 1 to 4, Simon and Schuster, Inc., New York, 1956. This is a very useful anthology of a wide variety of "classic" expositions about basic mathematics and its applications.

Ogilvy, C. S.: *Tomorrow's Mathematics,* 2d ed., Oxford University Press, London, 1972. In nontechnical language, Ogilvy describes a number of unsolved problems for amateur mathematicians.

Schaaf, W. L.: *A Bibliography of Recreational Mathematics,* vols. 1 and 2, National Council of Teachers of Mathematics, Washington D.C. 1970.

Smith, D. E., and J. Ginsburg: *Numbers and Numerals,* National Council of Teachers of Mathematics, Washington, D.C. 1937.

Smith, D. E.: *Number Stories of Long Ago,* National Council of Teachers of Mathematics, Washington, D.C. 1969.

Stein, S.: *Mathematics: The Man-made Universe,* 2nd ed., W. H. Freeman and Company, San Francisco, 1963. This book presents a number of different mathematical topics emphasizing the "spirit of mathematics"—its structure, beauty, and vitality.

Struik, D. J. (ed.): *A Source Book in Mathematics, 1200–1800,* Harvard University Press, Cambridge, Mass., 1969.

Tanur, J., et al. (eds.): *Statistics: A Guide to the Unknown,* W. H. Freeman and Company, San Francisco, 1972. No mathematical or statistical background is required to enjoy this interesting book of brief essays about a wide variety of uses of statistics in medicine, law, government, literature, sports, and many other places.

Van der Waerden, B. L.: *Science Awakening,* Cambridge University Press, London, 1960.

The Way Things Work: An Illustrated Encyclopedia of Technology, Simon and Schuster, New York, 1967. Extraordinarily clear and concise descriptions of the way many machines, technical processes, and appliances work; accompanied by more than 1,000 simple drawings. Topics range from the ball-point pen to the computer, from dry ice to nuclear reactors, from television to sailing. This book helps any lay person to understand our technological world better.

Zaslavsky, C.: *Africa Counts,* Prindle, Weber & Schmidt, Incorporated, Boston, 1973.

B. BOOKS ABOUT TEACHING MATHEMATICS TO CHILDREN

Ashlock, R. B.: *Error Patterns in Computation,* Charles E. Merrill Books, Inc., Columbus, Ohio, 1972. Ashlock focuses on possible causes of computational errors, and suggests remedial activities.

Berger, E. (ed.): *Instructional Aids in Mathematics,* Thirty-fourth Yearbook of the National Council of Teachers of Mathematics. National Council of Teachers of Mathematics, Reston, Va. 1973. This NCTM yearbook contains valuable information about manipulatives, sources of manipulatives, and references about manipulatives.

Biggs, E. E., and J. R. MacLean: *Freedom to Learn,* Addison-Wesley, Canada, 1969. *Freedom to Learn* describes an active learning approach to learning and describes how such a learning environment can be created. Biggs and Mac-Lean have been associated with the Nuffield Project (British primary schools).

British Association of Teachers of Mathematics, *Notes on Mathematics in Primary Schools,* Cambridge University Press, London, 1969. The material in this book is for teachers who are looking for interesting ideas to challenge their pupils.

School Mathematics Project (SMP): *Teachers Guide for Books A–H, X, Y, and Z,* Cambridge University Press, London, 1969–1973. Although the SMP books contain Nuffield-like activities that were written especially for junior high–level students, many of the materials are also appropriate for upper elementary school children.

Chandler, A. M. (ed.): *Experiences in Mathematical Ideas,* vols. 1 and 2, National Council of Teachers of Mathematics, Washington, D. C., 1970.

Charbonneau, M. P.: *Learning to Think in a Mathematics Laboratory.* National Association of Independent Schools, Boston, 1971. Charbonneau is an experienced teacher who gives practical "teacher-to-teacher" advice to those who are interested in trying a laboratory approach to instruction.

Copeland, R. W.: *Diagnostic and Learning Activities in Mathematics for Children,* The Macmillan Company, New York, 1974. The diagnostic activities that are described in this book are related to instructional activities that are described in Copeland's *How Children Learn Mathematics.*

Copeland, R. W.: *How Children Learn Mathematics,* 2d ed., The Macmillan Company, New York, 1974. Copeland gives an interpretation of Piaget's theory of cognitive development as it applies to the acquisition of mathematical concepts.

Davis, R. B.: *Discovery in Mathematics: A Text for Teachers.* Addison-Wesley Publishing Company, Inc., Redding, Mass., 1964. Davis describes short "Madison Project" lessons of activities concerning a variety of mathematical topics. Although the book focuses primarily on middle grades, most of the ideas and techniques can be easily adapted to other grade levels.

Dienes, Z. P.: *Building up Mathematics,* Hutchinson Educational Ltd., London, 1960. This book gives examples to illustrate some of the principles which underlie Dienes' "mathematics laboratory" mode of instruction.

_____: *Exploration of Space and Practical Measurement,* McGraw-Hill Book Company, New York, 1966. Activities for exploring topological space and for measuring length, weight, capacity, and time are contained in this book aimed for children from kindergarten through grade three.

_____: *Learning Logic: Logical Games,* McGraw-Hill Book Company, New York, 1966. This handbook for teachers of young children contains many activities with attribute blocks.

_____: *Modern Mathematics for Young Children.* McGraw-Hill Book Company, New York, 1966. Sets, logical operations, number and notation, place value, and applications of grouping concepts are introduced through games.

_____: *Teacher's Guide: Mathematics Experience Program,* McGraw-Hill Book Company, Webster Division, New York, 1973. The guide gives references to specific activities in many other books by Dienes, and it provides an outline for an entire elementary school curriculum.

Dumas, E.: *Math Activities for Child Involvement,* Allyn and Bacon, Inc., Boston, 1971.

Frédérique, *Mathematics and the Child, 1.* Montreal, Algonquin, 1971. Both books contain actual commentaries describing elementary school classes that were conducted at the Centre Belge de Pédagogie de la Mathématique. Lesson descriptions are accompanied by a discussion about pedagogical and mathematical issues that were involved in the lessons.

_____ Frédérique and Papy: *Graphs and the Child,* Algonquin, Montreal, Canada, 1970.

Genise, J. R., and J. Kunz: *Opening Doors in Mathematics,* Cuisenaire Company of America, Inc., New Rochelle, N.Y., 1971. A basic manual about the use of rods.

Hardgrove, C. E., and H. F. Miller: *The Mathematics Library: Elementary and Junior High School,* National Council of Teachers of Mathematics, Reston, Va., 1973.

Howson, A. G. (ed.): *Developments in Mathematics Education,* Cambridge University Press, London, 1973. This book is a report on the proceedings of the Second International Congress on Mathematical Education.

Kidd, K. P., S. Myers, and D. Cilley: *The Laboratory Approach to Mathemat-*

ics, Science Research Associates, Chicago, 1970. This book provides helpful information about implementing a mathematics laboratory. The focus is on upper elementary school grades.

Laycock, M., and G. Watson: *The Fabric of Mathematics,* Activity Resources Company, Hayward, Calif., 1971. A description of mathematical concepts, and laboratory materials and sources to use in teaching these concepts.

Lorton, M. B.: *Workjobs,* Addison-Wesley Publishing Company, Inc., Menlo Park, Calif., 1972. *Workjobs* focuses on the development of mathematical skills and language. Suggested experiences actively involve primary and preschool children in mathematical tasks.

Macdonald Educational, *Science $5/13$ Project,* London. (Also handled by Purnell Educational, New York.) An excellent series of paperback resource guides for teachers concerning science for children between the ages of five and thirteen. Innumerable mathematics applications are contained in these books. Some of the titles are:

Working with Wood, 1972.
Time, 1972.
Early Experiences, 1972.
Science from Toys, 1972.
Structures and Forces, 1972.
Change, 1973.
Minibeasts, 1973.
Holes, Gaps, and Cavities, 1973.
Metals, 1973.
Ourselves, 1973.
Like and Unlike, 1973.
Science, Models and Toys, 1973.
Children and Plastics, 1973.
Trees, 1973.
Colored Things, 1973.

Nuffield Mathematics Materials, *Checking Up I and Checking Up II,* John Wiley and Sons, Inc., New York, 1970 and 1973.

Nuffield Mathematics Materials, John Wiley and Sons, Inc., New York. The Nuffield materials were developed for use in British primary schools. They suggest many ways to make mathematics more interesting and enjoyable for youngsters.

I Do and I Understand (Introductory Guide), 1967.
Your Child and Mathematics (A Guide for Parents), 1968.
Into Secondary School (For Teachers of Older Children), 1970.
Maths with Everything (For Teachers of Infants), 1971.
The Story so Far (Index to the Early Guides), 1969.
Mathematics—The First Three Years (For Teachers of the First Three Primary Grades), 1970.
Mathematics—The Later Primary Years (For Teachers of the Later Primary Grades), 1972.
The Core Guides:
Mathematics Begins—1967

Computation and Structure 2 (six–eight years), 1967.
Computation and Structure 3 (seven–eleven years), 1968.
Computation and Structure 4 (ten–thirteen years), 1969.
Computation and Structure 5 (ten–thirteen years), 1972.
Beginnings – 1967
Shape and Size 2 (six–nine years), 1967.
Shape and Size 3 (seven–eleven years), 1968.
Shape and Size 4 (eleven–thirteen years), 1969.
Pictorial Representation – 1967
Graphs Leading to Algebra 2 (eight–thirteen years), 1969.
Graphs Leading to Algebra 3 (eleven–thirteen years), 1972.
Weaving Guides
Desk Calculators, 1967
How to Build a Pond, 1967
Environmental Geometry, 1969
Probability and Statistics, 1969
Computers and Young Children, 1972
Logic, 1972.

Modules of Work
Speed and Gradient, 1974.
Decimals, 1974.
Number Patterns, 1974.
Symmetry, 1974.
Angles, Courses, and Bearings, 1974.

Reys, R. E., and T. R. Post: *The Mathematics Laboratory,* Prindle, Weber & Schmidt, Incorporated, Boston, 1973. Reys and Post explain some of the psychological foundations and aims of a mathematics laboratory. The book also contains many helpful pragmatic suggestions about how to implement a mathematics laboratory – including many helpful references to books and equipment.

Trivett, J. V.: *Mathematical Awareness,* Cuisenaire Company of America, Inc., New Rochelle, N.Y., 1962. Basic ways of using rods in teaching arithmetic.

University of Illinois Committee on School Mathematics, *Stretchers and Shrinkers,* Harper & Row, Publishers, Incorporated, New York, 1969. Some novel ways of teaching about fractions.

C. MISCELLANEOUS BOOKS FOR CHILDREN

Adler, I.: *Giant Golden Book of Mathematics,* Golden Press, New York, 1960.

Seymour, D. G.: *Aftermath 1,* rev. ed.; *Aftermath 2; Aftermath 3; Aftermath 4,* Creative Publications, Palo Alto, 1971.

—— and S. Gidley: *Eureka,* rev. ed., Creative Publications, Palo Alto, Calif., 1972. *Eureka* and the *Aftermath* books emphasize problem-solving activities and recreational mathematics for upper elementary or junior high school youngsters.

Wirtz, Botel, and Sawyer Beberman: *Math Workshop for Children,* Encyclopedia Britannica, Inc., Chicago, 1965.

D. JOURNALS FOR ELEMENTARY SCHOOL TEACHERS

National Council of Teachers of Mathematics (NCTM), *The Arithmetic Teacher,* vol. 21, no. 5, 1974. *Arithmetic Teacher* contains a variety of different kinds of articles for elementary school mathematics teachers, including suggestions for specific classroom activities.

Quarterly British Math Journal, *Mathematics Teaching,* Association of Teachers of Mathematics. Among other things, *Mathematics Teaching* contains reports of new teaching methods that are currently being introduced in British primary schools.

Scientific American. Contains a number of different kinds of readable scientific articles for curious adults.

index

This book was designed by Jules Perlmutter of A Good Thing, Inc., New York, New York. The art was rendered by J & R Services, New York, New York. The text was set in 10 point Times Roman Linofilm by Progressive Typographers, York, Pennsylvania.

Printed and bound in the U.S.A. by Halliday Lithograph.